A Critical
Cinema 2

A Critical Cinema 2

Interviews with Independent Filmmakers

Scott MacDonald

University of California Press

Berkeley / Los Angeles / Oxford

This book is a print-on-demand volume. It is manufactured
using toner in place of ink. Type and images may be less
sharp than the same material seen in traditionally printed
University of California Press editions.

University of California Press
Berkeley and Los Angeles, California

University of California Press
Oxford, England

Copyright © 1992 by The Regents of the University of California

Library of Congress Cataloging-in-Publication Data

MacDonald, Scott, 1942–
     A critical cinema.

     Includes bibliographical references and index.
     Filmography: p. 423–435.
     1. Experimental films—United States—History and
criticism.   2. Motion picture producers and directors
—United States—Interviews.   I. Title.
PN1995.9.E96M34   1988   791.43′75′0973   87-6004
ISBN 0-520-05800-3 (v. 1 : cloth)
ISBN 0-520-05801-1 (v. 1 : pbk.)
ISBN 0-520-07917-5 (v. 2 : cloth)
ISBN 0-520-07918-3 (v. 2 : pbk.)

Printed in the United States of America

To my best teachers:
Patricia O'Connor, Peter Watkins,
J. J. Murphy, Bob Huot, Morgan Fisher,
Frank Bergmann, Su Friedrich, Ian MacDonald

Contents

Acknowledgments

Thanks to the following journals for permission to reprint interviews and, in some cases, my introductory comments:

Film Quarterly, for "Southern Exposure: An Interview with Ross McElwee," vol. 41, no. 4 (Summer 1988), pp. 13–23; "Yoko Ono: Ideas on Film (Interview/Scripts)," vol. 43, no. 1 (Fall 1989), pp. 2–23; "Illuminations: An Interview with Andrew Noren," vol. 44, no. 3 (Spring 1991), pp. 30–43; "Demystifying the Female Body—Two Interviews: Anne Severson—*Near the Big Chakra*/Yvonne Rainer—*Privilege,*" vol. 45, no. 1 (Fall 1991), pp. 18–32.

Afterimage, for "Interview with James Benning," vol. 9, no. 5 (December 1981), pp. 12–19; "Interview with Anthony McCall," vol. 15, no. 5 (December 1987), pp. 6–9; "Damned If You Don't: An Interview with Su Friedrich," vol. 15, no. 10 (May 1988), pp. 6–10.

The Independent, for "The Nuclear War Film: Peter Watkins Interviewed," vol. 7, no. 9 (October 1984), pp. 22–24, 32; "Daddy Dearest: Su Friedrich Talks about Filmmaking, Family, Feminism," vol. 13, no. 10 (December 1990), pp. 28–34.

Cinematograph, for "A Picture a Day Keeps the Doctor Away: An Interview with Anne Robertson," vol. 4 (1991), pp. 53–66.

Feminist Studies, for "Interview with Lizzie Borden." Article reprinted from *Feminist Studies,* vol. 15, no. 2 (Summer 1989), pp. 327–345, by permission of the publisher, Feminist Studies, Inc., c/o Women's Studies Program, University of Maryland, College Park, MD, 20742.

Journal of Film and Video (Journal of the University Film Associa-

tion), for "Interview with Peter Watkins," vol. 34, no. 3 (Summer 1982), pp. 47–55.

October, for "Interview with Jonas Mekas," no. 29 (Summer 1984), pp. 82–116.

The Velvet Light Trap, for "But First a Little Ru Ru: An Interview with Robert Breer—Recent Films," no. 24 (Fall 1989), pp. 75–84. *The Velvet Light Trap* is published by the University of Texas Press.

Thanks to Utica College of Syracuse University for several research grants, and to my typist Carol Fobes.

Introduction

Since nearly all of us are acculturated to expect certain types of experiences in movie theaters and on television, one of the valuable functions of the multifaceted independent cinema that has developed alongside the popular cinema during most of its history is to challenge our expectations. When we see a film that surprises or shocks us, we are forced to question the implicit assumptions about cinema our expectations encode. Of course, this process is inevitable within any area of film history. Even in the standard genres of commercial film, viewers are inevitably comparing each new instance of horror film, Western, and suspense thriller with previous instances and with the sense of the genre's history they have developed. What gives some forms, and some particular instances, of independent film their "critical" edge is the *extent* to which they force us to question our psychological/social/political investment in the conventional. A new instance of a horror film usually confronts, at most, a limited number of the expectations we bring to the genre—the way in which characters are developed or plots resolved, or the type of special effects used, or the overall look of the events dramatized—but an independent film with a powerful critical edge might challenge our assumption that a film must include characters and plot or must present events within images that confirm Western perspectival conventions or must include recognizable imagery at all. Indeed, one of the signals that one is experiencing a powerfully critical film is the conviction that what we're seeing isn't a *real* movie, even though it is obviously being projected by a movie projector in a movie theater.

A particular critical film can relate to the conventional cinema in various ways. My distinctions in Volume 1 were determined by the degree to which a particular film, or the work of a particular filmmaker, invokes the conventions in order to challenge them. In some instances, filmmakers use just enough of the elements employed in conventional movies to create an aura of the conventional, but use these elements in a consistently challenging way. George Kuchar's films often reveal characters enacting melodramatic plots, but his articulation of conventional elements—the acting, the costumes and sets, the continuity, the characters' motivations—is so unlike big-budget Hollywood films that for most viewers Kuchar's films are as much about the disparity between the two levels of film practice as about the issues he pretends to explore. Not only do we realize the limits of Kuchar's economic means and see the effects of these limitations in his films—we are also reminded that the very extensiveness of the resources available to Hollywood directors constricts what big-budget directors can express and how they can express it.

Other filmmakers invoke fewer cinematic conventions. Some replace the interest in fictional characters and scripted plots with personal explorations of their own lives, particularly dimensions of their lives usually considered unfilmic—too mundane or too outrageous for a conventional film. Carolee Schneemann's frank, erotic revelations of her sexual interactions with lover James Tenney (in *Fuses*, 1967) exposed—and continue to expose—not only her own personal life, but the limitations of the conventional cinema's portrayal of heterosexual eroticism. Still other filmmakers bring forward dimensions of the conventional cinema that are so fundamental that most moviegoers have rarely, if ever, been conscious of them as conventions. In his films of the early seventies, Taka Iimura eliminates all photographic imagery and explores the impact of durations of time in the movie theater, using a variety of systems of measurement. Iimura's films simultaneously create new, "minimal" forms of film experience, and they focus on the issue of duration in a way that enables us to think more extensively about the nature and implications of the conventional cinema's manipulations of time.

The critical dimension of the films discussed in *A Critical Cinema* is certainly not the only interesting aspect of those films. The long history of independent cinema has produced hundreds of films that can sustain a viewer's fascination regardless of whatever relationships exist between these films and the commercial cinema. While some independent filmmakers admit their interest in critiquing what they've experienced in commercial movie theaters and on television, others see their work as developing out of traditions that have little or nothing to do with the movie industry and its products. In fact, some of the filmmakers I include under the rubric of "critical" have never been regular moviegoers.

My investment in the idea of critical cinema comes from being a teacher. Indeed, "critical cinema" is not meant as a descriptive term that distinguishes some intrinsic dimension of the particular films it is used in connection with; it's a pragmatic term meant to suggest a way of using a broad spectrum of independent films that, in general, remain one of film history's most underutilized educational resources. I cannot imagine teaching effectively without exposing students to an intertextual discourse of the broadest possible variety of film experiences, including those "avant-garde" or "experimental" films that provide the most extensive and deepest shocks to viewers whose definition of cinema is primarily a product of commercial entertainments in the theater and on television. Of course, another practical value of including a range of independent film in film courses at all levels of formal film study (and in the many other sectors of academe that can profit from them) is the maintenance of forms of film production that remain financially marginal: the more often independent films are rented—for whatever reason—the more vital independent film production is likely to be.

My decision to become involved in an ongoing interview project developed from my recognition that those who are interested in using independent film as a critique of mainstream cinema and television are likely to appreciate the historical and ideological context extensive interviews with filmmakers can provide. Because "critical films" are unconventional, they almost inevitably create problems for audiences, even audiences that consider themselves open to new film experiences. And while comments by filmmakers about the particular films they make can never be the final word—as Hollis Frampton says in Volume 1, "It's obvious that there are things that spectators can know about a work, any work, that the person who made it can ever know" (p. 57)—their attitudes about what they've made and their revelations of the personal, social, and theoretical contexts out of which particular works developed can be of considerable interest and use to the viewer trying to come to terms with difficult films. Further, discussions with filmmakers usually reveal the degree to which the critical edge of particular films is the result of conscious decisions by filmmakers interested in cinematically confronting the conventional and to what degree it is a projection by programmers or teachers interested in mining the intertextual potential of the films. And finally, in-depth interviews with filmmakers over several years help to develop a sense of the ongoing history of independent filmmaking and the people and institutions that sustain it.

Volume 2 of *A Critical Cinema* extends the general approach initiated in Volume 1. All the filmmakers interviewed for this volume could be categorized in terms of how fully or how minimally they invoke the conventional cinema and the system of expectations it has created, or to be more precise—since nearly all the filmmakers I interview make various types of films—each film discussed in this volume could be ranged along an axis that extends from films that invoke many conventions—films like James Benning's *11 × 14* (1976), Laura Mulvey and Peter Wollen's *Riddles of the Sphinx* (1977), Lizzie Borden's *Working Girls* (1986), and Su Friedrich's *Damned If You Don't* (1987)—only to undercut the expectations they've created, to films that seem to have almost no connection with the conventional cinema, but nevertheless explore a dimension of the film experience that underlies both conventional and alternative film practice: Anthony McCall's *Line Describing a Cone* (1973), which focuses on the cone of light between projector and wall, is a good example.

My method as an interviewer has also remained the same. I have sought out filmmakers whose work challenges the conventional cinema, whose films pose problems for viewers. Whenever it has seemed both necessary and possible, I have explored all the films of a filmmaker in detail and have discussed them, one by one, in as much depth as has seemed useful. In a few recent instances, however, my interest in interviewing a filmmaker has been spurred by the accomplishments of a single film. I interviewed Anne Severson (now Alice Anne Parker) about *Near the Big Chakra* (1972) and Laura Mulvey about *Riddles of the Sphinx* because of the excitement of using these films in classes and the many questions raised about them in class discussions. In most cases, I have traveled to filmmakers' homes or mutually agreed-upon locations and have taped our discussions, subsequently transcribing and editing the discussions and returning them to the filmmakers for corrections. My editing of the transcribed tapes is usually quite extensive: the goal is always to remain as true to the fundamental ideas and attitudes of filmmakers as possible, not simply to present their spoken statements verbatim, though I do attempt to provide a flavor of each filmmaker's way of speaking. The interviews in *A Critical Cinema* are in no instance conceived as exposés; they are attempts to facilitate a communication to actual and potential viewers of what the filmmakers would like viewers to understand about their work, in words they are comfortable with.

While my general approach as an interviewer has remained the same, the implicit structure of Volume 2 differs from that of Volume 1, in which the interviews are arranged roughly in the order I conducted and completed them. In Volume 2 the arrangement of the interviews has nothing to do with the order in which they were conducted. Rather, the volume is organized so as to suggest general historical dimensions of the film careers explored in the interviews and to highlight the potential of the work of individual independent filmmakers not only to critique the conventional cinema but to function within an ongoing discourse with the work of other critical filmmakers.

The audience investigates the projector beam during McCall's Line Describing a Cone *(1973).*

In general, the interviews collected here provide a chronological overview of independent filmmaking since 1950, especially in North America. The first three interviewees—Robert Breer, Michael Snow, Jonas Mekas—discuss developments from the early fifties and conclude in the late seventies (Mekas), the early eighties (Breer), and 1990 (Snow). The next two interviewees—Bruce Baillie, Yoko Ono—review developments beginning in the late fifties (Baillie) and early sixties (Ono). Anthony McCall and Andrew Noren discuss their emergence as filmmakers in the early seventies and the mid sixties, respectively. The Anne Robertson and James Benning interviews begin in the mid seventies and end very recently. And so on.

Another historical trajectory implicit in the order of the eighteen interviews has to do with the types of critique developed from one decade to the next. Of course, the complexity of the history of North American independent cinema makes any simple chronology of approaches impossible. Indeed, each decade of independent film production has been characterized by the simultaneous development of widely varying forms of critique. And yet, having said this, I would also argue that certain general changes in focus are discernible. One of these is the increasingly explicit political engagement of filmmakers. The films of Breer and Snow emphasize fundamental issues of perception, especially film perception. From time to time, one of their films reveals evidence of the filmmaker's awareness of the larger social/political developments of which their work is inevitably a part, but in general they focus on the cinematic worlds created by their films. The focus of the films of Mekas, Baillie, Ono, and McCall is broader: the worlds *in* their films are somewhat more directly engaged with social/political developments outside their work. In several of Mekas's major films, for example, the filmmaker's real homeland (Lithuania) is ultimately "replaced" by the creation of an "aesthetic homeland" that exists within the films themselves and within the social and institutional world documented by the films. Mekas may "really live only in my editing room," but his life there is, as his films make clear, contextualized by the personal/ethnic/political history out of which this current "real life" developed.

With few exceptions, the remaining interviews in Volume 2 reveal a growing interest in national and global concerns. Some interviewees—Benning, for example, and Ross McElwee and Su Friedrich—make films that reveal in some detail how their personal lives are affected by larger social and political developments; Friedrich, in particular, uses the process of filmmaking as a means of responding to these developments. Severson, Mulvey, Yvonne Rainer, and Trinh T. Minh-ha have used filmmaking to explore the gender politics that underlie contemporary life and thus inform much of the popular cinema, and Trinh and Rainer in particular relate the disenfranchisement implicit in these gender politics to other forms of disenfranchisement: to the undervaluing of ethnic heritages within the United States and of the cultural practices of "Third World" peoples. Godfrey Reggio and Peter Watkins explore the possibility of a global cinematic perspective, in films that attempt to demonstrate the interconnectedness of all cultures and their parallel problems and aspirations.

The other general organizational principle that informs *A Critical Cinema 2* is my arrangement of the interviews so that each successive pair of interviews (the mini-interviews with Severson, Mulvey, and Rainer are treated as a single piece) reveals a general type of response to the conventional cinema *and* articulates a set of similarities and differences between the work of the paired filmmakers. My hope is that the implicit double-leveled interplay will make clear that the contributions of the filmmakers interviewed are not a series of isolated critiques of the conventional film experience but are parts of an explicit and/or implicit discourse about the nature of cinema. For those interested in teaching or programming a broader range of film practice, a brief review of the implications of a few of my pairings might make the complex and simulating nature of this discourse more apparent.

Breer and Snow came to filmmaking from the fine arts, having already established themselves as painters and sculptors (Snow was also a musician). Neither uses filmmaking as a means of developing narratives peopled by characters with whom viewers do and don't identify. There are, at most, references to conventional narrative and character development in their films—in some instances, just reference enough to make clear that the conventions are being defied. The focus of Breer's and Snow's films is the nature of human perception. Breer's animations continually toy with our way of making sense of moving lines and shapes. At one moment, we see a two-dimensional abstraction, and a moment later a shift of a line or a shape will suddenly transform this abstraction into a portion of a representational scene that disappears almost as soon as we grasp it. In *Wavelength* (1967) and *Back and Forth* [←→] (1969), Snow sets up systematic procedures that allow him to reveal that certain types of events, or filmstocks, or camera speeds cause the same filmed spaces to flatten or deepen, to be seen as abstract or representational. Both filmmakers confront the conventional viewer's expectations with considerable wit and frequent good humor.

But while Breer and Snow critique some of the same viewer assumptions in some of the same general ways, their films are also very different. Nearly all of Breer's films are brief animations of drawings and still photographs. Indeed, Breer is a central figure in the tradition of experimental animation, which has functioned as an alternative to the commercial cartoon and its replication of the live-action commercial cinema. With the exception of his first film, Snow has made live-action films, some of them very long. While Breer's films move so quickly as to continually befuddle us, Snow's films often move so slowly as to challenge our patience. Both filmmakers confront our expectations about what can happen in a certain amount of film time, but they do so in nearly opposite ways.

The second pair of interviewees mount a very different kind of critique of conventional cinema. Mekas was a poet before coming to the United States after World War II, and once he arrived here, he transposed his free-form approach to written verse into a visually poetic film style (a style that often includes written text). Baillie, too, came to see himself as a visual poet, translating traditional literary stories and rituals (the legend of the Holy Grail, the Catholic Mass, *Don Quixote*) into new, cinematic forms. Both filmmakers were, and remain, appalled by the conformist tendencies of American society, by what they see as the denigration of the spiritual in popular culture, and by the more militaristic dimensions of modern technology—tendencies so often reflected in the popular cinema. Both have produced a body of films that sing the nobility of the individual, of the simple beauties of the natural world, and of peaceful forms of human interaction. And both have embodied their personal ideologies in institutions (Mekas: the New York Cinematheque, the New York Film-makers' Cooperative, *Film Culture*, Anthology Film Archives; Baillie: Canyon Cinema) that have attempted to maintain the presence of alternative cinema in a nation dominated by the commercial movie and television industries.

While they have a good deal in common, their work is also quite distinct. Mekas has made a permanent home in New York. His primary influences are European; indeed, one of the central quests of his films has been to maintain his Lithuanian heritage and his contact with European culture. His film style is often wildly free-form; his gestural camera movements, quick editing, and single-framing create a sense of childlike excitement about the people and places he records. His films are sensual but avoid the erotic, and in recent years they have celebrated the joys of the conventional nuclear family. Baillie's filmmaking began when he moved to San Francisco and often reflects the Eastern influences that were so pervasive on the West Coast during the sixties. While he too developed a hand-held personal style, its tendency has always been toward the meditative. Indeed, with Yoko Ono, he was probably the first modern filmmaker to explore the potential of the single-shot film, in *All My Life* (1966) and *Still Life* (1966). Baillie's films are both sensual and erotic; they seem less involved with searching for a homeland and a home than with chronicling the film poet's physical, spiritual, and erotic travels.

Neither Yoko Ono nor Anthony McCall have made films in over a decade, but their films of the late sixties and seventies use minimalist tactics as a means of providing new forms of film experience. Ono's earliest films are either single-shot slow motion portraits of actions that challenge viewers' assumptions about the correct "velocity" of film action, or serial examinations of the body that challenge the commercial film industry's fetishization of "filmic" (i.e., erotically marketable) parts of the body for periods of screen time that conform to conventional audiences' film-erotic "needs." McCall's early films are as minimalist as

Ono's. In *Line Describing a Cone* (1973) and his other "Cone films," as well as in *Long Film for Four Projectors* (1974) and *Four Projected Movements* (1975), McCall focuses the moviegoer's attention on the projector beam (the movie projector is located in the room during these films) for relatively long periods—*Line Describing a Cone* lasts thirty minutes; *Long Film for Four Projectors,* six hours—as a means of calling attention to the cinema environment and its sociopolitical implications: what does it mean that nearly all of our public film viewing involves our sitting in rigid rows of chairs looking up at the shadow products of an apparatus kept out of the view, and control, of the audience? Both Ono and McCall later collaborated with others on films that had quite overt political agendas: Ono and John Lennon made *Bed-In* (1969), a documentation of their Bed-In for peace in Montreal; McCall worked with Andrew Tyndall on *Argument* (1978), a feature-length exploration of the political implications of men's fashion advertising and of mass market media practice in general, and with several women and men on *Sigmund Freud's Dora* (1979), an examination of the gender-politics of a famous Freudian case.

Ono and McCall differ in the specifics of their politics—Ono's films are internationalist, McCall's implicitly or explicitly Marxist—and in terms of the viewership they address in their films. At the beginning of her career, Ono was part of Fluxus, an international group of artists functioning outside the mass media and in defiance of accepted art practice and institutions, but as her resources grew, so did her interest in addressing a much larger audience: *No. 4 (Bottoms)* (1966) was a widely reported happening in England, and the later Lennon-Ono collaborations aimed at the huge pop music audience and beyond. *Line Describing a Cone* and McCall's other early films were designed for small groups in art gallery contexts (indeed, the Cone films and *Long Film for Four Projectors* can be understood as "light sculptures"), and his collaborative films were designed as catalysts for small discussion groups in big-city art-ghetto screening spaces, or in academic settings.

The volume's final pairing reveals similarities and differences in two filmmakers who have worked toward a "global" approach to filmmaking: Watkins most obviously in the 14½-hour *The Journey* (1987) and Reggio in a trilogy of films, the first two of which—*Koyaanisqatsi* (1983) and *Powaqqatsi* (1988)—have been completed. Both filmmakers have explored the relationships of industrialized and "developing" nations and have emphasized the degree to which modern industrialized society has tended to undervalue regional and ethnic heritages, the natural environment, and the meaningful participation of the individual. Both filmmakers have circled the globe to create a far broader spectrum of people and places than the commercial cinema provides and to focus

Ross McElwee and his father (Dr. Ross McElwee) during the shooting of Back-yard *(1984).*

their viewers on these people not as backdrops for the fictional adven-tures of Western swashbucklers, but as individuals with concerns, ideas, and accomplishments worthy of our sustained attention.

Reggio and Watkins differ radically in their understanding of the "correct" production process for such work, and in their assumptions about how their finished films should engage viewers. Reggio functions in the main like a conventional, commercial director: he raises adequate capital to finance his films, then travels to locations with his crew to record the societies that interest him. The individual films are cut so as to fit comfortably into the commercial exhibition system (indeed, he has received distribution assistance from industry luminaries Francis Ford Coppola and George Lucas). Reggio does not assume that viewing his films will initiate change in any direct fashion, but assumes that the images he presents and the implicit ideology of this imagery will affect at least some viewers' assumptions about the societies depicted. Watkins's central concern in making *The Journey* was to demonstrate an alterna-tive to current media practice. The film was shot by local crews assem-bled in locations around the world, with financing raised locally by production groups. And Watkins's hope—a hope that, thus far, has not come to fruition—was that the unusual nature of his film might instigate an international, activist network of those who had produced *The Jour-*

Su Friedrich and her mother (Lore Friedrich), during the shooting of The Ties That Bind *(1984).*

ney and those who came to see it which would directly address the problems articulated in the film.

There is no point in trying to enumerate the similarities and differences between the filmmakers in all eight pairings. Indeed, none of the summaries I have included does justice either to the many ways in which the pairs of filmmakers critique conventional cinema or to the conceptual fertility of the individual pairings. Additional relationships will be evident in the introductions to the particular interviews, as well as in the interviews themselves. And in any case, my pairings provide only one way of thinking through the work of the filmmakers interviewed. Many other arrangements of the filmmakers could instigate similar discussions.

While the interviews in this volume of *A Critical Cinema,* and indeed in the two volumes together, document a considerable variety of film-making approaches and offer a composite perspective on a substantial period of independent film history, the limitations of the project are, no doubt, obvious. For one thing, my interviewing has been confined to North America and, with the single exception of Michael Snow, to the United States. This is not to say that no other nationalities are represented: Snow, Mekas, Ono, McCall, Mulvey, Trinh, and Watkins are not of American extraction. Nevertheless, nearly all these filmmakers made most of the work we discuss while living in the United States, and many have become citizens or long-time residents. Further, even if one were to accept the idea of an interview project that confined itself to the United States, my failure thus far to interview African-Americans remains problematic.

This general limitation of *A Critical Cinema* is a function of the history of my personal development as a chronicler of independent film history. My choice of interviewees has always been motivated by the difficulty I have had, and that I assume others must also have, understanding particular films and kinds of films, or to be more precise, by a combination of fascination and confusion strong enough to energize me to examine all the work of a given filmmaker in detail. That for a time nearly all the filmmakers whose work challenged me in this way were Americans is, to some extent, a function of the limited opportunities for seeing non-American independent cinema in this country and of my limited access to (and energy for) foreign travel, but it is also a result of the remarkable productivity of American independent filmmakers: as consistent as my interest has been, I am continually embarrassed by the many apparently noteworthy films produced in this country that I've still not had the opportunity to see.

That so many of the filmmakers I have finished interviews with are European-Americans does, of course, reflect issues of race and class—most generally, perhaps, the implicit access or lack of access of various groups to the time, money, and equipment necessary for producing even low-budget films (though, of course, some of the filmmakers I have interviewed were and remain economically marginal). Fortunately, the ethnic diversity of independent filmmaking has expanded in recent decades, as has our awareness of earlier contributions ignored or marginalized. Like many people, I am struggling to develop an increasingly complete sense of what has been, and is, going on. This struggle has had a major impact on the final definition of this general project. My assumption now is that ultimately *A Critical Cinema* will be a three-volume investigation, and that the third volume will complete a passage from the local to the international: "international" meaning multinational *and* intranational. In the modern world, after all, every geographic region is international in the sense that it includes people of a variety of ethnic heritages. Currently, several interviews for Volume 3 are underway, including discussions with John Porter (Canada), William Greaves (U.S.A.: African-American), Yervant Gianikian/Angela Ricci Lucchi (Italy), and Artavazd Peleshyan (Armenian). In the coming years I expect to interview filmmakers of an increasingly broad range of heritages and perspectives.

Of course, no survey of critical filmmaking—especially one produced by a single individual—can ever hope to be "complete." The immensity of this field and its continual expansion in so many directions is what made this project intriguing at the outset and what continues to make it exciting for me. My goals are simple: to share my fascination with some of the many remarkable contributors to critical moviemaking I have had access to, as a means of piquing the interest of filmgoers, film exhibitors, and teachers, especially those who can bring a remarkable body of films to a larger audience, and to provide those who have already developed a serious interest in critical forms of film with a more complete context for this interest.

Robert Breer

Robert Breer is the most accomplished contemporary in a tradition of experimental animation that begins with Emile Cohl and Winsor McCay and includes, among others, Hans Richter, Viking Eggeling, Oskar Fischinger, Len Lye, the Whitney brothers, and Jordan Belson. What distinguishes Breer's work, however, is his decision to use frame-by-frame filmmaking to conduct explorations of the viewer's perceptual and conceptual thresholds. Breer's gift is to be able to do exploratory film work with a wit, a technical dexterity, and a knowledgeability that make his films accessible to a much broader audience than most experimental/ avant-garde filmmakers can attract. During the middle part of his career he was also a sculptor, designing and building elegant (and amusing) "floats" that move very, very slowly along the floor or ground. The largest of these were made for the Pepsi-Cola Pavilion, designed for Expo '70 in Osaka by the Experiments in Art and Technology group. In fact, one of the more fruitful ways of thinking of Breer is to see him as an artist fascinated with making things move and with the ways in which their motion can affect those who perceive it.

Breer's first films—*Form Phases I* (1952), *Form Phases II, III* (1953), *Form Phases IV* (1954)—seem closely related to Richter's *Rhythm 21* and some of Fischinger's work: shapes of colored paper are moved around to create continually changing abstract configurations that intermittently draw the viewer's awareness to the materials and processes used. The films seem to flip back and forth between exercises in two-dimensional design and indices of the three-dimensional materials and processes being used. As he became increasingly interested in film (before beginning to make films he was a painter living in Paris), Breer began to explore a variety of techniques. For *Un Miracle* (1954) he cartooned with paper cutouts to create a tiny satire of Pope Pius XII. In *Image by Images* (1956), *A Man and His Dog Out for Air* (1957), and *Inner and Outer Space* (1960), the focus is the drawn line and Breer's ability to use it to create a continuous metamorphosis of two-dimensional abstract design and three-dimensional illusionism.

To define Breer as an animator, as I have done, is misleading, for beginning with *Recreation* (1956) and *Jamestown Baloos* (1957) he began to explore the impact of radically altering the imagery in successive frames in a manner that has more in common with Peter Kubelka's films and theoretical writings than with any area in the history of animation up to that point. If Breer's earliest films can be seen, in part, as an attempt by a painter to add motion to his work, these films seem an attempt to reveal film's potential in the area of collage. Instead of creating a homogeneous, conventional film space into which our eyes and minds can peer, *Recreation* and *Jamestown Baloos* create retinal collages that our minds subsequently synthesize and/or decipher. In *Eyewash* (1959) and later in *Fist Fight* (1964), Breer used his single-frame procedure to move out of his workspace and into the world in a manner that seems related to the hand-held, single-framing style Jonas Mekas was using by the time he made *Walden* (1968). In many of these films, Breer includes not only drawing and the movements of cutout shapes but imagery borrowed from magazines and objects collected from around the home. One is as likely to see a real pencil as a drawn pencil; in fact, the inclusion of one kind of image of a particular subject is almost sure to be followed by other kinds: a drawn mouse by a real mouse or a wind-up mouse, for example. Of all the films of Breer's middle period, *Fist Fight* seems the most ambitious. Thousands of photographs, drawings, and objects are animated into a fascinating diary of Breer's environment, his background, and his aesthetic repertoire.

By the mid sixties Breer was moving away from collage and back toward abstraction in *66* (1966), *69* (1968), *70* (1970), and *77* (1977). Not only is *69* the most impressive of these (among other things it creates a remarkably subtle palette of shimmering color); its paradoxical structure enacts a procedure which seems basic to much of Breer's work. *69* begins as a rigorously formal work: a series of perspectival geometric shapes move through the image again and again, each time with slight color, texture, and design variations. But as soon as we begin to become familiar with the various shapes and their movements, Breer begins to add details that undercut the hard-edged formalist look and rhythm established in the opening minutes. By the end, *69* seems to have turned, at least in part, into its opposite: the shapes continue to rotate through the frame, but they sometimes "wilt" into flat, two-dimensional, cartoonlike shapes. For Breer, the homogeneity of most film experiences—the seemingly almost automatic tendency for commercial narrative films, as well as for documentary and experimental films, to establish a particular look and procedure and to rigorously maintain it throughout the duration of the presentation—represents a failure of imagination that needs to be filmically challenged.

During the seventies and eighties Breer produced films that bring together many of the procedures explored in earlier work while continually trying out new procedures, new attacks on filmic homogeneity: *Gulls and Buoys* (1972), *Fuji* (1974), *Rubber Cement* (1975), *LMNO* (1978), *TZ* (1978), *Swiss Army Knife with Rats and Pigeons* (1980), *Trial Balloons* (1982), *Bang!* (1987), *A Frog on the Swing* (1988) . . .

I talked with Breer in January and February 1985.

MacDonald: One influence that seems clear in your first films, *Form Phases I* and *Form Phases II* is Emile Cohl.

Breer: I hadn't seen Cohl's films at that point. After I did *A Man and His Dog Out for Air,* Noel Burch, who was also in Paris at that time, asked me if I'd seen Cohl. When I said no, he took me over to the Cinematheque, and we saw Cohl's films there.

MacDonald: The similarity I see is the idea of animation being primarily about metamorphosis, rather than storytelling.

Breer: I did what I've always done. I skipped cinema history and started at the beginning. I used very peculiar techniques because I didn't know how to animate. That I would do what Cohl did makes sense. You know Santayana's line about how, if you don't know something, you're doomed to relive it. I'm still working out things that people worked out years ago. My rationale is to not risk being influenced, but in truth it might just be laziness. I think it makes sense to do research. My old man was in charge of research at an engineering firm. The word was part of his title, and he used the word all the time. But I always associated it with the academy and with institutions and didn't want any part of it. I remember seeing a book, *How to Animate,* put out by Kodak I think. The kind of cartooning it was pushing turned me off so badly that I didn't want to learn *anything* they had to offer. I was afraid it would contaminate me.

MacDonald: In *Form Phases I* you were already doing sophisticated work with figure and ground, and with the way the eye identifies and understands what it sees.

Breer: Oh sure. That comes out of my paintings. *Form Phases I* was a painting before it was a film. I used its composition for the film. I moved the shapes around and had them grow and replace each other. I went from making paintings to animating paintings. For me, that was the whole point of making a film.

I was very involved with the abstract, geometric, post-Cubist ortho-doxy: a painting is an object and its illusions have to acknowledge its surface as a reality. The tricks you use to do that are Cubist tricks: figure/ground reversals, intersections, overlappings. Of course, [Hans] Richter did all this in 1921 in *Rhythm 21.* I guess it's pretty obvious that I'd seen that film by the time I made *Form Phases IV.* I got to know Richter later in New York, but I remember that film having a big impact. I lifted stuff right out of it.

MacDonald: How long had you been painting in Paris before you began to make films?

Breer: I went to Paris in 1949. I started abstract concrete painting in 1950, about six months after I arrived. Until then I had painted every-thing from sad clowns to landscapes. The first film was finished in 1952.

MacDonald: In *Fist Fight* there's an image of a gallery with Mondrian-esque paintings . . .

Breer: Those are mine. That was my gallery, though by that time I wasn't rectilinear the way Mondrian is. The Neoplastic movement with [Victor] Vasarely and [Alberto] Magnelli had happened, and I was aware of their new take on constructivism.

MacDonald: I was going to ask you about Vasarely. There are places in *Form Phases IV* and also in *Image by Images* [1956] and *Motion Pictures* (1956) where one striped design passes over another to create an optical effect that reminds me of Vasarely.

Breer: My earliest paintings in Paris were influenced by early Vasa-rely—not by what got to be called "op art," but by his earlier paint-ings, which were very simple and much less systematic than the later op works. By the time I was making films, I wasn't interested in Vasarely, though maybe there's some residue.

The movement show at Denise René Gallery opened in 1955. And to go along with it, Pontus Hulten was supposed to organize a film show. He's an art historian and until recently was the director of the Beauborg Art Museum in Paris. He did the Machine show at MoMA [The Ma-chine as Seen at the End of the Mechanical Age, 1968]. Pontus got sick, and I picked up the pieces a little bit and helped him. We were drinking buddies in Paris. He was a collaborator on my Pope Pius film [*Un Mira-cle*], and he used my camera to make an abstract film called *X.* He also made *A Day in Town* [1956], a Dada-surrealist film that ends with a fire engine burning. Anyhow, the two of us made a document of Denise

René's movement show. Denise bought a couple rolls of film for us, and we used my camera. Later I did the editing. That show was the first time Vasarely showed those grids that would swing in front of one another. Maybe that was the first gallery show of exclusively kinetic art, although, of course, Denise was preceded in general by the futurists. But after the war, kineticism was one of the things she picked up on. [Jean] Tinguely was incorporated into her gallery after his first show.

On a visit home in 1951–52, I went to an art supply store in downtown Detroit and saw this device—"Slidecraft" I think it was called. You could rent a projector and buy a bunch of frosted three-by-three-inch slides and draw on them. I made sequences and projected them singly onto a screen, and then filmed them off the screen, one at a time. That's how I made *Form Phases I*. Strange way to work, but I didn't know about using an animation stand yet. In some ways though, by seeing my images projected on a screen before they were shot, I could better visualize the end result. I still have a flipbook made up of those slides bolted together in sequence.

MacDonald: Did film grab you right away?

Breer: By the time of *Jamestown Baloos* I was enthusiastic. But at first I was scared of the camera. I had an aversion to photography, partly, I suppose, because of my father's enthusiasm for it. The only big fight I ever had with him was over his taking pictures of me, and of stopping things to take pictures of the family. He came to visit me in Europe, and we'd go to a restaurant, and he'd stand on the next table and take pictures. It was embarrassing. It seemed to me then that he photographed everything before he reacted and could only react *after* he'd developed his pictures. That was counter to my feeling of how life should be experienced. I didn't like the idea of the lens between me and what I was looking at. I wouldn't even wear sunglasses. It's a wonder I ever got into film.

MacDonald: From what you say, I assume that the history of film was not particularly interesting to you. Film simply became a way of doing things with painting that you couldn't do on a still canvas. And the filmmakers whose work seems related to your early films tend to have come to film for the same reason. Fischinger, for example.

Breer: In a way, I suppose that's true, but somebody I always mention as having a powerful influence on me was Jean Vigo, who didn't make animated abstract films. His spirit of free association in *A propos de Nice* [1930], for instance, and the kind of cutting he does there, moved me. And I liked *Zéro de Conduite* [1933], his anarchism, his humor, and his esprit. I could identify with him. I have an aversion to just purely abstract films. That's why I have trouble with Fischinger. I admire him in some ways and find him something of an abomination in others.

I did bring to those early films all these post-Cubist notions of space. Making *Form Phases I,* I realized that whatever moves destroys everything else. You have to counter one movement with another. If you have one thing moving in an otherwise static field, the static field dies. You know the usual opening shot of a conventional film, the helicopter shot of a car going down a highway seen from above—you watch that car. It's a tiny dot on a huge screen, but you're glued to that one thing and everything else is peripheral. Once I was making films, I learned that I couldn't work with the stable kinds of relationships I'd worked with in my painting. I had to rethink things completely. And that's when I went for an all-over active screen and for real hectic films. Then I could play with the agitation itself in dosages, rather than try to think in terms of static compositions in which elements move.

MacDonald: Most of your films are not about particular topics. Was there a specific incident involving Pope Pius XII that caused you to do *Un Miracle?*

Breer: It must have been inspired by something I saw, but I'll be damned if I know what. I had had this vision of doing a film based on *The Metamorphosis,* the Kafka story where the main character changes into an insect. I wasn't interested in illustrating Kafka, but in using the notion of metamorphosis. I had my camera set up in Montparnasse. It was Sunday, I remember, and I was going to shoot film. I walked to the kiosk in Montparnasse and bought a *Paris Match.* In this *Paris Match* there was an essay on Pope Pius XII, with a lot of photographs. My vision was that this film would go from live action into animation or vice versa, and back again. The idea was just as general as that. But after buying the *Paris Match,* I saw the possibility of doing a number on Pope Pius. My anti-Catholicism was pretty fervent in those days. Pius XII was accused of reneging on allowing Jews to escape from Germany and was generally very aloof and removed—pious in the worst sense. So with all these pictures in my hand I went to the studio. I picked up Hulten on the way and talked to him about what I wanted to do. He suggested a way of organizing a little sequence, and I cut the photos out and put the thing together. He helped me conceive narratively, which I don't think I would have done normally. But the sacrilegious part was all mine. Pontus and I had gotten drunk together around that time and I went into the church in Montparnasse to slip goldfish into the holy water. Hulten was the lookout. I got the fish into the basin, but it was shallow, and they went out the other side, and onto the floor. I scooped them up, got them into the plastic bag, and we took off. I remember writing a letter to the pope asking how much it would cost to be excommunicated. That was the mood behind that film. The actual esthetic had to do with transformation. It ended up being the pope juggling his head. It wasn't what I had expected it to be.

MacDonald: While metamorphosis is usually central in your films—we watch the constant shifting of one thing into another—during the early part of your film career it was already taking two different forms, each of which tended to be primary in one film or another. In some cases you worked with generalized shapes: *Form Phases I, II,* and *IV* are examples. In other cases—*Image by Images, Inner and Outer Space,* and *A Man and His Dog Out for Air,* for example—the metamorphosis of the drawn line is the focus.

Breer: Well, the linear ones come from my wanting to be simple, wanting to make a film with a pencil, or in this case, with Flomaster pens. I really got to be an expert with those pens. I called myself a Flo Master. Anyhow, I liked the idea that all I needed to make a film was paper and ink, or pretty close to it. *A Man and His Dog Out for Air* was a popular success, relatively speaking. It wasn't the first time I got noticed, but it had a large audience in New York, including people who wouldn't normally have reacted to avant-garde painting or avant-garde anything else. I thought maybe this was a special way of expressing myself simply, directly, and primitively, that could get a broader audience. And it was agreeable to sit and draw on cards or paper all day long. Those films came more from sitting at a drawing table or a desk, looking out the window, and having a nice time. And later committing it to film.

When I was making the collage films, I was more involved with what I was going to see on the screen at the end, which had more to do with editing and with thinking in terms of that big rectangle up on the wall with people looking at it. I alternated methods. I'd get tired of doing film one way, and the next time I'd do it the other way.

I just had a flash about something you said about metamorphosis. Metamorphosis is just a natural thing. In animation you make each frame, and for something not to be dead on the screen, it has to change. One of my tricks used to be to see if I could trace an image as exactly as possible. I knew it would still vary a little bit and that that variation would give it a sort of breathing presence on the screen. *Breathing* [1963] is an example. In trying to copy, I found I couldn't, and I liked the idea that it was impossible. Whether I tried to hold the images absolutely still or let them fly off in every direction, metamorphosis was what was going to happen anyway.

The tendency for someone who's just starting to animate will be to begin on the left side of the page and move something very laboriously a little bit at a time over to the right side. As you get more sophisticated, you plan ahead so that you know where the thing is going to be on the other side long before it gets there. And instead of starting at point A, maybe you'll start at point O or point L, somewhere in the middle of an action, and work it backward and forward. But if you choose to be simple, naive, direct, open, and follow your nose, your nose will take you places you can't foresee, and that leads to so-called metamorphosis. That's where the spirit of spontaneity comes in. In my films spontaneity is mostly in the beginning stages; then in the editing I contradict my spontaneity by encapsulating these bursts of spontaneity in a structure of some kind. A structure can come either through the editing or the planning; in my case, it usually comes through editing.

MacDonald: You always seem at pains to show figuration and narrative as one of a very large number of possibilities that an animator can work with. We always know that you could do conventional animation if you wanted to.

Breer: One thing about narration is its effect on figure-ground relationship. One common form of narration is to have a surrogate self on the screen that people can identify with. In cartooning it's a cartoon figure. Grotesque as he or she might be, the figure becomes an identity you follow. If that figure is anthropomorphic or animal, it has a face, and that face will dominate, the way an active ingredient in a passive landscape dominates the field. It sets up a constant visual hierarchy that to me is impoverished. I want every square inch of the screen potentially active, alive—the whole damned screen. I don't want any one thing to take over. The problem with narration is that the figures always dominate the ground. In the theater, the actors have their feet planted on the stage, and there's a large space above them. That space is justified because the actors are three-dimensional, living, breathing, sweating human beings who make sound when they move and have real physical presence. It doesn't matter that gravity keeps them all at the bottom of the stage. But when it comes to a flat screen, I don't have to have gravity dominate, and I don't want it to dominate.

Felix the Cat is an interesting case. It was one of the first times cels were used. They drew the background on the cels and the animation on paper—just the reverse of what the cel process was finally used for. So that meant that Felix was on paper *underneath* his background. If he went over to a tree he'd have to go behind the tree. There was no way for him to go in front of the tree because the tree was on a cel on top of him. I think that made for a nice, agreeable tension between the background and the foreground. The foreground (which would normally be the background) fought back against the domination of the figure. And, of course, with Felix the foreground was very busy: everything was animated in those films. That's a case where all eyes were on Felix, but there was a nice playoff between the physical, plastic environment and the narrative of this little creature.

It came naturally to those early cartoonists to see narrative as a skeleton you could hang things on. Nevertheless, there was always anthropomorphism involved. I wanted to play with all those questions, but to avoid falling into them. Sometimes I succeeded, sometimes not. Sometimes I guess I'm showing off my confidence that I can do conventional animation if I want to. But a nicer way to think of it is to see the figurative and narrative elements in my films as establishing norms from which to depart.

MacDonald: Image by Images is the earliest of your films where you use actual photographed images of reality. Your hand appears in that film, and part of a face.

Breer: And the eyeglasses, right. At a flea market one time we walked by a blanket on which this old lady—she must have been a widow—was selling what looked to be parts of her husband. She had his teeth and his glasses and other parts of him out on this blanket. I think that's where that idea came from. It was a way of having a human presence without it taking over.

MacDonald: Why did you begin to use sound? The first four films were silent.

Breer: Well, sound was too big a deal to think about in the first films. But once I saw my films in public, I began to think about it. I had my first one-person show of paintings in Brussels in 1955, right after I got married, at Gallery Aujourd'hui. Opening in Brussels instead of Paris was sort of like opening in New Haven instead of New York. The idea was that I was then going to open at Denise René Gallery, but we had a falling out. Anyhow, I took *Form Phases IV* to Brussels, and Jacques LeDoux (I didn't know him then) arranged a screening of it in the gallery. The public at the gallery seemed indifferent to my paintings, but they reacted to the film. It was the first time I heard laughter, and then applause! As a painter I'd never encountered that. Suddenly there was a tangible, collective reaction. Here was a new ingredient, *sound,* even though it was coming from the audience, and not the film. I had to deal with it.

MacDonald: Do you feel comfortable with sound? For some filmmakers—Kubelka in *Our African Journey* [1966], Len Lye in his direct animations—sound is central to the making of the film.

Breer: For me the most exquisite parts of a film have to do with some kind of plastic event that's silent. Generally I think that sound is padding in a predominantly visual experience, and necessary at times and fine, cathartic. Sometimes I'll use some sound just to announce that there is a sound track, so don't be uneasy, you're not going to have to suffer in silence and be afraid to cough, or whatever. But then once I've established some sound, I'll go into long periods of silence (especially in those earlier films), because looking at the images in silence is very important to visual concentration. I've always been aware of how sound can take away from the image. That's what I hated about Fischinger for a long time: there was never a moment in his films when your eyes could just look. But the problem, of course, is that silence is an illusion. John Cage went into that anechoic room at Bell Telephone, where all sounds are absorbed. He said he could hear his nervous system and his blood flowing, or something like that. Anyhow, I knew I had to deal with sound in some way.

MacDonald: Are you a music lover? The motif structure you often use in the films seems musical.

Breer: Well, if I said I'm a music lover, I'd have to make good on that claim with great erudition. When I painted in Paris, I used to listen to Mozart every morning on the radio. But after a while I found it intolerable. I couldn't listen to organized sound, because it would confuse my signals. I couldn't make useful decisions on color. If I was listening to blues music, I'd have to go blue. When it comes time to make sound for the films, then I concentrate on it.

MacDonald: So you finish the visuals and then look for sounds?

Breer: Always. I feel the visual thing is very fragile and subtle and has to be nurtured and put exactly in place. When it's strong, then you can inflict it with sound. I've always put sound on later, though recently when I cut a film I allow spaces for sound to substitute for events or relate to events. I have the word "bang" in the film I'm working on right now [*Bang!* (1986)]. And obviously that'll call for an asynchronous event of the same kind. When the telephone rings in *TZ*, you hear the voice saying, "Hello," first, and *then* the phone ringing. It always gets a giggle. It's deliberate that the sound-picture relationship is obverse, perverse, and sometimes absolutely synch.

Have you seen *70* recently? I decided to leave it silent, and I had the option of a black sound track or a clear one. For some reason I decided on a clear track, which, it turns out, picks up dirt and glitches, so that if you leave the audio on, there's sound. I show *70* now with instructions to leave the projector sound on. There's a breathing quality to the soundtrack, and it dispels the uncomfortableness of a nonsound film.

MacDonald: Certain films seem pivotal for you. *Jamestown Baloos,* for example, and *Recreation.*

Breer: Well, the only reason *Recreation* isn't pivotal is that I did a film before it which got lost. It was a little loop that looked like *Recreation.* Discovering the possibilities of the collision of single frames was a breakthrough for me. The loop got worn out, and I had to throw it away. I made *Recreation* trying to do the same thing, but longer, so it could be on a reel and be practical to show. *Jamestown Baloos* was more a matter of trying to control what I had discovered.

MacDonald: Recreation was made in France?

Breer: Right. I could tell from feedback at cine clubs that it was pretty outrageous.

MacDonald: Another aspect of *Recreation* and *Jamestown Baloos* that seems new to you is a kind of self-reflexivity about filmmaking.

Breer: I wrote a manifesto during *Jamestown.* I thought I was developing a whole new language (I didn't realize at the time how influenced I'd been by Fernand Leger's *Ballet Méchanique,* [1924]). Anyhow, the manifesto was about painting being fossilized action, whereas film was real action, real kinesis. Rather than a diagram or a plan for change, film *was* change. And that was the exciting new thing about it. At the time, I was thinking of Rauschenberg in particular, who was doing what I thought were essentially post-Schwitters [Kurt Schwitters] combine paintings, not something new. Rauschenberg was being touted, but I felt I was doing *real* collages that had all the Rauschenberg combinations but were also dynamic and rhythmic, a real step forward from Schwitters, who I admired very much.

MacDonald: It's also another step in the development of metamorphosis. When you begin using imagery recognizable from pop culture in a new context, you're changing its meaning and impact. And also, in terms of timing, the viewer's mind is always behind in understanding what's just been presented: in both *Jamestown Baloos* and *Recreation* we're often seeing something new, and at the same time trying to think of the implications (original and new) of what we just saw.

Breer: There's another thing too, that has to do with trajectory, with cutting on motion. If you have something continuing across the screen so that the continuity of the action itself dominates the content of what that thing is, you can change the thing that's moving, from one frame to the next. I've heard that old cartoonists used to play with that as a gag. As a bird would fly across the screen, they'd replace one of the images of the bird with a brick. Because of the motion of the bird, nobody would see the brick. That's an option you don't have in a static picture.

MacDonald: An obvious example is in *Gulls and Buoys,* where the character riding the bicycle changes continually.

Breer: That's me riding the bike, rotoscoped. I change radically each time. Some of this has to do with a psychological phenomenon: the eye oscillates, wiggles, at the rate of twenty-five or thirty times a second. They've discovered that the retina teases an image out of the void by oscillating over perceptual thresholds. In an experiment, a gadget was fixed to the subject's face so that it could read this very fine oscillation of the eye and translate it mechanically to the target image the person was looking at. The image would move every time the eye moved, in other words, remain fixed in relation to the retina. The image consisted of a green rectangle with a red circle inside. As soon as that image got stabilized in terms of the retina, as soon as the retina wasn't oscillating over the surface anymore, the red circle dropped out. The color differentiation was gone. That physiological process goes on all the time. It's interesting that it's almost the same rate as twenty-four frames a second, but maybe that's not related. The important thing is that the thresholds are needed. In order to establish *this,* you have to have *that.* I had a scientist following me around at one point. He got excited by my films because he hadn't thought of the consequences of this kind of rapid change. And *I* never thought about consequences; I just thought about how it looked to compose this way. But in teaching it over time I've picked up on what's going on.

MacDonald: What was Noel Burch's commentary in *Recreation?* I don't know enough French to understand it.

Breer: It's nonsense poetry: the words are puns that refer to the images. I made the film silent, as usual. I showed it that way for a while, but speculated on a soundtrack, and Noel got interested somehow. I don't remember the exact circumstances, but he went off and typed up a text, brought it back to me, and I suggested he record it. In those days I usually used a microphone on the projector: I'd record on the sound strip. In this case, though, I edited the sound so that I could synch the words exactly with the events. After it was recorded, Noel had second thoughts, so I didn't use the soundtrack out of deference to him. Then later, after I moved back here, I asked him about it, and he said he liked the track after all. So I added the sound and a credit, "Text by Noel Burch."

MacDonald: Recreation 2 [1956] seems like an afterthought.

Breer: I never show that film. I should've ditched it. I learned from doing it not to try and do sequels. I was just using up the leftover energy from *Recreation.*

MacDonald: Jamestown Baloos is an antimilitaristic film. In your earlier work you had been into abstraction. Here you're more directly political.

Breer: I have mixed feelings about that. For one thing, there are some figures in *Jamestown Baloos* who are no longer known. Arkansas Governor Orval Faubus walks through with his briefcase and dark glasses. Governor Soapy Williams of Michigan rams his finger up the nose of the horse that a nun is sitting on: the horse lurches and the nun falls off—something like that. They called him "Soapy" because the Williams family had a soap company. I had no particular contention with Soapy Williams. It's just that at the time he was a familiar figure. After I made that film, I realized that a lot of those political allusions were gone, irrelevant. I'd begun with an assumption that is no longer valid: that there's a logical progression from figurative to abstract in the history of art, and that this progression was unidirectional; fine art had to be abstract, and illustration or illusionism—including topical satire—was a step backward or a step down, a slightly lower form of expression. In this hierarchy political film is lower as an art experience than abstract film, because it quickly becomes irrelevant. Abstract art film wasn't subject to aging, and therefore was a higher form that could address itself to all humanity and all situations. Now I see that idea as another chimaera, a delusion. But in *Jamestown* I thought I could escape this supposed truth by having lower and higher forms in the same film: I could combine all levels of experience and all levels of ambition, from low vaudeville to high art, to make an analogy for real life. It was a great rationale for combining all my urges: to cartoon, to allude to my experiences in various degrees of depth and penetration, and to integrate all that stuff into a unit of experience by means of pacing, rhythm, and texture.

MacDonald: I guess I assumed that the more obvious politicalness of it had something to do with your coming back to this country and becoming reimmersed in American political life.

Breer: Well my politics were extremely simplistic. For all of my Marxist artist friends, Marxism didn't really take seriously on me. I had conventional liberal views—I still have them, I guess—which *are* pretty cool on capitalism. I'm very antiauthoritarian, but I've never sorted out my politics, and I'm always embarrassed to put politics up front in a film.

At one time I was hired to do twenty political cartoons for PBL [Public Broadcast Laboratory], when they had their Sunday night prime time series on big issues: birth, death, and so forth. David Brenner was the producer. Two of the cartoons got done: *PBL 2* [1968], the one about racism; and *PBL 3* [1968], about television. I have only a magnetic striped copy of *PBL 3*. The series was promising, but it got axed. The fourth show was going to deal with the Pentagon, and it was going to be a fairly critical, liberal view of the Pentagon. Word came from Washington that all the footage had to be prescreened, and everybody was embarrassed. That, along with the roasting the series got in the public press, ended the project.

I found that those little cartoons came easily, but I also suspected myself. I suspect pieties; I suspect the motivation behind the pieties. So I'm always a little embarrassed and suspicious of myself when I do polemical projects. I've gone South without *PBL 2* just so I wouldn't trade on easy political emotion. A really political person gets off on relationships to large social movements. That's not my thing, and yet I feel that at times the elitism of Pure Art needs to be questioned too, and put in its place.

MacDonald: Jamestown and *Recreation* use a lot of junk art, trash art, assemblage in a way that moves the films in a diaristic direction. We get a sense of your environment. *Eyewash,* which was made right after those films, uses a highly edited, gestural style, with obviously personal imagery, a method exploited so effectively by Stan Brakhage and Jonas Mekas. *Fist Fight* has some of that feeling too, but in *Eyewash* the feeling of you moving *through* an environment seems more powerful.

Breer: Eyewash was the last film I did in Paris. I was back here when I made the soundtrack. I wanted to send it to a festival in Germany that wouldn't accept films without soundtracks. That annoyed me, just as an idea. So I did a soundtrack but kept it separate from the film. I planned to send the two things to them separately, and say, "Here's my fucking soundtrack; play that, *then* show the film," but I never sent it.

The soundtrack is called "Earwash," by the way; it's exactly the same length as the film. This was a case where I thought I'd use a collaborator, get in touch with musique concrète—just a vague idea. I found out about a guy who ran a series of new music events at the YMCA on Ninety-second Street, New Music for Our Time, something like that. It might still be going. Max Polakoff his name was. He was a violinist. I called him explaining that I had a little film and was looking for somebody to do the sound track. He met with me and saw the film and wanted to do it. I don't know, violin didn't seem appropriate to me, but I figured I could edit what he did. We went to [D. A.] Pennebaker's studio and Polakoff improvised on a violin while he looked at the film. I thought, "Oh shit." But he was a good musician and respected in New York, and there was no way I could politely disengage myself. Later, he wanted to show the film at the music series. I hadn't yet heard the mix; we'd just gotten it back from the studio. As things turned out, it'd been overmodulated. It was too loud and sounded like a cat being pulled through a knothole. We didn't hear it until we played it that night for the audience, a full house. Before the presentation Polakoff dragged me onto the stage. I muttered something about keeping the sound separate from the picture because I didn't want the sound to interfere with the movie. Everybody giggled when they heard that, except Max. What I was saying must have seemed aggressive to him. Anyhow, we played the track and it sounded awful; then watched my film, and went on with the rest of the program. The next day newspapers wrote up the event. The music critics didn't give a shit about the film, but really roasted Max. I called to apologize for the lousy reproduction of the sound, but he didn't want to speak to me, and I haven't seen him since. And I haven't used the sound since.

MacDonald: How did you come to do mutoscopes?

One of Breer's mutoscopes.

Breer: When I was back here in America in 1957, I was thinking about buying a mutoscope. Somebody told me to look up this guy on Tenth Avenue who had a big collection of them, along with pinball machines and other penny arcade stuff. I went to see him and got a price on a mutoscope. I think it was twenty-five dollars, which was a lot of money in those days. I had to go home and think about it. When I called him up, he told me that while I'd hesitated, Disney people had bought almost all of them for Disneyland. The price of the few he had left had gone up to seventy-five dollars. I said the hell with it, and decided to make my own.

Shortly after I went back to France, I started making mutoscopes. The first was made out of a cigar box: paper was glued in a cross section of a broomstick with slots in it—probably a hundred images in all. It was restored by Pontus Hulten a while ago: it's become a museum relic. Anyhow, I made a bunch. They were big contraptions, sculpted on the edges so that just sitting there they were interesting as shapes. When you cranked them, the shapes would make for a kind of flowing change. I still have one. The rest fell apart.

When I got back to America, I was interested in having a show of films and objects. I found a vinyl that looked and felt just like paper, but was a lot tougher, so the subsequent mutoscopes were made with vinyl leaves, and I improved the mechanism too. I mass-produced a bunch of boxes and cranks for them, and I showed them [in 1965] at the Bonino Gallery, along with a lot of other kinetic sculpture (an earlier show of the paper mutoscopes had been scheduled in a Paris gallery in the spring of 1958 but never happened). I never made any more mutoscopes after that.

One guy wanted to exploit the mutoscopes as toys. He thought he could peddle them as a do-it-yourself kit for children. He did a patent search on his own and found out that I had come up with a couple of patentable items. I'd made some improvements on the 1898 model. Of course, I didn't have any delusion that I was inventing anything entirely new. I just thought I could explore my ideas about continuity and discontinuity. One of the advantages of the mutoscope was that you could sit there cranking the same cycle over and over and, through subjective changes, you would discover new images, so the piece would seem to be constantly renewing itself. I never thought of the mutoscopes as replacements for cinema. They were a way to get the magic of flip cards out of the flip-book into a contraption that was easier to work with, could be nailed down in an art gallery, and could work in daylight. I also liked that you could stop on a frame and study it. Mutoscopes had certain advantages over just plain film. I also did a few wall pieces that you riffle your hand along, a variation.

MacDonald: How was it, coming back here?

Breer: When I came back in 1960, we had two kids and a house on loan up in Rhode Island, near Jamestown (where we'd stayed a few years before, and I'd made *Jamestown Baloos*). The house wasn't heated, so we could only stay there until the end of October. Then I rented an old farmhouse in Westchester that had rats in the basement, which is where I worked on film. I used to chase them around with a broom. I made *Inner and Outer Space* there and also the Tinguely film [*Homage to Jean Tinguely's Homage to New York,* 1960].

I began to hang out with pop artists. I didn't know many of the independent filmmakers. I had met some in Brussels in 1959, but I didn't connect very strongly with them yet, though Amos [Vogel] must have been throwing us together at his Cinema 16 screenings.

When I got back here originally, I thought I had a connection. In France someone had sent me to Henri Langlois. He was enthusiastic about my films—he and Lotte Reiniger who was there too. Langlois said they were the best experimental films he'd seen since 1928. He wrote a letter to Richard Griffith at MoMA in New York, and sent a reel of my films ahead. A lunch was arranged with me, Griffith, and John Adams, Griffith's assistant; after lunch they went back to the museum to look at the films. Three or four days went by and no word. I went by the museum, and another assistant came out, handed me the films, and said, "Mr. Griffith really prefers Westerns." It was a real cheeky thing to say, and I didn't know whether it was a put down of my films or of Griffith. Then somebody sent me to Margareta Akermark, who was in charge of film circulation at MoMA. She was very skeptical, but she sent me to a woman who ran an educational film distribution company. I can't remember the name. I do remember she went into a frenzy. She couldn't decide whether my films were good or awful, but finally she decided they were awful. She sent me back to Akermark.

I went back with my hat in my hand, and Akermark sent me to Amos. He was the only one who could deal with this kind of film. Amos wanted to drive a hard bargain, sign a contract, exclusive this, can't do that—and didn't promise me much return. But he would show the films, and it's all I had and so it was fine: I went with Amos.

MacDonald: Who else did you meet?

Breer: Brakhage was gone [to Colorado] by then. I met Madeline Tourtelot. She made films in Chicago, including a documentary about Harry Partch (he designed his own musical instruments and composed music for them). I'd met Marie Menken in 1958 in Brussels at the experimental film festival that Jacques LeDoux created, and I'd met Kenneth Anger there too. He was kind of silly and very gay and private. I also met Agnes Varda. And Peter Kubelka. He and I got along; there were similarities in our films—by that time he had done *Adebar* [1957] and *Schwechater* [1958]—that made them different from anybody else's.

MacDonald: Blazes [1961] was the first collage film you made after returning to the United States. It seems a bit more systematic than your earlier collage films.

Breer: Blazes was an attempt to put my money where my mouth was. I'd written a piece on abstract expressionism as being just fossilized evidence that some action had taken place previously and that film could actually give you the action while you were looking at it; you didn't have to look at streaks of dried paint anymore, you could look at streaks of live action. It was a thin argument, but it made me think about what I was doing. I was adding up what I could do with film that painters couldn't do. I wasn't competing with painting; I was legitimizing film. Uniqueness enhances the market value of art, but I didn't want to participate in that way of thinking. I had my democratic idealism to justify working in film—and I didn't even need that: film was just fun. But I also had a romantic bittersweet attitude about the limited commercial possibilities of working my way. The gap between the legitimacy of painting and of film art was so wide that I couldn't help openly challenging it. Anality makes the art world survive: the guy who's anal retentive and wants to have a better art collection than the next guy. You can get anal about paintings, but how can you get anal about film? It's an endless run that you can keep printing and reprinting.

MacDonald: What led to *Pat's Birthday* [1962], the live-action film you made with Claes Oldenburg?

Breer: After I did that film, I seriously debated going into live-action filmmaking. But I didn't think I could deal with production, especially with getting the money. I had four kids. And I didn't want to quit working on film until I had the money. I guess the thing that bothered me most was having to get involved with other people on an artistic level. With Oldenburg there was no problem because we were on the same wavelength.

Actually, before *Pat's Birthday,* I shot a live-action film that became a segment on the first installment of *David Brinkley's Journal.* I had moved into a little house in Palisades that had been owned by this TV producer, Ted Yates. When Maya Deren's Creative Film Foundation awards were announced in the *New York Times,* and he saw my name, he decided to look me up [Breer won the Award of Distinction for *Inner and Outer Space* from the Creative Film Foundation in 1961; in 1957 he had won a Special Citation for *Recreation*]. He looked at some films and signed me up to edit some footage that was part of a gangster film he was doing with Ben Hecht. I forget how that project fizzled, but anyhow, he got himself hired to produce *David Brinkley's Journal,* a spin-off from *The Huntley/Brinkley Report.* I told him about the massive kinetic art show in Stockholm, which had been put together by Pontus Hulten, who at that time was director of the Moderna Museet in Stockholm. I was taking part in that show, and I guess he thought it would be an interesting subject. He hired me as a coproducer. It was a hurry-up job, and suddenly I found myself in Stockholm in the middle of the museum with a five-person crew who didn't speak English—all these people waiting for me to say the fatal words: "Lights, camera, action!" I didn't know how to say them in English, much less in Swedish, but I shot the film—or rather my cameraman shot it on a new Arriflex which, we found out a month later, he couldn't focus. The stuff was developed in New York, and it wasn't until I got back here that I realized that most of this guy's footage couldn't be used. Fortunately, I'd taken my Bolex and shot a lot of footage. That became the backbone of a fifteen-minute *Brinkley Journal* segment. I hired Mimi Arshum, a friend of Sasha Hammid's, and a good editor, because I didn't know what the hell I was doing. She helped me put together a tentative assemblage, which we took to Washington. As soon as Brinkley started watching, he said, "Where's the establishing shot?" I knew I was in trouble. I'd syncopated everything. I even had a pixilated sequence of the king of Sweden arriving at the museum and jerking through the whole exhibit shaking hands rapid fire with all the other dignitaries. Brinkley looked at the whole thing, said some patronizing word to me, and we knew that was that. The assemblage was eventually given over to their editors, over my not quite dead body, and they cut the film. It appeared on television, with a conventional talking-heads interview with Hulten which they'd gone back to Stockholm to shoot. It was my footage, cut along the lines of my assemblage, but without the rhythms. I sat there watching it, cringing, with my parents in Michigan. They were proud: my name was in the credits. I did get paid, but I felt like I'd been raped. When I tried to get the footage later, they wouldn't cough it up. I *was* able to buy that new Bolex, the Rex model. Up until then I'd been using an old non-reflex model that belonged to my father. I shot *Pat's Birthday* with that new camera, and I still have it. At the rate of ten minutes of film a year, I haven't worn it out yet.

After I got my new Bolex, I took to loaning out the old one. One of the first borrowers was Carolee Schneemann. She went away with Jim Tenney for the summer and came back with the footage later used for *Fuses* [1967]. I remember her showing me this film of her and Tenney endlessly fucking, and wanting to know how I felt about it. Finally I realized that they'd had to stop and wash clothes and cook food and do other things in between the fucking, just like the rest of us, and I got over my depression.

Anyway, to get back to *Pat's Birthday:* when I'd gotten to New York, I'd met Oldenburg and other pop artists. We used to go to parties and hang out. I was on the fringe. Then they came to some of my films. I'd been introduced to Oldenburg as a guy who owned a movie camera, and he wanted to employ me (for no pay) to shoot his happenings. This is 1961, 1962. I said nix. I'd just done that film with Tinguely [*Homage to Jean Tinguely's Homage to New York*] and realized, once again, that I didn't like to use my camera as a substitute witness for myself. And I'm not a good live cameraperson anyway. But I went to all the happenings. In the spring when he'd finished them, we talked about making a real film together. I suggested doing it out in my neighborhood in Palisades, in Piermont, where *The Great Train Robbery* [1903] was shot and where Woody Allen shot *The Purple Rose of Cairo* [1985]. Allen turned that little town into a Depression town. The local joke is that he had to upgrade it about ten years to make it look right.

So Oldenburg and I hung out there and talked, and then on our appointed day a week or so later he arrived with Lucas Samaras, and Pat [Oldenburg], and one or two other people. He had a big duffel bag full of props, which he dumped on the floor, and we started from there. We shot for a week or ten days, about three thousand feet. I just followed him around with my camera. The golf scene was my one contribution to the action.

As we were shooting, I'd get the rushes every morning and everybody would show up to see them, which was a big mistake. I didn't know enough to realize that you don't show actors their rushes because when you cut out their best scenes—and I was pretty ruthless about that—they hate you.

I took about six months to edit the film. I agonized over it, though it was also thrilling. I developed an elaborate theory, which I won't bore you with, called "discontinuity," having to do with cutting on the basis of the interior feel of the shot rather than on either the plastic or the rational explanation of the sequence. It was no giant breakthrough, except for me. Also, I cut so as to obfuscate narrative. I did realize that if you're going to cut against narrative, it's got to be a positive thing. When you're disrupting the narrative expectations of the audience, you've got to do it in a way that makes interior sense of some kind. It was a matter of making a structure that had consecutive form, where one thing certainly led to the next, but where the specifics were chosen in ways other than story. You might go from a light frame with a lot of angular action to a lush dark one with rather static images as a matter of counterpoint. In a sense you do build up expectations and you've got to make good on them in the terms you finally set up.

I wrote something about those ideas, saying that time doesn't move forward, that things *are* going, but sideways, obliquely, down, and backward, not necessarily ahead. The sense of motion is the issue. That idea seems hard to defend, because our locomotion drives us forward with our face looking toward new things. But since that movement is toward oblivion, in my philosophy anyhow, it might as well be backward. It's a delusion to think that you're getting anywhere. Of course, there is an accumulation of experience.

When I finished editing *Pat's Birthday,* we opened it at the Charles Theater at midnight, and I took Claes with me. I'd shown *Horse Over Teakettle* [1962] there at midnight a few months before and got a big ovation for it, partly because it was about the atomic bomb and everybody had atomic bombs on the mind. But for some reason the audience for *Pat's Birthday* was antipathetic. In fact, there was some hissing, which I told Claes was the radiators, but he didn't believe me. Since then, it's slowly gathered a little momentum.

MacDonald: The cool, deadpan, arty mood of the action seems very much of that period. The animations seem less dated.

Breer: At the time, there was a sincere feeling that the only valid approach to life's absurdities was to have a certain Zen distance on everything, to be above it. To make it obvious that you *were* above it all, you would set up outrageous situations that you'd go through without batting an eye.

Anyhow, I didn't see much difference between shooting live action and animating, because in both the emphasis was on cutting. For me editing isn't just the perfunctory business of filling out the plan; editing is where I make the crucial decisions that make or break the film. It doesn't matter how good the shooting is if the editing isn't good.

MacDonald: I've always assumed that when you animate, you prepare your cards more or less chronologically and then simply record them.

Breer: Hell no! I don't know what I've got until I start cutting. I don't know how things are going to play off each other. When I'm shooting, I can flip a handful of cards and see five seconds of continuity. But until I get it all shot, I don't know how it's going to work. When I was a painter, the process was very different. I used to lie in bed in the morning (which I do still) and daydream, fantasize a creation of some kind. But as soon as I put my foot on the cold floor and took one step toward the easel, that feeling, that image, whatever, would start to evaporate. Every step toward the easel would kill off part of the dream. At the same time, I learned to discipline myself to replace it with equivalents. Every one of those evaporations would be replaced by some more solid idea that would allow me to unscrew the cap of the paint, squeeze it out onto the pallet, put the brush in it, and hit the canvas. It was a matter of using the original inspiration as a motor, but forgetting about the particulars I'd started out with. It's the same thing with filmmaking, but even more so. There are so many mechanical tasks to perform that the concrete replaces the ephemeral. The inspiration gets you moving, but the concrete is what you get at the end. To pretend that I can write down my dream fantasy in words and then transfer it to film later is unrealistic as far as I'm concerned and would be an unfair imposition on the editing process, which really should be as creative as the other stages.

MacDonald: So how do you shoot? Do you get a general idea and explore it for a while, knowing that later on—much later—you'll make a film with it?

Breer: That's right. Sometimes I've got a strong enough idea to carry me a year. The idea has to be able to accept a lot of definitions, even contradictory definitions, and at the same time survive the attacks I make on it. It might be something as stupid as a particular image or a feeling that the next film will be all crisp and clear. But that's how I work. I'll get a theme for the year and start drawing around it (or I'll start drawing and in the drawing I'll see how I feel that year and what it's going to be like).

MacDonald: Breathing is a tour de force of drawing. It reminds me of Lye's scratched imagery in *Free Radicals* [1958] and of the directly scratched jazz passage in the middle of [Norman] McLaren's *Hen Hop* [1942].

Breer: I was sent a copy of *Hen Hop* in 35mm, and I turned it into a mutoscope as a gift to McLaren for this big tribute they had for him in Canada. I cut up his hen so it hipped more than it hopped.

Breathing is 35mm. I drew the whole thing, and then shot it in 16mm several times, until I got all of the images lined up in their proper order. I didn't want to waste the 35mm time.

MacDonald: Why did you make this particular film in 35mm?

Breer: Because I wanted absolutely the sharpest, best image I could get. I wanted to do *A Man and His Dog Out for Air* better. *Breathing* is kind of a throwback in that sense. I wanted to use high contrast film and the sharpest lens possible and the most stable camera. The drawback with my Bolex windup camera is that the shutter exposures are not consistent; there are slight variations, flicker. Shooting in 35mm gives you just that much more resolution. I wanted a super slick film for very simple drawing. I used soundtrack film, which is absolute black or white, and I rented a 35mm Oxbury for a day, at ten dollars an hour, which seemed like a hundred dollars an hour at the time, from Al Stahl, who had about six of them in a row down at 1600 Broadway. I went in there one morning with boxes of cards and by nighttime I'd shot eight thousand of them. I couldn't stand. I couldn't walk. But when I got the film back, I had to make only one cut. The result was so good that the film was used to focus the projectors at Lincoln Center.

When I started making that film, we were in this little summer house in Rhode Island. I'd rented a barn space. I put a sign on the wall, saying "This film is what it is what it is." In fact I had several of those signs on the walls to keep me on target and not allow me to digress from line drawing into craziness.

MacDonald: At times, it's hard to believe that the imagery isn't rotoscoped.

Breer: I didn't know from rotoscoping. I do remember the exquisite pleasure in taking a flat line and making it come at you. Rudy Burckhardt mentioned to me one time that that was his favorite film of mine, and especially when that elbow shape suddenly comes into 3-D and swings around.

MacDonald: That's the movement that reminded me of *Free Radicals*.

Breer: Lye made *Free Radicals* by laying the strips out on a table and scratching and listening to the music. He didn't have the advantage I had of being able to see consecutive images, so his film really is a tour de

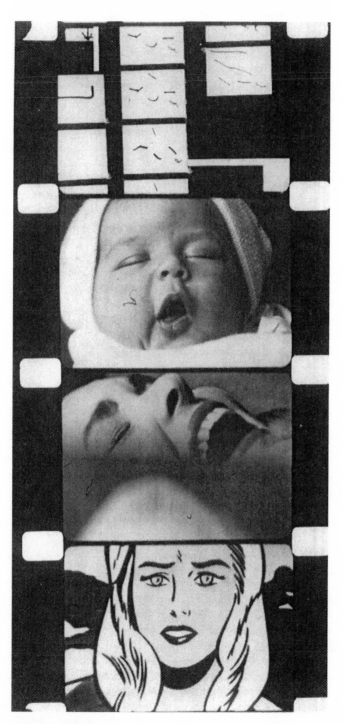

Successive frames from Breer's Fist Fight *(1964).*

force. He was so sure of his continuity that he didn't have to see it, though he must have played it back to himself on a viewer or something.

MacDonald: Fist Fight seems like a personal scrapbook.

Breer: It started out as an openly souvenir film, using family memorabilia. I had seen some of the personal films people had made, and I decided I could deal with my own personal material unsentimentally, that it would be a challenge to use family snapshots and items from my own life and yet to keep the film cold and public—to have it both ways, in other words. Then I got sidetracked by [Karlheinz] Stockhausen. He wanted me to make a film for his theater piece *Originale.* I'd shot and edited most of *Fist Fight* by then. He had a scenario that required a little preface to the film which would consist of snapshots of the people in the theater piece, so I decided I would turn this film into his film. I asked all the participants to send me snapshots of themselves, and that's how the finished film starts, with Stockhausen himself upside down on the screen, then all the people in the performance: Nam June Paik, Charlotte Moorman, Alvin Lucier, David Berman, and Mary Lucier, all in bed together with a blanket pulled up to their chins, Letty Lou Eisenhouer, Max Newhaus, Alan Kaprow, and Olga Klüver. I made a composition out of all those stills, moving them and blowing smoke across them, spinning them around and so forth. That preface stopped the film from being a personal film in terms of content, although snapshots of my brothers and myself appear later.

At the Stockhausen performance, my role called for me to open up the scene with closed-circuit television. I had a video camera, and we had two monitors in the audience. As people came in, I shot them so they could see themselves on the screens. That got the audience involved right away, or at least self-conscious. This was at the Judson Hall across from Carnegie Hall, in a kind of arena theater. Later on, in the middle of the piece (all kinds of things were going on: there was even a chimpanzee in it) I turned on a projector that was hidden in the scaffolding on one side of the set and it threw the image onto a screen on the other side of the set, across all the actors, who by that time were directed to lie down on the floor. Around six minutes into the film (which lasts about eleven minutes) I walked over to the screen with another screen, a hoop, and carried the image back to the projector—put it away in a sense. We did this for five evenings, I think.

Fist Fight is almost twice as long as any film I'd made—because of John Cage. I'd been going to Cage concerts. Cage didn't cater to the public at all. Whatever his program for the evening was, it went on interminably. He didn't seem to have any theatrical sense of time or timing. I found that very refreshing and thought maybe I could apply it to the film. It was one of the few times I deliberately did something that wasn't an aesthetic reaction to the material I was working with. I made an arbitrary, intellectual decision that the film would be twice as long as I thought it should be. I figured that for the first six minutes people would be resisting the onslaught of imagery, but if I kept on going, they'd give in and relax and begin to look at it the way I wanted them to. I think it's a specious bit of theorizing, but that's how the film got to be so long. I thought I could drive it home by dint of overkill.

I'm uneasy when I see the film now, since most people project it at its full length. Kubelka tried to solve the same dilemma by showing his films over and over. Kubelka's obsession is that people have to know everything about his work. It's a little totalitarian to insist that people look at your work over and over, but that's a matter of style. I'd like the same thing, only I wouldn't want to force you into it.

To get the audience to look at films that are proposing different conventions, you first have to disabuse people of their ordinary conventions. Then you have to introduce them to the new conventions. Only then can they see the film the way the artist expressed it. Filmmakers of our ilk have to wait for the public to get educated to the conventions of this kind of filmmaking, but while we wait, our conventions are usurped and absorbed into mainstream cinema. I think most of the pioneer filmmakers of this kind of filmmaking have been fucked. They were pioneers and didn't get to cash in. Some of them are bitter and disappointed.

On the other hand, I think it's fatuous to set yourself up as a pioneer and point at yourself narcissistically and assume everybody's going to congratulate you. It's a self-serving attention-getting process that doesn't guarantee good art. You just look around, see what nobody else has done, and do it. In itself that's not something to be appreciated.

Another Cage idea I picked up on and have used as moral support is that you have to do what you perceive to be the *next* thing. That can get you into the position where you're doing something that nobody's ready for, so that you get dumped on. But it's excusable that way. If it's just an attention-getting process, you deserve oblivion.

MacDonald: I think the problem with setting oneself up as a pioneer is that so much is always going on in so many places. There are precedents for just about everything.

Breer: Absolutely. There's always a context for what you do. Ideas float in the air like the flu, and a lot of people get them at the same time. The reason for doing something new is the simple excitement of getting new life out of an old form. And that's enough of a reason.

When I said that I thought that many film artists have gotten fucked, I was referring to the enormous power of consumerism. Take the use of dense groups of different single frames that I came up with in *Recreation*. I've never claimed any firsts for that, and I became aware of precedents maybe subconsciously before and consciously afterward, in Leger and [Dimitri] Kirsanov, and occasionally in [Dziga] Vertov. I've never made any case for that device in itself. It's basically a gimmick, but if you carry a gimmick as far as I did, it becomes a style of sorts. In the sixties I was watching the Smothers Brothers on TV. On one of their shows they introduced some guy who then proceeded to show the history of art in thirty seconds with a single-frame kaleidoscope of images of paintings. Well, I had done that in *Jamestown Baloos,* specifically with art history and a series of images of landscape paintings. It was just one ingredient of *Jamestown Baloos.* But here was the device on the Smothers Brothers show, with some kind of crappy music to go with it. The whole thing was one big joke, and it made me very unhappy. It wasn't so much an envy/greed reaction. It was that the newness of that feeling had been simultaneously introduced and disposed of, totally thrown out the window and on a grand scale. I could never imagine myself reaching all those people across the country with more serious work using that device, so it was depressing.

Recently a case has been made on our behalf. Birgit and Wilhelm Hein put together a show of so-called pioneering films and special effects for the Berlin Film Festival, to show how these special effects have been absorbed. I haven't seen any program notes, but they asked for *Recreation.* I don't know what the other films are.

MacDonald: Of course, it goes the other way too: a lot of things in avant-garde film were done first by totally anonymous commercial people, who did their work without any long-term recognition either.

Breer: Good point. I went to an advertising agency one time, and they said, "We like your stuff a lot, but our clients are very conservative." The guy there cited the case of Len Lye and his little Chrysler film: Lye was given an award for the best advertising film of the year, by whatever society or committee does that, but the award was withdrawn because Chrysler hadn't accepted the ad, which wasn't broadcast and so wasn't eligible for the prize. Lye was very bitter about it. He thought he deserved that award, and then he had to be contemptuous of it at the same time. Lye had had big audiences at the beginning; his films ran in first-run theaters, and then later he had to become this "elitist," far removed from all that.

MacDonald: On the *Fist Fight* sound track there are voices apparently talking about the Stockhausen performance.

Breer: I took stuff out of the actual performances; you hear the participants. The voice at the end criticizing the film was an English actor.

Stockhausen hadn't been there for the performances, so he hadn't seen the finished film. Later he came out to my house with Mary

Bauermeister (they were married at the time), and he was enthusiastic about the film and claimed to be enthusiastic about the sound track. He said he was inspired to make a new sound track for it by chopping up all of his sound compositions collage-style to fit the film. I was flattered, and we talked a little bit about it, but it never happened. I always wondered whether he just wanted to get rid of that critical voice. He was a famous, impossible egotist, though in spite of that we were friends— although I found him intolerable at times: my own egotism versus his, maybe. At the world's fair in Osaka in 1970 he did the German pavilion. We were staying in the same hotel and ran into each other. I described our Pepsi pavilion, with thirty-seven speakers around our dome, and he said he had forty-seven, or whatever—more. It got to be ludicrous, that kind of jockeying for superiority.

MacDonald: 66 seems a logical film to come after *Fist Fight,* which seems almost its opposite. *Fist Fight* seems to have emptied out a whole collage part of you.

Breer: Exactly. First effulgence, then something dry and astringent. I think that, to survive, an artwork has to have excessive input. You've got to put everything into it each time. You can't ride on past laurels. You've got to start from scratch again and on a tack that'll identify the new thing as clearly different from the old thing, and quite often it is almost the opposite. For *66* I had practically a gimmick: long static shots of slick, crisp imagery, with very short gunbursts of interruption.

I guess you go through stages. First of all, you're worried about your identity as an artist. In a sense you don't know who you are and what you're going to do. After a while you're happy that you've discovered what you can do best and are milking this vein, and then a while after that, you realize you're trapped, and you can't get out no matter how fucking hard you try. I'm in that last stage. But I still try. That's the only thing worth doing. There's no point in repeating myself, so I still try to change. I might use a gimmick to get into another vein, as I did with those three abstract films following *Fist Fight, 66, 69, 70,* and later *77.* In the last few years I've combined things more and more. I no longer do a collage film, then an abstract film, then a collage. These days I might take the middle of an abstract film and turn it into a lyrical landscape film. Who's to say I can't? I'm the boss of my films.

MacDonald: Individual films also reflect this need for change. For a while, *69* is a consistently hard-edged film; then it shifts into something else.

Breer: Do you know the joke about the two explorers who get captured by the natives and tied to trees? The chief tells the first one, "You have two choices: death or ru-ru." The explorer thinks a bit and says, "Well, ru-ru." "Wise decision," says the chief, who unties him. Then the

Successive frames from Breer's 69 (1968).

whole tribe beats him up and abuses him sexually and completely destroys him and throws him down dead in front of the other explorer. The chief asks the second explorer which *he* prefers, death or ru-ru? The second explorer is very shaken up by what he's seen and finally says, "Death." And the chief says, "Very wise decision—death it is—but *first,* a little ru-ru." I love that joke. In my work there's always a little ru-ru.

69 undoes itself. It starts out like a system, then the system breaks down and goes to hell. During the editing I came up with the idea that it should break down, so I shuffled the cards. I thought it served me right to undo my own pretense at formal purity.

MacDonald: When exactly did you shuffle the cards?

Breer: First I shot each sequence several times. I was thinking of serial repetitions and building a texture. But I got bored with that, so I said "What if." I started shuffling the cards and shooting them in random sequences and shuffling more and more.

Also, there were some accidents. This was before dimmers were available and I had a parallel circuit for the lights and a double-throw switch, so I could put them on half-light (Stan Vanderbeek had shown me how to do that). I shot a sequence on the low light by accident, and it was brown and dismal looking, but somewhere during that scene I had turned the lights on for a second and there was a flash of proper lighting embedded within this dark stuff. Instead of dismissing all that material, I took advantage of it in the best tradition of experimental filmmaking. I went back and deliberately shot a lot of stuff at half-light, with a few sprinklings of properly lit imagery.

MacDonald: You're very early in experimenting with flicker effects. They're an element in some of the earliest films, and you come back to flicker often.

Breer: If you question everything, you'll question why you have to eliminate flicker. Flicker is disturbing, but it has an impact, and it doesn't make you have flat feet, or burn your retina. It's just another tool we've overlooked. I question all the time. It started out with my questioning the existence of God when I was a little kid. I read something by Sinclair Lewis when I was twelve or thirteen years old and challenged God to strike me dead. I gave him about fifteen minutes, thinking if he was all that powerful, that'd be plenty of time. And nothing happened, and I went down and told my parents I wasn't going to church anymore. I never had believed in God, but I'd been too scared to announce it. Of course, I had some awful experiences as a little kid at Catholic school, so I already had bad vibes about religion. But I questioned and got away with it.

In film a lot of things have been repressed for so long that they're fresh. I explore the medium for that kind of thing. There's an awful lot

of conformism. That's the natural tendency, just for the sake of conve-
nience and safety. You learn what doesn't kill you; you play it safe. But
when it comes to art, you can do stuff that'll "kill" you. A basic example
of that is the oscillation of light and dark in the projector. Of course, the
modern cinema device was designed to eliminate flicker, but you can
bring it back and play around with it.

MacDonald: During the late sixties you began to make a new kind of
kinetic sculpture—what you call "floats." How do you see them relating
to your film work?

Breer: In my films, I deal with a medium designed for motion and
bring it to a point where things go by so fast that they start standing still:
the interruption of continuity is so great that finally there isn't much, if
any, continuity, and I have what amounts to a static picture where everything is on the brink of flowing into motion but never quite does. With
the floats, it's the same and in another sense the opposite. Sculptures are
"not supposed" to move, but these do, just barely. In each case I'm
challenging the limits of the medium, or confusing the expectations that
one might normally have.

And there's something more to it. Since childhood model airplane
days, I've always had a great satisfaction in putting things together,
pounding nails, sawing wood, sandpapering. My brain had gotten me
into a kind of painting that didn't have a hell of a lot to it past the
conceptual stage. In my geometric paintings I just had to cover vast
areas of canvas: it was like house painting. When I started doing films,
there was a lot more involvement with making things. There was the
camera apparatus itself, and making thousands of images for a film put a
demand on my imagination that doing one painting didn't. Starting to
make sculptures had a workshop satisfaction that filmmaking didn't. It
got me involved in the world of switches, wheels, electricity. It made me
feel good. I could even listen to the radio when I worked. And I got high
on the idea that when I was through with them, these things had their
own autonomy. I didn't think I was Pygmalion, but the idea of making
art objects that were restless was intriguing to me. I was trying to create
a sort of gallery presence with them and didn't want their activities
reduced to anecdotal events, so that people would wait to see what
happened when they bumped into each other. But I did get a certain
pleasure in the unconventional behavior (in any behavior at all!) of
these art objects.

One collector who was being persuaded to buy one of the floats was
very worried. She asked me what would happen if one of them went
across the room and ran into one of her paintings. Bob Rauschenberg,
who did buy a bunch of them, was worried that his dog would take after
them, but his dog never showed any interest at all. There were some

Breer's floats on the move.

junior high kids who used to come to the gallery after school. They'd lie down on the floor of the gallery and wait until the floats would nudge up to them. Those kids understood that the floats were atmospheric, which was the point as far as I'm concerned.

MacDonald: Why did you start working with the rotoscope in *Gulls and Buoys*?

Breer: Gulls and Buoys started in the South of France. We took four kids down to an apartment in a chateau that we rented for eighty dollars a week. I was supposed to be on vacation for once. I had gotten this heavy number about not always working, but I still wanted to. The place was very bare. There was a desk and a desk lamp. The desk had a deep drawer, and I put the lamp in it and made a light table with a piece of broken glass. I bought cards in a little stationary store. I'd buy them out every day—fifty cards. I just started drawing. I outlined my hand, and then I took the key out of the desk and outlined that. I guess from that I got the idea that since I'm outlining the reality anyway, I could do the same thing with a projected image. When I got back to the States, I dug up this footage of gulls I'd shot from the back of a ferry boat, and the footage of swans. It was all good stuff I had shot when I was trying to make a film after I did the NBC thing for Brinkley. I'd gotten a lot of 7252 stock, but I was so ignorant that I couldn't get the lighting right and the stuff looked flat. Of course 7252 stock does look flat in the original. It's only a printing stock. But I was very slow coming to this, and I was so disappointed in the live action material that I abandoned the whole project. Anyhow, I decided I'd use that footage, but that I could draw those gulls better than I'd photographed them. For the rotoscoping I just remade my old Craig viewer. I took the top off it and enlarged the screen to four by six, bought index cards that would fit, and started tracing and cranking through the images one at a time. It was very crude. I couldn't see the gulls sharply at all and realized that it would be silly to pursue it in too much detail. I decided to be sketchy about it and assume that the general movement would show. I could enjoy myself with drawing for a change and not have to worry about the relationships from one image to the next.

Three or four years ago I rotoscoped David Bowie.

MacDonald: How did that happen?

Breer: Pennebaker asked me to do it for that film he made with Bowie in his last incarnation as Ziggy [*Ziggy Stardust and the Spiders from Mars*, 1983]. I did some sample sequences that were sent to Bowie, who liked them, though as things turned out that material was never used. But at one point Bowie decided he wanted to learn animation and wanted me to teach him. Pennebaker sent him a tape of my films and Bowie's ten-year-old son ended up using *Fuji* to teach himself how to animate.

MacDonald: Fuji seems the most conventional narrative you've done. We experience a particular, chronological train ride. Did you shoot the original footage of that trip with this film in mind?

Breer: No. I had a neat little fifty-dollar Super-8 Kodak camera, which I still use. The handle folds up, and you can slip it in your pocket. A no-focus, idiot camera. I shot the footage out the window of the Tokaido Express, a 135-mile-an-hour train. You can't go to an exotic place like Japan and not record your trip to show the folks, so that's what it was, just a mindless bunch of footage out the window, without the possibility of refined focus and with no thought of the future. I didn't dig that film up until three years later when I was fishing around for an excuse to do some more rotoscoping. What attracted me to the footage was the mountain in the background and the possibility for motion perspective in the foreground. The film plays with deep space and the flat picture plane of the screen.

MacDonald: Maybe what makes *Fuji* seem more conventional than the other films is the sound of the train, which is more continual than the sound in many other films, and has a clear, direct relationship with the visuals.

Breer: The sound was put on six months after I finished the film. Actually, I showed *Fuji* in Pittsburgh as a silent film and realized there that maybe it should have some sound. I used all kinds of contraptions in my studio to create the train ride noises. Of course the Tokaido Express doesn't sound anything like my clackity clack, but the soundtrack does evoke "train," and it's the rhythm I thought I needed for that film. One trick that I was real happy with is the interruption of the sound near the end. After using the relentless clackity clack at various paces and pitches, I stopped it right at the climax of the film, or I should say I created the climax of the film with this sudden drop into total silence. Then just at the end the sound creeps back in as a little coda, and we see the person on the train [Frannie Breer] in live action. I withheld the sound in a couple of other places too.

MacDonald: Rubber Cement uses a lot of collage; it seems a return to the sensibility of *Fist Fight* or *Jamestown Baloos.*

Breer: I hadn't thought of that. I do have a tendency to pick up on neglected practices. It's possible that I had become collage starved.

MacDonald: How did your involvement with Xerox in *Rubber Cement* come about?

Breer: I was invited to be a member of a seven-member NYSCA panel that was formed to give artists access to Xerox machines. Part of the privilege of being a panelist consisted of getting an identity card to go into the Xerox Company. They'd just come out with a color machine. I had to share the time with some of the artists we selected: Bob Whitman was one and Steven Antonakis another. Anyhow, I didn't have a lot of time on the machine, but I generated a bunch of images by playing around with frames from some of my old films (*70,* for one). I was hoping that if Xerox looked at my film, they might think I was worthy of a little more indulgence, but I had a negative reaction from their PR people; they weren't even curious to see the film. So when I realized later that I had misspelled the company name in my title tribute, "Thanks to Zerox," I was happy to leave it that way.

MacDonald: 77 is in the mold of *69.* Like the earlier film, it explores color: the early part centers rigorously on primary colors, then at the end there's a dispersal of that control into a crescendo of color.

Breer: I intended to make a black-and-white film, to reduce elements and simplify everything. But DuArt informed me that it would cost more to shoot in black and white than in color. I had always secretly admired the effect of black-and-white images in color film, and this discovery made it easy for me to decide to shoot on color stock. Then I thought, it's a shame not to let the stock see some color once in a while. I had thousands of black-and-white images, and the idea of now adding color to the images had coloring book qualities I didn't think too highly of: the color would have had a passive, ornamental role. My answer was to add color to the film by hand, which I'd done once before, in *Eyewash*. Only this time I decided to hand color the original. What this means in an animated film is that if you screw up and overpaint, you're undoing weeks of work. You can't correct. It was a situation I liked, a challenge to the predictability of my techniques. It heightened the intensity of making the film. It was a way of reversing the usual progression toward greater control and less risk. I hoped some of my excitement would rub off on the whole film. In the same spirit, I spray painted the ending of *LMNO* a year later. I looked at *77* the other day and thought that, while the film does have a mix of extreme control and some out-of-control stuff, there's too much of the former.

MacDonald: LMNO (and *TZ,* too) uses a lot of sexual imagery, more than most of the other films.

Breer: In *LMNO* there are these tiny objects that rain across the screen from top to bottom. Some look like sets of cocks and balls. The others look like upside-down coffee cups. The origin of those is pretty complicated. They were made with rubber stamps sent to me by Claes Oldenburg, one ordinary rubber stamp very carefully divided down the middle. One side had this giant lipstick on it (in the scribble form it looks like cock and balls, which is typical of Oldenburg: he's always dealing in phalluses and so forth); the upside-down coffee cup shape doesn't quite fit as the opposite of his phallus—it's not quite the vagina shape, but it relates. Anyhow, I play with those shapes in *LMNO* and in *Rubber Cement*.

Those rubber stamps were the culmination of a drawing contest Oldenburg and I had during a period when we both were having sculptures made up in a big sculpture factory in Westhaven. Mine was a big float, now in Stockholm, that you can sit on and ride. Every time I'd go up there there'd be a drawing of his lipstick on caterpillar treads; it looked like a tank and was aimed aggressively at a sketch of my coffee cup–shaped "rider float." I had to retaliate with a drawing that had my float getting underneath his sculpture and driving off with it—my point being that my sculpture was motorized and really worked, while his only *looked* like it would move. When I came back the next time, I found a drawing of the two of these things going over a cliff—his point being that while my float was motorized, it didn't know where it was going. At the bottom of the cliff, the lipstick is stuck in the ground and the treads are up in the air. My sculpture was cradled in the treads of his as though on a pedestal of his sculpture, and there was a guy standing there scratching his head, wondering what kind of sculpture *this* was. My reply to that was to have the cliff that they had gone over collapse and create an avalanche that covered both of them completely. He came back and had a helicopter with a magnet fly over and pull them out of the debris. I retaliated with the same helicopter flying too close to the sun: the blades dropped (in another version it was hit by lightning), and the two pieces fell into the ocean and disappeared. His retaliation was to have the ocean turn into the contents of a pop bottle, and the two sculptures became bubbles going to the surface in huge numbers. I didn't know how to answer that. I ended up making vast numbers of little sculptures half his and half mine out of Play-doh. I put them in cotton, in a box, and sent them to him. His answer was the rubber stamp, and of course you send a rubber stamp to an animator and it's going to get into his films. All that time I never saw Oldenburg.

MacDonald: TZ, LMNO, Swiss Army Knife, and *Trial Balloons* seem to be blends of collage and animation with bits of live action. Do you still see each film as a new experience or is the newness now in the particular mixes of techniques you've already explored?

Breer: You didn't use the word "rehash" but that might be your question. New wine in old bottles, or is it old wine and new bottles? I forget. I'm always hoping for a totally new kind of image, but I've been around long enough to know that repeating myself is something I can't help. I don't think you fall into ruts; I think you're born into them, but that every effort to break out is a healthy one and should be nurtured. When I was a kid, I thought style was going to be forever elusive, and that it was something some people had and others didn't. Now I realize that style is something everybody has in spite of themselves. Anyhow, the way I'd put it is that in those films I was looking for a maximum range of technique.

MacDonald: Have you ever thought about making a feature-length animation? That's been the fantasy, and in some cases more than a fantasy, for a number of serious animators.

Breer: To do an animated feature is reminiscent of fakirism, beds of nails, and other activities where you try to extend your normal capacities beyond the ordinary. The idea of filling up twenty-four frames every second for an hour or two hours sounds pretty dreary to me and, unless it was one of these full-blooded collective efforts like the Disney features were (which I'm not interested in anyway because in the long run that sort of collective process usually takes all the corners off the film so that it's no longer very expressive), everything would get stretched thin, and you'd see the stretch marks. At the rate of ten minutes a year, it would take me six years. So, no, I don't have any feature film yearnings, certainly not for films that would look like the shorter films I've made.

MacDonald: What else have you been working on?

Breer: Well, I've been sawing wood and painting window frames for what seems like years. I have six hundred feet of new material I haven't told anybody about; it hasn't congealed into a film and might never. I play with words on the screen and do some rotoscoping—usual techniques, but with a different look maybe. I got interrupted so many times last year in the middle of this film that it might be lost forever. I do have plans to make a new film dealing more with the soundtrack-picture relationship than I have in the past. At least that's my concept now: anything can happen to change my mind. As far as how the future looks: from where I sit it looks compressed. As a little kid, I was told there was a Beyond, but I never got a convincing picture of it. So without a Beyond, I have a kind of trapezoidal vision of eternity. It's like looking at the table I'm sitting at; the table tilts away in perspective, but it's sawed off at the end: it doesn't go to an infinity point. My sense of time compressing does make life a little more savory, though I don't know if it was ever unsavory. Right now I've got a couple of shoe boxes full of index cards and half an urge to go up and fiddle them into a sequence, and I follow my urges pretty much. They don't always take me into doing a film, but I'll return to the euphoria of putting out a work of art because it's a high you can't get any other way that I know of.

Michael Snow

Very few filmmakers have had as powerful an impact on North American independent cinema as Michael Snow. Indeed, five of this volume's interviewees (Ono, McCall, Noren, Benning, and Mulvey) talk specifically about him, as do several of the interviewees in Volume 1. The impact of Snow's work—and of the breakthrough *Wavelength* (1967), in particular—is a function of the fact that Snow came to filmmaking, not with extensive experience as a moviegoer—conventional cinema never seems to have been of particular interest to him—but as an accomplished musician, painter, sculptor, and photographer, for whom the movie camera and projection space were new artistic tools to explore. While it was not his first extended film—that was *New York Eye and Ear Control* (1964)—*Wavelength* established him as a major contributor to the development of critical cinema.

In *Wavelength,* Snow demonstrated a new approach to cinematic space and time, and, at least by implication, declared his independence from the reliance on narrative in both conventional and independent cinema, as well as from the exploration of the personal that was characteristic of so many of the films of the sixties. *Wavelength* defined a new kind of "plot," one closer to the geometric sense of the term than to its conventional meaning in film. Snow divided the focal length of his zoom lens into approximately equal increments and zoomed, at intervals, from the most wide-angle view of a New York City loft space to a close-up of a photograph on the far wall. The relentlessness of the viewer's journey across the loft is wittily confirmed by periodic nods in the direction of conventional narrative: near the beginning of the film, a woman (Amy

Taubin) directs two men who move a bookcase into the space; they leave and the woman reenters with another woman; later, a man (Hollis Frampton) staggers into the loft and falls dead in front of the camera; he is discovered by Amy near the end of the film. This series of events allows *Wavelength* to critique the cinema's traditional reliance on story. While a mysterious death in a film would normally be a lynchpin for melodrama, in *Wavelength* the death is enacted precisely so that it can be ignored during the remainder of the film. Not only does the camera fail to stop for the death, the film overwhelms whatever interest we might have in the fledgling narrative by providing the eye and ear with continued stimulation of a very different order: as we cross the space by means of the periodically adjusted zoom lens, Snow continually changes film stocks, filters, and the camera's aperture, so that the loft becomes a visual phantasmagoria. And after the opening passage during which we hear "Strawberry Fields Forever" ("Living is easy with eyes closed") on Amy's radio, the sound of a sine wave increasingly dominates the soundtrack, ironically building toward the "climax" of our recognition that *this* film relentlessly refuses to conform to the "rules" engendered by the tradition of narrative cinema.

In the years since *Wavelength,* Snow has continued to make films that defy conventional expectations (and he has continued to work in a variety of other media). In film after film, he has explored the capabilities of the camera and the screening space and has emphasized dimensions of the viewer's perceptual and conceptual experience with cinema by systematically articulating the gap between the experience of reality and the various ways in which a film artist can depict it.

In *Back and Forth* [←→] (1969) the pan is the central organizational principle. The continual motion of the camera from right to left to right across the same classroom space (during the body of the film) becomes a grid within which Snow demonstrates the wide range of options panning offers. *One Second in Montreal* (1969) uses a set of still photographs of potential sculpture sites in Montreal as a silent grid within which Snow can focus on the viewer's sense of duration: we see each photograph in a single, continuous shot for a different period of time—at first for longer and longer, then shorter and shorter durations. *Side Seat Paintings Slides Sound Film* (1970) uses the repeated presentation of slides of early Snow paintings, filmed from the side of the auditorium in which they're projected, as a grid within which he can dramatize the "interference" created when artworks in one medium are reproduced in another medium. *La Région Centrale* (1971) extends Snow's interest in the moving camera. A complex machine designed by Snow enabled him to move the camera in any direction and at nearly any speed he could imagine as he filmed the wild, empty terrain north of Montreal: the resulting film immerses the audience for three hours ten minutes in an experience halfway between a landscape film and an amusement park ride. The epic *"Rameau's Nephew" by Diderot (Thanx to Dennis Young) by Wilma Schoen* (1974) uses a set of individual filmic actions to explore as many variations on the concept of synch sound as Snow could imagine. *Presents* (1980) compares different ways of composing film imagery with a moving camera. In *So Is This* (1982) Snow uses a grid of one printed word per shot to develop a fascinating exploration of the distinctions between reading a text and experiencing a movie. *Seated Figures* (1988) is a landscape film made up of repeated tracking shots of landscapes filmed from a camera looking vertically down from a position a few inches from the ground. And in *See You Later/Au Revoir* (1990) extreme slow motion transforms Snow's standing up and walking out of an office into a gorgeous motion study. Together, Snow's films provide one of avant-garde film's most elaborate critiques of cinematic convention. They are an inventive and productive artist's revenge on film habit.

While Snow remains known primarily as a filmmaker in the United States, he has continued to demonstrate that he is, above all, an *artist* for whom the cinematic apparatus is one of many sets of tools with which art can be made. Even during his most prolific years as a film-maker (1964–1974), Snow maintained his interest and productivity in other media, and in intersections between media. The confrontation of audience expectations and assumptions so important in *Wavelength* and other films remains central in *The Audience* (1989), a set of sculptures commissioned by Toronto's new Skydome stadium: the individual char-acters in the two groupings of representational figures (baseball fans) confront the patrons entering the arena in a variety of provocative ways.

I spoke with Snow in Montreal twice, in early June 1989 and in late May 1990. The two sessions were combined into a single discussion.

MacDonald: I want to start with *The Audience.* My guess is that people who know you solely or primarily as an avant-garde filmmaker will say the Skydome gargoyles are something new for you. I can even imagine somebody saying, "Oh, another formalist filmmaker selling out." And yet, on many levels, the gargoyles are in keeping with work you've done all along. From very early in your career, you've been drawn to the public arena and to the idea of confronting expectations. A central premise of the "Walking Woman" paintings, sculptures, and

Gargoyles in Snow's sculpture, The Audience *(1989), gesture down at those entering Toronto's Skydome Stadium.*

mixed media pieces was that they were located all over New York (and later other places), so that people—mostly people who hadn't planned on looking at or thinking about art—would be running into them. And, of course, film is a public arena, too. Your early films were powerful interruptions of what audiences had come to expect—even from what was then called "underground film." They remind me of the old gesture in Hollywood films of slapping people across the face to bring them out of a daze. When Pat [Pat O'Connor, MacDonald's wife] and I were driving in on the expressway the other day, our eyes were immediately drawn to the gargoyles (this is before I realized that the new work you had mentioned on the phone wasn't a film). Out of the whole panorama of the Toronto skyline we were noticing these funny things hanging out of the Skydome. Everything else is rectangles and planes, so this interruption in the city's geometry can't be ignored. Even at a considerable distance, the gargoyles confront the spectator. So, for me, this new piece seems very closely related to your early work.

Snow: I think that's really true. The big departure in the new piece for some people, at least people who know my sculpture and gallery work, is that it's figurative. I haven't done that before, except with *The Walking Woman,* but *The Walking Woman* had a whole other kind of premise. In 1953 I did a painting called *Colin Curd about to Play.* It was one of my first big oil paintings. Colin Curd was a flute player I had met. The painting shows this person and a group of people, faces. It's rather Paul Klee-ish. The focus of the painting is the relationship between the audience and the artist or the audience and the work.

There's also some early sculpture, which people would generally call abstract, that includes the spectators. There's *Scope* [1967], which was originally shown in New York in the late sixties. Actually, it's one of a series of sculptures I've continued. They're framers and directors of the spectator's attention. *Scope* is kind of a giant periscope on its side, an illusory straight ahead, made by a couple of right angles. If you look in one end, you see this tunnel and—if someone else is looking into the other end—another person at the end of the tunnel. There's also *De La,* a video installation work (owned by the National Gallery of Canada) which uses the apparatus I made to film *La Région Centrale.* The spectators are part of the image.

Another connection—though I didn't think about it at the time—is in *Seated Figures,* the film I made during the same period when I was working on the Skydome piece: the sound is the sound of an audience. The connection is obvious now, but when I made the soundtrack for the film, I was just trying to figure out what kind of sound was going to do the best job in connection with the imagery. So, yes, the Skydome piece is in some ways a continuation of my earlier work.

MacDonald: What originally drew you to film?

Snow: Confusion. I decided to go to art school from high school because I was given the art prize, which surprised me. I knew I was sort of interested in art, but I was still trying to figure out what to do, so I went to the Ontario College of Art to study design. I started to paint, more or less on my own. A teacher, John Martin, the head of that department, was very, very helpful (he's dead now). He suggested what books to read and made comments on my work. He was fantastic. He suggested that I put a couple of paintings in a juried show, put on by a group called the Ontario Society of Artists. This was a big group show that happened every year, for members and other people. I was still a student, but my two paintings got accepted. It was a big deal because a student had never been in the show. It was very encouraging.

I had already started to play music. During high school I had met a bunch of ne'er-do-wells and started to play jazz. It was a fantastic part of my life. At school I had been rebelling (mildly) against everything. But when I found music, I really found something. I started to play a lot, and a band formed, and by the time I went to O.C.A., I was playing occasional jobs. So I was simultaneously getting into music and into painting and sculpture, mostly painting. I was influenced by a lot of people: Matisse, Mondrian, Picasso, Klee. I liked Klee very much.

When I got out of O.C.A., I found a job in an advertising firm that did catalogues and stuff like that. And I was miserable and really terrible at the job. I made stupid mistakes. I thought, "Is this life on the other side of school?" So I saved what money I could and quit the job and went to Europe to find myself. I was miserable. Fortunately, I went with Bob Hackborn, who had been at O.C.A. with me. He was a drummer; we had played in some of the same bands. And some other musicians I knew at the time also went to Europe. I ran into some jobs with them, though not just with them: I played with the band at the Club Méditerranée (now known as Club Med), which had started just two or three years before. An amazing band. The guys were from French colonies or former French colonies like Guadalupe and Martinique—black guys studying dentistry in Paris. They were looking for a trumpet player and a drummer, and we were in Paris trying to figure out how to live on two hundred dollars for a year . . .

MacDonald: Two hundred dollars?

Snow: That's about what I had.

I had started to play trumpet about three months before I went (I played piano before that) and knew a couple of tunes. Anyway, we did an audition. I played "Lady Be Good," one of the few tunes I knew, and these guys really liked it. So I got this job and went from Paris to Italy, where the Club Méditerranée had a place on the coast of Tuscany and another on the island of Elba. We were paid our board and drink tickets. They'd give us a book of tickets, so we were plastered every night.

I also traveled around during the year; I went to all the museums and churches. And I did thousands of drawings and some paintings, including *Colin Curd about to Play.* It's quite a big painting, at least for then, and for the circumstances.

When I came back, somehow or other, I was asked to exhibit some of the drawings I had made while I was away, along with Graham Koftree, another artist who had also been in Europe and was a friend of mine—at Hart House, a University of Toronto gallery. When the show was on, I got a call from a guy who said, "I'd be interested to meet you. When I saw your work, I thought that whoever did those drawings was very interested in film." In fact, I wasn't. I didn't know what he was talking about! I went to meet him and it was George Dunning, who later directed the Beatles film *Yellow Submarine* [1968]. He said, "Do you want a job?" I didn't know what the hell to do with my life. I told him frankly that I had no special interest in film, but I certainly would be interested to try and do something. He and some other people who had been at the National Film Board had just started a film company called Graphic Films, and he was hiring people whose main interest or training was so-called fine art. So I took the job.

I met Joyce Wieland there and we eventually married.

MacDonald: Had you been a film-goer as a kid?

Snow: No, not especially. That was a very strange observation on Dunning's part. In those drawings there is some inadvertent interest in movement. They're not futurist or cubist, but sometimes they include different positions of arms, of objects. Well anyway, he liked the work and saw something he thought could be applicable to film.

Graphic Films was the first company in Canada, or one of the first, to do television commercials. They were animated. Everybody, except for the cameraman, Warren Collins, was learning how to do the work. And it's hard! It was my introduction to film.

MacDonald: Your first film, *A to Z* [1956], is an animation.

Snow: It had nothing to do with the work. It was just that the camera was available and Warren Collins was willing to help me shoot. Some of the other people working there also made their own films: that's when Joyce got started.

Then Graphic Films collapsed. I had been playing music all along, occasionally with a guy named Mike White. He put a band together, and all of a sudden we got a hell of a lot of work. We were playing at the Westover every night for a year; this is 1961–62. The band became quite popular, and the Westover brought in a lot of Dixieland stars. I was playing with the former Ellingtonians, Cootie Williams and Rex Stewart; and Buck Clayton, a really great trumpet player; Pee Wee Russell, a genius of a clarinetist. It was a fabulous job. We played in a lot of other places in Toronto, and sometimes in other parts of Ontario. And we made some records. I also started to play with my own groups occasionally because I had started to get interested in what were called "more modern" directions. I played Thelonious Monk pieces, stuff like that. And some of the musicians I met with the Mike White band asked me to play with them. I played with Jimmy Rushing, the great blues singer, in Detroit and a couple of places in New York State. There's a Film Board film, *Toronto Jazz* [1963], by Don Owen, that I appear in with my quartet (it's called the Alf Jones Quartet in the film, can't remember why—Alf was the trombone player).

It was a beautiful time for me. The music was wonderful and lots was happening. I was able to get to my studio every day to do painting and sculpture. During 1959 I had done a series of abstract paintings that I'm quite proud of. In them I gradually did this flip into working with the outline of a figure. *The Walking Woman* started in 1961.

MacDonald: Are those abstract paintings the ones in *Side Seat Paintings Slides Sound Film*?

Snow: Some that I did in Europe are in that film and some of the abstract ones. But I hope you wouldn't make any judgment of the paintings from their appearance in that film!

MacDonald: Things were going so well here. What drew you to New York?

Snow: Well, I had been following what was going on in New York very closely. For a long time, I had been moved (and still am) by the accomplishments of Willem De Kooning, Mark Rothko, Barnett Newman, Arshile Gorky, and Franz Kline. That's fantastic work, and I was carrying on my own dialogue with it, trying to define what *I* could do, what *I* could contribute, and after a while it seemed that doing this via magazines and occasional trips to the Albright Knox (in Buffalo) or to New York was not enough. I decided I should just get there. I was scared shitless, and Joyce was even more scared—so we went.

All during this period I kept thinking that in order to get somewhere and get something out of myself, I should make a choice. It seemed like the lesson was that Willem De Kooning *paints* and that's why it's so good. That's what he does; he does just that. And there's really a lot in that argument. So I tried not to play when I first went to New York. Mind you, I didn't know how I was going to make a living. It turned out that I did play a couple of times to make a couple of bucks, but basically, I was trying to get rid of music, to make it a hobby.

But when I got to New York, I had something I hadn't counted on, a contact with the most inventive music that was going on at that time, the "free musicians." I already knew about Ornette Coleman and Cecil Taylor. I had their records. But I met a guy named Roswell Rudd, a great trombone player, through a Dixieland clarinetist named Kenny Divern, another fabulous musician. I had a studio with a piano in it that I made available. There was no place for them to play, and the public antipathy was incredible. Cecil was considered a total nut. It certainly seemed that way the first time you heard him, but he was, and is, amazing.

Anyway, music wouldn't go away. But I was trying to be a painter. I was working on *The Walking Woman,* which, as you said earlier, involved works of many kinds in many places. A lot of it was what I call lost works: making things that were outside, in public spaces—on subways, in the street, in bookstores . . . it had a lot of range, despite the fact that it was concerned with this single outline.

The main thing I was trying to do was concentrate on visual art and get a gallery. I watched everything that was going on and gradually met people. That's when I met Hollis Frampton. I first noticed him at openings at Green Gallery. He was very noticeable! And he was at every opening. Gradually, I started talking to him, and at first I only knew that he was a photographer who was interested in art. I guess when I first met him he hadn't made any films.

MacDonald: When did you meet him?

Snow's Walking Woman out for a stroll.

Snow: Probably 1963, 1964. I went to New York in 1963.

MacDonald: In *The Walking Woman Works* you were putting the same figure in place after place, in serial fashion, which has a good deal in common with film. Were you conscious of that connection at the time?

Snow: Well, in the work itself there was a lot of sequential stuff. There are several pieces that are, say, four or five variations of the same figure. And, yeah, I did think there was something filmic about it. And then in 1964 I made *New York Eye and Ear Control.* I had had the idea for that film in Toronto.

When I first went to New York, I met Ben Park, who worked for one of the television stations I think, though he also produced films in a small way, I guess. I told him my ideas for *New York Eye and Ear Control,* and he said that he'd finance it. So we shot quite a bit of stuff, including a sequence of Marcel Duchamp and Joyce walking across the street, seen through a mask cutout of the Walking Woman. Anyway, Park finally decided against going ahead with the project and kept what I had shot. There wasn't too much enmity there, the film just stopped. Later on, I decided to try to do it myself.

MacDonald: New York Eye and Ear Control combines your fascination with music and *The Walking Woman Works.* It's as if you were learning how to work with film as a means of getting this other work down, but then, when you were done with that film, you were ready to be involved with film at a level comparable to what you'd achieved in music, painting, and sculpture.

Snow: Yeah, although *New York Eye and Ear Control* was interesting in itself. As far as I know, I invented the idea of putting art works—parts of *The Walking Woman Works*—out in the world, and then documenting the results in another work. The photographic piece, *Four to Five* [1962], was the very first time I did this, and the film expanded the idea. The business of making a work by documenting some action that you take hadn't happened yet, as far as I know, and I'm kind of proud of the priority of it. On one hand, *New York Eye and Ear Control* was another transformation of *The Walking Woman,* but I was also trying to work with the possibilities of the medium, especially with duration.

One of the things I wanted to do in the film was to bring two aspects of myself together. I used to refer to it as a classical side and a romantic side, or Apollonian and Dionysian. At the time, I felt I was rather schizophrenic. At any rate, the imagery is measured and calm, but beside it is this expressionist, romantic music. Most of the action is in the sound.

I already felt objections to the general use of sound in films, especially to the way music is subordinated to image. Even the greatest work of the greatest artist, J. S. Bach, is often used to set up a certain attitude in commercial films, and I've hated that for years. I wanted to do something where the music could *survive* and not only be support for the image. I think I accomplished that in *New York Eye and Ear Control.*

MacDonald: Was *New York Eye and Ear Control* shown a lot? At what point did you become part of the New York underground film scene?

Snow: Before Joyce and I got to New York, Bob Cowan was already there. He's from Toronto. In fact, he went to the high school I went to, Upper Canada College. And when Joyce and I went to New York on visits, we would see him occasionally. Sometimes we'd drive all night, and we'd park outside his place in Brooklyn and have a nap, then wake him up at eight o'clock. We used to get stoned and start driving, it was very nice. One time I drove all the way from Toronto to New York whistling Charlie Parker and Thelonious Monk tunes. But anyway, on one of these visits Bob said, "There's two friends of mine coming over with a film they just made. Do you want to see it?" And it was George and Mike Kuchar. They were nineteen. They had just made *A Town Called Tempest* [1963].

MacDonald: A wonderful film!

Snow: Their accents knocked us out. Anyway, we set up this little 8mm projector and showed the film. And Joyce and I were amazed. It was really, really inspiring. After that—it might have been through Bob—we discovered the Cinematheque screenings. When we were in Toronto, we didn't know there was a genre called "experimental film." We had seen Norman McLaren's films and not much else. When we were making our own films, we didn't feel like they were part of a big development. Anyway, we started to go to the Cinematheque and to meet people. Ken Jacobs was one of the first. And he was fabulous in those days, really an amazing man.

I was still saying to myself, "You should stop this and just do that, or you're just gonna be a dilettante all your life." I had thought that going to New York would clarify that. In fact, it didn't. I just kept on multiplying my interests.

MacDonald: You and Joyce were beginning to make films at the same time, and in one instance [*Dripping Water,* 1969] you did collaborate. Was there a reason why you didn't collaborate more often?

Snow: Our work was always independent. We discussed, and looked at work, and helped each other, but we never thought about doing things together. She had her own direction. She was affected by the Kuchar experience in a way that I wasn't. Their work was close to her sensibility in a lot of ways. I was very affected by *A Town Called Tempest* and their other films because I liked the freedom of it and the fact that George and Mike just went ahead and *did* it. It's wonderful, but it wasn't my kind of thing. I think it really opened up things for Joyce. She didn't imitate them, but she had a kinship with their work. I don't know whether you've seen any of her 8mm films, but they're really terrific. I don't know what's happened to them. She was going to get some blown up, but I don't know whether she ever did. When I was starting the first attempt at *Eye and Ear Control,* she was already shooting in 8mm.

MacDonald: Where does *Short Shave* [1965] fit into all this?

Snow: I did it before *Wavelength,* and after *Eye and Ear Control.*

MacDonald: It's a nice film.

Snow: You like it? I think you know I said in the Co-op Catalogue that it was my worst film. I saw it recently and I think it's good, too. I had worked with the Walking Woman concept from 1961 to 1967. I still had ideas for it, but I decided that it had to stop. And making that film, shaving that beard off, was part of trying to make the change. Actually, I had a big commission, the first I ever had—for Expo '67 in Montreal. And I decided that would be a nice way to end *The Walking Woman Works.* The Expo '67 piece grew out of the dispersed things that I'd done before, but this was more monumental, in stainless steel. There were eleven parts scattered all over the Expo area. They fit together, perhaps, in your memory; they couldn't all be seen together. So anyway, that was the last of *The Walking Woman Works,* except for her bow-out in *Wave-*

length, which was shot in the same year: 1966. I finished it in January 1967.

MacDonald: Her appearance in *Wavelength* reminds me of Koko the Clown's appearances in some early Betty Boop cartoons: he's a star in the silent Fleischer Brothers' animations, but in the early Betty Boop sound cartoons, he becomes a bit player and moves into the background.

Wavelength has become a crucial film in people's writing about the history of avant-garde work. And yet, by the time you made it, you'd done a lot of work of a lot of different kinds, much of which is related to it. When you were making *Wavelength,* did it seem to you that it was pivotal, or was it just another of many comparable moments in your work?

Snow: It was very important to me. I spent a year thinking about it and making notes before I started shooting. I've always oscillated between an incredible lack of confidence and conceit. I was going through a stage where, as usual, I was trying to clarify myself and get rid of some of what I had been doing before. I was trying to make something that would benefit from what I'd done, but to work *in time* in a new way. What came to be *Wavelength* did feel like some sort of do-or-die thing. That's the kind of mood I was in. I wanted to prove something to myself. *Wavelength* was an attempt to concentrate a lot of stuff in one piece. I had come to feel that some of *The Walking Woman Works* had stretched. Individual works were strong, but others were just part of the series: if you didn't see the series, they didn't have strength in themselves. I wanted *Wavelength* to be very strong.

I don't know where the money came from because those years were pretty poor. But everybody else involved in the film scene, which was really tiny then, was scraping together a couple of cents to do a film. So I felt I could do it, too.

MacDonald: The idea of concentrating is interesting because a lot of the earlier work disperses outward. *Wavelength* is literally a narrowing in.

Snow: Precisely. You start with a wide field and move into this specific point.

MacDonald: How much did you envision the film in terms of its impact on an audience?

Snow: At that time, I didn't think there was an audience other than at the Cinematheque. When *Wavelength* was finished, I had a little private screening, which I thought might be the *only* screening. There's a nice photograph of the people who were there.

MacDonald: Who was there?

Snow: Richard Foreman and Amy Taubin, who were married then; Jonas [Mekas], Shirley Clarke, Bob Cowan, Nam June Paik, Ken and Flo Jacobs, a few others.

The loft in Snow's Wavelength *(1967). By permission of the Museum of Modern Art Film Stills Archive.*

MacDonald: What was their reaction?

Snow: They thought it was good!

MacDonald: It's still a remarkable film. And it still works as an effective subversion of conventional film expectations. If I want to make my students furious, *Wavelength* is the perfect film. The duration of *Wavelength* has been much talked about. What kind of thinking did you do about how long *Wavelength* would be, and how you would control the duration? It's a long film for that period, particularly given the fact that no one had much money.

Snow: Well, it's hard to post facto these things. I knew I wanted to expand something—a zoom—that normally happens fast, and to allow myself or the spectator to be sort of inside it for a long period. You'd get to know this device which normally just gets you from one space to another. I started to think about so-called film vocabulary before I made *Wavelength*—with *Eye and Ear Control.* You know, what *are* all these devices and how can you get to *see* them, instead of just using them? So that was part of it.

And the other thing is that a lot of the work that I was doing, including the music, had to do with variations within systems. One of the pieces of classical music which I've always liked (I got one of Wanda Landowska's records of it in 1950) is J. S. Bach's *Goldberg Variations,* which is a statement of theme, followed by a number of variations (I'm oversimplifying). That was the basis of a lot of my work, like *The Walking Woman*. I wanted to make this film a unified unfolding of a number of variations with the zoom as the container for the variations. The process had to have a certain length of time. It could be fifty minutes and it could be thirty minutes—maybe thirty would be too short—but that's how I thought about it. I did want to make a temporal place "to stay in," as you've properly put it.

I'd noticed something like this happening in another way, in *Eye and Ear Control*. Sometimes when the music is at its most passionate or frenetic, there's a feeling of being in a space that's made by the continuity of the music and the picture. Other people might not feel this, but it gave me my first taste of a kind of temporal control I was able to elaborate in *Wavelength*.

MacDonald: Another thing that's very important in *Wavelength* is the way it deals with narrative. It sets up its direction, and what would be considered the conventional narrative moves in and out from the edges. Hollis Frampton comes in and falls dead and the camera just continues on its way. One is tempted to say, "There's no plot," and yet there *is* a "plot," in a number of senses, including the mathematical: you plot straight ahead on an axis toward the far side of the loft. At any rate, *Wavelength* comments on conventional narrative, especially on mystery and suspense.

Snow: Yeah, but you know, I had no background in that at all. I just wanted to set up a temporal container of different kinds of events. In the sections where you don't see anybody in the space, it becomes much more a two-dimensional picture. When it's peopled, it's a whole other thing. And the memory of the space seen one way affects our other views of it. The space and duration of the film allow for all kinds and classes of events. There is a life-and-death story, but on another level, the whole thing is sexual. And there are a lot of other considerations, like making a reference outside with the phone, having something come in from outside through the radio. There are all these different symbolic implications of the room. It can be the head, with the windows as eyes, and the senses feeding into the consciousness . . .

MacDonald: Or a camera with the windows as apertures . . .

Snow: All those things. I was aware of a lot of them, and there are things I can see now that I didn't know about then, that's for sure. But a lot of it *was* conscious. A lot of the color effects weren't preconceived because I didn't know what the hell I was doing. Actually, Ken Jacobs was very, very helpful. He lent me the camera and he gave me some old rolls of stock. I used this stuff and didn't know what it would look like.

MacDonald: Over the years, the perception of *Wavelength* has changed. When I interviewed Anthony McCall, he mentioned that he was profoundly influenced by written descriptions of *Wavelength* when he made *Line Describing a Cone* [1973]. When he finally saw *Wavelength,* he discovered it was completely different from what had influenced him, and that he had developed a relationship to something that actually didn't exist.

Snow: In your mind, the shape of the zoom is the same as the shape of a projector beam. I was thinking about that at the time, too. All the imagery issues from still photographs, frames that are amplified in one direction, while the zoom narrows your view in the opposite direction. Maybe that's part of what he was thinking of.

MacDonald: What surprised him is that the zoom wasn't consistent, smooth, and even. In fact, *Wavelength* is a very rough film in many ways.

Snow: The zoom was hand done. The imagery was shot out of order. Originally I thought I might make the film without editing. Later, I realized I'd need to edit. I shot reel three and that had to be at a particular place on the lens, which I'd marked out. Then I shot reel one, then reel five. And I moved the zoom lens by hand, so it's very uneven. And I really like that a lot. There are cuts in the film, too, to get from reel to reel, and sometimes there's editing where I took something out. It's not a continuous zoom by any means. There's a lot of nuance to the fact that it was hand done, not in the tactile sense of, say, Brakhage's films, but as a nice by-product of the process.

MacDonald: There's a surprise at the end where viewers discover they're not going toward the photograph of the Walking Woman.

Snow: Well, there are a couple of mistakes at the end of *Wavelength,* because I had to move the camera. Almost all of the film was shot from a platform. I put the camera up high because I figured that would provide a certain kind of view. But then to finish the zoom I had to move the camera down. I wanted to move it on the same horizontal line, but I made a mistake: it's a little off. This is toward the end where you've got the photographs sort of in the middle and an equal amount of space around them. Every time I see it, I think, Jesus, that's *bad* [laughter]. Sometimes I think it's good.

MacDonald: Well, it's what it *is,* now.

Snow: [Laughter] It certainly is.

MacDonald: I'm always struck by the textural dimension of *Wavelength,* by the variation in grain. In fact, there's so much to look at in the film that I'm amazed when it's called a minimal film.

Snow: Oh, I don't understand that at all. Every time I read that, I'm amazed—though it hasn't happened all that often. It's also described as a "conceptual" piece, sometimes. Certainly a lot of thinking went into it and I hope it provokes thinking, but that it's sometimes identified with the art style called "conceptual" seems peculiar, too.

MacDonald: You were friends with Taubin and Frampton at the time when you made *Wavelength.* Was there a reason beyond just knowing them and their being available that they show up in the film? Was Frampton's appearance related to his being a particular kind of artist?

Snow: No. They were friends and we had talked about what I was doing. I knew that Amy had acted, and I wanted an actress. She'd been in *The Prime of Miss Jean Brodie,* a popular Broadway play. Hollis volunteered. I was going around saying, "I want somebody to die for me," and he said, "Oh, *I'll* do that."

MacDonald: When you first showed it to this small group of friends, they liked it very much. How was it received when it was first shown to a larger New York audience?

Snow: It wasn't shown in New York at first. You know what happened? When Jonas saw it, he said, "You know, you should send *Wavelength* to this festival coming up in Knokke-Le-Zoute [Belgium, 1967]." But I didn't have enough money to finish the film: when I first showed it, the sound was on tape. I had decided I wanted to have the sine wave sound, the glissando, on reel-to-reel tape: it was better sound. But then I realized that was impractical, and if I wanted to show the film again I'd have to have an optical track. Anyway, Jonas—wonderful Jonas!—found the money to make this new print and he sent it to Knokke-Le-Zoute and it won first prize, and all these things happened as a result.

MacDonald: Was *Standard Time* [1967] done as a sketch for *Back and Forth* [←→]? In some ways they're very different, and yet when one sees them in succession, the question is almost inevitable since both center on the panning camera.

Snow: Well, no, because I didn't really know that *Back and Forth* was ever going to exist. *Standard Time* was exploratory. I wanted to find out about circular pans on a fixed base and about what happens at different speeds. And when the film was finished, I got the idea for *Back and Forth.* I decided I wanted to work with back-and-forth and up-and-down pans of a limited angle.

MacDonald: Standard Time has a diaristic element.

Snow: Yes. It's my home movie in the sense that that was where we were living—123 Chambers Street—and Joyce is in it.

MacDonald: I assume *Back and Forth* was scored but that part of it was exploratory.

Snow: Yes, that's right. Before I started shooting, I worked out the speeds with a metronome. I knew it would start with a medium tempo and slow down. And I guess that's the slowest point, actually. Then it would gradually speed up to its fastest and then cut to the vertical pans and finally slow down. I made these two sides to the tripod, so that when I panned, I couldn't go further than a certain point, which would define the arc I wanted. I tried making a little machine with a display motor, but it was uncontrollable, so I did it by hand.

My use of that space was similar to my use of the space in *Wavelength*: there's a difference in the space when there are people in it and when it's empty. Before shooting, I had set up places where certain kinds of things would happen, and I wanted them all to relate to the idea of back and forthness, or reciprocity, or exchange.

MacDonald: More fully than in *Wavelength,* every action that happens in front of the camera seems to be specifically referential to the process of the back-and-forth panning.

Snow: That's right. It's more integrated into one set of issues than *Wavelength.* I did *Back and Forth* during the summer of 1968. A number of artists were invited to Fairleigh Dickinson University in New Jersey over a period of a month. I decided to shoot it there in a classroom that had the interesting situation of being right on the street, so that would allow the imagery to be inside and outside, another kind of back and forth. *Back and Forth* was also shot out of order, depending on who was available when.

MacDonald: Both films start slowly and build to a kind of climactic fast motion, and then calm down during a denouement. This is particularly evident in *Back and Forth.* In fact, after the credits there's a passage of "reminiscence" about earlier moments in the film. Was that a conscious play on conventional narrative?

Snow: Well, no, though, as you say, the shape *is* climactic. *Wavelength* literally "cums" at the end: the last thing you see is liquid. I was and am interested in sex and so I suppose maybe that's the source of the shape, at least in those two films, though that's not the only way to think of that shape. As I told you, I really have no background in the development of narrative film and have never had any particular interest. I'm not consciously trying to subvert the movies. The structure you mention is just one way of moving in time, as far as I'm concerned.

The main problem with narrative in film is that when you become emotionally involved, it becomes difficult to see the picture as picture. Of course, the laughing and crying and suspense can be a positive element, but it's oddly nonvisual and gradually destroys your capacity to see. There's really no narrative in *Back and Forth.* There are isolated incidents that are called for partly by the kind of space you see, but no narrative connection between them.

MacDonald: One Second in Montreal followed *Back and Forth.* Whereas *Wavelength* and *Back and Forth* have often been called minimal, *One Second in Montreal* really is minimal: you subtract out almost everything except duration itself.

Snow: I have been influenced by reductive work—maybe that's not the right word. I like Mondrian a lot. And I like Donald Judd's first work. In fact, I had a piece from his first show.

In *One Second in Montreal* I wanted to concentrate again, and I was interested to see what it would be like to live through a film that, as purely as possible, had to do with duration. I didn't want what I put on the screen to be too interesting, which is a funny situation. I wanted each image to be different—otherwise there would be no measurement. But they couldn't be *too* different because I didn't want to have any peaks or checkerboarding of interest: I wanted the viewer to be aware of the time passing, of how long the shot was there. I finally decided on these bad offset-printing images I'd gotten years earlier for a competition to put sculpture in parks in Montreal. I'd put them away because I liked them, though I didn't know *what* I liked about them.

MacDonald: On a certain level they continue the idea in *Back and Forth* of making the figurative action that happens in front of the camera refer to the process of the film itself. The viewer is looking at spaces that are there because they're empty of what they're trying to draw into them. They're places where sculptures *could be,* just as the photographic imagery in your film is where action or event would be, were there any.

Snow: I suppose that's true, though you wouldn't know that from the film itself. They're just these bleak photographs of parks and public spaces. It is Montreal, but you don't need to know that either.

I think the film worked very well. And I think that people do recognize after a while what it's about. Yvonne Rainer told me one time that she got very, very fidgety as the shots got longer and longer, and was really mad. And then, when they started to go fast and the film ended, she was really mad that it ended. She wanted more. I'm happy that the film could do that. It's an interesting range of response that's *not* produced by an imitation of real life as in narrative film.

MacDonald: There was a period during the early seventies when there was some acceptance of the idea that film is a temporal space within which you can meditate. This film has that dimension.

Snow: Also the silence is interesting. It's a silence that I don't think I've ever felt before in films. Sometimes silence is beautiful, and everybody's concentrating. That happens with some of Stan Brakhage's films. In this film the silence is almost meditational, partly because the snow-blanketed scenes have a mute quality. The imagery affects your feeling about the silence.

MacDonald: It's a pun, too, in that we're sitting in the audience "frozen" within this experience. In that way, *One Second in Montreal* prefigures *Seated Figures.*

Snow: I just remembered that originally I had the idea to mark the cuts with sound. I didn't, but I used that idea later in *Presents.*

MacDonald: Dripping Water is another reductive, "minimal" film, though it's more complex, more subtle than it first appears. It seems to be one shot long, but if you're watching and listening carefully, you realize that it's not a single shot. A drop of water sometimes doesn't make it to the sink, for instance. And a multilayered space is created outside the frame by the soundtrack.

Snow: I made the tape first as music. I just happened to notice this drip, and started to listen to it. And it's really fantastic. So I made a tape just to listen to that sound amplified. The original tape was longer than the film. Mike Sahl, wonderful guy, a composer who at that time did a new music program on WBAI, played the entire tape on the radio. That dripping sound on the radio: fabulous! Joyce had the idea that maybe we should make a film of it.

MacDonald: There's an irony in the fact that *Dripping Water* announces that it's a collaboration of two filmmakers, and yet there's precious little to collaborate on.

Snow: We just set the camera up together; and I guess we put the dish into the sink together [laughter].

MacDonald: Side Seat Paintings Slides Sound Film has grown on me. It's a quirky film, but very interesting. If I remember the photographic piece *Glares* [1973] correctly, *Side Seat Paintings* has in common with it the idea that the process of recording something inevitably creates interference, which everybody normally labors to avoid, or at pretending it can be avoided. In *Side Seat Paintings* the many levels of interference, of distortion, become the primary subject of the work.

Snow: That's certainly true. I think you could say that representations are all abstractions from some original given, whether they're photographic or verbal or whatever. *Side Seat Paintings* is a Chinese box, one abstraction within another, within another . . . until you get a new form. I've always tried to make the recognition of exactly what's happening part of the experience of seeing a film. In this case, the projection of the slides of the paintings becomes the film, and I think it really *is* transformed into a film.

MacDonald: Of the films, *Back and Forth* seems the furthest from the other arts that have fascinated you. *Eye and Ear Control* combines music, painting, sculpture, photography *in* film. *Wavelength* has a musical element and, at the end, references to photography and *The Walking Woman.* By *Back and Forth,* you're really into film at a very intense level with, at most, vestiges of music on the soundtrack. Then with *One*

Second in Montreal, you move back toward photography and with *Side Seat Paintings* you combine photography (in the slides) and painting and sound in a kind of artist's autobiography.

Snow: Yes. It's not exactly autobiographical, since you can't really see the paintings. It's really a redigesting or a recycling of earlier work. But it is true that other kinds of work come and go during various periods.

MacDonald: I think of *Side Seat Paintings* as autobiographical in the sense that, as a *visual* artist, you were first a painter, then a photographer, then a filmmaker. In the film, the paintings are recorded in the slides, which are recorded in the film. Did you and Hollis ever talk about the similarities between that film and *nostalgia* [1971]?

Snow: Well, actually *nostalgia* is more similar to *A Casing Shelved* [1970], a slide and tape piece, my only 35mm "film." It's a slide of bookshelves I had in my studio, loaded with all kinds of stuff. And the sound is a voice, my voice, discussing what's on the shelves from various points of view: what it is or what it was and where it came from. The bookshelf has many small things on it and the text is written to move your eyes around on this big image. There's a plan in the text that moves you over the whole space of the image, and through time, because some of the things and events referred to are recent and some are older. Some are art related and some are related to my so-called private life. But it is very autobiographical. And it's similar to what Hollis did in *nostalgia,* although there's no destruction involved.

MacDonald: What strikes me as similar in *nostalgia* and *Side Seat Paintings* is that both are look-backs at the past, and in both the earlier work is "destroyed." In yours the destruction isn't literal [actually, it isn't in *nostalgia* either, since only *prints* are being burned and since they're exhibited in the film before the burning "destroys" them], but because of the processes of recording those paintings have gone through, there's no way to know what they actually looked like: what we know is that we *can't* see exactly what they were.

Snow: That's interesting. And in both films, the works discussed are two-dimensional surfaces.

MacDonald: There's been a tendency, at least among some people I talk to, to think of you as an old-fashioned guy who has a problem accepting women and women's independence and that this problem is embedded in *Presents.*

Snow: Well, I am an old guy, but I've never had any problem accepting women's independence. In fact, I was very much interested in women's independence before this current wave of feminism. I was always very supportive of Joyce in her work. Everybody should have the possibility of going as far as they can with whatever they do. It's not an

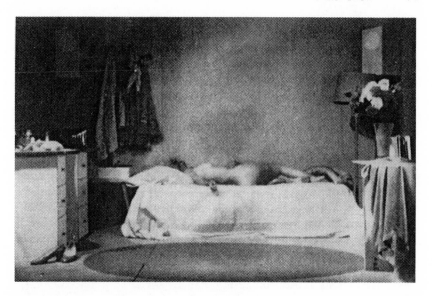

Nude in opening section of Snow's Presents *(1980).*

issue for me. However, exactly how "independent" anyone can be is a question we'd better not try to get into now.

MacDonald: I suppose it surfaced in the case of *Presents* because the film came out at a time when everyone was talking about the eroticized female body as the subject of the male gaze. This film seemed to rebel against that concern: it focuses in on a naked woman's body at the beginning, and then in the third long section where you jump from one shot to the next, naked women's bodies are used often. Were you addressing that issue or . . .

Snow: Yes, I guess I was. It was probably the first time I'd done something specifically as a means of entering a current dialogue. The way you said "rebel against that concern" is interesting. It reminds me of that horrifying phrase "politically correct." Is having *some* differences of opinion with *some* feminist/social theory "rebelling"? Is the "concern" so defined that it can't be discussed, only approved?

Looking for "what does this mean?" first and not experiencing what is happening in its sensual complexity is a terribly wasteful, ass-backwards way of experiencing my films or any other work of art. I have never made a work to convey *a* meaning. I work with areas of meaning and know that there are as many meanings as there are viewers. What is *there* in the concrete, phenomenological sense is of first importance. You seem to see all my other films, except this one, that way and I appreciate your observations. The problems here seem to be as much yours as the film's.

On one level I was asking the spectator to consider the relationship between separate, or seemingly separate, parts of this one film to each other, and in that light to consider the relation between the two parts of the human species. After the opening where the image, which is electronically shaped, focuses on the nude woman, there's a section that's totally staged: there's a fixed camera and the set moves. The longer, third section is the opposite of the first two in terms of what is done to make the image.

The first image sequence is made by shaping, molding, manipulating the entire frame. In the second, what was photographed was staged, constructed, the way a play or most narrative fiction films are made. The camera is fixed on a tripod and what one first reads as a series of side-to-side trucking shots is soon revealed as the opposite: the entire set is being moved. This sequence is audibly directed by the director. Then the camera dollies into the set, destroying it and knocking down a wall, which starts the third and longest section: a montage of images taken from life that's quasi-documentary and diaristic. It's important that I shot all these images: the surgery, May Day in Poland, the Arctic hunt, et cetera. All the shots are hand-held panning shots, the movement of the camera always being derived from an aspect of the scene: following a line, moving with, or against a motion . . .

I wanted to make a dialogue between these systems. Aspects of the film are male: it's made by a heterosexual man. Some of this is conscious, for *this* film, and some of it's inevitable. Aspects of the film have to do with experiencing the inherent nature of the camera, and then, seeing with the camera within the different systems used in the film, which includes man seeing women with the camera. It so happens that I do occasionally lust and while I didn't try to shoot only that way, I do *see* women. I noticed in working on the film that women's magazines always have women on the cover, which is very interesting. There are a lot of photographs of women's magazines in the film. There's some so-called pornography. And there's some intimately personal stuff.

These images involve my sexual life as an artist in some respects, but they're interwoven with many, many other things that are all thematically announced in the first section. For example, the room is pink and the film gradually develops into a discourse on red: the symbolism of red, which, at least in the West, has to do with "stop" and red-light district, blood, sugar, passion—all those things and, of course, communism too. That's all in there. It demonstrates the multiplicity of readings there can be for any word or image.

The word "presents" has incredibly varied meanings and uses, including the use in zoological literature that females *present* to males. Biology is as important to the film as psychoanalysis. Entertainment advertising says So and So Presents Such and Such. I like that my title is an abstraction of this. It doesn't say who presents what, it says that "Presents" will be the subject of this film, so "presentation," then "re-presentation," is invoked. A mostly feminine use is: "is so and so presentable?" But of course the film is also "presents" or "nows," and also "gifts."

Interwoven with all *that* is this business about how things are made. There are three different ways of making things. You can shape something, squeeze material into a certain form. Or you can add this to that. Or you can subtract this from that. And those are the *only* ways you can make anything. The film is involved with those options, and with a latent aspect of them, which is the unfortunate truth that in order to make something, you have to destroy something else, or at least change its form. And that crisscrosses with the sexual themes in some ways, but again, it doesn't attribute any one way of making to one gender or the other. So much is interwoven in the film in so many ways that it's almost the opposite of *Wavelength*. *Presents'* references get wider and wider. It closes with the fading out of the red and a drum roll, which is either military or funereal, the death of the film.

MacDonald: I understand that *Presents* had some hostile audiences, at least at first.

Snow: One of the worst was at the Collective in New York, where some women were furious in a way I found really obtuse. One question was, "How come there's so much tits and ass in this film?" I was tempted to say, "I can tell from your voice that you are the possessor of tits and ass." The assumption seemed to be that tits and ass *can't be seen.* It was brought up that you *can't* photograph so-called pornography—for *any* purpose. That's amazing. I don't necessarily have anything against so-called pornography. I'm aware that there are aspects of it that are extremely questionable—involving children and cruelty for example—but I like, sometimes, some of what's called "pornography." I say "so-called pornography" because that's always a question, too. What do you mean by "pornography"? You mean it's what doesn't turn you on? Or what does? Another amazing question that night was, belligerently, from a male voice, "How come there's no men's asses in this film?" I thought the discussion at the Collective didn't have much to do with the film.

It's true that *Presents* was prompted by the debate about eroticism and the depiction of women that was going on. I had been thinking about those issues for quite a while.

I think it was at that Milwaukee conference [Cinema Histories/ Cinema Practices II, held at the University of Wisconsin, Milwaukee, November 1982] that, after the screening of *Presents,* Christian Metz asked, with a certain amount of puzzlement, "What is the relationship between the two parts?" What *I* want that film to do is to force the spectator to *think* about the relationship between the two parts. All I could say to him was, "The relationship between the two parts is a splice." How *do* they relate? How are they part of the same organism? The point is that there are *a lot* of answers.

MacDonald: So Is This has been very useful for me—especially in thinking about the relationship of film experience and film criticism. Film criticism is almost always considered to be a *written* text about a *visual* experience. But there's an inevitable gap between what writing can communicate and the multi-dimensional experience of film. It strikes me that a lot of what passes for complexity in writing about film is interference that results from the inability of the word to really come to grips with the visual/auditory experience of film. *So Is This* is about these issues; it turns film onto language in the way that language is normally turned loose on film.

Early in the film you pay homage to independent filmmakers who have used text in inventive ways: Marcel Duchamp, Hollis Frampton, Su Friedrich. . . . Had you been thinking about working with text for a long time or did the recent spate of this kind of work inspire you?

Snow: I wrote the original part of that text around 1975 and made the film almost ten years later. It came out of the text for the Chatham Square album [*Michael Snow: Musics for Piano, Whistling, Microphone and Tape Recorder,* Chatham Square, 1975] and out of *One Second in Montreal,* as another way of controlling duration. Since then, I've been asked whether I knew Jenny Holzer's work, but I didn't at that time. The things she's done have some relationship, although there's no timing involved in her work, as far as I can tell.

MacDonald: So Is This is poetic justice for people who make a fetish of the ability to write and read sentences. Is that what you had in mind?

Snow: That's part of it, yes. Another thing is the business of using the art object, in this case film, as a pretext for arguments that the writer considers of more interest. That's valid in some senses, but sometimes it seems like a misuse of the stimuli, the film. It's as if you're producing these things for other people to advance their own interests and arguments.

MacDonald: The way in which text is used in *So Is This* makes a comment on language-based approaches to film. The formal design of showing one word at a time with the same margins, regardless of the size of the word, results in the little words being large, which of course grammatically they often are in the language, and the big words being much smaller. This is precisely the opposite of what a lot of academic writing does. At academic conferences, using complex vocabulary often becomes a performance. *So Is This* seems to critique that kind of linguistic performance with a different kind of performance.

Snow: It does, yes.

MacDonald: There's sometimes a tendency in academe to see film-makers as laboratory animals who don't really know what they're doing, but whose doings can be explained by theorists. Have you read much theory?

Snow: I've read lots of Michel Foucault, Roland Barthes, Jean-François Lyotard, Jacques Derrida, Gilles Deleuze, Jean Baudrillard. Some of those people have become deified. I think Derrida is one of the most interesting.

Barthes's writing is unctuous. He seems often to be defining a new category of the object under observation, but when you start to examine what he says, you find that it isn't as essential as the revelatory tone of the writing suggests it is. And some of the ideas are really ludicrous. "The Death of the Author" [in Barthes, *Image-Music-Text* (New York: Hill and Wang, 1977, translated by Stephen Heath)] is this essay written by a very distinctive stylist, with a name, and *he* says that the individual writer is subsumed in the totality of writing, that there really is no writer. It's an arch little essay by a famous author! A lot of "theory" is like that. And in Barthes's *A Lover's Discourse,* the supposedly revolutionary tack is that there's no reference to gender. It's sex with no body. The book becomes this vapor of extraordinary style, perfume. *Mythologies* is interesting, but pretty strange, too.

There's a fashionable idea now, especially among academic theorists, that the person—or the subject, as they say these days—is totally cultur-ally shaped. I don't believe that at all. I think somebody is born, that there is an organism that has functions. It can be twisted; it can be hurt; but there's still a specific person there. Every person is born with a certain complicated set of possibilities. Of course, there's a lot of breadth to that, but I don't believe that culture totally shapes the per-son. Individual people also shape culture, which is, after all, one of the functions of art. Those who have commented on the way in which domi-nant ideologies totally shape people often seem to assume *they've* been able to escape that process. Very mysterious!

Philosophy has been very important to me: Plato, Aristotle, Nietz-sche, [Maurice] Merleau-Ponty, many many commentaries like Have-lock's *Preface to Plato.* One of my favorite books is Heidegger's *Early Greek Thinking.* I've read everything by Wittgenstein, I think. Derrida is very interesting, a kind of Hegel/Mallarmé. Lacan is medieval Chris-tian Zen. Laura Mulvey seems a university student in this context. Years ago I read a lot of Paul Valery and was quite affected by his writing, though sometimes he's arch in a way similar to Barthes.

My feminist reading is fairly wide. I've even read books by Andrea Dworkin! Joyce Carol Oates is terrific, Germaine Greer too. I like

Fernand Braudel, Norbert Elias, George Steiner. I'm reading Mandelbrot on fractals and Jack Chambers's *Milestones* (on Miles Davis) right now. I read *October* and *Critical Inquiry* and other journals, and various art and film magazines. I've thought of my film work as a kind of philosophy.

Jonas Mekas

Jonas Mekas has made substantial contributions to film history as an organizer, as an editor and writer, and as a filmmaker. The driving force behind the New American Cinema Group, Mekas sought to change the film society model of noncommercial exhibition and distribution epitomized (in the United States) by Amos Vogel's Cinema 16. In place of what he called the "potpourri" approach to programming standard at Cinema 16 (on any given program, Vogel might present an experimental animation, a scientific documentary, a cartoon, a psychodrama—all by different filmmakers), Mekas established the single film-artist show, first at New American Cinema Group presentations, and later at the New York Cinematheque and Anthology Film Archives, which under his leadership became and has remained a leading institution devoted to the maintenance of the heritage of independent cinema. In place of Cinema 16's selective distribution policy (Vogel decided which films by an independent filmmaker he would distribute), Mekas promoted the cooperative distribution system in which filmmakers decide which of their films to distribute and receive all rentals minus the basic expenses of keeping the cooperative afloat. The result was the New York Filmmakers' Cooperative.

Mekas's commitment to making a cultural space for avant-garde film also energized his editorship of *Film Culture,* which published several issues a year, beginning in 1955 and continuing into the seventies (in more recent years, the journal has appeared irregularly). *Film Culture* remains a remarkable compendium of information and commentary about many forms of cinema. Mekas may have had his broadest influence as a polemicist for independent cinema in "Movie Journal," the weekly column he wrote for *The Village Voice* from 1959 to 1971 (selected columns are available in *Movie Journal* (New York: Collier, 1972) and subsequently for *The Soho Weekly News*. No writer has written with more passionate insight about avant-garde film.

Mekas's dogged labors on behalf of independent cinema would have assured him a place in film history, had he never made a film of his own, but in fact he has been a prolific and influential filmmaker. At first, filmmaking was Mekas's primary means of dealing with his status as a refugee in the United States. Mekas and his brother Adolfas had fled Lithuania in 1944, as the Nazis took over (their pro-Lithuanian newspaper had made them a potential danger to Nazi control). They spent eight months in a German forced labor camp; then, after the war, four years in displaced persons camp (the experiences of these years were chronicled in regular diary entries, available now in *I Had Nowhere to Go* (New York: Black Thistle Press, 1991).

In 1949, the Mekas brothers arrived in New York, found a tiny apartment in Brooklyn and bought a 16mm camera. During the fifties Jonas Mekas documented the Brooklyn community of displaced Lithuanians at their meetings and on their outings. Later, when he had broken away from that community and moved to Manhattan, he chronicled the film and art scene he discovered there. In 1960, he completed the angst-ridden experimental feature narrative, *Guns of the Trees*. In 1963, hoping it would be the first installment of an alternative film "periodical," he recorded aspects of the New York art scene for *Film Magazine of the Arts*. And in 1964, he critiqued cinéma-vérité style by documenting the Living Theater's off-off-Broadway production of *The Brig* as though it were a real event.

By the end of the sixties, Mekas had developed an erratic, hand-held filmmaking style and a sense of imagery roughly analogous to the poetry he had written in Lithuania (Mekas remains a well-known literary figure in his native land), and he had completed *Walden* (1968), the first of a series of films called, for a time, *Diaries, Notes & Sketches*. *Walden* is an epic chronicle of Mekas's personal experiences, of the daily life and seasonal cycle of New York City, and of the cultural scene as Mekas observed it from 1964 to 1968, including portraits and evocations of Tony Conrad, P. Adams Sitney, Stan Brakhage, Carl Theodor Dreyer, Timothy Leary, Marie Menken, Gregory Markopoulos, Allen Ginsberg, Andy Warhol, the Velvet Underground, Ken Jacobs, John Lennon, Yoko Ono, and many others. And it announces what had become Mekas's credo: "I make home movies—therefore I live. I live—therefore I make home movies." For Mekas, "Walden" is a state of mind open to the inevitability of natural process, regardless of where or how one experiences it. The film is "dedicated to LUMIÈRE," dramatizing Mekas's rejection of conventional theatrical narrative and its highly determined rhetoric, in favor of what he perceived as a return to cinematic basics and origins.

Since 1968, Mekas has completed a series of films that articulate the style and approach of *Walden*. *Reminiscences of a Journey to Lithuania* (1972) chronicles his first visit to Lithuania since 1944, framing his dramatic reunion with family with imagery shot soon after he arrived in the United States, and—after a "parenthesis" during which he and Adolfas visit the site of the forced labor camp near Hamburg—with then-recent imagery of his new "art-family," Peter Kubelka, Annette Michelson, Ken and Flo Jacobs. Mekas's loss of a homeland and his subsequent discovery of an "aesthetic homeland" where he could again live creatively within a community is also the theme of *Lost Lost Lost* (1975, two hours, fifty-eight minutes). The beautiful opening reels focus on the early years in the United States, particularly Mekas's involvement with the displaced Lithuanian community in Brooklyn. The middle pair of reels recall the first, lonely years in Manhattan; and the final two reels document his discovery of a world of friends and fellow artists who ultimately allow him to emerge, reborn, as a personal filmmaker and "warrior" for film art: in the final reel Mekas, Ken and Flo Jacobs, and Tony Conrad invade the Flaherty Film Seminar in Vermont on behalf of the New American Cinema.

In Between (1978) presents imagery and sound recorded from 1964 to 1968, but not included in *Walden*. *Notes for Jerome* (1978) recounts Mekas's visits with filmmaker/friend Jerome Hill (*Albert Schweitzer* [1957], *Film Portrait* [1970]), whose inheritance has been a major source of support for Anthology Film Archives and other organizations devoted to independent film. *Paradise Not Yet Lost* (*a/k/a Oona's Third Year*) (1979) focuses on 1977, the third year of Mekas's first child, Oona. *He Stands in a Desert Counting the Seconds of His Life* (1985) chronicles the years 1969–1984, by means of 124 brief sketches: "portraits of people I have spent time with [including Hans Richter, Roberto Rossellini, Marcel Hanoun, Henri Langlois, Alberto Cavalcanti, Kenneth Anger, the Kuchar brothers, Robert Breer, Hollis Frampton, John Lennon, Jackie Onassis, the Kennedy children, Andy Warhol, Yoko Ono, and George Maciunas], places, seasons of the year, weather," as Mekas explains in the Film-makers' Cooperative Catalogue, No. 7. Other films document performances by the Living Theater (*Street Songs,* filmed in 1966, completed 1983), by Erick Hawkins and Lucia Dlugoszewski (*Erick Hawkins: Excerpts from "Here and Now with Watchers"/Lucia Dlugoszewski Performs,* filmed in 1963, completed 1983), and by Kenneth King and Phoebe Neville (*Cup/Saucer/Two Dancers/Radio,* filmed in 1965, completed 1983). Mekas's most recent film is *Scenes from the Life of Andy Warhol* (1990).

I spoke with Mekas in December 1982 and January 1983. I had decided in advance to focus on his filmmaking, rather than on his activities as organizer, editor, writer, and administrator.

MacDonald: Though *Lost Lost Lost* wasn't finished until 1975, it has the earliest footage I've seen in any of your films.

Mekas: The earliest footage in that film comes from late 1949. *Lost Lost Lost* was edited in 1975 because I couldn't deal with it until then. I couldn't figure out how to edit the early footage.

MacDonald: When you were recording that material, were you just putting it onto reels and storing it?

Mekas: I had prepared a short film from that footage in late 1950. It was about twenty minutes long and was called *Grand Street.* Grand Street is one of the main streets in Williamsburg, Brooklyn, populated mainly by immigrants, where we spent a lot of time. Around 1960 I took that film apart. It doesn't exist anymore. Otherwise, I didn't do anything with that footage. Occasionally I looked at it, thinking how I would edit it. I could not make up my mind what to eliminate and what to leave in. But in 1975 it was much easier.

MacDonald: Is that opening passage in *Lost Lost Lost,* where you and Adolfas are fooling around with the Bolex, really your first experience with a camera?

Mekas: What you see there is our very first footage, shot on Lorimer Street, in Williamsburg, Brooklyn.

MacDonald: Were you involved at all with film before you got to this country?

Mekas: The end of the war found us in Germany. Two shabby, naive Lithuanian boys, just out of forced labor camp. We spent four years in various displaced persons camps—Flensburg, Hamburg, Wiesbaden, Kassel, et cetera—first in the British zone, then in the American zone. There was nothing to do and a lot of time. What we could do was read, write, and go to movies. Movies were shown in the camps free, by the American army. Whatever money we could get we spent on books, or we went into town and saw the postwar German productions. Later, when we went to study at the University of Mainz, which was in the French zone—we commuted from Wiesbaden—we saw a lot of French films.

The movies that really got us interested in film were not the French productions, but the postwar, neorealistic German films. They are not known here—films by Helmut Käutner, Josef V. Baky, Wolfgang Liebeneiner, and others. The only way they could make films after the war in Germany was by shooting on actual locations. The war had ended, but the realities were still all around. Though the stories were fictional and melodramatic, their visual texture was drab reality, the same as in the postwar Italian films.

Then we started reading the literature on film, and we began writing scripts. What caused us to write our first script was a film—I do not remember the title or who made it, but it was about displaced persons. We thought it was so melodramatic and had so little understanding of what life in postwar Europe was like that we got very mad and decided we should make a film. My brother wrote a script. Nothing ever was done with it. We had no means, we had no contacts, we were two zeroes.

MacDonald: When you were first starting to shoot here, did you feel that you were primarily a recorder of displaced persons and their struggle, or were you already thinking about becoming a filmmaker of another sort?

Mekas: The very first script that we wrote when we arrived in late 1949, and which was called *Lost Lost Lost Lost* (that is, four *Lost*'s as opposed to the three of the 1975 version), was for a documentary on the life of displaced persons here. We wanted to bring some facts to people's attention. It did not have to do so much with the fact that we were displaced persons, or that there were displaced persons. It had more to do with the fact that the Baltic republics—Estonia, Latvia, Lithuania—were sacrificed by the West to the Soviet Union at Yalta just before the end of the war and ended up as occupied countries to which we could not return. We were taking a stand for the three Baltic countries that the West had betrayed. Our script was an angry outcry. We sent it to [Robert] Flaherty, thinking he could help us produce it, but he wrote back that though he liked the script and found it full of passion, he could not help us. This was at a time when he couldn't find money to produce even his own films.

We did start shooting nevertheless. Actually, two or three shots at the beginning of *Lost Lost Lost* are from the footage we shot for that film. A slow-motion shot of a soldier (actually, Adolfas) and one or two others (a family reading a newspaper, a skating rink, a tree in Central Park) were meant for that film. But my brother was drafted and so we abandoned the project. When he came back from the army a year or so later, things had changed.

MacDonald: During all the intervening time you were recording other material?

Mekas: Yes, I was collecting, documenting, without a clear plan or purpose, the activities of displaced persons—mainly Lithuanians. I shot footage of New York immigrant communities, and I did some weekend traveling to record communities in Chicago, Toronto, Philadelphia, Boston. I worked in Brooklyn factories and spent all my money on film.

MacDonald: A lot of the footage that ended up in the first reel of *Lost Lost Lost* is compositionally and texturally very beautiful. When you were shooting originally, were you thinking about the camera as a potential poetic instrument?

Mekas: The intention was to capture the situations very directly, with the simple means that we had at our disposal. All the indoor footage was taken with just one or two flood lamps. We made no attempt to light the "scenes" "correctly" or "artistically." Sometimes we were at meetings— actually, most of the time—where we couldn't interfere, or we were too shy to interfere.

During the first weeks after our arrival here, we had read Pudovkin and Eisenstein, so in the back of our minds there was probably something else, a different ambition, but I don't think that that footage reveals much. In Germany we had bought a still camera and had taken a lot of stills. Maybe that affected how we saw and the look of some of the footage. We also looked at a lot of still photography. In 1953 or so I began working at a place called Graphic Studios, a commercial photography studio, where I stayed for five or six years. The studio was run by Lenard Perskie, from whom I learned a great deal. All the great photographers used to drop in, and some artists, like Alexander Archipenko.

In 1950 we began attending Cinema 16 screenings. By this I mean absolutely every screening of the so-called experimental films. It became my Sunday church, my university. We also attended every screening of the Theodore Huff Society, which was run at that time by the young Bill Everson. He showed mostly early Hollywood and European films that were unavailable commercially. I think it's still going on, but I haven't been there for years. It's one of the noble, dedicated undertakings of William Everson, who has performed a great educational role for nearly three decades.

MacDonald: I asked the question about your using the camera as a poetic device because by the second reel there are shots in which it's clear that more is happening than documentation. I'm thinking of the beautiful sequence of the woman pruning trees, and the shot of Adolfas in front of the merry-go-round.

Mekas: That shot of Adolfas was intended for our first "poetic" film: *A Silent Journey.* We never finished it and some of the footage appears in reel three of *Lost Lost Lost*—the film within the film about the car crash.

MacDonald: Were you collecting sound at this time too?

Mekas: We were collecting sound, but between 1950 and 1955 this amounted to very little. After 1955 I collected more and more sounds from the situations I filmed.

MacDonald: The early reels are punctuated by images of typed pages. Were you writing a record of your feelings during that time?

Mekas: Those pages are from my written diaries which I kept regularly from the time I left Lithuania [1944] until maybe 1960. Later I got too involved in other activities—the Film-makers' Cooperative, *Film Culture,* the Cinematheque, et cetera—and the written diaries became more and more infrequent.

MacDonald: Did you know English when you arrived here?

Mekas: I could read. I remember reading Hemingway's *A Farewell to Arms* on the boat as we came over. Hemingway is one of the easiest writers to read because of the simplicity and directness of his language. He is still one of my favorite writers. So I could read and communicate, but writing took another few years. To write in an acquired language is more difficult than to read, as you know, and I am still learning. Until the mid fifties I kept all my notes in Lithuanian. For another two to three years there is a slow dissolve: on some days my notes were in Lithuanian and on other days in English. By 1957 all the diaries and notes are in English.

My poetry remains in Lithuanian. I have tried—mostly fooling around—to write "poetry" in English, but I do not believe that one can write poetry in any language but the one in which one grew up as a child. One can never master all the nuances of words and groupings of words that are necessary for poetry. Certain kinds of prose can be written, though, as Nabokov has shown.

My brother mastered English much faster than I because he found himself in the army with no Lithuanians around. Of course, I am not talking about our accents. The Eastern European pronunciation requires a completely different mouth muscle structure than that of the English language. And it takes a lot of time for the mouth muscles to rearrange themselves.

MacDonald: When you came to put *Lost Lost Lost* together in its present form, did you then go back to the journals and film pages with that film in mind or had those pages been filmed much earlier?

Mekas: I filmed the pages during the editing. When I felt that some aspect of that period was missing from the images, I would go through the audio tapes and the written diaries. They often contained what my footage did not.

Also, as it developed into its final form, *Lost Lost Lost* became autobiographical: I became the center. The immigrant community is there, but it's shown through my eyes. Not unconsciously, but consciously, formally. When I originally filmed that footage, I did not make myself the center. I tried to film in a way that would make the community central. I thought of myself only as the recording eye. My attitude was still that of an old-fashioned documentary filmmaker of the forties or fifties and so I purposely kept the personal element out as much as I could. By the time of the editing, in 1975, however, I was preoccupied by the autobiographical. The written diaries allowed me to add a personal dimension to an otherwise routine, documentary recording.

MacDonald: Your detachment from the Lithuanian community in reels one and two seems to go beyond the documentarian's "objective" stance.

Mekas: I was already detached from the Lithuanian community—not from Lithuania, but from the immigrant community, which had written us off probably as early as 1948 or even earlier, when we were still in Germany, in the DP camps. The nationalists—there were many military people among the displaced persons—thought we were Communists and that we should be thrown out of the displaced persons camp. The main reason for that, I think, was that we always hated the army. We were very antimilitaristic. We always laughed and made jokes about the military. Another thing that seemed to separate us from the Lithuanian community was that we did not follow the accepted literary styles of that time. We were publishing a literary magazine in Lithuanian, which was, as far as they were concerned, an extreme, modernist manifestation. So we were outcasts. That was one of the reasons why we moved out of Brooklyn into Manhattan. I was recording the Lithuanian community, but I was already seeing it as an outsider. I was still sympathetic to its plight, but my strongest interests already were film and literature. We'd finish our work in a factory in Long Island City at five P.M. and without washing our faces, we'd rush to the subway to catch the five-thirty screening at the Museum of Modern Art. To the other Lithuanians we were totally crazy.

MacDonald: You begin *Lost Lost Lost* with your buying the camera, which does end up recording the Lithuanian community, but the camera is also suggestive of an interest that has come *between* you and that community.

Mekas: Yes, recording the community was part of mastering new tools. It was practice. If one has a camera and wants to master it, then one begins to film in the street or in the apartment. We figured, if we were going to film the streets, why not collect some useful material about the lives of the Lithuanian immigrants. We had several scripts that called for documentary material. One of them required footage from many countries. My brother took a lot of footage for that film in Europe, while he was in the army.

But, basically, at that time our dream was Hollywood. Fictional, theatrical film—not documentary. We thought in terms of making movies for everybody. In those days if one thought about making films for neighborhood theaters, one thought in terms of Hollywood. We dreamed we would earn some money, and borrow some from friends, and would be able to make our films, our "Hollywood" films. Very soon we discovered that nobody wanted to lend us any money. So we began to send our scripts to Hollywood. I remember sending one to Fred Zinnemann and another to Stanley Kramer. We got them back; I don't know whether they were ever read. Now one can see that our first scripts were not Hollywood scripts at all; they were avant-garde scripts. But we naively thought we could get backing for the films we were dreaming of.

Luckily, just around that time, in New York, there were some people, like Morris Engel and Sidney Meyers, who were beginning to make a different kind of cinema, who began breaking away from Hollywood. We saw *The Little Fugitive* [1953] and it made us aware of other possibilities. Before we arrived here, we were completely unaware of anything other than commercial film. As we were entering adolescence, when we might have become interested in such things, the war came, and the occupations by the Soviets, then the Germans, then the Soviets again. There was no information, no possibility at all for us to become aware of the other kind of cinema. The Russians came with their official cinema; then the Germans with theirs. After the war the United States army came with Tarzan and melodrama. Our film education was very slow. In late 1947, and in 1948, when we were studying at the University of Mainz, we were excited by *Beauty and the Beast* [1946] and a few other French films. But that's about it.

MacDonald: Is there some reason why you included almost no explicit information about your film interest in those first two reels—other than the obvious fact of your making the footage we're seeing? When I originally saw reel three and the intertitle, "FILM CULTURE IS ROLLING ON LAFAYETTE STREET," I was surprised: it seemed to come out of nowhere.

Mekas: I have no real explanation for that. I figure, the professional life, even if it's a filmmaker's, is not photogenic. There are certain crafts, professions, that are photogenic—to me—such as, for instance, bread making, farming, fishing, street works, cutting wood, coal mining, et cetera. Technological crafts and professions are not photogenic. Another reason is that until 1960 or so, no filmmaker was really filming his or her own life. Whatever one was filming was always outside of one's life—in my case, the Lithuanian community or New York streets. The diaristic, autobiographical preoccupations did not really exist. The personal lives of the whole first wave of American experimental filmmakers are not recorded on film. There is a little bit of Dwinell Grant, fooling in front of the camera. Francis Lee has footage of himself and some of his friends. But the personal had not yet become a concern. As a result, in *Lost Lost Lost* you do not see much of my own life until later. One didn't go to parties with the camera. If I had taken my Bolex to any of Maya Deren's parties and started filming, they would have laughed. Serious filmmaking was still scripted filmmaking.

MacDonald: Who were the first people you ran into who were using film in more personal ways?

Mekas: My first contacts with the New York film-viewing community began very early. The second or third evening after I arrived here, I went to a screening of *The Cabinet of Dr. Caligari* [1920] and Epstein's *The Fall of the House of Usher* [1928], sponsored by the New York Film Society, run at that time by Rudolf Arnheim. Then we went to Cinema 16, but we did not meet any filmmakers there: we were just two shabby DPs watching films. When I heard that Hans Richter was in New York, running the film department at City College, I wrote him a letter saying that I had no money, but would like to attend some classes. He wrote back, "Sure, come!" So I did and I met Hans Richter. I did not take any of his classes—actually, he did not teach any classes that winter—but I met many people: Shirley Clarke, Gideon Bachmann, Frank Kuenstler (the poet), and others. I continued seeing Gideon, and we decided—it was his idea—to start our own film group. It was called The Film Group. Beginning in 1951 we had screenings once a month, sometimes more often. We rented films, mostly experimental, avant-garde films. I wrote many of the program notes. Through those screenings we met other people interested in filmmaking. Another person very active during those years (between 1950 and 1955) was Perry Miller, who has lately made several important documentaries—*Gertrude Stein, When This You See, Remember Me* [1970]. She was running an international festival of films on art, a very big event, at Hunter College. She held at least three of these events, in 1952, 1953, and, I think, 1954. I saw Alain Resnais's early films there, and some films by local filmmakers. I remember a pattern film by John Arvonio, who filmed reflections in the rain in Times Square. Nobody knows that film anymore. I don't know if it still exists. Also, no one seems to hear any longer of Wheaton Galentine or Joe Slavin, or Peter Hollander, who distributed early films by Jordan Belson and others through a distribution center called Kinesis.

We undertook two or three documentary film projects with Gideon Bachmann. One was about modern architecture in a community not far outside of New York called Usonia. I shot two or three rolls on the Frank Lloyd Wright buildings there. I think Gideon has that footage; I don't. In 1953 I ran a short film series at the Gallery East, on First Street and

Avenue B, a gallery run by Joel Baxter and Louis Brigante. In 1954 my brother and I started our own film society called Film Forum. George Capsis was the third member. We had screenings for two years. At one of our first shows—a Jordan Belson show, with Belson present—we clashed with the projectionists' union. They came and cut off the electricity. When we wanted to continue, they threatened to beat us up, so we had to stop the screening.

MacDonald: The color in the first two reels of *Lost Lost Lost* is gorgeous.

Mekas: Much of it is time's effect on the early Kodachrome. I didn't like it in the original color. As it began aging, I liked it much more and decided to use it. I remember having a similar experience with Gregory Markopoulos's trilogy, *Psyche, Charmides, Lysis* [all 1948]. It seemed to me to become more and more wonderful as time went on. When some people looked at it later, they said, "It's horrible, what's happened to the color." But I found the later color superior to the original.

MacDonald: That process will continue.

Mekas: Yes. Even though I have a master now, on Ektachrome, the Ektachrome itself changes rapidly. The print stocks keep changing. And, of course, the color changed in the transfer from the original Kodachrome into the Ektachrome master. So there is no such thing as original color anymore. Every stage is original, in a way.

MacDonald: It seems to me that your varied use of intertitles has always been a strong formal element in your films.

Mekas: I was always faced with the problem of how to structure, how to formalize the personal material, which seems just to run on and on. It's so close to me that I have to use abstract devices, numbers, or descriptive intertitles, to make it more distant, easier for me to deal with, to make the footage seem more as if someone else—maybe Lumière—were recording it.

MacDonald: You mentioned that you feel that you can't be a poet in English, and yet both in the spoken narrative passages (in *Lost Lost Lost* especially, but also as early as *Walden*) and also in the printed intertitles, your spoken or visual phrasing evokes several American poets—William Carlos Williams, for example, and Walt Whitman.

Mekas: But those passages are not poetry. They are poetic, yes, which is a different thing. By the way, I wanted to make a documentary about William Carlos Williams. In 1954 or 1955 I made some notes, visited Williams in Paterson, and discussed the film with him. I wanted to make a film about his life there in Paterson. He was supposed to prepare some notes about what he wanted to have in the film. I lost my notes; probably his estate would know if his still exist, if, that is, he made any. I took LeRoi Jones with me. He may remember more about that trip.

MacDonald: Had you read Whitman by this time?

Mekas: I had read Whitman in German translation in 1946 or 1947. Later I read some in English. By 1950 I had read it all. I had even translated some of his poems, or rather, had tried to translate them into Lithuanian. During those periods Whitman *was* important to me, along with Sandburg and Auden. Later I gravitated toward other preferences. I haven't read Sandburg for decades, but there's a lot in him that is very appealing.

MacDonald: Lost Lost Lost seems to be divided not only into six reels but into three pairs of two reels, each of which has the same general organization: the first tends to be about personal and family life, the second about the political context of that personal and family life.

Mekas: That footage is largely in chronological order, though I took some liberties here and there. I worked with it as one huge piece. I kept looking at it, eliminating bits and dividing it up in one way and another. I didn't plan on six reels originally, in fact I had seven or eight at one point, but figured that that was too much to view in one sitting. I considered three hours the maximum for a single sitting.

MacDonald: When the unfinished film-within-the-film that you show at the beginning of reel three was originally made, did you conceive of it as a sort of parable of your own experience as a displaced person?

Mekas: No. That film was very much influenced by my viewing experimental films at Cinema 16. I wanted to make my first consciously "poetic" little film. At that point I thought it was totally invented and outside of me. All I wanted was that it be very, very simple, just one moment from somebody's life, a memory.

MacDonald: In that passage, as it appears in *Lost Lost Lost,* you seem to be developing a parallel between yourself and the protagonist. Both of you go to the woods to walk off the pain of your losses.

Mekas: Now, from the perspective of years, I can see that connection.

MacDonald: In reel three you begin to develop the more gestural camera style with which many people identify you. In later reels the gestural camera becomes increasingly evident, so that the film as a whole seems, in part, about the emergence of that style.

Mekas: It's more complicated than that. My first major work in Lithuanian, which to some of my Lithuanian friends is still the best thing I've done, was a cycle of twenty-odd idylls I wrote in 1946. I used long lines and an epic pace to portray my childhood in the village. I described the people in the village and their various activities during the four seasons, as factually and prosaically as I could. I avoided what was accepted as poetic Lithuanian language. My aim at that time—I talk about this in my written diaries—was to achieve "a documentary poetry." When I began filming, that interest did not leave me, but it was pushed aside as I got

caught up in the documentary film traditions. I was reading John Grier-
son and Paul Rotha and looking at the British and American documentary films of the thirties and forties. I feel now that their influence
detoured me from my own inclination. Later, I had to shake this influence in order to return to the approach with which I began.

Now that I am transcribing all my written diaries, I notice that already
in the forties there are pages and pages of observations of what I've seen
through windows, what I've heard in the street—a series of disconnected, collaged impressions. If one compares my camera work with
those pages, one sees that they are almost identical. I only changed my
tools.

MacDonald: I had assumed that your gestural camera represented the
development of an American film style, growing out of your progressive
acculturation.

In reels two and three of *Lost Lost Lost,* you seem very lonely, and
yet you were obviously very busy with many people.

Mekas: When I read my written diaries, I see that I was very, very
lonely during those early years, more so than, say, the average Italian
immigrant. There's an established Italian community here which one
can become part of. It's lonely, but not that lonely. Italian immigrants
know they can go back to Italy if things don't work out. Once we left
what Lithuanian community there was in New York, and moved to
Orchard Street, we were very much alone. One of the reasons why I
went to City College for a few months was to meet new people. I could
not stand just walking the streets by myself. My brother was in the army.
For two years I had no friends, nobody. If I had been a communicative,
friendly person, it might have been different. But I was never that kind
of person. I was always very closed and extremely shy. Actually, I still
am, but I have learned techniques to cover it. At thirteen or fourteen I
was so shy that when finally, for some reason, I began speaking to
people—other than members of my family—everybody was amazed:
"He speaks! He speaks! Really, he speaks!" This shyness did not disappear all at once. Even though we started publishing *Film Culture* and
went to film screenings, we'd go home and be alone. We were still
thinking about Lithuania. Our mother was there, our father, and all our
brothers. Until Stalin died we could not even correspond.

I did a lot of walking in this new country, but as yet I had no memories
from it. It takes years and years to build and collect new memories.
After a while the streets begin to talk back to you and you are not a
stranger any longer, but this takes years. That experience is not pleasant
to go through and so it's not always reflected in my footage, though it's
in the diaries. I put it into the film later, by means of my "narration," or,
more correctly, my "talking."

I walked downtown, and
I thought about my child-
hood, and Lithuania, the
forests, and all the smells
and all the sounds, and I
asked myself, what was I
doing here.

Jonas Mekas walking New York streets in Lost Lost Lost *(1976).*

MacDonald: Some of it comes through in the mood of those images.

Mekas: Some, yes.

MacDonald: I showed Menken's *Notebook* [1963] recently, and noticed not only a feeling similar to the one in your work, but a similar use of tiny passages of text as a means of contextualizing and distancing personal footage.

Mekas: Oh, yes. I liked what she did and I thought it worked. She helped me make up my mind about how to structure my films. Besides, Marie Menken was Lithuanian. Her mother and father were Lithuanian immigrants, and she still spoke some Lithuanian. We used to get together and sing Lithuanian folk songs. When she'd sing them, she'd go back to the old country completely. So there might also be some similarities in our sensibilities because of that. But definitely Marie Menken helped me to be at peace enough to leave much of the original material just as it was.

And John Cage. From him I learned that chance is one of the great editors. You shoot something one day, forget it, shoot something the next day and forget the details of that. . . . When you finally string it all together, you discover all sorts of connections. I thought at first that I should do more editing and not rely on chance. But I came to realize that, of course, there is no chance: whenever you film, you make certain decisions, even when you don't know that you do. The most essential, the most important editing takes place during the shooting as a result of these decisions.

Before 1960 I tried to edit the material from 1949 to 1955. But I practically destroyed it by tampering with it too much. Later, in 1960 or 1961, I spent a long time putting it *back* to the way it was originally. After that I was afraid to touch it, and I didn't touch it until 1975.

MacDonald: It's in the fifth reel of *Lost Lost Lost* that you seem, for the first time, to be back in touch with rural life and with the land.

Mekas: Yes, that's where the "lost lost lost" ends. I'm beginning to feel at home again. By reel six one cannot say that I feel lost anymore; paradise has been regained through cinema.

MacDonald: It's the paradise of having a place where you can work and struggle for something that you care about?

Mekas: When you enter a whole world where you feel at home. A world for which you care. Or, a world which takes you over, possesses you, obsesses you, and pushes all the other worlds into the shadow. Still, I don't think that I'll ever be able, really and completely, to detach myself from what I really am, somewhere very deep: a Lithuanian.

MacDonald: Reel five is exhilarating in its use of light and texture. And you take some chances by allowing yourself to be very vulnerable: you allow yourself to look foolish.

Mekas: I realized I was taking chances. I have to give credit here again—one is always taking lessons—to Gregory Markopoulos. Gregory had taken chances that I thought wouldn't work, but he always managed to pull through. I don't know how familiar you are with Markopoulos's work; it's practically impossible to see these days—he doesn't show it in America. I learned from Gregory that what seems embarrassingly personal soon after a film is made, later comes to be part of the content, and not embarrassing at all.

Another lesson came from Dostoyevsky, from a statement of his that I read when I was fifteen or sixteen and which I have never forgotten. A young writer complained to Dostoyevsky that his own writing was too subjective, too personal, and that he would give anything to learn to write more objectively. Dostoyevsky replied—this is my memory; I may have adapted it totally to my own purpose; it's not a quotation—"The main problem of the writer is not how to escape subjectivity, but rather how to be subjective, how really to write from one's self, to be oneself in language, form, and content. I challenge you to be subjective!" It is very difficult to be openly subjective. One has to keep it within formal limits, of course; one must not wallow in subjectivity. Perhaps I come very close to that sometimes. . . .

MacDonald: Did the fact that 1976 was the American Bicentennial year have any impact on the making of *Lost Lost Lost?* It does tell a quintessentially American story.

Mekas: Lost Lost Lost was completed because the New York State Council on the Arts (maybe because of the Bicentennial) decided to give four very special twenty-thousand-dollar grants. Harry Smith got one too. Suddenly I had enough money and I said, "This is my chance."

It's amazing, when one thinks about it: everybody says—and it's quite true—that this country is made of immigrants, that America is a melting pot. But it's not reflected very often in American literature. There is no major work that really documents the immigrant experience. Sinclair's *The Jungle* is the closest we have that I know of. *Lost Lost Lost* is a record of certain immigrant realities that have been largely ignored in art.

MacDonald: Guns of the Trees [1961] is probably the closest of your films to a recognizably commercial narrative. What was the background of that project?

Mekas: First I wrote a sketchy, poetic script that consisted of thirty sequences. I wanted to improvise around those sketches, and that's what we set out to do. "We" means Adolfas and me. We had agreed to assist each other on our own productions: first I'd make a film, and he'd help; next he'd make a film, and I'd help. He helped me on *Guns,* and I helped him on *Hallelujah the Hills* [1963]. The only thing that went wrong, and really very badly wrong was that at that time we had a friend, Edouard de Laurot, who wanted very much to be involved in the film as well. From solidarity and friendship, we decided to invite him to work with us. He was a brilliant person, but very self-centered and very dictatorial. Edouard's position was that absolutely every movement, every word, every thing that appeared in the film should be totally controlled and politically meaningful. I tended, even at that time, to be much more open; I was interested in improvisation, chance, accidents. I was too inexperienced and unsure of myself to push through with my own shy vision. So often I did things Edouard's way. It came to the point, finally, that we had to part, to end the friendship. This was an important lesson for me: it was clear that I had to work alone in the future. I was never happy with that film.

MacDonald: How did you come to make *The Brig* [1964]?

Mekas: I wanted to make a film in which sound was about as important as the image. I was attracted by the sounds of *The Brig*—the stamping and running and shouting. It was a staged reality that was very much like life itself. I thought I could go into it the way a news cameraman would go into a situation in real life. Cinéma vérité was very much in the air at that time. People connected truth to cinema verité camera technique; style produced an illusion of truth. I made the film, in a sense, as a critique of cinema verité.

At that time the most widely used newsreel camera was the single system Auricon. You could record the sound in the camera during the shooting on magnetic sound-striped film stock. I rented three cameras and shot the film in one session, in ten-minute takes. Two days earlier, when I went to see the play on stage, the idea of making the film shot through my mind so fast that I decided not to see the play through to the end. That way, when I filmed I would not know what was coming next: the opposite of the usual situation in which the filmmaker studies and maps the action in an attempt to catch the essence of the play. I went to Julian Beck and told him that I wanted to film the play. He said this would be impossible since it was being closed the next day. The police had ordered it closed on the pretext that the taxes had not been paid. I decided that I wanted to do it anyway; I only needed a day to collect the equipment. We concocted a plan to sneak into the building after the play had been closed and begin shooting.

It was so sudden, an obsession. The cast got into the building at night, through the coal chute. So did we, my little crew—Ed Emshwiller, Louis Brigante, with our equipment. Shooting was very intense. I had to film and watch the play at the same time. Most of the time I did not even look through the camera. I'd finish with one camera, grab the next one, and continue. I'd have to yell out to the actors to stop while I changed cameras. Ed and Louis loaded the cameras while I shot.

From Mekas's The Brig *(1964).*

MacDonald: Did you assume that people who saw the film would not know the play?

Mekas: No. Some of the people who later saw the film had seen the play. Some people who were not familiar with the play were actually fooled by the "amateur" style. They thought that the United States army had permitted me to go into a real brig and make the film. This was the case with some Italian newspapers.

MacDonald: The credits say that you shot the film and Adolfas edited it. How much was edited out? Was the play just an hour long?

Mekas: The editing involved was technical work. When I would run out of film and grab another camera, the actors would stop and overlap a little bit. I liked the film with the overlaps, and actually the first screening included them. The Living Theater liked it that way too. But David and Barbara Stone, who were at that point beginning to get involved in distribution, agreed to distribute it, and for distribution's sake, we decided to eliminate the overlappings. My brother took care of this. He had just come back from Chicago, where he did the editing and salvaging of *Goldstein.* Also, though I shot the sound on film, I had a separate tape recorder running independently, for safety's sake. We decided to intensify the sound in certain places by merging the two soundtracks. My brother did that. Also, one camera was always slowing down towards the end of a roll, so we had to replace those parts of sound with the separate recording, or resplice it practically frame by frame. There was a lot of that kind of subtle technical work, which my brother does very well.

As far as the play itself is concerned, I filmed the whole thing. There were parts, however, which worked on stage, but didn't work so well on film. As in real life—some of it was just too boring to film. As documentary as the play is, towards the end it becomes more theatrical: acting and melodramatic lines I couldn't do anything with. I decided to cut those parts out. The people from the Living Theater were not too happy about this decision at first, but eventually they accepted the changes, and now they're very happy with the film. The play ran approximately ninety minutes. I cut out about twenty minutes.

MacDonald: There's a weird dimension to the play: it has to be as rigorously unrelenting in its production as a real brig would be. The people who "play" the marines were, I assume, as demanding on themselves and each other as real marines would be—maybe more so, depending on how long the play ran.

Mekas: I think the play ran for about a year. All those punches were real; they were rehearsed, but real. Every actor had to know the parts of all the other actors so that they could rotate roles. I'll be punched tonight, and you'll be punched tomorrow. They were incredibly dedicated to their theater.

MacDonald: What's interesting to me is that it's the same performance as the real thing. It's just in a different context.

Mekas: That's why I wanted to film it. It could be treated as reality, though actually the play was not as intense as the film. I intensified it by picking out certain details, by cutting out dead spaces, and by the movements of the camera. Still, for the theatergoer of that period, *The Brig* was a very intense experience. In 1967 or 1968 I was invited to the University of Delaware to see their production of *The Brig*. Kenneth Brown, the author of the play, was there too. The production, from all I remember, was pretty intense. But it didn't have the same impact on the audience as the original performances did. To have the same effect in 1968 you had to be two or three times more shocking. Society had become more brutalized.

I should add another footnote here. In the late sixties, a TV station in Berlin did their own version of the play. They planned it all very carefully, spent a lot of money on it, took a month to make it—and it was a total dud. It didn't work.

MacDonald: The sound in the film is somewhat rhythmic. Over and over it starts relatively quietly and then builds, finally going past the point of audibility. Was the distortion done on purpose?

Mekas: In one track there was distortion because I was too close to the sound with my camera mike. Also, one camera distorted the sound when it slowed down. But I decided to keep the distortions. More than that: I combined the tracks to intensify it. That was one of the major objections at the time I made the film, and I had to overrule it. Noise is very much part of that film. The noise is more important than what's being said.

MacDonald: It's like some kind of horrible music.

Mekas: It's not a pleasant film to see. You don't want to see it twice. You might say, "Oh, I liked it," but you don't want to see it twice.

MacDonald: What was the nature of your collaboration with Markopoulos on *Award Presentation to Andy Warhol* [1964]?

Mekas: I wanted to give that year's Independent Film Award to Andy Warhol. I had arranged a series of screenings, including Warhol films, at the New Yorker Theater. But he said he didn't want to be on stage or do anything as public as that, so I suggested that we make the award in his studio and that I'd film it. He said that would be okay. We collected some of his superstars of that period and two rolls of film and set it all up. On my way to the studio, I suddenly remembered that I would actually have to award him with something, so I bought a basket of fruit at the corner store. During the actual presentation, I needed someone to operate the camera, which was a motorized Bolex. Gregory happened to be there and said he'd do it. Much of the time he's actually in the film, on the set; and the rest of the time he was operating the camera. I slowed down the film in the printing as a form of tribute to Andy: most of his films—actually all the films from that period—were projected at sixteen frames per second, though they were shot at twenty-four. I did the same thing, but I had to do it by means of optical reprinting because I wanted to have the sound on the film.

MacDonald: How did you get involved with *Show Magazine,* and *Film Magazine of the Arts* [1963]?

Mekas: Did you see that one?

MacDonald: Yes, it's a nice little film.

Mekas: Show Magazine needed a promotional film, and somebody suggested to them that I make it. I agreed to do it. They paid well. I conceived the film as a serial film magazine that would come out once a month, or once every three months. We shot a lot of footage, with *Show Magazine* people always present, taking us to various places. When I was shooting, I noticed that they were always dropping issues of *Show Magazine* on the floor everywhere. When I screened the first draft of the film for them, they were shocked to see that I had eliminated all those magazines and much of the footage of fashion models they had me shoot (although you see some of that at the very end of the film). So that was the end of that project. I think that the concept of a film magazine, had they really supported me, was a good one and would have received much better publicity than the kind of thing they wanted.

MacDonald: I think that's the first film of yours I saw.

Mekas: There are some parts I like very much; I like the whole thing, really. They seized the original right after the screening. They were planning to hire their own editor to reedit the film their way. They also took all the outtakes, but decided finally not to do anything with it. All my prints are from the work print.

MacDonald: Was the greenish tone of the black-and-white imagery caused by printing black-and-white footage on color stock?

Mekas: That particular tint was my choice.

MacDonald: You used some interesting music by Storm De Hirsch and others.

Mekas: The section with Lucia Dlugoszewski is unique. I think she's an exceptional composer and performer.

MacDonald: Walden is the film of yours I've seen most often. When I first saw it, I was conscious primarily of the diaristic aspects. But, more recently I've been just as aware of the changing film stocks and the different tintings of the black-and-white footage. It now seems simultaneously an exploration of your personal environment *and* of film materials.

Mekas: Those are all controlled accidents. Some of the stock was used because it was available when I ran out of film. When I was filming the part now entitled "A Visit to Brakhages," I ran out of film, and Stan found some outdated Kodachrome under his bed. It was a very different texture than the surrounding material. Sometimes I ran out of color, so I used black and white. I had no plan to explore film stocks. But once you have all those different stocks, then you begin to structure with color; you pay attention to their qualities. The aspect you notice had also to do with my whole approach to film laboratories. You know how paranoid and careful some filmmakers are about labs. Usually the filmmaker tries to supervise the lab work closely, checking one print and another, refusing prints, switching labs. . . . I don't do that. I consider that whatever happens at the lab is what I want. I don't indicate that they should make this part lighter and that darker. I do my work in the camera, and all I ask from the lab is to make a straight, what's known as "one light" print, with no special timing, no anything. Usually I get results that I like. I have never rejected a print. If something goes really wrong, then of course I indicate on the next print that it should be corrected. I think that I have complete control over my materials; I don't leave anything for the labs to do or undo.

MacDonald: You must have had a tremendous amount of diary footage by the time you made *Walden.* How did you come to make that particular film?

Mekas: The Albright-Knox Gallery in Buffalo had a special celebration—I don't remember the occasion—and they commissioned new works in the fields of music, dance, and film, and maybe some other arts. Film was included at Gerald O'Grady's request; he was the adviser there. I was invited to make a film and given ten months to work on it. I used the material that was easiest for me to put together. The gallery helped to make a print and paid the expenses. The version I screened in Buffalo had sound on tape; it was also slightly shorter than the present version. Later I decided to finish the film and to include some other material.

MacDonald: For me the strongest reel of the four has always been the first. Several sections from that reel are distributed separately.

Mekas: Yes, *Cassis, Notes on the Circus, Report from Millbrook,* and *Hare Krishna,* all filmed in 1966.

MacDonald: It led me to wonder whether you edited it reel by reel or . . .

Mekas: I worked on the thing as a whole. I put those particular parts into distribution, however, before the rest was finished and before the invitation from Buffalo. Eventually I think I will pull them out of distribution, except for *Cassis*—which is different from the version you see in *Walden*—and *Report from Millbrook,* which is also different.

MacDonald: When did you become familiar with Thoreau's *Walden?*

Mekas: It's one of the books that Peter Beard is obsessed with. During the shooting of *Hallelujah the Hills* he gave me a copy, and when I was editing *Walden,* I always had it around. For a long time I thought that that was the first time I read it. But recently, while retyping my early diaries from 1948, I discovered that I was reading *Walden* then, in German.

MacDonald: It's sometimes thought of as a book about country living, but Thoreau was living just outside of town. In that sense your use of Central Park as your "Walden Pond" strikes me as particularly appropriate.

Mekas: Not only Central Park. To me Walden exists throughout the city. You can reduce the city to your own very small world that others may never see. The usual reaction after seeing *Walden* is a question: "Is this New York?" Their New York is ugly buildings and depressing, morbid blocks of concrete and glass. That is not my New York. In my New York there is a lot of nature. *Walden* is made up of bits of memories of what I wanted to see. I eliminated what I didn't want to see.

MacDonald: Is New York the first big city you've spent a lot of time in?

Mekas: Yes, the first big *modern* city. All other cities I had been in before coming here—cities like Hamburg or Frankfurt or Kassel—had been destroyed in the war. There wasn't very much of the city left.

MacDonald: By the time you made *Walden* you'd been filming for a long time. Had it gotten to the point where you were deciding in advance that you wanted to go film this or that for a specific film? It's clear that you decided to go to the circus several times for *Notes on the Circus.*

Mekas: No, I didn't plan. I just recorded my reactions to what was happening around me. *Notes on the Circus*—originally I thought I'd get it all the first time. But I got involved in the circus and went three or four times. I decided in advance to film Peter Beard's wedding, but when I arrived, I discovered that my Bolex wasn't working. Peter happened to have a Baulieux camera, so I used that. I had never used it before, so it was very risky.

MacDonald: What is your connection with Peter Beard? He's very prominent in the diaries.

Mekas: I had met him before *Hallelujah the Hills.* He was the cousin of Jerome Hill, whom I knew by that time. We became friends during the shooting of *Hallelujah the Hills,* and the friendship has continued.

MacDonald: In the first reel you say, "I make home movies— therefore I live," a line that's quoted a lot. Had you seen much home-movie making?

Mekas: No. I hadn't seen much 8mm until the Kuchars came on the scene. They brought a few others out into the open. Many millions of cameras were floating around in the country for home-movie making, but no one saw the footage. We did attend amateur club screenings in the late fifties.

MacDonald: All your films are involved with social rituals, but *Walden* seems particularly involved with the specific social rituals that are often the material of home movies: weddings especially.

Mekas: There are a lot of weddings in my diaries. A wedding is a big event in anybody's life; it's colorful and there's always a lot of celebration. As a child, I remembered for years my sister's wedding. Where I come from, weddings go on for a week or two. Occasions like that attract me. There are, of course, no such weddings here. But I film them anyway, hoping to find the wedding of my memory. There are also places to which I keep coming back. One is the Metropolitan Museum. On Saturday and Sunday lots of people sit on its front steps. There is something unique about this and for years I've kept going back, trying to capture the mood that pervades it. I think I finally decided I've gotten what I wanted and I'm not going back again. The autumn in Central Park is also something unique and for years I kept going back to it, but now I think I've gotten that. Winter in Central Park also. And I've filmed a lot of New York rains.

During the period when I was shooting the *Walden* material, I wanted to make a diary film of a teenage girl just leaving childhood and entering adolescence. I was collecting diaries and letters of girls of that age, and making many notes. I wanted to make a film—actually, a series of three or four films, one of a girl fifteen, one of a woman and a man twenty-five; then forty-five; then sixty-five. I never progressed beyond the notes. But on several occasions I took some shots with three or four girls whom I thought I would use in that film. I always filmed them in the park. Some of the young women were friends of friends. I don't even know some of their names. But that's the reason for the repeated shots or sequences of young women in the park.

MacDonald: During the making of *Walden* did you try different types of music with different imagery?

Mekas: By then I was carrying my Nagra or my Sony and picking up sounds from the situations I filmed. There is a long stretch where I did not have any sounds, so I had John Cale play some background music. It's very insistent, constant sound that goes on for fifteen or twenty minutes. There is no climax; it's continuous, with some small variations.

MacDonald: It works very intricately with the imagery. There are all sorts of subtle connections. Even within the slight variations, a slight motion in the sound may be matched by a parallel motion in the imagery.

Mekas: I should reveal a secret: that John Cale sound is tampered with. I doubled the speed. It didn't work as it was. I tried different sounds for different parts. I made many different attempts. Sometimes I had two or three televisions going simultaneously, plus phonograph records and a radio. As I was editing, I was listening and trying to hit on chance connections. The tape recorder was always ready so I could immediately record what might come up.

MacDonald: Walden begins with the sound of the subway.

Mekas: There's a lot of subway and street noise in *Walden*. It's a general background in which all the other sounds are planted.

MacDonald: The opening subway sound goes on for a very long time and suggests a rush through time. Then it stops abruptly and the doors open, just as you're waking up and as spring is waking out of winter.

Mekas: I like that noise. It has continued through all the volumes of my film diaries. Also, that was a period when I did a lot of walking, and the street noise was always present.

MacDonald: I assume that, as was true in *Lost Lost Lost,* the material is more or less chronological, though not completely.

Mekas: Yes. I had to shift some parts for simple structural reasons. I did not want two long stretches like Notes on the Circus and Trip to Millbrook right next to each other. That would be too much; it would throw the structure out of balance. There had to be some separations. I shifted those longer passages around, but in most cases I didn't touch the shorter scenes; they are in chronological order.

MacDonald: The last reel has the John Lennon/Yoko Ono passage. Did you know them?

Mekas: Yes, I knew Lennon. I'd known Yoko since 1959 or 1960 perhaps. Around 1962 she left for Japan, then decided to come back to New York. But she needed a job, for immigration, so *Film Culture* gave her her first official job in this country. We have been friends ever since. I met John after he married Yoko. When they came back from London to settle in New York, they were quite lonely. On their first night I took them for coffee, very late. We could find nothing that was open until eventually we came to Emilio's on Sixth Avenue. We sat and drank Irish coffee. John was very happy that nobody knew him there, nobody bothered him. But just as we were about to leave, a shy, young waitress gave John a scrap of paper and asked for his autograph. She had known all along who he was.

MacDonald: Am I correct in saying that at the time of *Walden* you had a sense of the increasing fragility of the things that mattered most to you?

Mekas: There is a very pessimistic passage of "narration" or "talking" in the Central Park sequence where I say that perhaps before too long there won't be any trees or flowers. But I don't mean for that attitude to dominate the entire film. In general I would say that I feel there will always be Walden for those who really want it. Each of us lives on a small island, in a very small circle of reality, which is our own reality. I made up a joke about a Zen monk standing in Times Square with people asking, "So what do you think about New York—the noise, the traffic?" The monk says, "What noise? What traffic?" You *can* cut it all out. No, it's not that we can have all this today, but tomorrow it will be gone. It *is* threatened, but in the end it's up to us to keep those little bits of paradise alive and defend them and see that they survive and grow.

Of course, there is another side to this, another danger. Even in concentration camps, in forced labor camps, people could still find enjoyment in certain things. Not everybody in the forced labor camps sat with his or her nose to the floor, saying, "How dreadful! How dreadful!" There are moments of feeling, happiness, friendships, and even beauty, no matter where you are. So what I said before could be seen as a justification and acceptance of any status quo. I wouldn't want what I say interpreted that way. Somewhere I would put a limit to what I, or a human being in general, would or should accept. As Gandhi did.

The question is how one is to counteract the destruction. Should one walk around with posters and placards or should one retreat and grow natural food in Vermont and hope that by producing something good, and sharing it with others, one can persuade those others to see the value of what you're doing and to move in a similar direction?

Change can't come from the top. The top, which is occupied by various governments, is totally rotten. This civilization cannot be revolutionized, changed: it has to be *replaced.*

MacDonald: The titles of *Walden* and your other films have evolved.

Mekas: Yes. *Walden* was originally titled *Diaries, Notes & Sketches (also known as Walden).* But now, since I have many other reels of diary material, there is a confusion—at least for the labs. When I was using the title *Diaries, Notes & Sketches: Lost Lost Lost,* they kept writing on the cans *Diaries, Notes & Sketches* and skipping the rest. I had no choice but to rethink the titles. All of my film diaries are *Diaries, Notes & Sketches,* but now I call the individual parts only by their specific names: *Walden, Lost Lost Lost, In Between, Notes for Jerome,* et cetera.

MacDonald: How does what we see in *In Between* relate to *Walden* in terms of time period?

Mekas: The *In Between* material is from "in between" *Lost Lost Lost* and *Walden.*

MacDonald: I had thought of the title as a reference to your situation of being partially rooted here, but still Lithuanian . . .

Mekas: Yes, that may be true. It's amazing how much one can hide, unconsciously.

MacDonald: *Walden* is very involved with traveling, whereas in *In Between* there's more home life. And there's a sense of a relationship with a woman.

Mekas: I did not want to make *Walden* too long, and there was a certain pace established there. Several of the sequences in *In Between* are much slower. They're not single framed. I did not want to put that material into *Walden.* After finishing *Walden,* I still thought that I would like to use that footage so I collected it and put it into *In Between.*

I made several versions of *In Between,* one of which I put into distribution, then reedited. It was a difficult film to structure because of the Salvador Dali footage, which was very different from the other material. I decided finally to separate that part; I put Dali in his place, so to speak, and I used numbering to break it up a bit. It's now one of my favorite films.

MacDonald: You mentioned last time that there was a tremendous amount of material collected in the fifties, only a small portion of which was used in *Lost Lost Lost.* Is the same thing true for the sixties?

Mekas: Maybe a little bit less. In *Lost Lost Lost* I used about one-seventh of the footage I had; in *Walden* and *In Between* I used perhaps a third. *Reminiscences of a Journey to Lithuania* was shot about one-to-one. I used everything in the film.

MacDonald: You still have the unused material?

Mekas: I have it all. I may go back some day and make something else with some of it. Some material is not at all bad. But so far it hasn't belonged anywhere. Much of what was not used in the early reels of *Lost Lost Lost* is not so interesting, though it's material of historical importance about immigrant life. It should not be destroyed, though it's slowly rotting away . . .

MacDonald: My first experience with *Reminiscences of a Journey to Lithuania* was at Hampshire College in 1973. After the screening some guy in the back row screamed at you, "Why can't you leave anything alone!" At the time it was sort of jolting. I'd watched the same film and to me it seemed quite lovely, but it had produced this violent response from this other person. Was that unusual?

Mekas: Until ten years ago, that was a very common reaction to single-frame shooting and to short takes, to the use of overexposures or underexposures, and in general to the work of independent filmmakers. There is less and less of that now, since people have gotten used to this type of film language.

MacDonald: Reminiscences of a Journey to Lithuania is the earliest edited film in which you seem primarily involved with time, in which your return to the past is one of the major themes. There are mentions of the past in *Walden,* but not a direct concentrated involvement with it. Was it that you were going to be able to go back to Lithuania, so the whole issue became more frontal for you?

Mekas: You may be correct. I don't know. It's complicated. The official reaction in the Soviet Union, and all the republics there, is to have no contact with any refugee, exile, DP who left during the war, unless that person is potentially useful to them. I had written already for *Isskustvo Kino,* a film journal in Moscow. Some Soviets had seen *The Brig* in Venice, and the editor of *Pravda,* who saw it in New York, wrote a glowing review. The film was invited to the Moscow Film Festival and presented there as an important antimilitary, anticapitalist work. They sent correspondents from Moscow to interview me here, and interviewed my mother in Lithuania. Suddenly I felt I had enough clout to apply for a visa to visit Lithuania. Since I had been invited to the Moscow Film Festival, I thought I would ask to be permitted to go to Lithuania also, to visit my mother.

For over a decade I had not been allowed even to correspond with my mother. I had written some poems against Stalin, so I was a criminal. My brothers were thrown into jail because of me, and my father died earlier than he would have, because of that. My mother's house was watched for years by the secret police. They hoped that one day I'd come home and they'd get me. My mother told me that in 1971. There was not a night, during my visit home, when I wasn't prepared to jump out the window, to run from the police if they decided to come after me. And this in 1971, many years after Stalin's death.

The Lithuanian government, that part which deals with the arts, saw that I had been favorably received by Moscow, from *Pravda* to *Literaturnaya Gazeta.* So they figured it was okay for them to permit me not only to visit my mother, but, as it turned out, to publish my collected poems. Until then I did not exist for them, officially, that is. Actually, they had mocked me in some articles in the official party paper. They had presented me as an example of a sick and corrupt mind, printing some paragraphs from my writings with words omitted, sentences turned around. That was around 1965. But once Moscow became favorable to me, Lithuania immediately followed suit. Suddenly I could film whatever I wanted. Usually visitors are not permitted to go into villages; they stay around their hotels. I was offered an official film crew to do whatever I wanted, but I said, "I will be using my Bolex; I don't want any film crews." They found it strange, but they gave in. They had their own crews around much of the time, making their own film about me and my mother—in Cinemascope. They sent me a print, which I have.

I also shot some Moscow footage on that trip, but I haven't used it so far.

MacDonald: When you came to Utica in 1974 or 1975 to show *Reminiscences,* a woman of Lithuanian background came to the film and seemed very upset about it.

Mekas: In general, the attitude among the older generation of immigrants is that if you go to visit one of those countries, you are a member of the Communist party, or at best you are a spiritual Communist, you are betraying the cause of those who are fighting for the liberation of Baltic countries. The younger generation, however, go for cultural exchange, on the assumption that the only way to help Lithuania is to go there and inform the people. Otherwise they know nothing, they live in controlled ignorance. So you send books, whatever you can, and when something you send gets there—which is a miracle—somebody sees it and something happens. The older generation of immigrants is for a complete cutoff, which doesn't help either side.

MacDonald: In *Reminiscences* Lithuania under Soviet domination seems relatively comfortable. There are a couple of instances where your brothers joke about what Americans will think; their mood seems to be, "We're doing pretty well; things are okay."

Mekas: Yes. Lithuania is an agricultural republic which produces a lot of food for the rest of the Soviet Union. So it's in a privileged position. To a degree, that is. As long as we do not confuse food with liberty. . . . There, they do not confuse the two. They eat, but they also want liberty. Only Moscow and Washington confuse bread and economic prosperity with liberty.

When the Soviet film representative here in New York insisted on seeing the film, I showed it to him; he hit the ceiling. "How do you dare to make and show a film like this to the world! Why didn't you show the factories? Why didn't you show the progress?" I said, "In this film I'm interested only in my mother and my childhood memories, that's all. This is my past." But he couldn't understand it. He thought it was outrageous and an insult. Even a bottle of vodka didn't improve his mood. The star of *Solaris* [1972], Donatas Banionis, saw the film with him and he thought it was great. The two of them almost got into a fist fight. Only another bottle of vodka and a few songs calmed things down.

MacDonald: Did you have a time restriction? How long were you allowed to stay in Lithuania?

Mekas: There was no limit. They said, "Why don't you stay here forever?" And so did my mother; she was already looking for a wife for me there. But I had to come back.

MacDonald: At one point during the second half of the film, you say, "the morning of the fourth day." It comes as a shock because it seems as if we've been there a very long time. By the way, an intertitle at the beginning promises "100 GLIMPSES OF LITHUANIA." Why do you stop after the ninety-first section?

Mekas: Only ninety-one? I thought I went up to ninety-four or ninety-six. Anyway, I decided to take pity on the audience, to give them only ninety-one. On the other hand, what is "100"? It's just an idea; the film shows 100 glimpses in a loose sense.

MacDonald: There's also one missing, number seventy-one.

Mekas: I did not like that segment. I cut it out, never replaced it with other footage, and never corrected the number. Too much work involved. I figured most people wouldn't notice. Maybe eventually I'll put something there.

MacDonald: The time structure of that film is very complex. The first part opens with the end of your period of uprootedness. Then it goes back to the earliest part of your American experience. In the second part a similar thing happens: by visiting Lithuania, you're simultaneously moving forward in terms of your personal development, and going back to the time, or at least the place, where you were before the 1950 material. In the third part your life with your American cultural family—Ken and Flo Jacobs, Annette Michelson—continues, and you visit Kremsmuenster, a centuries-old center for the maintenance of culture.

Mekas: That developed organically. It's not that I sat and thought about time or about the past. I went directly to Austria from Lithuania; that's the way the footage was shot also. Originally I thought I would just use the Lithuanian material, but as I thought more about it, I liked the way the Austrian material complicated everything. Then I decided to complicate it further, give it more angles, more directions, by adding the Brooklyn section. Later I added some Hamburg footage. It just devel-

Elzbieta Mekas, mother of Jonas and Adolfas Mekas, in Reminiscences of a Journey to Lithuania *(1972).*

oped as I worked on it. Time became very integral, time and culture. Culture, as represented by Kubelka, Jacobs, Annette, [Hermann] Nitsch, had become my home. It was clear already at that time that there was no going back to Lithuania for me.

MacDonald: Your mother is spectacular in that film.

Mekas: She's still in very good shape. She's ninety-six now [Elzbieta Mekas died on January 12, 1983, at the age of ninety-seven].

MacDonald: Notes for Jerome has a very different kind of organization than the other films. It's more involved with a specific place, Jerome Hill's environment in Cassis. Was that material made intermittently during this period?

Mekas: The whole film is about forty-five minutes long. Thirty-eight minutes or so are from the 1966 trip. There's also about three minutes from the trip the following year. Ten years later, in 1977, I made another visit. I used about two minutes of that footage.

MacDonald: There's a very different use of intertitles. Sometimes they're repeated and become motifs.

Mekas: In all the other diary volumes most of the titles are used very factually to describe what will be coming up. In this film many of the titles are not descriptive. They make statements which are not connected with any image. I was experimenting with a different use of titles.

MacDonald: The sound is different too. There's no narration.

Mekas: There's very little of my voice, maybe because I did a lot of taping there and had enough other sounds.

MacDonald: Were you drawn to Cassis just because of the friendship with Jerome Hill?

Mekas: Jerome Hill had a little outdoor theater there on the shore of the Mediterranean. Usually he brought over some musicians, like the Julliard Quartet. But in 1966 he persuaded the city of Cassis to cosponsor—he sponsored part of it himself—the Living Theater's production of *Frankenstein.* A special theater was built outdoors for the performance. Jerome wanted somebody to record the event; I agreed to help him. I filmed *Frankenstein* and *The Mysteries. Frankenstein* was the greatest performance I have ever seen. Not the one that was brought to New York, but the one in Cassis.

MacDonald: Was the *Cassis* section in *Walden* done at another time?

Mekas: That was done in 1966.

MacDonald: Is *Paradise Not Yet Lost* finished, or is it part of a larger film?

Mekas: I am not sure. I have been thinking of changing it. I may make it into a two-screen film.

MacDonald: Is the amount of material that you have for all the other years similar to what you had for *Paradise Not Yet Lost*? That's a pretty big film.

Mekas: I have as much material from every year. There is a whole Cincinnati film.

MacDonald: Cincinnati?

Mekas: Yes. I stayed there for a while. Also, I spent a lot of time around Jackie Kennedy's and Lee Radziwill's children. I have a lot of footage from that period.

MacDonald: How did that come about?

Mekas: After Kennedy's death Jackie went through some difficult years during which she was concerned about the children. She wanted to give them something to do. Peter Beard was tutoring them in art history at the time. He suggested that I teach them some filmmaking. I got them simple cameras and made up some basic examples, which they had great fun executing. It proved to be just the thing they needed. Caroline has since turned to photography and cinema. When John was still in school, he made some very exciting four-screen 8mm films—actually one of the most exciting four-screen films I've ever seen, almost as good as Harry Smith's.

MacDonald: Are you to the point where the footage feels like a weight you carry, or is getting back to it something you look forward to?

Mekas: I really live only in my editing room. Or when I film. The rest of my life is slavery. But I am afraid that most of my early material—and my early films too—are fading, going. It would take about forty thousand dollars to preserve my films. That's a lot of money. Money—or dust. Money against the dust of time into which all our works eventually disappear.

Bruce Baillie

In the world of film studies, one often senses a suspicion of beautiful imagery, a suspicion based on the assumption that the apparatus of the movie camera is so constructed that it produces beautiful images almost automatically. Bruce Baillie's films are full of beautiful imagery, but they are anything but "eye candy." For Baillie, the filmstrip is a space where the physical world around him and the spiritual world within him can intersect; the screening room is a place where cinema devotees can share moments of illumination. The remarkable textures and colors of Baillie's films are not the products of a movie camera doing what it does automatically; they are achieved by means of home-spun technologies Baillie devises to modify the camera so that it can be true to what his inner vision reveals to him, rather than to conventional visual and narrative expectations.

In his earliest films Baillie explored ways of visualizing his own mental states and of capturing something of the lovely simplicity of the people around him he saw as most deeply spiritual. Increasingly, his films became characterized by a tendency to layer or combine multiple images and by an unusual sensitivity to texture, color, and light. Each of these tendencies can be understood as an emblem of a particular understanding Baillie had developed. The layering and combining of imagery—most memorable, perhaps, in *Mass for the Dakota Sioux* (1964), *Tung* (1966), and *Castro Street* (1966)—became a way of expressing the complexity of experience, the discovery that reality is not simply a set of surfaces available to perception and intelligence, but a composite of surface and of spirit that flows beneath the surface and behind our perception of it. Baillie's dexterity in capturing the sensuous textures of the world—particularly notable in *Valentin de las Sierras* (1968), *Quick Billy* (1970), and the recent video *The P-38 Pilot* (1990)—is an emblem of the degree to which he sees the perceivable world as invigorated by spirit. And his fascination with color and light in such films as *Still Life* (1966), *Quick Billy,* and *Roslyn Romance* (1977) is a function of his desire for spiritual enlightenment; it connects his work with that of such predecessors and contemporaries as Oskar Fischinger, Jordan Belson, James Whitney, Stan Brakhage, and Tom Chomont, who have used film as a way of visualizing the colors of the soul on its journey toward spiritual regeneration.

For Baillie, the very idea of making his films is so out of synch with the mainstream history of film and the commoditized world it reflects and reconfirms that it renders him an anomaly, an outcast, a "pure fool" like Parsifal and Don Quixote. Indeed, modern society is encoded in the very tools a filmmaker must work with. Achieving the spiritual by means of filmmaking—a mechanical/chemical process—simply "can't be done," and *therefore* is worth doing as a means of demonstrating the ability of film artists to transcend their means. In *To Parsifal* [1963], *Mass for the Dakota Sioux,* and *Quixote* [1965] Baillie becomes the spiritual knight-errant not only in terms of what he trains his camera on and how he uses it but by being willing to enter the field and make films at all.

His refusal to betray his cine-spiritual quest, despite the resistance that surrounded him, became a demonstration of the spiritual integrity of his work. Throughout the sixties, Baillie functioned as both film artist and as organizer. He was the catalyst for the Canyon Cinema exhibition programs that finally resulted in Canyon Cinema distribution, now (along with the Museum of Modern Art's Circulating Film Program) the most successful American distributor of a wide range of critical forms of cinema.

I spoke with Baillie in June 1989 at his home on Camano Island in Washington State.

MacDonald: How did you get started?

Baillie: What led me toward making films in the beginning, in 1960 or even a little before, was an interest in theater and the need to function in the world through art. When I was a kid, in sixth or seventh grade in Aberdeen, South Dakota, we messed up one time and the principal's punishment was that we had to give a play for an assembly. At first, we thought this was a severe penalty, but pretty soon we liked the idea.

Later, we asked him could we give a play every assembly; we had formed a little theater group called "The Acme Company" I stayed involved with theater all through high school and into college (and I refer to it in the introduction to *Quick Billy,* Part Four). Then when I was alone, I thought, well, now that I'm without all these guys, I'll do it on the big screen. I went to the University of Minnesota. A professor there recommended I go to the London School of Film Technique, which was just starting: it was a small operation and they didn't have much equipment, but there were several very good teachers.

MacDonald: This is when?

Baillie: 1958 or 1959. We were an international group of university graduates, ambitious, impatient, and mostly poor, except for the Arabs, who lived in Chelsea hotels and who had numerous English and German girlfriends. We couldn't do much there and were very discouraged. I was sick: the London fog and the poor food made me weak. So I just left in the middle of the term. I went down to Yugoslavia, where I remember seeing a sculpture by the best-known Yugoslavian sculptor: a relief depicting the cycle of life circling a traditional well in the Austro-Hungarian center of Zagreb, where people came for water and to meet each other and gossip. I thought, "This relief is at the source; it's an essential part of everyday life." I liked that, and decided I wanted to do something similar with film.

I came back and thought, "Well, I'll just figure out how to make films." By then I was in San Francisco. I tried to figure out how sound got onto film. I couldn't. There weren't any manuals on it. And nobody could tell me! Finally, I met Marvin Becker, who was making travel and educational films. He was a real expert in 16mm (35mm, too) and had a big studio in San Francisco. He'd hire a few free-lance people for big jobs. I told him, "I'll work eight hours a day, for as long as my unemployment lasts—three more months—and without salary." So he says, "Well, you can't beat that! When can you start?" I parked my '49 Chevy under the Bay Bridge every day, after the long drive from Canyon, where I lived with Kikuko Kawasaki, who was one of my real mentors and a dearly beloved. I got the Chevy from a wrecker for twenty-five dollars; it had to have its brake fluid refilled for every crossing of the bridge!

Marvin started me out rolling up sound film outs that were lying all over the studio. I'd play them through a little sound reader and label them with a grease pencil. So I got acquainted with how film feels and how it works. Later, a free-lance editor was splicing the track for a film for the Horseless Carriage Clubs, and I hung around behind him and saw how he organized footage, cut and spliced it with Mylar tape. Then I got to go out and shoot with another man, from Bechtel Associates, as his assistant; I took a few shots with his Bell and Howell which he was able to use. And then I started making a film with my dogs and my dear friend, Miss Wong. I remember Mr. McKinney at Multichrome Lab, on Gough Street, helping me out during this time—later his son, "Mac," took over the lab and was a friend to many of us.

MacDonald: Was the film with Miss Wong *On Sundays* [1961]?

Baillie: On Sundays—a typical early sixties film where someone gets chased and you go through old buildings and all that.

MacDonald: There are some nice moments in that film.

Baillie: Oh, there might be. I can't tell you how hard it was for me to edit. I had started to learn cinematography—that was hard enough. I had never used a still camera in my life before I picked up the Bolex, but after I was getting used to it, I tried editing and couldn't manage it. So I just hung around the studio and kept practicing. I would take a scene with the dogs and I would cut it one way, then another. It took me forever to develop a little bit of freedom. For quite some time, I was like a gymnast without any grace.

The issue of poverty and art was very important then, and it has always been of special interest to me. I had a friend in Berkeley, a very fine commercial artist, Jeff Belcher. He lived in an attic: everybody was living in somebody's shed, or in an attic or in the back of a car—a lot of skilled people. I don't know how it is now, in the world at large, or among American intellectuals and poets, but then there were *many* people with skill and sensitivity but no place to live and no place to apply their gifts. Jeff was the only guy I knew at the time who had tried cinema, and when I announced to him that I was going to try it, he said, "No, don't! You cannot make films by yourself, because one person can't do that many jobs, learn that many skills, alone, and without an income, and without a place to live. And where would you find the equipment and the materials? None of it's available to you. Never will be. You can't afford it, never will be able to. Don't do it, I don't want to see you broken!" Well, I had a lot of strength then, and I decided that was how I was going to use it. Later, I invited him to my first show.

I was discovering the principles of working. I saw myself going over the Oakland-San Francisco Bridge on the mission of the day like a knight. I wasn't twenty, I was thirty and headed toward forty, mature enough to learn, and to move toward consciousness at last. One of the many things I discovered was that what my friend had said in the very beginning was obviously true, and that as a result, there were not many of us trying to do this, and very few who understood that attempt. It was close to a one-hundred-percent effort. It was like war.

For me, poverty was really the mother or the sister of our craft and of our lives. Our aesthetic came from Sister Poverty, as Saint Francis used to say. Ron Rice was a good example of a poor guy, dead poor. He used machine-gun-camera film that half the time wouldn't respond to the lab developer. I remember him coming through town in the early Canyon days with two beautiful young ladies. He found some back room in Berkeley with these two lovely ladies. We were curious about the relationships, naturally, but we never asked him. He was kind of a severe guy, I thought. He was on his way to Mexico, and as you know, he never returned. He was working on a film, had it hanging up with the women's underwear on strings across his borrowed room.

I find that when we [Baillie and Lorie, his Filipina wife] go to the Philippines, in some ways we find the spirit we had at Canyon Cinema in the sixties. The key was, and is, *simplicity.* At Canyon we recognized that one of the essential ingredients was necessity, and that to be heard you have to be needed. When we're in Lorie's village in Bobol, anything we can offer is needed. In a Philippine village, there's no such thing as Mom and Dad who live in a middle-class house, commute to work, and love their children, and when their child has a birthday, they have a little birthday party. In a village, everyone's a brother or a sister or a cousin, and all children are mine and my children are yours, and when they have a birthday, there's plenty of time because nobody's commuting, we're all unemployed. We had a dance last night for somebody who got married and today the daughter is having her fifth birthday and people cry and laugh and there's music and cake and all kinds of stuff is happening. Christmas takes two months! That was film art for ten years in America. We needed each other and enjoyed the process, regardless of its difficulties. It was hungry people making cookies all day!

MacDonald: How did Canyon get started?

Baillie: We started Canyon Cinema about 1960, in Canyon, California, over the hills from Oakland and Berkeley. Kikuko was paying the rent and giving me the chance to free up my time to make films. Immediately, I realized that making films and showing films must go hand in hand, so I got a job at Safeway, took out a loan, and bought a projector. We got an army surplus screen and hung it up real nice in the backyard of this house we were renting. Then we'd find whatever films we could, including our own little things that were in progress—"we," there wasn't really any we, just myself for a while—and show them.

So I made a *thing* of it. I had no occupation. I couldn't get a job anywhere. So, I thought, I'll invent my own occupation. I set up a little part of the house as an office. I had to call it something: I put up a little sign, and it turned out to be "Canyon Cinema" with a light bulb next to it. Fairly soon, we had weekly showings. Kikuko made popcorn. The kids around the neighborhood gathered the community benches and chairs, and we'd sit under the trees in the summer with all the dogs and people and watch French or Canadian Embassy films and National Film Board of Canada stuff, along with our own. I let it be known immediately that I had a place to show films, if any filmmakers were coming through town. I let Jonas [Mekas] know right away. At first we were in touch with only Larry Jordan, and later, Jordan Belson.

Stan Brakhage came to town after a while and tried to make a home in San Francisco with Jane. And other filmmakers were scattered here and there; we didn't really see each other very much. There weren't many films to show, but toward 1962 it began to build up rapidly. We'd send out postcards, and soon the mailing list was too long. Then Chickie Strand was in town, at Berkeley, and we got together and ran Canyon together. There were a few other people around: her husband, Paul Strand, took care of the screen and the Volkswagen bus, and later Emery Menefee joined us. Chickie was working at the university, and we would show in Berkeley at various places, whatever was available. By then we were showing our newsreel and everything else we could find: Brakhage's films, and Mekas's . . .

MacDonald: There was a generation of Bay Area filmmakers in the late forties: Peterson and Broughton . . .

Baillie: We would order those films from the Audio Film Center catalogue and show them. James Broughton was a kind of father figure. He didn't come around much, but we knew he was in the area. We'd show all his films. Marie Menken, Sidney Peterson, Maya Deren, Frank Stauffacher—we'd have a festival once in a while. Later, we showed in North Beach in San Francisco, in the late beatnik era. So we were pretty busy, putting up signs everywhere, keeping our equipment in shape, and renting films and trying to pay for them, shipping them, returning chairs to the mortuaries, sending announcements to the paper, which they'd *never* print. Nobody would ever write anything about us. But the Berkeley police would come constantly and run us out, right at the last minute, as a fire hazard or something.

MacDonald: Why?

Baillie: I don't know. This was in prerevolution times. Berkeley was quite conservative in the early sixties. They just didn't like the spirit of it. We'd have the Finnish Hall as a backup and a bunch of Volkswagen buses out front (Paul Strand in charge). The police would come and tell us to leave, and we'd say OK, and everybody would get on the bus, go to the next place, and we'd set up again. It was like von Richthofen's Flying Circus. We got really adept at setting up a nice theater anywhere. It was never sloppy. We taught all the people who would come to work for us— volunteers—to set everything up precisely, the right way. We had a good projector and good programs, and we tried to pay attention to the timing of the interludes between films.

MacDonald: How many people came to screenings?

Baillie: At the University of California, or nearby, we'd always have from twenty-five to seventy people. I'd guess the average was thirty-five to forty-five. Over in North Beach, there might be twenty people. We showed all over the Bay Area. We were very concerned about the tone of the events.

MacDonald: What tone were you looking for?

Baillie: We wanted a nice family mood. We knew we were going to show things that were likely to upset people's expectations. They were prepared for the conventions of a literary kind of movie, *real movies,* and they weren't going to be seeing much of that. So we wanted to be kind to them. Mainly, we wanted them to relax. That's why we had pies and fruit and door prizes.

One time I gave a show in Los Angeles, with our normal relaxed mood, but people came in expecting a lot of excitement: "Experimental Films!" Since they weren't getting that out of *Parsifal,* they threw food at me! I had spent months collecting my old paintings for a show in the lobby, and they drew moustaches on them! If you get 'em worked up, it can go the wrong way. But we always tried to work with the audience.

Choosing programs, however, was like making films: we didn't take audience preference into consideration. Our decisions were totally personal and aesthetic. Putting a program together is like making art. It's one of the few places where a person can function without damage to others, with personal power, self-centeredness, ego, whatever—their own vision. Our theater was like that. During the tea ceremony in the old Japan, nobody would ever ask could you bring out the *other* scroll, please? [laughter]. Or could we maybe have some *other* tea? No, you'd come and there it was, and because the master of the ceremony, the master of ceremonies, is a particular person, with all the limitations of being particular, the master would do it his or her way. And as a result, this particular ceremony would have a universal touch.

Teaching for me should be done the same way. If a student approaches me, implicitly assuming that I should be concerned with the same politics she is, or he is—some fashionable dogma—I always fade out immediately. That's not education. I don't like to please students and I don't like to please audiences. If I did, I'd make Coke ads or porn films, and right now we'd have a fat income. College students are so fashion conscious. These days, they're very concerned about how you're supposed to treat each other, "correct politics." I've always taken to the Zen way, where you make a big joke of what everybody thinks is serious and you're very serious about what everybody thinks is not. You mix it all together and throw it out backward. It stays new that way.

MacDonald: What else do you remember about the early Canyon days?

Baillie: After we moved over the hill from Canyon to Berkeley, we were a small, impoverished, but very alive collective, a few people who put together some equipment that other people could borrow (and that we could use to make our own films). We came up with *The News,* the Canyon Cinema newsreel. It was like in the old days at the movies when they had a feature and a cartoon and a serial—and a newsreel. We used outdated, reversal, black-and-white 16mm film. Ernest Callenbach [editor at University of California Press and of *Film Quarterly;* author of *Ectopia* (New York: Bantam Books, 1975)] had a little house in back of his place that we used. We couldn't mix sound at that point, so we made wild sound and used a quarter-inch tape recorder. The news itself would sometimes be the guys laying some pipe somewhere, mundane information, or it might be a totally cinematic piece. When new people came through, we'd tell them, "Don't feel obliged, but if you want to make a newsreel, just make whatever you want to make, and we'll call it "The News."

MacDonald: Termination [1966], the film about Indians in Laytonville, and *Mr. Hayashi* [1961] were "news items," right?

Baillie: Yes.

MacDonald: Mr. Hayashi is like an ad. It gives Mr. Hayashi's hourly rate, a dollar twenty-five an hour.

Baillie: It had an immediate basis in necessity.

MacDonald: When I was going through *The Pleasure Dome,* the catalogue for the Swedish show of American experimental film put together by Jonas Mekas and Claes Söderqvist for the Modern Museum in Stockholm in 1980, I noticed that your filmography lists several films not included in the Canyon or Film-makers' Cooperative catalogues: *David Lynn's Sculpture* [1961], *Friend Fleeing* [1962], *Everyman* [1962], *The News No. 3* [1962], *Here I Am* [1962], *The Brookfield Recreation Center* [1964], and *Port Chicago Vigil* [1966]. Were those Canyon newsreels?

Baillie: Mostly. Those are either in my negative archive box in the house here or were part of what I shipped to Jonas to be stored at Anthology. *David Lynn's Sculpture* was one of my first films, a newsreel of David Lynn's *big* log sculpture, made for the first Canyon Cinema up in Canyon. I was leaving Canyon one day to go on a little trip, so I made a little film for everybody: *Friend Fleeing.* I think *News No. 3* is about the testing of the bomb on one of the South Seas Islands during the early sixties. *Here I Am* was made in the early days for an Oakland school for children with mental disorders of various sorts. It was quite a nice film. I gave them one print, and I made a print for myself. I don't know if I ever got the original reversal back; the San Francisco lab folded. The Brookfield Recreation Center was another school, and I made them a looser, rougher film than *Here I Am. Port Chicago Vigil* was made at a time when we used to stand out by the naval base when they were shipping napalm to Vietnam. At first I went out there just to film the demonstrators, but then I joined them. People who had sons or brothers in the war would come by and throw stuff at us from their cars or shoot at us. I don't remember too much about that film. *Everyman*—I don't know! It's funny to forget my own films! I think there's at least one print of all of those films. Some of them were with Willard Morrison, a friend who loved films and for a time was the manager of the San Francisco Audio Film Center. He moved to Costa Rica, I haven't heard from him. His distribution became Macmillan Films in Mount Vernon, New York.

MacDonald: How long did you do the filmed newsreel?

Baillie: Maybe two years—it gradually merged with/into our personal filmmaking. A little later, Chick [Ernest] Callenbach invented the written and printed *Canyon Cinemanews.* My mother took over the business of it and it grew fast. Chick had his own job, so Chickie Strand and I edited it, and later Paul Tulley and I. We discovered a great logo, the front and back pen drawing of a beautiful guy from a nineteenth-century medicine catalogue: The Exothematic Method of Cure. It was a little kit with platinum tipped needles: you punctured yourself and used the "Olium" that came with the needles. By this *advanced method* you were supposed to be able to rid yourself of "morbid matter." We really loved that; we had the image reproduced and it went on our news. Later, we had it made into stamps, stickers, and it went on the reels of film the Coop distributed.

MacDonald: When did distribution begin? And who was involved?

Baillie: First, there was a woman who ran it over in Sausalito, and Bob Nelson ran it for a while. And Bruce Conner, Larry Jordan, Edith Kramer. It took me a long time to back out of it. So much was dependent on the manager.

MacDonald: When did you get out?

Baillie: Oh gosh, I guess in the mid or late sixties, when I made *Castro Street* and the other more difficult films. I was at Morningstar, a commune near Santa Rosa. Lou Gottlieb was the owner. He was a Limelighter [the Limelighters were a popular folk group during the sixties], a real neat guy who opened up forty acres. A friend named Ramon Sender, a San Francisco composer, moved up there, and a great painter, Wilder Bentley; a lot of people were coming and going. I made my strongest films there. We all lived outdoors in the woods, alone in different spots. I lived with my dog in a homemade canvas tent with a kerosene lamp. We had a building where we ate and took turns cooking. I could not have been directing Canyon Cinema then. It was about this time I met Will Hindle, who was to have quite an influence on me, and Scott Bartlett, another great friend.

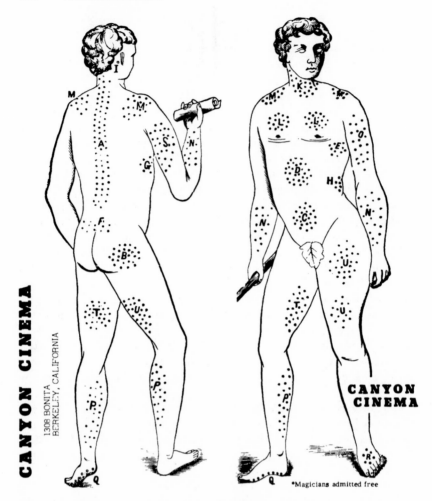

The Exothematic Man: Canyon Cinema's first logo.

MacDonald: What do you think are your strongest films?

Baillie: Castro Street, All My Life [1966], *Quixote, Quick Billy,* and even though *Mr. Hayashi* is a very crude film, I love it because of the person *in* it. I like *To Parsifal.* It's a little awkward, but mostly good. And *Mass.* I suppose that's it . . . oh gee, I like *Roslyn Romance* quite a bit, the introduction especially. And *Valentin of the Mountains* [*Valentin de las Sierras*] I like very much.

An odd thing about filmmaking is that you don't practice like a pianist; you make a film every time. So a lot of the films were practice.

MacDonald: About *On Sundays.* You said something last night that reminded me of that film. You said that if your parents hadn't left this house to you, you'd probably be on Skid Row.

Baillie: Like the guy in *On Sundays,* yes. I met him living in an abandoned car under the Bay Bridge.

MacDonald: It struck me that there was an interesting prescience in that film: there's this Skid Row guy chasing this young Asian woman . . .

Baillie: Oh yeah! Just like me and Lorie. [laughter]

MacDonald: Obviously, you're not homeless, but the thought of that seems to have been in your head a long time.

Baillie: Well, it hasn't, actually, at least not that I'm aware of. Only in recent years when I came to realize what the result of not following the "American Plan" can be and usually is: you have nothing when you get older, after you've used your energy. All the systems are designed, more and more, to take care of *employees.* I've only been an employee occasionally to earn a little more to go on being an unemployed artist. In the American value scheme, people who are not employed are not holding up their end.

But whatever someone else might see in *On Sundays* must be there for the seeing.

MacDonald: While not a conventional narrative, it has a lot of conventional narrative elements, and it's interesting that the next two—*The Gymnasts* [1961] and *Have You Thought of Talking to the Director?* [1962]—are a little different: they're both narratives, but the story seems only a pretext for a trip into a mental state. There's a development from learning how to tell a story to learning how to externalize what you're thinking or feeling. Could you talk about those early developments?

Baillie: Hard to recall. Generally, each film showed me what *it* wanted, as the Eskimo carvers say. I was slowly coming to understand more about my medium. I do recall deciding to proceed slowly with this huge task and to proceed in a conventional way, meanwhile looking around and seeing others going off into modern art and expressing themselves in their own unique ways. I simply couldn't at first.

I was just pushing on to uncover hidden ground. Looking back on that time, I think of a Japanese garden with all the neatly laid stones you walk along that emulate the randomness of nature and yet have the exactness of the Zen Buddhist's mind. I look back and see that each step, each stone, was something I laid of necessity, my own necessity, the necessity to know myself. I would make each film as it came along, I'd smell in the air when the time had come again.

I remember more clearly what started me to work on the later films. In *Castro Street* it was the color quality of the Standard Oil tanks in Richmond, California, on a particular rainy day. For *All My Life,* it was the quality of the light for three summer days in Casper, California, up the

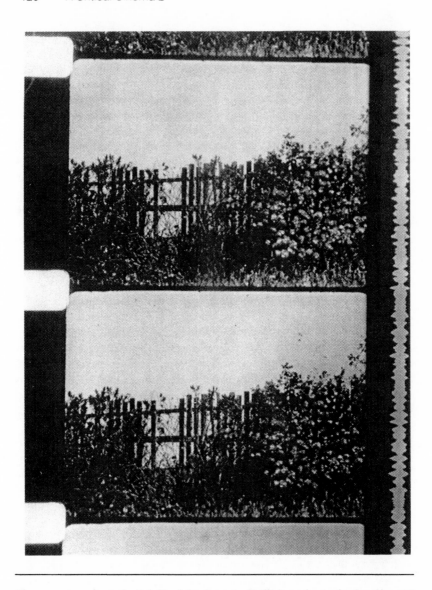

Flowers grow along the "clef" of the fence in Baillie's early single-shot film, All My Life *(1966).*

coast where Tulley lived. It looks like Cork, Ireland, used to. The managerial class, as usual, invaded that lovely little place and neutralized it. But it was a beautiful place for a while. There were three days: the peak day was the first day I noticed the light. I had this outdated Ansco film I wanted to use. But I didn't want to make a film. By that time, I knew the toll making a film can take. But the second day the light was still marvelous. A friend was with me, and we started to drive back to San Francisco, and suddenly I said, "No, I can*not* turn my back on this!" We stopped, and I got the tripod, fixed it real solid. Then I practiced and had her call off the minutes: we had about three minutes to get up into the sky in one roll, one continuous shot. Then we shot it and it went as smoothly as possible—I panned with the three-inch telephoto lens and pulled focus as I panned. *All My Life* came out well. It was inspired by the light (every day is unique as you know), and by the early Teddy Wilson/Ella Fitzgerald recording ["All My Life"], which was always playing in Tulley's little cabin, with its condemnation sign on it (one evening, we were having supper and heard "tack tack." We went out and looked at the door. The sign said, "You are required to leave these premises by twelve o'clock tomorrow!"). I knew that song had to be the track and that it had to have the same sound it had at Paul's, with a potato sack over the speaker. It's supposed to sound a little scratchy. When I got back to the commune, I put the music and the image together.

MacDonald: A Hurrah for Soldiers [1963] is dedicated to Alfred Verbrugge because his wife was killed; why wasn't the film dedicated to her?

Baillie: Well, generally, I'm not political—especially then I was not. And I did not keep myself very well informed about the world, history, events. But all of a sudden in *Life* magazine there was this terrible, tragic picture of a man, Verbrugge, screaming: these soldiers had murdered his wife, by mistake. It was a horrifying picture. I couldn't stand that human beings could do such things to one another. I just couldn't contain it, so I immediately set out to make a film, my first color film. Somebody'd given me a few rolls. The light was so pretty in the lower sky and made such nice grays and blacks. It was almost a-chromatic. That interested me.

So it was a tribute to a man who had lost his beloved through the savagery of total obedience to an idea. Krishnamurti abhors that we follow ideas, not to mention ideologies, like little puppy dogs, or *soldiers*. He often admonishes his students to try to learn to transcend ideas. An idea is fixed; it's a nonexistent point in the continuity of the moving spirit: the essential infinite life we seek in all our thinking, feeling, acting. I just hated that these soldiers were obedient to a command that resulted in this tragic moment that reverberates forever in the universe: murder never stops, and I wanted to have some say about that kind of ignorance, that obedience to authority. I was a newcomer to the medium and that film was probably the best I'd done with it. By then, I had a little equipment to work with, though I had to borrow or rent things every time I wanted to make a movie. I recall the tears, the total frustration, at not being able to work when it was time!

A Hurrah for Soldiers was also inspired by a seemingly completely different event. I was down by the beach, and on the sea wall was written one of those things that odd mentalities will write privately in public places: "I want to be beaten up by girl gangs." That interested me, too, so I got a "girl gang" together—all my girl and women friends who were part of Canyon Cinema, and said, "I want to see some guy joyfully getting beaten up by a bunch of females." It didn't have any particular implications or complications for me at the time. I didn't read much into it; I was just amused by that statement out there on the wall. Before we shot, I repainted it over so it'd be darker, more obvious, and [laughter] a neighbor came along and said, "So *you're* the one writing this crap on the wall! I'm calling the police!" So we had to get out rather quickly. I don't think we ever photographed the words. For the beating, we found an old rubber tire and beat on that, out of frame. I don't know where I got that strange Mexican choir of children singing "Maria." *A Hurrah for Soldiers* was an odd mishmash. My father played the priest.

MacDonald: When I was looking at your films chronologically and came to *To Parsifal,* it seemed as though you had reached a point where it was enough just to look at something gorgeous in the world. It was as though you had realized, "Oh, this can be a film. I don't need to put this *into* anything else."

Baillie: I remember the exact process of making that film. That was probably the first film where I felt I was starting to get a hold of the medium. There are some awkwardnesses, especially a few still cuts between trees, that remain disturbing to me, but for the most part it's a pretty interesting tribute to Wagner and the myth of the Holy Grail and the Parsifalian hero.

I was out on a fishing boat, and I knew a new film was cooking in me and that it was spring and a tribute to the loveliness of spring was coming, and I heard this music on the boat and had my camera. An old friend, Willard Morrison of Audio Film Center, in San Francisco, had given me the first rolls of new color film I ever had, about seven rolls of the old Ektachrome—so beautiful. ASA 15 or 16. It was like liquid gold in my camera. Like silver bullets. I had a couple rolls of that with me, so I listened to the music coming in over a little speaker up on the mast as we rolled along in the Pacific Ocean off the Golden Gate—we were very low to the ocean because of the way the boat was designed—and you could really feel the sea, and so I just shot it the way it was. Then I thought, "Well, what's this music: it's got to go in there," and it was *Parsifal,* by Richard Wagner. I didn't know anything about him or his music at the time, though I was familiar with the Grail legend. So it all mixed together—the magic sword and the wound given Amfortas, the result of his own indiscretions or imperfections.

You're given a certain responsibility and a gift or grace, a certain unique capability, which can turn against you if it's not attended to properly. Even the king who possessed this emblem of purity or perfection, this divine weapon, was heir to temptation, and the weapon fell into the hands of his nemesis. The wound was ultimately mortal. Though he was still alive, still functioning, he was incapable of carrying on this essential divine mission to celebrate Infinite Truth, embodied in the Holy Grail, so it was foretold that there would be a successor who would come along, a "pure fool" as Wagner called him—whether the original name was Parsifal or Percivil, it really meant "pure fool."

MacDonald: So you saw yourself as cinema's Parsifal?

Baillie: Parsifal was object and subject all at once, an objectified depiction *and* a reflection of my subjective pursuit of an identity, my recognition of myself. To try to make *my* own films against enormous resistance was perhaps Parsifal-ian: to be out there in the woods and on the ocean with a movie camera, unemployed, not doing the usual things— marrying, making children, setting up the pension plan, carrying the mail.

MacDonald: At the beginning of the film a superimposed text says "Part One," but there's no "Part Two." Did you have in mind another film that would be Part Two of *To Parsifal*?

Baillie: No. That film, as it is, was conceived as being in two parts: the sea and the Sierra Nevada. Even though I didn't say "Part Two," evidently, there is a definite closing of one section and an opening of the other. Perhaps, I said, "Part One" just to indicate that it *was* in parts. That first part was shot off of Steve Brenner's boat. We hear the sounds of the VHF radio and the fishermen talking to one another, early morning. Sort of beautiful, isn't it? And then up in the cliffs the wind was blowing through those grasses that grow along the Northern California coast.

MacDonald: That gorgeous shot of the wind in the grasses is a motif all through your work and apparently your life—even your child [Baillie had a baby girl in March 1989] is named Wind.

Baillie: The horses, the grasses blowing in the wind, the sea, the flesh of young girls' faces, edges of bodies, movement . . . those are my motifs.

MacDonald: You know, it's very hard to verbalize about your work.

Baillie: But it's kind of fun, isn't it, to verbalize around things, because each person gets a chance to see for him- or herself! *Parsifal* isn't closed down like a Coke ad. It gives a lot of room to the viewer. I think there are lovers of the medium who are more amorous perhaps than some of the filmmakers. I like to make analogies between filmmaker and the man of arms. The man of arms becomes so much *of* his/her weaponry that he can become inured to that pure love, which is his/her source.

MacDonald: You mention the openness of *To Parsifal.* Some years ago, there was a tendency to see that film as having a clear, almost polemical message: people who ran trains were bad and people who looked at nature were good. In the film the issues seem more complicated. You seem simultaneously a person in love with the purity of nature and fascinated with these processes that people engage in— partly because they're *also* drawn to nature—in order to exploit nature. I want to go up into the mountains near here, and I'll use an automobile to do it: I have to bring *with* me the opposite of the mountains in order to get to the mountains to enjoy this illusion of purity!

Baillie: That's right: the combination of ingredients which seems to transcend good and evil *and* at the same time, the clear continuing theme of good versus evil that began with *On Sundays.* There's always the simpleminded theme of what's good and what's bad, but it isn't carried on in a simpleminded way.

MacDonald: That's certainly true of *Mass.*

Baillie: Yeah.

MacDonald: The hero of *Mass* is the guy on the motorcycle—his "noble steed"—which on one level is distinct from the tract houses he passes and what they seem to mean; but on another level the motorcycle is part of the same consumer culture. The people coming to take care of the guy lying in the street is a parable of taking action within a society where the tendency is to ignore the suffering of others.

Baillie: Disposable people, as Tulley says. *Mass* is a requiem, conceived on the occasion of President Kennedy's murder. A sad time for many people. I had just come back from a long lonely trip to where I'd been born in the Dakotas. I don't remember if I shot anything on that trip—I think not—but I knew I was into a film. One night after I was back I stayed up all night—one of those rare times when I stay up all night—and listened to the requiem masses being played on the radio, especially Mozart's. It was so beautiful. You know, Celtic people love to weep over the beauty of things. One of the many really nice ways to respond to the world is through sadness. It's very deeply rooted in me, and maybe you too. The requiem mass is a non-Celtic way of celebrating death joyfully. So I knew I was making a mass, but again it was new information for me. I'll run into Catholics who think I'm a Catholic. But I only studied the mass for a short time in order to do my work, and then I forgot it. I have almost no data stored in my brain. My life and my art are entirely "noninformative."

The film has a very strong critical thesis: it's *against* contemporary society, buildings, pollution—all the rest of it—and it's *for* the at least implied joy of nature and selfhood and being human!

MacDonald: Mass is full of layered imagery, superimpositions. That's a stylistic way of expressing the fact that things are more complex than they first seemed to you. As your films develop in the years after *Mass,* layering becomes more and more important, even characteristic.

Baillie: Perhaps.

We can't leave out of this discussion of *Mass* the tribute to the American aborigine, the original people who were considered by the celebrants of the Holy Mass as unholy savages. The hero in the film was a tribute to the native people of Dakota, the Lakota Sioux in general and all their tribes, and it was a tribute to the best of man who lies on the sidewalk, dead already at the beginning of the film and hauled off later by the celebrants: the body of Everyman taken away in the celebration of the Holy Eucharist. It was also a tribute to *the poet* (and specifically to Jean Cocteau). I portrayed the gift of poetry as deceased, gone. The film is a celebration of what has passed away from our hysterical milieu of materialism and technological redneckery!

MacDonald: Though paradoxically it hasn't passed away because you're making film poetry.

Baillie: Right. I am that very person, or if it isn't me, it's others. I'm making this film and portraying myself, betraying myself, uncovering the self, expressing Every Person's dilemma.

MacDonald: At times, *Mass* has a strange sheen to it, especially on the bridge . . .

Baillie: I did a couple of things to get that. A lot of times I used a green filter in the summer sun. It gave an odd flatness to a pretty good, contrasty reversal film. And then I put Vaseline on my clear filter for the diffusion. A lot of times I would shoot and wind back and shoot again— as people did in those days—making double images *in* the camera, taking what happened and declaring that another clue to what was developing, discovering the film as I went.

MacDonald: Quixote was the biggest film you'd done up to that point and still is, except for *Quick Billy* and *Roslyn Romance* (if one counts all the sections of those two films). In many ways, it's an extension of *Mass.*

Baillie: I was living with my folks. I never could afford my own room or anything, and by this time my father was saying, "You're getting to be thirty-whatever and you're doing these films, and you're getting nowhere. You just can't live here anymore." I had to quit in the middle of *Mass* about three times 'cause I had no place to house it. I was always living in someone's back room, where I couldn't work. Finally, I went home to my folks' house where the film was, and walked quietly back into my room and went to work on the *Mass,* and no one said anything, and I finished it. Ultimately, it was my father and mother whose support made this period [of creativity] possible. All the films and my life are thanks to my mother, Gladys, and my father, E. Kenneth Baillie.

Well, anyway, all these critical personal issues were hitting me. Where was all this going? How long could I keep it up? I don't know when I first got a grant, but I remember I couldn't go another inch. I'd got myself way in debt. No income. I didn't have any equipment, and I had all this work to do. And then my friend Ramon Sender from the San Francisco Tape Music Center told me a fellow from the Rockefeller Foundation was coming out to find western artists, possibly to give them grants. I got to talk to him, and he looked at my work.

A little while later, I was on my way to Eugene, Oregon, to give a show, and the Volkswagen broke down. I put a pin in it somewhere and got a little further down the road to a phone, and I called this Rockefeller guy and said, "What about the grant? Can you do it or not, because I'm either going to quit right now or push ahead; it depends on what you say right now, because my car's broken down, I'm in debt, I can't go any further." And he said, "Yeah, we're going to give you a grant." And I said, "Well, can I pay my debts off?" He said, "No, you can't use a grant that way. You have to spend it on your films." And I thought for a minute and said, "Well, that's OK." Because when it came, that's what I did: I paid all my debts, and bought a little equipment. So I was able to push ahead through the middle sixties and get *All My Life* finished and *Still Life, Castro Street, Valentin,* and *Tung*—some of my very nicest films.

But *Quixote* was before all this, when poverty was really facing me. The first phase was the Southwest. I went with a friend of mine from Kowloon, named Tseng Ching. She was a wonderful girl who'd finished college, and her visa was almost up. She gave me two hundred dollars that her uncle had given her. I've never gotten over that. I told her "Absolutely not!" when she offered it; I couldn't believe it, and as time went on, I couldn't raise a penny. So I took her money and she came with me, and my dog—Mama Dog—a big shepherd. I was reading *Don Quixote* as I went. I was aware of the structure of Cervantes's work; the transitions, in particular, were important to me. Also, I'd studied some of John Cage's notes and his music and some of Stan Brakhage's films and writings, and some e.e. cummings. But especially, Cervantes. I liked how he would get out of one chapter and into the next. There'd be the name of a chapter and then a subtitle would say, "Of what was said when on the road to. . . ." Then there'd be submaterial indented with space around it where, say, the shepherd's song would be. I liked that shape. I knew I was going to have very unique, disparate materials that had to fit together, and it was going to be quite an assignment. I felt up to it 'cause I had made quite a few films now, and I wanted to make a long film with an interesting form. I wanted to show how in the conquest of our environment in the New World, Americans have isolated themselves from nature and from one another. As you may remember, in the Southwest sequences I go way away from the town and film it from out among the cacti and cicadas.

The passage about the pigs in South Dakota being herded around and the guys eating dinner was *not* supposed to be an obvious pun on "piggish eating," which would never have occurred to me. I never think of pigs in that common sense of "piggish" . . .

MacDonald: You mean you wouldn't insult pigs by comparing them with those guys?

Baillie: Yeah. So I made a mistake there, because it's always taken that way. It was really just another one of many little devices in that movie to enforce the contradistinction between the guys back here in town, the City Fathers, doing whatever they do to perpetuate this characteristic defensive wall against nature. Anyway, Tseng Ching and I went out and had some adventures, and I recorded a lot of it. We found an old schoolhouse out in Arizona somewhere, where there used to be trails for the stagecoaches and the cavalry, and I found an old out-of-tune piano that she played and I recorded—stuff like that.

Then Tseng Ching had to leave for China. I never saw her again. I went back to my folks' house for a while and winter came and that's when I went over the mountains and started the black-and-white section. I used film I had stolen in Hollywood: Tseng Ching and I had gone down to Hollywood before going to the Southwest and shot some film which I never used, and we found some stacks of that old film that Ron Rice used to use, in an alley in a big box. I immediately knew it was for me. So I hit the road with that film and over the mountains from San Francisco it was winter. I'd almost forgotten! I arrived in my Volkswagen with a weak battery, and it snowed and we were stuck in Nevada somewhere. The dog and I had to sleep together to survive! The next morning we ran into an Indian guy who was living with his pony in the basement of a hotel. He got a guy to come out and jump start us. There are so many stories in that film!

Technically speaking, I knew I wanted to have a more sophisticated way of combining imagery, which would somehow be accomplished *after* the original shooting. And I decided this was going to be a long film for two projectors. I didn't like the simple effect of in-camera superimposition. That was just too elementary. I shot a long section in the hills of the San Bernardino Valley one foggy morning. We were camped out. Later, when I started editing, it was used as a separate piece to be projected alongside the other material. I practiced that for a while, then I put it away. In the archives with the *Quixote* material are long segments that were made to go side by side with the material that's in the distribution version of the film. But in the end I didn't combine imagery that way.

Instead, to make a combined image, I used black Mylar tape. I'd lay stuff down side by side on a light table, and mask parts of the frame, so that later the frame would share two disparate scenes *without* the effect of superimposition. I had to do it manually because I didn't have access to optical printers. And a lot of that had to be taken off again, gradually, because it was a mess, but that's how some of those little effects were done. Lots of the material was put aside because it just wouldn't match up: lots of segments weren't used.

Finally I got the car running better and went north. I wanted to go up to Cutbank, Montana, 'cause that always had the coldest weather; I wanted to be there in the middle of winter. It was so cold that I broke the handle on my tripod while panning in a blizzard. It was crazy. I got up into the Indian reservations and then headed east. I wanted to do something in New York City, but Selma was happening, so I borrowed some money and flew to Selma. I was a day or two behind the terrible beating days that had sent me down there. I got what I could.

MacDonald: You had no sense at the beginning of the overall route you would take?

Baillie: I went wherever my knight errantry took me, like Don Quixote.

MacDonald: It's like a feature-length newsreel. It seems to come out of *Mr. Hayashi* and the early Canyon newsreels.

Baillie: Yes.

MacDonald: Castro Street uses still another method of combining imagery.

Baillie: Castro Street took about three months of solid work. To go into the process at length would take us all day, but there are a lot of notes about the film, some at Anthology Film Archives. The notes were very important. After I had finished *Castro Street,* there was a long period of going back to my tent at night and writing notes on the lessons I had learned from having made it. The film was still teaching me.

Castro Street was made by the most horrendous effort of intellectualization and intuition combined, using the back and the front of the brain simultaneously, which blew my fuses for life. When I was editing *Castro Street,* I would come out of my morning editing session around noon to lie in the sun and eat, and people I lived with in the commune would pass by, and I couldn't recognize them. I didn't know who they were. I was like someone with Alzheimer's disease. I just blew my brains out every morning editing that film. Now, I try to dissuade my students from this kind of suicidal single-mindedness!

Technically, when I made *Castro Street,* I went into the field again with my "weapon," my tools. I collected a couple of prisms and a lot of

From Baillie's Castro Street *(1966). Still courtesy of Anthology Film Archives.*

glasses from my mom's kitchen, various things, and tried them all in the Berkeley backyard one day. I knew I wouldn't have access to a laboratory that would allow me to combine black-and-white and color, and I was determined to do it by myself. I went after the soft color on one side of Castro Street where the Standard Oil towers were; the other side was the black and white, the railroad switching yards. I was making mattes by using high contrast black-and-white film that was used normally for making titles. I kept my mind available so that as much as one can know, I knew about the scene I had *just* shot when I made the *next* color shot. What was white would be black in my negative, and that would allow me to matte the reversal color so that the two layers would not be superimposed but combined.

I shot the railroad material in shorter shots, as "masculine." The "feminine" was the longer, more continuous, simpler, steady color. So one side of the street was feminine for me; the other side masculine. I discovered that I had in my archives some music from Southern India that was based on that idea, and although I didn't particularly recognize why it was that way, I enjoyed the music, and I needed inspiration so I always played it while I edited. I wanted to visualize that ancient, universal fact of opposites that are one, both in conflict and harmony—opposing each other *and* abiding together and requiring each other.

MacDonald: On one level it would seem strange to make a beautiful film about an industrial landscape, and yet, if you're combining opposites, it seems very logical. It's like taking the place where one might think there's nothing to look at, or at least nothing of a poetic sort, and then making the opposite thing from it. Your film is a kind of magic.

Baillie: That sounds good to me. At that time my work was recognized mostly as social criticism: the theme of modern systems as evil always seemed to be there. I remember thinking, "Well, I'm just dropping all that; I'm going to make a *film* film." And then I began to recognize the inner meaning of it. Naturally that *would be* the foundation of it, since it was clear to me always that my purpose in making each film was to find myself, and each film took me further, until finally I was beyond the necessity of making films. Originally, I showed *Castro Street* with stereo sound. I'd take a little Ampex speaker and amplifier along. We'd have the one optical track, and we'd play the magnetic B track on the tape recorder. That was the original plan. Then it got to be too much trouble, and it went around with only the monaural optical track.

MacDonald: Who was Tung in *Tung*?

Baillie: Well, she still is a close friend who lives in San Francisco. At the time, we were very close. I think it was one New Year's that I found myself in love with her again, feeling so much love for her. I remember sleeping on the floor in my room at my folks' house, waking with a momentary impression—that *was* an idea that preceded the images—and getting right up and making myself work before it was gone, to capture exactly what I had seen in just a half an instant. I'd trained myself for a lifetime to catch *some* of those instances—not only visualizations, but thought-stuff.

I remember my folks were going to church, and I went up on the roof of the house. I had a blue glass that I'd brought back from Japan, which I taped over my lens and did that long pan around the house, diffusing and giving that purple-blue to everything, shooting the sun as though it were the moon. We shot the material of Tung herself out by the Berkeley horseracing track where there was nothing disturbing the horizon line. I shot at a low angle against the sky with black-and-white copy film, high contrast, so that if I used the negative as a reversal, the black sky would in effect be a matte with her against it. I shot her on roller skates in slow motion to get the image that had come to me that morning.

MacDonald: Did the little poem come in that early morning impression?

Baillie: I had written the poem the night before, I think, as I went to sleep. It was one film that only needed to be assembled. Later, I found myself down in my mother's flower garden getting some reds. I did an A, B, C roll, like I did for *Castro Street*. My technique was the most successful that I know about, aside from using optical printers. I laid out the A, B, and C rolls, doing the dissolves between A and C (I had a spring motor then that could do, at most, twenty-five-second runs), dissolving from one shot of the sky to another, to make it look like one long shot. And B would fade in smoothly to bring in the black-and-white material of Tung. I could see where to fade her in, or fade her out, by just looking at the film on a light table. That was the nice thing about working in reversal.

Now there are no film stocks left! They removed them one at a time, like they remove everything else that's beautiful in our world. They take away all the nice old buildings and the old fences, all the visually beautiful stuff. They modified the old Ektachrome three times I think; then they withdrew it. They had an Ektachrome 50, ASA 50, reversal. That was pretty decent. Nobody used it a lot, but it was real nice. And the Kodachrome before it was very interesting, but that disappeared right in the beginning. Then they got into these flat, uninteresting TV newsreel stocks and that's all they had left for a while.

This society has a way of homogenizing every goddamn thing. It's terrifying. I just can't tell you how I feel about it. When I moved to Olympia, there were a few little alternative corners left in town. Within five years, they were all destroyed, all the old docks, the alleys, the berry bushes, the crazy sailors, all gone. Horrible. And now we have the New World Order, the storm troops, a world of "winners."

MacDonald: When I interviewed Yoko Ono, she had an idea for a travelogue of Japan, where everything would be in super close-up: you wouldn't have to leave your room to make a travelogue. You could talk about noodles and have an extreme close-up of noodles . . .

Baillie: [laughter]

MacDonald: Her idea reminds me of *Valentin de las Sierras*.

Baillie: Yeah.

MacDonald: Which is like an ethnographic film made up of textures.

Baillie: That's right.

MacDonald: How did you end up in Mexico? Did you always carry a camera with you when you traveled?

Baillie: That was one of the banners of the sixties, filmmakers carrying their cameras. They got too heavy after a while.

In *Valentin* I just shot simply but used a telephoto lens with an extension tube on the back, which gives you a very limited focal plane, a few inches. No one I know ever uses it with a long lens, especially with a moving subject, but I really liked the way it looked. I had to get into the flesh of that town, with the merciless sun beating into the bricks of the street and all the death—every night there'd be something or somebody killed, lying in the street in the morning. I had met up with this (archetypal) young girl, riding her pony. And I was afraid to meet her father. I'd sent word out trying to see her, and *he* sent word back to come meet him, and I thought, "Oh, God!" But he turned out to be a very nice fellow: Manuel Sasa Zamora, of Jalisco. They were very poor and lived behind a big gate and had a horse and a dog named Penquina. That horse didn't like me and would not let me film. I had to give it up for a while. Later, I named my horse after the film—*Valentina*.

MacDonald: When I was looking through your films, the biggest discovery for me was *Quick Billy*. It's a pretty amazing film, and certainly begs for questions because it's so diverse. Reel one is very much about morning and creation.

Baillie: I think that beginning section is one of the most beautiful things I've ever seen in the movies. I had to get out of bed to make every one of those takes. I was really sick, with hepatitis. Tulley would come over, and I would tell him what part of the house I had to go to, and he would help me up. I'd tie a knot in a big beach towel and pull in my liver with it. He'd walk me over to, say, the fish tank, and set the tripod up and load the camera. Then I'd do the take and go back to bed.

MacDonald: The opening shot of Part One is very mysterious. The spectator never actually sees anything, just a shade of pink that gets a little more dense, then less, over a period of about two and a half minutes. And I'm not sure what I'm hearing: sometimes it sounds like traffic, sometimes like the ocean.

Baillie: It's the ocean. Later, there are the sounds of passing timber trucks.

That opening is supposed to be the highest moment of illumination in the whole work. I was following the Tibetan description of the time between life and death, and that's either the illumined memory of perfection or the illumined moment of discovery. It can go either way. I never played the film backward, but it was designed so it could run backward or forward.

MacDonald: You mean the whole film, all four parts?

Baillie: Let's see, the last reel was in narrative form so that would always run forward. Then would come the end of Part Three, from the end to the beginning; then the end of Part Two would come, then the end of Part One. The end of the whole film would be the beginning shot with that pure light.

MacDonald: So that version would move from the mundanery of conventional narrative toward this moment of supreme illumination, like a journey up the chakras?

Baillie: I don't remember the whole story. I was describing my own death experience through the catalyst of hepatitis. I had studied *The Tibetan Book of the Dead*. There the deceased is on a journey, "the time of uncertainty." The specters come to us as our own personal cinema: we are obliged to confront the results of our own deeds. It becomes more and more frightening. As I pursued the experience, I found this delightful moment in the beginning which was so lovely; it degenerated into a terrifying but lovely cosmic storm. In *The Tibetan Book of the Dead* each moment has an opposite side, and there's a color for every aspect. I forget their phraseology, but green, for example, on the positive side might be the jewel from the knowledge of equality (or some such Buddhist term), and on the opposite, negative side, the fearful aspect, jealousy.

In all the segments of *Quick Billy* I had a ruling form or deity. One was an old, wise horse named Amber that lived with us. I shot her mane against the black stormy sky. Then there'd be another form, another creature or person. Their opposite would appear in the second reel, all in the same order exactly, with the opposite meaning. So those first two reels were mates; they ran almost the same length. There's a continuing gradual degeneration, and the beasts of light become the terrifying beasts of darkness that are the guiding entities of the second reel.

The assignment the first time, given to me by the conditions of making the film, was not to make a beautiful film, but rather to make a *document* about this inner passage, a little-described, but very common—in fact universal—phase of being human: the evolution of consciousness through which every man and woman eventually must go. There's hardly any information about it in our modern age, but it's common in some of the old civilizations, perhaps in all of them: information as to how to make that passage. In contemporary culture we have the ball-game or warfare scores on TV, the homogenized newscasters all reading the same news.

I think my concept for *Quick Billy* is almost identical to Stan Brakhage's *Scenes from Under Childhood* [1967–70], which explores the "scenes" prior to childhood—the scenes so near that time between being and being. Brakhage was sending me those films at the time I was going through all this, and they were essentially identical to what I was making, I thought.

MacDonald: Do you see reels three and four at all as mates?

Baillie: No. I just saw reel three through my own sequential experience, almost like lessons in a course. I went from presexuality into sexuality, using recollections of boys I grew up with, the athletes I admired so much, out of the yearbooks. That wasn't too well shot.

MacDonald: Were you an athlete?

Baillie: No. I was underdeveloped in high school, this little punky guy with a cute haircut. I really admired athletes a lot; they were big, muscular, and hairy. I was born to be an artist, and I had an artistic way of seeing. I looked at every basketball game as a great symphony: the changes of movement, the rhythms, the nice coordination and musculature young athletes have. That finally came out in reel three in that moment of the Bardo, No Man's Land. I was studying it all and putting it down as I saw it. The sun went down in the ocean at the end of reel three. And then reel four was entirely separate and different, but it continued the same themes. Paul, Charlotte, and I scripted this little story and filmed it as we went along. The film ended with the phrase "Ever Westward, Eternal Rider," a kind of Celtic farewell, which I have written into my will—a tribute to myself, to life! One must do these things for oneself, I think, given the monumental indifference of the modern mind.

MacDonald: The beginning of reel three, the scene where you and the woman make love, is very sexy.

Baillie: Oh, yeah.

MacDonald: I wondered if you were thinking of three and four as a pair because the personalized, direct experience of life at the beginning of reel three is the opposite of the Hollywood-ized Western in reel four, which certainly isn't very romantic—certainly not for the woman. Reel three puts reel four into a funny perspective.

Baillie: A lot of people just *couldn't* see that reel four belonged to the film at all.

It was nice to work that hard in those years, to have the blessing from the gods to allow me to manage it. That film just seemed to go on endlessly, like a pregnancy, and then the baby bursts out with such pain! Whew! It was so taxing, so that now, twenty-five years later, I'm living a half life.

I have to rest a lot just to get up and talk to people now. Many people just don't understand these things *at all,* haven't the *slightest* idea, with the longest unendurable explanation, what I'm saying: "Oh, you mean you're retired!?" It's so far from the simple fact that you've used yourself so ruthlessly in order to be a channel for something beautiful. But it is wonderful that such a limited fragile creature as a person, a human being, *can make* a beautiful thing!

MacDonald: I'm puzzled about the numbering of the short, "extra" reels of *Quick Billy.* There are numbers fourteen, forty-one, forty-three, forty-six, forty-seven, and fifty-two. Is there a system?

Baillie: I always just number the reels from one on. I shot *Quick Billy* on ASA 25 outdoor Kodachrome, I believe. I think it was about the last they had. And I numbered the rolls from one on, just to keep track of them when they went to the lab. That sunlight image that opens Part One was the first roll I shot. I didn't use number fourteen in the film.

Then I used all the rolls from fourteen up to forty-one. And so on. And I shot after I knew I was done making the main body of the film. I had to let it keep going since there was so much vitality in what I was shooting. Finally, it got to be like the Greek Golden Age passing when everything got too elaborate and touched up and didn't have the newness of the earlier stuff. So I stopped. Later, I selected the best "rolls" and released them as such. I consider them as artifacts, essentially, as in an archeological dig.

MacDonald: Roslyn Romance is also made up of a lot of little rolls.

Baillie: Yes. They're not all small, but generally they have the roll concept, or they're like "postcards," as the intro explains. They're all separate but have the basic connection of belonging to the Romance. I use "romance" in the French sense, of story, and also in the sense that the human mind seems to prefer inventing, rather than accepting, from moment to moment, the *what is* of life/reality.

Roslyn, Washington, was one of the few remaining examples in North America of the kind of Old Europe village life that ended at the beginning of the twentieth century and was to a degree transported over here. I found myself in that town, with people from the "Old World." For them, reality was, "Well, I'm here in this house and I have a job and I'm respectable and I feed my children and love and protect them; I built this house to defend myself, my family, and this town from others and from the wilderness around us." That was the life I recorded in infinite detail in *Roslyn,* and a major theme of *Quixote* which preceded it.

I wanted to know, like Stendhal, *is that all there is?* I did ask them this question constantly. Every day I would leave my house and walk down the street like anyone else in the village and be stopped and invited in for Italian pastry or some other treat and an hour's gossip, on the way to the post office. I would ask myself, "Is it really true?"—the subtitle of the work. The unanswered question works itself through lots of rolls and reels after the formal introduction, which I just barely managed to finish in the seventies while at Bard College before I had to move again. The rolls and notes to *Roslyn Romance* remain in my Washington archivery waiting to be finished and released.

The concluding part, which is called "The Cardinal's Visit," is a narrative film, conceived with my close friend and filmmaker Elliot Caplan. I shot it with the last grant I had (an NEA) with the help of Elliot and a lovely apprentice and friend, Ms. Harley, who stayed in my little trailer in Upstate New York, between 1979 and 1981. We worked very hard for a while. I was the cardinal (I still have the costume). We shot about four hours of really pretty color negative with very elaborate lighting setups. We'd do two or three setups a day, just about like a Hollywood film. There were usually three of us: me, the young woman, and the man who played the young priest. I took a lot of the immediate dramatic detail from our everyday lives. For example, in real life the young guy fell in love with the girl. He didn't recognize the cardinal's interest in her, and I didn't want to tell him about it. There wasn't any reason to tell him. But he was getting romantic about her, and he would call every night, was rejected as often. The cardinal represented the church, but he was/is also a sensualist. His red cloth represents holy office *and* the fires of hell, the torments of time and mortality.

I spent a lot of money on the film. It's almost done. A friend of mine, Bonnie Jones, painted beautiful medieval title cards because there are a lot of booklike segments with chapter headings. I'm looking for a serious graduate film student who wants to finish the film as an M.A. project or something. We could select what goes with what and edit it. Or he or she could put it together. I don't want to do all that anymore. I'm too tired.

Because *movies* are viewed as popular art and thus the property of the twentieth-century masses. Implicitly, it's part of our thinking that anyone who uses film seriously, poetically, experimentally is transgressing on sacred convention—like asking the "tree cutters," who identify with "free enterprise," to use restraint in destroying our common environment. For the neighbors it can't be explained: "Who are you: What do you *do*? You waste your time all day! Why don't you get a *job*? You've got a wife and children!" God, there's no *end* to it. Or you come into town and you're filming something, and you try to explain, but if you're not making a profit, it's inexplicable to people, it doesn't compute. It's so exhausting. It's like being a pugilist: you can only do it so long. And when you're finally broke and broken, no one—truly very few—care at all.

I heard Peter Kubelka talk about it at Bard College. He's standing up front, and an innocent young man asks him, "Gosh, Peter, it must be fun to take a camera out and turn it onto the world and make art and show it to people." Kubelka's quiet for a minute, then he says, "Well, on ze contrary, it's *zo* exhausting, I cannot tell you!"—in that high voice of his—"To take a heavy camera out in the world and carry the bloody thing under your arm for twenty years and be obliged to *record* everything instead of simply living it—it's zo telling on your soul, zo exhausting in your bones and muscles. It's impossible to do it, *impossible*—the places it takes you, into the nether world constantly. It's zo distressing to your merely human frame, I can't tell you. Don't do zis thing!"

I was once a free-wheeling artist among other artists, all of us on the move, giving everything we could, taking a lot as well. In those days Ann Arbor was one of our centers, because of the Film Festival and George Manupelli. We'd all stay at his house; and then later, Sally

Dixon made a center for us in her house in Pittsburgh and arranged many shows. I usually stayed, by preference, in her basement, by the washer and dryer. I've always preferred small, private spaces (I still hanker for the simple life in a cardboard box). Later, Sally moved to Saint Paul. I haven't heard from her in years.

I met Robert Haller in Pittsburgh. He's now in New York City with Anthology Film Archives. And there was Gerry O'Grady in Buffalo of whom I hear nothing anymore. My last time through there, I publicly awarded him a general's star (from the collection I had as a kid) for his efforts on behalf of the art of cinema. He lived like a modern Basho—briefcase, suit, one pair of shoes, three ties, three shirts, three shorts. Don't know what's become of him or George Manupelli: sent a new work to Ann Arbor this year, but never heard from them!

In New York City I would always stay with Charles Levine—his mom made chicken soup for us, especially when I needed energy to give a show. We usually bought champagne, cheese, and crackers for those Millennium and other shows in the sixties and seventies. My wife at the time (mid seventies), Gigi Alinre, a wonderful artist, and I started doing little theater routines. I still have in my archives Danny Scheine's stills of me changing on stage into the Cardinal. The last run through New York, before the recent [February 1991] Maya Deren Award visit—where my two-year-old daughter, Wind, and I did a few small routines—was in 1986 with my friend and filmmaker Nabuko Yomashita of Kyoto. We came up via Texas, through New York City, and up into Connecticut and Vermont. And there were Layne, Ed, Tom, Dan, Helen, and others at SWAMP [The Southwest Alternative Media Project] in Houston. Ray Foery, teacher of film history, and the Farrells of Vermont, filmmaker Tom Brener and the folks of Rokeby, Rhinecliff, New York. In Minneapolis, the Sutherlands; Bill and Sylvia Wees, Montreal; Kerryi and Kumi Yianesaka, Tokyo; Dominic Angerame and all the people of Canyon and Film-makers' Cooperative. I mention these particular places and people because they (among many others) were essential in my own life and in the creation of the various films we have discussed.

Some of it disintegrated, at least for me. Many of those who have supported us have been so unselfish that I wouldn't want to speak critically about them. All I know is that I don't know who they are anymore, or where they are. I don't hear from them. There's no more exchange. Canyon, the successful little cooperative that I fathered, lost a certain spiritual feel—perhaps it's coming back. For a time it was like the Methodist church; they have voted out all the peculiarities—the poetic craziness. But it's the way of the age. At the same time, I am very grateful it functions so well! We received nice royalties from Canyon this year—amazing really. I don't know who rents those films or why, but they continue to do so. But they don't want to see the artist; they don't want him or her in their living rooms or classrooms. So I'm here with a small family, doing my little Dr. Bish radio shows, photographing Cambodian girls, writing notes, and making some video.

My gift has been imagination. It's always alive and working; it loves *theater*. It seems to me that someone who's born to do that, should be doing that because all people benefit when creativity is alive. Just like a guy who's born to be a great pugilist should do *that*. He shouldn't have to go through some system where there's a bunch of application forms and say, "Well, I would like to box, and I'm a potential champion," and be told, "Your application will be held on file. We appreciate your interest." You should be able to say, "Here's what I do, this is the time to do it!" Instead of all the nonsense of politics and "managerial policy": the film business and the academic business are merely managers talking to managers. They're a caste who too often control the creative, which, as Joseph Campbell says, is so essential to society. It is art and myth that reflect our identity, our process, and our history. It is the path of the poet we follow: lonely tracks in the black snowy places of memory and an unknown horizon.

Yoko Ono

Yoko Ono's relationship and partnership with John Lennon have given her access and opportunities she might never have achieved on her own, but her status as pop icon has largely obscured her own achievements as an artist. Nowhere is this more obvious than in the area of filmmaking. Between 1966 and 1971, Ono made substantial contributions to avant-garde cinema, most of which are now a vague memory, even for those generally cognizant of developments in this field. With a few exceptions, her films have been out of circulation for years, but fortunately this situation seems to be changing: in the spring of 1989 the Whitney Museum of American Art presented a film retrospective along with a small show of objects—eighties versions of conceptual objects Ono had exhibited in 1966 and 1967—and the American Federation of Arts re-released Ono's films in the spring of 1991.

Except as a film-goer, Ono was not involved with film until the 1960s, though by the time she began to make her own films, she was an established artist. At the end of the fifties, after studying poetry and music at Sarah Lawrence College, she became part of a circle of avant-garde musicians (including John Cage and Merce Cunningham): in fact the "Chambers Street Series," an influential concert series organized by LaMonte Young, was held at Ono's loft at 112 Chambers. Ono's activities in music led to her first public concert, *A Grapefruit in the World of Park* (at the Village Gate, 1961) and later that same year to an evening of performance events at Carnegie Hall, including *A Piece for Strawberries and Violins* in which Yvonne Rainer stood up and sat down before a table stacked with dishes for ten minutes, then smashed the dishes "accompanied by a rhythmic background of repeated syllables, a tape recording of moans and words spoken backwards, and by an aria of high-pitched wails sung by Ono" (Barbara Haskell's description in *Yoko Ono: Objects, Films,* the catalogue for the 1989 Whitney Museum show).

In the early sixties Ono was part of what became known as Fluxus, an art movement with roots in Dada, in Marcel Duchamp and John Cage, and energized by George Maciunas. The Fluxus artists were dedicated to challenging conventional definitions in the fine arts, and conventional relationships between artwork and viewer. In the early sixties, Ono made such works as *Painting to See the Room Through* (1961), a canvas with an almost invisible hole in the center through which one peered to see the room, and *Painting to Hammer a Nail In* (1961), a white wood panel that "viewers" were instructed to hammer nails into with an attached hammer. Instructions for dozens of these early pieces, and for later ones, are reprinted in Ono's *Grapefruit,* which has appeared several times in several different editions—most recently in a Simon and Schuster/Touchstone paperback edition, reprinted in 1979.

By the mid sixties, Ono had become interested in film, as a writer of mini film scripts (sixteen are reprinted in the Fall 1989 *Film Quarterly*), and as a contributor of three films to the *Fluxfilm Program* coordinated by Maciunas in 1966: two one-shot films shot at 2000 frames per second, *Eyeblink* and *Match,* and *No. 4,* a sequence of buttocks of walking males and females. Along with several other films in the *Fluxfilm Program* (and two 1966 films by Bruce Baillie), *Eyeblink* and *No. 4* are, so far as I know, the first instances of what was to become a mini-genre of avant-garde cinema: the single-shot film (films that are or appear to be precisely one shot long). *No. 4* is interesting primarily as a sketch for her first long film, *No. 4 (Bottoms)* (1966).

For the eighty minutes of *No. 4 (Bottoms),* all we see are human buttocks in the act of walking, filmed in black and white, in close-up, so that each buttocks fills the screen: the crack between the cheeks and the crease between hams and legs divide the frame into four approximately equal sectors; we cannot see around the edges of the walking bodies. Each buttocks is filmed for a few seconds (often for fifteen seconds or so; sometimes for less than ten seconds), and is then followed immediately by the next buttocks. The sound track consists of interviews with people whose buttocks we see and with other people considering whether to allow themselves to be filmed; they talk about the project in general, and they raise the issue of the film's probable boredom, which becomes a comment on viewers' actual experience of the film. The sound track also includes segments of television news coverage of the project (which had considerable visibility in London in 1966), including an interview with Ono, who discusses the conceptual design of the film.

No. 4 (Bottoms) is fascinating and entertaining, especially in its revelation of the human body. Because Ono's structuring of the visuals is rigorously serial, *No. 4 (Bottoms)* is reminiscent of Eadweard Muybridge's motion studies, though in this instance the "grid" against which we measure the motion is temporal, as well as implicitly spatial: though there's no literal grid behind the bottoms, each bottom is framed in precisely the same way. What we realize from seeing these bottoms, and inevitably comparing them with one another—and with our idea of "bottom"—is both obvious and startling. Not only are people's bottoms remarkably varied in their shape, coloring, and texture, but no two bottoms move in the same way.

On a more formal level *No. 4 (Bottoms)* is interesting both as an early instance of the serial structuring that was to become so common in avant-garde film by the end of the sixties (in Snow's *Wavelength* and Ernie Gehr's *Serene Velocity,* 1970; Hollis Frampton's *Zorns Lemma,* 1970 and Robert Huot's *Rolls: 1971,* 1972; J. J. Murphy's *Print Generation,* 1974 . . .) and because Ono's editing makes the experience of *No. 4 (Bottoms)* more complex than simple descriptions of the film seem to suggest. As the film develops, particular bottoms and comments on the sound track are sometimes repeated, often in new contexts; and a variety of subtle interconnections between image and sound occur.

Like *No. 4 (Bottoms),* Ono's next long film, *Film No. 5 (Smile)* (1968, fifty-one minutes), was an extension of work included in the *Fluxfilm Program.* Like her *Eyeblink* and *Match*—and like Chieko Shiomi's *Disappearing Music for Face* (in which Ono's smile gradually "disappears"), also on the *Fluxfilm Program*—*Film No. 5 (Smile)* was shot with a high-speed camera. Unlike these earlier films, all of which filmed simple actions in black and white, indoors, at 2000 frames per second, *Film No. 5 (Smile)* reveals John Lennon's face, recorded at 333 frames per second for an extended duration, outdoors, in color, and accompanied by a sound track of outdoor sounds recorded at the same time the imagery was recorded. *Film No. 5 (Smile)* divides roughly into two halves, one continuous shot each. During the first half, the film is a meditation on Lennon's face, which is so still that on first viewing I wasn't entirely sure for a while that the film was live action and not an optically printed photograph of Lennon smiling slightly. Though almost nothing happens in any conventional sense, the intersection of the high-speed filming and our extended gaze creates continuous, subtle transformations: it is as if we can see Lennon's expression evolve in conjunction with the flow of his thoughts. Well into the first shot, Lennon forms his lips into an "O"—a kiss perhaps—and then slowly returns to the slight smile with which the shot opens. During the second shot of *Film No. 5 (Smile),* which differs from the first in subtleties of color and texture (both shots are lovely), Lennon's face is more active; he blinks several times, sticks his tongue out, smiles broadly twice, and seems to say "Ah!" Of course, while the second shot is more active than the first, the amount of activity remains minimal by conventional standards (and unusually so even for avant-garde film). It is as though those of us in the theater and Lennon are meditating on each other from opposite sides of the cinematic apparatus, joined together by Ono in a lovely, hypnotic stasis.

The excitement Ono and Lennon were discovering living and working together fueled *Two Virgins* (1968) and *Bed-In* (1969), both of which were collaborations. *Two Virgins* enacts two metaphors for the two artists' interaction. First, we see a long passage of Ono's and Lennon's faces superimposed, often with a third layer of leaves, sky, and water; then we see an extended shot of Ono and Lennon looking at each other, then kissing. *Bed-In* is a relatively conventional record of the Montreal performance; it includes a number of remarkable moments, most noteworthy among them, perhaps, Al Capp's blatantly mean-spirited, passive-aggressive visit, and the song "Give Peace a Chance." Nearly all of Ono's remaining films were collaborations with John Lennon.

When the Whitney Museum presented Ono's films at its 1989 retrospective, *Rape* (1969) provoked the most extensive critical commentary. The relentless seventy-seven–minute feature elaborates the single action of a small filmmaking crew coming upon a woman in a London park and following her through the park, along streets, and into her apartment where she becomes increasingly isolated by her cinematic tormentors. (Her isolation is a theme from the beginning since the woman speaks German; because the film isn't subtitled, even *we* don't know what she's saying in any detail.) The film was, according to Ono, a candid recording by cinematographer Nic Knowland of a woman who was not willingly a part of this project. When *Rape* was first released, it was widely seen as a comment on Ono's experience of being in the media spotlight with Lennon. Two decades later, the film seems more a parable about the implicit victimization of women by the institution of cinema.

Fly (1970) has a number of historical precedents—Willard Maas's *Geography of the Body* (1943), most obviously—but it remains powerful and fascinating. At first, a fly is seen, in extreme close-up, as it "explores" the body of a nude woman (she's identified as "Virginia Lust" in the credits); later more and more flies are seen crawling on the body, which now looks more like a corpse; and at the end, the camera pans up and "flies" out the window of the room. The remarkable sound track is a combination of excerpts from Ono's vocal piece, *Fly*, and music composed by Lennon.

Up Your Legs Forever (1970) is basically a remake of *No. 4 (Bottoms)*, using legs, rather than buttocks: the camera continually pans up

A fly explores a woman's body in Ono's Fly *(1970). By permission of Ono.*

from the feet to the upper thighs of hundreds of men and women, as we listen to the sound of the panning apparatus and a variety of conversations about the project. Though *Up Your Legs Forever* has some interesting moments, it doesn't have the drama or the humor of *No. 4 (Bottoms)*.

Ono and Lennon also collaborated on two Lennon films (whether a film is a "Lennon film" or an "Ono film" depends on whose basic concept instigated the project). *Apotheosis* (1970) is one of the most ingenious single-shot films ever made. A camera pans up the cloaked bodies of Lennon and Ono, then on up into the sky above a village, higher and higher across snow-covered fields (the camera was mounted in a hot-air balloon, which we never see—though we hear the device that heats the air) and then up into the clouds; the screen remains completely white for several minutes, and finally, once many members of the audience have given up on the film, the camera rises out into the sunny skyscape above the clouds. The film is a test and reward of viewer patience and serenity. For *Erection,* a camera was mounted so that we can watch the construction of a building, in time-lapse dissolves from one image to another, several hours or days later. The film is not so much about the action of constructing a building (as a pixilated film of such a subject might be), as it is about the subtle, sometimes magical changes that take place between the dissolves. *Erection* is more mystery than documentation.

Imagine (1971)—not to be confused with the recent *Imagine: John Lennon* (1988, directed by Andrew Solt)—was the final Ono/Lennon cinematic collaboration: it's a series of sketches accompanied by their music. Since 1971 Ono has made no films, though she did make a seven-minute video documenting the response to a conceptual event at the Museum of Modern Art: *Museum of Modern Art Show* (1971). She has also made several music videos that document her process of recovering from Lennon's death—*Walking on Thin Ice* (1981), *Woman* (1981), *Goodbye Sadness* (1982)—as well as records and art objects.

Of course, she remains one of the world's most visible public figures and the most widely known conceptual artist.

I spoke with Ono at her office at the Dakota in May 1989.

MacDonald: Were you a moviegoer as a child?

Ono: I was a movie buff, yes. In prep school in Tokyo you were supposed to go directly home after school. But most of us kids often went to the movies. We used to hide our school badges and sneak into the theater.

MacDonald: Do you remember what you saw?

Ono: Yes, I mostly saw French films. There was a group of kids who liked American films—Jimmy Stewart and Katharine Hepburn, Doris Day and Rock Hudson, Bob Hope and Bing Crosby—and there was another crowd of girls who thought they were intellectuals, and went to French films. I was in the French film group. We would go to see *The Children of Paradise* [1945], that sort of thing. It was a very exciting time. I loved those films.

MacDonald: Did you see some of the early French surrealist films from the twenties?

Ono: Those things I saw much later. We're talking about when I was in high school in the late forties. I saw the surrealist films in the sixties in New York and Paris.

The films I saw in high school that were closest to surrealism were the Cocteau films, *Beauty and the Beast* and *Orpheus* [1950]. Those films really gave me some ideas.

MacDonald: The earliest I know of you in connection with film is the sound track you did for Taka Iimura's *Love* in 1963 by hanging the microphone out the window. I know the later *Fluxfilm* reels that were made in 1966, but did the Fluxus group get involved with film before that?

Ono: No. I think that one of the reasons why we couldn't make films or didn't think of making films was that we felt that it was an enormously expensive venture. At that time, I didn't even have the money to buy canvas. I'd go to army surplus shops and get that canvas that's rolled up. During that period, I felt that getting a camera to do a film was unrealistic.

MacDonald: Grapefruit includes three tiny descriptions of conceptual film projects that are identified as excerpts from "Six Film Scripts by Yoko Ono." Were there others, or was the indication that there were six scripts a conceptual joke?

Ono: No, there were six at first; then later there were others. At the time I wrote those scripts, I sent most of them to Jonas Mekas, to document them. Actually, that's why I have copies of them now.

MacDonald: There seems to be confusion about the names and numbers of the films on the *Fluxfilm Program,* and about who did them. I assume you made the two slow-motion films, *Eyeblink* and *Match,* and the first film about buttocks, *No. 4.*

Ono: Those are mine, yes.

MacDonald: Did people collaborate in making those films, or did everybody work individually and then just put the films onto those two Fluxus reels?

Ono: One day George [Maciunas] called me and said he's got the use of a high-speed camera and it's a good opportunity, so just come over [to Peter Moore's apartment on East 36th Street] and make some films. So I went there, and the high-speed camera was set up and he said, "Give me some ideas! Think of some ideas for films!" There weren't many people around, at the beginning just George and . . .

MacDonald: Peter Moore is credited on a lot of the slow-motion films.

Ono: Yeah, Peter Moore was there, and Barbara Moore came too. And other people were coming in—I forget who they were—but not many. When I arrived, I was the only person there, outside of George. I don't know how George managed to get the high-speed camera. I don't think he paid for it. But it was the kind of opportunity that if you can get it, you grab it. So I'm there, and I got the idea of *Match* and *Eyeblink* and we shot these. *Eyeblink* didn't come out too well. It was my eye, and I didn't like my eye.

MacDonald: I like that film a lot. Framed the way it is, the eye becomes erotic; it's suggestive of body parts normally considered more erotic.

Ono: The one of those high-speed films I liked best was one you didn't mention: *Smoking.*

MacDonald: The one by Joe Jones.

Ono: Yes. I thought that one was amazing, so beautiful; it was like frozen smoke.

MacDonald: There's a film on that reel called *Disappearing Music for Face* . . .

Ono: Chieko Shiomi's film, yeah.

MacDonald: I understand you were involved in that one too.

Ono: Well, that was my smile. That was me. What happened was that Chieko Shiomi was in Japan at the time. She was coming here often; it wasn't like she was stationed in Japan all the time, but at the time I think she had just left to go to Japan. Then this high-speed camera idea came up, and when George was saying, "Quick, quick, ideas," I said, "Well, how about *smile*"; and he said, "No, that you can't do, think of something else." "But," I said, "Smile is a very important one. I really want to do it," because I always had that idea, but George keeps saying, "No you can't do that one." Finally, he said, "Well, OK, actually I wanted to save that for Chieko Shiomi because she had the same idea. But I will let you perform." So that's me smiling. Later I found out that her concept was totally different from what I wanted to do. Chieko Shiomi's idea is beautiful; she catches the *disappearance* of a smile. At the time I didn't know what her title was.

MacDonald: I assume *No. 4* was shot at a different time.

Ono: Yes. At the time I was living at 1 West 100th Street. It was shot in my apartment. My then husband Tony Cox and Jeff Perkins helped.

MacDonald: The long version of the buttocks film, *No. 4 (Bottoms)*, is still amazing.

Ono: I think that film had a social impact at the time because of what was going on in the world and also because of what was going on in the film world. It's a pretty interesting film really.

Do you know the statement I wrote about taking any film and burying it underground for fifty years [See *Grapefruit* (New York: Simon and Schuster/Touchstone, 1971), Section 9, "On Film No. 4," paragraph 3, and "On Film No. 5 and Two Virgins," paragraph 2]? It's like wine. Any film, any cheap film, if you put it underground for fifty years, becomes interesting [laughter]. You just take a shot of people walking, and that's enough: the weight of history is so incredible.

MacDonald: When *No. 4 (Bottoms)* was made, the idea of showing a lot of asses was completely outrageous. Bottoms were a less-respected, less-revealed part of the anatomy. These days things have changed. Now bottoms are OK—certain bottoms. What I found exhilarating about watching the film (maybe because I've always been insecure about *my* bottom!) is that after you see hundreds of bottoms, you realize that during the whole time you watched the film, you never saw the "correct," marketable jean-ad bottom. You realize that nobody's bottom is the way bottoms are supposed to be: they droop, or there are pimples—something is "wrong." I think the film has almost as much impact now as it did then—though in a different way.

Ono: Well, you see, it's not just to do with bottoms. For me the film is less about bottoms than about a certain beat, a beat you didn't see in films, even in avant-garde films, then.

This is something else, but I remember one beautiful film where the stationary camera just keeps zooming toward a wall . . .

MacDonald: Wavelength? Michael Snow's film?

Ono: Right, Michael Snow. That's an incredibly beautiful film, a revolution in itself really. Bottoms film was a different thing, but just as revolutionary I think. It was about a beat, about movement. The beat in bottoms film is comparable to a rock beat. Even in the music world there wasn't that beat until rock came. It's the closest thing to the heartbeat. I tried to capture that again with *Up Your Legs Forever.* But in *No. 4 (Bottoms)* it worked much better. Maybe it was the bottoms. That film has a *basic* energy. I couldn't capture it in *Up Your Legs Forever.*

MacDonald: No. 4 (Bottoms) plays with perceptions and memory in different ways. For a while it seems like a simple, serial structure, one bottom after another. Then at a certain point you realize, Oh I've seen that bottom before . . . but was it with this sound? No, I don't think so. Later you may see another bottom a second time, clearly with the same sound. A new kind of viewing experience develops. Did you record all the bottoms and the spoken material for the track, and then later, using that material, develop a structure? It seems almost scored.

Ono: Yes. I spent a lot of hours editing. It wasn't just put together. The sequence was important. A sympathetic studio said that I could come at midnight or whenever no one was using the facilities, to do the editing. I got a lot of editing time free; that's how I was able to finish it.

MacDonald: On the sound track some of the participants talk about the process of getting people to show up to have their bottoms recorded, but I'm not completely sure what the process was. You put an ad in a theatrical paper apparently.

Ono: Well, we had an ad, yes, but most of the people were friends of friends. It became a fantastic event. You have to understand, the minute the announcement was made, there was a new joke about it in the newspapers everyday, and everybody was into it. We filmed at Victor Musgrave's place; he was a very good friend who was very generous in letting me use his townhouse.

MacDonald: Did you select bottoms or did you use everybody that was filmed? Were there really 365 bottoms involved?

Ono: I didn't select bottoms. There was not enough for 365 anyway.

And the impact of the film as a happening was already getting lost from filming for so long. And there was the rental of the camera and the practical aspect of the shooting schedule. At a certain point I just said, "Oh well, the number's conceptual anyway, so who cares. It's enough!"

MacDonald: I assume that when you did the early Fluxus version of *No. 4,* you just followed people walking across an apartment. For the long film you'd built a machine to do the filming, which allowed you to film in more controlled close-up; we can't see around the sides of the bodies the way we can in the earlier film.

Ono: Well, in the first *No. 4* I was pretty close too. But, as you say, it wasn't really perfect. In London we did it almost perfectly. My idea both times was very visual. All my films had very visual concepts behind them in the beginning. I mean *No. 4 (Bottoms)* has many levels of impact— one being political—but originally I simply wanted to cover the screen with one object, with something that was moving constantly. In the course of seeing films, I had never seen a film where an object was covering the screen all the way through. There's always a background. The closest you get to what I mean is like some macho guy, a cowboy or something, standing with his back to the screen, but you always see a little background. The screen is never covered; so I thought, if you don't leave a background it might be like the whole screen is moving. I just wanted to have that experience. As you say, it didn't work in the early version, but it was the first idea I had for the film actually.

And also, the juxtaposition of the movement of the four sections of the bottoms was fascinating, I thought.

MacDonald: No. 4 (Bottoms) reminds me of Eadweard Muybridge's motion photographs.

Ono: Oh I see, yeah.

MacDonald: Was the finished film shown a lot?

Ono: Well, I finally got an OK from the censor and we showed it in Charing Cross Road. Then some American Hollywood producer came and said he wanted to buy it and take it to the United States. Also, he wanted me to make 365 breasts, and I said, if we're going to do breasts, then I will do a sequence of one breast, you know, fill the screen with a single breast over and over, but I don't think that was erotic enough for him. He was thinking eroticism; I was thinking about visual, graphic concepts—a totally different thing. I was too proud to make two breasts [laughter]. I think there was an attempt to take the bottoms film to the United States, but it was promptly confiscated by the censor.

MacDonald: At customs?

Ono! Yes.

MacDonald: There's a mention on the sound track that you were planning to do other versions of that film in other countries, and the film ends with the phrase, "To Be Continued." Was that a concept for other films, or were there some specific plans for follow-ups?

Ono: Well you see, all my films do have a conceptual side. I have all these scripts, and I get excited just to show them to people because my hope is that maybe they will want to make some of them. That would be great. I mean most of my films are film instructions; they were never made actually. Just as film instructions, I think they are valid, but it wouldn't be very good if somebody makes them. I don't have to make them myself. And also, each film I made had a projection of future plans built into the idea. If somebody picks up on one of them, that's great.

At the time I was making films, what I felt I was doing was similar to what *The Rocky Horror Picture Show* [1975] did later. I wanted to involve the audience directly in new ways.

MacDonald: How did *Film No. 5 (Smile)* come about?

Ono: When I went to London, I still kept thinking about the idea of smile, so when I had the chance, I decided to do my version. Of course, until John and I got together, I could never have rented a high-speed camera. Well, maybe if I'd looked into it, I could have. I don't know, but I thought it would be too expensive.

MacDonald: Did you know Lennon well at the point when you did *Film No. 5 (Smile)*?

Ono: Yes.

MacDonald: Because I wondered whether you made the film because you wanted to capture a certain complexity in him, or whether the complexity that's revealed in that seemingly simple image is a result of what the high-speed camera reveals, or creates, as it films.

Ono: Well, certainly I knew John was a complex person. But the film wasn't so much about his complexity as a person. I was trying to capture the complexity of a visual experience. What you see in that film is very similar to how you perceive somebody when you are on acid. We had done acid trips together, and that gave me the idea. I wondered how do you capture this?

MacDonald: It's a beautiful film.

Ono: Well, of course, you know from the statements I made about *Smile* [See Ono, *Grapefruit,* "On Film No. 5 & Two Virgins"] that my idea was really very different from the film I finally made. My idea was to do *everybody's* smile. But when I met John, I thought, doing *everybody's* smile is going to be impossible; and he can *represent* everybody's smile.

MacDonald: What I find incredible about *Smile* is that as you watch John's face, it's almost as though you can see his mind working. I don't know whether it's an optical illusion, maybe it's created by the way that the camera works. But it's almost as though as you watch, the expression is changing every second.

Ono: I know. It's incredible, isn't it? Of course I didn't know what exactly a high-speed camera would do. I knew in general, but I didn't know what the exact effect would be. And, of course, I never would have known unless George Maciunas had rented a high-speed camera and called me up. George was a very interesting person. He had a very artistic mind. I never knew why he didn't create his own art; he always wanted to take the role of helping create other people's work. But that combination was very good; he not only executed what we wanted, he gave us the opportunity to look into the areas we would never have looked into. He had that kind of mind.

MacDonald: With *Two Virgins* you and John began collaborating on films and in the next few years there was a whole series of collaborations. Judging from the credits on the films, I assume that one or the other of you would get an idea and then both of you would work the idea out, and whoever had the original idea for a particular film—that film was theirs. Normally, the directorial credit is considered the most important one, but on these films there's a more basic credit. It might be "Film by Yoko Ono," then "Directed and produced by John and Yoko." Am I correct: was it that whoever had the original *concept* for the film, that's whose film it was?

Ono: Yes.

MacDonald: I remember reading years ago in a collection of *Rolling Stone* interviews that when you and John got involved with politics and in particular with the Bed-In, it was partly because Peter Watkins had written you a letter. Is that how you remember it?

Ono: Well, yes, Peter Watkins's letter was a confrontation to us, and at the time we had a conversation about what we felt we had been doing politically: "Well, I was doing this. Yes, I was doing that." As a Beatle, John was always asked, "What is your position about the Vietnam War," or something else; and I think that their manager, Brian Epstein, was very concerned that they wouldn't make any statements, and so they didn't make any direct statements. But a covert statement was made through an album cover that was censored, as you know. And I was standing in Trafalgar Square, in a bag, for peace and all that. So separately we had that awareness, and we were expressing it in the ways that we could. I was doing it more freely because it was easier for me. So we were comparing notes after getting the letter, and then we were saying, "Well what about doing something together," which was the Bed-In (and the film *Bed-In*), so Peter Watkins's letter definitely did mean something to us.

MacDonald: How much control did you (or you and John) have over the way *Bed-In* looks? You credit a large crew on that film. What was your part in the final film, other than as performers?

Ono: We always maintained careful control over the finished films. I was generally in charge of editing, which I did for that film, and for others, frame by frame. I mean I would have a film editor working with me—I don't know the technology—but I would be very specific about what I wanted. When Jonas [Mekas] did the John and Yoko screenings at Anthology [Anthology Film Archives], I had three editing machines and editors brought into our hotel room, and I edited *Bed-In* there because of the deadline.

I enjoy the editing part of filmmaking most of all; that's where the films really get made.

MacDonald: Rape is often talked about as a parable of the media intruding into your lives, but when I saw it again the other week, it struck me as very similar to pieces in *Grapefruit*.

Ono: Well, they keep saying that. I'll tell you what happened. By the time that I actually got to make the film, John and I were together, and the reporters were hounding us, but the *Rape* concept was something that I thought of before John and I got together.

MacDonald: In *Grapefruit* there's "Back Piece II," a part of which is "Walk behind a person for four hours."

Ono: It was that kind of thing, right. But it was also a film script ["Film No. 5 (Rape, or Chase)"].

MacDonald: How candid is the *Rape* footage? It no longer *looks* candid to me.

Ono: It was completely candid—except for the effects we did later in the editing. The girl in the film did not know what was happening. Her sister was in on it, so when she calls her sister on the phone, her sister is just laughing at her and the girl doesn't understand why. Nic Knowland did the actual shooting. I wasn't there. Everything was candid, but I kept pushing him to bring back better material. The type of material he brought back at first was something like he would be standing on the street, and when a group of girls passed by, he would direct the camera to them. The girls would just giggle and run away, and he wouldn't follow. I kept saying he could do better than that, but he actually had a personal problem doing the film because he was a Buddhist and a peacenik: he didn't want to intrude on people's privacy. I remember John saying later that no actress could have given a performance that real.

I've done tons of work, and I don't have time to check it all out, but I wish I could check about this strange thing, which is that a lot of my works have been a projection of my future fate. It frightens me. It simply frightens me. I don't want to see *Rape* now. I haven't seen the *Rape* film in a long time, but just thinking about the concept of it frightens me because now I'm in that position, the position of the woman in the film.

Production still from Ono's Rape *(1969). By permission of Ono.*

MacDonald: In the video *Walking on Thin Ice*, we see a similar scene, but with you.

Ono: I know. And why did I think of *that* song? After I wrote that song all sorts of trouble started to happen, all of which was somehow related to the song, that feeling of walking on thin ice. Sometimes I intentionally try to write something positive. But in a situation like that, art comes first. I really thought "Walking on Thin Ice" was a good song when it came to me. I had no qualms about recording it. The artistic desire of expressing something supersedes the worry, I suppose, and you think, ah it's nothing, it's fine, it's just a nice song or something; and then it turns out that it becomes my life and I *don't* want that.

Just recently I was in this film where I performed as a bag lady [*Homeless,* by Yukihiko Tsutsumi, unreleased at time of interview]. I was a bit concerned what it might mean to enact a bag lady, in terms of future projections. But I reasoned that there are actors who die many times in films, but live long lives, so actually enacting death makes their real lives longer. Well, in the first scene it was a beautiful April day, one of those I'm-glad-to-be-in-New-York days, and I'm wearing these rags and I'm pushing an empty baby carriage in this beautiful green environment. And as I was doing it, I remembered the song "Greenfield Morning" and the line, "I pushed an empty baby carriage all over the city." That was the first song we recorded for Yoko Ono's Plastic Ono Band, and I think it's in *Grapefruit,* too—I mean the instruction "Push an empty baby carriage all over the city" [See "City Piece: Walk all over the city with an empty baby carriage" (Winter, 1961) near the end of the first section (Music) of *Grapefruit*]. So I'm pushing the baby carriage and I'm thinking I don't want to *know* about this. That aspect of projection is interesting, isn't it?

MacDonald: Yes.

Ono: If you are somebody who makes films with a commercial concern or other concerns, other than just inspiration, maybe that sort of thing wouldn't happen. I don't know. But inspiration is very much connected with your life in the past and future.

MacDonald: Apotheosis is a gorgeous film. It's one of the collaborations that's listed as John's film, though the idea of stripping things away until you've got a white screen is very much like some of your work.

Ono: Well, I'll tell you what happened. I think some of the instructions are already there in *Grapefruit,* or maybe not, maybe it's one of the instructions that haven't been published [Ono is referring to the second version of her film script, "Film No. 1 (A Walk to the Taj Mahal)"]. There was a constant feeling of wanting to take an object that's on the ground—not necessarily an object, could be a person—in fact the original idea was a drunken guy walking in a snowy field; you don't see the drunken guy, but the camera suggests that he's drunk because of the way it moves. So he walks and sways, and finally the camera goes up in the sky. When we did the cover for the "Two Virgins" album, where we were both naked, one of us said, "Why don't we make a film where the camera moves from the ground up, shooting our naked bodies, and then just goes up in the air." Later, John said, "Well, let's make one where the camera goes up." So the idea stemmed from that. What happened, of course, was that we didn't expect the balloon film to be the way it turned out. We went up in the balloon, and it happened to be a snowy day.

MacDonald: You were in the balloon with the camera?

Ono: Up to a certain point. The part where you go into the cloud, and then break out of the cloud, was taken later. The footage that came back from the lab was beautiful. It was just something that happened naturally, the dogs barking, everything that happened—it was an incredible experience. We didn't expect it was going to be that beautiful. A lot of things just happen, you know.

MacDonald: If you allow them to, I guess.

Ono: Yes!

MacDonald: Fly seems almost the opposite of *Apotheosis* in a way; it seems . . .

Ono: Very much intentionally calculated?

MacDonald: Right.

Ono: It's true.

MacDonald: You did the sound [for the vocal piece *Fly*] before you did the film. Had you had the idea in mind then?

Ono: I was always thinking about the idea of fly. Actually, I was always fascinated with the pun "fly" and "fly" in English. There was also a conceptual event about flies and where they fly to.

MacDonald: The piece you did for the Museum of Modern Art?

Ono: Yes. Did you see that Museum of Modern Art catalogue? [A 112-page, one foot by one foot catalogue—the title seems to be *Museum of Modern FArt* (Ono is carrying a shopping bag with the letter "F" directly beneath the Museum of Modern Art marquee)—which details her concept at length; the catalogue was designed by Ono and produced by Michael Gross.] At the end of that, I talk about how to fly.

MacDonald: I know the video with the sandwich-board guy in front of the Museum of Modern Art who interviews people about the Yoko Ono show that "isn't there" [*The Museum of Modern Art Show*]. In the text for that piece, you explain how some flies were exposed to your perfume and let loose and that people are following those flies around to see where they land.

Ono: The catalogue was made for that event; it had all sorts of interesting stuff in it, about how to fly and all that. All the pages are post-cards that you could mail, so the catalogue and *Fly* piece could fly all over the place.

MacDonald: So MoMA had this on sale?

Ono: No, no, no, no! MoMA would not do it. MoMA was busy saying to people, "There's no Yoko Ono show here." People would come in and ask, is there a Yoko Ono show, and they would say *no*. They were very upset; they didn't know what was going on. I couldn't sell the book anywhere. Nobody bought it, so I have piles of it.

MacDonald: Earlier, in the mid sixties, you did a number of descriptions of environmental boxes that the viewer would go inside of and images would be projected on the outside. *Eyeblink* was involved in a number of those descriptions, and another was called "Fly." I guess the idea was that a viewer would go inside the box and on all sides you would project images that would create the sensation that the viewer was flying.

Ono: How do you know about these boxes?

MacDonald: I found the descriptions in the *Fluxus Codex*, in the Yoko Ono section [See Jon Hendricks, *Fluxus Codex* (New York: Harry N. Abrams, 1988), p. 418 for the descriptions]. Was either piece ever built?

Ono: They were never built. I haven't seen these ideas since I did them. Whenever I had an idea, I sent it to George Maciunas. He probably kept them. I don't even have the originals for those. I'll have to get this book. You know, I have this thing about reading about me. When something about me is in a book, I mostly don't want to know about it.

MacDonald: One of the interesting things about watching the film *Fly* is that one's sense of what the body we're seeing is about, and what the film is about, is constantly changing.

Ono: A cartoon in a newspaper gave me the idea. There's this woman with a low-cut dress, and a guy is looking at her, and the guy's wife says, "What are you looking at!" and the guy says, "Oh, I'm looking at a fly on her." I wanted the film to be an experience where you're always wondering, am I following the movement of fly or am I looking at the body? I think that life is full of that kind of thing. We're always sort of deceiving ourselves about what we're really seeing.

MacDonald: Do you know the Willard Maas film, *Geography of the Body*? It's all close-ups of bodies, framed so that you can't quite tell what body part you're looking at—but they all look erotic. *Eyeblink* is a little like that, and *Fly* is full of that effect. If you go close enough, every part of the body looks the same, and they're all equally erotic.

Ono: Oh, there's an incredible film instruction that has to do with that close-up idea. It's a travelogue ["Film No. 13 (Travelogue)"]. You have a travelogue to Japan or somewhere, and you say, "Well, now I'm on Mount Fuji," and there's an incredible close-up of stones; and then, "We bathed in a mixed bath," and you see just steam—you get it?—and then, "We ate noodles," and you see an incredible close-up of noodles . . . so in effect you can make a travelogue of any country without going out of your apartment! "Then we saw geisha girls," and you see an incredible close-up of hair [laughter]. I wanted to make that, but I just never got around to it.

MacDonald: *Freedom* [1970], the little one-minute film of you trying to take your bra off, was made the same year as *Fly.*

Ono: Yeah, isn't that a great little film?

MacDonald: It's so paradoxical. You show freedom as the ability to try to break free, which implies that you're never really free.

Ono: Right, exactly.

MacDonald: You mentioned earlier that you didn't think *Up Your Legs Forever* worked as well as *No. 4 (Bottoms).* I thought it was interesting to see that people's one leg is very different from their other leg.

Ono: The best thing about that film is the title, I think. My first vision for that film was like going up all the legs, up, up, up, to eternity ["Film No. 12 (Esstacy)"—the misspelling of "ecstasy" is left as it was in the original film script, at Ono's request]. But in making it, that vision got lost because of what was necessary to film the legs. I don't know how you can do what I originally had in mind.

MacDonald: Jonas and Adolfas Mekas are thanked at the end of *Up Your Legs Forever.*

Ono: Because they did the editing. That was one of the few films I didn't edit myself.

MacDonald: Somebody mentioned to me the other day, and I assume it's not true, that *Erection* was originally a film about John's penis. Was there a film like that?

Ono: Yes, there was. But it wasn't called *Erection.* I think it was called *Self Portrait,* and it wasn't an erection, it was just a long shot of his penis. That was his idea. The funny thing was that *Self Portrait* was never questioned by customs because of its title, and *Erection,* which was about the erection of a building, was questioned.

MacDonald: Is there a relation between the 1971 version of *Imagine* and the recent *Imagine: John Lennon*?

Ono: There's no relationship. We wanted to make a surrealistic film in the tradition of Luis Buñuel and Jean Cocteau. It was John's idea to say just one or two words at the beginning, and make the rest of the film silent, like a silent movie. I liked that idea and we did it. I think that now it's more or less known as a forefather of MTV. Each scene came from some idea John or I had. It was really a collaboration between John and me.

MacDonald: Are you involved in film now? Are you planning to make films? You made several videos in the early eighties, but it's been a while since you've made a film.

Ono: I don't know; it might get to that. I'm one of those people who can't do something unless I'm totally motivated. That's one of the reasons I jump from one medium to another. I did the Whitney Museum show, and suddenly all the inspiration is sculptural; and then last night or the night before, I went to the studio to do some music. But I'm not getting that feeling like I gotta make a film—except for *The Tea Party* [the film script "Film No. 7 (Tea Party)"]: for years I've been wanting to make that one, but because of the technical difficulties I don't seem to be able to get it together. I think one of the reasons I'm not making more films is that I've done so many film scripts. I'd like to see one of them made by somebody else. Maybe one day out of the blue I'll feel it so strongly that I'll make a film myself again.

Anthony McCall

During the years Anthony McCall has been living and working in the United States (he moved from Great Britain in January 1973), he has made relatively few films, but those he has made are dense with idea, particularly about the construction of the film audience and about the situation of independent filmmaking within the larger commercial culture. McCall's filmwork can be divided roughly into two periods.

During 1973–75, he completed a series of "solid-light" films, which seemed a natural development of his earlier interest in environmental sculpture. The first of these was *Line Describing a Cone* (1973), which was followed by three other "Cone" films—*Partial Cone* (1974), *Conical Solid* (1974), *Cone of Variable Volume* (1974)—and then by *Long Film for Four Projectors* (1974), *Long Film for Ambient Light* (1975), and *Four Projected Movements* (1975). The solid-light films were attempts to provide a new form of thought-provoking film pleasure. They are presented in an open gallery space, not a movie theater, and viewer attention is directed not to imagery on a screen (no screen is used), but to the light beam between the projector and the wall. During the thirty minutes of *Line Describing a Cone,* a single strand of light slowly grows into—"describes"—a hollow cone. Perhaps the most obvious dimension of *Line Describing a Cone* and of the other "Cone" films is their simple, beautiful elegance as light sculptures. But for McCall this beauty was as much a means as an end. By presenting the "Cone" films in an open gallery space, McCall means to instigate a new kind of interaction between members of the film audience. As *Line Describing a Cone* develops, audience members don't merely look at it, they interact with the

Cone and with each other, crawling under the Cone, telling other viewers about particularly engaging spots to see it from, and blowing smoke through it. (In order to keep the Cone's thin shaft of light visible, McCall usually makes sure the screening space is smoky before the film begins, or asks that viewers smoke during the presentation.) Often, groups who experience the film lose their self-consciousness and, by the end, are interacting freely. As McCall explains in his program notes for *Line Describing a Cone,* the audience experience generated by the film is a way of throwing into relief the implied politic of the normal screening situation, with its rigid rows of seats and "hidden" projection booth.

By the mid seventies McCall had become dissatisfied that the interactive process explored in *Line Describing a Cone* and other early films was available only to a very small audience in rather cloistered situations: colleges, art galleries in a few major cities. He began to consider the relationship of experimental art making to the larger, commercial society. One result was his involvement with *an anticatalogue* (New York: Catalogue Committee of Artists Meeting for Cultural Change, 1977), an anthology of articles exposing the implicit political agenda encoded in the power structures of contemporary art museums and in the art shows generated by these institutions. Another result was a pair of collaborative films: *Argument* (1978) and *Sigmund Freud's Dora* (1979).

Argument was a collaboration with Andrew Tyndall, who had come to the art world with a background in journalism and commercial film reviewing. Their idea was to use the fact that the audience for experimental forms of filmmaking was small (albeit educated, intelligent, sophisticated) *as a resource.* They proposed their ninety-minute feature as a catalyst for an extended discussion among the members of the Downtown art community (and related communities in other areas) about the position of such communities vis-à-vis Western consumer culture. In order to contextualize the plight of the serious film artist, they decided to use *Argument* to conduct a filmic examination of the aesthetic, economic, and political implications of using printed text and still photography in the world of mass-market commercial media—as exemplified specifically by the September 18, 1977, issue of the *New York Times Magazine* (devoted to men's fashion), the November 14, 1977, issue of *Time,* and the July 1977 issue of *Esquire.*

Argument is serially organized into five differently structured units, each of which presents the viewer with a different balance of text and imagery. These structural units are arranged A, B, C, D, E, A, C, D, B, E, D, C, B, A. For many viewers, *Argument* is a frustrating and annoying experience. We are asked to read and hear the same or similar information over and over, always in contexts that frustrate our ability to completely grasp it. During structural unit B, for example, we must read a text that moves physically while listening to a second continuous text read by continually changing voices. The irony is that the frustration *Argument* creates is an essential part of its central goal: to use the methods of commercial culture to provide a critique of that culture. Despite the information overload, we have a clear sense of the filmmakers' fundamental message by the conclusion of *Argument,* just as we always get the message of the commercial culture ("You deserve a break today!" "Aren't you hungry?") through the barrage of conflicting and partial information that characterizes the commercial television hour and the newspaper and magazine page. *Argument* uses manipulative tactics, not to entertain and market, but to jar the intelligence into a more thorough recognition that our culture's most pervasive and powerful uses of "communications" technologies have more to do with the maintenance of economic and political power than with the exchange of ideas in a free society.

McCall's second collaborative film, *Sigmund Freud's Dora,* developed out of the discussions that *Argument* generated. In fact, the two women listed along with McCall and Tyndall as directorial collaborators on *Sigmund Freud's Dora*—Claire Pajaczkowski and Jane Weinstock (Babette Mangolte did the camera work)—had written critiques of *Argument* that were published in the final edition of the workbook McCall and Tyndall designed for the seminarlike presentations of *Argument.* Like *Argument, Sigmund Freud's Dora* uses a complex balance of enacted imagery, still photographs, and printed text, but in this case to suggest that Freudian psychoanalysis functions—or in the particular case of Dora, failed to function—as a means of controlling female psyches in the interests of male ideological and economic goals.

McCall has not completed a film since *Sigmund Freud's Dora,* though he has written scripts for film and television, including a version of the Frankenstein story. My interview with McCall began in 1983, with revisions continuing through 1986. Our conversation covers McCall's films up through *Argument* (Tyndall was present when *Argument* was discussed).

MacDonald: Where did your interest in film begin?

McCall: I went to art school [Ravensbourne College of Art], where I studied art history, graphic design, and photography. I was part of a mixed-media performance group called Jacob's Ladder: we used film and slide projections, live music, and dance within an open structure.

There was a film department at Ravensbourne, but I didn't have much to do with it, except for a bit during my last year (I was there for four years—1964–1968). For two years after leaving art school, I worked collaboratively with a friend (John McNulty) who was a computer scientist. Our work culminated in an exhibit for an international computer exhibition, which involved an interactive game and a 360-degree slide presentation. It might seem strange to be working with a scientist, but at that time we were quite captivated with the possibility of marrying art and technology. It was happening in New York [City], too: there were those nine evenings of Rauschenberg, Billy Klüver, and the Bell Telephone Labs. It's also around the time of Expo '67 in Montreal and the love affair there with mixed media.

Having completed work on this two-year project, I made my first film, a very short piece to open Bob Cohan's *Stages,* a dance performance at the London Contemporary Dance Theatre. That hooked me. I began to do photographic pieces based on performances, or, really, actions made to be photographed. One of those was an elaborate landscape event that took place in the middle of the countryside. It was too big to be still photographed, so I made a film, and with the aid of friends taught myself how to edit it. That was *Landscape for Fire* [1972]. Increasingly—and partly because of my interest in the work at the Co-op [The London Film-makers' Co-operative]—I got more and more interested in film itself, and less and less in the events I was making to be photographed. I began to think about the possibility of a film that was only a film. What were the irreducible elements for a film? My interest in that question was certainly influenced by Peter Gidal's early writing about the films of Andy Warhol. Also, during the early seventies there was a stress on the idea of process and on the implications of the medium itself.

The specific question that interested me was, how does an audience look at a film? How does an audience relate to a film? Was sitting and looking at a conventional narrative film a passive or an active experience? At the time it seemed as if a conventional Hollywood film could be faulted for the way in which it constructed a passive audience. That position, of course, was later discredited, but at the time it did lend some justification to the quite pared-down films we were making. In any case, the question of how an audience relates to a film was one which I felt could be explored through the film object, with an audience. My particular circumstances, and those of friends, made it a given that this work had to be cheap, which tended to mean that the films were silent (8mm was not used a great deal at that time; we were mostly working in 16mm). The specific idea that I was working on was that the projector's light beam was not only visible, but physical and space-occupying, and it could be shaped, both in space and in time, using film as the medium. I conceived *Line Describing a Cone* in the mid-Atlantic, two and a half days out of Southampton, when Carolee [Carolee Schneemann, with whom McCall lived from 1971 to 1976] and I moved to New York. This was January 1973. I made the film in August.

MacDonald: I usually show *Line Describing a Cone* at the front of a movie theater, across the space, so that it makes a specific reference to the normal projection situation.

McCall: It was designed to be shown in an empty room, at an independent film showcase like the London Co-op or the Collective in New York or in a museum space or gallery. And always in an empty space, free of chairs.

There was never a showing of the film where it was necessary to do more than make a simple announcement, something like, "This film asks to be viewed in a rather unusual way. You'll find out the best way for you to look at it, but I recommend that to start with, you stand where there would normally be a screen, looking back toward the projector." People who weren't expecting this would be intrigued, annoyed, whatever, but usually they did what I suggested, and then, after ten or fifteen minutes, they'd be finding their way to look at it.

MacDonald: On one level, the film is a product of serious, analytical thinking about the structure of film exhibition. On another, it's close to a spiritual experience. Are some presentations of *Line Describing a Cone* particularly memorable for you?

McCall: I love *Line Describing a Cone.* I saw it for the first time in Sweden. Carolee and I had been invited to Fylkingen in Stockholm to do performances: I was still doing my fire performances at that time. I picked the film up at the lab the day I was leaving, threw it into the suitcase as I left, and had it tucked under my arm when I arrived in Stockholm. I hadn't seen it. I told people there about the film, and they arranged a screening. None of us knew what to expect, really. There was a polite audience of about thirty people. The room was darkened, the projector turned on, and the film began. I was astonished, mostly by the physical beauty of the shape that came into being. The film did all the things that I wanted it to do. I had anticipated that the audience would go about looking at it in a way that was quite different from looking at a picture on a screen. And I had expected to see a light beam shaped in space. But all that I'd expected seemed less important than what was going on in the room: the physical event seemed bigger than the idea. I was rather awed by it.

I suppose *Line Describing a Cone* achieved its most perfect scale for me when, after seven or eight screenings in friends' houses or in screening rooms like Artists Space in New York, a joint presentation was arranged by Film Forum, which at that time was on the Upper West Side in a small upstairs screening room, and the Collective, which was also on the Upper West Side. The two groups decided to have the event at the Collective's screening room, which was larger: a hundred feet long or so and fifty feet wide, with a high ceiling. There was an audience of 120, and the projector had an extra-bright bulb. The distance from the wall to the projector was about eighty feet, and the height of the circle on the wall was about ten feet. It seemed to me like a hymn; it did have a spiritual quality—and absolutely *nothing* to do with the work I had consciously made. I felt as though I was seeing the film for the first time.

MacDonald: Is *Line Describing a Cone* shown a lot?

McCall: It's rented a few times a year, and I do get orders for prints. It's in the Museum of Modern Art's permanent collection, and in the Royal Belgian Film Archive's permanent collection, and in the collection for the Arts Council of Great Britain.

MacDonald: Its value and relevance is so broad that I'm surprised it's not shown a great deal more than it is.

McCall: My regret is that it didn't get shown much outside the avant-garde film world. It had quite good exposure at international art events, but it didn't really get seen very much by people whose concerns were related to other areas.

MacDonald: How did you decide to do the other "Cone" films?

McCall: In 1974 I made *Partial Cone, Conical Solid,* and *Cone of Variable Volume.* They were attempts to find out a bit more about the beam of light. In them I developed a small vocabulary of tremoring and flickering which I was able to use to most effect in the largest of the films after *Line Describing a Cone: Long Film for Four Projectors.* You haven't seen that, have you?

MacDonald: No.

McCall: In *Long Film* I extended the single axis I had used in *Line Describing a Cone* into a rectangular field of activity. There was a projector in each corner of the room, pointing inward. Great flat planes of light floated across the room intersecting and passing one another. Wherever you stood in the room, you were *inside* the film, surrounded by it. The best screening of that film, the most perfect scale, was realized at Millennium Film Workshop, in a basement space something like seventy feet by fifty feet.

Long Film has only been shown three times: once at the 1977 Documenta in Kassel, West Germany, once at Millennium, and once in the Neue Galerie in Aachen, Belgium. It requires four projectors, and they're running for six hours. There's quite a lot of maintenance. The beams sweep at different speeds, and the surfaces of the planes of light vary.

It was the last big film following from the "Cone" series. It's made of four forty-minute reels, and the six hours results from showing all the possible permutations of those reels; each reel can go through the projector backwards and forwards, inside out and right way around. Each reel has four ways of being put through the projector.

MacDonald: Was *Four Projected Movements* made as a study for *Long Film for Four Projectors,* but released later?

McCall: No. *Four Projected Movements* was in a way a précis of *Long Film for Four Projectors.* You make something on a large scale, then you want to make something much finer, simpler. *Four Projected Movements* clarified that idea of permutation. It was one fifteen-minute reel of film, put through the projector four ways. The other change was that instead of existing in an open empty space, it was presented against a wall, so that the plane of light was always experienced in relation to the wall or the floor: it "pushed" people against the wall, away from the wall, down onto the floor . . .

MacDonald: I've only shown it once, but it has the same kind of impact that *Line Describing a Cone* has.

McCall: It's a simple film, and, unlike *Long Film for Four Projectors,* easy to send through the mail with instructions.

MacDonald: A number of people have done work related to your projected-light films. Some of Taka Iimura's work in the early seventies is related in a general sense, as is Tony Conrad's *The Flicker* [1966], though in other ways, *The Flicker* is nearly the opposite of *Line Describing a Cone.*

McCall: I didn't see a lot of the films that, I suppose I could say, influenced me. I didn't see Michael Snow's *Wavelength* until 1976, but I'd read about it, and other films, in David Curtis's *Experimental Cinema* [London: Studio Vista Ltd., 1971]. I was intrigued by his description of *Wavelength.* The idea of creating a rule that would generate a film—a continuous zoom in this case—was fascinating. It was a surprise to me when I finally saw *Wavelength,* because it didn't have anything like the precision and cleanliness I had assumed from Curtis's description. It stopped and started; it jumped; light came in and out; and people arrived and left. It's quite funny to think that one can be influenced by a description of something which doesn't accurately represent the thing itself.

I didn't see *The Flicker*—although again I had read about it—until 1975 at Anthology [Anthology Film Archives]. People talked as though *Line Describing a Cone* were a three-dimensional version of *The Flicker.* They are both about light, but, as you say, they're also very different. Tony Conrad rented *Line Describing a Cone* sight unseen from a description he had read. He was teaching at Antioch. Then he called me and invited me out there. We had a great time together.

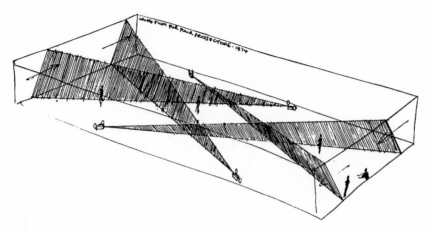

Sketch for McCall's Long Film for Four Projectors *(1974).*

MacDonald: When I showed *Line Describing a Cone* during the mid seventies, people loved getting into the mysterious smoky space it created. Now with the health backlash against smoke, many people won't stay in the room with the film.

McCall: Actually I consider the use of smoke a problem. But it's a necessary contingency. I've shown the film in city spaces where there's a lot of dust, and it works there. But I showed it in Sweden once without smoke or dust, and it was completely invisible. Personally I don't like the perfume smell of incense, which is the most convenient way to make smoke. Somebody at the Chicago Art Institute told me that when they decided to show it, they consulted their chemistry department and came up with a completely odorless, safe smoke. I wrote the method down and then lost it. It's always with a little regret that I use the incense method. And when you have a film as long as *Long Film for Four Projectors,* cigarette smoke is a real problem.

MacDonald: With the later "Cone" films it matters less; they're more visible without smoke.

McCall: When I drew the lines for those, I made them a bit thicker. The line of *Line Describing a Cone* is delicate; it could have done with a little strengthening.

MacDonald: In a sense there's an irony in the fact that the implicit politic of the film—the idea of using film to communitize the film audience—is undercut by the presumptions of the spaces or the institutions in which it's usually shown.

McCall: Well, that's always going to be true. Every context you show a film in is always going to imply a whole set of assumptions. If American independent film has found a home, it's definitely in colleges. That's where it's still alive and viewed regularly. That's where the rentals come from. At this point, art museums have lost interest in avant-garde cinema, and I think there's a much smaller audience for it than there was in the seventies.

MacDonald: Line Describing a Cone was made with a grant, wasn't it?

McCall: No. *Line Describing a Cone* was made independently. It only cost me a hundred dollars. The later "Cone" films were made with a CAPS grant from New York State and an NEA. CAPS and NEA were creations of the seventies. It may be that we've seen the end of subsidized filmmaking. I know there were no grants when Carolee was beginning to make films, and it would appear that there are precious few now. That's something that will be interesting to look at later. Historically, what was created by those grants? What did they make possible? There weren't a huge number of them, but there were a few; and one looked forward to applying for them. The NEA was expanded enormously during the seventies and created all sorts of cultural institutions and funding for new programs in museums, which had film curators for the first time. That had an important effect.

MacDonald: I suppose *Long Film for Ambient Light* is the ultimate minimal film, or one of them. It's an installation, without a projector or a screen or film, which *refers* to conventional cinema—a single electric light bulb reflects on the white paper covering the installation windows ("screens") during a twenty-four-hour installation period—from the greatest possible distance. It's as though filmmaking had led you out of film.

McCall: Yes.

MacDonald: How often did you do *Long Film for Ambient Light?*

McCall: I did it three times: once at Galerie Saint Petri in Lund, Sweden, once at the Idea Warehouse in New York, and once at the Neue Galerie in Aachen.

MacDonald: You're an important part of Carolee's *Kitch's Last Meal* [1978], which was being made during the same period. What was the relationship between you as artists?

McCall: As far as *Kitch's Last Meal* is concerned, I did pick up the camera sometimes and use it—always according to her instructions. She'd say, I want you to shoot this or do that—and I'd do it. But that film was completely her project. I really had very little influence, except as an actor in it and as a very occasional cinematographer.

I met Carolee when she and Joan Lifton came to my big computer exhibit in 1970. We became friends, and I think I derived a lot of inspiration from stories she told me about New York performance. I think you'd agree that the aesthetic of *Line Describing a Cone* is the polar opposite to the expressionistic aesthetic Carolee was exploring. There was absolutely no confusing our work at any time.

MacDonald: To an extent, the consciousness of audience and the willingness to confront audience expectations give *Line Describing a Cone* and *Fuses* [Schneemann's landmark erotic film was completed in 1967] one common dimension. Both create a new audience space, where people are very conscious of each other.

McCall: The brilliant thing about *Fuses* is that it's silent. My memory of seeing that film in an audience is the constant sense of tension created by the subject matter of the film. One can feel and hear the tension because there is no sound track to cover it. However, the word you used was "confront," which is something I never felt in terms of the "Cone" series. The "Cone" films are rather ethereal in a way. If they're aggressive and confrontational, it's because they're *passive*. They ask to be found; they don't set out to root you to the spot.

MacDonald: I know you do free-lance design work. Is that how you've supported yourself?

McCall: I have a small graphic-design business with which I've supported myself since I left art school. These days it's more full-time than it was when I first was here.

MacDonald: Is it fair to ask you what sort of clients you have?

McCall: Sure. A large proportion of them are galleries. What I do for them is design their general look and everything they need, including announcements, posters, catalogues, the ads they put in art magazines, business cards, stationery . . .

MacDonald: Which galleries?

McCall: The Mary Boone Gallery, the Delahunty Gallery, Blum Helman, Sherry French, Pace, Rosenberg, and many others.

MacDonald: Do you think of your experience as a designer as separate from your films?

McCall: I'd always considered it to be completely separate from my filmmaking, a way of filling in the gaps between grants. But gradually my attitude toward it changed. You begin to feel very strange if you spend three-quarters of your time doing work to make money, but describe yourself in terms of work that only takes twenty to twenty-five percent of your time.

The relationship between money and the making of art is complex. Grants were supposed to work like this: You got grants as a young artist to help you through that difficult period. By the time you were in your thirties, you were supposed to have a gallery to sell your work and give you a living. But though painters and filmmakers in New York shared a social and intellectual space in the seventies, their economic structure was utterly different. Painting is supported by a smaller number of people paying large sums of money; filmmaking is supported by large numbers of people paying small sums of money. So as a filmmaker one had to make a choice: you could teach, you could enter the film industry proper, you could make your money in some other not-film-related area. I did teach for a semester at NYU. I enjoyed it, but I don't feel particularly comfortable teaching. What I finally did—what I do now— is to think of graphic design as my business and of filmmaking as my career.

It's very difficult to make film independently. One could conceivably write the great American novel while working in a bank; one could conceivably paint a painting whilst doing other things. But filmmaking requires not just money, but capital, quite large sums of money. Another advantage of the minimalist aesthetic was it aesthetically justified making films that were very cheap. Since I've become fascinated by stories— narrative—things are very different. You can work pretty cheaply in Super-8. But it takes so long to make a narrative film and requires so much effort and the assistance of so many people, that to make it in Super-8 seems absurd to me. It was thinking like this that led Andrew [Tyndall] and me to consider ways in which we could make our work viable commercially on some level. I look forward to the time when my filmmaking can take a place next to my graphic-design work and be self-supporting.

MacDonald: One thing I've noticed with *Line Describing a Cone* and other minimal films is that they do create a narrative experience, but they change its location: *Line Describing a Cone* takes the narrative off the screen and locates it in the theater space.

McCall: Yes, *Line Describing a Cone* is a type of narrative film.

MacDonald: And not only narrative, but structurally conventional. There's a sort of climax of activity and then a period of denouement near the end.

McCall: When one looks again at the films that at one point seemed so radical because of their structural rigor, one invariably finds other elements at work. When I finally saw *Wavelength,* I was astonished that there was a story in it. I'd had no idea that was there; no one had mentioned it. There's even a murder! I was a bit shocked: I thought, "That shouldn't be there; it ruins the simplicity of the structure." Now I think it's interesting.

MacDonald: I assume that the films you admire have changed along with your assumptions about your own films.

McCall: Yes, absolutely. The films that I have come to like a lot contain a strong narrative element but fall to the side of both "big narrative features" and "narrative features" and "New American Cinema."

MacDonald: What films are you thinking of?

McCall: Films like *Chronicle of Anna Magdalena Bach* [1967], the

Straub/Huillet film, Syberberg's *Ludwig* [1974], Fassbinder's *In the Year of the Thirteen Moons* [1979], Godard's *Two or Three Things I Know About her* [1966], Apted's television project *28 Up* [1985].

MacDonald: In "Film as a Connective Catalyst" [a paper delivered at the International Forum of Avant-Garde Film, Edinburgh Film Festival, 1976], you talk about home-moviemaking as a potential model for film practice. Do you make home movies?

McCall: I had a CAPS grant in 1976 and with it I bought one of the first Super-8 sound cameras. I developed the idea of making Super-8 letters, where I could deal with a specific issue and a specific person very directly.

Also, I did a number of very short films during some of which I developed the formal ideas we began to play with in *Argument,* like the device of printing a word whilst saying something related but contradictory. Also, I was the cinematographer on what I think was one of the first Super-8 sound features: *Carnage* [1976] by the Australian Tim Burns. He was a friend, I had the camera, and he wanted somebody to shoot it. *Carnage* was made over a year and was immensely enjoyable to me. I started to experience lots of pleasures that I hadn't experienced for a while, such as constructing a fiction out of photography: I suppose that's when I began to be interested in fiction again, and in acting.

Andrew and I met a year or so after this. Andrew had a strong background in commercial film. He had studied it formally and was beginning to get interested in avant-garde film just at the time when I was getting interested in narrative. Also, he followed political events quite carefully. We had quite a lot to talk about. We were just friends for a while, and then as we talked more and more, our talking turned into working together. One day we were looking through a color supplement about men's fashion in the *New York Times,* and we got caught up with how many things were conveyed in the supplement.

Tyndall: I was a journalist when I left school. I'd been very interested in film. I'd worked on a local paper, doing film reviews. I'm of the same generation that found *Screen* important when they were coming out of school. I had friends who were very interested in structuralism and in semiotic theory. In England I was aware of what was called "independent cinema." When I came to New York, I discovered what in those days was called the "avant-garde" film scene, which was much closer to the art world than the British independent cinema was. Anthony and I started meeting during the summer of 1977, when all sorts of things in the art world and in avant-garde cinema and independent cinema and in the theory of cinema were being moved around and readjusted. We were in the middle of that readjustment—of people stepping back and starting to think about different strategies for making independent films.

And, of course, *Argument* addressed precisely that problem—and probably no other. *Argument* is a film about the strategies for making independent films.

McCall: And a film that was made to function as part of that discussion within the community of people who made films. It was a film that had no audience other than people who made films, which was quite deliberate on our part. *Argument* was conceived as an analysis of the place of avant-garde cinema in the art world. As we saw it, avant-garde cinema was a little ghetto, a very small group, and there didn't seem any way out of that. We decided to take that weakness, that problem, and turn it into a strength by making a film that spoke to that audience directly. Later, *Dora* was made specifically to bring together a number of different audiences that previously had had no connection with one another: an avant-garde film audience; a politically feminist audience; an audience interested in psychoanalysis; and, in addition, interested members of the public. *Dora* was extremely successful as a strategy. It has been seen a great deal. But actually where it led was out of the art world and into the academy. *Dora* finds itself in the same circuit as other avant-garde film—except that it ends up in a different academic department.

MacDonald: I came to one of the seminars you held at the Collective when you were first presenting *Argument* and at the time I was struck by what seemed a paradox: The film was made for an audience that already knew a good deal about the way in which information was constructed in film and what its impact on audiences was. The audience most likely to benefit from *Argument* (an academic audience, classes in communications) didn't see it, and the audiences that did seemed to resent it.

McCall: Looking back, I think we would locate the resentment at those early screenings not in what was being said by the film, but in the way the film was saying it. When I see and hear the film now, I find that it jars. Its tone is pretty strident and a bit smug. But I don't agree (although it's what people said; I remember Bill Brand saying it at the Collective seminar you were at) that everybody was familiar with all the issues the film raised. And even if the terms of the argument were familiar, it was useful to put them into a work that drew people together, that organized a situation where people could talk about them. I'm quite sure the resentment about the film was about the tone in which it spoke. You did feel assaulted, and with an incredibly dense amount of information. And it never let up, and it repeated itself, and it spoke very loudly. It didn't have very much light or shade—it just kept talking.

Tyndall: I think there were people on the Left who went one step further than Bill Brand. They said, OK, we understand all these problems you have in the area of an independent filmmaking practice and the politics of ideology, but where's your program? This film gets turned in

The twin principles of modernism and marketing: seeing fresh promise in familiar things

Text from McCall and Tyndall's Argument *(1978).*

on itself too often, and it can't allow a program. Also, I remember that Scott and Beth B turned up at one of the final seminars. They were just starting to make Super-8 films. I remember them saying, "Why do you insist on films being boring?" That was the only thing they said at one of these meetings, and of all the comments we heard, that one stuck with me, because it suggested to me that one response to our dilemma was to go back to storytelling.

  McCall: I don't think that was the dilemma they were responding to. I had many conversations with Scott years ago, because he used to be around this neighborhood quite a bit. I think he and Beth were part of the generation that was at art school when conceptual art was big, when it wasn't necessary to paint in order to be an artist. Any medium was OK and as good as any other. An enormous number of people came to New York at about that time from different art schools, all of them doing different creative things in different mediums. I think the Bs chose film because at the time when Super-8 became available, there was no longer any gallery space for all this conceptual art. There was room for only a few people, but there were hundreds of people who were trained as artists. Super-8 film proved to be a very useful way of getting work seen.

It was a year or two later, January 1979, that Becky Johnston, James Nares, and Eric Mitchell founded the "New Cinema" on Saint Mark's Place, which lasted one year. Every Saturday evening they showed what someone had made that week. Most of the films were shown as soon as they were done. I went to those screenings quite regularly. It wasn't that the work itself was so remarkable, but it made you think again about filmmaking. After seeing and hearing films in which people talked, there was no going back to silent minimal films, or abstract films.

Tyndall: There's another factor. For a while, the only place where you could see X-rated movies was in an art environment. As a result, there was all sorts of audience subsidy for independent avant-garde film through the box office. You could mix your experimental films and foreign imports in the programming.

McCall: In fact, *Fuses* was supposed to be shown as a short with *I Am Curious (Yellow)* [1968], though I believe the exhibitor got cold feet at the last minute. He didn't think he wanted two court cases on his hands. But that was a perfectly possible idea then. Once the law changed, what had been protected as part of the avant-garde suddenly vacated. I looked at some of the sixties films in the American New Wave show organized by Bruce Jenkins and the Walker Art Center, and I was struck by how time had changed their meaning. The sexuality that was exhibited freely in a lot of these films, which Jonas Mekas praised in his writing and was very important to a lot of people at the time, is no longer an issue; and so the films seem lame. Often they're structurally not very interesting. When you go back and read a lot of the writing on underground cinema—whether it's Jonas or Parker Tyler—there's a hymn to the freedom to talk about sex and to illustrate then illegal acts, such as homosexuality, on film. That was a major part of the importance of underground cinema. The avant-garde got busted a lot; it was like a testing ground. We were at a screening of Warhol's *I, a Man* [1967] at the Bleecker Street last year with Tom Baker. He was talking about how some of the Warhol films were made, quite consciously, to test the obscenity laws.

Tyndall: So to jump back to 1976, '77, '78, what had happened was that the independent experimental cinema had split: one part went into a commercially viable industry—hard core—and another went into relatively sanitized, relatively unexciting, relatively arty, government-funded showplaces, which mushroomed once the NEA was founded, and which dealt with independent film as another fine art.

McCall: I think that's a little unfair. Certainly that was something of the flavor one got from Anthology, which for a number of years struggled to get a lot of films recognized that had actually been made earlier. But I think that was only one tendency.

Tyndall: I'm looking not at the kinds of films being made, but at the institutions. In my opinion, a lot of the places that show independent film nowadays exist because of the bureaucracies that have supported them in the past, rather than because they've got a vibrant audience that's supporting them through the box office. And it's a major question to ask about independent filmmaking: are you making films to please bureaucrats or to please people in the seats?

MacDonald: Ironically, *Argument* seems more an analysis of content than of the spaces in which films are shown. From what you say, the idea of using *Argument* in a particular context was one of the main things that was new. But in the content of *Argument* that's not so clear. The film itself seems more about the ideology of commercial advertising and of the *New York Times.*

McCall: We saw it as a political film with certain aims. The simple aim, as we said in our book [*Argument,* a pamphlet with statements and imagery from the film and with essays about the film and the issues it raised, was published in three editions in 1978–79], was to create a precondition whereby the problems that the film describes can be worked on. That meant using the film as a way of bringing together the community of filmmakers we had found ourselves part of.

MacDonald: But you seem to have had it both ways in that decision. You wanted to show a ninety-minute film as a catalyst for a community dialogue about the issues raised by the film. Everybody was supposed to come in and watch *your* film, and *then* talk about the issues. Why not just hold the meeting and discuss the issues? And after the film, you two were in front to talk about it. The experience claimed to be about community, but it functioned more as performance.

Tyndall: OK, remember that at the time *Argument* was made, the usual model in the places where you showed avant-garde film was that the person stood up afterwards and answered questions. We said, OK, we'll show the film and then stand up afterwards and answer questions, but we're going to limit the number of people to thirty, give them a book to read first so they're prepared for the film, and tell them this is a *discussion,* rather than a question/answer session. Our presentation was a reaction to *that* situation, rather than a reaction to the commercial cinema, where it would be a "radical" idea just to bring the filmmaker in after the film.

MacDonald: Well, I respected and admired the idea then—and still do—and yet as an experience *Argument* seems to have undercut its own modus operandi.

McCall: Yes. As a political project, I don't think it worked out at all. It caused us to revise our ideas about the way people see film.

MacDonald: At the time, I had what seemed like a common reaction.

The film seemed strident, overbearing. Now it seems much less a polemic than a labyrinth. I find it poignant and personal.

In the credit sequence you mention that it's an autobiographical account of your years as avant-garde filmmakers.

McCall: That was one of a number of contradictory descriptions. They were all true.

Tyndall: I think it is personal myself, but we wouldn't have dared recognize that at the time we were making it. At the time, we wanted a film that would be *against* personal cinema. We wanted to look at cinema as a collective experience, not one where the individual artist donates his work to an audience.

MacDonald: I don't know any film that dramatizes more clearly how difficult it is to make a serious, meaningful, politically active film. Those conversations where the one person will go through this whole explanation/justification and then review how the person he was talking to responded with an equally convincing but opposite explanation/ justification are tremendously revealing.

McCall: We were quite fond of those monologues. They're probably pretty close to everyone's experience, including our own.

Tyndall: The film that we quote the most from is Godard's *Letter to Jane* [1972], which has that same sort of tormented concern with how to make a politically correct film.

MacDonald: It may be that one of the problems people had with *Argument* is that it understood so completely, and rejected, the lines of defense for bodies of work that were popular in the mid seventies. In some ways, it's a remarkable chronicle of that moment in downtown Manhattan filmmaking. It's also gorgeous to look at. At the original screening all I saw was the information coming at me. Now the color and design elements are more obvious.

McCall: It is good-looking. It's got very rich color. We only have one print, which is too bad, because we can never make a print that looked like the one you saw. There's no Kodachrome printing left, so those reds are gone forever.

MacDonald: The whole minimal background that you brought to it works quite powerfully in the film. In the credit passage, the guy changes his clothing in a single, long continuous shot; there are long passages of clear leader, and so on.

McCall: Yes. In a way, nothing got left behind.

MacDonald: Even the text has a certain graphic elegance though the three texts we see superimposed on the advertisements are not exactly precise. There are slight inconsistencies, which give the film a hand-crafted feel. It seems like a subtle vestige of the New American Cinema's concern with the personal.

McCall: Well, actually, they were mistakes. We were using a huge amount of animation in that film, and you know how time-consuming and complex that is. We did it as best we could.

Tyndall: Our constraints were financial as well. The hands-on process was prescribed by budget.

McCall: We were borrowing George Griffin's animation stand. It's in the middle of his living room. Andrew had a full-time job and I was intermittently doing free-lance work. We sometimes had to go there at six o'clock in the evening and work all night until it was time to go to work again. We had to work on nights when George and Karen [Cooper] were out, or out of town. We did make some total errors, and it was miserable to go back in there and shoot for another fifteen hours because the calibration was off.

Anyway, there were a lot of reasons why we decided that it was absolutely fine that the film looks the way it does, and that those mistakes were all right.

MacDonald: How much did you show *Argument?*

McCall: We did three seminars at the Collective, four or five at Millennium Film Workshop. We showed it at Center for Media Studies in Buffalo; at NAME in Chicago; at the International Film Theory Conference at the University of Wisconsin; at the Edinburgh Film Festival; and at the London Film-makers' Co-operative. Andrew and I were present at those screenings. But since that first year when we were working with it quite a lot, it hasn't been rented on a regular basis.

We saw it again about two years ago and I think we were both quite disappointed. I think we both realized how differently we would do it if we remade it.

MacDonald: What would you do?

Tyndall: First, we'd do it on video, rather than on film. It really belongs on video.

McCall: That amount of information and talking would seem much more normal on television than it does when you're waiting for it up on the screen. The last time we talked about it, we agreed that we'd put much more on the visual level and take a lot of the talking out.

Tyndall: Or maybe just take a cut. The film does play long. Of course, now we can stand outside it and have a look, but it was never made for that sort of detached reaction.

McCall: We made the film on ready credit at Citibank. We each borrowed five-thousand dollars, which was like a car loan. My debt is still about forty-five hundred dollars. Citibank is doing well on their investment. The principal hasn't changed, and we've been paying ever since.

Andrew Noren

Andrew Noren has been making contributions to North American independent film since the mid sixties. As interesting as his early films seem to have been, few survive, as a result of a fire in 1970. Noren began with a Godard-inspired experimental narrative, *A Change of Heart* (1965, lost in the fire), and then—perhaps as a reaction to his day job as an apprentice editor at a network news department—began making films characterized by long, continuous shots. *The New York Miseries* (c. 1965 to c. 1967) was made up of single-take, 100-foot rolls of 16mm film (each approximately three minutes long) in which Noren documented "absolutely every aspect of my life." Though *The New York Miseries* was destroyed in the fire, Noren's quest to capture his own experience was dramatized in Jim McBride's *David Holzman's Diary* (1967). L. M. Kit Carson, who played David Holzman, later described Noren and his influence on McBride: "The un-camera-shy Noren—in America, where most filmmakers either fear or worship the camera—this Noren who unscrewed the lens from the camera and pushed his fingers into the guts of the camera while it was running, he was onto something. . . . And when Jim talked to Noren now, Noren kept kicking Jim's imagination in the ass" (from the introduction to the screenplay of *David Holzman's Diary,* pp. viii–ix). An unpublished interview McBride and Carson had conducted with Noren had already raised the question of cinema "truth," a central topic not only of *David Holzman's Diary,* but of *Say Nothing* (1965), the one surviving instance of a series of thirty-minute, single-shot films. *Say Nothing* is an "interrogation" of an actress/character by the filmmaker that hovers between fiction and documentary.

In 1968, Noren finished *The Wind Variations*—a meditation on the winter light flowing through two windows, as it is modulated and transformed by the window curtains blowing in the breeze—and *Huge Pupils,* the first of a series of films that have become known as *The Adventures of the Exquisite Corpse. Huge Pupils* (originally entitled "Kodak Ghost Poems") is a compilation of domestic moments, often tender, sometimes meditative, consistently lovely, and sometimes startling in their openness about sexuality. Other than Carolee Schneemann's *Fuses* (1967), I know of no instance where a viewer shares so openly and directly in a filmmaker's experiences with a lover.

Since the completion of *Huge Pupils* (reworked in 1977), Noren has completed four sections of *The Adventures of the Exquisite Corpse:* these are *False Pretenses* (1974) and *The Phantom Enthusiast* (1975), both currently out of distribution, being reworked, and the two most recent films: *Charmed Particles* (1978) and *The Lighted Field* (1987). Increasingly, Noren's interest is light itself, as it is captured and manipulated by camera and filmmaker. After his exploration of color in *The Wind Variations, Huge Pupils,* and *False Pretenses,* Noren returned to black and white and has proved himself a master of black-and-white filmmaking. Of course, other contemporary independents have done remarkable work with black and white (Su Friedrich and Peter Hutton, for example), but if one thinks of the movie camera as an instrument with which a filmmaker can compose and perform visual music, Noren may well be the most accomplished visual musician we have. *The Lighted Field* reveals that Noren is at the peak of his form: the film is a visual phantasmagoria—exquisite, scintillating, sensual, sometimes nearly overwhelming.

My interview with Noren was conducted in an unusual way. Once he had agreed to do an interview, Noren asked me to send him a list of questions, which I did in the summer of 1990. He labored for some months on answers, and we worked together, by mail and phone, condensing and refining the interchange.

MacDonald: When I learned you're originally from Santa Fe, and that you continue to visit New Mexico regularly, I was surprised. It helps account for your fascination with light, but I'm amazed that you've not used that section of the country as a subject for a film.

Noren: The light there had a great influence on me and still does. There's a sense in which it made me. I was drawn to it very strongly, early in my life, a natural and very powerful attraction. An early memory is of sitting under a cottonwood tree behind my parents' house, September afternoon light of great clarity with a wind blowing—you know how cottonwood leaves shiver and tremble in the wind. I sat there watching the light and the leaf shadows dancing on the dust, listening to the wind in the leaves. It was my first movie and a great one. I was bewitched by it.

At night out there the stars are so vivid and immense that the existence of other suns and other worlds is made very apparent, commonplace. I couldn't have expressed it at the time, but I came to realize back then that light is alive and intelligent . . . the living thought of the sun, you might say . . . and what could be more intelligent than the sun? There's a very real sense, a very literal, unmystical sense in which this world and everything in it is made of the sun and by it. We are part of it. So my interest in light is quite natural; there's nothing esoteric about it. It's been one of the great passions of my life.

Over the years I've shot a great deal of material out there; some of it has been included in the films I've released, but there's more in existence that I haven't used yet.

MacDonald: Were movies an early interest?

Noren: Yes. At the time I lived in New Mexico it was still very wild, as though the twentieth century hadn't happened yet . . . in spite of Los Alamos. I didn't get to see many films, but I loved them. The communication of thoughts by means of pictures interested me very early. I taught myself how to read by means of comic books, studying the pictures and then asking what the words meant. I was fascinated by the way that words, which are literal pictures themselves, form pictures on the imaginary screen of the mind; and fascinated by spoken words and by sound itself and by music for the same reason, their power to conjure pictures. Radio and comics were most important to me. I was a passionate fan of "The Shadow" and of Krazy Kat. Later on, I fought my way to books and records in quantity and devoured them; I was starving for them. Blake and Stravinsky, Scriabin and Raymond Chandler, Swedenborg and Django Reinhardt, John Donne and Jerry Lee Lewis, Yeats and Wolfman Jack from down on the border, who blasted out the international rock-and-roll beat to the backwoods.

MacDonald: When did you come to New York?

Noren: The mid sixties. Left home and caught the first thing smoking for the imperial city, where I hoped to find fame, money, and the love of beautiful women . . . all of which have continued to elude me . . . just kidding, all of which I found in one degree or another.

MacDonald: How did you support yourself?

Noren: Got a job in the news department of one of the television networks as an apprentice editor. And I started making films. At a certain age, anything in the world seems possible, and I leapt into it without a second thought. My first film was *A Change of Heart,* 16mm, black and white, sound, feature length, influenced by *Breathless* [1959]. I worked in the news department during the day and worked on the film at night and on weekends, a pattern that continues to this day. My first show came about through Louis Brigante, who worked beside me in the news department and who was associated with *Film Culture* and knew Jonas Mekas. He was a very kind and good person who helped many young filmmakers. Jonas at that time was showing a lot of independent features, like *Shadows* [1957], *Guns of the Trees, Twice a Man* [1963], *The Flower Thief* [1960], and many other things in the various fugitive venues of the Cinematheque, which was literally at that time a fly-by-night operation. Sometimes the location would change from week to week with Jonas dodging corrupt cops, avaricious fire marshalls looking for payoffs, and various other harassments. It was a true guerrilla activity. Through his "Movie Journal" column in *The Village Voice,* Jonas was a revolutionary commandante, operating from the hills, striking at night and vanishing before the "authorities" could get there. It was exciting.

Also, I worked at the Film-makers' Co-op for a while, and that was interesting because I got to meet many filmmakers. There was much exchange of ideas and clash of raging egos. For a while at least, there was a strong sense of revolutionary possibility, that anything could happen and was likely to happen. A rough and unrefined situation in many ways. At that time there were no university courses in avant-garde film, no doctoral candidates, no wildest dreams of tenured positions. With a few exceptions, most were poor, cold, and hungry, not to mention insulted and injured and angry. I remember discussions about whether to buy film or food. There were also dilettantes, as there always are: rich kids looking for something to do.

MacDonald: Are there filmmakers you especially remember? Did you know Brakhage? Frampton?

Noren: Brakhage would descend on New York from the mountains once a year or so, grandiloquent and Promethean, lightning bolts in one hand and film cans in the other, talking everyone under the table—what a talker! And in general burning the place to the ground. It's impossible to overestimate his influence on absolutely everyone: you could run, but you couldn't hide. I remember thinking *Mothlight* [1963] was one of the best films I'd ever seen, and I still think so. I was very impressed by Michael Snow and Joyce Wieland, who were both hilariously intelligent, clear-minded, and highly elevated. They couldn't help but laugh, and it was very contagious. They loved jokes and puns. I often felt they were on the verge of levitation by laughter.

Harry Smith interested me also. I spent many hours back then puzzling over *Heaven and Earth Magic* [1960]. He'd drop by the Co-op from time to time in various states of altered awareness and was often brilliant in conversation; Cabala and Bach, peyote songs and Haida masks, string games and dreamtime, riddles of the Rosy Cross. He was tiny, hunched, gnomic, wizardly, and I was young enough to be in awe of his occult erudition.

Hollis Frampton I met through Michael Snow. He and I had next to nothing in common, and so I saw very little of him.

Jack Smith was around a lot. He was at the height of his infamy then, because of *Flaming Creatures*. A strange figure . . . tall, gawky, long-beaked, storklike. I didn't care for *Flaming Creatures* [1963], but I'd often go to his slide show/performances at the Plaster Foundation of Atlantis, which was wherever Jack happened to be living at the time. They were often wonderful. There was absolutely no demarcation between what was "performance" and his "real" life. He was notorious for taking hours getting started . . . in fact things never really did get started. He just lived and you could share that.

He would show things that he'd dragged in off the street, play his favorite records, read aloud from books and newspapers, musing and brooding. You had the feeling that he'd be doing the same thing whether there was an audience or not. He was very political in the truest sense, and the only true socialist I ever met. *The Secret of Rented Island* and *Sacred Landlordism of Lucky Paradise* were political art of a very high order.

MacDonald: I'm unclear about the chronology of your work, but from what you've said to me, there were a good many films, made at the beginning of your activity as a filmmaker, that no longer exist. I remember you telling me about a number of early single-shot films, made as a series.

Noren: A lot of my earlier films were destroyed accidentally in 1970; I was working in film as early as 1965. I made *A Change of Heart* then, a long narrative film with sound, and *Say Nothing,* which still survives. I did several similar one-take thirty-minute films. One was an "interview" with a former concentration camp guard; another was an interview with a pair of twin brothers who were idiot-savants; and a number of other things in that format. Also, a very long film, *The New York Miseries,* which was made up of "one-take," three-minute, one-hundred-foot sections. This was the precursor of *The Exquisite Corpse* and was inspired in a way by the Lumière brothers, by Balzac, who I was reading at the time, and also by news reportage.

One of my first film fascinations was with newsreels. I was crazy about them. This was before television, if you can imagine that. I think what attracted me was that the people in them were not "acting," or so it was supposed to seem. This was the real stuff, a window on the way things really were in the Big World, which I was dying to get to. It was thrilling actuality, glares and flashes of "reality," what people really *did*. And I loved the style—simple, straightforward, direct—and the basic idea of "witness": eyes and ears of the world you might say, Buddhalike, nonjudgmental eye on suffering and on joy. Every conceivable human emotion would be engaged in the seven or eight minutes of the format. And they were strangely innocent, elegant, and severe. The cameramen and editors were studio-trained and knew all the tricks of classical composition and montage ("Russian cutting," they called it). Newsreels were an endless source of innocent, unintentional surrealism. Sex, disguised, and death, made plain, were the great themes. Buñuel himself once said that on his best day he couldn't hope to create images as bizarre as one could see every day in the newsreels.

Of course, they were all produced and controlled by the major movie studios (Hearst Metrotone was the exception) and issued each week as part of an entertainment package, carefully calibrated to the comprehension level of some mythical hick in Indiana, and they were all hysterically patriotic, and fundamentally fascist and manipulative, but they were great all the same, and they affected me greatly. Not so strange that over the years I've always made my living working around "news" in one form or another.

(There's an amusing passage in a novel by Harry Crews where the narrator delays orgasm by remembering newsreels he has seen of death, disasters, and various horrors. He recommends Pathe News as a specific for premature ejaculation and for birth control in general.)

MacDonald: What was *The New York Miseries*?

Noren: The New York Miseries was meant to be a personal "newsreel," to document absolutely every aspect of my life, starting with the small domestic things and then moving out into the larger social context. I would try to shoot a one-hundred-foot roll each week, if I could afford to buy and develop a roll—I was very poor. I filmed virtually every person that I knew then; I filmed family, landlord, employer, police. And I filmed myself cooking, eating, sleeping, lovemaking. I filmed in the supermarket, bank, and my workplace . . . you get the idea. Each roll was sort of a core-sample extracted directly from the heart of my life. The style was very simple and straightforward—minimum of artifice. I would simply focus on the situation, turn on the camera and let the roll run out. I was naive enough to believe that there was an objective "truth" that could be "captured" in this way. I later accepted "version," instead of truth. There's some commentary on this period in my life in the published screenplay of *David Holzman's Diary*, by Jim McBride.

   Another project that occupied a lot of my time then was a script for a feature. The working title was *The Big Picture,* and of course, there was no chance of it getting made, but it still interests me in a way. The basic idea was simple enough: a movie crew shooting a movie about a movie crew that was shooting a movie about a movie crew that was shoot-ing . . . film within a film within a film to infinity.

   Another "truth" operation. The cardinal rule was that every last foot of film that was shot would be used, and used in the order in which it was shot. For example, if the "A" crew shot fifteen takes of Scene 7A, in order to get the "right" one, then all fifteen would be included in the final film. If the "B" crew shot ten takes of the "A" crew filming the fifteen takes of Scene 7A, then all of those takes would be included, and so on. If a total of two hundred hours of film were shot, the final version of *The Big Picture* would be two hundred hours long. Mind you, the "A" crew would be filming actors pretend-ing to be filming other actors who would be pretending to film other actors, et cetera. Much use was to have been made of "takes" and "mistakes" and "out-takes." Everything would be included. I've always been fascinated by out-takes, by what goes "wrong." An actor forget-ting his lines or looking at the camera by accident, one fiction collaps-ing instantly into another; the shot at that moment changing from an "acted fiction" into a document, which of course it was all along; all narrative films are really documentaries about actors pretending. Any-way, it was to be about the impossibility of ever getting "behind the scenes." I was working on several other scripts at that time as well. It was the next best thing to actually making the films.

   MacDonald: Were there other kinds of work?

   Noren: I worked with loops for a while, using found footage. I did some cut-up films under the influence of [William S.] Burroughs/[Brion] Gysin. I would raid the waste containers at the Film Center Building on trash pickup day. There were a lot of film labs in the building and you could find thousands of feet of imperfect prints, rejects of all kinds: "educational" films, nature documentaries, pornography, military train-ing films, everything. So I took all of this material and cut it up at random into uniform lengths—I think it was twenty-four-frame sections—and then put the pieces into a large box and tossed them until any selection would be totally random. Then without looking to identify the pieces, I would splice them all together and recut the whole thing, starting in the middle of the original twenty-four-frame piece, jumping the first splice, and ending in the middle of the next twenty-four-frame piece. Then I would recut and retoss these pieces and randomly splice them together so that each piece was now twelve frames long and so on. I ended up with shots that were about four frames long and thousands of splices. When it was physically impossible to continue I would print the result. This was very laborious and time consuming, needless to say, and very difficult to print, but they were interesting, especially the relation of the sound to the picture. At the time I sort of scorned them, I think because of the "found" nature of the material; my feeling was that because I didn't shoot the images myself, the process was invalid. I think they'd be very interesting today.

Anyway, all of the early films were shown, usually once or twice, at the Cinematheque when it was in the basement of the Wurlitzer Building on Forty-first street. If my memory serves, this would be around 1965–66.

I also did a series of ten-minute, one-take films of people bathing, stationary camera—a meditative stare at the act itself. The fascinations were, of course, the beauty of the human body and the peculiar, dreamy, self-absorption that comes over humans when they're submerged in warm amnioticlike liquid. Defenses drop and more private and vulnerable aspects of personality emerge. An interesting section from this series was of George and Mike Kuchar, twins, bathing together. George insisted on wearing a three-piece business suit in the tub because he was shy. Somehow a puppy got in there with them. I doubt if anyone got clean, but it turned into a strange and tender document. I always liked George because of his kindness to animals.

MacDonald: So far as I know, *Say Nothing* is the earliest of your films still in distribution. It's an unusual single-shot film, thirty minutes long, and dramatic. Could you talk about the genesis of that project? [For some years one other relatively early Noren film was available from Film-makers' Cooperative: *Scenes from Life: Golden Brain Mantra* (1972), a double projection of buildings exploding in slow motion, in forward and reverse, that "was intended as mantra, to run perpetually, viewer to enter/leave at any point. Originally B&W on color stock. On occasion I provided live piano accompaniment, extempore, a la 'perils of . . .' " (letter to author, April 4, 1989).]

Noren: Say Nothing was made in half an hour one afternoon in 1965. I was able to borrow an Old Auricon synch-sound news camera for the weekend. Great cameras, by the way; you used to see them around all the time. This one had a twelve-hundred-foot magazine, so that determined the length of the film. I thought of the film one Saturday morning over coffee and shot it the next week. It was shot on 16mm Tri-X reversal, a continuous twelve-hundred-foot take, optical sound on film.

Many fascinations were at work there. I was interested in the idea of the "screen test" as a form in itself and wanted to work with that. Also, I had a mischievous interest in subverting the cinema-verité ideas that had such currency then. [Jean-Luc] Godard's definition of film as "truth twenty-four times a second" was much quoted. One of the first things I ask the actress in the film is, "Does the camera lie?" And then, "Do you lie?" The answer is, "Yes." I was playing with that and was also fascinated with the idea of identity or personality being a series of masks—a young man's fascination—and I was curious to see if it were possible to set up a mask-removal procedure, and finally discover the "real" person behind all the smoke and mirrors that constitute an "official" personality. Another interest was in interrogation as a form, "confession" extracted under duress, the Truth.

MacDonald: How well did you know that woman? And how fully did you plan the interaction between the two of you?

Noren: I chose a young actress named Miriam, whom I had met once before in connection with another film. Of course, I was also interested in the fact that she was an actress—when are we ever not acting?—and wanted to see if perhaps I could register that borderline transfiguration of "real" person into actor/actress and back again. I think that aspect of the film is successful and interesting still. So, Miriam came for her screen test, and we talked and performed and acted while the half-hour of film ran through the camera. It left us both bewildered and exhausted, questions hanging in the air.

MacDonald: Several photographs hang on the wall behind the woman; two of these—a photo of an aborigine looking at a movie camera, a news photo of a woman in Vietnam—suggest that you were dramatizing problematic elements of the conventional uses of cameras, and the conventional functioning of the media. Is that a correct assumption? Do you see the parallel between the exploitation of aborigines and the exploitation of women? Both have often functioned as exotics for the voyeuristic movie viewer.

Noren: The photo of the aborigine and the Arriflex on the wall had nothing to do with "exploitation"; it was a humorous comment on my own absolute lack of expertise in using that camera, nothing else. On the wall behind her also is a photograph of [Piero Paolo] Pasolini. I was interested in him at the time because of his efforts at making "fictional" documentaries, which *Say Nothing* certainly is. There is also an absolutely up-to-the-minute news photograph, which was taken from the front page of that day's *New York Times,* which sort of localizes the film in time.

MacDonald: These days, especially, the film raises issues with regard to the camera as an instrument of the "male gaze." In fact, it seems a particularly vivid instance of the use of the camera to exert power over a female subject.

Noren: The camera is an instrument of the "gaze" of the person controlling it, male or female. Your question suggests that the male gaze is inherently exploitative and manipulative, while the female gaze is somehow, by definition, pure and free of such faults. I doubt if that would ever stand up to analysis. Any filming or photographing of anyone or anything, by a man or woman, is an attempt to exert power and to gain control.

The natural act of looking and seeing is an assertion of power and the desire for control. That is why we see in the first place, why we have eyes. It didn't happen by accident. Power and force in their many disguises rule this world absolutely. It is not a charm school. All human motivation and behavior is about power and control. This is not necessarily bad or undesirable. Every living thing has its own version of what is and what should be, and all of these versions are usually in conflict. The stronger ones survive and prevail. It's not difficult to imagine a better world than this one, but that does seem be what obtains here, at this time.

Filming by its nature is voyeuristic—so is natural looking and seeing—both unavoidably involve a privileged spectator observing an "other." There's no way around this. You are no less voyeuristic looking out from inside the camera obscura of your own skull than you are peeping through a viewfinder or keyhole or watching a film or any other visual spectacle. Any seeing of another person, or seeing of anything, automatically makes that person or thing "exotic" simply because they are "other"—not "you." The entire world and everything in it is "exotic," except for "you."

There was no real planned interaction. I made some notes about questions and chose a few texts I was interested in. The professorial tone at the beginning, which I meant to maintain throughout the film, but didn't, was a mocking of the "authority" behind the camera. In general there is a rather elaborate mockery going on in the entire film as it's being made. There are moments of what I still think are good poetry: one of them is when the actress/ghost on screen tells what will happen to her when she dies.

Much was made of the moment when she comes forward to touch the lens of the camera, but no one has ever noted that it was one of the very first instances in experimental, avant-garde films, of the self-reflection that became so prevalent in the seventies.

MacDonald: A minor question. What is that moaning sound during the early part of *Say Nothing*? It certainly gives the film an eerie feel, almost a horror-film feel.

Noren: The moaning sound came from some defect in the camera magazine . . . I think the drive belt on the take-up reel was out of alignment, or something like that. But you're quite right. It is a horror film, and also a sit-com, melodrama, documentary, and poetry of a strange sort.

MacDonald: Say Nothing is your only sound film so far as I know.

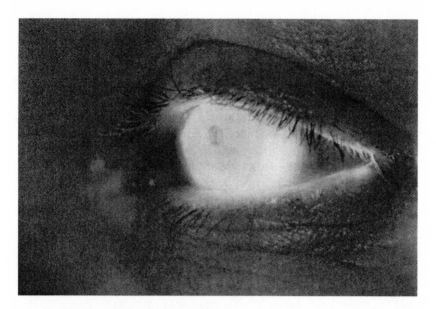

From Noren's The Lighted Field *(1987).*

Noren: No, *Change of Heart* was a sound film and all of the early one-take films I mentioned were sound on film. Also, I'm working on one right now.

I'm interested in how the mind manufactures pictures in response to sound, how it converts sound into imaginary light, so to speak, imaginary images. What exactly are these images, what are they made of, how are they made, where do they come from? A curious thing is that I always have a strong sense of a "projected" image, and of a "spectator." So where, exactly, is this image being projected, who is the spectator, who is the projectionist, and where and what is the screen? Of course, the mind does this all the time, even without sound stimulus, as in memory and in dream images. And, as every child knows, sit in the dark with your eyes closed and you will be presented with an automatic "movie" of considerable vividness and detail.

We don't really "see" anyway, so much as "imagine." Our sight is imaginary, as R. L. Gregory demonstrated some twenty years ago. Each eye is separately informed, and the information supplied to each eye is constantly being synthesized and interpreted and processed into imaginary constructs. This is the continuous natural movie of the world, which each of us is busily engaged in creating all the time, even in sleep.

MacDonald: The Wind Variations was the first of your films I ever saw. I was at the Whitney Museum screening room, with a small audience from the Museum. Within a few minutes, there was an argument between those who were annoyed by the pace of the film and those who—whatever their reaction to the film—were annoyed by the arrogance of the others. There was almost a fight. Through all of this, I found the film long, but gorgeous, beautifully meditative. Do you remember early reactions to that film?

Noren: I remember a fistfight. It was at the Modern [Museum of Modern Art], where the audience was sometimes unruly. Someone was talking during the film, and the person in front of him stood up and hit him. Somehow, several other people got involved, and it turned into quite a brawl, a hot-blooded, two-fisted dukeroo in defense of meditative silence and beauty.

MacDonald: I assume you were in a period of experimenting with color. Was this your first color film?

Noren: No, the first color shooting I did was the bathing series I mentioned. *The Wind Variations* was made while I was working on *Huge Pupils,* although I didn't release it until a couple of years later. All of that was simultaneous. Up until this time I couldn't afford to shoot in color. I remember a golden age of black and white when it was incredibly cheap; you could buy and develop a one-hundred-foot roll of black and white for five or six dollars. It was almost like [Alexandre] Astruc's ideal of the camera-stylo, of film being as cheap as pen and paper. That was some time ago, but it's now possible again, or almost, with video.

MacDonald: Each of the film's six sections is, I believe, done in a different location, and each explores somewhat different sets of variables, within the general subject of light/shadow and the movement of the wind in the waving curtains. Is the order in which we see the six rolls the order in which they were shot? If not, what was the logic behind your choice of order?

Noren: I made *The Wind Variations* in a few hours on two winter days, two different windows, in a rapture. I shot eight one-hundred-foot rolls, later rejected two of them, and arranged the remaining six in the order in which they were shot. As you can see from *The Lighted Field,* the subject still fascinates me.

MacDonald: During the late sixties, a number of people were beginning to do films that provide meditative experiences. Were you in touch with other filmmakers working in similar areas?

Noren: Not really. I was aware of Bruce Baillie's *Still Life,* which I liked a lot, though I haven't seen it for years. And Michael Snow and Joyce Wieland's *Dripping Water.* But you have to remember, the meditative stare was in the air, so to speak, at that time.

MacDonald: This is also the earliest film in which your fascination with light—I'm tempted to say your fetishization of light—is evident. At what point did light become the focus of your filmmaking?

Noren: Around the time of *Huge Pupils* I suppose, although it's very hard to say. I don't care for "fetishization"; it suggests irrational obsession, and that is inaccurate.

I've described my feelings about light earlier. There is nothing mystical or arcane or irrational about it. We are made of the sun. That's where we came from. Anything less than a consuming interest in light seems strange to me.

I was very amused recently when I came across a line of John Milton's in which he defines light as "darkness made visible." Not surprising from a blind man, but what a wiseguy!

At the risk of having my poetic license revoked, you could say that *The Wind Variations* is the solar wind made visible.

MacDonald: Like *The Wind Variations, Huge Pupils* seems an experiment in broadening your dexterity with the camera. What led you to the diary form?

Noren: I never thought of it as "diary"; in fact, I doubt if I was consciously thinking in terms of any particular form at all. Jonas Mekas described it as such after the fact, I think because he *was* consciously working that form and saw some affinities, but that concept was never useful to me. I think what was really at work was my old fascination with "news," in this case news of what I took to be heaven. The style and stance are there, hand-held and eye-level, steadfast and innocent of artifice and mortality—innocent, period. Trying to "record" that light storm of ghostly beauty blowing around me, doomed in the attempt, as we always are. And ghosts they were and are: the people by now aged to unrecognizability, the animals dust long since, the rooms themselves demolished; the only remaining trace is a length of decaying plastic with a few inaccurate shadows, rapidly fading. But I was sincere.

The shooting was improvisatory in the extreme. It was very important to me to be able to respond immediately and completely to whatever moved me at a given moment, with a minimum of art thought. It was the Code of the West . . . shoot first and ask questions later. I never used a light meter or tripod. My fond wish at the time was for a cinema of pure telepathy . . . transmission of visual energy direct from mind to mind, no fooling around with machinery. Everything was done in-camera at the moment of filming, complete trust of intuition, "first thought, best thought," thinking that being "right-minded" in the given moment would assure a successful outcome.

I was trying for a direct life-energy transmission, unrestricted by culture and by intellectualization about art.

MacDonald: When was the title changed from "Kodak Ghost Poems" to "Huge Pupils"? And why?

Noren: The title was changed because I was threatened with a lawsuit by Eastman Kodak for copyright infringement over the use of "Kodak." I'm sure they would have won, since they did invent that word. After that, the film was referred to as *The Ghost Poems* for a while, until it became *Huge Pupils,* Part One of *The Adventures of the Exquisite Corpse.* This would have been 1974, I believe. There was some feeling that I should have resisted and gone to court over this, but of course, those who felt that way weren't about to pay the legal fees, and I wasn't about to be a martyr over it. I could hardly pay the rent at the time. Actually, the title worked better without "Kodak," anyway, because it reflected my feelings more exactly.

MacDonald: I wonder if the second title was a pun, on the "huge pupils" of the filmmaker entranced with light and the sensuality of things, and the "huge pupils" of the viewers in their surprise at the film's openness about things normally kept personal. In one sense, the film seems a quintessential sixties film—sexuality, the human body, become subjects to be revealed, reveled in, explored, whether they're one's own body or the body of one's lover or those of others.

Noren: It was a pun, sure, many of my titles are. I enjoy ambiguity. The erotic aspects of the film now seem incredibly innocent and naive in view of what has happened in the intervening years, but life has a way of doing that about everything.

MacDonald: How did you decide on "The Adventures of the Exquisite Corpse" as a title?

Noren: I first used that title in 1972, and later Part Two was shown at the Whitney under that title in 1974. As you know, it was the name of a parlor game popular among the surrealists in the twenties, although it has a long occult history as a divinatory tool. The game takes a number of people to play. The trick is that a piece of clean paper is given to one person who draws a human head on the top, and then folds that over so that it can't be seen. The second participant then draws the neck and shoulders and folds that over and passes it to the third person, et cetera. At the end, the paper is unfolded and behold!—the exquisite corpse. Of course, any imagery can be substituted for the human body.

I was attracted to it as a title, first of all, because it's a perfect analogy for my own process of working: shooting "blind" without really consciously knowing why, or knowing how what I'm shooting connects with material already shot, or what I will shoot. Seeing the material assembled chronologically, I see many connections and couplings I might have been unaware of earlier, and by repeating this process, the shape of the finished film is finally "revealed."

MacDonald: When I first saw *Huge Pupils,* I was jealous of the erotic pleasure you seemed to be having!

Noren: Carnality was most important to me then, as it is for all healthy and amorous young animals. And, of course, it is the most important part of the "trick" that life is: it's the lure, the bait. What animal can resist orgasmic pleasure? We don't learn until later that the other part of the trick is more sinister and ominous, at least as far as our cheerful and bright-eyed "personal identity" is concerned. If we could see the entire trick from beginning to end, we wouldn't play, would we? The bad news is revealed in stages, broken to us gently. The trick has fatal consequences.

I had moved from uptown bourgeois restriction and rectitude down to the Lower East Side and *la vie bohème.* Life more abundant! I imagined myself to be free, as we all do at that age. I lived with the Canadian actress Margaret LaMarre on Essex Street above Bernstein's Kosher Chinese Restaurant and made the film there. Big windows that got the morning sun. We were lovers in the way you can be only when very young, and I wanted to celebrate this. So, very simply and in the most straightforward fashion I could manage, I made pictures of my strongest delights and joys, reveling in flesh and in light with great appetite, and in the ghost of flesh on film. No one really seemed to be dealing directly with erotic matters in film at that time. The general psychic climate was still very repressive and puritanical. Brakhage was working with sexual imagery, of course, and Carolee Schneemann, but they both seemed to be disguising the substance of it with "art."

I thought that perhaps more honesty and directness were possible, and I tried to work along those lines. Someone once described the film as being in "beast language," which I took as a compliment, and still do. And, of course, the mythic "beauty and the beast" elements are now quite evident, although I wasn't conscious of that at the time. You might even say that the film is the beast's version of the story. You will find echoes of this near the end of *The Lighted Field.* It was made in a state of innocent wonder and even joy, much in the spirit of Blake's painting "Glad Day," the human beast in unashamed glory of body.

Looking back, I can see lots of influences, although I was unaware of them at the time. I discovered [Gustave] Courbet and Kodachrome II simultaneously. Courbet was very important to me. I still think highly of some of his work, but seeing *La Belle Irlandais* and *Girl with a Parrot* for the first time really knocked me over. I also admired [Pierre] Bonnard and Stanley Spencer. I'd seen Spencer's various *Resurrections* at the Tate in 1964 or so and was very moved by them. I'm still in awe of them. Kodachrome II was wonderful; it was the only film stock ever made that could render flesh with any kind of accuracy. I'm told that Kodachrome I was even better, but that was before my time.

I remember that Christopher Smart was on my mind. I found out about him from Benjamin Britten's working of *Rejoice in the Lamb*. And John Clare—I picked up a ragged old copy of his poems in a London bookstall for fifty cents. No one had ever heard of him over here. I admired them both for their incredible openness. Neither of them was a very good poet technically, and both were as mad as March hares, but they both got the full lethal high-voltage jolt of life straight, without protection or defense, the undiluted juice right from the source. And it killed them both, of course, but for their few luminous moments they got it right, as Blake did. Smart was incarcerated for stopping people on the street and asking them to join him in kneeling on the pavement to thank God for the miraculous beauties of the world.

Anyway, I was a kid and aspired to such openness, and I had all the things I loved around me in those ghost rooms, now gone. Ghost-woman and ghost-light, and my familiars, ghost-dog and ghost-cat, beauteous apparencies, and I tried to catch them, with my little shadow catcher, to stop their vanishing, but they vanished anyway.

MacDonald: In terms of technique, you seem to be exploring new areas in these films. Was this your first use of single framing?

Noren: I think so. After a period of very long takes, I got interested in the possibility of twenty-four different images in a projected second, working with the individual frame as the basic unit.

There were a few people working in single frames then, but for the most part they all seemed to be trying to force techniques from other art forms onto film, which never seemed to work too well, that is, each frame as a word or syllable, or each frame as a musical note or a brush stroke, trying for a synthesis that was never really possible. I was interested in using single framing to convey kinetic energy. If it's done right, it can evoke states of high energy in the mind. Also, for me it's a much more accurate graphing of the flow of my own visual energy while shooting, more like a true picture of how I perceive. My seeing, at least while shooting, tends to operate in pulses and spurts of intensity, where thought and feeling and raw perceptual material coalesce and come into focus for distinct instants. Single framing is very attractive for that reason. I've refined my use of that technique over the years, and I think it came to real fruition in *Charmed Particles* and *The Lighted Field*, and I'm working with it now in other ways.

The long, Lumièrelike stare brings the mind to an attention of unnatural duration and intensity . . . an altered state, and that's the source of its power. With single framing, the constant interruption of focused attention forces you to a kind of heightened perception because the mind is racing to absorb a great deal of information very quickly; the power here is constant surprise, which compels unusual alertness and the exhilaration that comes with that.

Most of us can't really deal with a situation where every frame is different. The mind tends to superimpose them, group them together into more manageable units for easier comprehension, so that individual frames aren't really seen individually. A two-frame image has a much better chance of standing on its own, and three- and four-frame images are workable, practical units; almost anyone can perceive them.

MacDonald: How widely was *Huge Pupils* seen? Were there extreme reactions? Were screenings shut down?

Noren: It was shown a great deal and was considered very scandalous, although that was never my intention. Things were still incredibly repressive then. People who didn't live through it can't really imagine how much so. *Naked Lunch* and Henry Miller's books were still going through the courts, and I routinely had material seized by the labs. I remember once going to pick up some material at a lab and being told by the manager that they had destroyed it. I was outraged, but curious too, and asked him what they had done with it. It turned out that they had dropped the rolls in boiling water!

I think it was in 1967 that I showed the film at Notre Dame, of all places, at a conference on eroticism in the arts. The administration told the students not to show the film, so of course they immediately set up a secret screening in an out-of-the-way classroom. At least three quarters of the student body showed up and tried to squeeze into the room. About five minutes into the film, the police broke the door open and tried to seize the print. Some students got hold of it first and took off, police in pursuit, waving night sticks and mace cans. Meanwhile the print had come loose and was unreeling all over the campus as they ran with it. Finally, the police cornered them. Wild punches, bloody heads, girl's screaming, film flying—a living defense of the Constitution. The print was literally ripped to pieces—the body of Dionysus. That was an extreme case, but there were several other incidents in the heartland. In New York things were more civilized. A well-placed twenty-dollar bill assured your right to free expression.

MacDonald: It has been years since I saw *False Pretenses* and *The Phantom Enthusiast,* the next two sections of *The Adventures of the Exquisite Corpse,* and I confess I remember very little. You've told me that the films are out of distribution, being reworked. Recently, I heard that your reworking them has to do with the demand of the women filmed not to be seen in the films. *Is* that the issue? Also, according to your filmography, *Huge Pupils* was reworked in 1977. How was it reworked? And why?

Noren: I can't imagine why anyone would say that to you. No one I've ever filmed has objected to the way in which it was done, and certainly no one has ever demanded changes.

The reworking of *False Pretenses* and *The Phantom Enthusiast* is a matter of reorchestration: expanding the films in some ways and condensing them in others. There's also a large amount of material from that time that I want to include if I can.

Unfortunately, the time available to me to do this work is very limited. Don't forget that I work for a living [Noren works at Sherman Grinberg Film Libraries, Inc. in New York City], with punishing expenditures of energy. Also, I'm working on a new film, shooting and editing almost simultaneously, and I'm working on several other projects as well, so it would be hard to say when the reworking of those films will be completed.

MacDonald: Charmed Particles puts the viewer—I assume by design—in an unusual situation: the film is full of visual pleasure. I'm "oooohing" and "wowing" all the time as I watch it. And yet, because of the way you use single framing, there's battering of the eye that reminds me of Tony Conrad's *The Flicker.* It causes the viewer to continually fight exhaustion.

Noren: By "viewer," you mean yourself in this case because not everyone has had that problem. The film presents an energy field of a particular intensity. It's possible to enter into it and be energized by it up to that intensity, if you want to. The pulsation of light and shadow, single framing plus sixteen to eighteen fps projection, exerts a hypnosis of a certain kind which tempts you to surrender conscious control of the proceedings. Loss of control is scary to that part of the mind responsible for it, so that part resists and fights to maintain control, and since the film is long, grows fatigued. But, of course, nothing bad will happen to you, in this case at least, if you lose control. The worst thing that can happen is that for an hour or so you'll see the way I see, rather than how you normally see. Also, since the energy level of that film is high, attempts to analyze it while it is in progress are frustrated, and that can produce fatigue. Various people have told me that the film is "too short," "too long," and exactly the "right" length. Who am I to say?

I never consciously think of viewers' reactions. It's something you can never predict or anticipate, and I'm certainly not trying to manipulate reactions. What I'm interested in is strong and clear transmission of the energies at hand.

It's interesting that many people see color in *Charmed Particles,* since it's the blackest of blacks and whitest of whites. I remember speaking to someone after a screening who was convinced that the entire film was in color with a few black and white insertions, and wanted to know why I had included the black-and-white.

MacDonald: Charmed Particles is, as I remember, a physics term, referring to particles of matter so small that they can be said to exist half way between matter and energy. I assume your use of the title here has to do with this film's hovering between being a record of the everyday, of what surrounds you in your daily life, and abstract, mysterious fields of visual energy. Often you begin with a recognizable scene, then "riff" into a wildly energetic set of abstractions. Is that the primary sense of the title for you?

Noren: It is a physics term, and what attracted me to it as a title is that it describes the point at which energy becomes matter, intangible "nothing" becoming somehow "something." What lies at the heart of each atom is nothing, the beast at the heart of the labyrinth, and from that nothing, the great black hole, comes the something we call the world. Being emanates from nothing and vice versa.

Also, the film is particles being "charmed" into form, the grains conjured into images.

MacDonald: You seem less interested in overall conceptualization—either before you shoot, in the structuring of your films, or after you shoot, in terms of editing what you've captured/discovered—than in "being in the *now,*" in "playing" the camera as a musician plays a musical instrument.

Noren: That's certainly true of *Charmed Particles,* which was totally improvised, starting with the very first image that appears in the finished film and continuing on from there. It was shot over a period of several years and the operating rule was that I would shoot every day, if at all possible and if the light was good, working with light and shadow and whatever was around me, not knowing in advance what I would be shooting, trusting that in the end, everything would cohere and come to meaning, which it did. Risé [Risé Hall-Noren] and I were living at that time in a tiny apartment on West Tenth Street, so small it was like living in a camera, although it got splendid light, and I took the basic elements of our life there and worked to see what improvisation and variations were possible, to see if I could charm the disparate elements into form. Being able to invent and improvise and consciously shape material in a given moment has always been important to me, and I've always felt that, given good light, even the commonest, most mundane things are wonderfully rich in possibilities, if you have the eyes for it. It's the old story of working to reveal the "ordinary" as being extraordinary, which in fact it is. I was very interested at the time in improvisational music of all kinds. Jazz, particularly Cecil Taylor and Charlie Parker, and Tibetan Buddhist music—bone trumpets and skull-drums—the Mazatec mushroom songs and Morrocan Sufi music. Also, animal songs: wolves, whales, birds, crickets—this was a special inter-

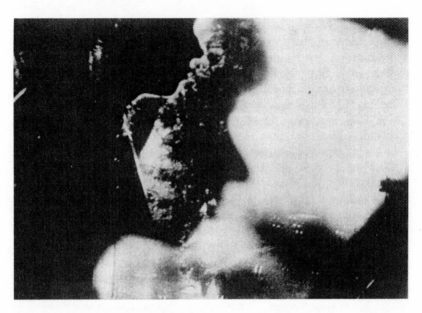

From Noren's Charmed Particles *(1979).*

est, since music doesn't get more sincere than that, and animals are great improvisers.

MacDonald: How much preplanning do you do? How much editing do you do, once you've shot the material? And how often do you make imagery?

Noren: There's preplanning only in the sense that I'm always thinking about images, thinking with images, always wanting to make images. Always "working." By this time it's a natural function. I seldom look at anything without thinking of how it can be transformed into an "image." It's automatic, I'm not even conscious of doing it.

Preparation is mostly keeping the materials at hand and maintaining the correct frame of mind, which makes working possible. A delicate balance between energy and circumstance. This is much harder to do than it sounds. But, of course, the basic, vital thing is good light where everything is revealed in its miraculousness. That is my passion. I love it physically, as I would a beautiful animal. October light is my favorite, and the raw spring light that always seems "new," somehow, but I take whatever I can get. I love it all, and I shoot whenever I can.

At its best, this is done in a special state of mind. It's not a trance state, and certainly not the taking of angelic dictation as [Rainer Maria] Rilke meant it. I think of it as a state of "health," where thought and feeling are one and the same. The response to light: the process of seeing and feeling and thinking about it, and "capturing" it, is harmonious and simple and direct, without doubt or hesitation. In this condition I know exactly what to do and how to do it, no questions. This state sometimes lasts for a long time before diminishing. I'm superstitious about forcing it, so when I feel it start to lessen, I stop working.

In editing, I gather material shot over a period of time and assemble it more or less in the order in which it was shot, chronologically, and then I study it until I begin to see how things belong together, what connections to make. This is always difficult. In theory, there are thousands of possible combinations, but in theory only. There is only one "right" way for it to go. It's very much as though the film were already "made" in a part of my mind, and the working is simply letting it reveal itself. This is a very painstaking process. It's frustrating and extremely exhilarating at the same time, and it's very hard work.

MacDonald: For you, all surfaces of reality seem equal, and shadow is as real as either light or the objects making the shadows. At times in fact you seem to offer an implicit polemic about this: I'm thinking of the section in *Charmed Particles* when you explore the surface of the TV screen, elaborating what you see there, but in a way that makes clear that for you the TV is no more interesting *visually* than any other surface of comparable size. You avoid commenting about reality—about politics, social relations, whatever—in favor of exploring visual surfaces. Do you see your filmmaking as an end in itself—the production of a new set of visual experiences—or as a visual training that includes moral or political implications in the long run?

Noren: I'm not sure I know what you mean by "reality." There is no human act that is not political—the "personal" *is* political—so in that sense my films are political. I wouldn't presume to advise anyone on their moral conduct or their spiritual condition. I'm not qualified. All I can hope to do is to send out my best and highest energies. If they are received and made use of, then I'm delighted.

If I had the time and the means there are many things I would like to propagandize on behalf of, like animal rights and ecological preservation, for example. But I hardly have time to do what I'm doing already, and I honestly don't think it does much good. How can you hope to "explain" to someone why they shouldn't torture an innocent animal? I thought at one time that most of our evils were a result of ignorance and that education could bring enlightenment and change. I no longer think this is true.

MacDonald: These days a good many filmmakers have been moving to video, either as a means of disseminating their films (videos, not films, are sent to prospective programmers) and/or as a new form capable of expressing much of what they want to express in their films, but more accessibly and less expensively. In a very basic sense, your films are *about* film and what an artist can accomplish with it. I can't imagine them on video.

Noren: The problem I have with video is the way it registers natural light; it's crude, insensitive, inaccurate, and barbaric. I don't know if this can be improved. The technology is fascinating and attractive in many ways. It is much easier and less expensive to work with, and the possibility of being able to inexpensively distribute many copies of a work is very exciting. As it is now, I'm lucky to have three or four prints of a film in circulation at any one time because they're so expensive. I'm not a snob about it—if the light problem were solved I'd start working with it immediately, but I don't think it can be. Probably video will replace film altogether in the future—a dreadful thought, but probably true. As for transferring film to video, I've never seen an example in which the film wasn't diminished.

MacDonald: Can you give me a sense of how often your films are rented? Years ago, when I talked with Diana Barrie, she felt that the issue of her films being seen or ignored wasn't all that important: for her, the pleasure was in making the films, and worrying about screenings was the downside of the process. If her films weren't seen, in fact, that'd be OK, so long as she could continue making work. In some senses, her films (especially her early Super-8 films) remind me of yours. Do you share her attitude?

Noren: My films are rented fairly often, seemingly more as time passes. I have a certain following, and I certainly don't feel "ignored." I don't know if I would continue to make films if they were never seen by anyone; that's too problematic. I'm interested in echos, I like to get energy back in exchange for the energy I send out; in fact, it's a necessity.

The situation is very frustrating, to the point of despair sometimes, but then it always has been, going back twenty years or so. The audience for the kind of films we're talking about here is larger than it ever was, and there are more places for the films to be seen and more outlets for scholarly writing about the films than at any point I can remember. But still you can spend years working on a film, putting your lifeblood and best mind into it, and then when it's released, you are very fortunate if it's seen by a total of two thousand people. After it's made the circuit of the places that show this kind of work, it can sit unseen for years, no matter how well-received it was. My films are complex and intricate; there's no way they can be completely understood in a single viewing, and this is true of many films, many filmmakers. I can't count the number of times I've seen interesting work, knowing at the time that I would very likely never see it again.

The obvious answer is high quality, inexpensive copies, like books, records, and tapes, so that thousands of copies of a given work can be in circulation at any one time and can be found by their true audience. But this will never happen with film; the economics are against it.

MacDonald: When I showed *The Lighted Field* at Utica College this past spring, Pat [MacDonald's wife, Patricia O'Connor] leaned over to me at one point and said, "He must love magic." It struck me as an astute comment; in a sense you're in the Georges Méliès tradition; for you the camera is the magician's top hat.

Noren: True in the sense that everything in that film was done in the camera at the moment of shooting. That's always been a point of pride with me, it's true of all my films. No optical printers or special processes. All invention in the moment of shooting itself. I stress this so that you'll fully appreciate my virtuosity—and my humility.

The Lighted Field is a magic trick, prestidigitatious resurrection of the dead, animation of the inert. That's the metaphorical nexus of the entire film. We all love magic, at least as children. That's basic good health.

I once spent some time studying occult matters, but in the end all of that just gets in your way. It's a trap like any other systematized way of thinking.

I still get a great deal of pleasure from alchemical thought and imagery. There's some wonderful cinematic poetry there and also some very sound, commonsensical advice about how to live.

I always liked this quote from "The Exposition of the Typical Figures":

> As the first substance of your work, seek the Water of Life that flows beside the Tree, and keep its counsel, and the counsel of the Wind and counsel of the Earth and counsel of the Sun. For while you anxiously look about in out-of-the-way places and long for extraordinary events to come to you, while you are desirous of witches brews and love potions and instant cures, you pass by the clear motions of the Blessed Stream. While you gather in groups to see unprecedented lights and colors in the night-time sky, and while you await incredible assignations of power on earthly lands . . . the Stone of Heaven lies directly at your feet . . . it is that upon which you stand.

MacDonald: The Lighted Field has a very different mood from your earlier films. In fact, the clarity of its mood helped me see that, while many of your visual concerns may have remained consistent since *Huge Pupils* and *The Wind Variations,* each film feels the way it does because of your overall mental state during the period when you were shooting. *The Lighted Field* showed me that the films are more personally expressionistic than I had realized. Specifically, *The Lighted Field* seems a very happy film; you seem happy as a filmmaker, as a family man, as husband and father; a certain psychological darkness seems to have lifted. I have

Successive frames from Noren's The Lighted Field *(1987).*

a feeling that this is just the sort of thing you don't like to discuss, but is this how the film seems to you?

Noren: Perhaps, although it's a little more complicated than that. But in general you're right, and you're right that I don't like to talk about it.

I began the film just after my marriage to Risé, which was extreme good fortune for me, for many, many reasons. It was made in a period of intense hard work, apart from work on the film, in which we tried to make a home. I was able to reprioritize things and to gather and focus my energies in a way I hadn't been able to before. It brought about a kind of very practical, utilitarian down-home "enlightenment." I don't really care to say more.

MacDonald: The Lighted Field also refers directly to your work as an archivist and researcher, in the found-footage passages. Could you talk about your work at Sherman Grinberg?

Noren: I work with news images daily, both modern material and material going back to the twenties and earlier, and that's how I came upon those shots. They were all originally shot on nitrate film and were in the process of decay when I found them, quite literally turning to dust, as nitrate does, so it wasn't really a question of appropriation but of rescue. I saved what I could of them and transferred them to safety finegrain. I found them very resonant and beautiful in themselves, and so I employed them, as though they were actors under my direction, frequently portraying me or acting as stand-ins for me. In their original commercial usage some fifty years ago, they were projected maybe twice at most. Some of them were never used at all and buried in the vaults and left to rot. So I was glad to be able to recirculate them, put them back into the light again.

I've worked as an archivist for a long time. My expertise is in knowledge of news, the ability to know about and locate very specific news images on request, very quickly and efficiently under intense pressure. And I'm extremely good at it. I also deal in the licensing of this material and in rights and clearances. I work on all kinds of projects: documentaries, features, television commercials, music videos, industrials, you name it. The stock in trade is war, murder, death, destruction, grief and weeping, disaster and degradation, greed, starvation, intense suffering, horrible human activities, crazed apes mad with blood lust! In short, news. Have you ever wondered why the news you get from TV and newspapers is all bad? Have I got news for you: there is no good news, none. The news *is* bad.

One aspect of the job is dealing with raw news material from the field, which is very interesting indeed. What you see on the evening news, compared to the raw material, is a very carefully constructed entertainment, disguised as reportage. This has always been true of news. The raw material is the real thing, and it is frequently horrifying. If you were appalled by the aired reports of the Valdez oil spill, or the Ethiopia famine, for example, wait until you see the field tapes. It was a hundred times worse than the media would have you believe. Working with this kind of material on a daily basis can have a profound effect on a person. It's an education of a very special kind, and in its way a very expensive one. It's not something you can buy at the Harvard Business School.

I also work regularly with a certain government agency that uses news material to make informational presentations to the president of the United States. I hope you're duly impressed.

MacDonald: The particular archival imagery in *The Lighted Field*— the dogs diving into the water and later "undiving"; the man who is put into the block of ice at the beginning and removed at the end; the boy and dog in bed; the X-ray material; the imagery of the laser—seems to be used in a metaphoric way. The man going into and coming out of the block of ice is particularly suggestive, since it's a framing device for the film. I'm tempted to see it as a comment on your moving into and out of the filmmaking process; but I confess also to a more sentimental interpretation: that the warmth and happiness of *The Lighted Field* is a function of your coming out of a "colder" period as person/filmmaker.

Noren: My use of those found images was metaphorical. There's a metaphorical progression from the first image to the last. This is something I rarely permit myself, although you can say that any film image is a metaphor, just by its very nature. Whatever else it is, *The Lighted Field* is a narrative, a carefully constructed one, the telling of a tale. Of course, every film is a narrative, isn't it, whatever other pretensions it might have, simply by virtue of the fact that one frame must follow another in time. Our minds are such that we are obliged to make a story out of everything we experience, obliged to frame things to make them comprehensible. We are constantly telling ourselves stories that allegedly interpret the play of light and shadow on the retina screen, and the play of imaginary light on the screen of the "mind," or "the lighted field," if you will. I think we probably became conscious in the first place by struggling to tell ourselves stories, to make meaning of the chaos of sensory input that afflicts us. "Story" is the absolute basic essential of thinking. Our minds consist of a "teller" and a "listener." Consciousness is the mind communicating with itself about itself, telling itself the story of itself, story of past, future, now. We have to have "story" to survive.

And our "story" of consciousness is dream by definition. We live in a dream of waking, we dream that we're "awake," imagining past and future, telling ourselves elaborate stories about both. We flatter ourselves that we recognize a delusional present moment, not past or future but the reality of "now." But of course we no sooner apprehend this present moment than it is past. (I read somewhere that the average person thinks that the "present" lasts for about three seconds.)

We invented cinema deliberately as a device to allow us to dream while waking, and to give us access to areas of the mind that were previously only available in sleep. It was no accident that the first film-makers immediately seized on dream device and method as the first, essential film "language," as though the cinema was specifically invented for the objectification and articulation of those things.

Anyway, in *The Lighted Field* "dream of story" and "story of dream" are closely interwoven as themes. It is also a ghost story in a sense. It was calculated in a way to be a posthumous work, a tale told from the grave, and of course, in time it will become exactly that. That's another narrative element in the film, an elaborate memento mori. This isn't unduly morbid. The best possible mental state to be in is one in which you are clearly conscious of your personal mortality. Clear and constant recognition of this will energize you in a way that nothing else can. At the very least, it keeps you alert. A friend of mine once calculated that since the speed of the revolution of the earth around its own axis is some 877 miles per hour, that is the exact speed at which your grave approaches.

In general, *The Adventures of the Exquisite Corpse* is a reworking of what has to be the world's oldest story, "the fool's progress," how the fool became wise. There are hundreds of versions and variations, but the story is always essentially the same: the young fool leaves home to set off down the road of the world, hoping to find the great treasure that is hidden behind the veil of the world's illusions, behind the screen of the movie of the world, as it were. After many dangers and hardships, and by the exercise of strength and cunning, the fool tears away the veil and discovers that what is behind it is "nothing." This is valuable knowledge: it *is* the treasure, the "Pearl of Great Price," and in recognizing this, the fool becomes wise, a wise fool, and can see the world for what it is. That is the larger framework of *The Adventures of the Exquisite Corpse*: the individual parts function as lesser wheels that move within the larger wheel of the whole.

Another narrative aspect of the film is about the famous journey to the "other world." In my program notes when I released the film, I identified the "other world" as being "this world," which I hope is self-explanatory. And yet another narrative level is that of the entire film as after-death hallucination, in the tradition of *Sunset Boulevard* [1950] and a great novel by Flann O'Brien, *The Third Policeman*.

MacDonald: Unlike *Charmed Particles*, *The Lighted Field* is not arranged seasonally; at times you play with winter and summer views out your window; each time we track past the window, the view outside has changed dramatically—sometimes jumping through months. The visual extravaganza of this film makes it difficult to be thinking of overall structural devices, though I have a sense that in general we move from what I'd call camera performances of one kind or another into a period of domestic portraits (of your wife, the kids, the cats, the wash, the garden . . .) then back to camera performances—all of which is framed by the found footage material. Could you talk a bit about what you had in mind for the film's overall structure.

Noren: It is carefully constructed and works on many levels simultaneously. There's a straightforward "documentary" level on which it's "about" being at home, going to work, and being at home again. That is the basic rhythm of my life, after all, so that's the "ground." I described it best in the original program notes: "the Ghost in love, at work, at play with bright companions in the Lighted Field." It's a tale of a dreamer, who dreams what you, viewer and also dreamer, "see," and *is* what he sees and what you see. It's a film about dreaming and is literally, physically a dream. This is a dream of sleep and waking, death and resurrection, which is the central theme of the film, and is of course the central theme of anyone's life, manifest on a daily basis, the "dream-film" of consciousness, of which we are solitary spectators in the theaters of our own skulls. I have little interest in psychoanalytical dream-interpretation by the way, which I've always found to be incredibly cynical. My interest is more in the mechanics of the process.

MacDonald: Having just recovered—at forty-six years—from turning forty, I feel very close to *The Lighted Field*; it feels to me, the way *my* life feels to me: "Hey! being middle aged is OK, it's better in many ways than being young!"

Noren: Measuring your life in terms of time will make you old. Time as we speak of it here is a dubious hallucination of sequence and cause and effect. In many ways I feel younger now than I did at twenty. Personal force is what matters. Most people do their best work as they get older. It takes a long time to be good. There aren't many Mozarts around.

This is from Hokusai, who was wise: "I drew some pictures I thought fairly good when I was fifty, but really nothing I did before the age of seventy was of any value at all. At seventy-three I have at last caught every aspect of nature . . . birds, fish, animals, insects, trees, grasses, all. When I am eighty I will have developed still further, and I will really master the secrets of art at ninety. When I reach a hundred my work will be truly sublime and my final goal will be attained around the age of one hundred and ten, when every line I draw will be imbued with life."

MacDonald: There's always been an element of performance in your films—always, at least, in the films I'm aware of. *Say Nothing* was very much about performance, as *The Exquisite Corpse* films have been. But in *The Lighted Field* this performance dimension seems more overt, more frank. I'm thinking of those sequences when you put your feet, or your shadow into a spin, or into high-speed motion along the street. We can see how you do it; but we're astonished at the results. It's like juggling: you pick up the camera, the way a juggler picks up bowling pins.

Noren: There's no animal behavior that is not performance. That's all we do. Whether you're in front of the camera or behind it, you're always acting, always performing. I've sometimes employed my image as an actor on the screen, an actor portraying my-"self." Who is better qualified, after all? Performance art as such doesn't really interest me.

In the sequences you mention, what's really at work is extracting visual power from something quite common and ordinary. Motto: "make it jump!" Con brio!

MacDonald: The Lighted Field seems, even more than earlier films, a demonstration of the range possible for a 16mm camera and black-and-white filming. What have you been doing since that film? It feels so much like a culmination of your career as filmmaker that I can't help but wonder whether it presages a major pivot in your direction, back toward color perhaps.

Noren: It's not a culmination, at least I hope not. It's a good piece of work. A lot of my life went into it. Taken with *Charmed Particles,* it's almost an encyclopedia of black-and-white possibilities, but the possibilities are endless. In a way, I feel I've just begun to work in that medium. There are many, many more things I want to do. I love black and white for its severity. By comparison color seems almost sentimental, and the range of color stocks that are available now is very limited. I'm still mourning Kodachrome II. Most of the things I've seen in color recently would have been much more interesting in black and white. Anyway, I'm very sensitive to color, and I have very strong feelings about individual colors, so that working in black and white frees me from a lot of restrictions.

Since finishing *The Lighted Field* I've been working on a long black-and-white film with sound, called *Imaginary Light.* It seems like all I do is work. There isn't any occasion when I'm not working in one sense or another, and there's no such thing as finished.

MacDonald: At times during *The Lighted Field,* I get the sense that you're consciously demonstrating that cinema can do, comparatively easily, much of what the other arts struggle to accomplish. Sometimes, particular segments of the film remind me of the work of particular painters and kinds of painting—the sequence of light on the drinking glasses reminds me of certain superrealist painters (Janet Fish, for example); the street corner sequences where we see multiple layers of imagery through the glass and reflected in it remind me of, say, Richard Estes; the sequences along the sidewalks, sometimes of Ray K. Metzker. I don't claim any expertise in the contemporary fine arts, but I wonder if you keep up with what's going on in painting, photography, the arts in general, and whether to some extent, sequences in *The Lighted Field* were homages or challenges to particular artists or kinds of work?

Noren: I try to keep up. I have a great appetite for images of all kinds, so I'm always looking for what I might devour. Like any other food, there's a lot of poor quality and very little that's really good. You can starve in the midst of plenty.

I'm aware of the work of some of the people you mention, and I think that some of it is pretty good, but certainly no homage was intended. Living in a city like New York, multiple reflections in windows are an everyday occurrence, all you have to do is look. The light on the glasses I saw one day when I was washing dishes and simply shot it, no more and no less.

MacDonald: At the end of *The Lighted Field,* there's a funny little coda, where we see the shadow of your arm as you flex your muscle. It seems a fitting conclusion to the film, which, so far as I'm concerned, proves that you can "play" the 16mm camera and black-and-white film with more ingenuity and dexterity than any other filmmaker. The making of the muscle seems a frank recognition of what you have indeed been able to accomplish; there's nothing in it of youthful ego—it's more a simple refusal to be falsely modest, almost as if to say to the viewer: "I'm a little amazed at what I can do, too, but there's no point in my pretending that I'm not excited about what I've learned over the years and what I can accomplish with this camera!" Is that what you had in mind in the final shot?

Noren: No, although you're most gracious and generous! That gesture was actually made by the limb of the tree whose shadow you see in that shot, not by me. It was an unusual occurrence, to be sure, and I was fortunate to be standing there with my camera.

MacDonald: Some general questions: Do you go to conventional films often? Are there particular commercial films or filmmakers you especially admire?

Noren: Rarely, these days. I live some distance from the city, and it's difficult for me. I still enjoy Robert Bresson. *Au Hasard Balthazar* [1970] is one of my favorite films. I like *Une Femme Douce* [1969] a lot, too. And I'm still interested in Godard. I thought *Hail Mary* [1985] was good. And Wim Wenders—*Wings of Desire* [1987] was interesting.

MacDonald: How much avant-garde film do you see? Are there particular filmmakers you make a point of keeping up with?

Noren: In theory I'm interested in almost everyone. I simply don't have enough time to see nearly as much as I would like to. A lot of what I do see is discouraging because it's silly.

There's a fashion right now for work that is allegedly "transgressive," which is supposed to be liberating, but it's really middle-class adolescent petulance, art as an arena for revenge against parents. This is okay in kindergarten, but doesn't do much good elsewhere. A lot of work I see seems to revel in pathology, which isn't especially useful either. Monu-mentalizing alienation and personal misery and grievance is a waste of everyone's time. There's also a lot of "clever" work from victims of art schools, which is depressing indeed. I do see good things from time to time, but as I've said, getting to see them more than once is a major effort.

The absolute best thing I've seen recently and certainly the most avant-garde was a lightning storm over southern New Jersey. It was so spectacular and sophisticated and surely one of the all-time great mov-ies. It was incredibly powerful and intricate and intelligent and terrify-ing. It blasted us awake at two A.M., and we watched it through the black frame of the back door: vivid, intense, electric presentation of every last single detail of each bush, tree, leaf of grass. Vibrating out of absolute blackness in blinding, blue-white light, figure and ground switching places several times a second. Violent dimensional collisions, macro-scopic magnification of the smallest things. Then everything vanishing into blackness so intense that the after-images were almost as strong as the original. And sound! Earth-shattering contrapuntal booms and blasts of such power I was sure the house would be blown away. I wish I could begin to describe it. It was wonderful, and as avant-garde as it gets. We were enchanted.

Anne Robertson

I first became interested in Anne Robertson because of her unusual relationship to her films. At the time when her *Diary* was shown, complete, at the American Museum of the Moving Image in 1988, it was over forty hours long, and was shown in a room that Robertson had decorated with childhood artifacts. The extended screening invited viewers out of their lives and prearranged schedules and into hers. Robertson's use of three sources of sound during the screening—sound-on-film, sound-on-tape, and in-person commentary—confirmed the viewer's immersion in Robertson's experience. That the diary reels were often startlingly beautiful was an unexpected surprise.

As this is written in July 1990, the film continues to grow, though some reels have recently been censored by Robertson (see her comments in the interview). The diary is essentially every film she's made: even films listed under separate titles in her filmography—*Magazine Mouth* (1983), for example—are sometimes included in presentations of the diary. As I've grown more familiar with Robertson's work (to date, I've seen about eight hours of the diary), I've come to understand that the relationship of this filmmaker's life and work is even more unusual than I had guessed. For Robertson, whose manic-depressiveness has resulted in frequent hospitalizations, making and showing the diary has become a central means for maintaining psychic balance, her primary activity whenever she is free of the mental hospital and free enough of drug therapy to be able to produce imagery.

Robertson's *Diary* can be experienced in a variety of ways. She most likes to present it as a "marathon": complete and as continuous as possible. But in recent years, she has also begun to fashion shorter programs (the most recent I've attended was four hours long). The scheduled show date has become a means for sampling from the diary. If Robertson schedules a show for April 25, for example, she may show all the reels that were shot during April: viewers are able to see the development (or lack of it) in her life from year to year. In general, we see Robertson simultaneously from the outside (within her recorded imagery and sound, and usually as the in-person narrator) and from the inside, as she expresses her moments of clarity and delusion in her handling of the camera and her juxtapositions of sound and image.

While my original interest in Robertson was a function of the fascinating and troubling interplay between her filmmaking and her illness, my decision to interview her was determined both by the compelling nature of her presentation (particularly her courage in submitting her films and herself to public audiences) and by her frequently breathtaking imagery. The single-framing of her activities in her tiny Boston apartment in early reels—she flutters around the rooms and through the weeks like a frenzied moth—and her precise meditations on her physical environment make her *Diary* intermittently one of the most visually impressive Super-8 films I've seen. And the way in which she enacts contemporary compulsions about the correct appearance of the body (her weighing and measuring herself, nude, is a motif) and about the importance of meeting "the right guy" provide a poignant instance of those contemporary gender patterns so problematic for many women. Robertson's *Diary*—along with films by Su Friedrich, Diana Barrie, Michelle Fleming, Ann Marie Fleming, and others—has re-personalized many of the issues raised by the feminist writers and filmmakers of the seventies.

I talked with Robertson in April 1990.

MacDonald: You remind me of a line in Jonas Mekas's *Walden*: "I make home movies—therefore I live." For Mekas, the ongoing documentation of his life is very important. But as important as his filmmaking is to him, I think the line is metaphoric, rather than literal: Mekas has a busy organizational life, as well as a filmmaking life. His statement seems more applicable to you. When you're not able to make films, your life seems in crisis. Could you talk about the relationship between your films and your life? Perhaps you could begin with how you got started making films.

Robertson: I started the diary November 3, 1981, which, it turns out, is Saul Levine's birthday. Sort of a psychic tribute there. He was one of the people who encouraged me to continue making films. I started the diary about a month after I began sitting in on classes at the Massachusetts College of Art. I'd made eleven short films before that, the first in 1976.

When I began the diary, I bought five rolls of film. I thought I'd film myself, one scene every day, moving around my apartment. And I would go on a strict diet: I knew of a photographer in New York [Eleanor Antin] who had simply taken a still of herself nude every day while she was on a diet. I wanted to do that, but at first, I wanted to be clothed, I wore a leotard. Every day I'd do one more scene.

Five rolls of film—it wasn't enough. Sometime in late November, 1981, my father told me to tell a story. I didn't really have a story to tell, except to expand more on my day-to-day life inside my apartment. The whole film starts out with me carrying some grocery bags into the apartment and then emptying out a huge bag full of produce from my garden and from the co-op. Then I take off a black coat, hang it up, go into the living room, and get myself a dictionary—a 1936 dictionary, which has fantastic definitions for the word "fat." In the thirties, "fat" meant something good. It meant plump, pleasing—the best part of your work is a "fat" job—and "thin" had a lot of opprobrium attached: meager, of slender means.

Anyway, I started filming myself in this black coat over yellow leotards—I wore yellow because the *I Ching* says that to wear a yellow undergarment brings good fortune. And yellow was the closest to flesh color I could get (yellow is also the color of fat). But instead of losing weight, I was gaining weight. I kept bingeing so I started taking more frames of that. Later, I filmed the actual makings of a binge, and street signs of food. It was all going to be about food. I didn't really have any goal—just to lose the weight.

I would do things like lay out the black clothing on the bed, a full suit, black pocketbook, black gloves, black coat, black dress, black stockings (this is after I had mended the black coat and put it away—because I was against wool: I was getting rid of animal products in my life, to become a vegan—not just a vegetarian, but a vegan).

Well, my father died January 10, about two months after the film had begun, and well, that laying out of the black clothing went, "Bong!" And, as if that wasn't enough, I'd just finished weaving a big yellow banner on a loom I had built myself. I had had it on the loom for ten years. *The next day,* my father died. I felt like I'd predicted my father's death. And the reason he died was because he was a hundred pounds overweight when I was a kid—at least a hundred pounds. He had a heart attack and strokes.

After that, the film just sort of came. I started doing striptease, kicking breadsticks around on the kitchen table; I read *The Tibetan Book of the Dead* and started taking long strings of pictures of lights, because *The Tibetan Book of the Dead* says to stare into the bright light.

MacDonald: When you say "pictures," you mean single frames?

Robertson: Frames, images—just a lot of pictures of lights, lights, lights, lights, lights, lights, lights in the city, lights outside. I used to have *The Tibetan Book of the Dead* as a soundtrack for the film, but I discarded it because, though the Tibetans say it's good for people who are alive to hear it, it has an amazing capacity for being used to hypnotize someone. Too many demons, also. I got into a lot of worry about future technologies and people resuscitating brains or keeping people in comas, making them think they're dead. When you die, if *The Tibetan Book of the Dead is* true, you first see the white light and then the four bright-colored lights. I'm supposed to warn you: don't look at any of the soft lights.

I took a lot of pictures inside my studio and gradually started taking pictures more and more of people, of my family, of day-to-day life. Sometimes I'd introduce the film by saying, "It's true, so, it's a trousseau": it's the only gift I have for the guy who will come along and be my partner and say, "What have you been doing with the rest of your life?"

Eventually, I just sort of discarded the costume, and filmed myself naked. Last fall, I got very paranoid, and I cut out a lot of the naked parts. A lot of pans down my body were cut out. I left all the shots that were at a distance, but I cut out a lot of the ones that I felt really looked seductive. I wanted to take all that seductiveness out of the film, but I discovered you couldn't really do that. You take a picture of a naked body: it's seductive. But I did take out some of the best scenes, several hours of film. Eventually it went from being ninety reels last fall to about eighty-two. I took out nakedness and irreligious statements. I felt I couldn't leave them in anymore (my films of myself naked—*Talking to Myself* [1987], et cetera—are available only for shows with small, trusted audiences and at legitimate artistic venues).

I also took out a certain amount of obscurity, although I did want to leave as much obscurity as possible, because I am hoping that there is a man in the world (whether he's a video or film artist I kind of doubt; I think he's more likely someone like this actor, Tom Baker [Baker played Dr. Who on *Dr. Who*], I'm interested in)—someone who has a burning desire to study parapsychology, and who's in synchrony with me. For several years I kept a dream diary and I would write down in my diaries all the dreams I had. I'm looking for someone who has done the same thing with random thoughts, poems, images that have come to mind—dream images. *Somebody* might have written a poem that said, "My love is kicking breadsticks across the table and reading the definition of 'fat' from a 1936 dictionary."

I've got notes in my film log for the first two hundred rolls of my film. I've got starting and stopping dates, right down to the minute I took a picture. I know Allen Ginsberg dates his diaries down to the minute. I thought that would be a good thing to do, so that later I could prove synchrony with somebody who was willing to keep a notebook with *him* and make jottings of images or the thoughts that come unbidden and you have no way of tying them to anything.

Tom Baker was born in 1934. Tom Baker has two hundred dictionaries. If I can predict my father's death, I might as well believe I've predicted that there's this guy who is interested in me, who happens to have a collection of dictionaries. The whole diary started when I became fascinated with this old dictionary and its crazy definitions.

Sometimes I think I'm going to go back and reinsert the naked parts back into my diary, but I have a feeling probably I won't. I kept them all on reels. Supposedly, they're in order. Some reels got so mishmashed by my paranoia last fall, I could never put them back in order again.

When I started the film, I thought I'd lose weight; and the second thing I thought was that I'd try to tell a story, as my father told me to; and the third thing I thought was that the film would be a trousseau; and the fourth thing was my realizing that my children would be watching.

MacDonald: One of the things that struck me last night when you showed sections of the diary at Utica College (I don't remember this so much from when I saw the film at the Museum of the Moving Image; I guess it depends on which sections you're showing) was your startling openness about your hospitalization.

Robertson: Well, I've got to be! Otherwise, as Kate Millett says, you're a "ghost in the closet."

MacDonald: Is the history of your being institutionalized simultaneous with your making of the diary? How do *you* see the two things relating?

Robertson: Well, I think Mekas's comment, "I make home movies—therefore I live," *is* really apt for me. You see, I didn't have any way of explaining why I was into bingeing, but I knew the bingeing was going to go at the beginning of the film. The film had a theme. The theme was I wanted to lose weight, because I didn't want to die like my father had. Yet, I couldn't explain why I had gotten into overeating, eating literally until I got sick, until I had to lie down because it was too painful to stand up.

MacDonald: You said last night that you had never been a bulimic, that you never purged.

Robertson: No, that's true. I wouldn't do that. But there's such a thing as making eight dozen cookies and eating four dozen and then just feeling sick. This was after a whole day of being so very, very careful with food. The mental hospitalizations that had happened to me by 1981—I had been hospitalized three times—happened every fall. For three months each year, I was in a mental hospital. Mostly, I'd fight the drugs they gave me, but I would have to give in eventually because they'd say they'd take me to court: they'd inject me.

I had no way of explaining why I had breakdowns. It was another inexplicable thing in my life. When I was a kid growing up, I never thought I'd be having delusions, and be hospitalized. In 1981 I started the diary, and in 1981 I didn't have a breakdown. I think it might be because I was going to film school: I had somewhere to go, I had a camera to borrow. I made several other short films the fall of 1981 and then began the diary.

One short film was called *Locomotion* [1981]. It shows me against a blue wall, screaming and exhibiting the side effects of medication I had observed in the hospitals. The first real breakdown that I got on film was in 1982. I showed my delusions. I showed that I was afraid that root vegetables suffered, so I was going to take them back to the garden and replant them. You can see me getting on my big rain slicker and getting out the beets and carrots and onions and preparing to take them back, making sign language in front of the camera.

In fact, that first breakdown occurred shortly after a person at school threatened he'd call the cops and take the camera away from me. Losing that camera, I lost my mind. Every time there's a breakdown, I try to take pictures of it. My problem with a film diary (and with a written diary) is that sometimes I become so paranoid and obnoxious. Voices in my head become so frightening, and I cannot bring myself to document them. It's just too terrifying.

I believe in film being necessary every day. Monet did his haystacks and I have done the gazebo in the backyard. This winter I was so depressed, after getting out of the hospital and being put under a whole lot of restrictions, I was taking pictures every day of the gazebo in all kinds of weather. In fact, just this last week I stopped.

So for a while in the diary there are pictures of the gazebo, and of Tom Baker on *Dr. Who*. Daylight is the gazebo, where I'd hoped to get married someday (I've discarded that notion since I think a justice of the peace is just about as good). Evening is *Dr. Who*.

Anyway, I had so much trouble from my paranoia of the people across the pond—the neighbors. My problem is that a lot of my paranoia is warranted. I can't say the voices in my head are warranted, but I'm *damned* if I'm going to say they come from me! When a person starts getting third-person stories, more hideous than they've ever heard before, or ever read before, the psychiatric establishment says, "You invented that," and everybody else says, "You thought of that." Nobody, not even the psychiatrists, want to know how horrible the stories in your head are. I have never had a psychiatrist ask me, "And what do the voices say to you?" No one has ever said, "What do you mean by the insane monologue in your head?" Nobody wants to know because they're too scared. They think that the person who is insane and hears voices is making them up and is in some way as evil as the voices.

It's a real old thing. Instead of putting you in iron chains, they put you in drug chains. They've done a lot of drug pushing over the years. Speaking of drugs, another thing that's in the diary is the drugs I've chosen to use at times—a lot of pictures of alcohol, of cigarettes, of pot smoking, a few of cocaine, and the prescription drugs. I thought I'd focus on all the things I ever did that were wrong, and then I'd put them, one by one, into the films, along with the bingeing, and get perspective so I could shed bad habits.

So far every subject I come up with—excess apologies, thoughts about suicide (for three years, from 1976 to 1979, I heard voices saying, "I want to kill myself"—it was my voice) . . . every subject has been affected by being included in a film. I made a film about suicide [*Suicide, 1979*] illustrating some of the ways I thought I'd kill myself, and literally edited it in about an hour and a half and screened it, and as I watched the film, the suicide voices stopped in my head and they haven't come back since.

MacDonald: Did that happen with bingeing, too?

Robertson: Yeah, it happened with bingeing, when I made *Magazine Mouth,* which we watched last night. I was taking Polaroid pictures of myself with my mouth wide open, and closed but bulging like I had a lot of food in my mouth. I filmed all the objects going into my open mouth—food, fish, baubles of the rich . . . all kinds of things going into my mouth. And bingeing stopped being a major subject in my life soon after.

MacDonald: When you had the breakdown last year . . .

Robertson: In September and then again in November.

MacDonald: Did it have to do with preparing for the show we had scheduled? Are there passages in the films that create problems for you when you watch them?

Robertson: I can handle things once they're on film. But it's hard to know what I can have others see.

MacDonald: You're remarkably good with a Super-8 camera. I don't believe I've ever seen more beautiful Super-8 footage. Sometimes it's very subtle and precise. When you're looking through the camera, how fully are you thinking in terms of texture and color and framing—what the image will look like?

Robertson: I'm trying to take a pretty picture, if that's what you mean.

MacDonald: I was surprised to hear you say that you shot for a long time before you even looked at the footage.

Robertson: I still do! I don't look at it for at least a year! I just do assembly editing. Everything I take is in the film. The only alteration I've made is the taking out I've been doing lately, and I really regret that in a way. I thought that with the diary it would be great if *everything* was included, if I left overexposed or underexposed film in. Then the guy who is in synchrony with me somewhere in the world would have plenty of room to put in *his* words. But lately I've been taking more and more out of the diary so that he has less and less space to put his own words over. Mostly I just take out anything that's not visually comprehensible, that's completely black or completely overexposed (thinking ahead to video transfer). Almost everything else stays in.

The idea of not looking at what I take is so that I always have a naive idea. I don't take a picture deliberately and then take another picture deliberately. I take pictures when I find something I really like. Recently I noticed that an image of John Lennon and Yoko Ono, naked (I saw it on MTV), had gotten paired up with a picture of myself standing nude in front of my closet where my measurements and weight are printed on the side of the door. So there's probably subconscious memory and association involved with some of my images.

MacDonald: How much other avant-garde film have you seen?

Robertson: I saw a fair amount when I was at Massachusetts College of Art, but I've gotten out of going to a lot of films. I've got to put going to see film back in my life. I'm trying to rebuild into my life things that I let go when I was really depressed—like reading.

I started reading last fall in order to counteract the boredom of the mental hospital. I read voraciously and I've been reading ever since, which is good, because about a year ago, and at times over the last few years, I've found it difficult sometimes even to read a newspaper. So I've been building reading back into my life.

And I've built exercise back into my life. They say a person who wants to lose weight should gradually increase their physical exercise. Well, I'm running every day now. I think the next thing is going to films.

The problem is that I moved back home with my mother, to save money for film and get out of the city. It costs about fourteen cents a second just to shoot and process original film, without making prints. Then my mother decided to be the guardian of my mental health. She used to be in the habit of going out to film festivals with me. At the moment, I hardly have anyone to go with except her. And I'm kind of afraid to say, "Mom, I'm going out to a film": she'd be disappointed that

Robertson self-portrait, December 1991.
Top to bottom: "Depressive," "Normal,"
"Manic."

I wasn't going with her. I'm dependent on my mother for transportation, since at the moment, I'm not working full-time. But I don't want her to think she has to be my moviegoing companion.

At least I keep the camera going when I'm depressed. It's only been one or two times that I've let the camera go for two months. When I first began the diary, I used to carry the camera every day and take a picture almost every hour. It's less, lately—between one and four scenes a day.

I'm sorry, you asked a question?

MacDonald: About other avant-garde filmmakers. One reason I asked is because the reel about your cat Amy's death reminds me very much of Carolee Schneemann's *Kitch's Last Meal* [1973–78].

Robertson: I saw part of that at Massachusetts College of Art—about three or four hours. I remember the scene of her holding her cat and weeping. I felt really guilty when Amy died, and I took a picture of my guilt. When Carolee was filming her diary, she followed everywhere that Kitch walked. I remember coming up to Carolee and saying, "I must go for a walk with my cat." I never did that, until Amy was dying. And it came back to me that Carolee had done it. I feel guilty, really guilty about that. Amy was a good old cat.

MacDonald: That's a powerful part of your film.

Robertson: It does come off well in screening, it's a true story.

MacDonald: I think what comes through in your screenings is your openness. A lot of filmmakers think they're open, but you reveal agony in a way that goes much further than what's usually called "openness"— especially on the soundtrack (your in-person narration is less emotional).

Robertson: Well, the sound is from that time. It's real. Sometimes I use three sound sources. There's sound on the film, and there's sound on tape at the same time, and I narrate in person. I do worry about saying too much in person because to hear two sound sources might be okay, but three is pretty hard. Usually, I interrupt the flow when the sound is from tape that was done at the same time the images were made. Then it's like you're looking at a photo album with someone, explaining certain pictures you know he or she won't understand.

MacDonald: When you've shown the diary, have you always combined sound-on-film, tape, and in-person narration?

Robertson: Yes, but at the beginning I was using unedited stretches of original tapes. I didn't know I could take samples from recorded sound. I'm afraid of mixers and fancy laboratories. People were telling me how you have to go very complex with films, and make finely tuned, synchronized soundtracks. I don't do that. If I have tapes for a period of time, I'll simply go through them and pull out anything I find interesting. Then I play that over the stretch of film and see if anything happens that's so completely off that I have to cut out a piece of sound. If you don't go trying to make things match up, they'll match up anyway. It's like fate. It's happened to me when I've just played a whole stretch of unedited tape, and it's happened to me with dubbed excerpts. You put little pieces of tape next to film, without looking at the film, and synchrony happens—or an interesting contrast.

The sound that goes with Amy's reel is an original stretch of a tape I made when I was just keeping the diary tape along with the diary film. But most of the tapes I've been making lately are dubs of the best of the best.

I have several hundred hours of tape. My problem is that in the last couple of years I've been sending most of my diary tapes away to a guy—Tom Baker again.

This last year the sound on my camera broke down, but I didn't know because, as usual, I didn't look at the film until a year later. Consequently, in 1989 I have stretches of film and no sound to put over them. I figure I'll read some of my political letters. A fifty-one page letter should cover up several reels! And the audience will get an idea of the verbal delusions I have. Well, I don't know if they're all delusions. But some of them are pretty farfetched, I'd say.

MacDonald: Who do you send those letters to?

Robertson: I send them to the United Nations, to representatives, congressmen, governors. The first batch were sent to women representatives. I've sent them to show-business figures and music stars, Susan Sontag—a whole bunch of people. I've sent them to the president of the United States—that was probably my biggest mistake. Mostly, they're just sort of your all-purpose liberal-green-politics letters.

MacDonald: How many times have you shown the whole diary?

Robertson: I've only done the marathon three times: at the Massachusetts College of Art as my thesis, at Event Works in Boston, and in New York at the American Museum of the Moving Image. I'd like to do it a lot more.

Last night was the third or fourth time I've done a sample show, using a cross section of time, sampling from reels that cover the same time period each year.

MacDonald: That's an interesting way to show it.

Robertson: Yeah, it is, except this spring show I did last night was really full of breakdowns. Actually, probably the whole film is! I don't know how many people have documented breakdowns. I understand Carolee [Schneemann] did.

MacDonald: In *Plumb Line* [1971] she documents a breakdown.

Can your films be rented anyplace but from you?

Robertson: I don't have any copies. I don't make prints of any of my films.

MacDonald: You're showing originals all the time?

Robertson: I'm showing originals. Every time I see a scratch, I wonder if it's a new one. I can't afford to make prints. It's cost me twenty-four thousand dollars to make the diary so far. I don't have twenty-four thousand dollars to make a print of the whole thing. No way! I don't make prints of the shorter films either. All I can afford is originals.

MacDonald: Have you applied for grants?

Robertson: Well, I'm planning to do that, retroactively—to do a video transfer. The problem is you have to make a copy to show people in order to make money to make copies! It's possible that if I made video copies, I could get the money afterward to cover the cost of the video copy, and film prints.

I've applied for grants. I was a semifinalist once. But they don't really want a diary of a mad woman.

MacDonald: Well, this is a very beautiful diary of a mad woman. Of course, New England has a long history of quirky women artists: Emily Dickinson . . .

Robertson: Oh yeah! I read all of her poems last spring. She wrote 1,775 poems in her lifetime and put them in little books and put them in a box. I read somewhere that she asked to have them burned when she died. They didn't do it, and they didn't do it to Kafka's things either. I've thought sometimes of killing myself. But it's interesting, I've got myself trapped now. I *can't* commit suicide. I have all my written diaries, which fill about four fruit crates, and ninety reels of film, plus a box of edited-out stuff, and several boxes of audio tapes. How could I possibly jump off a boat with all that? It's too heavy to carry! Then I thought maybe I could just jump with the edited-out stuff. But then my family would be confronted. They would come upstairs and see all this film. It would be the most depressing thing in their lives because there would be all these home movies of the family growing up that they'd never be able to touch again because they'd be too melancholy to rent a projector. I've saddled myself with something, in effect, that prevents me from committing suicide. So it's another way of saying that the film has kept me alive.

MacDonald: I was thinking the other day that the diary is sort of like your skin.

Robertson: You were thinking that about my film?!

MacDonald: The celluloid is like an outer skin.

Robertson: There was a lot of skin in it! This last spring [1990], when I edited some of the nude material out, I discovered I'd accomplished one of my goals, which was to look at myself naked and like myself at all the different weights. I discovered it was true that a person who is thirty pounds overweight can be quite beautiful and that there was no reason for me to dislike the way I looked. I sent a ten-minute excerpt of the best of the naked that I was still too paranoid to keep in the film to . . .

MacDonald: Tom Baker?

Robertson: Yes. (He had written to me in 1989, thanking me for films of myself, my cats, and my family.) He's a plausible nut. He's a plausible nut. He might be The Guy. The thing is, if he *isn't,* I've boxed myself into a corner. I've said I'd give all this to my husband. If I meet some other guy, and *he's* the one, he's going to say, "Where's the film for me?" I'm going to have to say, "I've already sent it away to some other man."

Earlier, I was sitting out here [I interviewed Robertson on my back porch], and I set the camera up on the tripod and took a picture of me in the corner of your house. Luckily, your house is a nice neutral color, like a lot of other houses.

I don't like taking pictures of other people in my film, because I've been a target. Someone has been breaking into my family's house. They've stolen from my garden, and left, really, some of the weirdest things. They've dug holes the size of a coffin, four feet deep, at the side of my garden. They've left piles of sand with feathers arranged on them. I've found a pile of something that looked awfully like human excrement in my garden. They've broken into my house; they've taken my cats overnight; they've left food and lace panties. They took film and then returned it to my house. I feel my letters have made me a target, and I don't want to get anybody else targeted.

MacDonald: What do the "experts" you deal with psychiatrically tell you about yourself?

Robertson: I'm a manic depressive. Sometimes they call it "bipolar syndrome." That's just the label for it.

MacDonald: It sounded last night like you've been through a whole evolution of ways in which they think they're dealing with it.

Robertson: Now they think the miracle drug is lithium. It's not a miracle drug; it doesn't stop you from having grandiose ideas. I left naked parts in my film and irreligious things that I can't even look at now. I was on lithium, and they seemed like perfectly fine pieces of film. When I went off of lithium just this last summer, I went into my film and felt I was looking at it with brand new eyes, with my own eyes, rather than drugged eyes. They told me I had to be on lithium the rest of my life. They've told me that about a number of drugs that have made me feel like a zombie. Every time they give me a drug, they tell me I have to be on it for the rest of my life.

I would be carefully monitored if I were pregnant. They would withdraw me from the drug and put me in a mental hospital. I've seen women who were pregnant in mental hospitals. There was one woman I knew who was convinced they were going to give her electroconvulsive shock treatment while she was pregnant. I kind of doubt that's possible, but I really wouldn't put it past a psychiatrist. I don't have any confidence in psychiatrists anymore—not a single one of them. They're almost all of them drug pushers. Right now, I'm in a situation where I take the antipsychotic drugs and they do a blood test every two weeks and see if I've got it in me. That's all they want to know.

MacDonald: But they would want you to take it, ideally, every day?

Robertson: Every day and twice the dosage I'm taking.

MacDonald: When you're on it, is it more difficult to make a film? Or is it just a different kind of film you're making?

Robertson: I don't think I take as many pictures on lithium. I think my mind kind of closes down. What would have happened if van Gogh had taken lithium? They would have prescribed it for him. They probably would have prescribed Thorazine for van Gogh, too. They like to make people take a "chemical stew." I don't think he would have taken it. I think he would have had the same problem a lot of mental patients do: they just want to be off all their drugs. There's no one to talk to about it except the doctors, who say, "Take the drug; that's all you need." The patients have no way out.

Sometimes, the act of taking a picture every day has kept me sane. I believe in it. I have to take a picture every day. It's true with tapes, too, though diary tapes don't help as much—except when I started sending tapes to Tom Baker, *that* helped (I began in spring of 1986). There was a crisis one winter, when I was so depressed and so agonized because my family kept staring at me. I was the nut in the family and had to be carefully monitored, and I had no friends because the friends had left me because of the mental breakdowns and subsequent depressions. The only thing I could talk about was my films, and they just didn't want to hear about it. I found myself becoming autistic. If my mother said something to me, I'd stammer, and I wouldn't be able to say anything. The only thing that kept me going was taping for Tom every day. I gradually began to be able to talk again. And I still talk to him more than to any other human being. I talk on tape and I'm normal. I have to *lie* to my shrink.

I have to work part-time in order to make my mother think I'm sane. I can't talk to the people I work with. The last few jobs I've had have been extremely paranoid-building. I have hassles as soon as I emerge from a depression and try to pick up the real world again. A lot of people are crazy out there in the nine-to-five world, but they lay it onto me and say *I'm* the crazy one.

James Benning

In the mid seventies James Benning was making films that combine elements of "structural" cinema—long single-shot takes; highly formalized compositions—with elements of conventional narrative. A period of intense activity from 1974 to 1976 saw the completion of three collaborations with Bette Gordon—*Michigan Avenue* (1974), *I-94* (1975), and *The United States of America* (1975)—as well as Benning's *8½ X 11* (1974), *11 X 14* (1976), and *9-1-75* (1975). All six films introduce characters, or at least human situations, but handle them in unconventional ways.

Michigan Avenue is a short, sensuous triptych: one woman walks on a busy city street; she and a second woman pose for a portrait; and the two women lie naked together on a bed. All three moments are manipulated on an optical printer; each is a meditation on the miraculous seam between stillness and motion that recalls Muybridge. *I-94* alternates individual frames of a naked woman (Gordon) walking away from the camera and a naked man (Benning) walking toward the camera, creating a thaumatrope-in-motion. On the soundtrack Gordon and Benning talk simultaneously: the volume of Gordon's comments about her frustration at not being taken seriously is progressively lowered, as the volume of Benning's comments about changes he's been going through is raised. For *The United States of America* Benning and Gordon mounted a camera in the back of a car, then traveled from the Brooklyn Bridge to the Pacific Ocean, periodically recording imagery and sound. The windshield becomes a movie screen within the movie.

8½ X 11 and *11 X 14* seem to have been a major breakthrough for

Benning. In *8½ X 11* a series of twenty-eight vignettes intercut between two narratives: two women drive along interstate highways, pick up two male hitchhikers, go to a motel with them to have sex, then continue their trip; a farmworker hitchhikes to a job, works, rests, then hitchhikes on. The two narratives intersect only in the final shot: as the farmworker takes a bath in a creek, we see the women's car pass over the bridge that spans the creek. This unusual narrative structure and Benning's seemingly detached attitude toward his material are reminiscent of such John Dos Passos novels as *Manhattan Transfer* and *U.S.A.*, where characters the reader has grown to know pass each other without making any contact other than to have been in the same place at the same time.

For *11 X 14* Benning expanded *8½ X 11* using some of the skeletal plot elements—and some of the actual shots—of the earlier film in a longer (eighty-three minutes), more complex structure. *11 X 14* develops at least three plot strands—a middle-aged man apparently involved in an affair; two lesbians traveling; a farm worker hitchhiking to jobs—but as the film develops, the original coherence of these plot strands begins to disperse, and at times the characters even seem to change identities. In fact, though *11 X 14* may seem at first to reveal a decision to make a more conventional kind of film, the balance between narrative and formal elements remains the reverse of what we normally find in commercial movies. While conventional films use formal elements to help us interpret the meaning of the plots the characters enact, *11 X 14* uses character/plot primarily as a means for maintaining our interest in formal elements. The fifty-eight sections of *11 X 14* provide visually elegant compositions memorable for their frequently playful, formally reflexive explorations of composition and perspective and of relationships between sound and image.

One Way Boogie Woogie (1977) is Benning's most fully formal film to date. Within a system of rigorous spatial/temporal parameters—each of the sixty sections of the film is a single, frontally-composed shot, exactly sixty seconds long—Benning explores composition, perspective, and sound/image relationships, without developing narrative continuity from one shot to the next. Generally, the film allows us to become accustomed to a particular composition, then supplies an event that forces us to see the composition in a new way. Benning's particular focus on depopulated industrial landscapes creates a mood reminiscent of Giorgio de Chirico's metaphysical paintings.

In his next three features—*Grand Opera* (1978), *Him and Me* (1982), and *American Dreams* (1984)—Benning attempted to find ways of adding human content back into his films without using conventional approaches to character and narrative. In *Grand Opera* he develops various autobiographical motifs, including a history of the mathematical concept of pi (autobiographical because for a time Benning studied and taught mathematics), which is used as a means for organizing passages of film time, and a set of allusions to important contributions to North American independent film that have influenced Benning: the title, in fact, comes from a comment by Brakhage—"I'm not against sound film though I rather think of it as grand opera."

Him and Me was made not long after Benning moved to New York City and is as deeply involved with Manhattan cityscapes as *11 X 14* is involved with the upper Midwest, and *Grand Opera* with Oklahoma. Unlike Benning's earlier features, however, *Him and Me* centers on a single, carefully developed plot, though it's arranged in an unconventional way. We don't find out about the central event of the plot—the unexpected death of a man ("him") as he slept with his lover ("me": the female protagonist of the film)—until the very end of the film. The actions and statements of characters are not "justified" until *after* we've experienced them.

American Dreams combines three simultaneous levels of development, each of which adds a narrative progression to a film that *looks* less like a conventional narrative than any other long Benning work: the first is a front-and-back chronological presentation of items in Benning's extensive collection of Hank Aaron memorabilia (baseball cards, pins, soft-drink container tops); the second is a handwritten text that runs across the bottom of the image from right to left; the third involves the soundtrack, which alternates between brief excerpts from notable speeches made during the years Benning was growing up and brief passages from popular songs of the era. Superimposed texts regularly identify the speechmaker, the occasion, and the date; the name of the song and the singer; and regularly provide us with the grand total of home runs Aaron had hit by the end of each year.

That *American Dreams* is a film for multiple viewings is obvious the moment one discovers at the conclusion of the film that the diarist is Arthur Bremer, the man who dreamed of becoming famous by killing a public figure (first Richard Nixon, then George Wallace) and finally shot Wallace in Laurel, Maryland, on May 15, 1972. In isolation, Aaron's relentless quest of Ruth's home-run record seems natural and heroic, and symbolic of the black pursuit of full recognition by the majority society. But as wonderful as Aaron's accomplishments were, their meaning is altered by the Bremer text. While Aaron's dream may be positive and Bremer's negative—they represent the polar opposites of American dreaming—Benning's juxtaposition brings out the parallels: both men seem involved in the same set of assumptions about how men demonstrate their worth as men.

The Aaron/Bremer parallel is further confirmed and extended by Benning's recognition of his own involvement with these assumptions: his choice of a continuous, relentlessly regular, minimal structure for *American Dreams* is implicitly a critique of the male-dominated structural cinema that was developing during the years of Aaron's and Bremer's final achievements. Of course, just as Aaron's accomplishments strengthened the position of blacks in American life, the accomplishments the structural filmmakers opened new territory for feminist filmmakers concerned with confronting Western consumer culture's imaging of women and men.

Benning's most recent features, *Landscape Suicide* (1986) and *Used Innocence* (1988), use rigorous, unconventional structures as a context for examining three people convicted of murder. *Landscape Suicide* explores the ways in which the crimes of Ed Gein (the prototype for Norman Bates in *Psycho* [1960], as well as a source for the butchers in *The Texas Chainsaw Massacre* [1974] and for Buffalo Bill in *Silence of the Lambs* [1991]) and Bernadette Protti (a teenager who killed a classmate in a posh suburb of San Francisco) reflect the landscapes in which the crimes occurred. *Used Innocence* is a portrait of Lawrencia Bembenek, who is currently serving time in Wisconsin for murdering her husband's ex-wife.

My interview with Benning began in March and June of 1980. I asked Bette Gordon to be present when we discussed the films she and Benning collaborated on. In November 1986, Benning and I updated the interview. I have left the update separate: so much time passed between the discussions that combining them would have resulted in distortions.

Part 1

MacDonald: How did you get into filmmaking?

Benning: I was in graduate school studying mathematics, but painting and drawing a lot. I decided I didn't like school anymore, and ended up in a half-black, half-white hillbilly ghetto in Springfield, Missouri. I bought a camera—a regular 8mm Bolex—not to document the area, but to use as a kind of paintbrush. I didn't do much, though. Then I moved to a farm and started to do little shots of flowers and things like that.

Actually, what motivated me to buy a camera was *Meshes of the Afternoon* [Maya Deren, 1943], which I had seen about seven years before on public TV. My whole vocabulary came from watching TV or going to the local theater, so I had no idea what *Meshes* was about. It just stuck in the back of my mind, and finally I bought a camera. I went back to school to finish my masters in math [1970]. Actually I wish I'd gone on to a Ph.D. I'd love to teach math. Then I got a job teaching at Paul Smith's College—a small, very conservative school in upstate New York. I lost my job. The circumstances were strange—somebody burned a building down, and I was one of the people who got investigated. Scary stuff. I went back to the University of Wisconsin at Madison, thinking I couldn't do anything but hide. I was going to go for one semester, but I stayed for three years and got an M.F.A. in film and graphic arts [1975].

MacDonald: Time and a Half [1972], the earliest film you list for distribution, is very different from your later films—it's a conventional narrative, a grim day-in-the-life of a drill press operator—though your interest in framing and in working with sound are already clear.

Benning: It was the second 16mm film I made. I hadn't seen much except theatrical film, so it was logical for me to begin with scripted, fictional, documentary narrative.

MacDonald: The way you go in and out of fantasy material is reminiscent of the foreign films that were popular during the sixties.

Benning: Time and a Half was what I remembered of working on a drill press: it was boring, and the speed of the machine regulated you. You'd get bored and try to daydream, but the lengths of the daydreams were dictated by the machine. It's dangerous—if you stick your hand in at the wrong time, you put a drill through it—so you have to have short thoughts and get back to work. I put that into the film.

MacDonald: The soundtrack is unusual.

Benning: It's a combination of two tracks: one was noises that would synch with what was happening, not necessarily generated by something in the frame but which seemed to fit the visuals; the other was the slowed-down sound of a big cylinder being ground. I wanted the noise to be repetitive and circular, because I was trying to get at a way of life where every day seems the same. Everything was post-synched.

MacDonald: It was shot in black and white and printed on color stock?

Benning: Yes. At first I worked with a small lab in Milwaukee. They didn't do black and white. Earlier, I had made a one-minute film, which they printed on color stock. I liked the way it looked, so when I did *Time and a Half,* I had certain scenes tinted a little green, a little brown.

MacDonald [*to Gordon*]: What was the nature of your collaboration on *Michigan Avenue?*

Gordon: The collaboration happened spontaneously. We'd been talking about ways of getting things across on film: I would say one thing,

James would say another, and somehow this film developed. We both conceived of it, and we both worked on it. Even then I was interested in forcing narrative away from simple story-line and character identification toward problems of representation, language, and the reading of the film text. The minimal narrative in *Michigan Avenue* contains a beginning, middle, and end, but an active viewer is required to fill in the spaces.

Benning: I remember that Bette was going to make a narrative film about two women. I can't remember the details. She started the film, but somehow it changed from a somewhat straightforward narrative to an optically-printed film—an optical printer arrived in Madison, and I was familiar with it. I kind of horned in.

MacDonald: As the film goes on, the women's actions seem increasingly performed for the camera.

Gordon: It's very much a conscious performance. The two women stare straight at the camera and the implied spectator, confronting the voyeuristic gaze.

Benning: I think one reason for Scott's observation is the actual change in technique. The first section was shot in slow motion (fifty frames per second); every frame was copied fifty-eight times, then dissolved into the next frame with a twenty-four-frame dissolve. It looks like a still at first, and as you watch the frame, different areas seem to move. Cars are the most obvious, then you see that people are slowly moving up and down. The second scene was shot at twenty-four frames per second, and every frame was copied once. The last scene was shot at twenty-four frames, and we copied either every third or fifth frame. The jump in the action is larger there, so you become more aware of the optical printing. In the third scene, the action is fast enough so that you actually start to see the freeze frames dissolving into each other. I think the changes make you concentrate more on the formal elements.

Gordon: It's a metaphor for the workings of persistence of vision in film.

MacDonald: *I-94* seems to have been, among other things, an attempt to assess where you were vis-à-vis each other.

Gordon: Hmmmm.

Benning: I think once we started making the soundtrack, the assessment just happened. We had decided to expose each other—literally. We were thinking about the sound, and I gave Bette the microphone and said, "Tell me something intimate," and she did. As soon as she finished, she said, "You tell me." I wasn't ready either. The film wasn't preplanned; we were driving along with our camera and just decided to make a film together.

Gordon: It was spontaneous. Of course, now I realize some of the problems the film raises, especially the body and voice of the woman being consumed by the body and voice of the man. As his voice gets louder, and his image gets larger, the female voice gets more muffled. This gets right to the point of women in the cinema being consumed by the male voice, women's images as a male projection. Our spontaneity revealed, once the film was finished, the basic condition of women in the cinema.

MacDonald: I assumed that the idea was that many women in the mid seventies, though in touch with their feelings on a personal level, were dealing with the emotions that come from moving out into the world, whereas men were trying to get in touch with their feelings. Your movement away from the camera and James's toward the camera, are interlocked—as though each is the context for the other.

Gordon: That's very interesting. Actually, we were trying to combat the art historical tradition of the female body depicted nude and frontally, while the male body is always covered.

Benning: I don't think there were any politics behind the film, except the idea of collaboration. The initial idea was that we'd each act, each do camera work, each do optical printing, and each do sound. I think it's probably the closest you can get to a perfect collaboration, in terms of equality of the partners.

Gordon: I disagree. I think the politics of sexuality were there whether or not they were completely articulated during the making of the film.

Benning: It's very electric when we pass through each other.

Gordon: It's like intercourse. The two shots were made ten minutes apart, late in the day, and the shadows under the bridges were different enough to cause a strobe effect. We cut back and forth, one frame to the next, so that, in fact, the man and woman are never on screen at the same time.

MacDonald: How did you choose the location?

Benning: Mostly by accident. The trucks passing over the highway create a lateral movement, compared to the way we move perpendicularly through the frame. Certainly, we were aware of superhighways and railroad tracks as American public symbols. We chose extremely loaded images, not knowing everything about how they might be read.

Gordon: We didn't say, "Let's make a film about sexuality," but I think intention should be seen as separate from the reading of the images. Jim has gone on to do his kind of films, but I got more and more intrigued with the idea of sex and sexuality—how I, as a woman, would present my own sexual images without being exploitative, though the cinema *is,* in part, the pleasure of looking at the body of a woman.

MacDonald: When I first saw *The United States of America,* I had a

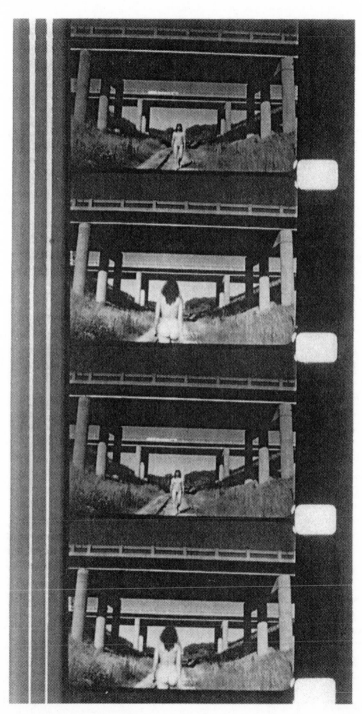

Successive frames of James Benning and Bette Gordon in their I-94 *(1974).*

sense that you might have had mixed feelings about what kind of film-making career you wanted. The specifics of the route, particularly the fact that it ends in Hollywood, and the entertainment value of a lot of the juxtapositions of sound and image made me wonder whether you were thinking of going into commercial filmmaking.

Benning: Not at all, although now I'm closer to that than I've ever been. At that time, I was interested in defining new ways of using narrative. *The United States of America* is very formal, but we used the radio to develop stories: recurring songs tie scenes together; there's a whole thread about the Vietnam War ending: as we get closer to the West Coast, the Communist troops get closer to Saigon.

Gordon: I think that film is more interesting as you get further from 1975—its historical nature becomes more evident. When we finished the film we were disappointed—somehow it wasn't what we had conceived. Now it's more powerful because those events are part of this country's past.

MacDonald: I assume you decided on the route in advance.

Benning: Pretty much. We were living in Madison, Wisconsin, at the time, so one weekend we drove to New York and back in four days. About a week later, we drove to Los Angeles and back in a week. We made the film in eleven days. Eight thousand miles of driving! It was awful.

MacDonald: You look relaxed in the film.

Benning: It was fun, but it was awful.

Gordon: Most people who travel take a camera to make "home movies." We went on this trip to make the inverse of a home movie. The trip was created *for* the film. The viewer never knows anything about the people in the car, except what can be assumed from where they go, what they look like from the back, and what they listen to on the radio. There's really no consistency of time or space in the film; it's the editing that creates a linear whole. It's creative geography, like Kuleshov. [Soviet filmmaker and theoretician Lev Kuleshov was a pioneer in the exploration of the potentials of film editing. Among his explorations was the combination of imagery from different locations to create the illusion of a single place: "creative geography."]

MacDonald: Were the sounds and visuals recorded at the same time and put together later?

Benning: We didn't have a synch-sound camera. We had a switch so that we could turn on the camera, which was mounted in the back. Periodically we'd pull over and record things from the radio. Then we'd write down approximately where those things were. When we put the film together, we put sounds recorded in an area with images from the same area.

One of the things we were interested in was comparing radio announcers' voices. Even though they all sound alike—they've been trained to sound alike—their voices change slightly as you move across the country.

MacDonald: Another interesting formal aspect is the way in which the film reverses foreground and background. Normally, the viewer looks past you through the window. The things closest to the viewer, the things inside the car, become—psychologically—the background.

Benning: And in the frame we seem to be continuous, whereas things outside the car are discontinuous with each dissolve. There's always a continuous space *and* a discontinuous space.

Gordon: And the constant actions—changing drivers, eating, pulling over, switching hats and scarves—alter the viewers' perception of and relationship to the image, which is actually a very complex frame.

Benning: In a sense the car is the main character. You get a real sense of a nation built on automobiles.

MacDonald: Do you two plan to collaborate again?

Benning: No.

Gordon: I thought the collaborations were fruitful, though. We never had any large disagreements about what we were doing. The disagreements we did have, and James can correct me if I'm wrong, had to do with working time, which I think is an interesting issue. I can't work late at night, and I can't work and work and work for hours. That's one reason we stopped collaborating. It also had to do with the credit that was going to him but not to me.

Benning: It was more my decision to stop than yours.

Gordon: Definitely. But ending the collaboration pushed me to go in a specific direction with my work, and I'm pleased about the new level of experimentation and questioning. I would collaborate again, with someone who had cinematic interests similar to mine.

MacDonald [to Benning]: 8½ X 11 is the earliest of your films that looks like what came to be thought of as a "Benning film."

Benning: I began by writing a detailed script about two women and a man traveling in different parts of the country; the women would somehow pick up the man. I wasn't sure what style I would use. I just thought I'd use the ideas that came from the optical printed films in a narrative. I did decide to change from a barrage of images to long takes. I tried to develop the space by moving objects within the frame. After it was finished, I realized that I was using a minimal narrative as a context for the formal elements of film itself. Now that I look back, it seems like there's a direct correlation between *I-94*, for instance, and the story idea for *8½ X 11*, though I did occasionally break up that regular alternation, so that it wouldn't be too predictable.

I took the script and scratched out certain scenes that helped to explain events, deliberately leaving it open-ended. I wanted the viewer to be able to add to the basic information: if forty people watch the film, they'll have forty different stories. That interested me.

MacDonald: Why the title?

Benning: It was supposed to refer to the fact that the script was typed on eight-and-one-half-by-eleven paper, and it also refers to a perimeter or an area, text and form at once. "8½ X 11" is more obviously a dimension than a reference to typing paper, and that's the way the film is supposed to work: the narrative is removed and the formal elements come forward. So many people ask me what the title means that I think [laughter] I'm the only one who understands it. *11 X 14,* of course, came out of this film. It's something of a joke that the title refers to a larger format and that film is longer; but at the same time it isn't a joke because I thought of *11 X 14* as being less narrative and more photographic [11 X 14 is a photograph paper size] than *8½ X 11,* even though there are more stories in it.

MacDonald: In one section of *8½ X 11* you handhold the camera. Why only one?

Benning: Those pans across the bodies in *8½ X 11* are so different from the rest of the film that I don't like it. I wanted the film to pivot around that point, but it does more than pivot around it: the scene jumps off the screen at you. When I filmed two people in bed for *11 X 14,* I used a static camera. My approach to film is generally conservative. I don't think of the camera as an extension of my eye. I don't have that kind of romance with the camera. I use it as a precise tool.

MacDonald: 9-1-75 uses the illusion of a candid, continuous shot filmed in a busy campground, but it's as fully fabricated as *8½ X 11.*

Benning: Yes. Usually I choreograph the movements of the characters within the frame, but at the same time I like to incorporate the random movements of unaware passersby. *9-1-75* has no controlled actors, only "documented" campers. However, the soundtrack is completely contrived and post-synched.

MacDonald: It creates an illusion that is immediately recognizable as an illusion, particularly since you're tracking through the campground in slow motion and the sound is played at a normal speed.

Benning: The day before I shot the film I recorded about four or five hours' worth of sound at the campground; different parts of conversations and a lot of ambient noise—people putting up tents and things like that. I also manufactured sound: I wrote little lines and had people say them; I used some sound-effect records that I knew would be recognized as such. I wanted to combine "real" and "manufactured" sounds, so that the audience would question each sound.

MacDonald: There are funny sections, like the orgasm when you pass the little pup tent. Do you set out to make funny films?

Benning: I've probably been holding back. I want to make a much funnier film. Some of my humor is so dumb though—puns that I should resist, but don't.

MacDonald: Where was the film shot?

Benning: Mothy Lake, about forty miles from Milwaukee. When I was small, there would be about five or six other people. Now, since it's so close to Milwaukee and Chicago, there are miles of people.

MacDonald: It's a funny situation—thousands of people "getting away from it all."

Benning: They rebuild a suburb.

MacDonald: In many of your films you seem aware of a certain kind of Americana—Niagara Falls, Las Vegas, Mount Rushmore . . .

Benning: I hate a lot of that stuff, but I also like it. It has a certain political meaning to me.

I used to be active in local politics, working with people trying to figure out how to live. The last time I did that was in Springfield, Missouri, where I helped set up a dropout school [in 1967] and helped people try to get jobs. I knew that I could quit whenever I wanted and that the people I was working with couldn't. It got to be a twenty-four-hour-a-day job, and I finally decided that you either give your whole life to working for political change or you don't. I wasn't sure what my own life was about, and I had to try to define it, so I quit working there and tried to define my life by being an artist.

When I started to make art, I realized I still had a lot of political concerns. Was I or was I not going to put those into my films, or my drawings and paintings? I was trying to experiment, and if you're experimenting, by definition, you don't communicate with a large audience. I thought it was rather silly to try to put political issues into an esoteric context. If you're trying to make political changes, you should use the language that is easiest to understand. But I was trying to develop my own language. Little things creep into my films that suggest I hold certain political beliefs, but they're not meant to change the audience's beliefs.

I suppose if I think of my films as dealing with politics, it's with the way you look at the screen. If you look at things differently aesthetically, maybe you'll look at things differently politically. I do feel I'm doing something that isn't totally self-serving.

MacDonald: One difference between *8½ X 11* and *11 X 14* is that in the latter at least three plot strands are followed: the women driving, the guy hitchhiking, and the older white-haired man who's out sometimes and home at others. After a certain point, because there's no regular alternation, you're not sure whether the next image will connect with any of those strands. The viewer has to examine every image to see if and where it fits.

Benning: You don't really know those three strands exist until the film is over. It's a totally different film on second viewing. You might need three or four viewings to sort out the different narratives. And there are interjected scenes that deal with formal issues. Maybe that's a fourth narrative.

MacDonald: Also, even if you do follow the strands, things get ambiguous. In the Mount Rushmore scene, we see characters who look like the two women. One wears a red blouse like the woman in the car. In a narrative sense, though, she almost can't be the same woman.

Benning: She *is* the same woman. The other woman is a new companion, though she *looks* just like the first. Two different women play the same part. And the older man wears that blouse in one shot. I change clothes among the characters, so the narrative gets confused. Every time you see that man, he's dressed differently and he seems to be defined differently: you see him saying good-bye to a woman; you see him in a kitchen with a family; you see him working at a gas station; you see him in front of a poster of Lenin; and finally, you see him playing golf. The scenes don't seem to match.

MacDonald: As in *9-1-75,* most of the individual images look candid and recorded in synch, but the more closely you look, the more evident are the clues that indicate that the images can*not* have been recorded the way they first appear. The film is a training ground for nonillusionistic seeing.

Benning: That was a major concern when I was making *11 X 14.* When you start to watch the smokestack scene it's obviously a smokestack, and you can apply particular meanings to that—even cliched meanings like pollution or a phallic symbol—but since it's on for seven and a half minutes, eventually you have to deal with it as swirling grain on a screen. Near the end of the scene, however, a plane comes through, so that after you've begun to look at the image formally, it's reintroduced into the narrative: in the scene before a plane takes off, and in the next scene a plane lands. Hopefully, the film teaches you how to watch the film.

MacDonald: One image that particularly struck me was the one with the two women in bed. You hear the Dylan song and see the record going around on the turntable. But, since the women are moving in slow motion, the music can't be coming from that record. And there's the image with the moon, where everything looks fine until you look away slightly and the moon shakes.

Benning: The blatant scenes—like the ones we've just mentioned— make you look carefully at scenes that aren't as blatant. Eventually, you question the reality of every image.

MacDonald: A lot of the shots in *8½ X 11* are fairly long, and, of

course, *9-1-75* is a continuous take, but in *11 X 14* you use three extremely long shots—the Evanston Express ride into downtown Chicago,
the smokestack, and the two women in bed. Were you conscious of other
filmmakers who have worked with long takes?

Benning: I was conscious of the early Warhol. I think he made it
easier for people to make films like I make. My idea in those scenes was
to use duration in three different ways. The first three scenes in the film
are the man and the woman saying good-bye; the man walking down the
street; then the man entering an el station. Next, there's the shot of the
express ride. Although the three shots aren't traditional, a somewhat
traditional narrative seems to be developing. A man says good-bye to a
woman, and he leaves on the el, but then the fourth shot holds for
eleven minutes (it's a four-hundred-foot reel), all the way to the end of
the el ride. As the minutes go by, you relate to the image differently: at
first it seems to be part of the narrative; then it becomes formalistic.
That shot is a key to the whole film. In the smokestack shot I do the
opposite: I start formalistically and then reintroduce the narrative. The
bedroom scene is the same length as the smokestack scene. I wanted to
use the same music and see how it would relate to different imagery.

MacDonald: One other question. When I studied the film, it occurred
to me that the black guy running the train literally becomes a shadow,
which is a major theme in black American literature: the idea that
whites just don't see blacks. And the Evanston Express goes over some
impoverished black neighborhoods. Is this connection accidental?

Benning: The man in the front of the car was an actor. I realized,
though, that people who take the Evanston Express to Chicago can get
on in Evanston and get off in downtown Chicago, without dealing with
anything in between. As I said before, politics creep into my films.

MacDonald: When Larry Gottheim made *Horizons* [1973], he collected images before he had conceived a structure. Did you start *11 X 14*
with a structure in mind?

Benning: It was scripted. About eighty percent of it was on paper.
Sometimes interesting things happened that weren't scripted, but it
didn't grow out of collecting images. That *is* how I made *Grand Opera.*

MacDonald: In both *8½ X 11* and *11 X 14* and in *One Way Boogie
Woogie,* too, you include a shot of the Dad's Root Beer Factory. Were
you purposely creating continuity from film to film?

Benning: That started when I was writing *11 X 14* and realized that it
was an extension of *8½ X 11.* I thought, why not take some of those
scenes and weave them into *11 X 14*? How would you read those scenes
if you had seen both films? Would they seem the same? Would they
suggest déjà vu?

MacDonald: You make small changes, too. In *8½ X 11* there's the shot where a truck goes by on a country road and you pan and follow it, then the shadow of a plane comes through the image. In *11 X 14*, the middle section was eliminated, and the viewer sees two shots.

Benning: That's the only different one. The others are lifted right out of *8½ X 11* and put into *11 X 14*.

MacDonald: Chicago Loop [1976] seems an attempt to combine techniques explored in Ernie Gehr's *Serene Velocity* and Michael Snow's *Standard Time* and *Back and Forth*.

Benning: I was probably influenced by both people. I made *Chicago Loop* while I was making *11 X 14*, to take my mind off it—it's the exact opposite of *11 X 14*. *Chicago Loop* is actually three small, separate films: they were going to be called *Chicago Loop, Chicago River, Chicago Cubs*, but I never made the titles so it's just called *Chicago Loop* from the title of the first film. They were made a week apart, all in the camera. The film is made to play forward and backward. When you get to the end, you can play it in reverse.

MacDonald: In *One Way Boogie Woogie* narrative elements have almost completely disappeared.

Benning: There are, however, cross references between the sixty shots. Hopefully, by the end it becomes more spherical than linear and you remember the film as a coherent whole. Color schemes run through the film. Smokestacks punctuate it. Three Volkswagens appear in all the possible permutations—you see each one by itself, you see all the possible pairs, and then you see them together. And three shots refer directly to filmmaking. One starts with the aperture closed. It slowly opens, giving the effect of walking into a dark theater and sitting down: you slowly define the theater as your eyes adjust to the darkness. Finally, as the aperture continues to open, the image washes out. The second shot involves color separation. It's a shot of some old oil tanks—just a triple exposure in the camera. Each time I used a different color filter—cyan, magenta, and yellow—so that anything that's recorded all three times becomes a normal color, and anything recorded only once will be the color of that filter. Then there's the negative shot of smoke coming out of a factory. Other than those three shots, there's not much manipulation. And there are recurring jokes. As you say, the film almost dispenses with narrative as a context for form, and uses form as a context for itself. The overall structure is defined very tightly: the film began with the idea that there would be sixty one-minute shots.

MacDonald: The title's reference to Piet Mondrian's *Broadway Boogie-Woogie,* and *Victory Boogie-Woogie* is pretty hard to miss since somebody carries a Mondrian across one of the images. But why "One Way"?

Benning: There are a lot of one-way signs and one-way streets. It's

shot one way: there's no camera movement, always a static frame. Movement was generally kept at a minimum, so that any particular movement
would draw attention to itself.

MacDonald: I first saw *One Way Boogie Woogie* at the Whitney,
where photographs similar to the various shots were mounted on the
walls of the auditorium. Were they meant to be a separate work?

Benning: I had shot the color slides to study different framings, since
I knew I wanted to do sixty static shots. Then I liked a lot of the slides,
and made them into eight-by-ten color prints.

MacDonald: The film was shot in Milwaukee?

Benning: Yes. I used to play in that section of Milwaukee as a kid. We
would hop freights and take them to the baseball games at County
Stadium. It's a rather romantic place for me, though I didn't want to
romanticize the factories. Generally I would film on Sunday morning,
when no one was there.

MacDonald: I first saw it with J. J. Murphy. He kept responding in a
way that suggested you were doing unusual things with the camera. I was
unsure what he was seeing.

Benning: Basically I was using a wide-angle lens, which gives the
image greater depth, but also tends to distort the axis. If there is movement away from the camera, things get smaller more quickly, which
points out the illusion of three dimensions. I shoot perpendicularly to a
flat surface, so that there generally aren't any depth clues to allow you to
deduce the length of the lens. For instance, the shot of the two workmen
carrying the Mondrian painting into the frame has a flat wall as a background. When they walk through, they're right next to the wall, so that
the frame is very flat. The street in the foreground seems vertical, but
then, at the end of the shot, a forklift comes by very close to the camera,
in very sharp focus. It gives you a new depth cue that, by defining the
distance between itself and the wall, almost flips the street straight out.
As soon as the forklift disappears, the scene flattens. I use that technique constantly.

A lot of the compositions look like Mondrian paintings. The very first
image has a blue square in the corner, some red garage doors, and a
green fence. If you squint, you get blocks of colors. It's a green fence,
and Mondrian rarely used green, but it's related. Red, green, and
blue—the primary colors of light. Then my daughter [Sadie Benning]
runs through dragging a stick on the fence, She's dressed in red, yellow,
and blue—the primary colors of pigment. If you're not used to looking
at a film that way, you'll look for a narrative, while the shot deals with
colors and sound. The off-screen sound of the stick against the fence
goes on for almost a minute, giving you the sense that that fence is a half
mile long. You hear it getting louder as you watch, and assume that the

source of the sound is getting closer. Actually, I recorded the sound five weeks later at a different location. Everything in the film is post-synched. That's true of all my films, except for *Grand Opera,* which has a few synch scenes.

MacDonald: There's a lot of mystery in *One Way Boogie Woogie.* It reminds me of de Chirico, partly because of the sound track. Things that we can't quite identify seem to hover around the image.

Benning: When I set up the structure of sixty one-minute scenes, I thought it would be very demanding on an audience. My idea was to make it a little more accessible by making it more like a game. I built mysteries into it, along with "clues." For instance, the structure of the film is spelled out in the shot with somebody doing jumping jacks, counting from one to sixty. Another puzzle happens in the shot where you hear a woman speaking French, reading a mathematics problem I made up. The idea was that if you didn't know French and wanted to know more about the film, you'd have to have somebody translate. But, you still wouldn't have the answer, because it's a problem, and you'd have to figure the problem out. But the problem is written in such a way that you assume it's going to ask a certain question, and the question at the end isn't the question you'd expect, so you have to go back and rework all the information. That's the extreme of the game-playing aspect of the film.

MacDonald: There's a scene where a person's gagged and lying in the middle of the street. Also, at the end, a car stops and the person slumps over the horn. In a conventional narrative those scenes might be serious, but since there is no sequence, they declare themselves as humor.

Benning: The image of the woman tied up has been criticized as sexist. The scene before that is the baby carriage rolling down the street, a reference to Eisenstein and the Odessa Steps sequence—a silly film joke—and in the background somebody with an accent is speaking about capitalism and the working class. The next shot is the woman who's tied up and gagged, which I meant as a reference to the working class.

MacDonald: Grand Opera seems to be your first attempt to come to grips, at least in film, with your own history as a filmmaker.

Benning: Of course, it's also distanced. It's an attempt to use my past, but not to explore it. I do show all the houses I ever lived in, and I include stories that are true, or that I think are true, about things that happened when I was in those houses. But they're read by a woman, which distances them.

I started *Grand Opera* in 1977. There was no real script. I just did things that suggested other things. When I edited, I rearranged it and pared it down. The blowing up of the Biltmore Hotel in Oklahoma City was the first shot I made: it became a metaphor for the end of my structural concerns. Then I thought, why not tell a little more about my life, about what brought me to that point? I wrote the short story that's printed at the beginning of the film as a continuous sentence. The story of the young boy memorizing the digits of pi seemed like a metaphor for my life as an artist and for my decision to become a structuralist film-maker. He's like an artist trying to define something indefinable, something you can get lost in.

I was also thinking about doing short performances. Two got into *Grand Opera*. One was to visit every house I'd ever lived in and measure my feelings against what I had thought the houses would suggest. I did the other performances in Oklahoma. I went to the same river every three or four days, from the shortest day of the year to the longest day, again trying to measure my own feelings—how *I* changed from day to day compared to something that was itself both the same and different. Those performances don't give the audience the same feeling they give me. At the time I felt that my films were getting too academic, too far from a personal meaning that might be more important.

MacDonald: Did you modify your memories of the places where you lived?

Benning: That section is about storytelling: basically they're true stories, but they have little twists, either to make them funny, or more interesting, or to give a clue to the way I perceive things. When they're not true, they're metaphors for truth. I did find somebody dead in the backyard, and I did find a cow that was dying, and I did fall through the ice.

MacDonald: Though *One Way Boogie Woogie* is probably the film one would most identify with structural film, *Grand Opera* is so full of allusions to structural filmmaking and filmmakers that unless you know that tradition, it would be hard to catch all the implications.

Benning: I would rather show it to a group that doesn't know of Snow, Rainer, and the others. The laughter then comes at entirely different places. I suppose I was thinking of my own audience when I made it, though—people who have seen my films, and other films that I like.

MacDonald: Did you decide to use Frampton, [George] Landow, Rainer, and Snow because they were especially important in your development?

Benning: I like all four of them, but the way I used them changed as I made the film. I started *Grand Opera* right after *One Way Boogie Woogie,* when I really did believe in Minimalism and felt that less was more. By the time I finished it, my feeling was more like the Bob Huot postcard you sent me: "Less Is More . . . But, It's Not Enough" [Huot, postcard of *Billboard for Former Formalists,* 1978].

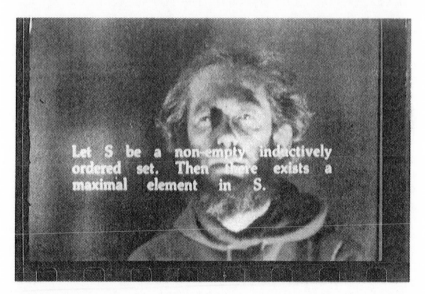

Homages to Yvonne Rainer, Michael Snow, George Landow (Owen Land), and Hollis Frampton in Benning's Grand Opera *(1978).*

It doesn't make total sense to have Yvonne [Rainer] in the film, except that I like her and her films. The other people have been called structuralists, and I refer to structure throughout the film, so it made more sense to include them.

MacDonald: There are also many allusions to other films. *Grand Opera* begins with the body discovery scene from *Wavelength*. The circular pans of the houses juxtaposed with the stories about your life read by someone else remind me of Frampton's *nostalgia,* and so on.

Benning: I'd meant to make reference to a lot of works, but people point out references I had no idea I was making. Once you start, you can read almost every scene as a reference.

MacDonald: Stan Brakhage is the source of the title. He thinks that sound competes with the visuals, but in your case sound constantly adds something different.

Benning: I agree with what he says, basically that you can't see and hear at the same time. It made him decide to work visually, but I concluded the opposite. I wanted to use sound *because* it makes you look at things differently. I've also worked with no sound as a sound, or at least as another option. *Grand Opera* starts with black leader, and you hear a voice—the speech from *Wavelength.* Then you see a notebook, and you don't hear any sound. Next, you see and hear somebody singing. The film begins by cataloging those possibilities; what follows is about sound-image relationships, among other things.

MacDonald: During the film you review the history of pi, and present pi in various ways. At one point, you talk about the person who calculated pi to 607 digits and found out that it was incorrect after 527. This is followed by a passage that "visualizes" the digits, but you included only 525 (yes, I counted them!). Why didn't you go to 527?

Benning: Pi is represented three times in the film. First, a voice with an Argentine accent talks about somebody who derived pi to thirty-five places. Then there's a black-and-white flicker film: three white frames, then a punch hole for the decimal point, then one white, four black, one white, five black, nine white . . . to thirty-five places. It's silent, so it's suggestive of the early history of cinema, as well as a reference to the flicker films of Tony Conrad and Peter Kubelka. The next time somebody talks about pi, you see a color flicker film with sound, again suggesting the progression of film history. I think I go to 100 digits that time. The third time is when I take *One Way Boogie Woogie* and re-edit ten scenes, assigning a digit to each scene. It was supposed to go to 527, and if it is short, the other two digits might happen in the soundtrack. The sound continues after the picture to give the dot-dot-dot effect of infinity.

The idea of the 527-part representation was to take my last film, which was highly formal, and restructure it by using the digits of pi, which can be proven to be random. I wanted to see what that would do to those ten scenes: what new juxtapositions would occur and how that might change your perception of the original image. It's a tedious part of the film, but I like the sound that's derived from the random positioning and certain juxtapositions.

MacDonald: A specific question about the long continuous shot of the sign on top of the building that reviews some of the history of pi. Halfway through, a guy comes out and almost gets hit by a car.

Benning: He's carrying a pie—another stupid pun.

MacDonald: It was too obvious for me! But once you start reading that sign, it's hard to look at anything else.

Benning: That was the idea behind putting the one little narrative element down below. I wanted you to wonder whether something happened earlier that you missed while reading. There's competition: should you read or should you watch the image?

MacDonald: Can you say a bit more about the film you're working on now?

Benning: I've written a script [the working title was "New York, 1980"; it became *Him and Me* (1982)]. It has dialogue, and I'm going to try to use actors. I'm not sure how it's going to be stylistically, probably something like *11 X 14,* but with a stronger narrative.

MacDonald: Are you going to continue to work in 16mm?

Benning: Yes, but my fear is that this could be my last film. Film's getting so expensive that we're going to have to raise rental prices. The people who rent our films now are so marginal that any increase could put them out of business. There has to be a larger market. Maybe I'm ready to stop making films. I don't know. I've been doing installations. They're more fun, they're quicker, and you get to use tools and build stuff.

I still like the films I made in the past, but I'm past all those issues, and I'm starting to react against a lot of avant-garde film. One thing that's affected me a lot is the films of Vivienne Dick and a few other Super-8 filmmakers. The whole mentality of making the film, finding your own showcase, renting a storefront if you have to, is very exciting. It's like the early Warhol factory. I'm thinking about making films that are much more accessible.

Part 2

MacDonald: This may be a strange question, but it seems an obvious one. In the films you've made since you woke up in bed with a friend of yours who had died—I'm not sure exactly when that was . . .

Benning: It's easy to remember because it's the day the hostages were taken in Iran: November 4, 1979.

MacDonald: Since then, all your films—*Him and Me, American Dreams, Landscape Suicide*—have dealt with crime or death. I assume that incident was pivotal for you. Did anyone question your innocence?

Benning: Only the police department when they talked to me in the morning. I'm not worried about anybody's suspicions about me. For a while I did have a huge amount of guilt: if I had awakened at the right moment, I could have saved her. It's interesting that you ask that though, because I've been talking about that incident with a woman in prison [Lawrencia Bembenek, subject of *Used Innocence*] who says she's innocent of the murder she's serving time for. She told me, "All it would have taken to convict you would have been a jealous boyfriend who said, 'Yeah, they were having a big fight before it happened.' " I could have ended up in prison like she did. I'd never thought of that.

The making of those films, starting with *Him and Me,* was a way of dealing with how I felt about discovering death so close to me. It certainly changed my life. As you say, all my films since have dealt with some kind of death—even *O Panama* [1985], and I didn't write that script [Bert Barr did].

MacDonald: When I've shown *American Dreams* and *Landscape Suicide,* I've found them accessible even to people not acquainted with unusual forms of films. My audiences have a harder time with *11 X 14* and your other early work. Were you trying to be more accessible?

Benning: Not at all. I would love to be more accessible just because I would like to make enough money with my films to support myself. But it isn't really a concern. The change you mention is just a by-product of adding more narrative information. Probably parts of the films still aren't accessible. In fact, I worry that people aren't seeing those parts of the films. At least in the older works the audiences were confronted directly with the major formal issues. In these new films they might miss half of what's going on, but maybe I'm not giving the audience enough credit.

MacDonald: When I saw *American Dreams* for the first time, I was frightened of missing some of the text that moves across the bottom. Perhaps because of the sexual hooks in the narrative that unfolds in the text, it quickly became the primary focus.

Benning: I think that's mainly a function of our educational system, where so much importance is put on reading and hardly any on visual thinking. Also, if you're watching TV and something runs across the bottom of the screen, it's generally a storm warning or some emergency, so you have to read it. Text is always given more importance than image. Even when *I've* watched *American Dreams*—and I know what the film's about and all the images, everything—I always read the text from beginning to end.

The text *is* very strong, of course. I chose as strong a text as I could think of at the time I was making the film. And the images are just these flat, two-dimensional baseball cards. At first glance, they don't seem to offer much information, though they do change, and I think that they're quite beautiful as objects. They also represent the innocence of youth.

Anyway, I wanted to play down the images and play up the text. Also, at some points the sound track is probably more interesting than the image or the text.

MacDonald: The issue of gender seems very central in *American Dreams,* which offers a comment on a certain kind of macho engagement with the world. Hank Aaron's understandable but compulsive need to pass Babe Ruth; Arthur Bremer's less understandable but not totally mysterious compulsion to kill Nixon (or some other public figure); and your compulsiveness on one hand in revealing your baseball card collection, and on the other in maintaining a rigorous formal structure throughout the film—all of these activities seem parallel instances of a particular male way of functioning in the world.

Benning: That's exactly what I was trying to suggest! When Bremer talks about how the danger of driving over eighty miles per hour with a bad front tire gave him an erection, the speech on the soundtrack is LBJ talking about escalating the Vietnam War. The main point of the film is that this kind of maleness is causing problems.

MacDonald: How did your collaboration with Bert Barr on *O Panama* come about?

Benning: O Panama was made because Susan Dowling at WGBH liked my films and Bert's writing and got us together. At the time, I was trying to raise money for *Landscape Suicide*. I had part of it, but not all, so I thought I'd take that project on. As it turned out, it took a year to do and cost more than *Landscape Suicide*. I hadn't collaborated in a number of years, so just going through the process was interesting. Bert and I worked well together because we thought a lot alike, but neither of us liked compromising. I probably won't collaborate again for a while; it's difficult. But I like the film.

MacDonald: What got you into the *Landscape Suicide* project? What drew you to Ed Gein and Bernadette Protti?

Benning: I had written a script about Ed Gein, Charles Evers (Medgar Evers's brother), and an ambulance driver in World War II. I was going to have each of those people deliver a monologue reflecting on the particular acts of violence they experienced. Gein would do what he does in *Landscape Suicide*; Charles Evers would talk about his brother's death on their front porch; the ambulance driver would talk about her experiences in

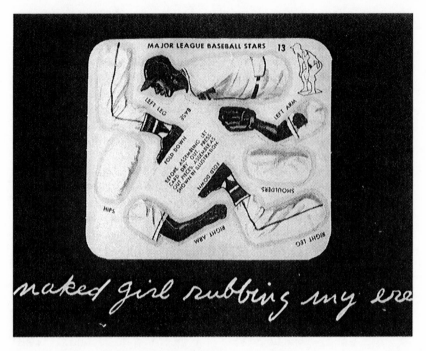

From Benning's American Dreams *(1984).*

World War II. As I was writing that script (this is explained in *Landscape Suicide*), my twelve-year-old daughter [Sadie Benning] and I were taking a train from Chicago to New York, and she was reading a *Rolling Stone* article on Bernadette Protti. It bothered her, and she stopped reading. So I read it, and realized that this murder was having the same effect on her as the Gein murder had on my life in 1957, when I was fourteen.

The more I looked at the two very different murders—one occurs in snowy, central Wisconsin in the fifties; the other in the eighties in lush, green California—the more I liked the idea of comparing them. There were also interesting similarities in how the communities reacted. Also, each murderer had an "out of body" experience when the murder occurred, and neither remembered what had happened.

MacDonald: Your way of meditating on the two murders seems unusual, given the way murder is usually sensationalized in the media.

Benning: My idea wasn't to dwell on violent acts, but to focus on how people look at themselves when they commit violent acts, and how they perceive what happened later. That's more interesting to me.

MacDonald: Is the Gein case one you've followed? *Psycho* and other films have kept that case alive.

Benning: No, not really. I remember the jokes people told about Gein when I was fourteen. When something as sensational as cannibalism happens in your own backyard, the only way kids have to deal with it— and adults too, I suppose—is with humor. There were lots of Gein jokes.

I can relate to Protti. There have been moments in my life when I could do something like she did. And maybe I can enter Gein sometimes, too. That's frightening, but true. Our minds are capable of strange things.

MacDonald: One of the things that's interesting about Hitchcock is his awareness that both he and the viewer aren't so different from his murderers. In *Psycho* we look through the peephole at Marian with Norman. And Hitchcock "kills her" in the shower as much as "mother" does. In both *American Dreams* and *Landscape Suicide,* you define yourself closely with criminals. In *American Dreams* you handwrite Bremer's diary. People who don't know that diary (and that's most people who see the film) probably assume it's your diary. In fact, about halfway through the film, when Bremer begins to focus on killing Nixon, the viewer wonders, "Did Jim Benning spend some time following Nixon?"

Benning: Yes, especially since Bremer's from Milwaukee. He lived on the Southside; I lived on the Northside. But we both grew up in similar working-class neighborhoods.

MacDonald: In *Landscape Suicide* there's a similar and maybe unconscious identification with Gein. One of the things we learn about Gein is that in the instances when he butchered people, he seems to have tried to become his mother, although he doesn't remember it (which is the element Hitchcock focused on in *Psycho,* of course). You use a woman to narrate the film. She becomes your alter ego, the way Gein's mother was his.

Benning: I hadn't thought about that. I've used a woman's voice for my voice in a number of films. I think I began doing that just to question gender and to explore how you hear stories differently if they're told by a man's voice or a woman's voice. Also, I don't like the sound of my own voice. And I want to distance myself from the personal things that I put into my films.

MacDonald: Landscape Suicide also points to the economic distance between rural Wisconsin (as it's portrayed in the film, it's on the skids: buildings are dilapidated, everything looks old) and suburban Orinda County, where even the prison looks like a condominium.

Benning: There's a Porsche out front.

MacDonald: The shots of the power lines in the Orinda County section and the noise they make seems like a metaphor for power of all kinds.

Benning: When I went back to film in Wisconsin in 1985, I wanted what I shot to look like 1957, and there was no trouble doing that. If you bring in some old cars, it looks like 1957, 1940, 1930. The actual store where the murder took place had been redone, so I didn't film that. Orinda County feels brand new.

MacDonald: There's a certain woodenness in the way the lines are delivered by the Gein and Protti characters. After our screening last night, the people from our Criminal Justice Program said that delivery was absolutely in keeping with the way they've seen people confess. Did you research that aspect of the film?

Benning: No. But I had a feel for it. I knew I was going to be shooting these close-ups and I wanted the language to be delivered matter-of-factly. I knew any little emotion would really show on the screen. By playing it down, I could play it up. So that was my direction to both actors. I think they did a wonderful job, and Rhonda [Bell] had never acted before!

MacDonald: When Protti and Gein are being interviewed, the voice that asks the questions is clearly in a different space from the room in which they're confessing. That reminds me of your experimentation with on- and off-screen sound in the earlier films.

Benning: I wanted a detached, off-screen voice because I wanted to focus on the confession itself. I like the separation you mention, but mainly it's a way of having the confessions seem like monologues rather than dialogues, even though the original texts I quote are questions and answers.

MacDonald: Also, in the shots of Orinda, even when it's clear that the sounds that accompany the landscape images are the kinds of sounds you might hear in those spaces, they're either a little too loud, or there's something that detaches them just a bit from the place we're seeing.

Benning: I've always been interested in that. I don't re-create reality, I create a metaphor that suggests reality. Within that metaphor I make things a little hyper-real, or surreal, just off balance.

MacDonald: In this film that approach seems especially appropriate. It's the separation between what Gein and Protti did and who they were perceived to be that's so creepy. Also, they don't remember doing these things, so they're disconnected from themselves.

How much did *Landscape Suicide* cost?

Benning: About sixteen thousand dollars. That's just material costs. I do all the camerawork, the editing—all those types of things—and I don't pay myself a salary. My actors work almost for free.

MacDonald: Is the computer piece, *Pascal's Lemma* [1985], an homage to Hollis Frampton and *Zorns Lemma?*

Benning: There's a general reference to Hollis because of his interest in computers and because I've always admired his work. And I liked him.

MacDonald: Why did you focus on Pascal?

Benning: Well, he's an interesting person. He would work on a project and quickly get to the center of things, but then he'd get bored and go on to something else. He invented the first digital calculator; he almost discovered the calculus. He made contributions to fluid studies; he invented the syringe. Then he had this religious experience, dropped science, and started writing theoretical essays on religion. He became quite mad in the latter part of his life, obsessive about punishing himself for impious thoughts. He had a wall with spikes on it and every time he'd have an impious thought, he'd slam his fist into it!

Pascal was the starting point of that piece and provided the overall narrative structure. And then I added other things, about computers, about art, about how technology and art function together and apart. I like the piece. I want to do much more with computers.

Also, there's a computer language called Pascal.

MacDonald: Why didn't you use Pascal for the piece?

Benning: I should have. It's just that the NEC BASIC language is a little higher powered and so I could write fewer statements and get the same job done.

MacDonald: How much has *Pascal's Lemma* been shown?

Benning: I've shown it to a couple hundred people who have visited my loft—friends or people who call up and come over to see it. The only public screenings have been at the Kitchen and at the Museum School in Boston. Lots of people came to the Kitchen to see it.

MacDonald: I remember seeing Laurie Anderson there.

Benning: I just talked with her this past week. She had been going to my films at the Whitney retrospective. I think we have some similar ideas, especially about technology.

MacDonald: You've mentioned a new project [*Used Innocence*] about a person who may or may not have killed somebody. What's the state of that project?

Benning: I've been doing research: basically, getting acquainted with Lawrencia Bembenek, who's been in prison for four years. I've visited her and written letters. I'm interested in how she feels about being in prison and in what she says happened when she was a police officer. And I'm very attracted to her.

MacDonald: Why is she in prison?

Benning: She was convicted—on the most circumstantial evidence one could possibly be prosecuted under—of murdering her husband's ex-wife. I can't say she's innocent. There's no evidence to show that she didn't do it. She doesn't have an alibi. She was home alone when it happened. It's too complicated to get into here. At this point my idea is to film her telling her own story, and she's agreed to do that. I'll have to work through the prison officials to get permission. I'd like to film eight to ten hours of her talking and then work with that footage until it suggests images. I don't really want to tell if she's innocent or guilty. I want to see where her life has been, where it's going.

In the four years she's been in prison, she's been active politically. She corresponded with male prisoners at the Wisconsin State Prison to find out what their rights were, and discovered that women prisoners were allowed to do much less than the men—in terms of the number of phone calls they could make, the amount of exercise equipment available, things like that. She filed suit against the state and won, upgrading the rights of women prisoners in Wisconsin.

MacDonald: How do you plan to get funding for the film?

Benning: Well, that's always a problem. I do want to film her; I'm going to get that done even if I have to borrow. I think once I have her on film, there'll be no problem raising money to finish the film. She's so interesting. At times she's naive, the twenty-one-year-old girl she was when the murder was committed. And since that time, she's become a well-read, self-taught Marxist/feminist with experience working with the system. And she's been in prison for four years, so she's also a hard-core lifer. Her three languages mix and separate from moment to moment. I meet with her four hours at a time and it seems to go by in minutes. I think I've developed a rapport with her, and I think she's pretty honest, but like I said, I can't tell what the truth is about her case. I finally asked her if she was innocent, and she said, "Of course, I am."

MacDonald: You said earlier you'd like to make enough money from your films to support yourself. What's the state of your film rentals?

Benning: They get rented more every year, but more doesn't mean it's enough to live on. I've pretty much exhausted the grant possibilities. At the moment, I have no income, except for rentals and visiting-artists fees, which I probably could get by on, except that I wouldn't have any money to make films. I'm at the peak of my career. I just had a retrospective at the Whitney. And I have the least money I've ever had. It seems like at some point you shouldn't have to talk like this. Other kinds of artists don't. I don't mean to sound like I'm complaining. I'm very happy. It's just frustrating to be at this point in my career and not know if I'm going to have rent money next month.

Lizzie Borden

One of the commonplaces of film theory is that the traditional Hollywood narrative has been devoted to the maintenance of a male vision of the world, a world in which women function as the central focus of men's erotic gaze. Many of the most discussed feminist films (Yvonne Rainer's *Film About a Woman Who . . .* , 1974, Laura Mulvey and Peter Wollen's *Riddles of the Sphinx,* 1977, Jackie Raynal's *Deux Fois,* 1970, Sally Potter's *Thriller,* 1979) have attempted to interrupt this gaze and provide more progressive depictions of women. In recent years, Lizzie Borden (her original first name was Linda: "everybody always called me Lizzie because of my last name. My parents hated it!") has made important contributions to this process, in two films: *Born in Flames* (1983) and *Working Girls* (1986).

Born in Flames is a feminist "sci-fi" feature that uses an approach reminiscent of Peter Watkins: nonactors portray scenes from a not-too-distant future in which women struggle within a postrevolutionary American society where they continue to be oppressed by men. Borden's decision to cast nonactors in roles that might allow them to psychodramatize new forms of collaborative action was ingenious and progressive. And to a degree, what Borden calls its "bargain basement" look functions for the film: the trashy production values enhance the lower Manhattan milieu in which most of the action occurs. Nevertheless, as a narrative experience, *Born in Flames* is only intermittently convincing.

In *Working Girls,* Borden finds a way of redirecting conventional film pleasure so that it can reveal the conditions within which the standard erotic gaze functions. By enabling us to share the vision of the prostitutes in her film, Borden helps us recognize the sad romanticism of conventional macho, the sexual self-delusions under which it functions, and the institutions that have developed to maintain it. *Working Girls* allows us a sense not only of the realities of women's bodies, and the ways in which they must be disguised for conventional sex roles to be enacted, but also of the vulnerability of men's bodies and the childish obliviousness of the "needs" that bring men to the brothel.

Despite the fact that *Working Girls* exposes men in a manner analogous to the way women have normally been exposed in film, it is anything but anti-male. Borden creates a sense that women and men are doomed to struggle through the world in relation to each other, but that, ironically, absurdly, the genders continue to exist at the expense of each other—despite all the damage it does and all the time it wastes. Nevertheless, as is clear in the interchanges between the women in *Working Girls* and between some of the women and men, the possibility remains for a mutually rewarding synergy of the genders. Instead of spending our energies acting out cliched "erotic" scenes in order to fulfill gender images relentlessly promoted by the commercial cinema and mass media marketing, we need to have a more effective sense of what the real experiences of the genders are. Borden seems to assume that if we develop a stronger empathy with what "eroticism" is like for the women who do prostitution and for the men who use them, we might begin to see each other so clearly that abandoning our relentless cycle of mutual exploitation would seem like common sense.

In the following interview with Borden, *Working Girls* is the catalyst for a discussion of issues relating to the sex industry, including the depiction of prostitution and other forms of sexuality in cinema, and the ambiguities of female and male responses to pornographic films. When I first saw *Working Girls* at the 1986 Festival of Festivals in Toronto, I was simultaneously shocked and exhilarated; as a man, I felt exposed—but in a healthy, useful way. I also felt in tune with the sensibility of *Working Girls,* enough to send Borden a copy of my "Confessions of a Feminist Porn Watcher" (*Film Quarterly* 36, Spring 1983: 10–17) and to suggest we discuss the issues raised by her film and my article. She kindly agreed. We talked in January 1987.

MacDonald: One of the interesting dimensions of recent independent film is that body of work, mostly by women, which attempts to interrupt the conventional way of looking at women in movies: Yvonne Rainer's films, Sally Potter's, the Laura Mulvey/Peter Wollen collaborations. I've come to admire and enjoy some of these films very much. And yet, for the most part, they're not widely accessible to audiences. *Working Girls* seems based on an awareness of how women have traditionally functioned in commercial film, but it seems to have the potential for communicating very widely, especially to men who need to reconsider how they think about gender. Is that a goal you had in mind?

Borden: Yes. After *Born in Flames,* I realized a lot about how the structure of a movie affects an audience. That movie was structured the way it was for various reasons: lack of money, having to shoot things over five years as opposed to being able to do it all at one time. A lot of the complaints I got about *Born in Flames*—I got complaints about everything—had to do with the structure. People felt it should have been more of a story. They found it hard to understand. Also, I was trying to reach black women and various other groups of women. I think I accomplished that to a degree, but the film had limited access because of the structure: it got shown mostly in places where many of the people I wanted to reach don't go.

When I started *Working Girls,* I wanted to begin with a whole different aesthetic that had to do with telling a story very simply. I didn't want to make a voyeuristic film, but I wanted to create curiosity in the viewer, *almost* voyeurism, about what it's actually like to be in a house of prostitution. I wanted to convey that as directly as possible and not exclude the possibility of the male eye. I wanted to make a film that would not deny men visual access to anything and yet would not be an erotic stimulation for them.

There are all these famous stories about *Not a Love Story* [1982], the documentary on pornography, which I didn't like at all. Supposedly, it's an attack on pornography. It shows pornographic footage, then presents women and men talking about how bad the footage is. At the end of the film this one stripper is leaping around on the beach, completely "unified in herself" again. But, in fact, the daytime audience for the film— for all its political bullshit—would be single men, who obviously could ignore the bullshit and deal with the film on a voyeuristic level.

MacDonald: I disliked that film because it pretended that pornography and sex shows are simply exploitation *by* men *of* women. It seems obvious to me that these institutions are systems of *mutual* exploitation based on a whole set of cultural values and expectations.

Borden: See, that's exactly what *Working Girls* is about. Everyone assumes that the men have the power because they have the money. And that, therefore, the women are victimized. But it's really an equal exchange and a very parallel one. And in *Working Girls* I wanted to show that. Except for the session with Paul the musician and maybe a little bit with the Asian guy, Molly's relationship with her clients is very even. The relationship with Lucy, the employer, is the exploitative one. In stripping and to an extent in pornography, and in prostitution, women often feel an enormous sense of power. This isn't to say that women aren't victimized. Obviously, there are as many kinds of prostitution as there are women or kinds of jobs. And it's so class divided. The problem is that all kinds of prostitution get lumped together in one massive moral judgment.

MacDonald: I'm sure many people would have a hard time seeing how prostitutes have power over their tricks. I don't see it myself.

Borden: Within middle-class prostitution, particularly, there is a lot of control on the part of the women, because on some levels it's men who become vulnerable by walking into a brothel, a place where women are basically calling the shots. The woman is the one who decides when to go into the bedroom, when to begin the session, how much time to give, when to talk, when to not talk—of course, she's following cues, trying to read the guy very carefully—when to pull out the condom, when to put it on, how much more talk to have. Within a half-hour session, there's maybe ten to fifteen minutes of sex at most, and there's a powerful sense of men's vulnerability during the entire time.

One of the reasons I think there's such a sense of power is that the women see how vulnerable the male sex organ is. Men need an affirmation of their masculinity, need to feel they're still in full working order, or whatever. And that's such a vulnerable thing. An erection can happen or not happen. Actual prostitution is so much a woman coaxing it to work or controlling it or making sex into an experience that somehow is professionally complete. If a man goes to a prostitute, he knows he's going to get satisfaction on some level—whatever that means. Whereas, if he picks up a woman any other place, he may spend a fortune, not knowing what the outcome will be or how he's going to respond if sex does happen. In prostitution, the notion of a complete sex act is some-what guaranteed. I think a lot of the reason men get so attached to prostitutes—attached on some level—is because there's an understanding and appreciation of that professional service.

In the movies, prostitutes in every class of prostitution—working-class prostitution, middle-class prostitution—are made to pay for having been prostitutes. How they pay is determined by how much they did it for the money, how much they did it for the thrill, where they started in the first place, whether they had daddy problems.

MacDonald: You're talking about conventional films . . .

Borden: Yes. Conventional films, and some women's films. Marlene Gorris's *Broken Mirrors* [1987] is an instance: women working in a house get assaulted and beaten up and slashed.

In reality, while there are thousands of women prostitutes, doing a job where they seem very vulnerable, relatively little happens to them. The women who do prostitution don't do it because they were abused children who now need the affection of all these different men or something like that. And they're not just people with drug problems. In most cases, prostitutes are people who, at a certain point in their lives, choose not to take another economic alternative, one which is debilitating in its own way, but less remunerative.

In this culture one hears constantly about the sacrifice you have to make for doing prostitution. I've been attacked by everyone: by feminists who say, "You're soft-peddling prostitution; prostitution is *wrong*," and by spiritual women who say you can't have all these sexual encounters without doing damage to your soul. But nobody criticizes the forty-hour workweek. Nobody criticizes the fact that for the most part people are trained into positive thinking about jobs that don't make use of half their talents. There are bad things about prostitution, but they're not the ones you see in the movies. It's not that the women get diseases or anything like that. Women who work in a brothel are probably safer from AIDS than anyone else, because they always use condoms. Street prostitution is different because it's tied up with heroin, and there are a lot of other factors. But the point is that the kinds of women *Working Girls* is about are very healthy. And they're not busted by the police, and they don't get hurt.

MacDonald: What *are* the bad things?

Borden: There's the difficulty with relationships. Either you're lying about being a prostitute or you're not lying. Both have consequences. It's really hard for some women to do prostitution and have a boyfriend. If he accepts it, he becomes like a pimp. If he doesn't, then there's a battle every time. So, one bad thing is a bit of schizophrenia. A lot of the women have double names and double identities. But schizophrenia happens in other work, too; it's just never talked about. "Normal" work is usually romanticized or ignored.

There's also a lot of damage if a woman does prostitution too long. She ends up buying into a fake world and, finally, has no alternative for that work and ages within it. The only alternative then is to become a madam or to work within the business in some other way, as a phone operator or something like that.

I can't stress enough how important it was for me to see how unsexual it is for women to be doing prostitution. Very few of them have any sexual response, and that can lead to problems. There was this one woman who was in a session and came out doubled over. People thought that somebody had hurt her. She called her gynecologist; it turned out that her resistance to feeling anything sexual during her sessions created a spasm in her body.

The idea that prostitution is unsexual for these women is hard for people to believe. What strikes me is that people who would morally judge sex without feeling during prostitution don't judge the same act in other circumstances: for example, a woman decides to give her husband a quick fuck because otherwise he's going to be pushing up against her all night, not letting her sleep; she's not into it, but it's quicker and easier to get him off, to get it over with, than to be continually dealing with it. How many times does that happen in this culture? And there are cases where a woman has gone too far with a man: he's bought her a million things, and she's made out with him, and she realizes, "I don't want to be with this person," but it's too late. It's either a fight or she goes along with it.

MacDonald: You obviously know a great deal about prostitution. How did you learn so much?

Borden: I was interested in prostitution theoretically. And then I found I knew more and more women who worked. I encountered women who knew I was interested, and I got brought to these different houses and hung out with them. The result was that I had to transform my way of seeing prostitution. It hit really close to home. These were women within the art world, and there are so many, you can't even imagine. I'm sure you've known women who've worked in the sex industry at one time or another.

So what happened is that the minute I went from theory to actual practice, I saw that the women who do prostitution are people who are like me in absolutely every other way. I knew I had to use what I was discovering. I just didn't know how. I've been frustrated with all the documentaries I've seen on prostitution because they never go far enough.

MacDonald: Have you seen Vivienne Dick's *Liberty's Booty* [1980]? In some ways her film gives me the same sense of prostitution as *Working Girls* does.

Borden: Oh, yeah. It's funny because some of the people in her film were people I knew. She actually did her film about one of the same places that I did *Working Girls* about. I was writing my script at about the same time she was doing that movie. The two films share some things—especially the sense of prostitution going on downtown in the art world and being very accessible. The problem with Vivienne's film is that it's hard to separate what her vision of prostitution is from these women just hanging around in messy lofts and carrying on about one thing or another. And since there's zero production quality in her film, it was kind of hard to locate the women within any class framework. I was really anxious to see her film. When other people are working in the same area as I am, I always wonder, does this mean I don't have to do this film? So I saw *Liberty's Booty,* and I thought, "Oh, no, there's still room for what I want to do." I had the same experience with Bette Gordon's *Variety* [1984] and with *Broken Mirrors.*

MacDonald: One thing that seems different about *Working Girls* is your openness about what goes on in the bedroom.

Borden: One of the reasons I felt it was really important to go into the bedroom in *Working Girls* was to demystify what happens. So often, movies about prostitution stop before you get to see what actually goes on. In *Broken Mirrors,* all you see is the man's back approaching a woman. Then it cuts to the next scene where she looks bruised and battered, and you wonder, what on earth did he do? Vivienne didn't really deal with the act itself in *Liberty's Booty,* either. *Crimes of Passion* [1984] did a little bit, which was what I found interesting about it. That part seemed exaggerated, but real. *Klute* [1971], a tiny bit. *Sessions* [1983] with Veronica Hamill a little bit. But not enough really.

In the bedroom I wanted to focus on the economics of prostitution, as the economics work out *visually* in this ritualistic exchange of goods: the condom, the exchange of money, putting the sheets on the bed. These ritual elements also have implications for other activities that women and men engage in normally. How many times has a husband stood in a room as his wife was throwing a sheet on the bed or getting him a drink or doing something to control the mechanics of sex or birth control? I meant for the things you see in the film to have a reference to standard married life, or singles bars, to any sexual situation which involves a code whereby women are treating men in very routinized ways.

There are some things I doubt men ever see: a woman lying on the floor putting in the diaphragm or washing blood out of it. I'd always been curious about how a prostitute deals with periods. And the issue of hygiene was interesting. A prostitute is constantly washing all these men off, gargling with Listerine and brushing her teeth. Those were the things that fascinated me.

The demystification of sex was important for me in relation to the male audience. But I felt that an informative look at it would also desexualize it for the women. I wanted to show women that, no, these rituals aren't really about sex. When I was interviewing actresses, I talked to them about prostitution, and I wouldn't even give them a reading if they gave me a really judgmental answer: "How can you spread your legs for anyone but someone you love?"—that kind of thing. And I made all the women go to real houses and apply for a job. They'd come to rehearsals dressed like conventional street hookers! I made them go to real places and see how people dressed. They came back very chastened, realizing that all these girls looked like their college roommates. The madams were just like the women who would hire them in other businesses, in the fashion industry, or on Wall Street. They had to change their attitudes.

MacDonald: I haven't looked at prostitute movies as carefully as you have, but what you're saying may be an extension of something I've been thinking about. It seems to me that pornography has primarily to do with men's hatred of their own bodies. It may be that the apparent need to see women punished in movies for being prostitutes is a function of their being so dirty as to have been with so many men.

Borden: Well, it relates to any of the kinds of postcarnal hatred of women that are so typical of men. It would be fascinating to explore those feelings. I did talk to a lot of clients when I was doing research for the film, but men are so reluctant to analyze their feelings, and the feelings are so complex (and so many men are living a web of lies anyway) that it's hard to get much out of them. But it's interesting that (at least this is what I've gathered from reading and watching movies and talking to people) regardless of the intensity of a guy's desire for a woman, the minute he has her, the minute he comes, there's some kind of hatred. There's a sense of having to throw it off, put it away. I'm not talking about when people are in love; I mean sex for itself or as part of long-term relationships—*most* sex. Anyway, that pattern does seem accentuated in prostitution.

But it's the other thing as well. A lot of clients want to see the women on the outside. For a lot of men there's this inability to separate a sexual act from something more. There's a desire to maintain something. Also, there's this need to feel different from the other clients, so different that a woman would give him the privilege of seeing him on the outside (so that of course he wouldn't have to pay for it!). There's that fantasy constantly. And there's this whole thing of regulars, which is how small places like the one in my film run. A lot of men like to see the same girl over and over again. There's a sense of having a kind of girlfriend.

But I think what you said is true, that men may have a hatred and mistrust of their bodies. Have *you* felt that way?

MacDonald: Yes, but in a way the feeling is buried, taken for granted. I certainly know that as I was growing up, I was internalizing the cultural teaching that, for example, semen is a gross substance, almost the definition of what is gross. It is produced at this moment where, theoretically, you're supposed to be ecstatic (or released, *something*), and yet the physical evidence of this ecstatic moment is a snotlike substance that everybody hates. The good news and the bad news arrive simultaneously. And there's not only a *witness* to the bad news, there's the process of women cleaning up afterward. Cleaning away the dirtiness—often right away. I mean, don't misunderstand me, I wouldn't like it either, probably. Here's this body not your own, unlike your own, squirting this stuff all over, *sliming* you . . .

Borden: Do you think also that that's why men have accused *women* of being dirty for so long and have had this horror of menstruation and women's body fluids, have called them dirty cunts? Do you think that that's a reaction against women's revulsion about semen?

MacDonald: I don't know. I suppose it's true that women are made to feel dirty about menstruation. It seems obvious enough in the compulsive neuroticism promoted by ads for tampons and sanitary napkins. But when I was growing up—I don't know what it's like growing up now—I didn't know *anything* about menstruation. And when I did find out about it, I never thought it was a *dirty* process—in the sense that semen was a dirty substance—it was blood: scary, but not dirty.

Borden: What's so interesting is the transformation of those feared fluids—in film—into fetishization. Every conventional porno movie I can think of has those slow-motion cum shots, beautiful arcing shots with symphonic sound behind them—at the finale. It never happens *like that.* This all relates to other forms of fetishization—golden showers, brown showers, the extremes, the desire for the most vulgar, hated substances.

MacDonald: The *fantasy* is to have these substances accepted, adored.

Borden: You know, in those sex fantasy phone calls you can charge to your credit card, the idea of men coming is treated in that way. The women transform semen into something very desirable, something very wonderful, to be waited for, to be coaxed out of men with a lot of adjectives as if they can't wait for it. There's a whole fantasy vocabulary for the penis, based on how men (clients) want their penises to be perceived.

I would say definitely that the reason the phallus has been so mythologized and symbolized as this mighty, powerful, steellike organ is that for the most part it's *not* like that. I mean if it *is,* it's for very short periods of time. Most of the time it's this vulnerable, very retiring organ that's easily hurt. In most rape cases men literally don't get it up. Violence happens *instead of* sex. Rape is about the inability to have an erection in any kind of framework of control.

Obviously, all of this evaporates in a case where two people are madly in love with each other. Then all these things become the most wonderful things in the world for a period of time.

MacDonald: After I got a VCR, I rented *The Devil in Miss Jones* [1972], *Deep Throat* [1972], and *Behind the Green Door* [1972]. I was planning to write an analysis of those films (or so I said to myself!) that explored my suspicion that the experiences many men have watching them are more complex than we usually think, that the nature of the gaze is not all that obvious. There's this very erotic scene in *The Devil in Miss Jones* that's terrifying in its implications for women. It's the first sex scene.

Borden: I don't remember it; I saw the film years ago.

MacDonald: Well, there's this incredibly long blow job during which Georgina Spelvin vocalizes tremendously. She's constantly affirming that she wants this, do it more, and then at the end of the sequence, she's saying, "Hurt me, hurt me, hurt me," and he fucks her in the ass. I believe that what's hiding behind that scene is a kind of homophobia. The character we identify with in that scene is Spelvin. I think the men who are excited by this scene have the repressed desire to be "feminine," to *be* fucked, but that since they cannot admit such a gender-confusing idea, the desire transmutes into a pain-giving experience.

Borden: A lot of people interested in film theory see the gaze of the camera as intrinsically male. But if you're a woman, who do you identify with? One of the things I've found to be true, for me, is that I identify with both men and women freely. But then, I've been bisexual, so that may change the way you experience these things. What's interesting to me, though, is how you can justify what you said earlier about men— that they hate their bodies—with the narcissism that goes along with the desire to fuck themselves.

MacDonald: I'd just say that when men look at women in pornography, what they want to see is women adoring having sex with men. What they're really looking for is an affirmation of themselves.

I saw all this at work when I looked at *Behind the Green Door*. The central character in the film is a woman (Marilyn Chambers). You meet her and follow her around, developing an identification with her. We *do* gaze at her quite a bit; she's very attractive. But she's also the only character in the film we know well enough to identify with. The male viewer "becomes" the female, who subsequently, during the sex scenes, has men (and women) come in to her. What they do to her—as the camera angles emphasize—is done "to you."

Borden: I saw all the famous porn films a long time ago because my aunt used to distribute them. That was about ten years ago. They're so old now. But I'll have to resee that one.

I think if enough men admitted that they identified with the female being fucked by the man, things would get better for both women and men. Because it wouldn't make them gay at all. It would just make them more empathetic.

I've always wanted to do a porno film for women. Something that women could see and really get excited about. It's funny, because *Working Girls* is the opposite. It's totally about *not* doing any of that. What I resent about the censorship of my film, the censorship in terms of ratings, is that basically *Working Girls* is not pornographic. Many different elements of this film have been affected by what people think of pornography, but this isn't pornography: it's *not* about turning men on.

MacDonald: Has the film been censored? I know when I first saw it in Toronto, the scene where Molly masturbates the Asian man who refuses to shower or wash was painted over (it was funny because you could see the shot through the paint). That shot is gone in the version of the film now available.

Borden: When I tried to get an R rating, I found out that so much would need to be cut to satisfy the MPAA [Motion Picture Association of America] that there'd hardly be a film left. I decided to distribute the film without an official rating. I did end up cutting the hand-job shot: it was six seconds. The only other changes I made were to revise the ending a bit and to change the prostitutes' names (to avoid a suit!). Also, I added a bit of conversation between Molly and the Ricky Leacock character at the end of their session.

Anyway, I'd like to make a porn film where you're aware that a woman is controlling the camera. I mean, is the cinema apparatus intrinsically male? Is the voyeurism that happens in film intrinsically a male approaching, attacking, a female? I guess I don't believe so.

It'd be funny too, to make a film about the awkwardness of sex. Sex is so awkward. It's always awkward; you can't get it in the right place, or whatever. When it's passionate, you laugh about the awkward parts and then forget them, but when it's not—and it's certainly not in pornography—the awkwardness is very extreme, because it's not two people who are attuned to each other. When it's not passionate, sex is pretty funny and funny not usually in the way that people want it to be.

In your article you talk about the experience of going to porn shops. Have you ever considered bringing Pat [Patricia O'Connor, MacDonald's wife], or somebody, to a porn shop?

MacDonald: No.

Borden: How would you feel if she were there?

MacDonald: Embarrassed.

Borden: Really?

MacDonald: When I wrote my article, I was trying to understand the experience for myself. It's embarrassing to realize what you're paying to look at. I certainly can't speak for all men, but I'd guess most men are embarrassed to know that there's actually something in these places, and in this imagery, that does turn them on, even briefly. Part of my embarrassment has to do with how porn shops must look to women. If I were a woman, I'm sure I'd feel that the imagery men see there is really horrible for women and must create images in the male psyche that feed into their real sex lives in debilitating ways. And yet, on another level, as a sometime experiencer of that material, I feel that there's more involved.

When I was first in love with Pat, totally passionately involved, and we were having lovely, exciting sex all the time, I went to these places more often than at any other time in my life. And all the time I went, I thought, this is really creepy, why am I here? I don't know why. But I know Pat would be grossed out by those places; it would hurt our sex life.

Borden: Wouldn't you bring her into it for some kind of erotic purpose? How long have you been together now?

MacDonald: Thirteen years.

Borden: Thirteen years! Oh, my God, that *is* a long time. That means you've gone through a lot of stages. It's funny because I've been to porn places with a guy that I was seeing, and there was a weird feeling about the experience. It was interesting to be a female there because nobody quite knew what to do. The men wouldn't look at me. And I had a hard time looking at the women. The women who perform live tried to bring me in in order to get more money out of the guy I was with. So there was that. But it was odd; I couldn't figure out what attitude to have in there. I was too curious. I felt like *really* looking at the women making these gestures and taking poses and doing these sexual things that are clearly right out of magazines. The women in *Working Girls* would *never* do those things. They would *never* dress like that or act like that. They would never be like the so-called bad girls in the sex shops, where it's all about something else. Then again, the women in the sex shops don't get touched (although they may do prostitution on the side). Or if they do get touched, it's just through windows. For the most part, they're guarded. The sex shop performance is all about women using their bodies as lures, which is the same thing as stripping. Women often feel a great sense of power seeing all those men panting away.

Men would prefer to be seen exploiting women because that gives the men the power. If you show the opposite, the men freak out. Men freak out in *Working Girls,* and in anything else that shows them not to have absolute power. In *Working Girls* there's no clear control one way or the other, but it's clear that the men are not simply the controllers.

MacDonald: For me, part of the power of *Working Girls* was in exposing men in a way that women are usually exposed. We hear men's sounds and see how *they* act in these situations. There were places in the film where I had to watch with my hands over my face, and the only place I do that is in horror films.

Borden: Really?

MacDonald: It was terrifying to see that sexual acts, kinds of sexual interchange I had thought were individual, *mine,* are not only *not* peculiar to me but are boringly automatic, clichés, with their own terminology!

Borden: Actually, I find it quite pathetic that a house and a prostitute could satisfy a man. He must be *so* sexually starved for any kind of real contact. Because the amount of sex that happens in a house is so minimal. That's all the more reason for examining the codes of heterosexual behavior within our culture, without moralization about men or women. Because men are victimized too by this culture. They're told, "You have to have a relationship with one woman; you have to have a family; you have to have a solid, steady job; you have to be heterosexual." And, on the other hand, there's this propoganda around about men having hot, various, wild sexual experience in their lives.

What is it about our culture, about the nuclear family and the way that male-female relationships are structured, and about the way in which sex is fetishized, that creates this situation where men can go into a place like this and be satisfied by what they get? That's what amazes me. A man wants "Around the World," or he wants to play out his little doctor fantasy, or he likes to pose in front of a mirror, or he likes straight sex for exactly five minutes and likes to do something exactly this way or push this, touch this, no, do it this way. The idea that things become so defined is what I find fascinating.

You know, a big problem for me in making *Working Girls* was how to shoot the sex. How could I shoot the bedroom scenes without making women sexual objects for the male gaze?

MacDonald: It's really tricky here, because you're working with conventionally attractive people, in a traditionally erotic setup. And yet it really is *not* erotic.

Borden: Yeah, I'm so happy about that.

MacDonald: Or am I kidding myself?

Borden: No. You're not kidding yourself. You're . . .

MacDonald: I'm sure somebody could say, "Well, you just want to have your eroticism and get spanked a little bit for it . . ."

Borden: No, no, no. It was meant *not* to be erotic, and I feel it's very successful in that.

MacDonald: So what did you do, to have that effect?

Borden: Well, let's see. I totally designed the bedroom shots. We [Borden and Director of Photography Judy Irola] collaborated a lot on the downstairs shooting, where there were a lot of dollies. Most of the angles in the bedroom scenes are not subjective camera, but they're from a woman's point of view. There's no shot in the film where you see Molly's body the way a man would frame her body to look at it, except when she's looking at herself that way, in the scene where she poses with the guy in front of the mirror, for example. But, even there, I set up the shot so that if we are looking at her body in that scene, we're also looking at her eyes looking at her body. The first time you see her without any clothes on, she's alone with herself, and our gaze is involved with her watching herself.

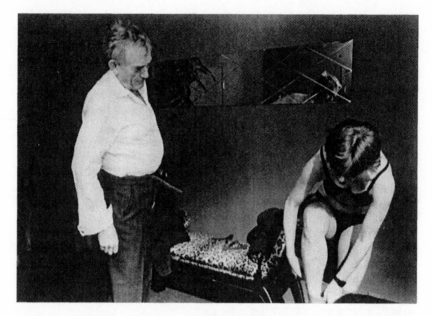

Molly (Louise Smith) and a trick (Ricky Leacock) in Working Girls *(1986).*

MacDonald: So our gaze is part of her gaze?

Borden: Exactly. You don't necessarily see exactly what she would see, but you see what you see, the way *she* would feel it.

Another thing that works against conventional eroticism is that by the end of the film, you see Molly take her clothes off fifty times. Her body becomes so familiar, it's like your own body after a while. That's what I hope happens. Her body is deromanticized.

Yes, it's true that the women are conventionally attractive, but they're not drop-dead gorgeous. And they don't have the kinds of bodies we see without clothes on in most movies. I wanted my main character to have a pretty face and a nice body, but not, "Wow! Look at that body!"

MacDonald: I understand *Working Girls* is the first film in which you've worked with professional actors. I would think that, given the subject matter, you had your work cut out for you.

Borden: Finding Louise to play Molly was very lucky. I had spoken to a couple of actresses. But nobody would do the role. There was too much nudity. It was hard to get women to even consider it. And then I met Louise. She was a nice Catholic girl who saw it as a challenge. She had never taken her clothes off before for a movie, but as it turned out, she was just great. And it was new for me. I knew I had to feel very comfortable. Actually, at times I felt a little like a madam myself. Louise had to act all the sex scenes, one right after the other, for a week. She *felt* like a prostitute by the end—which was great; that's how she was supposed to feel, though the sex is simulated.

MacDonald: I always find it interesting when what seem like limitations work positively for a film. In *Working Girls,* the awkwardness in the actors doing what they do seems perfect for the situation.

Borden: A lot of people have attacked the acting, especially the men. It was so much easier to find women who would take their clothes off than men. I got the Chinese guy from *Screw* magazine. He's not an actor. I could not find a Chinese man over forty who would take his clothes off. And I didn't want it to be a young man.

The way I dealt with the actors was parallel to the situation they were acting out. They'd come to work on the film, and they'd be uncomfortable. I had to keep the men happy; otherwise they were impossible to deal with. Because the women had longer parts, they were around more; and when a new male actor would come in, there'd be this uncomfortable exchange. I did the bedroom scenes first, actually. I knew what would happen if I didn't: they'd do their downstairs scenes, freak out, and not show up for the bedroom scenes. I wasn't paying very much. I paid the men more, the more clothes they took off and the more they would do. So it was a role reversal.

Many men think they can show themselves naked, and that they'll have perfect control. One guy assured me he could get an erection, but that never worked out. So I didn't do the scene the way I wanted to. In another scene a guy was *not* supposed to get an erection, but he got one. He was so embarrassed that he wouldn't take his towel off. So I said, "Great, great, great. Do you know what other men would do to get that?" But he hid in the towel. I said, "You've got to take your towel off. I don't want to have to shoot the scene from the waist up; lie on your stomach." But he was too embarrassed. I was furious. These men—they couldn't control their erections, but they had no sense of humor about it either! The two guys I found easiest to work with are Ricky Leacock and Fred Newman, who played Fantasy Fred. Both were very comfortable with themselves, and they had a great time doing the film. As a result, their scenes were fun to shoot, for the women as well.

MacDonald: How have men who have seen the film reacted?

Borden: I've been a bit depressed about some male reactions. One New York exhibitor said the film was done by a woman who obviously hated men, that the men were treated horrendously, that they're not real. And I thought, hey, wait a minute, don't you have a sense of humor? I wanted to make a film where the men would have to identify with *Molly* ultimately, where identifying with men would make them uncomfortable.

MacDonald: I think that kind of reaction has to do with the way you expose the men's sexuality, which is ironic since it's so "normal" in film to expose female sexuality. Men feel hated if they're exposed.

Borden: Maybe men feel hated if there's not a strong, wonderful male character in a film. There are some likable male characters in *Working Girls*: Elliot, her last client, maybe, and Neil, the sweet guy who just wants to talk. And it's clear that Molly doesn't hate men.

MacDonald: Working Girls is one of the few films I've seen where the men who are genuinely liked by the women are the opposite of the men who are theoretically attractive in more conventional films. They're sort of gentle, sweet people, and they have a better time than the more macho guys.

Borden: Yeah. Exactly.

There's also a myth about prostitutes hating men. What I found interesting and informative was that a lot of women who had been through prostitution for a short period of time ended up liking men more, not less. They felt less threatened by men, less in fear, and more able afterward to articulate their own sexual desires. Because they could see and be more skillful in providing what men wanted, they themselves could make sexual demands from their boyfriends or husbands.

By the way, I didn't mean to suggest that the "man-hating" charge is the only reaction the film gets. I've had a wide range of responses. In England, we did an audience survey at one point: young women and older men liked it. Older women didn't like it, and a lot of younger men said it turned them off. Of course, I don't want people to like the film necessarily; I want them to walk out *thinking* about prostitution.

Ross McElwee

During the Italian Renaissance, schools of painting came to be identified with particular cities. In recent decades something similar has been occurring in North America, where "schools" of independent filmmaking have become identified with specific places. San Francisco has been a center for surreal forms of avant-garde cinema. For a time, New York (and subsequently Buffalo/Toronto) was identified with what had come to be called "structural filmmaking." And for three decades, cinéma vérité has found a home in Boston. Many of the leading vérité filmmakers—Ricky Leacock, the Maysles Brothers, Frederick Wiseman, Ed Pincus—have had and continue to have crucial ties with Boston. Over the years, the cinéma vérité procedure (a hand-carried 16mm rig, hand-carried tape-recording equipment for synch sound, a one- or two-person crew) has been articulated in a variety of forms within a continually developing history. For a time, the assumption of a number of the prime movers of cinéma vérité was that the value of the procedure was precisely its ability to capture events without the intrusion of the filmmaker: the filmmaker's persona, either in a visual embodiment or in narration, was to be avoided at all costs.

By the seventies, however, a reaction to this position was occurring: men and women (Ed Pincus, Martha Coolidge, Amalie Rothschild, Alfred Guzzetti, others) were carrying 16mm cameras and tape recorders into their domestic environments to see what they could discover. Even within this more personalized kind of cinéma vérité, a good bit of articulation has been possible. One of the most interesting recent developments has occurred in a series of films by Ross McElwee, a native of

Charlotte, North Carolina, who studied filmmaking at MIT with Leacock and Pincus, and has taught at Harvard. Since arriving at MIT, McElwee has completed *Charleen* (1978), an extended portrait of Charleen Swansea, a friend and ex-teacher whose home became a haven for young painters, writers, and musicians—"a place like no other in the South I'd ever seen"; *Space Coast* (1978, co-made with Michel Negroponte), a portrait of three residents of Cape Canaveral, Florida: Mary Bubb, a local newspaper reporter who had witnessed sixteen hundred consecutive launches, "Papa" John Murphy, an ex-maintenance man turned motorcycle gang guru, and Willy Womak, small-time construction company owner and clown-host for a local kids show; *Resident Exile* (1981, also co-made with Negroponte), a portrait of an Iranian exile, tortured under the Shah's regime, living in the United States during the hostage crisis; *Backyard* (1982), McElwee's portrait of his home in Charlotte; *Sherman's March: A Meditation on the Possibility of Romantic Love in the South during an Era of Nuclear Weapons Proliferation* (1985), a record of McElwee's travels in the South, and the women he meets along the route General Sherman took during the Civil War; and *Something to Do with the Wall* (1990, co-made with Marilyn Levine), a meditation on the Berlin Wall.

In *Backyard,* McElwee's presence within the situations he records is, for the most part, similar to our sense of the filmmaker's presence in many earlier domestic cinéma vérité films: the world recorded simply surrounds the filmmaker and camera, and it's obvious that the people filmed are very aware of the camera's intrusion into their lives. But in some instances McElwee goes further: he introduces himself as a character within the imagery; we see him as we hear him comment about himself and his life. And just as important, he sometimes takes conversational actions that revise his relationships with the people he's talking with *as he is filming.* In other words, the camera is not simply recording McElwee's domestic life, it is witnessing changes in his life made possible, in part, by the camera's presence.

In *Sherman's March* this more complex presence is the central catalyst for the film. We get to know McElwee's (or McElwee's filmic persona's) hopes, concerns, nightmares; and we are behind the camera with McElwee as he uses the filmmaking process to forge new relationships and to revise previously important relationships. As is true in many literary first-person narratives, McElwee's approach in *Sherman's March* is simultaneously very revealing and somewhat mysterious: the candidness of the scenes is frequently startling, but the more the film—and McElwee-as-narrator—reveals, the more we realize that there are many aspects of the relationships he is recording that we are not privy to. We cannot help but wonder about the narrator as we experience things with him.

McElwee's films are also portraits of the contemporary South. *Charleen, Backyard,* and *Sherman's March* expose the complexity of Southern race relations from the inside, with a subtlety, a directness, and a humanity we rarely see in film or anywhere else. The oppression of black people is often obvious in the films, but so is the diversity of experiences blacks and whites share in this part of the nation where the races have lived longer and more intimately together than anywhere else on this continent.

McElwee and I talked on February 14, 1987, and subsequently fleshed out the interview by exchanging tapes.

MacDonald: Could you talk about your educational background and about how you got into filmmaking?

McElwee: When I was in high school and then in college as an undergraduate, creative writing was what I wanted to do. For a couple of semesters I worked with novelist John Hawkes, who teaches at Brown. Then during my last year in college I took still photography courses at the Rhode Island School of Design. I met students there who were making a film, and watched them work on the moviola. That got me thinking about the process of putting a film together. I went to student screenings at RISD, and I guess that's when I first thought about filmmaking as something an ordinary mortal could do. Also when I was in college, I saw *Primary* [1967], Richard Leacock's film about the 1960 Humphrey-Kennedy race in Minnesota, and Wiseman's *Titicut Follies* [1968] about the insane aslyum in Massachusetts. These two films stuck with me. They represented a very different approach to filmmaking. There was something gritty and startling about their attempts to capture real life. Also, the notion that there wasn't a large film crew, just two or three individuals out exploring the world and filming it, appealed to me in some vague sense. But I didn't really act on these feelings until close to two years later.

I saw *Touch of Evil* [1958] for the first time in Paris when I was twenty-two or twenty-three, at the Cinémathèque Française, and was dazzled by the opening shot where the camera tracks across the Mexican border. I suddenly had a kind of satori about the energy and magic of filmmaking. Later, I realized that by being a documentary filmmaker, I could satisfy my curiosity about the real world *and* I could indulge in that magical experience of presenting a film to that dark room full of people. It took awhile, but I got a summer job as a television cameraman at a station in Charlotte.

I quit that job after about a year and went to Stanford's summer film institute for three weeks of intensive filmmaking. I made a couple of short Super-8 films and a 16mm film there and then, through a producer friend, got a job as an assistant cameraman for *Bill Moyers' Journal,* on PBS. Basically all I did was load magazines for the cameraman. The shows weren't very exciting filmically (the Moyers series used a formula that centered on interviews and was heavily narrated), but I learned things and made a living for a year.

After that I applied to MIT's Film Section. MIT didn't have an official graduate program at the time, but Leacock was there, and so was Ed Pincus. Here were these two filmmakers, both doing unscripted, non-commercial documentaries, films that weren't intended to fit into the industry in a particular way. It appealed to me a lot. I ended up in the graduate program the following September.

Students were pretty much on their own. Leacock and Pincus were available, but the curriculum was pretty unstructured. We had access to lightweight portable 16mm rigs. They'd give us these rigs for a month at a time and say, "Get lost. Come back when you've got a film." That was terrific. Apparently it isn't that easy at all schools to have access to equipment for extended periods. For this kind of filmmaking you need to be able to shoot for weeks at a time in order to garner the kind of footage that can be shaped into a movie. By the end of two years I'd shot *Charleen,* which was my first real film.

I'd also shot footage for *Backyard* (which wasn't completed until a good bit later) and for *Space Coast,* which was finished after I officially left MIT. I was paranoid about not having access to camera equipment— not being able to afford it—once I left MIT, so I tried to stockpile footage for as many films as I could—thinking that somehow I could always wangle access to editing tables later.

MacDonald: Like several of your later films, *Charleen* seems, in part, a portrait of the South. Is that what you had in mind?

McElwee: I had originally thought that the film might be even more a portrait of the South, or at least of Charlotte, North Carolina, with Charleen as a witty tour guide. I wasn't at all sure that the film would be an intimate portrait of Charleen herself, though I hoped this would be the case. As it turned out, Charleen enjoyed being filmed and was a natural performer, in the sense that even though it was simply her own life that she was performing, she always performed it with a certain élan that was very "filmable." She enjoyed revealing her life to me and the camera. As a result, much of the Southern detail simply got eclipsed by Charleen herself.

Still, as you suggest, there is a latent portrait of the South in the film—maybe more a sketch than a portrait. I think the way interactions between blacks and whites are captured is interesting, with Charleen usually being the catalyst for such interaction. She repeatedly confronts whites with their own racism, and blacks with their sense of separateness from whites. She's always trying to break down the barriers between blacks and whites, but never politically. It's always done for art's sake, for poetry's sake, and out of an intense enthusiasm and love for her fellow human beings. And fortunately, it's nearly always done with a great sense of humor and verve, which prevents her passions from being self-righteously political or moralistic. She draws people out and confronts them with their own racial insecurities—and in the South, those insecurities are rampant for both blacks and whites.

MacDonald: By the time you made *Charleen,* there was already a group of films made in the early to mid seventies—Amalie Rothschild's *Nana, Mom and Me* [1974], Martha Coolidge's *David: Off and On* [1973], and others—in which the filmmakers took their cameras into their domestic environments. Had you seen these films?

McElwee: I saw *Nana, Mom and Me* after I left MIT, but there were other films that were much more important as influences. Jeff Kreines and Joel DeMott had spent time at MIT, and their films were definitely influential for me. And Pincus's later films, especially *Life and Other Anxieties* [1977] and *Diaries* [1976], which was a five-year portrait of his marriage.

MacDonald: Actually *Diaries* is in some ways the closest thing I know to *Sherman's March.*

McElwee: I'm sure I was influenced by it in all kinds of ways.

MacDonald: *Space Coast* is much more detached than *Charleen* since you don't know the people except while you're filming them. But the most interesting scene in it for me is when the young daughter (who looks much too young to ever have had a baby, anyway) is in the phone booth calling to try to get welfare. She suddenly says something to you . . .

McElwee: She asks me, "Have they hung up on me?" And I take the phone and listen at that point.

MacDonald: That moment is something special. But during much of the film I'm a little uneasy about the film's stance. There's a fine line between looking into the lives of these weird people, and laughing at them.

McElwee: Yes, that's the danger of this kind of filmmaking.

MacDonald: John Marshall's *N!ai, Portrait of a !Kung Woman* [1978], was made during the same period. How did you come to work on that film?

McElwee: There was the basic necessity to make a living. During those years [1977–80] I didn't have any steady source of income, so I continued to take jobs as a free-lance cameraman. I preferred opportunities where I could work with filmmakers I respected, such as John Marshall or D. A. Pennebaker. I'd never met John, but I'd seen his work. He had been filming a !Kung settlement for a month in Namibia, and though his cameraman was scheduled to leave, John felt that he did not have his film yet. I was recommended by Mark Erder, the original cinematographer, who was also from Boston. They cabled me, and I said I'd do it.

It was a complicated situation. John has a distinctive style, and I think at first he was nervous about having me shoot. He didn't know me at all; he'd never seen any of my work. Could he edit my camerawork with his and Mark's? Also, Namibia was his world, and I was coming into it cold. But it all worked out. I could tell you a hundred stories about the experience.

MacDonald: Tell me one.

McElwee: Well, the day I arrived (after an exhausting sixteen-hour flight through Frankfurt and then south to Namibia, where we finally landed on a stretch of dirt in the middle of the Kalahari Desert), John said, "Well, let's not shoot today. Let's just show you the layout." We started walking around, and suddenly we heard a commotion. A fight had broken out between one of the !Kung men and an Ovamba worker that John had brought with him to be a cook for the camp. They were accusing the cook of having an affair with this guy's wife. There had been tension between !Kung people and the Ovambas to begin with, so this was a volatile situation. The argument exploded to include every member of the village; people were screaming and yelling and chanting and crying. We simply had to film it, and I didn't even know who John felt the principal people were at this point. John said, "Just shoot, shoot whatever is happening."

The !Kung are very short people, and I had this odd sense of not being there, of being invisible. An angry !Kung rushed in my direction bandying a large stick, seemingly at me, but actually in pursuit of another !Kung who happened to be next to me. But my presence was never acknowledged. I saw a grass hut shaking wildly, and I held the shot of it, and pretty soon the allegedly cuckolded husband's head breaks through the wall, like a chicken emerging from an egg. He was being restrained by two people on each arm—relatives who were trying to keep him from murdering the Ovamba cook. Meanwhile, his wife was being slapped by her mother. And it was all based on nothing but rumor. Nobody was seriously hurt. We filmed for something like seven straight hours—all stages of the argument, its dissipation, and the lamenting that followed it . . . it was an amazing experience. Some of that footage was used in *N!ai,* but edited down.

MacDonald: Were you there when *The Gods Must Be Crazy* [1981] was being filmed?

McElwee: No. That was done before I arrived. It was wonderfully ironic that those two films were being made in the same place at the same time. They should be shown side by side. *The Gods Must Be Crazy* had its charming moments, but it was silly and condescending about the !Kung.

MacDonald: Backyard is your first full-fledged portrait of the South. It centers on two themes: the relationship of the two races and your relationship with your father and brother.

McElwee: How *Backyard* was conceived might be of interest to you. It started out as two separate films: a portrait of Clyde, the beekeeper; and a study of my brother's last summer at home before going away to medical school. I was thinking of doing a film about the difficulty of getting through four years of medical school. I felt pretty confident that my brother would return to North Carolina and practice with my father, which he eventually did, so there would be a kind of closure to a story filmed over five or six years.

What happened was that the two separate films kept pulling toward each other like magnets, and I found I couldn't separate them. There was this interwovenness between the lives of Clyde and the other black people who worked around our house and my father and my brother, and it seemed artificial to try to pry the two stories apart. Finally I realized I had to make a film that incorporated both elements. When you're making unscripted documentaries, your preconceptions about the film you're going to make usually start out very different from the film you end up making. Then, given that I didn't have much film stock, I decided to give the film a restricted area in which to work: to let it literally be confined to my backyard, with a couple of departures to other places in the neighborhood.

MacDonald: The panorama of relationships between black and white people is interesting. There's the scene where your brother walks into the kitchen and kisses Lucille, the cook, in such a natural, automatic, unconscious way that I'll bet many Yankees fall out of their chairs. Then there's a scene where the new bride surveys the people and says good-bye to them before she leaves on her honeymoon: she seems totally oblivious to this black guy who, on his part, is totally involved in an almost fawningly sentimental way with her leaving. In their juxtaposition these scenes capture the surreality of the social life of the South. Also there's that scene where you visit Lucille's brother (who's had a tracheotomy) in the hospital room. His total discomfort with your presence is obvious.

McElwee: Yes, he makes a gesture, a sideways move of the hand that's right on the border between being a wave, a perfectly innocent good-bye, and a somewhat hostile shooing me away. This man is very depressed, and a lot of the reason he's depressed is because he's oppressed. For whatever reason (I don't know the specifics of his history), his alcoholism, growing up black in the South, never having had anything of material value, starving himself—that's what Lucille said; he's suffering from malnutrition—that gesture is very important: it's emblematic of an anger that blacks in the South want to express, but can't really because of the mutual interdependency between blacks and whites, and because of an odd sense of family. And I don't mean "family" in a sentimental way: it's not a good situation. Lucille's brother won't get angry and say, "Get the hell out of here," but at the same time he's not going to smile at me. There are plenty of angry blacks in the South now, but you still find his kind of acquiescence, and it makes me feel terrible. Certainly there's the implication in that scene of the cameraman as one more white exploiter of the black class. I am victimizing the helpless, using them as fodder for my film. If I'd cut the shot before the gesture, I would have cleaned the scene up as far as implicating myself in this idea of white domination of blacks. But then it would have been dishonest. Godard's comment about every cut being political is very true.

MacDonald: The interactions between you and the black workers at the country club are loaded. Your talk with the guy you see at the flagpole in front of the Tara-looking country club building encapsulates a lot of Southern history, as does the moment where you film the black guys in the kitchen.

McElwee: I read some hostility in those black kids. They're seventeen or eighteen years old, washing dishes for the white folks, and they're really banging those dishes around. And then the chef comes in and cocks his head, and asks me if I'm "filming all the dirt here." It's one of those amazing little moments. It's fascinating that the black guy who has been sent out to lower the flag walks the entire distance and begins undoing the rope before he looks up and notices the flag isn't there. For me there's a lot of meaning in the downward gaze. Somehow he's learned not to look up very often. That's very sad. And then he walks back to the side of the building, crossing paths with the country club member in the white dinner jacket who goes in the front door . . . pure serendipity. It's the magic of these kinds of films that now and then, with a little patience, you get a very complicated scene, shot very simply, that unfolds like a flower right in front of you.

MacDonald: Your relationship with your father seems very problematic for you. Your father and brother seem very close because your brother is going into medicine and hopes to go into practice with your father. Your mother is no longer alive and you seem to feel left out, maybe a little bitter.

McElwee: It's complex. I myself would not describe my mood as bitterness, but I can see how other people could say that. In fact, I was not unhappy with my station outside the closest family orbital ring. Orbiting is important, and I want a connection to family, but in that film I was exploiting the humor and poignancy of being just one step removed as a result of choosing a life-style that my family couldn't quite relate to.

MacDonald: That opening passage where you talk about the various professions you were thinking about going into is very funny. Clearly, all the professions you list were chosen to infuriate your father's sense of what a good Southern boy ought to do. At the same time, your tone reflects your own awareness of and detachment from your earlier adolescent reaction.

McElwee: It seemed to be impossible to make that film without making myself a character.

MacDonald: Another thing that comes across in *Backyard* is a portrait of a certain sort of Southern Scottish Presbyterian life. You, your father, and your brother reveal an apparent inability, or a refusal, to really talk with each other about what's happening in your lives. There's a strange conversation with your brother at the end, when you ask him what he knows about your mother's death. It's a moment that prefigures *Sherman's March,* in that you seem to be using the camera to forge a new kind of relationship with your brother.

McElwee: That's an interesting observation.

MacDonald: Though he slams the door shut on the attempt.

McElwee: Well, he slams it shut, but not without revealing a startling fact: that my brother, with all of his medical background and his closeness to my father, doesn't know any of the details about my mother's death. He too has never talked to my father. There's some sort of strange Scottish Presbyterian existentialism operative here: why talk about the details of the death of someone one loves; who cares what the details are, we all understand the sorrow and the absence. Also, a certain politeness about not discussing unpleasant things is very Southern. I think it's partly the Scottish highlands heritage of a restraint in living, a feeling that men should not express emotions.

MacDonald: Would it be fair to say that because of this non-communicativeness, your family can live within this complicated society and its racial inequities without thinking much about it?

McElwee: The fact that they don't talk about it doesn't mean they don't think about it, or act upon it. I'm told that when my father set up his practice in Charlotte, after finishing medical school and his residency in New York City, he was the first doctor in the city to have a desegregated waiting room. There was no fanfare, no newspaper story. (I was not told this by him but by other people.) It seemed absurd to him that black people had to sit in one room and whites in another when he was going to be operating on all of them sooner or later. He's quietly done things like that all his life. I saw them throughout my childhood. Anyway, the fact that people don't talk about racism doesn't mean they don't have strong feelings and act to eliminate it. We tend to analyze things to death up here—especially in Cambridge, which must be the self-analysis capital of the eastern half of the United States. *Sherman's March* explores the paralysis that occurs when people are talking about their emotions rather than acting on them. That's a phenomenon we're saddled with in the Northeast.

MacDonald: Your particular presence as a narratorial persona in *Sherman's March* makes that film different from *Backyard*. I assume all the narratorial stuff in *Backyard* was recorded after the original footage.

McElwee: Yes. Painstakingly, with many, many revisions. The true chronology of when my films were finished is *Charlene, Space Coast, Resident Exile, Backyard,* and *Sherman's March*. But that's not the order in which they were shot. *Backyard* sat on the shelf for years and then was edited relatively recently. *Backyard* was a sketch for *Sherman's March*, an experiment in how I could approach the bigger film.

MacDonald: Sherman's March is often formally beautiful, which is part of what makes it sustainable for two and a half hours. *Backyard* is . . .

McElwee: Cruder. Part of the problem with *Backyard* was that I was just learning to shoot as a one-person crew. I was just getting over that odd sense of camera shyness in reverse. It takes awhile to summon the gumption to shoot people you know well, to be able to face them and talk to them as you're filming. Also, I was using a Nagra 4, a very large tape recorder: it weighs twenty pounds and I carried it slung over my shoulder. For *Sherman's March* I used a miniature Nagra SN, a very highly developed piece of recording equipment that could fit on my belt. This technological improvement made shooting much easier.

MacDonald: In Wiseman's films you can always see that everybody is conscious of the camera, but not so much of him personally, whereas in *Sherman's March* and *Backyard* you know the people and have fairly complex relationships with them: the camera is more a part of you, rather than you a part of the camera. Your subjects may respond to the camera being there, but they're primarily interacting to *you* having the camera pointed at them. The interaction is more complicated. Or complicated in a different way.

McElwee: In objective, detached, "classical" cinéma vérité, you may have very strong emotional feelings about what you're shooting, but basically the world plays itself out in front of you without any of your feelings being directly represented in what you're shooting. You're detached, separated. This enables you to develop levels of complexity within a single frame, foreground/background relationships for instance. In *Space Coast* there's a shot of Papa John sitting in a chair rambling on about how he can't get a job, while in the background you can see his wife struggling to load the refrigerator with groceries; all kinds of interesting ironies and complexities are set up in that shot. When you start taking on part of the burden of the narrative and the interactions yourself, you can lose this kind of complexity. The interaction begins to be more perpendicular to the camera. Often, you're giving up the observed detail that reflects the depth and multileveled complexities of the world, both visually and sociologically. What you're getting instead is a self-reflective complexity that turns back on itself. Occasionally in *Sherman's March,* however, there are moments when I was able to step back and observe what was going on. The scene with the survivalists is an instance of that. They're not really part of my world, so I can step back and film them objectively. Ideally, I want my films to phase in and out of these two kinds of experience.

MacDonald: I assume your use of Ricky Leacock to narrate the opening passage of *Sherman's March* is an homage to him.

McElwee: Yes, but it's an ironic homage because he pioneered a kind of filmmaking in which narration, didactic narration at any rate, was to be avoided at all costs. At the time, that was a break with the convention that had been established by Humphrey Jennings and the other British documentary filmmakers during World War II and to some degree by Robert Flaherty, for whom Ricky was a cameraman: Flaherty's films were narrated with title cards. When I was at MIT, Ricky was always irreverent, always encouraging us to do films for ourselves, to do films that were not conceived of as commercial entities. This is not what you hear in a lot of film schools, where you're encouraged to produce films that will get you jobs in public television, or in commercial television or Hollywood. Ricky was always very caustic and irreverent about those reasons for making films. I was really happy that he was willing to do the introduction. Ricky likes the film a lot. He's been very supportive. At one point, when my camera stopped functioning somewhere in Georgia, he airshipped me his.

MacDonald: When you were moving through *Sherman's March,* filming people, what did you set up in advance? What did you tell people about what you would do? Did you just walk in on them?

McElwee: Pretty much I always walked in on them. Obviously, I'd steer the conversation in a certain way, and indeed that's what human dialogue is anyway, so why not let it be part of the film? I guess what my conversations have that conventional interviews don't is a serendipitous quality, an emotional charge that has something to do with the personal connection between the subject and the filmmaker. I never came with a list of questions.

MacDonald: Did you call ahead and prepare people?

McElwee: Well, in the case of Karen, the lawyer, the last portrait in the film, I said, "Can I come and spend some time with you? I have my camera and I'll probably do some shooting. I'm making this film about women in the South and about my journey along Sherman's route." And she said, "Sure, come." In one sense she's startled when I walk in the door shooting; she hadn't quite expected that, but in general she's prepared. That scene on the porch when I'm asking her, "Where have you been for the last year? Why didn't you ever write?" is exactly as it happened. We didn't talk about it beforehand. In fact, if I had called ahead and told her I'd ask her about certain things, she'd have inevitably tried to preconceive what she was going to say, or would have said, "Well, I don't think I'm going to want to do this." It's just easier to go ahead and film.

MacDonald: What was the balance between how much you shot and didn't shoot when you were with people?

McElwee: I think a more accurate way to think about this is that I was almost always ready to shoot. I kept the camera within reaching distance, sometimes balanced on my shoulder. Maybe *Sherman's March* took five months of shooting. I never figured it out exactly. But even between major portraits, when I was on the road, I was totally open to filming whatever might happen in a gas station or in a restaurant, or wherever. So in one sense you can count all that time as "filming time."

I'd guess the total amount of footage I actually shot was about twenty-five hours. I don't remember exactly. In the finished film I ended up with two and a half hours of that—a ten or eleven to one filming ratio. But that other ratio, between five months and two and a half hours—that's astronomical.

I spent five or six days with Charleen [Swansea]. That was probably the shortest period overall that I spent with anybody. She's so intense, things happen so quickly with her, that I didn't need to be there long. Of course, there were also times when I'd go with her prepared to film, and film nothing because it wasn't interesting enough. I'd just relax and enjoy myself if I could.

MacDonald: *Sherman's March* is another portrait of the South, and like the other films, it includes moments of interrelationship between whites and blacks. Your conversation with the fellow whose daughter has died is especially memorable.

McElwee: It's an amazing moment. It happened totally unpredictably. I was there because the car with its mechanical woes was becoming a theme I thought I might be able to develop. It's pretty much a single unedited shot that takes you from a discussion of the car to his son to his daughter's death to my mother's death. To me, that's preferable to piecing together five different shots to create the same impression. This way you can see the emotional shift in his eyes, hear it in our voices, as we move from discussing something that's mundane to something that's of profound importance to both of us. It's the kind of thing you could never set up ahead of time because people will put up their defenses. If I'd said, "I'd like to talk a little bit with you about the death of your daughter," he might have done it, but it would not have happened organically the way it did. That's something I feel very strongly about. Another instance of this is when I'm talking to Mary, the fashion model, near the opening of the film. I haven't seen her since we were kids. We start off talking about something very superficial—where we used to play Superman—then the conversation turns to her kids, then to her feelings about divorce. Again, it's all one shot and you can track the development of the dialogue in her eyes. There's a moment of real sadness there that to me is absolutely amazing.

MacDonald: Did you assume from the beginning that the film was going to be a survey of Southern womanhood?

McElwee: I think that the way in which the film begins to put itself on track is fairly accurately described in the film itself. I knew I didn't want to make a *Space Coast*-like documentary of the South. I thought I would do a synthesis of *Backyard* and *Space Coast*: I would film some of my relatives, but basically the film would not be so much about me as about my homeland. I would have a personality, but initially I didn't know it would be as important to the film as it turned out to be. I began filming the Scottish games, thinking, "Well, here's an interesting event." The imagery was sort of bizarre: these guys tossing huge phallic poles around, guys in kilts wrestling on the ground—all of it in the American South. It had a surreal quality.

The breakthrough occurred with my sister on the following day, when she said—somewhat seriously, somewhat joking—"You should use the camera as a way to meet women." She's sincerely upset about my having ended my relationship with my girlfriend, and she's looking for ways to get me back on my feet. I think she perceived me as being incapable of resurrecting my life—a lot worse off than I really was. (Obviously I had the wherewithal to get a camera on my shoulder and start filming something.) But at the point when she gave me her advice about how to use the camera, I experienced a minor epiphany. The next thing that happened was the announcement that Mary was in the neighborhood. Why not look her up *with the camera* and see what happens? The miniportrait of Mary went well. She was gone the next day, so there was no potential for filming her more, but it was a start. And it was a microcosm of how the film might work.

Then I met Pat, who was a natural film subject. She loved being filmed, had no self-consciousness whatsoever, was somewhat outrageous, articulate, and had bizarre outlooks on life. And she had nothing to do but allow me to film her. It was perfect.

MacDonald: One complaint I've heard about *Sherman's March* is that you center on women who are bizarre, a little wacky, maybe objects of patronizing humor.

McElwee: I see them as being independent and intelligent for the most part. But eccentric, yes. I don't see anything wrong with having chosen women who are eccentric, who are unusual. Having decided to film women who are independent in the South means they're going to have to be somewhat eccentric. The fact that they decided not to embrace the more traditional conservative values of the South, nor to accept the roles that most Southern women seem to accept, made them by definition somewhat eccentric.

You know, I hear myself saying these things and immediately feel uncomfortable. I'm not sure I have the sociological background to even begin to define who's eccentric and who's not, who's conventional and who's not. And yet I feel somehow that the women I filmed are out of the norm, and that's why I decided to film them. I can only say that I wasn't attempting to make any statement about the status of women in the South or in the United States. I felt no obligation to select a group of women who were somehow representative of something. I think the women in the film are wonderfully individualistic; some are eccentric, some seem quite normal to me. A lot of them are struggling with life, and I'm interested in that kind of struggling. We all do it. *I'm* doing it in the film. I was interested in capturing some of that. A lot of documentaries try to package things very neatly from an ideological point of view. In some ways it leaves the viewer with a false sense that problems have been solved, points of view have been neatly defined. I think that's very dangerous. Life isn't like that.

A more valuable question to ask is, are we laughing with people or at them. Pat, the woman in search of Burt Reynolds, is an aspiring actress. Some of the things she says are quite outrageous, but she has a sense of self that in my view enables her to get away with saying the things she says. I think she's a fascinating and complicated and very unique person in the film, very entertaining, very funny; she knows that we're laughing at a lot of the things she says, but she's pleased with that fact. It's part of her way of presenting herself to the world. She's seen the film and is

Pat Rendleman in McElwee's Sherman's March *(1986).*

delighted by it. She's even had her agent circulate it to studios in California, hoping that she can get work.

It's true that a lot of the situations that I end up in or that the women end up in are humorous or comic, but it's important to have a sense of humor about life and about oneself. I see the situations as being funny, but not pathetic. I've made films that flirt with filming the pathetic in other people's lives, and it makes me very uncomfortable. I hope I've avoided doing it in *Sherman's March.*

MacDonald: Do you think of yourself as a Southern filmmaker? The South has not played a particularly conspicuous role in independent filmmaking.

McElwee: I don't feel a responsibility to film the South. When I made *Backyard* and *Sherman's March,* the South seemed very rich in possibilities, and as you say, not so many other people have explored it. I'm glad that you've asked this question because I do think that aspect of *Sherman's March* often gets overlooked. It's not merely an autobiographical film; it's a film about a region, to some degree about a way of life. I don't think I would be satisfied doing purely ethnographic films of the South. There are certainly filmmakers who choose to do that. There are a number of documentaries that deal with the customs, the rituals, and the arts and crafts of the South. These themes are a peripheral interest to me. But I continue to be very interested in the way the South resists the homogenization that seems to have made most other parts of the United States indistinguishable from one another.

As to whether I consider myself to be a particularly Southern film-maker: it's not important to me that I be described that way. I'm sure I could have gone to California and made a film that in some senses would have been an equally accurate portrait of California life. But because I am from the South, I have a particular slant on the South that non-Southerners might not have, which includes having access to people and places an outsider might not come across. I take advantage of the fact that I'm Southern in making my films, but I don't really think of myself as a Southern filmmaker, and I hope that the films I've made are of interest to people outside the South. Of course, there is a tradition of Southern fiction (Flannery O'Connor, William Faulkner, Thomas Wolfe . . .), and the label as used there to indicate a genre of literature that was created by writers from the South but transcends the region, transcends the label of "Southern," is what I'm striving for.

MacDonald: The parallel between Sherman's march through the South and yours suggests that you also think of yourself as a Northerner.

McElwee: I am trying to draw a parallel between Sherman and my-self, which is accurate in some ways and comically ironic (I hope) in other ways. I do have some things in common with Sherman although some of the parallels have been reversed. He's a Northerner who was coming down South; I'm a Southerner who went up North. But I also take it a step further and posit myself in the role of an exiled Southerner living up North who returns to the South again. I both identify with Sherman and find my personality and what my life stands for as being in contradistinction to what Sherman stood for. I both consider myself to be a Southerner *and* to no longer be a son of the South. In some sense the South is alien territory for me.

MacDonald: There's also a parallel in the fact that you and Sherman met mostly women.

McElwee: Yes, most of the Southern troops were in Virginia at the time, with Robert E. Lee, entrenched around Richmond. Left behind were women, children, and old people. There's also the basic difference between Sherman and me in that Sherman was quite successful in his campaign. He achieved his military objectives. If one considers the pur-pose of my journey finding an ideal Southern woman to marry, to fall in love with, whatever, I'm unsuccessful in my "campaign." Time and time again, I meet with outright defeat or at best there's a draw.

MacDonald: Is there a sense in which you use the camera as a weapon? Is that an implicit parallel?

McElwee: In no way am I really trying to use the camera as a weapon.

But, of course, the act of filming—no matter how gently, how sensitively it's done—takes advantage of people's vulnerability. The act of filming is an invasion of privacy, in a metaphorical sense perhaps a rape of some kind, pillage of some kind. In the scene when Karen, the attorney and ERA activist, tells me to stop filming, she has to tell me not once, but three times. That suggests an indictment of the act of filmmaking.

MacDonald: The scene of Burt Reynolds at work in Charlotte is interesting, both because Reynolds is a Southern star and, from my point of view, because—ironically, since you're not allowed on the set—*Sherman's March* is at least as interesting a film as he's appeared in. Did you originally plan to "invade" the set?

McElwee: At first, I did go through proper channels. Had I talked myself onto the set, I might have gotten some interesting imagery of Hollywood filmmaking and of the creation of the Southern hero as represented by Burt Reynolds. But even when I requested permission to be on the set, I understood that if they denied it, I would then explore the point of view of the outsider peering over the fence, or I might take a stab at going behind the scenes only to be stopped. As things turned out, I pursued both and ended up with the second, which seemed to me to work out fine. The scene is a successful emblem for the difference between two styles of filmmaking: the single-person documentary approach is posited against the very complicated Hollywood way of making films, where you have celebrity casts and large crews, and security forces to keep people at bay.

MacDonald: The way the Ross McElwee persona develops in *Sherman's March* reminds me more of the literary device of creating a narrating character whom the reader does not entirely identify with, or, at least, who is different from the writer. In *Sherman's March* there's a lot you don't reveal (information about whether or not you're sexually involved with the women, for example). We get an inside view of your life, *but* you as filmmaker shape what we see in such a way that we come to see you as a separate and somewhat mysterious character.

McElwee: In *Backyard* I am represented primarily through my subjective voice-over narration. You do see me in a mirror shot, and playing the piano, but those are the only times you see the filmmaker. In *Sherman's March* I go a step further. I deliver monologues; I try to create an almost literary voice-over. I think this enables the film to achieve a subjectivity it wouldn't have otherwise. I could have filmed the same people in the same situations without having said anything or revealed anything about my personality. That film might have been interesting, but I think not as interesting as when you hear something of what the filmmaker is thinking at a particular juncture in the film, and when you occasionally see the filmmaker in the setting where the film is unfolding (such as at the treehouse on the island when you see me in the bunk bed). It seems to me that these things are absolutely necessary to make the film work.

It's true that I'm not explicit about my sexual involvement with the women in the film, some of whom I slept with, some of whom I didn't. It seemed to me not the point of the film to graphically render that dimension of things, even if it had been possible to do so. I think that by being respectful of the women involved in the film vis-à-vis my sexual involvement with them, the film gains more than it loses. To have been more explicit would have pushed the film into sensationalism and solipsism that ultimately would have been alienating. Also, we have to keep in mind that this is a film about real people and real events. It's a documentary, not a fiction, and there are certain issues of privacy one simply has to respect. But the sexuality being alluded to and yet not directly revealed adds a subtle tension to the film that I hope works in its best interests.

It's also true that the Ross McElwee who's presented in the film is not a completely rendered Ross McElwee. I don't say everything about myself that I could be saying. I don't tell you everything that's on my mind. I am creating a deadpan persona. Perhaps I create a heightened sense of depression, heightened in an attempt to attain some sort of comic level. I'm creating a persona for the film that's based upon who I am, but it isn't exactly me. Of course, it's hard to make the judgment myself. It's like the problem Wittgenstein describes when he talks about how the eye can see the world but can't see itself. It's difficult to know yourself and to know how you're presenting yourself to the world.

Su Friedrich

The critique of conventional cinema that is articulated in Su Friedrich's films—*Cool Hands, Warm Heart* (1971), *Scar Tissue* (1980), *Gently Down the Stream* (1981), *But No One* (1982), *The Ties That Bind* (1984), *Damned If You Don't* (1987), *Sink or Swim* (1990), and *First Comes Love* (1991)—has roots in two different cultural projects: the development of North American avant-garde cinema and the recent feminist reassessment of modern society (and of the popular and independent cinema). Each of her films represents a different combination of these sources, and she has demonstrated her loyalty to both in her extra-film activities: she was instrumental in getting the 1990 *Film-makers' Co-operative Catalogue* finished and published and is a regular workshop leader at the Millennium Film Workshop, and for years she was an active member of the *Heresies* collective. Her particular gift has been to find ways of combining cinematically experimental means and a powerful feminist commitment in films that, increasingly, are accessible to a broad range of viewers, even to viewers unaccustomed to enjoying either experimental or feminist filmmaking. This accessibility is, to a large degree, a function of Friedrich's willingness to use her filmmaking to explore the particulars of her personal experience. And her success in reaching audiences represents a powerful attack on the assumption that viewers will only respond to conventional film rhetoric.

At the beginning of her filmmaking career, Friedrich's films were fueled by a grim feminism, personal only in the most general sense. *Cool Hands, Warm Heart* documents several women performing conventional, but normally private, women's rituals—one woman shaves her

legs; another, her armpits; and a third braids her hair—on a crowded
street on the Lower East Side, as a way of rebelling against canons of
"feminine modesty" in commercial media and against those independent
filmmakers who argue that films shouldn't polemicize an identifiable
politic. *Scar Tissue* uses footage recorded on New York City streets to
reveal the workings of patriarchy, in a mood of numbed horror.

The next two films, and especially *Gently Down the Stream*, are
more specific to Friedrich's personal experience. In preparation for
making *Gently Down the Stream*, Friedrich spent months collecting her
dreams, writing them down, and etching the most powerful and suggestive into the emulsion of black-and-white film, word by word. At times
there is no imagery except for the hand-scratched words; in other
instances, the words, which are always the foreground of the film, are
combined with photographed imagery, much of which provides metaphors for our voyage along Friedrich's "stream" of consciousness (a
woman exercises on a rowing machine, another swims). In general, the
dreams recorded in *Gently Down the Stream* reveal a conflict between
Friedrich's Roman Catholic upbringing and her lesbian desires. Indeed, the words that tell these dreams often seem to quiver with the
intensity of this conflict.

The Ties That Bind, Friedrich's first long film and her first 16mm film
with sound (an early Super-8 film, *Hot Water* [1978], no longer in distribution, had sound), combines elements of documentary (on the soundtrack
she interviews her German-born mother about her experiences growing
up in Germany during the thirties as an anti-Nazi German) with elements
familiar from avant-garde forms of cinema: the visuals are a mix of Friedrich's hand-scratched questions of her mother (we hear only her
mother's responses on the soundtrack, not the questions that provoke
them); photographic footage recorded with a hand-held Super-8 camera
during Friedrich's visit to Germany to investigate her roots (this material
has a gestural feel reminiscent of Jonas Mekas and Stan Brakhage); 16mm
footage of her mother in her current Chicago environment, and of her
own trip to a demonstration at the Seneca Army Depot in upstate New
York; archival footage recorded during the Second World War in Germany; and home movies made soon after Friedrich's mother arrived in
the United States with her GI husband at the end of the war. Diverse as
the film's sources of information are, they are bound tightly by Friedrich's
intricate editing, which develops a range of thematic and formal "ties"
between the various visual and auditory strands of the film. *The Ties That
Bind* is a consistently moving record of a filmmaker's coming to terms
with her mother's troubled past and her own threatened present.

Friedrich's decision to explore her German background confronts an
implicit cultural taboo. Like many of us who have German roots, Frie-

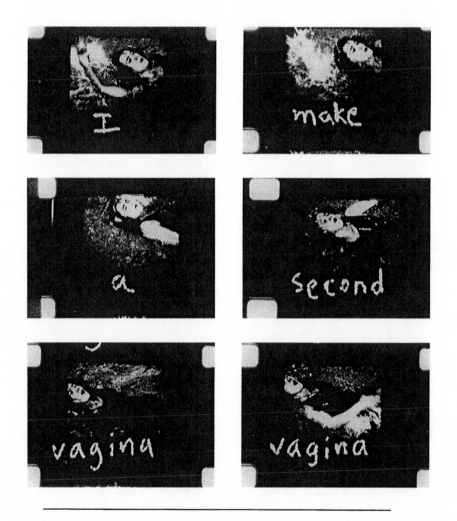

Part of one of the dreams from Friedrich's Gently Down the Stream *(1981) (frames should be read left to right).*

drich was/is haunted by the specter of the Holocaust: even if we grew up after the Holocaust ended, our genetic inheritance seems to condemn us. At the time when she talked with her mother, Friedrich could not be sure what her mother might reveal about herself—and by implication, about Friedrich. And even once she had learned of her mother's fervent disapproval of the Nazis and what this stance may have cost her, Friedrich had to have been well aware that whatever suffering her mother and the rest of her family endured was probably mild compared to what went on in the camps, and that therefore a film that tried to create sympathy for a German family could seem counterproductive. The finished film, however, is useful and revealing in many ways, not least of which is that it allows people of German heritage to admire the courageous example of some Germans in resisting the Nazi horror and, one hopes, to feel their own progressive urges reconfirmed. Of course, Friedrich's decision to use the production of a film as a "space" within which to try and resolve her personal conflicts with regard to her mother and their shared heritage is a departure from the detachment of conventional cinema and much independent cinema, as well.

Damned If You Don't returns to the issue of Catholicism and lesbian sexuality. But where *Gently Down the Stream* grimly dramatizes the psychic trauma this conflict seems to have created in Friedrich, *Damned If You Don't* is as good-humored as it is daring. Friedrich imbeds a narrative about a nun (played by Peggy Healey) pursued by another woman (played by Ela Troyano) within an informal investigation of some of the ways in which the issue of nuns and sexuality has played itself out in Western culture.

Like *The Ties That Bind, Damned If You Don't* is an amalgam of elements from disparate cinema traditions: the film begins with an amusing précis/critique of the Michael Powell–Emeric Pressburger melodrama *Black Narcissus* (1947), which the woman protagonist is watching on television. The woman's subsequent pursuit of the nun is interwoven with documentary imagery of nuns and convents, with formally lovely and metaphorically suggestive passages focusing on swans, snakes swimming in water, and white whales at the New York City Aquarium, and with a variety of information on the soundtrack: an interview with a high school friend (Makea McDonald), passages from Judith C. Brown's *Immodest Acts: The Life of a Lesbian Nun in Renaissance Italy* (New York: Oxford University Press, 1986), and moments of self-reflexive conversation. The beautifully choreographed final scene of the nun and the Troyano character making love is the culmination of the narrative.

Damned If You Don't is a courageous film on two different levels. Obviously, even to *seem* to attack nuns is highly unusual, and to do so with humor and in the name of an open expression of lesbian desire will be downright shocking for many viewers. The lovemaking scene where the Troyano character undresses the nun is as outrageous as it is sensual. The second level of Friedrich's courage is her rejection of what has often been seen as one of the central tenets of feminist filmmaking since the mid seventies. Once the filmic gaze was recognized as essentially (or at least traditionally) male, some filmmakers and critics came to see traditional film pleasure as an implicit acceptance of the workings of patriarchy, and it seemed necessary to expunge female sexuality and nudity from serious cinema in the service of progressive feminism. Other forms of film pleasure also seemed questionable: the sensuous rhythms, textures, and structures of personal and structural forms of avant-garde film were seen as self-indulgent. While some filmmakers refused to take such concerns seriously and continued to make films to be enjoyed, regardless of the implicit gender politics, other filmmakers eliminated or interrupted all conventional forms of film pleasure.

Friedrich may have originally been in sympathy with this feminist position (*Cool Hands, Warm Heart* and *Scar Tissue* suggest she was), but by *Damned If You Don't,* she had come to see it as a dead end, an attitude that implicitly reconfirms patriarchy. If male films are sensual and pleasurable, while female (or at least "feminist") films are rigorously unsensual and pleasureless, males are defined, once again, as having something females lack. Traditionally, women have been "damned" to function as cogs in an exploitative male cinema that thrives on female sensuality. In some feminist films, women are "damned" a second time, to wander through ideologically pure but pleasureless (or, at least, sexless) narratives. *Damned If You Don't* is Friedrich's declaration of independence from this pattern. It energizes the feminist response to patriarchal cinema by locating it within a context of two forms of reappropriated film pleasure: the excitement of melodramatic narrative and the sensuous enjoyment of cinematic texture, rhythm, and structure. Friedrich's decision not only to include a representation of female sexuality but to use it as the triumphant conclusion of the film is crucial. Friedrich has cinematically reappropriated the pleasure *of* women *for* women. Yet she is willing to share this pleasure with men (her use of imagery of a male and female tightrope walker to announce the lovemaking of the two women suggests that the sexual pleasure of women need not be confined to women): if men are fortunate enough to be able to take pleasure in the pleasure of women, so be it! Regardless of what men or women do, however, Friedrich can *not* be a nun, Catholic or filmic.

In *Sink or Swim,* which can easily be seen as a companion piece to *The Ties That Bind,* Friedrich returns to her family history to explore her relationship with her father, anthropologist/linguist Paul Friedrich, who left the family when Friedrich was a child. In *Sink or Swim,* Friedrich confronts the brutality built into the conventional nuclear family by virtue of societal gender assumptions, directly and personally, though with subtlety and thoughtfulness. Her goal is not simply to respond to the long-term effects of painful childhood experiences but to aid viewers—men and women—in thinking about their own experiences as children and their own approaches to parenting.

As is true in all Friedrich's longer films, her desire to enhance viewers' willingness to interact in humane ways is reflected by her cinematic approach, which is, on one hand, to bring together filmmaking traditions that are normally (at least in North America) considered distinct and, on the other, to edit her visuals and her sound track so that these separate sources of information intersect in a wide range of obvious and subtle ways. *Sink or Swim* is a personal narrative recorded in a gestural style, but its organization suggests "structural film," particularly Hollis Frampton's alphabetically arranged *Zorns Lemma*: the individual stories that make up *Sink or Swim* are presented in reverse alphabetical order, according to the first letters of their one-word titles: "Zygote," "Y Chromosome," "X Chromosome," . . . Friedrich tells her story clearly and powerfully enough to move a broad spectrum of filmgoers, but the interplay between sound and image can feed the eye and mind for many viewings.

First Comes Love is a meditation on marriage—on traditional heterosexual marriage and on the widespread illegality of same-sex marriage. The film begins with imagery of several couples arriving at New York City churches, with family and friends, to be married, accompanied on the sound track by a variety of musical homages to love and marriage. But once the various couples have arrived at the altar, Friedrich suddenly shifts to a rolling text (a ceremonial "scripture" of her own) that lists every country in the world where same-sex marriage is legally forbidden. When the long listing is complete, Friedrich returns to the marriage imagery and records the couples exiting the church, having their pictures taken, and leaving for receptions and honeymoons. At the very end of the film, Denmark is revealed as the only nation where same-sex marriage is currently legal. *First Comes Love* is a poignant combination of Friedrich's frustration with the conventional assumption that "first comes love, then comes marriage" (an idea clearly proven false by the worldwide resistance to same-sex lovers legalizing their bonds), of her recognition, often suggested by her editing, that conventional marriage continues to be about the consolidation of money and power, and of her sadness in being left out of a form of bonding that for many couples is deeply meaningful (this sadness is implicit in Friedrich's characteristically beautiful black-and-white imagery and in the subtlety of her interconnections between image and sound).

Friedrich and I discussed the films up through *Damned If You Don't* in March 1986 and again in September 1987. We discussed *Sink or Swim* in June 1990.

MacDonald: I find *Scar Tissue* and *Cool Hands, Warm Heart* hard to look at. They seem to have been made within a small circle of friends as feminist exercises. The change from those two films to *Gently Down the Stream* seems considerable, even though the style of all three films is related. I feel somewhat the same way about the jump from *Gently Down the Stream* and *But No One* to *The Ties That Bind*. Do you see big leaps in power from the earlier films to the later ones?

Friedrich: I think of those early films as being too obvious, or too much about a single issue or image. *Cool Hands* is about these acted-out women's rituals; *Scar Tissue* is about certain midtown men and women. *Scar Tissue* was made with a small audience in mind. I think it was made in part as a response to Dave Lee and his film *Remembering Clearing Space* [1976, 1979], which was made with black and clear leader and footage from the Margaret Mead film *Trance and Dance in Bali* [1952]. We'd had this ongoing debate about what happens when you use clear and black leader. When I made *Scar Tissue,* I was doing the opposite of what he did. We were very close then, and we talked a lot about film. I do tend to think of just one or two people when I'm working on a film. Actually, after I made *Scar Tissue,* I made a film that you haven't seen. It had two titles: first it was called *Someone Was Holding My Breath*; I changed it to *I Suggest Mine.* I didn't like that film; it was so personal, about such neurotic aspects of my self-image, that I re-edited it, but I still didn't like it. Then I started working on a film about excision in Africa.

MacDonald: That's the removal of the clitoris?

Friedrich: Yes. And sewing up the vagina and the labia. I was really freaked out about the subject. I'd seen Ann Poirier's film *Primal Fear* [1978]. In it there was this brief bit of footage of an excision being done on a little girl in Africa. When I saw that footage at the New York Film Festival, I screamed out, "No!" But then I got interested in doing a film about excision. I read lots of material, and I started doing scratched-word tests because I wanted to make the film a conversation. One voice would be the "experts," like Western doctors or African men and women who would talk about why it's done, and the other voice would be the women describing what it felt like and their memories of it. I did a lot of tests with scratched words, but then I realized that that was a completely inappropriate form for such a film, which would have to be a much more accessible sort of documentary. Since I didn't want to work in a documentary style, I gave it up.

I started working on *Gently Down the Stream* because I was having a lot of trouble, and I wanted to reread my journals and then burn them all. Instead I got interested in many of the dreams I'd recorded. I developed *Gently Down the Stream* from those dreams.

When I made *I Suggest Mine,* I thought I should try to do something very personal, entirely about me. I failed miserably. I was much too self-conscious about exposing myself. By the time I got around to *Gently Down the Stream,* I had accepted the idea of using personal material, but I had also found a way to work with it with some sort of distance. At first, when I was reading the dreams and thinking about them, I felt really embarrassed about revealing them. But by the time I began to see how they looked when they were scratched out and saw what images went with them, I had lost some of that personal investment.

When I was doing *Cool Hands* and *Scar Tissue,* I was much more rigid in my thinking, both about film and about myself as a woman. With *Scar Tissue,* especially, I wanted to be very extreme, to just use a few elements and be very aggressive with them. In both films I wanted to convince people of something; I wanted to show them some little corner of the world and say, "You see, this is the way it is, and it's not good that it's this way." When I made *Gently Down the Stream,* I felt differently. I had certain assumptions about what my dreams meant, and I certainly had ideas about what it meant to be involved with a woman and then involved with a man. I had ideas about how to work with dreams and how I felt they were useful. But I also liked the idea that, being less doctrinaire, I was leaving things more to chance. I wasn't saying that all women are good or that it's only good to be with women. I was saying, well, you know, things are kind of messy in our private lives and in our dream worlds and that's just the way it is. At first it seemed that if I was going to be a "good" feminist I should show the relationship with the woman to be a good one as compared to the relationship with a man. But I couldn't because the dreams that I had about the relationship with the woman revealed a lot of problems. The dreams revealed that both relationships were pretty much failures, and that seemed more realistic than trying to sell some theory about how relationships *should* be.

MacDonald: Are there a couple of shots from *Scar Tissue* in *The Ties That Bind?*

Friedrich: Yes. There's also a lot of footage from *Hot Water* [1978], my very first film, in *Gently Down the Stream*: the stuff of the woman swimming in the pool and the woman rowing on the rowing machine.

MacDonald: That material looks like found footage from another era.

Friedrich: Yes, it does. I really liked shooting that first film. It wasn't a very good film, but it was fun to do. I liked the footage in it, but I wasn't crazy about the way it was put together. I was low on footage when I was making *Gently Down the Stream,* and I figured I might as well use this stuff. Actually, I was thinking of using some outtakes from *But No One* in *Damned If You Don't.* I like the idea of recycling things and of finding new meanings, in a new context, for images that have appeared in earlier films.

MacDonald: There are some very weird dreams in *Gently Down the Stream.* The dream about making the second vagina and the image of the baby that crumbles are pretty powerful. I used the film in several classes this year, and the students found the film outrageous. They were riled up about it.

Friedrich: If people see the film without knowing it's made from dreams, they do tend to get very anxious. But if they recognize that the texts are dreams, they tend to accept the film. We all have weird dreams.

MacDonald: Well, there's also the question of admitting what you dream or feel. We may know we have embarrassing dreams, but publicly admitting what they are is something different. I'll bet most people repress confusing dreams very quickly.

Friedrich: I've been surprised when I've traveled with *Gently Down the Stream* how many people tell me that they never remember their dreams or if they do they never bother to write them down. They don't take them seriously. I find that I go through periods when I don't remember any of my dreams, and I feel terrible after a while because I feel like I really need to remember them and look at them. When I went through my journal to find dreams for *Gently Down the Stream,* I found great dreams I hadn't remembered—the one about making the second vagina was one of them. I thought, "What a great image. It's so loaded and says so much"—and I'd forgotten about it! I would never have come up with that image during a conscious moment; I feel grateful for the images we create while dreaming.

The dreams that ended up in the film are suggestive in different ways. Remember the dream where I say that the woman sitting on the stage asks a friend from the audience to come and make love to her? Every time I show the film and I'm in the audience, I think about how somebody in the audience feels. As a filmmaker, I'm doing just what the woman in the dream is doing. I think there's something about making work that has to do with your wanting to please people, to make love with the audience. This dream is a bald statement of a desire that I think is part of a lot of films.

MacDonald: How many dreams did you start with?

Friedrich: Ninety-four. I asked my current lover, who was a man, and a former lover, who was a woman, and one male friend and one female friend (both of whom are gay) to read all the dreams and tell me which ones they liked.

After I got all their responses, I studied them to see which ones the men liked and which ones the women liked. I didn't really use that as the basis for making a final decision about which to use but it did help me to think about the dreams. Finally, I chose to do the dreams about women with moving scratched words and the dreams about men with optically printed freeze-framed scratched words. I did about forty dreams, some with images, many without. I put it all together and showed it to a few people. They said, "It's just horrible; it's way too long! Nobody could ever make any sense of it." So I went through a painstaking process of cutting dreams out: each one I eliminated felt like such a great loss. But that experience was a crucial lesson for me because I learned that no matter how painful it is to let go of material, a film usually benefits from a very severe editing process. As I whittled the film down, I also started developing more ways to use images; I started combining images with dreams that hadn't had any before.

MacDonald: Your use of text reveals a strong sense of poetic timing. Do you read much poetry?

Friedrich: No. I read Walt Whitman one summer—almost nothing but him. The only other poets I've read closely are Sappho and Anna Ahkmatova. But I have trouble reading poetry. I get impatient with it.

MacDonald: There's something about the timing and the spacing in your films that reminds me of William Carlos Williams.

Friedrich: Well, the timing is important. I started out with each dream on an index card, and kept whittling down the phrasing until it was really succinct. Then I started breaking it up into lines to see how it should be phrased in the film. I heard the rhythm of each dream very clearly in my mind before I started scratching. I would scratch them onto the film and project the results. If something wasn't right, I'd cut out a few frames or add a few frames.

MacDonald: I remember Hollis Frampton saying that once you *can* read you can't *not* read. When the words appear, the viewer has no choice about reading them. You participate in this film on a different level from the way you participate in a conventional film.

Friedrich: I have a fantasy that one day I'll show *Gently Down the Stream* and the audience will say the whole thing out loud.

I'm at a strange point now, as far as using text goes. I had so much fun making *Gently Down the Stream* that I ended up making a second, similar film, *But No One.* I liked what I did in *But No One,* but I wasn't crazy about it. *But No One* is made out of a certain amount of repression and depression, and it shows.

MacDonald: Even the device of scratched texts doesn't work as well.

Friedrich: I feel very intimate with that device, but I also feel that I might not be able to use it much longer. Actually, I pushed it further in *Gently Down the Stream* than I did in *But No One* or *The Ties That Bind*.

MacDonald: You may articulate it more in *Gently Down the Stream* than in *The Ties That Bind*, but in the longer film you found a way of using it without its dominating the entire experience.

Friedrich: One large area that I haven't really worked with is scratching words over images. I mean I did that a little in *The Ties That Bind* (when I go to my mother's house, for example) and at the end of *Gently Down the Stream*, where "blindness" is spelled out over the water with that incredible movement. That's one area I'd like to explore more. I'm interested in what would happen if I started using scratched text to comment on the images that you're seeing, or to completely confuse the image, to have them be so contradictory that you couldn't, or wouldn't, want to be looking and reading at the same time.

MacDonald: What got you started on *The Ties That Bind*?

Friedrich: Well, I remember that I was in California on tour with Leslie Thornton, showing films. I wanted to make a movie, and I kept thinking of the phrase, "She built a house"—just the phrase. I was doing a lot of drawings and making little notes to myself about having a sense of home, and one day I suddenly thought of my mother. She was someone I thought of as without her own home—although she's lived in the United States since 1950 and is settled here, she'd always seemed a little bit uprooted to me, partly because I'd never met any of her relatives.

Suddenly, I thought that her life was something I absolutely had to find out about, something I had to work with. I went to Chicago to see her. I had to lie a little bit, to make it seem like this wasn't such a serious project. I was very diffident about it when I talked to her, and then I showed up with lots of equipment. I think she was suspicious. But she was great about the filming. She was so unself-conscious, and *I'm* the sort of person who *hates* to be in front of the camera, still or movie. I thought she would be very uptight; I thought she would worry about the way she looked, but she was completely indifferent. She just went about her business, paid no attention to me. One or two times, she said, "Oh, stop that filming for a minute." She'd be having a conversation with me, and I'd be behind this big camera grunting and saying, "Oh yeah? Oh yeah?" and I think after a while she felt uncomfortable with it. But she never refused to let me film anything.

MacDonald: You recorded the tapes later?

Friedrich: No. I did all the interviewing and some shooting on my first visit there, but the film was ruined because my filter holder wasn't completely in and the light was coming through. I went back about a month later and shot all the material you see in the film.

I felt really distressed about the project. I had started on it so quickly because I had such a passion about it, but I hadn't really thought it through. I was still insecure. When I saw the ruined footage, I felt *really* discouraged and almost didn't continue.

MacDonald: How much taping did you do?

Friedrich: I taped for five evenings. I was embarrassed about it. I had originally said to her that we were doing it so that the tapes could be transcribed, so that she could pass on her stories to her children. I was misleading her, and I was afraid that if I pushed certain issues too far, she might wonder what was going on. When I realized how upset she was becoming as a result of the discussions, I was worried. I thought she might just fall to pieces. Maybe suddenly I would say the wrong thing, and it would be the last straw for her, but she came out with a lot more than I expected.

MacDonald: She seems very at ease. She's a good storyteller.

Friedrich: Well, that might be my editing too. I did a lot of editing. There's always a certain artifice in even the most "natural" footage or sound of someone. For example, my mother became very upset when thinking and talking about certain experiences, and she tended to slow down and have long pauses between passages of a story. At first I thought those pauses should remain so that the viewer would feel her searching through her memories, but I realized that the effect would be boring, rather than moving. So I spent a lot of time cutting out silent passages.

MacDonald: The story itself is interesting—the idea of knowing what it felt like to be anti-Nazi in Germany in the thirties. Even if she wasn't a member of The White Rose [an anti-Nazi underground organization discussed in *The Ties That Bind*], it took nerve to be who she was. The audience can empathize with her and admire her. Is she pleased with the film?

Friedrich: If I ever hear myself on tape, I always think, "Oh my god, I sound like such a fool!" She had the same reaction at first, and she also felt that a lot of other people had suffered much more than her, or had been a lot more courageous, and that therefore she wasn't appropriate material for such a film. But the last time she saw the film, she seemed pretty comfortable with it.

Before I made *The Ties That Bind* I had such bad feelings about being German, being the daughter of a German; and my father is half German too. I don't think I really trusted the material I had. When I was working on the film, I told myself to stop worrying, to stop thinking I shouldn't be doing it, to stop disbelieving her, to trust her. I figured if the film was a failure in the long run I wouldn't show it. At some point I just stopped carrying on about it. It was strange to suddenly be thinking of my mother in this respectful way, to really be admiring her for what she did, for surviving. I had never thought of *her*.

MacDonald: She's a remarkable person.

Friedrich: Well, it took me a lot of time to figure that out. I think part of being a teenager is that you're so interested in forming your own identity and not being identified with your parents that you only see their bad side. One night when I was making this film, I was talking to Leslie [Thornton] about it, and said, "It just occurred to me that I learned some really good things from my parents." I was developing a better sense of myself; I was respecting myself more as a worker. I was proud that I could support myself, and I thought, "You know, this came from something; somebody taught me how to do this for myself, and it must have been them."

MacDonald: You said at the screening tonight that you edited *The Ties That Bind* section by section, for seven hundred hours. The subtle interconnections between the imagery, the text, and the sound make it an easy film to see again and again.

Friedrich: I was really scared about editing sound and picture. It was completely unknown territory for me. The temptation was to have this strong sound carry the image, but I was afraid of the image getting lost. I started with a forty-five-second bit (when she says she feels so horrible that she's a German) and inched my way along from there, going to a two-minute section, then to a five-minute section, and finally I could work on a ten-minute section comfortably.

I think part of my process as a filmmaker has been to start at a point where I think nothing is allowed, where you have to work with the barest minimum. I've needed to see what I can make from that minimum and then move in the other direction. I find I'm letting more and more things into my films now, and sometimes it worries me. I'm afraid I'm going to get to be too indulgent, too entertaining and engaging.

But I always want my films to be very sensuous. I want the rhythm and the images to be gratifying. I think it would be foolish, and false, for me to make a film simply in order to be "difficult," to respond to a certain part of the film world that expects that of a film. I enjoy going to films that are both sensual and entertaining, that engage me emotionally as well as intellectually. I'm so bored by most of the films that are made in response to current film theory, and I've never felt obliged to use that sort of language in my own work. I'm perfectly aware of all the pitfalls of the identification that happens when we watch narrative films, and I think that's an issue worthy of serious discussion. But I'd never deny the necessity and pleasure of storytelling, because I've learned so much from being engaged by other people's stories of their lives. I've always wanted to make films that are as emotionally honest as they can be, and then I hope that other people will learn something from seeing them or feel that a part of their own life is being honored in the films.

MacDonald: While I understand the resistance of some filmmakers to the idea that watching films should be a pleasure, I sometimes have a suspicion about the "moral purity" of this stance. I mean, if you're against sensuality in film, you don't have to go through the painstaking process of learning how to create a sensual experience.

Friedrich: Right, right. It's the same thing with humor. I really envy people who can make funny films. That's a great talent. I would love my next film to be funny to a certain degree, but that's very difficult to do. I think there's a difference between humor that you laugh at, and wit, where something is clever and surprising and pleasing in a more subtle way. I think there are witty moments in *Gently Down the Stream* and in *The Ties That Bind.*

MacDonald: One of the things I found really interesting about *The Ties That Bind* is your mother's perspective on the arrival of the liberating allies. She goes into some detail about how they destroyed her house; you can feel how violated she felt by that.

Friedrich: When I talked to my father about it, he said that as far as he was able to observe (and he was never in combat; he came in at the end of the war to work in the denazification program), the first soldiers to come in were the combat troops who had seen a lot of action and were just sick and tired of everything. They came through and went home. It was the service and supply guys who hadn't been in combat, who were looking for some kind of action, that caused trouble. The combat troops had probably gotten rid of a lot of the aggression they felt toward the Germans, but the supply guys were doing it this other way. My mother told me a story about two friends of hers, neighbors, who were raped and killed by American soldiers. I was going to use that story in the film, but I decided that what I had was strong enough. She had many stories about being harassed by American soldiers. She was almost raped one time but got away.

MacDonald: You mentioned earlier that you feel your parents gave you the skills you needed to be able to support yourself. How do you earn money?

Friedrich: I do pasteup. I haven't worked lately but when I do, I get eighteen dollars an hour. I hate it passionately, but I learned how to do it by pasting up the first couple of issues of *Heresies* (with some other women). You just take the text and the picture and set it all up for the printer. It's very exacting, mechanical manual labor. Actually, I think it's affected my filmmaking. My ability to be precise with the scratched texts is partly a result of my experience as a pasteup person. At this point I don't want it anymore as an influence, but I don't know what else I would do to earn a living. During the past two years, I've also been able to earn about twenty percent of my income by doing one-person shows at schools and museums. It gets pretty difficult at times to answer the same questions over and over, but it's important to make contact with the audience, to know the people "out there" who still support these sorts of films. I've also gotten a few grants, which were a real blessing; it would have taken me twice as long to make *Damned If You Don't* without them.

MacDonald: When you took on *The Ties That Bind,* did you assume its length would generate more shows?

Friedrich: I had no idea that *The Ties That Bind* was going to be as long as it was, and I also didn't think that people were going to be that interested in it. It just got longer and longer and more expensive, and then I found that because I had an hour-long film it *was* easier to get shows. Before that, I had always been in group shows. (Actually, I started out doing some programming myself, setting up shows in galleries in the East Village, in churches.) I had never really worried much about getting one-person shows because I kept making these short films and it didn't seem possible. But once I did *The Ties That Bind,* I got lots of invitations. It's always hard to be businesslike about your own art products, but I decided I had to force myself to accept that part of the filmmaking process, to deal with the hard work that comes *after* the hard work of getting the film made.

MacDonald: I would think *The Ties That Bind* could have a pretty good-sized audience, certainly more than just the avant-garde film audience.

Friedrich: I've shown it in a number of places where it seemed like a lot of people in the audience don't see experimental film. Afterward people would come up to me and say, "I've never seen a film like this. I was confused at first, but by the end I really understood and enjoyed it." When I was making the film, I was hard on myself about the relationship of sound and image. I wanted to be very precise, to push the two elements in a way that doesn't happen in a standard documentary, but I also wanted the film to be accessible to people. I respect people's intelligence enough to think that if they were shown this sort of film more often, they would be able to understand it. I don't think people will necessarily run screaming from experimental films, and I wish some programmers had more respect for their audience's intelligence.

And I think people might enjoy playing the games the film sets up. I certainly feel the difference between a film in which the person is trying to be communicative and one where a person is just trying to be obscure and go over everyone's head. I don't think *The Ties That Bind* feels deliberately obscure.

MacDonald: Avant-garde film is always going to have technical "weaknesses," compared to commercial cinema. The secret is to use them to your benefit. When the viewer of *The Ties That Bind* hears the mike bang on the couch, the home-movie feeling of the film is enhanced; it's as if we're sitting in somebody's den looking at the slides of their trip. Your film is technically screwed up just enough to make the viewer feel at ease; it's the polar opposite of Leni Riefenstahl's *Triumph of the Will* [1936], which I've juxtaposed it with in courses a number of times.

Friedrich: I have a very uneasy relationship with the technology of filmmaking. I think I'm careful only up to a point, and it's usually the point where redoing something would mean spending more money than I have. Past that point I think, "Fuck it."

MacDonald: Has *The Ties That Bind* been shown on TV? Has it earned income as a semicommercial theatrical film?

Friedrich: It was shown at a number of festivals, and it was shown on WNYC in New York.

MacDonald: Do you think your work suffers when it's transferred to video?

Friedrich: Scratched words don't look good on video. They lose the crisp articulation and rhythm that's there on film. And the material in *The Ties That Bind* that's blown up from Super-8 to 16mm looks terrible on video. It just falls to pieces. I have a horrible feeling about that because in the past—let's say five or ten years ago—when I would go to a screening of films by women, many of them would be technically poor. There would be this urgency about getting the film made and saying this important thing, and if you didn't expose the image right or if the sound was bad, well those were the breaks. When I've seen my film on video, I've thought, "My god, if somebody just turns this on and doesn't know me and hasn't seen the film projected, they'll think, 'Oh god, another film by a woman that looks like shit.' " Of course, these days many women are making technically competent films. And I think that that earlier period in our history—of making films out of a breathless sense of urgency despite technical limitations—was absolutely crucial. The same process happened in third-world countries when they were first developing their own film industries, and some incredibly powerful films were made despite the lack of technology.

MacDonald: One feminist reaction to conventional cinema has been to confront patriarchal exploitation by eliminating the kinds of pleasure that conventional films thrive on. I'm assuming that in *Damned If You Don't* you're taking the position that there's no reason why feminist films shouldn't be as sensuously pleasurable as conventional cinema.

Friedrich: I think I did have that plan when I started. I wanted to make something that I (and viewers) would enjoy. But I don't think I set out to contradict any other person's film or any other kind of filmmaking. It's true that when I go to films that are determined *not* to provide traditional pleasure, I end up being really frustrated or bored or angry. My reaction to such films has been building for a long time. Even when I was making *Gently Down the Stream,* I had a combative stance toward antipleasure films, but at that time I wasn't able to do as much as I wanted to do in terms of providing pleasure myself. And certainly there wasn't much place for pleasure in *The Ties That Bind.* It wasn't until I was actually into making *Damned If You Don't* that I realized I could create some of the visual (and aural) pleasures I had wanted to experience in other people's films. Maybe it took me this long to be able to begin to work with pleasurable material because I had my own reservations about it. As much as I was angry about what other people were doing, I knew that I wasn't prepared politically or emotionally to do something different. I had to overcome my own backlog of things I *shouldn't* do.

MacDonald: The subject of *Damned If You Don't* doesn't seem a very likely place for humor, and I'm sure to some people it isn't at all funny.

Friedrich: I have a tendency to look at things too seriously. When I made *Damned If You Don't,* I was particularly close to someone who has a really good sense of humor and who definitely pushed me into putting more humor into the film. Also, when I told my brother I was working on the film, he said, "Oh god, why don't you just once make a film about a light subject!" He imagined, rightly, that I was planning another anguished exposition. His saying that really stuck in my mind.

MacDonald: The woman who delivers the critique of *Black Narcissus,* Martina Siebert, does a terrific job.

Friedrich: I chose her partly because she's German and has a German accent. Initially I thought of it as a joke on the expert German scientist in fifties documentaries. But her delivery didn't come through that way. Her English is good, but she didn't always understand the cadence I intended, so a lot of times she said things in an odd way I couldn't have anticipated—which ended up working out for the best.

MacDonald: Another section of the film that's pretty funny, and I assume consciously so, is when the text from *Immodest Acts* is juxtaposed with the shots of the nuns walking around. When the reader says, "I saw Christ coming," one nun looks up as though she sees something coming. It's as if the nuns are unwittingly acting out the story. At the end of the film you apologize to those nuns. Was that because you felt you had made jokes at their expense?

Friedrich: Well, I started the film feeling very angry toward nuns and toward the Catholic church, and I wanted the film to be a condemnation of everything about the church.

MacDonald: Why were you angry at nuns in particular?

Friedrich: Priests had some influence too, but the nuns were more immediate for me because they were my teachers for eight years. And, of course, they're women and they set what I thought was a bad example for me as a woman. But as I worked on the film and remembered more about the nuns, I realized that there was also a very good side to them, and I found myself feeling a lot of affection for some of them. Later, when I had the footage, I just wanted to look at them and remember them somewhat affectionately through this footage.

In the passage you asked about, the nuns are just walking around on the street looking very ordinary. I would look at that material and think about the nun in *Immodest Acts* who's in a delirious state because Christ is supposedly removing her heart while another nun watches from behind a curtain. By combining that text with the footage of nuns looking like they lead a fairly normal life, I wanted to create an uneasy feeling. When you see the nuns, it's hard to imagine that they would go so far as to believe that their hearts could actually be taken out of their bodies. Yet there's an ambiguity: maybe they've all had that kind of experience.

But to answer your earlier question: I apologized at the end because I'd had to lie to the nuns at the convent so that they would let me shoot, and I felt guilty about it.

MacDonald: What did you tell them you were doing?

Friedrich: I said I was making a narrative film about a woman lawyer who's working on a case and struggling with some ethical problem that causes her to have a flashback about a nun she'd had in grade school who taught her an important moral lesson. They were very flattered and liked the idea of my filming. When we were there, they kept coming in and out of the convent and saying hello. If any of them had spent time watching what we were doing, they would have sensed that something else was going on. I mean, here was this nun looking out from behind a tree while another woman was walking by. I don't know if they figured anything out.

MacDonald: At the Flaherty seminar [Friedrich was a guest at the thirty-third Robert Flaherty Seminar in August 1987], after Johan van der Keuken's *The Way South* [1981], you were very angry at his manipulation of the people he filmed. I thought then and still think someone could ask a very similar question of you.

Friedrich: Of course, it's convenient for me to be able to see a distinction between the two.

MacDonald: I'm interested in hearing the distinction.

Friedrich: Well, I would never have interviewed any nuns on film or on tape and then have used the material without their knowing the complete context of the film. All the nuns I shot were in the public domain; they were out in the world. And I wasn't making a direct connection between any of those particular nuns and specific material in the film. I think it would be very different and completely unacceptable for me to interview nuns and then reveal their private lives, the way van der Keuken revealed the people in his film, without their permission. I gave my mother final approval of *The Ties That Bind.* I certainly could have thought, "Fuck her, she's my mother; I can do whatever I want with the material." But if she had said that any part of that film was not permissible to use, I would have removed it. When I filmed at the convent, I very deliberately didn't show the name. I tried not to create a context by which people could identify the convent. I wanted the material to be anonymous.

MacDonald: I would argue that were van der Keuken to explain his politics to the people he films, they would be comfortable about appearing in his film. On the other hand, if the nuns whose images you use knew what the politics of your film were, I'd guess they would be quite horrified.

Friedrich: Again, this may be splitting hairs, and the nuns definitely wouldn't be interested in my hair splitting, but I made a conscious choice not to use any images of them over any explicit sexual material. I thought that would be going too far. I'm sure you're right that they would all be incensed to find themselves in the film, but what can I do? There *are* nuns who have either come out or have gotten involved with men and left the convent, so the issue in the film is legitimate. I don't think it's sacrilegious or vulgar to suggest that some nuns might be sexually frustrated by their vows and might go to certain extremes to break away from their past beliefs and practices.

MacDonald: Damned If You Don't seems related to the tradition of psychodrama and trance film—what P. Adams Sitney has called "visionary film"—where an entranced character (a dreamer, a "seer"—in any case, a representative of the film artist) is pursuing Beauty, Vision, whatever. The Troyano character's pursuit of the nun strikes me as an emblem of your pursuing the subject of nuns as a filmmaker.

Friedrich: I haven't really thought about it that way. I had already shot a fair amount of footage about nuns during the spring and summer of 1986, but it wasn't narrative material. And then in the fall I went to London and was staying with someone who had a tape of *Black Narcissus.* That film pushed me into thinking about my film more in terms of a sexual confrontation between this nun and another woman, rather than as a personal documentary about my experiences growing up Catholic.

So in a way it is true that *Black Narcissus* functioned for me the way I had it function for Ela in the film.

I guess I thought when I was doing *Damned If You Don't* that it was really about my finally coming to terms with my own fear of sex and of dealing with people about sex. The film was going to be a celebration of sex. I guess I did identify with Ela as the aggressor, the one who represented sexual freedom. And I was a little bit scornful of the nun because she embodied my fear. I think that as I went along I felt more and more for the nun, and when I was finished with the film and some time had passed, I realized the film was very much about that fear. My fear must have been pretty great for me to make a film about it.

MacDonald: You know, both characters look a bit like you, but like different parts of you. It's almost like one part of you is being pursued by another part, and the goal of the film is to help you bring the two parts back together, to put them in balance. At first it looks like the sensual person is following the spiritual person, although as the film develops, you realize that if the nun weren't sensual, she wouldn't be having a conflict about sex, and if the Troyano character weren't spiritual, she wouldn't be putting dozens of candles around her bed before they have sex.

Friedrich: I think this kind of psychoanalyzing is a problem in public discourse. Audiences don't know that much about my character and shouldn't need to. The way I would talk about these issues is to focus on one abiding problem within Catholicism, the split between the spiritual and the sexual. One of the really profound lessons I learned as a Catholic—and I don't mean "lesson" in a good sense—was that on the one hand there's a general love for the world, a love that leads one to serve the world, to serve people and God. And then there's another kind of love, a sexual love for someone. The church always splits those two things. Within the context of loving an individual in a marriage with children you are expected to serve your community, but still there is married love and, distinct from it, the love that a person within the church—a nun or a priest—has with God and toward the world. I find that terribly schizophrenic. I think it really fucks people up. I chose Peggy Healey to play the nun character because she has a very sensual face, and I wanted someone who would embody a certain sensuality within a supposedly unsensual context.

MacDonald: It's interesting that you introduce the Other Woman alone, not as part of a community, whereas the nun implicitly does have a community.

Friedrich: That's true. Toward the end of the film, when Ela gets dressed up to go out to the party, I'd planned to show her within a community, and at one point, I thought of her having a friend or a lover.

But that sort of fell by the wayside. It is funny to have her be such a lone wolf. A very powerful thing about being a nun is that you're part of a community of like-minded souls.

To come back to the issue of sex for a moment, in a lot of public discourse sex is defined as something anarchistic and divisive. The sex drive is what ideally unites two people in a very intense way, but it creates a great discord in the world at large, in the form of jealousy, hysteria, whatever. Sex is allowed to function in people's lives when they're young, when they don't have responsibilities; but once responsibilities set in, somehow it gets put on the back burner. Once people are married or coupled, sex with a person outside the marriage creates a terrible problem. I think the church is very aware of that and controls it. It knows that if it were to say that God loves sex as much as he loves anything else—go right ahead and enjoy yourself—it wouldn't be as successful in convincing people to live in strictly monogamous marriages. This idea is implicit in the film. You have this one woman who is part of a coherent community where becoming sexual puts her at great risk. You don't see a context for the other woman so you can never be sure whether she's just picking this nun up or whether she's looking for love and romance and a life happily ever after. That they come together at the end and that sex is what unites them doesn't mean the problem is solved. Although the end is very celebratory within the context of the film, there's still the possibility that in the long run sex will create the same problems for these women that it's created for other people.

MacDonald: There's something almost sad about the fact that it takes so much conflict and self-questioning for this moment to happen. The bells going off at the end not only celebrate their union, but seem a campy way of laughing at our difficulties with sex: why is it so *difficult* all the time?

Friedrich: Right! [laughter] Actually, some people have said, "Well, that nun sure looked like she knew what she was doing." I guess they feel she should have looked more awkward or innocent. Obviously, it would have made the scene much less erotic if I'd shown her fumbling around and complaining and saying, "Oh, don't!" I wanted that final scene to be beautifully choreographed. But I think there's some truth to their lack of awkwardness. All of the stuff that leads up to the moment when you're finally in bed with somebody is where most of the awkwardness and hysteria happens. A lot of times, once you're there, you only think, "God, what a relief! Let's go!"

MacDonald: It's interesting that we see *Black Narcissus* within your black-and-white film. You may know that *Black Narcissus* won an Academy Award for best color.

Friedrich: Oh really? I didn't know that, but the color is beautiful.

The nun (Peggy Healey) is undressed by her lover (Ela Troyano) in Damned If You Don't *(1987).*

MacDonald: Your critique of the film in *Damned If You Don't* doesn't allow the viewer to experience that film's sensuous levels.

Friedrich: Well, that's not completely true. Or I hope it isn't. The way I frame the imagery, very close, is to me a way of appreciating the really high drama of *Black Narcissus*. A lot of narrative films seem to have some very exciting moments connected by a lot of filler, and it was fun to pare *Black Narcissus* down to the bone, to string the exciting moments together and really focus on the sexual hysteria at the core of the film. Powell and Pressburger used lighting to such great effect and created a lot of expression in the faces, which is all you have to work with when you're dealing with characters who are completely covered. I tried to bring some of that out.

Some people have reacted negatively to the roll bars that happen when you film from a TV screen. They think the roll bars are there because I had no control over the technology. When I saw *Black Narcissus* in London, I thought, "This is a fantastic film; I'm going to use it," and the next day I set up my camera and shot it. I came home, developed the film, and there were the roll bars. I thought, "Okay, I can either go back and work it so that there aren't roll bars or I can keep going the way I've begun." Once I had decided that the roll bars were part of the image, it became really interesting to edit for the rhythm of gestures within the shot, combined with the rhythm of the roll bars, combined with the cadence of the speech at the moment. It became an elaborate game to play, though my eyes were on the floor when I was done.

MacDonald: One of the things that draws me to your films is their precise rhythmic control, which I connect with a certain tradition of sixties film—Brakhage, for example.

Friedrich: Actually, a long time ago when Marjorie Keller first showed *Daughters of Chaos* [1980; at the Collective for Living Cinema in New York City], I saw it and liked it. I talked to somebody afterward who said, "It's one of those films that was made on a Steenbeck." At that point I had never worked on a Steenbeck, and so I didn't even know what he meant. He said, "Well you know, it all gets done in the editing." Part of me thought, "Well, that's an interesting criticism; maybe it is a problem," but on the other hand, I found myself thinking that I liked the film and wondered how the method could be so bad if it resulted in something so intricately woven together? I guess I do admire Brakhage's editing, though I don't always admire what he's making the film about. To me the most fantastic part of constructing a film is taking many disparate elements and making some sense out of them, making them work together and inform each other. That process was really hard in *Damned If You Don't* because I had shot so much for a more documentary film, and the more the narrative took shape, the less that other stuff worked with it.

Also, at times I felt really angry at myself for getting caught in this bind between narrative and experimental. That was something I had always warned myself about and critiqued other people for. I had felt that once you start dealing with narrative, there really isn't the room for serious experimentation that there is when you don't use narrative at all. I don't know what will happen the next time I make a film, but in *Damned If You Don't* I do manage to create certain moments I really enjoy, which are a result of the film's mixture of very different approaches.

MacDonald: You could say that the film reclaims certain kinds of pleasure that are the stuff of commercial cinema without accepting the commercial cinema's ideology *and* that the film reclaims certain kinds of pleasure that are particular to avant-garde film without necessarily accepting the ideology of the films in which these avant-garde pleasures are usually experienced.

Friedrich: It seems that the issue is always giving yourself the maximum amount of freedom. If you make narrative film, then—some people would argue—you have more freedom because you're making something that will be accessible to people and will get to more audiences. Other people would say that only if you're doing something extremely

experimental do you have absolute freedom, because you never have to
worry if anyone understands anything you're saying. There are draw-
backs to both positions, and advantages to both. Actually, I think when
they're good, experimental films are as accessible as good narrative
films.

MacDonald: Name some experimental films that you think compete
on an enjoyment level with commercial films.

Friedrich: I'd say a number of films by Brakhage or Frampton or
Maya Deren. Margie Keller's films. Leslie Thornton's. God, there are
so many.

I think that in the past my animosity toward narrative film had to do
with not having the usual experience of identification. This was partly
because I'm a woman (I saw a lot of films about interesting male characters and stupid female characters) and at times because I couldn't identify with the romantic line of the films. One of the things that changed
me was finally seeing Fassbinder's films. I certainly have my differences
with his style and with what some of his films are about, but I have a
strong identification with many of his films. When I first saw them, I had
the feeling that here finally was a narrative filmmaker who was talking
about stuff that I wanted talked about in films. Experimental films were
mind-expanding for me in other ways that related to my studying art
history, especially painting and sculpture.

It's tempting to want to work on every possible level in a film. Narrative is tempting in its way, but I can't imagine eliminating the footage
that deals with elements of the materiality of film. There *is* a danger.
You can make something that's terribly compromised, that doesn't do
either thing well. To me *Damned If You Don't* was risky because I didn't
know what I was going to end up with. One of my oldest friends, who
had once been an experimental filmmaker, was very critical of *Damned
If You Don't.* He saw it as a weak compromise.

MacDonald: I'd say that since conventional narrative cinema and
experimental cinema have been ghettoized away from each other, the
radical thing to do is to bring them together.

The critique of *Black Narcissus,* which is funny and precise and
which, I'm sure, nearly everyone enjoys, builds patience that allows the
more materially experimental elements to be accepted by the audience.
Because you begin by giving them elements of conventional pleasure,
you enable them to go with less conventional experiences.

Friedrich: What I felt I was doing by beginning with the *Black Narcissus* material was saying, "OK, you want a narrative; here, take it: you
can have it. And you can have it just for its high points; you don't have
to slog through all the bullshit, all the transitions." In a way it was a joke
on the conventional narrative "hook." I do think there's a real awkward-

ness for about five minutes after the *Black Narcissus* critique is over, when the audience has to shift out of this really safe, funny world into something that's less clear. And I did want the *Black Narcissus* critique to be interesting and amusing on its own terms.

MacDonald: Are Makea McDonald's reminiscences her own or did you write them?

Friedrich: I interviewed seven women who had gone to Catholic schools. One was my sister; four were women I've known from living in New York; and two were women I went to high school with. I had gone to school with Makea and met her again in New York after many years. Some of the other women were gay, but they didn't really talk about their relationship to nuns in terms of being gay. For a while I tried to collage their voices, but it got too confusing and so I settled on Makea. She was the only one who talked about having crushes on nuns, and I really identified with some of what she said, not just about nuns, but about other things too. I particularly love what she says during the Coney Island section, when she talks about her spirit splitting from her body when she had sex with a man. That was really beautiful. It was nice to discover her again and have her be such a crucial element in the film.

MacDonald: She enacts one of the conflicts that the film's about. She talks about being gay and yet she also sings the Lord's Prayer.

Friedrich: Yes. That ambivalence was very appropriate for the film. And since she's a trained soprano she has a powerful voice.

MacDonald: We see two motifs during *Damned If You Don't*: the black-and-white snake that curls through the water and the swan through the fence. On one level both are reminiscent of the nuns because of their formal coloring, but both are also traditional phallic images. I assume that you're reappropriating the imagery so that it represents female sexuality.

Friedrich: The first time the snake and the swan appear is when Ela has fallen asleep after seeing *Black Narcissus*. My alternating between them was meant to be a dream sequence of hers. I was thinking of the snake being the Ela character (its movements are very sensual but sort of dangerous) and the swan being the nun. But actually, I think it was just that I loved the footage and wanted to use it, and worked it in that way!

MacDonald: At the end you announce the women's sexual union by showing a routine between male and female tightrope walkers. It's a convenient metaphor for the nun's doing this chancy thing of coming to the other woman's room. But why did you use a heterosexual tightrope couple?

Friedrich: I liked the dance between them. I thought it was a wonderful ballet of a seduction. I certainly considered that it was a heterosexual moment right before a homosexual moment, but I don't see sex as exclusively heterosexual or homosexual. At a discussion of *Damned If You Don't,* somebody asked whether I was trying to imply that all nuns are lesbians. I really hope that people don't think that that's what I'm saying in the film; it's very important to me that people *don't* think that. To be provocative, I said, "Well, I think it would have happened exactly the same way if it had been a man and the nun." At the time I thought to myself, "That isn't entirely true!" But I wanted to make people think about it. I think the whole ritual of seduction works out to be pretty much the same thing between a man and a woman or between a woman and a woman—at least that's been my experience. There are differences, but there's also something universal about being attracted to somebody and trying to make something happen about it.

MacDonald: Sink or Swim is about your relationship with your father, but the way in which you present your struggle to come to grips with that relationship is unusual. Probably of all your films, *Sink or Swim* has the most rigorously formal organization. The only other film I know that uses the alphabet as a central structural device is Frampton's *Zorns Lemma.* Obviously, your film deals more directly and openly with personal material than Frampton's did, but I wonder, is there any conscious reference to cinematic fathers, as well as to your biological father?

Friedrich: That's a hard question to answer. Offhand, I'd say I wasn't making a conscious reference to any other filmmakers, but that the structure was determined more by the fact of my father's being a linguist. I thought that using the alphabet was an obvious choice for the overall structure. I've certainly been influenced by many filmmakers, including some of the so-called structural filmmakers, like Frampton or Ernie Gehr, but my films are never meant to be a direct comment on or a reworking of ideas from other people's films.

I tend to think of the structural film school as avoiding the use of personal, revealing subject matter; I think they're more concerned with how film affects one's perception of time and space than with how it can present a narrative. Whenever I set out to make a film, my primary motive is to create an emotionally charged, or resonant, experience—to work with stories from my own life that I feel the need to examine closely, and that I think are shared by many people. With that as the initial motive, I then try to find a form that will not only make the material accessible but will also give the viewer a certain amount of cinematic pleasure. In that I feel somewhat akin to the structural filmmakers, since I do like to play with the frame, the surface, the rhythm, with layering and repetition and text, and all the other filmic elements that are precluded when one is trying to do something more purely narrative or documentary.

In the text of *Sink or Swim,* I had to make a decision about form. I was using stories from my own life and began by writing them in the first person, but I got tired of that very quickly. I sounded too self-indulgent. Writing them over in the third person was quite liberating. The distance I got from speaking of "a girl" and "her father" gave me more courage, allowed me to say things I wouldn't dare say in the first person, and I think it also lets viewers identify more with the material, because they don't have to be constantly thinking of me while listening to the stories. Some people have told me afterward that they weren't even aware it was autobiographical, which I like. The point of the film is not to have people know about *me*; it's to have them think about what we all experience during childhood, in differing degrees.

On the other hand, it can sometimes be a problem to impose a structure on a story. I was happy to have thought about using the alphabet, but then that forced me to produce exactly twenty-six stories, no more, no less. I went into a panic at first, thinking that I had either seventy-five stories or only ten, and wasn't sure that I would be able to say all I wanted to say within the limits of the twenty-six. But that became a good disciplinary device; it forced me to edit, to select carefully for maximum effect.

MacDonald: I think the irony is that Hollis, for example, really thought his formal tactics were keeping his films from being personal (his use of Michael Snow to narrate *nostalgia* is similar to your use of the young girl to narrate the stories in *Sink or Swim*). When I talked with him about his films, he rarely mentioned any connection between what he made and his personal life—a conventionally "masculine" way of dealing with the personal in art. But from my point of view, his best films—*Zorns Lemma, nostalgia, Poetic Justice* [1972], *Critical Mass* [1971]—are always those in which the personal makes itself felt, despite his attempts to formally distance and control it.

Friedrich: The issue for me is to be more direct, or honest, about my experiences but also to be analytical. I think there's always a problem in people seeing my films and immediately applying the word "personal." *Sink or Swim is* personal, but it's also very analytical, or rigorously formal.

I don't like to generalize about anything, but I do think it's often the case that the more a person pretends or insists they're not dealing with their own feelings, the more those feelings come out in peculiar ways in their work. Historically, it's been the position of a lot of male artists to insist that they are speaking universally, that they're describing experiences outside of their own and thereby being transcendent. I think conversely that you get to something that's universal by being very specific. Of course, I think you can extend beyond your own experience; you can speak about your own experience while also describing the experience of other people you're close to or decide to know. But I think you have to start at home.

MacDonald: Maybe these things are cyclical. I'm sure those late sixties, early seventies filmmakers who avoided the personal—Frampton and Snow, Yvonne Rainer—were reacting against the sixties demand that art, including film art, had to be personal. You bring two things together—the sixties' emphasis on the personal *and* the reaction against it—and make the intersection into something that exploits the useful parts of both approaches.

Friedrich: I am a child of both worlds. When I was studying art history, I really responded to conceptual art, minimal art—those approaches which were very much about form and not about personal drama. But then, of course, I grew up through the women's movement and from the start really responded to the personal drama involved there. Not just that: I love fiction, I love to read about other people's lives, to learn about the choices people make and the ways in which they survive, or overcome, their personal histories. So I feel very much caught between the two approaches and I learn from both.

As an artist, it's important to me to keep both issues alive: to remember that my responsibility is to speak honestly about how it feels to be alive, and that my pleasure is to use my medium to its greatest advantage. I wouldn't be happy if I only let film tell a story in a conventional form, but I would feel that the heart of the work was missing if I only worked with the film as a material, if I only investigated its formal properties. The film scene is in a constant state of flux, and I think this effort to convey meaningful subject matter through unconventional form occupies a lot of filmmakers today. Hopefully, the lines between narrative, experimental, and documentary will continue to be broken down.

MacDonald: Now that you've made a film about your father, as well as the film about your mother, it's probably inevitable that the two films will be paired a lot. When you made *The Ties That Bind,* did you already assume that, sooner or later, you'd come back to your history with your father?

Friedrich: I know some people always have three or four projects in mind, but I never know what I'm going to do next until I'm completely finished with my current project. Certainly when I was interviewing my mother for *The Ties That Bind* and she got onto the subject of them getting divorced, it really struck a nerve and I thought it might be something to explore later.

One time a friend said it seemed like all of my films have been about my father—not really *about him,* exactly, but about reacting to his influence, or trying to get away from his influence, which is, in a larger sense, reacting to patriarchy. That was a pretty good observation, and I suspected there was going to come a time when I would have to deal with the question of patriarchy more directly, to look at how it happened closest to home, not *out there* somewhere.

MacDonald: This film is clearly going to have a larger audience than some of the other films, just because it's in synch with the pervasive, contemporary issue of child abuse. What's interesting about *Sink or Swim* is its focus not on the most extreme types of child abuse, but on the situations men create because they feel that in order to *be* men, they have to act in a certain way. On one hand, you uncover the brutality that's gendered into the family situation. On the other hand, as much as there are things your father did that you really dislike, even hate, the film suggests an ambivalence about him and about his influence on you.

Friedrich: Yes. I agree with what you said about gender, that abuse is more likely because of the inhuman situations that are intrinsic to a society that divides roles along gender lines. But *Sink or Swim* is also like *Mommie Dearest*: it's about the damage either parent can do when they're trying to shape their child in their own image. Most parents, either instinctively or consciously, try to instill their values in their child. They have a lot of ambitions themselves and, consequently, a lot of ambitions for their children. They force their children into activities or try to instill certain ideas in them that are not good, not natural for the child. I can see from watching the children of friends and relatives that part of who we are is formed by our parents and part of us is there from Day One. If you have a kid who's not naturally ambitious or aggressive and you try to make him that, you're just going to bend him out of shape. On the other hand, if you have ambitious children and don't encourage them, you can be very destructive.

To answer the second half of your question—about my ambivalence about my father: people have said to me, "It can't be all that bad, because look where you are," or "You're not a destroyed person; you're capable, you've made films, you've lived a relatively good life." I recognize that, and that's the source of my ambivalence. Certainly, I've learned to do things from him that have stood me in good stead over the years, just as I have from my mother.

Moreover, since the film is about how I've been affected by *my* childhood, it would have been grossly unfair not to acknowledge how my father was affected by his. I tried to speak to that by including the story about his younger sister drowning and showing how he spent many years afterward trying to overcome his guilt and loss. I put that story right before the one about him punishing my sister and me by holding our heads under water for too long, because I wanted to give a context to that punishment, to show that although we were devastated by his punishment, we were being punished by someone who had suffered his own childhood traumas.

One of the most painful things to realize in making the film was that we all inherit so much sorrow and hurt from our parents. We aren't the product of perfectly balanced adults; we are each created by people who have a legacy of their own, which goes back through each family line. On my good days, I try to believe that each generation rids itself of a bit of the violence of the prior generations, that with education and greater material well-being we wouldn't have such widespread abuse. But unfortunately I think the solutions are extremely complex, and I can see that simple notions like education are hardly an answer.

MacDonald: The most obvious example of your ambivalence is the source of the title, which refers to the incident of his throwing you into the pool for you to "sink or swim," since you wanted to learn to swim. At the end of that story, you admit you've remained an avid swimmer.

Friedrich: But the swimming was fraught with all kinds of anxiety, which is why at the end of the film I tell the story about wanting to swim all the way across the lake and realizing that maybe I'm not physically capable of it, and am certainly very frightened at the thought of doing it, but feel compelled to do it anyway, because of him. It's at that moment that I finally say, "No, I don't have to do that. I can enjoy swimming, but on my terms, and I won't take on his standards for what makes a good swimmer or a brave swimmer," and then I swim back to shore.

MacDonald: Although there's an irony there, too, because you swim halfway across the lake and then back, which means you actually swam as far as all the way across.

Friedrich: I think the ambivalence reveals a great deal about the stubbornness of human nature. Many children who are born into situations that undermine them in certain ways still manage to survive beyond the situations. The question is why parents build that degree of uncertainty and anxiety and fear into the family setup. If you want your children to learn something, why not teach them in a way that is constructive and supportive, rather than by terrorizing them? It's been standard practice for parents to get children to learn to do something by scaring them in one way or another about what will happen if they don't learn to do it. I don't think that's the way people learn. It's certainly not the way you learn to do something you later enjoy.

MacDonald: I think in his generation there was this feeling that unless you were capable of terrorizing your kids a little, you weren't a serious parent. Scaring them was almost a way of demonstrating how much you cared. As a young parent, I remember debating in many situations whether I was wimping out and doing my child damage by not being tough enough to do something that in the long run would be good, even if in the short run it was bad. And I think your father's generation felt this even more strongly.

Did you talk with your siblings when you were making this film?

Friedrich: Yes. My sister is a year older than I, and my brother six years younger, so I was interested in their different memories of childhood. My sister and I shared a lot of the experiences I mention in this film, and we lived longer with my father, so she was able to confirm many of my stories. She had other stories she wanted me to include in the film, but I stayed with those which had the most resonance for me. Since my brother was much younger, and was only five years old when my parents got divorced, he didn't know about, or hadn't shared, some of the events in the film, but I valued his perspective a great deal. He has slightly more distance from my father and was concerned that the material be presented fairly, that it not function simply as vendetta, which was also a concern of mine. In fact, he had a funny reaction to *The Ties That Bind.* He said, "Jesus, I hope you never make a film about me!" I certainly can't blame him for that sentiment; it's a weird and suspect process to make films based so openly on one's own family.

MacDonald: It seems inevitable that at some time or another your father will see the film. What do you think about that?

Friedrich: I dread it. When I first started working on the stories, I had a lot of anger, obviously—I even thought about sending a script to him. I had vengeful feelings. But the longer I worked on it, the less I wanted to punish him, and the more I felt I was not doing it so that *he* would finally acknowledge my experience, but so that *I* could acknowledge my experience.

The nuclear family is based on a relationship in which one person (the parent) has a lot more power and control than another (the child). Because of this, I think children are constantly having their feelings denied by their parents. If the child is unhappy and the parents can afford to acknowledge the unhappiness, they do it; but if the parents can't acknowledge the unhappiness because it reflects badly on them, they won't. For me, it was a matter of writing these stories so that I could finally say to myself, "This *did* happen to me, and this is the effect it had on me," regardless of his experience. I'm sure he has a very different interpretation of a lot of the stories, which is understandable—everyone sees things from their own perspective, their own history.

By the time I finished the film, I really felt that I was making it so I could understand what had happened *and* so other people who had the same experience could have that experience acknowledged. I don't think the sole purpose of art is to provide acknowledgment for people, but I think that's one of the things art can do. You can see a film or read a book that in some way corresponds to your experiences, good or bad, and you might feel stronger because you see yourself reflected in it. That's what being in the world is all about—having common experiences with other people. I hope that's the effect the film will have.

MacDonald: During the film's coda, we see a home movie image of you and hear you sing the ABC song. The last words of that song, and of the film, are, "Tell me what you think of me." Obviously, the song relates to the film in several ways, but is your use of it, on one level, a comment on the whole enterprise of making film? Do you mean that films are attempts to please whatever is left of the father in us and that the audience, which is now going to make a judgment of the film they've just seen, is an extension of patriarchy?

Friedrich: Well, in a way, but that was the joke end of it. When you make a film, you do it to get a response, and presumably most people want a good response. I surely can't imagine making a film and hoping everyone will *hate* it. The conclusion of *Sink or Swim* was more a way for me to acknowledge my absurd ambivalence. A lot of the stories in the film are about doing things to get my father's approval, and then at the end in the last story I decide I'm not going to swim across the lake to please him. I've made a sort of grand gesture of turning back to shore, swimming back to my friends who will hopefully treat me differently than my father has treated me. But then in the epilogue I turn right around and sing the ABC song, which asks him what he thinks of me! I believe that, to a certain extent, we can transcend our childhood, but in some way we always remain the child looking for love and approval.

MacDonald: I would guess that whether or not men like this film is going to have a lot to do with their ideologies about family. I'm sure it will make some men uncomfortable; it will expose them.

Friedrich: A surprising number of men have come up to me afterward and talked about the film from the vantage point of being fathers. That wasn't foremost in my mind when I was making it, but their responses have been interesting: the film brings up a lot of fear in them, a lot of concern about how they're treating their own children. Many of them express a profound hope that they won't do major damage to their kids.

MacDonald: At one point your father takes you to a movie theater and you see this film about people who didn't care about Western culture.

Friedrich: The Time Machine [1960]. I used that film because it was one I remember seeing, but also because I could address the issue of people who have abandoned civilization. In the story, the time machine transports the main character into the year 20,000 (or whatever). He goes into the library, which no one uses, and sees that the books are just rotting away. The people, oblivious to history, are living a life of pleasure and yet are slaves to green monsters who control them and finally

Shot from final alphabetized story ("Athena/Atalanta/Aphrodite") of Sink or Swim *(1990).*

eat them. In some ways, I feel critical of the idea of people living a hedonistic life, divorced from serious thought and ignorant of the consequences of history. On the other hand, my experience with my father was that he was absolutely indebted to Western civilization and to the world of books and theory. I wouldn't say that he would defend Western culture against other cultures—he's an anthropologist who's spent a lot of time studying other cultures—but in some more profound way his life is organized around the principles and institutions of Western civilization. If you've lived your life in an ivory tower at a university, if you've lived your life in books, that can exclude you from a lot of experiences.

In some ways I was trying indirectly to critique a certain kind of film practice that's been in vogue for the last ten or fifteen years, and a certain kind of film theory that is often quite divorced from normal experience (although I wonder about the word "normal"). The story later on in the film about the kind of articles my father was writing while my parents were getting divorced was meant to be a dig at a lot of the writing that's done about films that I think strips the life out of them. I'm interested in more direct speech, something more visceral, more emotionally honest. I wanted to touch on that, but not directly.

MacDonald: I assume this project was similar to *The Ties That Bind* in that you worked at great length on the editing.

Friedrich: I started editing in November 1989 and worked pretty steadily until April. I had some breaks of a week or two here and there, but I pretty much kept to it that whole time. It took a tremendous amount of juggling to decide what the order of the stories would be and what the overall visual theme of each section would be, and how to make the images move. As I've said before to you, when you're working with voiceover, you have to be extraordinarily careful about how your images work so you don't lose your audience. I think we tend to see more than we hear; I think we favor the sensual experience of images. I realized I had written a dense narration, and felt it would be drowned out by the barrage of images if I didn't work really carefully to keep the two elements informing each other.

Some people who have seen *Sink or Swim* have said that sometimes they spaced out, that they couldn't follow every word of every story. I understand that because I don't think I'd be able to either: the film presumes a second or third viewing. But that was something I really struggled with. I also didn't want the film to work just on a symbolic level, or to be completely literal, so I go back and forth between the two. For example, there's a story about going over to the neighbors' and making ice cream sundaes and then watching a circus on TV, which is synched with circus imagery; and the story of the chess game, which is illustrated by a chess game. But other stories are accompanied by more symbolic imagery, like the story about the poem my father wrote about going to Mexico, which you hear as you see a glass vase being filled with water and three roses. And there are stories that are somewhere between the two poles, which I like. I most prefer when something is both symbolic and literal, though it's hard to do.

MacDonald: I think probably the dimension that gets lost most easily in your films is the intricate network of connections between sound and image. In both *The Ties That Bind* and *Sink or Swim* the subject is so compelling that the subtleties of your presentation can easily be overlooked.

Friedrich: I think people might not be so articulate about that level of the films because, not being familiar with the field of avant-garde film, they might not have the language with which to describe those effects. But I do think there's an unconscious recognition of that level; that's why the film is working. If I wasn't editing well, if I was putting stupid images up against those stories, the stories might have a certain impact, but the images I use produce so many more meanings, and *that's* what people are really responding to, even if they think it's primarily the stories that are affecting them. If they come up afterward and say, "That was really powerful," I think, "Well, it's powerful because it's the right shape, the right texture, and the right rhythm—all those things."

There was a period when I thought it was important to deny myself everything, including all kinds of film pleasure, in order to be politically correct and save the world, but I think if you do that, you deplete yourself and then have nothing to offer the rest of the world. If you want to engage people, if you want them to care about what you're doing, you have to give them something. Of course, that doesn't mean making a Hollywood musical. The discussion tends to be so polarized: some people think that if you introduce the slightest bit of pleasure, whether it's visual or aural or whatever, you're in the other camp.

MacDonald: There's always an implicit debate between the people who seem to want to get rid of cinema altogether, because of what it has meant in terms of gender politics, and the people who want to change the direction of cinema, to make it progressively vital, rather than invisible.

Friedrich: Sometimes it's a case of "the harder they come, the harder they fall." When people hold out against a position—against cinematic pleasure for example—the urge is still there in them. If they hold out too long, they end up doing something that is so much about cinematic pleasure that in effect they've gone over to the other side without really acknowledging how or why. I think that happens a lot, and it disturbs me. I really believe in film. I believe in its power. I think it's going to be around for a long time, and if people can't accept their responsibility for producing cinematic pleasure in an alternative form, well, that's their problem, and everyone's loss.

MacDonald: Do you plan to tour with this film? I know you've been having some reservations about the usual way independent filmmakers present their work.

Friedrich: In the case of the last two films, I did go around the country (and a little bit in Europe), showing the films and talking about them. With *The Ties That Bind,* I was eager to do it. For the most part, touring with that film was interesting for me. With *Damned If You Don't,* touring was a way to earn part of my living, and I was curious about the audience's response: since it was about a lesbian nun, I was curious to see whether people would be scandalized or amused, if a lot of lesbians would come to it, whatever.

But I got really worn out from the experience of having to speak after *Damned If You Don't,* and I approach the prospect of doing it with this film with a lot of dread, for two reasons. Making a film that evokes such painful memories is risky; people sometimes look at me afterward as if I have a solution to all the problems, as if I know some way to cope with the pain one feels. I'm afraid I don't really have any answers to give. All I know right now is the importance of acknowledging those childhood expectations.

The other reason is more general: I think the whole setup of having a personal appearance by the filmmaker after the screening is obsolete. I think this structure grew in part out of a feeling in the sixties and seventies that, while there was an audience out there for avant-garde film, it wasn't big enough, and one way to make the film more accessible was to have the filmmaker there. If people were frustrated or confused during the viewing of the film, they would be relieved of their frustrations afterward by having the whole thing explained to them.

Avant-garde film is in a period of crisis. Many independent filmmakers are moving into feature narratives, and there's a feeling that the process of making "smaller" films is dying out. That might make some people think it's still important to go out and proselytize and educate, but I think that's a misguided response to the situation. The idea that I would go to a performance by John Zorn or whomever—some composer or musician—and he would have to get up afterward and explain how to hear his music, as opposed to how to hear Schönberg or Beethoven, is absurd. I think the film community is much too paranoid about the audience's alleged inability to understand avant-garde films.

My experience with *The Ties That Bind* proved this to me. Since it was about an older woman, I often had older people in the audience, people in their fifties and sixties who had never seen an experimental film. Sometimes they told me afterward that they were intimidated at the outset, but by the end of the film they were fine, they understood and enjoyed it. They're adults; they've got minds. There has to be more respect for the audience, and more trust.

Anne Severson (on *Near the Big Chakra*) Laura Mulvey (on *Riddles of the Sphinx*) Yvonne Rainer (on *Privilege*)

Probably the most important film critical development since 1970 has been fueled by the larger feminist revaluation of Western culture. Of course, there have been feminist films as long as there has been critical filmmaking: Germaine Dulac's *Theme and Variation* (1925) was a feminist response to *Ballet Méchanique*; her *The Smiling Madame Beudet* (1923) prefigures Chantal Akerman's *Jeanne Dielman . . .* (1975); and Maya Deren's *Meshes of the Afternoon* can easily be understood as a feminist response to marriage. But the renaissance of pop and theoretical feminist writing in the sixties and seventies inspired, and was inspired by, a significant increase in the production of films that had as their central agenda a critique of the conventional cinema's imaging of women. During the past twenty years women (and men) have devised a variety of feminist tactics for confronting sexist dimensions of the commercial cinema, especially its depiction of the female body. The three films discussed in the following mini-interviews with Anne Severson (now Alice Anne Parker), Laura Mulvey, and Yvonne Rainer reveal a variety of these tactics.

As a filmmaker, Anne Severson was (she has not made films since 1974) a product of the sixties, especially the sixties' reaction to an earlier puritanism about the human body. For many sixties artists the body was a territory in need of liberation, both from the residue of Hays Office demands that it be hidden in film (more recently known as the Motion Picture Association of America, the Hays Office was the Hollywood censorship organization from 1922 on), and from the more general cultural assumption that sexuality was a moral issue, rather than a natural process—an assumption that had been evident during much of conventional film history and that was equally evident in the new pornographic inversion of puritanism. Severson's earliest films confront these issues in several ways. In *I Change I Am the Same* (1969) a man and woman stand before the camera in brief alternating shots (the entire film is forty

319

seconds long), dressed or partially dressed in each others' clothes, or nude. *Riverbody* (1970) is a longer film (seven minutes) during which we see eighty-seven nude males and females, one by one, each dissolving into the next, to the accompaniment of the sound of lapping water. The two films implicitly polemicize the naturalness of the body and satirize the social control of the body by means of the gender (and other) roles encoded in dress.

By the time she made *Near the Big Chakra* (1972), Severson had come to realize that the politics of the body as image were different for the two genders. Of course, film had always marketed young, shapely female (and male) bodies, but as the strictures against nudity fell, women found themselves increasingly exposed. And more importantly, they continued to find themselves exposed as objects, icons, rather than as bodies in process: all dimensions of the female body as organism were routinely suppressed. For Severson, this pattern seemed increasingly problematic, and *Near the Big Chakra* was her response. *Near the Big Chakra* presents, in extreme close-up, the vulvas of thirty-seven women ranging in age from three months to fifty-six years. Each vulva is presented in a single continuous shot, though from time to time Severson adjusts the zoom lens; the shots are of varying lengths. The film lasts seventeen minutes and seems to most viewers substantially longer, especially since it's silent. The tradition of transforming female bodies into lifeless, conventionally "erotic" icons is continually subverted: from time to time tampon strings hang from vaginas; some of the women contract muscles; hands reach into the image to reveal the baby's vulva more clearly; and from time to time, there's evidence of an infection or of semen.

I've seen few films that demonstrate an audience's investment in the conventional imaging of women more dramatically than *Near the Big Chakra*. Indeed, the film is a way of measuring the degree to which our experiences with conventional film (and with the depiction of women's bodies in other media) have caused us to romanticize women. The extent of a viewer's shock or disgust at the film—and these are the standard reactions, even now—is a gauge of that viewer's investment in woman as beautiful (inorganic) object. Of course, one might argue that the enlargement of the vulvas affected by filming and projecting them is the cause of much of this response, and that any part of any real body, magnified to this extent, might shock viewers. But this only confirms Severson's essential quest: to liberate the body as part of a larger process of putting us in touch with reality. After all, the romanticized "perfect" bodies visually polemicized by the Hollywood industry are enlarged as well. Severson's shock tactic is simply a means for producing a more sensible view of reality unenlarged, human-scale.

For Laura Mulvey and Peter Wollen the conventional cinematic de-piction of women (and its exploitation of the female body) required a very different tactic, a tactic that no one could construe as participating in the gender-problematic patterns they meant to confront. As Severson makes clear in her interview, the ideology that produced *Near the Big Chakra* did not necessarily determine the way in which audiences re-sponded to it. She discusses more than one instance where men, seeing the film in what they assumed was a private situation, responded to the film in a manner counterproductive to what she had in mind. For Mulvey and Wollen, the issue was not the body itself—though *Riddles of the Sphinx* certainly avoids conventionally erotic imagery of the female body—but the many central dimensions of women's lives that are rou-tinely ignored in the commercial cinema's dedication to women as the objects of romantic/erotic, heterosexual quests. For their second collabo-ration (their first was *Penthesilea* [1974], a feature on Amazons currently out of distribution), they decided to focus on motherhood and daugh-terhood as it is experienced just before and during the interruption of what has been a thoroughly symbiotic relationship, without at any point requiring that either mother or daughter appeal to the erotic desires of the man in the film or of the "male" in the audience.

The mother-daughter story is explored in the film's central narrative, entitled "Louise's Story Told in Thirteen Shots." This narrative is framed by three beginning sections (a close-up of hands paging through a book of mythic images of women; "Laura Speaking," a passage that intercuts between images of the Egyptian and Greek sphinxes and Mulvey reading a paper on the history of the sphinx; and "Stones," a montage of rephotographed imagery of the Egyptian Sphinx) and three ending sections, each of which "mirrors" the corresponding opening section ("Acrobats," a montage of optically printed images of a juggler, a tumbler, and a trapeze artist—all women; "Laura Listening," where Mulvey rewinds and listens to a tape of her comments in "Laura Speak-ing"; and "Puzzle Ending," a long single-shot close-up of hands solving a maze game: it "mirrors" the maze of imagery of women revealed in the film's opening section). Louise's story is presented sequentially, in long continuous shots (the shortest is one minute, forty-two seconds; the longest, ten minutes, eight seconds), each is a 360-degree pan. Between each pair of 360-degree pans is a bit of intertext that expands on the story revealed in the pans. At the beginning we see Louise preparing breakfast for Anna, then in Anna's bedroom as Anna is going to sleep; in shot three, Chris, Louise's husband, moves out (his good-bye to her and Anna are the story's first synch sound); in shot four, Louise leaves Anna at day-care for the first time; in shot five, we see Louise at work at a telephone switchboard, and in shot six, at lunch with the other workers; in shot seven, she talks with other workers about child care as a union issue; in shot eight, we see Louise (with Anna) and her friend Maxine whom she met at the day-care center; in shot nine, Louise is at a playground with Anna; in shot ten, in Louise's mother's garden where her mother is looking after Anna while she and Maxine look at old photographs; in shot eleven, Louise and Maxine are at Chris's studio where he shows them his recent film and tapes (about artist Mary Kelly) and Louise tells him she wants to sell the house—she's moving in with Maxine; in shot twelve, Louise and Maxine talk about one of Maxine's dreams at Maxine's apartment; and in shot thirteen, Louise and Anna visit the Egyptian Room at the British Museum.

The activities revealed in "Louise's Story Told in Thirteen Shots" are the polar opposite of the activities that would be the focus of any conventional narrative film. Each shot focuses on a dimension of Louise's life that would be, at most, the background for erotic (and/or violent) adventures in a commercial movie. The film doesn't entirely eliminate the possibility of the erotic from Louise's life (her relationship with Maxine may be an erotic one, though we never see any direct evidence of erotic engagement between the two women), but at no point is the erotic the "hook" for viewer interest. The pleasures of this cinematic text are formal and intellectual: the brilliant and often exhilarating 360-degree pans that define a new kind of cinematic space and an entirely original narrative structure; the densely suggestive mise-en-scène, which in every instance elaborates the implications of Louise's story; and the intricate mirror structure—itself a reference to the "mirror" phase of childhood development—that informs the sections that frame "Louise's Story." For Mulvey and Wollen, the antidote to the conventional cinema's depiction of women's bodies and its narrow sense of women's lives is not shock, not a reductio ad absurdum of its tendency to fetishize particular sectors of the body as in *Near the Big Chakra,* but a thoroughly imaginative and accomplished alternative to traditional cinematic narrative, and perhaps, a catalyst for a new, progressively feminist genre.

Privilege (1990) is Yvonne Rainer's most recent addition to a filmmaking career of twenty years that has produced six feature films, a career that itself followed an influential career in dance/choreography/performance that began in the early sixties (see Rainer's *Work 1961–73* [New York and Halifax: New York University Press and Nova Scotia College of Art and Design, 1974]). Throughout her feature filmmaking, Rainer has attempted to respond to her audience's interest in melodrama without relying on the forms of cinematic pleasure that characterize industry films *and,* in the years since *Film About a Woman Who . . .* (1974), without relying either on the pleasures of sensuous image-making or of formal design—the mainstays of much of the independent cinema that critiques conventional moviemaking. Rainer has become identified with a filmmaking approach that provides narrative development by means of a variety of anti-illusionistic means: most obviously, she develops characters who enact scenes that are inevitably revealed as fabrications as they are presented: usually we see the scene and the filming of it, simultaneously; and she uses a variety of forms of printed or spoken text—some of it written by Rainer, much of it borrowed from other sources—that elaborate a weave of narrative actions that are "shot" in the mind of the viewer. *Privilege* uses Rainer's approach in order to explore the issues of menopause and racism.

The very idea of centering a feature film on menopause, which, as Rainer makes clear in *Privilege,* has been culturally defined as *un*pleasure—the tail end of youth and eroticism, the epitome of the uncinematic—is an explicit critique of the conventional cinema and its limited view of women. The fact that *Privilege* is an enjoyable film, fascinating even to rather conventional audiences (at least in my experience as an exhibitor), makes it a breakthrough, the ultimate cinematic magic trick, and a potential catalyst for the liberation of women and men from conventional definitions that have tended to constrict our lives in the most obvious ways.

The central narrative thread of *Privilege* is the reminiscences of Jenny, a white woman of middle age, about a particular, troubling moment early in her career as a dancer. In her "hot flashback" Jenny recalls moving into an apartment in a comparatively high-rent building next door to her less affluent Puerto Rican and African-American neighbors, Carlos, Digna, and Stew. Jenny lives directly above Brenda, who is a lesbian. Like other neighborhood residents, Jenny becomes accustomed to the fights between Carlos and Digna. Soon after Digna is arrested and taken to Bellevue after a particularly violent fight, Carlos enters Brenda's apartment late at night, naked, and when Brenda screams, Jenny comes to her rescue. Ultimately, Brenda presses charges and Jenny, annoyed at the defense attorney's attempts to categorize her as a loose woman, perjures herself, saying she actually saw Carlos in Brenda's apartment, and she becomes lovers with the assistant district attorney. This central episode is elaborated by Rainer in characteristically anti-illusionist fashion: throughout her flashback, Jenny remains her current, menopausal age; Digna becomes an invisible (to the other characters) commentator, particularly about Jenny's love affair with the wealthy assistant district attorney; and the narrative is regularly interrupted by other kinds of information, including dramatizations of dreams.

Interwoven with the basic melodramatic situation are numerous interviews about menopause with Jenny and with many women who are clearly not characters in the film's central fiction. The interviews are conducted by Rainer herself, with the exception of the interview with Jenny, which is conducted by "Yvonne Washington," Rainer's African-American alter ego. Essentially, the use of this alter ego allows Rainer to develop two levels of inquiry in the film. The first involves menopause, as it affects women of various economic and ethnic backgrounds, positively and negatively. The second involves race: "Yvonne Washington" is able to explore and critique Jenny's attitudes and the degree to which the shape of her thinking is determined not simply by her maturation as a woman, but by her privileged social status as a white woman with financial resources. Or to put this another way: since Jenny's flashback is based on Rainer's experiences after first moving to New York City, "Yvonne Washington" allows Rainer to interrogate herself as she questions other women. More fully than either *Near the Big Chakra* (which includes the vulvas of two black women among the thirty-seven) or *Riddles of the Sphinx* (where the relationship of Louise and Maxine crosses racial lines, without comment by either woman, and where the issue of the relationship of ethnic background and social class is raised only by implication—we see a black woman cooking for the telephone operators in the company lunchroom), *Privilege* explores the complex set of relationships and distinctions between the loss (and gain) of "privilege" as a result of menopause and as a function of ethnic background. For Rainer the issue is not simply the woman's body as an index of Western society's—and the Western camera's—attitudes about gender; it is also an index of attitudes about race and language (Digna's marginalization as a Spanish speaker and the marginalization of other forms of language—systems of signing employed by the deaf, for example— are also explored in the film).

As a trio of films, *Near the Big Chakra, Riddles of the Sphinx,* and *Privilege* chart a trajectory of feminist concern over the past two decades. In a sense, each film builds from and subsumes the concerns of the previous films: *Riddles of the Sphinx* is as much a response to the fetishization of a restricted sense of the female body as Severson's film is; and *Privilege* responds both to that issue and to the issue of women's economic marginalization within modern social structures (and in the films that reflect these social structures). Together, the three films reflect a growing awareness that our assumptions about the female body and the economic marginalization of women must be conditioned by an awareness of the ways in which our "local" experiences of such issues are contextualized, both *inter*nationally, by the experiences of women and men around the world, and *intra*nationally, by virtue of the fact that nearly every modern nation has become a nexus of racial and ethnic experiences.

My discussion with Severson was accomplished through an exchange of voice tapes in the summer of 1990. I interviewed Mulvey in November 1990 (the edited discussion was sent to Wollen; his additions are included within the text, in brackets), and Rainer in January 1991.

Anne Severson (Alice Anne Parker)

MacDonald: How did you originally conceive *Near the Big Chakra?*

Severson: I've been thinking about that movie a lot as I've worked on my new book [*Understand Your Dreams: 1,001 Basic Dream Images and How to Interpret Them,* published by H. J. Kramer in 1991]. I knew when I made that film that I was taking a big chance, that it might scandalize and disturb people. *Near the Big Chakra* was made in 1971, at the end of that first great wave of feminism, which certainly opened the door to a lot of forbidden thoughts and issues. I think as a film it created a certain space.

Janis Joplin was a neighbor of mine. She used to sing with Big Brother and the Holding Company at a ratty little bar in Berkeley called the Blind Lemon. I was living with a man from Texas at the time; he had been a student at the University of Texas when Janis was there. She had been much maligned because she violated a lot of ideas about how women were supposed to behave. They weren't supposed to be sloppy, loud, drunk; they were supposed to comb their hair, shave under their arms . . . looking back now, it doesn't seem so radical or unconventional. But when she was first performing, she was on the edge, and I really appreciated that. By taking such an extreme position, she made all the space in between available.

Eldridge Cleaver and the Black Panthers did a similar thing when they first started expressing that macho, potentially violent image of black men, holding big guns and wearing black leather. They created a much larger space for all black men, by taking an extreme position.

MacDonald: The film certainly makes sense in that context, but how did you come to the idea of filming vulvas in extreme close-up?

Severson: I told that story in the *Spare Rib* article ["Don't Get Too Near the Big Chakra," *Spare Rib,* No. 20 (February 1974); reprinted in *Spare Rib Reader,* ed. Marsha Rowe (London: Penguin Books, 1982), pp. 312–318]. I got the idea to make the movie one day in California when my teenage daughter was lounging nude in the sun after a bath, casually exposing herself. I found myself staring at her vagina. When she noticed me, she said, "Mother, for heaven's sakes!" We both felt a little embarrassed.

Later it seemed odd to me that, first, I had not looked at that part of her body since she was very small, and second, that my curiosity had made me uncomfortable, as though there was something wrong with my interest. I realized that I had never seen any woman's vagina except in crotch-shots in pornographic films and magazines or close-ups in birth films. I asked my women friends if they had ever looked at other women's vaginas. One or two, with bisexual experience, assured me they had; most hadn't. Few wanted to pursue the matter.

I started talking about making a film about vaginas. Men filmmaker friends listened to me with distaste. Bob Nelson was the first to support me. He became interested and, in a burst of enthusiasm, produced the title.

His wife, Diane, and I were taking a yoga class together and I was intrigued that the first chakra one gains control of, or "awakens" in yogic terms, was located between the genitals and the anus. "Chakra" is Sanskrit for wheels or centers of radiating life force. Joseph Campbell calls them "centers of consciousness." There are seven or eight, depending upon the system you follow. The first is located at the base of the spine. It's the chakra of pure physical being, survival—the place where you just hang on.

The second is where all psychological energy is erotic or creative. I was jokingly calling it the "big chakra" because in the early seventies we all seemed to be stuck at this level of development. It also seemed to me that the way out of this morass was to transform some of this energy into art. In the proposed film I wanted to focus on the same area that our energy was flowing from in the beginning yoga class. I also hoped to creatively release some of this energy for myself and other women in order to move on up the cerebrospinal ladder.

Anyway, enough people told me it was a terrible idea that I should not pursue under any circumstances that I definitely decided to do it. *Near the Big Chakra* assumes that it's a good idea to take a look at things, even if they're forbidden, or taboo, or frightening, or exciting, or mysterious, or dangerous. I guess that's one of my basic assumptions about what's interesting to do in the world and also what's interesting to do in art.

MacDonald: How did you find participants?

Severson: I went to Glide Methodist Church in San Francisco. At that time the church was very active in the area of human sexuality. Later, the group at Glide evolved into Multi Media Resource Center. They presented all kinds of sexuality seminars and classes.

I approached them and asked if they'd produce the film and, in fact,

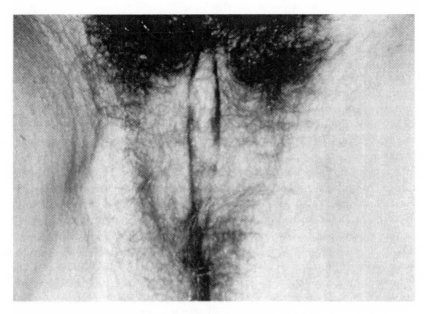

From Severson's Near the Big Chakra *(1972).*

they did. They paid for it and sent people from their courses to be in it. Then I did a flyer with a red rose—a good symbol for the vagina: spiritual unfolding, femininity, fecundity—coyly inviting women to be in a film about "women's parts."

I shot it at the San Francisco Art Institute, where I was teaching. A student of mine—a very maternal, comfortable, candid woman, met people in an anteroom near the room where I was filming. She described what I was doing and talked about the film. Also, there were women in the anteroom who had already been photographed. They would hang around and talk to other women who had come in to find out what was going on before they decided whether to be in the film or not. It was very relaxed, and I think almost everybody who came by that day was in the film. It turned out to be easy, although I had been a little nervous about it—fearing that not enough people would show up. Altogether, thirty-eight women appeared in the film. The age range was from three months to sixty-three years. There were two black women, one half-oriental girl, two lesbians, one prostitute, two virgins (I think), a lot of mothers, three mothers-to-be, three grandmothers, four women menstruating, one girl who discovered a week later that she had gonorrhea, and one woman who learned a month later that she had uterine cancer. None of these characteristics is evident in the film—except the women who are menstruating: you can see their tampon strings.

At that time in the Bay Area there was a certain willingness to experiment on every front, and I think most of the people in the film are people who were already known to me or who already knew my work. They had been my students at the Art Institute, or they were friends, or mothers of friends, or children of friends, or other artists. There was a certain level of trust. My films had been shown around town a lot, and at that point, independent filmmaking was an acknowledged art form in the Bay Area and received a lot of attention from the press. It was like going to a Be-in.

In general, that was of a time of casual nudity. There were often parties at the Art Institute where almost everybody was nude. Adam Bartlett was visiting us here in Hawaii last summer. He's the son of Scott Bartlett, who was one of the most successful filmmakers in the Bay Area in the sixties and seventies. Adam's twenty now, a student at Santa Cruz. I had taken him to a party given by some friends here, who recognized his name and were curious about what it was like to grow up in that milieu. He said, "My folks would get together with their friends and everybody would take off their clothes and they'd make a movie." He was right. Part of the process of social interaction at that point in history seemed to be casual nudity. Actually, at one point I had planned to make a film called "Casual Nudity," because the phenomenon was so widespread. *Chakra* is also part of that phenomenon.

MacDonald: In your *Spare Rib* article, you often use "cunt." Was the word more acceptable in that milieu than it is now?

Severson: Women *were* disturbed by my using "cunt." I was often questioned by feminists when I showed the film. My position at the time was that if a word was loaded for you, the best way to demystify it and disarm it was to make it your word and use it. So during that period I always referred to vaginas as "cunts," particularly when I was showing *Chakra* and talking about it. Then at some point I stopped doing it. It's not a word I use very often now.

MacDonald: My current students find *Chakra* the most shocking film I show them. I'm sure it shocks *them* more than it did the original audiences. But I'd be very interested to know what kinds of experiences you've had with the film.

Severson: There are a *lot* of stories.

I had been invited to show the film in London at a college of engineers. Now usually I showed at film societies, women's groups, or art schools, but for some reason I was invited to a college of engineers! It turned out that people there were relatively comfortable and interested in the movie. By this time, my daughter was fifteen or sixteen years old and in a love relationship with a delightful man, a good friend, Barney Boatman, who had grown up in a radical political household in London and was very smart, very articulate, very well-read. He had come to the film showing, never having seen my films. At the end of the screening, when I asked people for their responses, he said that he had found it very disturbing. I asked, "What was disturbing about it for you?" And he said, "Well, I found myself unconsciously thinking that this wasn't feminine. And *then* I thought, well, how can this *not* be feminine. I mean this is the female part of females! So I looked at my attitudes and realized that, without really knowing it, I had developed certain assumptions about femininity—that feminine means symmetrical and pink and pretty and delicate. I realized that even though I thought I was conscious, I still held unconscious attitudes about femininity." I really appreciated his comment and his willingness to share it publicly.

I had other, very different responses. At one point, I was invited to the University of Wales in Aberystwyth, which was presenting a fine arts festival. I couldn't resist the idea of a fine arts festival in Aberystwyth. I had also been invited to Cannes to show *I Change I Am the Same,* a stunning little forty-five second movie that's still out there making money for me, which is really satisfying. Both invitations were for the same dates. Being invited to Cannes was quite a *coup* for an independent filmmaker, but I decided to go to Wales instead. I discovered that the University of Wales in Aberystwyth was a hotbed of Charles Olson studies. I'm sure you know the American poet, Charles Olson, whom I had met a couple of times and really admired and loved. My boyfriend, D. V. John Dubberstein, and I were staying with a lecturer in the English department, who was much more interested in my anecdotal memories of Charles Olson than in my films.

Anyway, the first night of that festival was devoted to a showing of films by Stan Brakhage, also a friend of mine from California, and John's cousin. I think John actually owned some of Brakhage's films because we had a copy of *The Art of Seeing.* I was very familiar with Brakhage's work, so I took it upon myself to represent him at the screenings and answer some of the questions from the audience. *Window Water Baby Moving* [1959] was shown and a few other things, and there was general outcry and outrage—at *Window Water Baby Moving*! I remember one person in particular, an English professor, who objected *violently* to that movie, and said, among other very hostile things, "Would you film someone making toilet?" I remember thinking, "Does he mean putting on makeup? Is that some kind of eighteenth-century phrase he's using, or is he talking about someone going to the bathroom?" So, when I stood up, I said, "I found your comment very interesting although I wasn't sure if you were talking about someone putting on makeup or someone peeing or shitting." Of course, that created even more uproar, as I, I'm ashamed to say, intended it to. Later, I said in a very direct way that I was showing my films the next evening and that if anyone had been offended by Brakhage's *Window Water Baby Moving,* I would strongly recommend that they not come to my show, or at least that they wait until the second half hour.

The next day as I was walking through one of the university buildings in the early afternoon on my way to a panel discussion, I passed a room with a door ajar, through which I heard the soundtrack from *Riverbody.* I pushed the door open, and there was a little screen and a group of men watching my films by themselves, like at a private smoker. I stayed in the back. The next film on the reel was *Chakra* and the group watched what I then called the "Cunt Movie," yakking and making jokes: "What did you have for breakfast?" "That's your mother!"—that sort of thing. I waited until the program was over. Then I turned on the light, and looked very carefully to see who was there. Of course, the professor who had made the comment the day before was there. I looked at them and laughed and said, "Well, I'm certainly glad that you got to see this privately, because I know how difficult it would be for you to watch it in public!" And I quoted some of their remarks. It was wonderful. Of course, that evening I told the story to the entire community. I was also very pleased when a graduate student who had been with the all-male party that afternoon got up and talked about the difference between seeing the film in a mixed audience and as part of an all-male smoker.

MacDonald: Did you stay in England, or did you travel through Europe?

Severson: I showed the film as part of a program of my own films and films by others that David Boatwright and I took all over Europe for a year. If you were a recognized filmmaker, you could easily schedule a European tour and show your films all over. You didn't make much money, but enough to live on while you were traveling around with the films. And there were very interested, communicative, sophisticated people in Belgium, France, particularly in Holland, Scandinavia, and Germany. Hundreds of people would show up to see and discuss the films.

The film community in Holland at that time was very active, and I think the museum there had scheduled eighteen film showings for us in about three weeks. We would get on a train, travel to a new city, be met by people, be taken out to dinner, do a film showing that night. Sometimes we'd have a day in between, but usually the next morning we'd go someplace else. Sometimes there were small groups in basements with a little projector and screen, but often there were big auditoriums. David was in England when I went to The Hague for a show. I was met at the train station by three middle-aged businessmen, very serious—art collectors, very interested in independent film. We had a wonderful dinner together. Driving to the screening, we passed a cinema and there was a long line of people waiting out in front and a big marquee. I casually asked what the performance was that night. They said, "That's where *your* films are being shown." At the beginning of the show, I got up and did an introduction in English—most Dutch people speak English. As usual, it was a very attentive crowd. I was grateful that I had already been on the road for a while so that my presentation was quite polished. As usual, I said that there was a film about cunts and recommended that people who would be uncomfortable might at that point get up and leave. I also mentioned that it was a silent film, and then I went back and sat down in the middle of the theater with the three businessmen, one of whom was the minister of art or the equivalent for the Netherlands. The films came on—*Chakra* was fourth or fifth in the program. There were some wonderful movies in that program: Scott Bartlett's *Stand Up and Be Counted* [1969], Neal White's *Putting the Babies Back (Part II)*—a collection of great films from Canyon Cinema.

When *Chakra* came on, at first there was a total hush, no coughing, no movement, nothing at all happening. Then I could hear voices making jokes, though, of course, I couldn't understand them because they were in Dutch. Every once in a while you'd hear a deep male voice say something obviously obscene, and a ripple of laughter would move through the crowd. I didn't know where the voices were coming from. It turned out that the professional projectionists weren't used to projecting silent films, and they hadn't realized that when they made loud comments up in the projection booth, their comments would trickle down on everybody. I really loved that because the audience could sense the difference between their experience of the film and the experience of these guys up in the projection booth watching it and responding—they thought—privately. I was disappointed when the minister of art went up and made them stop.

At the end of that screening, I went up on stage to answer questions, and, of course, a lot of the questions were about *Chakra*. When I talked about *Chakra*, as usual, I used the word "cunt." Afterward, the minister and I were photographed, smiling and shaking hands—the classic newspaper photograph. It appeared in the paper the next day, quoting the minister as saying, "I, too, am very interested in cunt." [laughter] I wish I still had that clipping.

MacDonald: How was *Chakra* received in this country? Were there memorable screenings?

Severson: Oh yes! After I'd been traveling in Europe for a year, I came back to the States briefly and was invited to be a judge at Ann Arbor, which at that time was *the* big independent film festival. *Riverbody* had won first prize there in 1970. In fact, that's when I started taking myself seriously as a filmmaker. When I had finished *Chakra*, I sent it to Ann Arbor, and I hadn't heard anything about it. I assumed they didn't like it. The next year when I came to be a judge, I heard incredible stories about *Chakra* being screened there the year before. Apparently I had been invited to be a judge because the board of the festival wanted to see the person who made *that* movie.

I learned that at the previous festival the judges couldn't agree to give *Chakra* a prize, but they had decided to show it in the festival as the last film on the last night—a position traditionally reserved for exciting new movies. Everyone was curious about the fact that the exciting new film being shown last, made by someone who had won first prize before, had not won a prize and was not included on the Ann Arbor tour. There was a huge crowd. When the film came on the event turned into a riot. The theater had a projection booth above the audience that you got to by ladder. Someone in the audience was so outraged by the film that he had climbed up and tackled the projectionist, Peter Wilde. They wrestled on the floor, the guy determined to pull the film out of the projector. People were booing and yelling and leaving. A woman stood at the door and, as people tried to walk out, she would swing her long shoulder bag by the handle and hit them over the head. When I met her the next year, she said, "You know, I would kill for that film." I thought, "My god, how could this have created so much furor?" I loved hearing about it, but I'm also glad I missed that screening.

MacDonald: Did you show the film outside the standard avant-garde screening spaces?

Severson: Sometimes. One summer I showed *Chakra* in my home-town, Eugene, Oregon. I had wrongly assumed that this would be a straitlaced, middle-class crowd. What I had not anticipated was that Eugene (at that time) was the lesbian separatist capital of the world! I went through an elaborate presentation, trying to make people comfortable, making all the wrong assumptions about whom I was speaking to. After the program, I was answering questions, and someone asked about my intentions and whether I thought the film was erotic. I answered, "To my knowledge, no one has ever gotten a hard-on watching it." A woman in striped overalls stood up and said, "I did!" I loved that—but it was a tough screening; I completely miscalculated my audience.

I was also invited to show *Chakra*, along with my other films, to medical students at the University of Southern California Medical School. I'd had some warning that the young doctors might be abusive, so I went with a friend who had a three-month-old baby, and I insisted on holding the baby all through the screening and during the question-and-answer period after. I recommend that if you expect to find yourself in a similar situation.

Looking back, the only regret I have about *Chakra* is that the titles are so sloppy. I was teaching at the Art Institute when I made most of my movies. It was a macho kind of place. In general, it wasn't considered appropriate to be too concerned about the niceties of your production or your performance. Things being a little rough around the edges was not only acceptable, it was admired. Now I look back at those films and I like the ones where I did a really clean job on the titles. I should redo the titles on *Chakra* and make them clean and very cool, almost clinical.

MacDonald: Have you continued to make films? Nothing is listed in the Canyon Catalogue after 1974.

Severson: No. I made one or two more films in England; *Animals Running* [1974] and *The Struggle of the Meat* [1974] are still distributed. I stayed in England instead of returning to the Art Institute because I was driven (that's definitely the word!) to seek teachers to help me develop some psychic capacities that had been surfacing. It was clear to me that something was happening to me, and I had to find out what to do with it, how to direct it more effectively.

In England I started working on a videotape series on unorthodox healing methods. I believed this would provide me with a kind of cover while I observed different teachers and their work. The third healer I interviewed was Dr. Thomas Maughan, a homeopathic doctor and Chief of the Ancient Order of Druids. He effortlessly lured me into the Order with some very tasty information about dreams and dreamwork.

Now I'm working a lot with dreams again. Personal movies. I have a call-in radio show on dreams in Honolulu, and I write a dream column. I'm still interested in basically the same thing—finding a convenient vehicle that makes it easy and exciting for people to explore and expand their own awareness. I think that has been my own lifetime script. Originally I thought my movies, and particularly *Chakra,* had that value. Now I guess you could say I'm working with other people to improve the scripts of their own inner dramas. You should hear some of the wild and hairy dreams that are called in to the radio show. By comparison *Chakra* is pretty tame!

Laura Mulvey

MacDonald: What was the nature of the collaboration between you and Peter Wollen as you were developing *Riddles of the Sphinx*? I assume that both of you had been seeing conventional narrative film, as well as the reactions to it: the movement out of narrative convention by Godard and others who were questioning the politics of the commercial cinema, and the various approaches of avant-garde film—the two "schools" described in Peter's "Two Avant-Gardes" [originally published in the December 1975 *Studio International.* "The Two Avant-Gardes" is reprinted in Wollen, *Readings and Writings* (London: Verso, 1982), pp. 92–104].

Mulvey: "Two Avant-Gardes" came before *Riddles,* as did my "Visual Pleasure and Narrative Cinema" [Mulvey's essay has been widely reprinted. It is included in her *Visual and Other Pleasures* (Bloomington: Indiana University Press, 1989), pp. 14–26]. In a way, the film developed out of those two texts. But we were also trying to edge toward an avant-garde aesthetics that wasn't a pure aesthetics of negation. In those days, you remember, the avant-garde thought it could remodel the cinema. I think we all really believed it would be possible [laughter]. Godard had talked about a return to zero. For Peter and me, *Penthesilea* was our return to zero (these days I call it our "scorched earth" film)—a film that consciously denied spectators the usual pleasures of cinema. After that, we felt we could start to think about an aesthetic that didn't just get its signification from negation. We were still committed to an aesthetic that would negate the expected cinematic conventions, that would be surprising to spectators but could *also* give them a hold on the formal devices we were using, a formal sense of what was going on. We didn't want a system like Brakhage's, where the spectator is *either* fascinated *or* threatened. We were interested in trying to make a movie in which form and structure were clearly visible but which would also have a space for feeling and emotion, that would open up a cinematic meaning beyond dependence on negating the dominant cinema's conventions and inbred ways of seeing.

The theme of a mother and child seemed to offer the means of finding a "beyond negation." At the time, people were first becoming excited and fascinated by psychoanalytic theory. It offered a means of rethinking the world and its subjectivities in just the same way that we felt that we wanted to rethink cinema. We felt that by using psychoanalytic theory to analyze and investigate how subjectivity was constructed, how sexual difference signified in the social, it was possible to challenge its "politics of the unconscious." That was probably the grand aim of the film.

We weren't questioning oedipality. We weren't questioning Freud. We weren't questioning psychoanalysis. We were suggesting that *if* the oedipal could be symbolized differently, then perhaps the way in which it is inscribed in the social would be affected. The mother-child relationship has been so iconically and iconographically important in our society, without the space between the mother and child ever having been opened out. Traditionally, they're there as a unit, epitomized by the Virgin and Child, who necessarily close off and deny what the relationship means theoretically and also poetically and emotionally. And yet the mother-child relationship is one of the most important relationships people live through. Our poetry, our literature, our culture cannot *speak* the mother-child relationship; it's as though its "feeling" is beyond formal expression. Psychoanalytic theory does provide a language and concepts to analyze it and begin to "speak" it. So although we felt, politically, that motherhood had been silenced and should be given cultural space and a means of expression, at the same time, we recognized the difficulty of doing so within the language of the patriarchy. It was a challenge. And that challenge was the starting point for the film. We wanted to bring together theory, the avant-garde, political aspiration, and this emotional, but uncolonized, experience of motherhood.

MacDonald: To what extent did *Riddles of the Sphinx* grow out of your own direct experience?

Mulvey: Of being a mother?

MacDonald: Yes. I've always wondered to what degree Louise is based on Laura.

Mulvey: She wasn't, really. While we were developing the idea for the film I was conscious of the close relationship between my sister and her two-year-old daughter. Chad, my son, was by that time a strapping seven-or eight-year-old, and when he was very little, I would leave him with my mother a lot. So Louise's leaving Anna with her mother, the second stage of her development, *was* much closer to my experience. My grandmother had taken care of me and my favorite first cousin, so I thought babies should be brought up by their grandmothers. My sister and her daughter are in the film, in the playground sequence. The little girl with the blonde hair in the same sequence is Dinah's two-year-old daughter, Georgia (Dinah plays Louise). Diane, the camerawoman, also had a two-year-old daughter, who plays Anna in the film. So there were all these two-year-old girls around!

[*Wollen:* My mother is in the film too. She plays the grandmother in the garden scene.]

Mulvey: But I'd also been reading. Louise's story wasn't just based on observation. I'd read Maud Mannoni's account of the case history of a mother who refuses to abandon her child to the symbolic and tries to keep the child within the dyad. This is there to some extent, at the beginning of Louise's story: Anna is too big to be carried around and babied. We wanted to imply that she was being kept too long, artificially, within the pre-oedipal.

[*Wollen:* Maud Mannoni's books were very important. She's a child analyst, a Lacanian who later disagreed with Lacan when he began to emphasize his "mathemes" and topological diagrams. She stressed the importance of the positioning of each child within a system of "Law" (the "Symbolic" in Lacan's terms). The question that interested us was how the Law itself was constructed and whether it was possible to envis-

Louise (Dinah Stabb) and Maxine (Merdelle Jordine) look at old photographs while Louise's mother cares for Anna, in Mulvey and Wollen's Riddles of the Sphinx *(1977). By permission of the British Film Institute.*

age a nonpatriarchal Law, rather than trying to escape from the patriarchal Law by retreating back into the pre-oedipal (the "Imaginary" in Lacan's terms), the dyadic relationship between infant and mother. This psychoanalytic approach to the mother-child relationship is also what relates the film to Mary Kelly's *Post-Partum Document*, part of which we use in the editing room sequences.]

Mulvey: Historically speaking, just after *Riddles* came out, the psychoanalytic feminist world got very preoccupied with the question of essentialism, and because *Riddles* focused on mothers and daughters, on pre-oedipality, on the sphinx, and so on, it got very much tarred with the essentialist brush, which I think was unfair. The French feminists, like Hélène Cixous and Julia Kristeva, had been interested in exploring and analyzing the mother-daughter relationship in the pre-oedipal stage, within a feminist politics of psychoanalysis. They've been criticized for valorizing this sphere of the feminine pre-oedipal. Anyway, it was a complicated time, and *Riddles* seemed to come into the middle of it all, and was seen as an essentialist film. I thought that was also theoretically unfair from another point of view. While one could perfectly well write "correct theory" in articles, journals, lectures, one of the points of writing literature or poetry or making movies is to be more daring; you can push against the boundaries of theoretical correctness. This, perhaps, is how culture can change. You're not really going to *move* people by writing theory. If you want to *move* people, you can't always have correctness hanging over you like the sword of Damocles. When *Riddles* first came out, it was shown at the Other Cinema for two weeks. There were some very good discussions organized around it on the weekends. I don't think the question of essentialism came up in those first discussions, but later.

[*Wollen:* We also got criticized for casting a black actress as Maxine. We thought we were simply giving the part to a black actress, Merdelle Jordine, whose work we both admired. Of course, we were also aware of how difficult it was for black actresses to get parts, as a result of discrimination and stereotyping, and we wanted to do something toward breaking down that kind of prejudice.]

MacDonald: How did you and Peter divide up the work of making *Riddles*?

Mulvey: We tried to get everything possible organized beforehand and leave the narrowest margin for decision during the actual shooting. We worked things out endlessly on charts when we were thinking about the film. Later, when we were working on films where the collaboration was much more difficult, we thought about how avant-garde strategies, like those we used in *Riddles,* enable collaboration, because once we had determined a fixed, formal system, all we had to do was organize all the elements around the formal system. We could decide an enormous amount in advance.

We spent a really, really long time talking *Riddles* through. And all of that was completely both of us together. I don't think one could say that one thing came from Peter or me, rather than the other. There *was* a shift in responsibility in the writing. We collaborated on the voice "off" over the first three sequences, in the sense that although in the end Peter composed the text we both together collected the key words, making arbitrary associations and collecting a vocabulary. Then Peter arranged them as poems, but I was always looking and making suggestions. The last two sequences—the mirror sequence and the British Museum sequence—were written completely by Peter. I might have done a little editing. I think the voice-over in the British Museum sequence, in particular, is an astounding piece of writing. I've been working on the myth of Pandora and the box in recent months, and I find I'm thinking about things *now* that were already there in the British Museum voice-over. It continues to set off resonances for me. I think it is very brilliant, perhaps particularly the way Peter creates a fragmentation of subjectivity. The "she" shifts around and you realize that the voice represents the child's point of view at some time in the future. It encapsulates, in a few lines, the feminist commitment to a fragmentation of subjectivity. This isn't just an avant-garde or postmodern strategy, it is a result of the way that femininity is an enigma in patriarchal society. *Being* the "riddle," women must make use of the heterogeneous in theory and aesthetics to figure out their own incoherent subjectivity.

The dream passage in the mirror sequence was written with a dictionary. Peter was trying to get a completely arbitrary association of words. I think he even used a French dictionary. He would look up a word, then find that word in the English dictionary and use the word *next to it*— something like that, something to get a complete displacement of logical consistency, rather like Buñuel and Dali trying to break down personal associations in *Un Chien Andalou* [1929]. Out of that collection of words, he'd build up a series of fragments of images.

[*Wollen:* That's right. I took words from a French dictionary, according to an arbitrary system I had devised, and then incorporated them in sequence into a narrative. It's a technique that derives from Raymond Roussel. I also used some words from H. D. (pseudonym of poet Hilda Doolittle). When I wrote the earlier voice-off "poems" I was thinking of *Tender Buttons* by Gertrude Stein.]

MacDonald: At what point did the use of 360-degree pans become clear as an essential element in the formal design? I first saw the film in Syracuse, when Owen Shapiro showed it. I was puzzled for the first three sections, but the minute the Louise story began, I was enthralled. I've never felt more exhilaration about a strategy for revealing a dimension of reality—in this case, child care in a domestic setting—that conventional film didn't deal with.

Mulvey: You never got to see *Penthesilea,* did you? It's been out of distribution for years—though Peter and I are trying to change that.

MacDonald: No, I've not seen it.

Mulvey: In *Penthesilea,* each segment was two continuous 16mm rolls of film run together, roughly twenty minutes. That gave us a formal logic, a pattern to work with, a constraint and a sense that our form was conditioned by something outside us. So in *Penthesilea* it was the literal material length of the roll of film. For *Riddles* we wanted an equivalent formal strategy, so we could still use long takes, but in a different way. The point of the decision in any take is: when do you end it? Is it ended because something dramatic happens on the screen? Is it ended because of some relationship to the mise-en-scène? Is it ended just because of some arbitrary whim of the director? The circular camera movement solved that problem for us. I must ask Peter what he thinks about this, but so far as I can remember, that first idea was a truly formal one.

[*Wollen:* I think it was a formal idea. I would also like to pay tribute to the camerawoman, Diane Tammes. It is extremely difficult to take ten minutes to walk a few feet around a tripod at an ultra-slow speed, keeping your eye pressed to a viewfinder and turning a gear handle at a constant tempo. It is even more difficult to do this over and over, varying the timing for each pan and still getting it right. It also demands very precise timing from the actors. Actors and camera had to arrive at the same time at the same place.]

Mulvey: And *also,* I was still very involved with the question of the look and the relationship of the camera to the woman protagonist. *I* felt that the circular camera movement would inscribe the presence of the camera as apparatus into the film. I thought people would be conscious of the *place* of the camera and what it was doing. But I don't think that happened at all. Now, I'm really glad that that didn't work. The only time in our films that I feel we developed the consciousness of the presence of the camera I wanted in *Riddles,* the only place it worked really well, is in *Amy!* [1979]. When Amy is just back from her flight to Australia, the camera pursues her down a little alley. But in *Riddles* you're not particularly aware of the camera.

MacDonald: Amazingly not, given the unusual nature of the pans. In fact, later, when you do see the camera in the mirror sequence, it's shocking.

Mulvey: Yes.

MacDonald: I've always assumed that part of the motivation of the pans was to avoid a "phallic" entry into the image . . .

Mulvey: Yes, yes, I think that's true. The pans have that effect. Certainly, feminist filmmakers' resistance to the zoom lens has been an attempt to get away from a phallic experience of the image. The circular pans took on a resonance of the feminine. But that was subsidiary to the formal decisions.

We were also trying to give a sense of flatness to the image, the feeling of a frieze, rather than a space with depth that is then penetrated. That emphasis on flatness and horizontality was important.

MacDonald: I enjoy the fact that those pans also defy the traditional cinematic focus on males as the center of activity, of image and movement. Generally, what *they* do is decontextualized from the necessities of domestic life and labor. The camera movements are perfect for reuniting action with context. I'm surprised the 360-degree pans have not been copied much.

Mulvey: No. Of course, there are 360-degree pans that predate *Riddles.* There's one in *Weekend* [1968]. There's one in *Vivre sa Vie* [1962]. There might be one in one of [Max] Ophuls's films.

[*Wollen:* There are also 360-degree pans in Jean Renoir's *La Crime du Monsieur Lange* (1935) and Raoul Walsh's *High Sierra* (1941).]

MacDonald: The opening and closing sequences of *Riddles* are closer to the tradition of American avant-garde film than to the history of experimental narrative à la Godard. In Morgan Fisher's *Documentary Footage* [1967] a woman asks herself a series of questions, recording them on a tape recorder; she rewinds the tape recorder, then answers the questions—all in a single, continuous shot. Section Two of *Riddles*, where you record your lecture on the sphinx, and Section Six, where you listen to that conversation, remind me of that film. Were the "frame" sections of *Riddles* allusions to particular films or filmmakers, or just to standard avant-garde procedures?

Mulvey: I hadn't seen the Morgan Fisher film. Peter knew Morgan Fisher, I think, but I don't know if he'd seen the film. In the sphinx rephotography section (Section Three), we certainly had in mind American structural film and the importance of rephotography in that work. Probably, if there was a reference there, it would have been to Ken Jacobs's *Tom, Tom, the Piper's Son* [1969]. I'm not so sure where the acrobats came from, Eisenstein's montage of attractions, perhaps. That sequence was done by a lab; it was the one bit of the film that kept eluding our control. We didn't like a lot of things the lab did, but now I like the sequence more than I used to.

[*Wollen:* I thought of the "Sphinx" and "Acrobats" sequences as East Coast and West Coast, respectively. And yes, I had seen Morgan Fisher's film.]

MacDonald: I was surprised when you said at Hamilton College that you hadn't seen *Riddles* in years, and hadn't really talked much about it.

Mulvey: I hadn't seen it in I don't know how long. The film that I show and talk about a lot is *Amy!* It's only thirty minutes long.

MacDonald: How did it feel to see *Riddles* again?

Mulvey: Well, I still get anxious, but it felt much smoother than it used to. Right after we first made *Riddles*, Peter was in the United States, and I did a lecture tour that the British Film Institute had organized. In those days, there was a feeling that the difficult films of the seventies would be humanized by the director's appearance, and we had always thought of the film as having an agitational element, not only politically, but in that its experimental strategies should be discussed and explained. This was not to give the director's answer, or the author's privileged insight, but to give people a chance to talk about ideas and issues that were unfamiliar. Or, if they were familiar, to respond with their own ideas and reactions. This particular tour was around Southwest England. I showed the film at various colleges and film societies. Lots of quite unwitting people from small towns suddenly found themselves confronted with *Riddles of the Sphinx*. Well, that was anxiety-provoking. I did get an unusual sense of the shape of the film. Often, at experimental film screenings, when people realize what they're going to see, they walk out at once. With *Riddles* that didn't happen: people just sat, kind of bewildered and mesmerized, *until* synch sound came on. They would sit right through the rephotography of the sphinx, which is in many ways the most difficult part of the film. They would sit right through the opening three pans of Louise's story. And then they would leave during the telephone exchange shot. There would be a first walk-out exactly at that point which, strangely enough, is exactly one third through the film. There's a reel change just before that shot. There was something in the rhythm of the film that captured people at the start. And then, one third of the way into the film, people would leave.

[*Wollen:* That sequence is too demanding. I hate it myself. We should have done a mix of telephone conversations as a voice-over. Then it might have worked.]

MacDonald: My students are usually overwhelmed at first. They tend to be frightened until they can get a handle on the form and realize they can begin to make sense of the film.

Mulvey: They should be able to figure out that the film has a pattern, that it's symmetrical. That should be engaging and is, indeed, intended to be a "handle." That is one of the things that I always thought, and still think, is most important about its structure: that it has a symmetry that can help viewers orient themselves—even if that structure was originally chosen for formal reasons. Even if you can't figure out *Riddles* during the first viewing, afterward you can see that *this* matches *that,* that the two bits with me go together and that acrobats go with the sphinx, and so on.

The experience of *Riddles* relates to the work I've been doing on Pandora, where I develop a parallel between Pandora and the box. Pandora herself is like a film noir figure: inside, she's deception, but outside she's beautiful—like Rita Hayworth in *The Lady from Shanghai* [1947]. I argue that there is a "topographical" repetition between her structure and the box's structure. So, her opening the box is a figuration of woman trying to look at the secret of femininity, or the enigma of femininity, as Freud said. I've been arguing for an "aesthetics of the enigma," an aesthetics of the riddle, in order to get away from literalism about the body and the literalism of the look and into the look as curiosity, directed toward the deciphering of a sign. To go back to *Riddles*: organizing the film around a formal pattern gave it the structure of an enigma; the audience is then allowed to enjoy deciphering the shape or pattern of it, so that aspect of the riddle wouldn't be a frustrating obscurity but a form of play.

MacDonald: A form of play that models solving the social and psychological riddles that surround us.

Mulvey: Exactly. You see, Freud in *The Interpretation of Dreams* describes the dream as a rebus—a rebus being a riddle that has its solution actually inscribed into its form. It's not as if the solution were concealed inside by a mysterious space; it's actually concealed in the text itself, and the "reader" of the dream has to decipher the clues through intelligence and imagination, through curiosity engaged by a text. Thinking back to *Riddles* from the point of view of my work on Pandora, I've realized how important the formal pattern of the film was, in making this kind of engagement possible.

I started being theoretically interested in this means of engaging the spectator through thinking about *Wavelength* and through reading Sitney on "structural film," particularly on that aspect of structural film he called "participatory film" [See P. Adams Sitney, *Visionary Film* (New York: Oxford University Press, 1974), pp. 430–435]. *Wavelength,* Frampton's *nostalgia,* and of course, Frampton's *Zorns Lemma* set up a pattern or a system the audience has to engage with. It seemed to me then that this was an important approach, if you're thinking about the pleasure of the text and the pleasure of the look: it provides a way in which the pleasure of the look can become implicated with the pleasure of the rebus. It allows curiosity to be associated not only with narrativity, with wanting to know what happens next, but also with formal engagement where narrativity is transposed onto a kind of grid or pattern.

MacDonald: Recently, I was embarrassed to realize—after seeing the film all the times I've seen it—that I had never noticed how extensive the mirror structure is. Clearly, the opening three sections and the last three sections mirror each other, but it had never occurred to me to look at how the shots of "Louise's Story" mirror each other. Shots one and thirteen, and shots two and twelve, and so on *also* mirror each other . . .

Mulvey: Well, they do and they don't, Scott. The first two shots are indoors, no windows, no outside, a completely enclosed space . . .

MacDonald: Like the last two shots.

Mulvey: Actually that *does* work, doesn't it? But the very enclosed, nesting space at the beginning is the space of the emotional relationship between the mother and the child, and the space of the last two sequences is—it sounds pretentious to say—the space of fantasy, of the enigma of the unconscious, of the enigma of the construction of subjectivity. In the last section they're looking at hieroglyphics. They're not enclosed in their own space; the film has gone beyond their relationship.

[*Wollen:* Hieroglyphics are an exemplary case of a riddle needing to be deciphered. They are also a form of rebus and, of course, Freud saw dreams as structured like hieroglyphs.]

Mulvey: I remember it seemed important to have Louise and Anna walking down the central corridor of the British Museum, *across* the space, breaking the circularity which had been more or less completely controlling their movements up until then. The circularity is still there in the pan, but they make an angle into it. And the child is allowed to walk. And we introduced a new color, red, moving from blue (at the beginning of "Louise's Story") to red. Red is introduced in the mirror sequence, and Louise is wearing red in the British Museum.

MacDonald: I think one of the interesting things the film accomplishes, and I assume it was one of the things you talked a lot about, was showing a positive development, people becoming aware of themselves and aware of what their potential is, without acting as though the world has suddenly miraculously changed. The differences between the early and late shots in "Louise's Story" demonstrate that the relationship of Anna and Louise is changing, and that Louise is becoming more independent. And yet, the parallels between these shots imply that living in patriarchy has not only enclosed Louise and Anna in the world of shot one, but that even if they are now out of their enclosure in the home, what they must investigate is the long public history of patriarchy: the British Museum's exhibits are the *public* form of the same thing that they've experienced in private.

Mulvey: Yes. That was certainly an effect we wanted to get at the end, but in the British Museum shot we were most interested in giving the impression of a "detour through the unconscious." The intertext that precedes that shot is "detour through these texts, entombed now in glass, whose enigmatic script reminds her of a forgotten history and the power of a different language"—the language of the unconscious. This now, of course, seems very much in keeping with feminist discussion at the time . . .

MacDonald: Though not so much in film to that point . . .

Mulvey: Not so much in film. We were trying to put that question into film. We wanted to make an advance in cinema narrative by having a narrative that was a journey into the psyche, so its "resolution" was literally an "opening," rather than a closing down. It's the same kind of thing, perhaps—I hadn't thought of this before—that Buñuel and Dali tried to do by slitting open the eye in *Un Chien Andalou* and discovering a completely different space with a different kind of logic and a different relationship between figure and event. We didn't have *Un Chien Andalou* in mind at the time, but we were trying to move into a phantasmagoric space in the last two shots.

We used the British Museum not as a real live space where people go to see exhibits, but as an image of the enigmatic and historical nature of the unconscious. That's why there is no one else in the museum. The British Museum isn't on the same register as the shopping center is, or the streets, or even the playground. It's the final stage in the film's

movement from the space of Sirkian melodrama [melodrama as epitomized in the films of Douglas Sirk] into the space of the psyche.

Yvonne Rainer

MacDonald: In recent years every time there's a new Yvonne Rainer
film, I read someplace, "This is new and accessible work from Yvonne
Rainer . . ."

Rainer: Right. They said that about the last one, and I've heard it
about *Privilege*.

MacDonald: I didn't find *The Man Who Envied Women* [1985] more
accessible than earlier work—though there were elements of it I liked—
but I do find *Privilege* extremely accessible. I enjoyed it from beginning
to end, and when I screened it as part of my film series in Utica I
discovered it was accessible to a relatively general audience.

Rainer: This is a mainstream-geared audience?

MacDonald: Pretty much. My series has a reputation, so the audience usually expects something unusual, but they're certainly not shy
about leaving. At *Privilege,* I don't believe more than five people left,
out of seventy-five or eighty. I've always assumed that your refusal to
provide certain kinds of conventional pleasure was a defiance of what
the audience has come to expect. But this film includes the audience in
a new way.

Rainer: In Australia, someone asked me—after screening *Privilege*—
"Why are you so committed to depriving the audience of pleasure?"

MacDonald: They said that after *Privilege*?

Rainer: After *Privilege*.

MacDonald: That surprises me.

Rainer: I was astounded because I have never thought of myself as
depriving anyone of pleasure, unless a shot or a sequence had a specific
political agenda, like the tracking shot into the nude in *Film About a
Woman Who. . . .* There was a specific mission there. It was an arduous
experience for the audience to stay with that shot: *no* one could derive
pleasure from *that* image of the woman's body. But in the general course
of things, *I* always thought I was introducing *new* pleasures—the pleasure of the text, of reading.

MacDonald: It's true; there are pleasures in many of the stories told in
your films but not much *visual* pleasure, especially in the films after *Film
About a Woman Who . . .* : that film and *Lives of Performers* [1972] have
an unpretentious elegance and sensuality that's lacking in later films,
especially from *Journeys from Berlin/1971* [1980] and *The Man Who Envied Women*. So when *Privilege* struck me as thoroughly pleasurable, I
thought that since, as Jenny says at the beginning of the film, the subject

of menopause has come to *mean* unpleasure, you felt free to bring back other obvious kinds of cinematic pleasure as a defiance of the conventional attitude about menopause (and its implications for women), and as a way of modeling a new attitude about menopause (and about film).

Rainer: That may be a way of reading the progression of my films, but it was certainly not uppermost in my mind.

What *has* been on my mind is an ongoing relationship to narrative, be it about pleasure or nonpleasure. If narrative is a way of *engaging* the audience, I've gone further and further toward narrative conventions, such as *plot*: this is the first of my films that has a semblance of a plot; it's the first film to use so many professional actors. This is the first film that does not have some overly long passage that people just can't stay with—the theoretical lecture in *The Man Who Envied Women,* or the anecdotal, voice-over material in *Journeys From Berlin.* I have always thought of my films as containing dry moments, but compensating for those with offsetting moments—with animals or stories or irony, humor.

MacDonald: This is also the first film where you use extensive interviewing, isn't it?

Rainer: Well, there's the housing hearing in *The Man Who Envied Women,* but I didn't interview those people. It's talking heads, people giving testimony.

MacDonald: Women talking about their menopausal experiences is, actually, fascinating. Ironically, since it has been a taboo subject in movies, it has become as interesting as other taboo subjects that have to do with the body. The audience—at least the audience I saw the film with—seemed excited to hear these revelations.

Rainer: These are all young people?

MacDonald: About half of them were college people; half were older people from the community.

Rainer: I often get the question from men, Who's your audience? At one point I was saying, "It's young women and men, because young women don't *want* to know about menopause, and men have no reason to, have nothing at stake."

MacDonald: Unless a man is deeply involved with someone struggling with menopause.

Near the end, the Yvonne Washington character says,

I try to monitor when my hot flashes occur. I'm watching a video cassette of "Sweet Sweetback's Baadaass Song." "Why does an embodiment of black protest have to be a stud?" flashes through my mind, and along comes a hot flash. I'm on the subway thinking about a friend. "Forget that family crap," I think. *Flash* . . . Ready to leave, I put on my coat in an overheated room.

> Instantly I am so hot, I must tear it off . . . Reading about the Supreme
> Court's latest setback to civil rights. One of the justices is quoted as saying:
> "The fact that low-paying, unskilled jobs are overwhelmingly held by blacks
> is no proof of racism." *Flash* . . . Thinking about what I could have said,
> should have said: *Flash* . . . [quoted from Rainer's screenplay]

The implication seems to be that you question whether at least some of the symptoms of menopause have anything to do with the physical changes occurring.

Rainer: That was physiological license; it was a way of bringing together the body and the external, social issues: race, especially.

MacDonald: I ask because during a particularly stressful period of my relationship with Pat [O'Connor, MacDonald's wife], she felt her hot flashes were pretty closely related to the psychic stress caused by outside circumstances.

Rainer: I've heard of only one corroboration of this. It certainly isn't my experience, but it sounds plausible. In *Privilege* it was a way of bringing together everything in the film, a kind of unresolved conclusion.

There are other wild goose chases: Jenny's remark that postmenopausal women don't have REM sleep, for instance. It doesn't seem to be many older people's experience that they don't dream anymore.

MacDonald: How did you find your way to the people you interviewed?

Rainer: A number of them were old friends. Two of the women in California I've known since I was a teenager. Once I found one person, I found another.

MacDonald: Were there people interviewed that you didn't use?

Rainer: Yes. And the original interviews are much, much longer. When I first started, I thought, "My god, this film's going to be ten hours long!" Then as I got the other parts of the film together, particular segments of the interviews began to pop out and be relevant.

MacDonald: Have African-Americans or Puerto Ricans played any role in your earlier films? I don't remember any.

Rainer: Yes. Roles, but not *as* ethnic-Americans. Blondell Cummings was in *Kristina Talking Pictures* [1976]. David Diao, who's Chinese-American, is also in that film. I was interested in an "interesting"-looking bunch of people. But I had no idea of dealing with racial or ethnic social difference.

MacDonald: Was there a particular set of circumstances that led you to deal with race in *Privilege*?

Rainer: No single circumstance. It was a gradual awareness of, one, the limitations of feminist film theory, as it has circulated around Lacanian, neo-Freudian theory; and, two, this incident in my own past that constitutes the flashback in the film, which had been troubling to me. In the back of my mind, I always knew that I'd have to deal with it at some point. The so-called postcolonialist cultural writing of the last five years or so moved me toward thinking about a film around that incident.

MacDonald: So Jenny's story is pretty close to yours?

Rainer: Jenny's *flashback,* yes.

MacDonald: What in particular was it about the incident that made it stay with you so long?

Rainer: It had to do with a sense that in coming to New York I had been very oblivious to many things around me. Even though I had come from an anarchist background, when it came to self-development and realizing my own potential in the world, certain things got excluded: social inequities took a back seat, in terms of consciousness. Some of that had to do with my being in psychotherapy and coming out from under an oppressive marriage and having the chance to produce a lot of work. This incident occurred at the very beginning of this psychic and social advancement, and at first it had no effect on me. It was just something that happened and was very quickly forgotten. But twenty years later, it came back to haunt me with a lot of questions about the kind of life I led then.

MacDonald: One standard thing to say about you, and maybe it's something that you've said about yourself, is that you relentlessly avoid the personal, the autobiographical, and yet looking back now, it strikes me that your films reveal more about you than many of the films of the sixties that are *called* personal actually reveal about their makers. It's because you deal with what you're *thinking about* at any given time, which is always a large part of "who we are."

Rainer: Yes.

MacDonald: But I wonder, did you set out at the beginning with the idea of *not* making personal film?

Rainer: No. I certainly wasn't making "personal film" in the sense Brakhage does, in the way the New American Cinemists did—in terms of personal vision. I had no particular vision. And filmmakers complained about my films at the beginning because they weren't "visual"; they didn't play on the retina. My films weren't about making poetic or beautiful images. I got images where I could. And I didn't even do my own shooting! I didn't have a personal touch, in the sense of the painter's hand or a filmmaker's eye—although an eye was certainly there, in the way shots were framed. But my imagery was always at the service of a theatrical, emotional realm; *melodrama* was the perfect form for what I was after: the emotional life lived at an extreme of desperation and conflict. I wanted to explore the emotion of personal life, but it was equally important to me that the films be fictionalized in some way and that there would be no central person you identified with. There's always a lot of personal material in my films, but it's diffused, decentralized, contravened by antinarrative techniques.

MacDonald: There's a healthy recognition that even if something *is* personal to oneself that one's personality shares concerns, ideas, feelings, whatever with lots of other people.

Rainer: Right.

MacDonald: Your characteristic way of putting texts others have written into the mouths of your characters certainly diffuses—or makes more complex—our sense of their identity, *and* it provides the viewer with a précis of issues that you and many other people have been thinking about over a period of time. Did that technique come out of your performance work?

Rainer: It may be related to the separation of persona and speech in some of my early dances. A person would recite a story by someone else in the first person, but their body would not be expressing that story; the body would be involved in some other continuity. I was always working for disparities between sound and image. So yes, that carried over into the films. Also, quotation is an expedient way to produce characters: I don't have to worry about psychological credibility. And it gets certain texts out: *someone* has to speak these texts that I'm interested in. It's always a question in my films who's going to speak what, especially where the characters don't have a direct connection to what or the way in which they speak. In *Privilege* Carlos speaks a text that does reflect on his life, but a text that because of his class and education, he wouldn't normally speak. I've always used my actors as mouthpieces. It's a way of talking about the spoken and the speaker at the same time, and to alternate between them: when Carlos is speaking about color, sitting on the stoop, all of a sudden he says, "Hola! Brenda! Qué tal!" as she passes by, and there's a naturalistic scene where we see him as a street person making advances to his neighbor. It's not "realistic," but it can certainly be followed by the spectator. Everyone has that potential to "speak" themselves in some kind of detached way, and also to enact themselves.

MacDonald: I think it's only *semi*-unrealistic because we're always mouthing ideas that we get from other people . . .

Rainer: Yes, absolutely.

MacDonald: But mostly we disguise, or try to disguise, that we're doing it.

Rainer: Right. Right. It happens daily. You're impressed with something someone has said or that you've read and you incorporate it into your next conversation.

MacDonald: I remember reading about a show at the Collective that you and Bérénice Reynaud curated ["Sexism, Colonialism, Misrepresentation," the Collective for Living Cinema, April 25–May 8, 1988 (the program and related papers were published as the Summer/Autumn 1990 issue of *Motion Picture*)]. It was controversial.

Rainer: Because it covered feminist films and British black films and African films. It swept with a really wide brush. We were taken to task for that.

MacDonald: Who took you to task?

Rainer: Coco Fusco, in *Screen* and in *Afterimage*.

MacDonald: What was her take on the show?

Rainer: Well, the name of her piece was "Fantasies of Oppositionality" [*Afterimage*, vol. 16, no. 5 (December 1988), and *Screen*, vol. 29, no. 4 (Autumn 1988)]. The tack she took was that white experimental filmmakers and psychoanalytic feminists are trying to make a bridge between themselves and black filmmakers or blacks in general, in terms of marginalization, and that by not examining our own "otherness"—in the panel discussions—we "re-centered" our whiteness. It was a hard lesson, though I still feel Coco's overkill approach was not entirely justified.

MacDonald: In *Privilege,* the Yvonne Washington character makes that argument.

Rainer: Yes, she's taken up a version of that criticism.

MacDonald: Were you already at work on this project at that point?

Rainer: Yes. But the Yvonne Washington/Jenny face-off hadn't been written.

MacDonald: How much response to the film by African-Americans have you seen? In Utica the audience was about twenty percent African-American. It was pretty much the same audience that had, earlier in the fall, seen *Sidewalk Stories* [1990]. At that earlier screening, I was shocked to realize that some young African-Americans in the audience had a hard time watching the couple in *Sidewalk Stories* kiss, apparently because they weren't young and attractive enough for the movies. So I wondered how middle-aged women discussing menopause would affect a similar student clientele. As it turned out, there seemed to be an appreciation for the kinds of African-American women who show up in the film and the way in which they're presented, and present themselves.

Rainer: I've had very little response from nonwhites so far. I took the film to the Frederick Douglass Institute of African-American Studies at the University of Rochester. I expected at least a fifty-fifty balance of races in the audience, but it was an almost totally white crowd. Karen Fields, who is the head of that institute, was very appreciative of the film. In fact, I remember she said, "How did you come to deal with something as explosive as a black on white rape, with such restraint?"

When I go out with the film, it's pretty much white audiences. After this year is over, when I stop taking care of my official bookings, I'm going to do an outreach and try to bring the film to community groups. I have to find the black audience. The discussions have been really interesting, and there's no reason they wouldn't be equally interesting with black audiences.

MacDonald: You mentioned to Lynn Tillman in the *Voice* interview ["A Woman Called Yvonne," Jan. 15, 1991, p. 56] that Novella Nelson had an input into the film . . .

Rainer: I was giving Lynn an example of why the opening title credit says *Privilege,* a film by Yvonne Rainer *and many others.* I've never submitted a film to so many people or asked for so much criticism. So there was a contribution there. In rehearsal, Novella corrected my vernacular. She substituted "dude" for "guy"—things like that. And there were a couple of key moments like the one I mentioned to Lynn: Novella's response to Eldridge Cleaver, for example. She was very involved and made comments along the way.

MacDonald: At one point late in the film, there's a tussle where Jenny and Yvonne Washington laugh and wrestle about being in front of the camera. Jenny feels she's been on the hot seat long enough and that it's Yvonne's turn. Yvonne Washington ends up being in front of the camera and talking about her menopause. This raises the issue of the filmmaker exposing herself to the eye of the camera to the degree her interviewees are exposed. You are in front of the camera in the Helen Caldicott reading, but you're not identified. You never do talk openly about *your* menopause. There seems an implicit irony here.

Rainer: Well, the film is very artificial. It continually plays with the so-called "truth value" of documentary, and with the authenticity of identity. I'm split across any number of people in this film. You might say the whole film goes on in my own head. Anyone who knows anything about my life will recognize little bits and pieces here and there. But it's not a roman à clef, where you figure out, Oh that's this one, and that's that one. It's just a way of using material that has an authentic ring to it. Jenny's menopausal story comes from a particular source, but not from me. And it parallels the story of the Cuban woman at the end who is a real interviewee. My menopausal story is there, here and there, but it's not identified. Is this an issue for you?

MacDonald: Well, only on the level that the real filmmaker isn't revealed as clearly as the "filmmaker" in the film.

Rainer: I play Helen Caldicott because it was convenient, and I enjoy making these Hitchcock-like appearances. I also pop up later, making the comment about Brenda not being desired by men.

There *is* an irony in my flu-ravished face. I'm sick every time I shoot a film. Here, I pop up with this smeared lipstick and drawn, pallid face and talk about desirability to men! The same kind of irony comes with putting "My Funny Valentine" over my middle-aged face. Of course, it prefigures what is going to be discussed at much greater length in the film. When Novella came in, she actually thought she was going to be handling the camera and be filmed as she was shooting. I wasn't about to go that far in developing her as a literal alter ego. It suffices for me to say in the credits that she is the filmmaker, and to have said she's making a documentary film. You either take it or leave it.

I deliberately put Yvonne Washington on the edge of the frame until that key Marxist speech when the camera comes around the couch and finally frames her in close-up. That has a very specific metaphorical meaning about marginalization, as does the shot of the black signer, center screen, signing for the white speaker in the oval on the side.

MacDonald: It had never occurred to me how ludicrous the normal way of including a signer on the TV screen is: the person *signing* is in the small hard-to-see space at the corner of the image and the person *talking,* who we can hear without any image at all, in the big space.

Rainer: When it's important to *see* the signer!

MacDonald: It's like the moment in *The Man Who Envied Women* where you reposition the slicing of the eyeball from *Un Chien Andalou* so that we realize its violence against *women.* After decades of teaching that film, the gender implications of that shot had never occurred to me!

Rainer: Really! Wow. It's always been thought of as the "eye" of the camera, hasn't it?

MacDonald: I'm a little puzzled about the dream where there are two black men looking at the *New York Times* want ads and two black women in the bed underneath them.

Rainer: Well, Jenny and Yvonne Washington have just been talking about REM sleep. Jenny mentions that she's heard that older people don't have REM sleep anymore, and Yvonne Washington protests: "I don't believe that, I still dream. Just the other night I had the weirdest dream . . ." and we're into the dream—or actually it's preceded by another dream image, of Jenny running in terror from something *off*screen. Then we see the two black men looking at the *Times* help-wanted ads. The camera pulls away and there's a sign beneath the *Times* that you really can't read: it says, "Lost: memories, muscles, husbands, friends"—all the things that are lost in the aging process or *look* like possible losses. And then you see these two women entwined in bed. It happens too fast (and there's also a voice-over that doesn't quite jibe with what you see), but the two *women* in bed are a reference to lesbians not *needing* men: the men are looking for work!

MacDonald: [Laughter] Hmmm. I missed it.

Rainer: I don't think it's that obvious. But *then,* there's a reverse shot of Jenny looking down, suggesting a racial thing, the threat of the white woman coming between the black women. It's a dream within a dream.

MacDonald: The title "Privilege" was used by Peter Watkins in a 1967 film about rock musicians receiving privilege as a means of siphoning off the political energy of young people into the rock concert phenomenon.

Rainer: I don't remember that film.

MacDonald: How did you decide to use that title?

Rainer: It had to do with Jenny's status in the flashback event. She had privilege and didn't know it, and was also lacking privilege and didn't know it. To her neighbors the Jenny character represents a white norm and a privileged life-style. The aging process has put her in a different relationship to privilege.

Every character in the film can be seen as either having or not having privilege, depending on race, sex, class, age. If they didn't have it, I gave it *to* them. I privileged Digna to be the commentator, to be more omni-scient than Jenny, and to be able to follow Jenny around without being seen. "Privilege" is a crucial term in the film, a kind of prism through which all these issues—and techniques—can be observed.

MacDonald: At the end, you do an interesting thing with the credits, particularly given the line we see during the credits: "UTOPIA: the more impossible it seems, the more necessary it becomes." You intercut between the textual credits and what I assume is the wrap party for the film (you also include additional interview information). Do you see the party as a kind of momentary Utopia?

Rainer: Yeah.

MacDonald: Is the process of making a film your attempt to model Utopian interaction?

Rainer: Originally, the ending was going to be a dozen postmenopausal women in bright red lipstick and black leather jackets, pouring out of a bar, trying to zip up their jackets [laughter]. It was going to be some climactic moment attacking stereotypes: these raunchy, spunky women. And then I kind of abandoned that and thought, "Oh, well maybe there'll be a dance." I thought I'd show all these women dancing to "Sounds of Soweto" or something, and then that seemed too corny. And finally, I decided, why not document what was already going to happen. I invited all the interviewees to the party. Only a few could come. Actually, Shirley Triest, the tall thin woman, flew from California: it was the first time in her life she's been out of California. I was very touched by that.

MacDonald: At the end of the film, just before we see the wrap party, Yvonne asks Jenny, "So, did you ever make it with Brenda?" and Jenny says, "Hell, no! I was terrified of women." That, the two women in bed in the one dream, and a textual statement (it's quoted in one of the stills

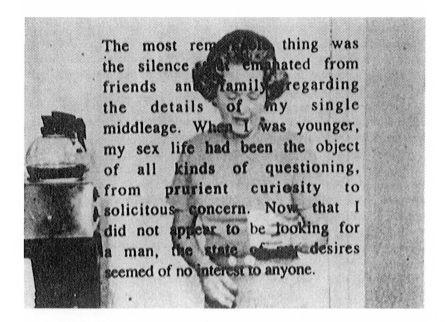

The most remarkable thing was the silence that emanated from friends and family regarding the details of my single middleage. When I was younger, my sex life had been the object of all kinds of questioning, from prurient curiosity to solicitous concern. Now that I did not appear to be looking for a man, the state of my desires seemed of no interest to anyone.

From Rainer's Privilege *(1990).*

you made for *Privilege*)—"The most remarkable thing was the silence that emanated from friends and family regarding details of my single middleage. When I was younger, my sex life had been the object of all kinds of questioning, from prurient curiosity to solicitous concern. Now that I did not appear to be looking for a man, the state of my desires seemed of no interest to anyone"—leads to my last question: What *is* the state of your desires?

Rainer: I've become a lesbian.

MacDonald: Ah.

Rainer: I mean I can only say that now because I'm deeply involved with someone. But for the last five years it's been on my mind. I've gone through these backbends to find some way of describing a state of nonactive, unrealized sexual identity. I did a lecture in Australia where I called myself "a lapsed heterosexual" and an "a-woman" and "a political lesbian." At the level of politics, and emotion, my empathy was with lesbians. But I was settling into a celibate life. I didn't know how to proceed.

That's something I want to learn more about in my next film. I want to interview lesbians who *became* lesbians in middle age. That's the stereotype: a woman is not wanted by men anymore; therefore, she turns to women.

MacDonald: That's a stereotype I've not heard, actually.

Rainer: Oh? It's in the culture. I don't think I invented it, and I really want to investigate it: *Is* it a stereotype? *Privilege* does raise all the stereotypes about desirability and women getting "old" before men get "old," and the old maid stereotype.

MacDonald: I guess the stereotype I've heard is that old maids are lesbians whether they know it or not—though I'm certainly not in touch with the conventional stereotyping of lesbians.

Rainer: What's very interesting to me is that the instant you get involved with someone of your own sex, it's like crossing the Rubicon! I mean, suddenly, I'm not a "political lesbian" (well, I *am* a political lesbian), I'm a lesbian. I felt I couldn't *say* that before, which was odd, because years ago, there was a time I couldn't say I was a feminist because I thought, "Oh a feminist is a political *activist,* not just someone who makes art." I got past that, and have been an avowed feminist for years.

You know, this is the first time I've uttered all this. No one has asked me directly.

MacDonald: Privilege gave me the sense you wanted to be asked, but I wasn't sure I'd have the nerve to ask you.

Rainer: I'm glad you did. It's the beginning—for me—of talking about it. Which means the beginning of fomenting a film.

Trinh T. Minh-ha

For Trinh T. Minh-ha, filmmaking has been a way of responding to the multicultural perspective she has developed as a result of growing up in Vietnam during the American military presence there and her subsequent experiences as teacher, writer, and artist in France, the United States, and in a variety of West African societies. At the time this interview was recorded, Trinh had completed three films: two—*Reassemblage* (1982) and *Naked Spaces—Living Is Round* (1985)—focus on West Africa; a third—*Surname Viêt Given Name Nam* (1989)—was made in the United States, about the experiences of Vietnamese women before, during, and after the recent war. Because Trinh uses a hand-held camera and a variety of other visual and auditory tactics familiar from North American and European independent cinema, her films can seem to be new instances of older critical approaches, but in fact, she accomplishes something relatively distinct. Her use of the hand-held camera in *Reassemblage* and *Naked Spaces—Living Is Round,* for example, is neither an expression of her emotions, as gestural camerawork is in such Brakhage films as *Window Water Baby Moving* or *Sirius Remembered* (1959), nor an expression of her understanding of some essential dimension of what she films. Rather, her seemingly awkward camera movements, and other obvious formal devices, function as a cinematic staff (in the musical sense) on which is encoded the interface between Trinh (and the cultural practices she represents/enacts) and the cultures within which she records imagery and sound.

Reassemblage is a cine-poem, or a suite, on the theme of Senegal, focusing particularly on the everyday activities of women. It is an immense (forty minutes) montage of visuals and sounds within which particular, unexplained sights and activities become motifs. Though the film developed out of Trinh's frustration with the ways in which Senegal is exploited and patronized by Western cultures, the film's focus and structure provide a film critical response not only to the depiction of African societies in the commercial cinema, but to the history of ethnographic filmmaking, which has often been seen as a critical corrective to the absurdities of cultural "representation" in mass-market entertainment. While we may appreciate the fact that such landmarks in the development of ethnographic cinema as Robert Flaherty's *Nanook of the North* (1922), John Marshall's *The Hunters* (1958), and Timothy Asch and Napoleon Chagnon's *Ax Fight* (1975) provide a more direct window on particular indigenous peoples than Hollywood film can even pretend to, *Reassemblage* reminds us of how fully such films participate in the formal procedures of the commercial cinema (in particular, its focus on adventure narrative and on the resolution of ambiguity) and the ideology embedded in these procedures.

While *Reassemblage* "reassembles" imagery in a particular society so that we see it from a less patronizing (and more feminist) perspective, *Naked Spaces—Living Is Round* provides a cross-cultural look—or set of looks—at living spaces and the people who inhabit them in a range of societies in West Africa: specifically, in Senegal, Mauritania, Togo, Mali, Burkina Faso, and Benin. The very breadth of Trinh's view in *Naked Spaces,* which is evident both in the variety of societies and living spaces recorded and in her consistent use of long, halting pans as a means of revealing both the living spaces and their spatial contexts, can be seen as a critique of the narrow focus of the depiction of African societies in both commercial film and documentary, and as a way of demonstrating that the diversity, ingenuity, and beauty of these societies are as cinematically worthy as the varieties of European or North American cultural expression. Trinh's unusual soundtrack confirms these implications. Rather than provide a single perspective on the cultures represented visually, Trinh weaves the sounds of the various West African cultures, statements by three different female voices—as she explains in the introduction to the text of the sound track, reprinted in *Cinematograph,* No. 3 (1988), a "low voice" remains "close to the villagers' sayings and statements, and quotes African writers' works"; a "high-range voice . . . informs according to Western logic and mainly quotes Western thinkers"; and a "medium-range voice" speaks "in the first person and relates personal feelings, and observations" (p. 65)—and periods of silence into an auditory montage that intersects in various ways at various times with the geographically organized visuals.

While *Reassemblage* and *Naked Spaces* can be understood as critiques

From Trinh's Naked Spaces—Living Is Round *(1985).*

of the conventional representations of particular indigenous societies, *Surname Viêt Given Name Nam* focuses more fully on the issue of translation: the translation of experiences in one culture into the verbal and visual languages of other cultures, and the "translation" of people from one nation to another. Again, Trinh refuses to participate in the conventional tendency to try to simplify and "clarify" complex cultural experiences for the film audience. During the first half of *Surname Viêt Given Name Nam,* a series of women discuss what, at first, most viewers probably assume are the women's own experiences in postwar Communist Vietnam. They speak in heavily accented English that intermittently is translated into superimposed printed text. Rather than simply clarifying the speakers' comments, however, the superimposed words suggest how translations tend to impede our willingness to actually listen to accented spoken English: we read the translation and cease listening to the people. The implications of this tendency are confirmed by the frequent disparities between what we hear and what we read: the very act of "translation," Trinh demonstrates, subverts our willingness to develop an ability to hear the expressions of people whose cultural difference is encoded in their accents.

During the second half of *Surname Viêt Given Name Nam,* we discover that the women interviewed in the first half are not current residents of Vietnam, but have been translated to the United States where they have acculturated themselves in varying degrees. Indeed, the Vietnamese experiences they have testified to are not even theirs: they are the reminiscences of other Vietnamese women translated first into French and subsequently into English for use in Trinh's film, which, we come to realize, has set us up to discover how fully our cultural (and film-cultural) training has led us to accept at face value simplistic renderings of the complex experiences of people in and from other cultures.

I spoke with Trinh while she was touring with *Surname Viêt Given Name Nam,* in Utica, in November 1989.

MacDonald: You grew up in Vietnam during the American presence there. This may be a strange question to ask about that period, but I'm curious about whether you were a moviegoer and what films you saw in those years.

Trinh: I was not at all a moviegoer. To go to the movies then was a real feast. A new film in town was always an overcrowded, exciting event. The number of films I got to see before coming to the States was rather limited, and I was barely introduced to TV before I left the country in 1970. Actually, it was only when the first television programs came to Vietnam that I learned to listen to English. Here also the experience was a collective one since you had to line up in the streets with everyone else to look at one of the TVs made available to the neighborhood. I had studied English at school, but to be able to follow the actual pace of spoken English was quite a different matter.

MacDonald: Did you see French films in school?

Trinh: No. A number of them were commercially shown, but during the last few years I was in Vietnam, there were more American than French films. My introduction to film culture is quite recent.

MacDonald: Reassemblage seems to critique traditional ethnographic movies—*Nanook of the North, Ax Fight, The Hunters* . . . I assume you made a conscious decision to take on the whole male-centered history of ethnographic moviemaking. At what point did you become familiar with that tradition? Did you have specific films in mind when you made *Reassemblage?*

Trinh: No, I didn't. You don't have to be a film connoisseur to be aware of the problems that permeate anthropology, although these problems do differ with the specific tools and the medium that one uses. The way one relates to the material that makes one a writer-anthropologist or an anthropological filmmaker needs to be radically questioned. A

Zen proverb says "A grain of sand contains all land and sea," and I think that whether you look at a film, attend a slide show, listen to a lecture, witness the fieldwork by either an expert anthropologist or by any person subjected to the authority of anthropological discourse, the problems of subject and of power relationship are all there. They saturate the entire field of anthropological activity.

I made *Reassemblage* after having lived in Senegal for three years [1977–80] and taught music at the Institut National des Arts in Dakar; in other words, after having time and again been made aware of the hegemony of anthropological discourse in every attempt by both local outsiders and by insiders to identify the culture observed. *Reassemblage* was shot in 1981 well after my stay there. Although I had by then seen quite a number of films and was familiar with the history of Western cinema, I can't say this was a determining factor. I had done a number of Super-8 films on diverse subjects before, but *Reassemblage* was my first 16mm.

MacDonald: You mentioned you were looking at films before you went to Senegal. Were you looking at the way in which Senegal or other African cultures were portrayed in film?

Trinh: No, not at all. Despite my having been exposed to a number of nonmainstream films from Europe and the States at the time, I must say I was then one of the more passive consumers of the film industry. It was when I started making films myself that I really came to realize how obscene the question of power and production of meaning is in filmic representation. I don't really work in terms of influence. I've never been able to recognize anything in my background that would allow me neatly to trace—even momentarily—my itinerary back to a single point of origin. Influences in my life have always happened in the most odd, disorderly way. Everything I've done comes from all kinds of directions, certainly not just from film. It seems rather clear to me that *Reassemblage* did not come from the films I looked at, but from what I had learned in Senegal. The film was not realized as a reaction to anything in particular, but more I would now say, as a desire not to simply *mean*. What seemed most important to me was to expose the transformations that occurred with the attempt to materialize on film and between the frames the impossible experience of "what" constituted Senegalese cultures. The resistance to anthropology was not a motivation for the making of the film. It came alongside other strong feelings, such as the love that one has for one's subjects of inquiry.

MacDonald: So the fact that you found a film form different from what has become conventional as a means of imaging culture was accidental . . .

Trinh: Not quite accidental, because there were a number of things I did not want to reproduce in my work: the kind of omniscience that pervades many films, not just through the way the narration is being told, but more generally, in their structure, editing, and cinematography, as well as in the effacement of the filmmakers, or the invisibility of their politics. But what I rejected and did not want to carry on came also *with* the making of *Reassemblage*. While I was filming, for example, I realized that my preoccupations often conformed to the norms of anthropology, and the challenge was to depart from them without merely resorting to self-censorship.

MacDonald: Often in *Reassemblage* there'll be an abrupt movement of the camera or a sudden cut in the middle of a motion that in a normal film would be allowed to have a sense of completion. Coming to the films from the arena of experimental moviemaking, I felt familiar with those kinds of tactics. Had you seen much of what in this country is called "avant-garde film" or "experimental film"? I'm sorry to be so persistent in trying to relate you to film! I can see it troubles you.

Trinh: [Laughter] I think it's an interesting problem because your attempt is to situate me somewhere in relation to a film tradition, whereas I feel that experimentation is an attitude that develops with the making process when one is plunged into a film. As one advances, one explores the different ways that one can do things without having to lug about heavy belongings. The term "experimental" becomes questionable when it refers to techniques and vocabularies that allow one to classify a film as "belonging" to the "avant-garde" category. Your observation that the film foregrounds certain strategies not foreign to experimental filmmakers is accurate, although I would add that when *Reassemblage* first came out, the experimental/avant-garde film world had as many problems with it as any other film milieu. A man who has been active in experimental filmmaking for decades, for example, said, "She doesn't know what she's doing."

So, while the techniques are not surprising to avant-garde filmmakers, the film still does not quite belong to that world of filmmaking. It differs perhaps because it exposes its politics of representation instead of seeking to transcend representation in favor of visionary presence and spontaneity, which often constitute the prime criteria for what the avant-garde considers to be Art. But it also differs because all the strategies I came up with in *Reassemblage* were directly generated by the material and the context that define the work. One example is the use of repetition as a transforming, as well as rhythmic and structural device. Since making the film, I have seen many more experimental films and have sat on a number of grant panels. Hence I have had many opportunities to recognize how difficult it is to reinvent anew or to defamiliarize what has become common practice among filmmakers. It was very sad to see, for example, how conventional the use of repetition proved to be in the realm of "experimental" filmmaking. This does not mean that one can no longer use it, but rather that the challenge in using it is more critical.

I still think that in *Reassemblage* repetition functions very differently than in many of the films I have seen. For me, it's not just a technique that one introduces for fragmenting or emphasizing effects. Very often people tend to repeat mechanically three or four times something said on the sound track. This technique of looping is also very common in experimental music. But looping is not of particular interest to me. What interests me is the way certain rhythms came back to me while I was traveling and filming across Senegal, and how the intonation and inflection of each of the diverse local languages informed me of where I was. For example, the film brought out the musical quality of the Serer language through untranslated snatches of a conversation among villagers and the varying repetition of certain sentences. Each language has its own music and its practice need not be reduced to the mere function of communicating meaning. The repetition I made use of has, accordingly, nuances and differences built within it, so that repetition here is not just the automatic reproduction of the same but rather the production of the same within differences.

MacDonald: When I had seen *Reassemblage* enough to see it in detail, rather than just letting it flow by, I noticed something that strikes me as very unusual. When you focus on a subject, you don't see it from a single plane. Instead, you move to different positions near and far and from side to side. You don't try to choose *a* view of the subject; you explore various ways of seeing it.

Trinh: This is a great description of what is happening with the *look* in *Reassemblage,* but I'll have to expand on it a little more. It is common practice among filmmakers and photographers to shoot the same thing more than once and to select only one shot—the "best" one—in the editing process. Otherwise, to show the subject from a more varied view, the favored formula is that of utilizing the all-powerful zoom or curvilinear traveling shot, whose totalizing effect is assured by the smooth operation of the camera.

Whereas in my case, the limits of the looker and of the camera are clearly exposed, not only through the repeated inclusion of a plurality of shots of the same subject from very slightly different distances or angles (hence the numerous jump-cut effects), but also through a visibly hesitant, or as you mentioned earlier, incomplete, sudden, and unstable camera work. (The zoom is avoided in both *Reassemblage* and *Naked Spaces,* and diversely acknowledged in the more recent films I have been making.) The exploratory movements of the camera—or structurally speaking, of the film itself—which some viewers have qualified as "disquieting," and others as "sloppy," is neither intentional nor unconscious.

It does not result from an (avant-garde) anti-aesthetic stance, but occurs, in my context, as a form of reflexive body writing. Its erratic and unassuming moves materialize those of the filming subject caught in a situation of trial, where the desire to capture on celluloid grows in a state of nonknowingness and with the understanding that no reality can be "captured" without transforming.

MacDonald: The subject stays in its world and you try to figure out what your relationship to it is. It's exactly the opposite of "taking a position": it's seeing what *different* positions reveal.

Trinh: That's a useful distinction.

MacDonald: Your interest in living spaces is obvious in *Reassemblage* and more obvious in *Naked Spaces*. You also did a book on living spaces.

Trinh: In Burkina Faso, yes. And in collaboration with Jean-Paul Bourdier.

MacDonald: Did your interest in living spaces precede making the films or did it develop by making them?

Trinh: The interest in the poetics of dwelling preceded *Reassemblage*. It was very much inspired by Jean-Paul, who loves vernacular architecture and has been doing research on rural houses across several Western and non-Western cultures. We have worked together as a team on many projects.

Reassemblage evolves around an "empty" subject. I did not have any preconceived idea for the film and was certainly not looking for a particularized subject that would allow me to speak *about* Senegal. In other words, there is no single center in the film—no central event, representative individual or individuals, or unifying theme and area of interest. And there is no single process of centering either. This does not mean that the experience of the film is not specific to Senegal. It is *entirely* related to Senegal. A viewer once asked me, "Can you do the same film in San Francisco?" And I said, "Sure, but it would be a totally different film." The strategies are, in a way, dictated by the materials that constitute the film. They are bound to the circumstances and the contexts unique to each situation and cultural frame.

In the processes of emptying out positions of authority linked to knowledge, competence, and qualifications, it was important for me in the film to constantly keep alive the question people usually ask when someone sets out to write a book or in this case, to make a film: "A film about Senegal, but what in Senegal?" By "keeping alive" I mean, refusing to package a culture, hence not settling down with any single answer, even when you know that each work generates its own constraints and limits. So what you see in *Reassemblage* are people's daily activities: nothing out of the ordinary, nothing "exotic," and nothing that constitutes the usual focal points of observation for anthropology's fetishistic approach to culture, such as rites, figures of worship, and artifacts, or in the narrow sense of the terms, ritualistic events and religious practices.

While shooting *Reassemblage,* I was both moved by the richness of the villagers' living spaces, and made aware of the difficulty of bringing on screen the different attitudes about dwelling implied. This was how the idea of making another film first appealed to me. *Naked Spaces* was shot three years later across six countries of West Africa, while *Reassemblage* involved five regions across Senegal.

MacDonald: Reassemblage takes individual subjects—people, actions, objects—and provides various perspectives on them; *Naked Spaces* enlarges the scope. You deal with a general topic—domestic living spaces—and explore its particular manifestations in one geographic area after another. And your view of particular spaces is enlarged too: you pan across a given space from different distances and angles (in *Reassemblage* the camera is generally still, though you filmed from different still positions). There's a tendency to move back and forth across the space in different directions to rediscover it over and over in new contexts.

Trinh: That is very close to how I felt in making *Naked Spaces.* Although I would say that the procedure is somewhat adverse (even while keeping a multiplicity of perspectives) rather than analogous, the immediate perception is certainly that of an enlarged scope, physically speaking, not only because of the duration of the film and the variety of cultural terrains it traverses, but also, as you point out, because ot its visual treatment. In *Reassemblage* I avoided going from one precise point to another in the cinematography. I was not preoccupied with depicting space. But when you shoot architecture and the spaces involved, you are even more acutely aware of the limit of your camera and how inadequate the fleeting pans and fractured still images used in *Reassemblage* are, in terms of showing spatial relationships.

One of the choices I made was to have many pans, but *not* smooth pans, and none that could give you the illusion that you're not looking through a frame. Each pan sets into relief the rectangular delineation of the frame. It never moves obliquely, for example.

MacDonald: It's always horizontal . . .

Trinh: Or vertical.

MacDonald: And it's always referring back to you as an individual filmmaker behind the camera. It never becomes this sort of Hitchcock motion through space that makes the camera feel so powerful.

Trinh: In someone else's space I cannot just roam about as I may like to. Roaming about with the camera is not value-free; on the contrary, it tells us much about the ideology of such a technique.

MacDonald: It's interesting too that the way you pan makes clear that the only thing we're going to find out about you personally is that you're interested in this place. Much hand-held camerawork is implicitly auto-biographical, emotionally self-expressive. In your films camera movement is *not* autobiographical except in the sense that it reveals you were in this place with these people for a time.

Trinh: There are many ways to treat the autobiographical. What is autobiographical can often be very political, but not everything is political in the autobiographical. One can do many things with elements of autobiography. However, I appreciate the distinction you make because in the realm of generalized media colonization, my films have too often been described as "personal film," as "personal documentary" or "subjective documentary." Although I accept these terms, I think they really need to be problematized, redefined, and expanded. Because personal in the context of my films does *not* mean an individual standpoint or the foregrounding of a self. I am not interested in using film to "express myself" but rather to expose the social self (and selves) that necessarily mediates the making as well as the viewing of the film.

MacDonald: "Personal," "subjective" suggest that something else is impersonal and objective.

Trinh: Right. As if anyone can produce objective documentary. There is nothing objective and truly impersonal in filmmaking, although there can be a formulaic, clichéd approach to film. What you often have is a mere abiding by the conventions of documentary practice, which is put forward as *the* "objective" way to document other cultures. It is as if the acknowledgement of the politics of the documentation and the documenting subject disturbs the interests of the guardians of norms.

MacDonald: In *Naked Spaces* we're inside the dwellings as much as we're outside. In fact, the movement from outside to inside, and vice versa, seems central to the film.

Trinh: Yes. When you walk from outside to the inside of most rural African houses, you come from a very bright sunlight to a very dark space where, for a moment, you are totally blind. It takes some time to get adjusted to the darkness inside. This experience is one of the conceptual bases of *Naked Spaces*. To move inside oneself, one has to be willing to go intermittently blind. Similarly, to move toward other people, one has to take the jump and move ahead blindly at certain moments of inquiry. If one is not even momentarily blind, if one remains as one is from the outside or from the inside, then it is unlikely that one can break through that moment where suddenly everything stops, one's luggage is emptied out, and one moves in a state of nonknowingness, where destabilizing encounters with the "unfamiliar" or "unknown" are multiplied and experienced anew.

MacDonald: Since as a technology, film captures light, the traditional

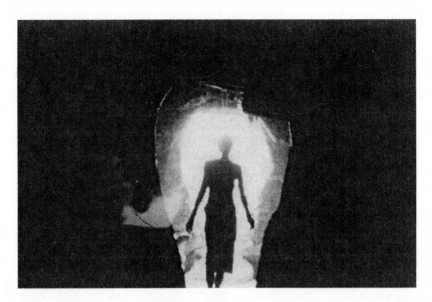

From Naked Spaces—Living Is Round *(1985)*.

assumption has been that anything that's dark is not worth looking at. At most, darkness is a context for romance and for danger. Even in a documentary, we'd either never see the types of dimly lit spaces you reveal, or they'd be lit artificially, which would allow the technology to record them, but in a way that would distort the real experience of such spaces. The technology determines what one can see about other cultures. You depart from this not only by recording indoor spaces in their own natural low-light conditions, but by revealing the beauty of these spaces.

Trinh: You can imagine these houses being shot with a light inside. The quality of solid darkness and the shafts of light that penetrate the inside spaces would totally be damaged.

MacDonald: Instead of intimate—if that's the right word—the spaces would become bare, empty.

Trinh: Yes, yes. The question of cinema and light is pivotal in *Naked Spaces.* Dwelling is both material and immaterial; it invites volume and shape, and it reflects a cosmology and a way of living creatively. In other words, to deal with architecture is to deal with the notion of light in space. To deal with the notion of light in space is to deal with color, and to deal with color is to deal with music, because the question of light in film is also a question of timing and rhythm. Such mutual accord of elements of daily existence is particularly striking in the built environments filmed and the way these materialize the multiple oneness of life.

There are a number of direct statements on color and color timing in the text of *Naked Spaces* ["Color is life / *Light becoming music*"; *"Orange and blue; warmer or colder; more luminosity, / more presence. Timing acts as a link between natural/and artificial light"*]. The look of a film and how people are represented depends so vitally on color timing. For me, it has always been crucial to work closely with the color timer, especially in *Naked Spaces.* Very often, when films shot in Africa reach the lab, they are treated the same way as films shot in Western cultures; that is, they are timed more on the blue side of the color chart for people with fair skin. Hence, the African people often come out with a skin color that is dull charcoal black. This is not the vibrant skin color that I saw and remembered, so I devoted much of my energy at the lab learning from and cooperating with the timer on "color correcting," insisting whenever appropriate, on the orange and warmer colors to obtain the usually missing vibrant quality of African skin tones.

The relationship I worked on between color and light was also the link I drew between architecture, music, and film. The connections that determine the structure of the film are those that I have experienced in the living spaces of the different peoples involved. The roundness of life is not only literally manifested in the round shape of many of the houses. It is also recognizable in all spheres of sociocultural activity, such as the various dances shown or even the way women work together. "The house opens onto the sky in a perfect circle," a voice states in *Naked Spaces,* and the subtitle of the film is "Living Is Round."

MacDonald: You were talking about music and architecture. Certainly one of the things that's unusual about both African films is the sound tracks: the movement back and forth between music, other everyday sounds, the various narrators, and silence. I assume this interweaving of different strands of sound and silence derives from your interest in music.

Trinh: I guess now I can come back to your earlier question about the film background I don't really have, by relating the way I work with film to my musical background. I fare with ease in the world of experimental music, perhaps because of the cultural hybridity of both its instrumentation and its deterritorialized space—the way it questions the boundaries of what is music and what is not. I really admired, for example, John Cage, whose Zen-inspired compositions and readings have effected radical change in all fields of the arts. I was very attracted to his work because it touched on something I was similarly groping for but had not articulated. The fact that Cage brought silence and the sounds of life into the consecrated realm of concert halls and out into the domain of public debate, was very liberating. "Experimental music" in this context is a constant exploration of sound as sound, rather than as a substitute for something else: a personal feeling or a psychological state. Narrative music is thus exposed in its ideology, its closures, and its link with power and knowledge.

Many viewers have, indeed, thought of my films as operating more like a musical score than like any traditional film structure. And I also tend to think of film montage and music composition as being very much alike (with the understanding that montage is not reduced to the editing stage, but can occur in the conception and shooting stages of the film as well). One can also argue that in poetry a very similar process happens in the play of words. For me, the exploration of new, complex subjectivity and the problematizing of the subject in contemporary theory can be best carried out through poetical language—as long as poetical language is not equated with a mere estheticizing tool or practiced as a place to consolidate a "subjective" self. In poetry, the "I" can *never* be said to simply personify an individual. It's amusing that the feedback I often get from my relatives or close friends on my book of poems tends to be something like: "We never suspected you could be what you are in your poetry!" For them all the feelings and situations depicted in poetry are *personally* true. They immediately associate me with the "I" who speaks in my poetry and assume it's "real," which is not wrong, but it's not accurate either. In poetical language, there is no "I" that just stands for *my*self. The "I" is there; it has to be there, but it is there as the site where all other "I's" can enter and cut across one another. This is an example of the strength and vitality of poetical language and of how it can radically contribute to the questioning of the relationship of subjects to power, language, and meaning in theory. Theory, as practiced by many, is often caught in a positioning where the theorist continues to stand in a "safe place" to theorize about others.

MacDonald: I've often felt that way about the little I know of theoretical film writing. Part of the reason I write articles is to consolidate a position for myself within an institution, to give myself a certain amount of economic and psychic security. Theorists talk about how the artist is situated within an economic system, but I rarely hear discussion of writing theory as a marketable activity.

Trinh: Exactly.

MacDonald: On the other hand, if I show *Nanook* and *Ax Fight* and then show *Reassemblage,* it's like film theory in action. Language has such a hard time grasping what's on the screen that it's just easier to put the films next to one another and let the audience discover what the juxtapositions reveal.

Trinh: There is a tendency in theorizing *about* film to see theorizing as one activity and filmmaking as another, which you can discuss with theory. This is an important question for me because I teach theory partly to people who come to a university department of cinema [Trinh teaches at San Francisco State University] primarily for film production. There's an antitheory tradition that runs deep among some of the "production people." I promote "bridge" courses and emphasize the indispensability of the mutual challenge of theory and practice, which can be summarized in an old statement by Marx: that theory cannot thrive without being rooted in practice, and that practice cannot liberate itself without theory. When one starts theorizing *about* film, one starts shutting in the field; it becomes a field of experts whose access is gained through authoritative knowledge of a demarcated body of "classical" films and legitimized ways of reading and speaking about films. That's the part I find most sterile in theory. It is necessary for me always to keep in mind that one cannot really theorize about film, but only *with* film. This is how the field can remain open.

MacDonald: The thing I find frustrating about the whole theory/practice issue as it has played itself out in the last ten or twelve years is that to make a film one has to take a chance with one's life and one's resources. It's true in Hollywood films and in independent film, where, if you're going to come up with thirty-five thousand dollars to make a movie, you have to restructure your life. You have to take a direct and dangerous part in whatever the national economy is that you live in. When I write about films—and I don't write theory, but I think it's also true there—you don't have to reorganize anything (at least in this country): you can remain within an institutional framework where you have a salary: you can critique without changing your life-style. I go to independent films to see what those people who are willing to put their lives on the line are able to discover. Theory can be brilliant and enlightening, but I rarely feel people's lives on the line in the same way.

Trinh: Well, I think there's such a resistance to theory because theory is often deployed from a very safe place. And I am not even talking about the other resistance that is found within the academic system itself, where theory can threaten the status quo and a distinction could be made between intellectual activities and academicizing pursuits. But I, myself, think of theory as a practice that changes your life entirely, because it acts on your conscience. Of course, theory becomes a mere accessory to practice when it speaks from a safe place, while practice merely illustrates theory when the relationship between the two remains one of domination-submission and of totalization. I see theory as a constant questioning of the framing of consciousness—a practice capable of informing another practice, such as film production. Hence theory always has the possibility, even the probability, of leading to "dangerous" places, and vice versa. I can't separate the two. The kind of film I make requires that economically, as you point out, I readjust my life, but

I am constantly questioning who I am, and making my films transform the way I see the world. You know, history is full of people who die for theory.

MacDonald: Can we go back to *Naked Spaces*? How did you decide on the order of the sections? Until I went to the atlas, I thought perhaps you traveled in a circle.

Trinh: Except for the end of the film, which leads us back to the opening sequences, *Naked Spaces* is organized in the geographical order of my itinerary: from one country, one region, to another. Each location is indicated by having the names of the people and the country appear briefly on the screen, more as a footnote than as a name tag or a validating marker. The sound track is, however, more playful: a statement made by a member of a specific group may be repeated in geographical contexts that are different. Needless to say, this strategy has not failed to provoke hostility among "experts" on African cultures, "liberal" media specialists, and other cultural documentarians.

Apparently, some "professional" viewers cannot distinguish between a signpost, whose presence only tells you where you are, and an arrangement that suggests more than one function at work. Depending on how one uses them, letters on an image have many functions, and viewers who abide by media formulas are often insensitive to this. For me, the footnotes or the names that appear on screen allow precisely the non-expert viewer to recognize that a few selected statements issued by one source or heard in one group are repeated *across* borderlines of ethnic specificities. Thus, the names also function as acknowledgment of the strategical play of the film, my manipulations as filmmaker.

The deliberate act of taking, for example, a Dogon [Mali] statement on adornment and desire or on the house as a woman, and juxtaposing it with specific images of dwellings among the Kabye [Togo] and then again, among the Birifor [Burkina Faso] is a taboo among experts. What one ethnic group says can absolutely not be reproduced in the context of another group. This is also applicable in the film to quotes from Westerners, such as Paul Éluard's "The earth is blue like an orange," which is heard in a sequence on the Oualatans [Mauritania] as well as in a sequence on the Fon [Benin]. And I use a similar strategy in the music: in both *Naked Spaces* and *Reassemblage,* music from one group is first heard with that very group and then repeated with variations within other groups. The viewer is made aware of such "violations" of borders.

There is a very interesting issue involved here. The peoples of third-world countries used to be lumped together in their undifferentiated otherness. And this is reflected pervasively in Western media discourses—radio, books, photos, films, television. You might have a program on Vietnam, for example, but you hear persistent Chinese music in the background. Even today, in many mainstream films on the Vietnam experience, the people cast in the Vietnamese roles are neighboring Southeast Asians who can hardly speak a word of Vietnamese. Of course, for many American viewers, it doesn't matter. Asians are Asians, and you can even take someone from the Philippines or from Korea to fill in the roles. Well, it's certainly the perpetuation of such attitudes that the cultural experts and anthropologists work against. And they should. But to rectify the master's colonialist mistakes, they have come up with disciplinarian guidelines and rules. One of them, for example, is that you always show the source of the music heard, and the music of one group must not be erroneously used in the context of another group. However, such rationalization also connotes a preoccupation with authenticity that supposes culture can be objectified and reified through "data" and "evidence." The use of synch sound becomes binding and its validation as the most truthful way of documenting is taken for granted.

It is fine for me if the master's heirs are now correcting his errors to raise their own consciousness of other cultures. But when circumstantial and history-bound methods and techniques become validated as the norms for *all* films, then they prove to be very dangerous: once more an established frame of thinking, a prevailing system of presentation, is naturalized and seen as the only truthful and "correct" way. Surely enough, these "rules" are particularly binding when it is a question of third-world people: films made on white American culture, for example, can use classical music from any European source and this hardly bothers any viewer. In *Naked Spaces*, I neither reproduce the master's mistakes nor abide by disciplinarian criteria of correct representation; hence the importance of the naming of the peoples to acknowledge the deliberate gesture of carrying certain cultural statements across ethnic boundaries.

MacDonald: So the imagery is a kind of grid against which the spectator can consider your manipulations of sound.

Trinh: Yes. One could certainly have a more restrained sound track, and let the images move back and forth across transcultural signs, but the choice here was to have that transgressive fluidity in the sound. The visuals, as we discussed earlier, have their own critical strategies. After all, boundaries are extremely arbitrary. Boundaries between nations are a recent phenomenon. The village people themselves refer to kinship boundaries, which are usually also the boundaries between different ethnic groups. And ethnic grouping cuts across geopolitical borderlines.

MacDonald: One activity that certainly confirms this idea is the pounding of grain, which we see in culture after culture.

Trinh: At five o'clock in the morning, I would wake up and listen to that sound in most villages, and it would go on late into the evening. The day begins and ends with women pounding to prepare the meals. And yes, it is a collective background sound that you'll recognize in villages across Africa.

MacDonald: At times you can't tell whether what you're hearing is daily labor or music.

Trinh: More than the music of labor, you also have the body rhythm of collective work. In the film, the way women bodily relate to each other while working is very rhythmic and musical. In other words, daily interactions among the people *are* music. You mentioned earlier the various aspects of the sound track: the silence, the commentary, the environmental sound, vocal and instrumental music. All these elements form the musical dimension of the film, but the relationship between and within the visuals is also rhythmically determined. The way an old woman spins cotton; the way a daughter and her mother move in syncopation while they pound or beat the grain together; the way a group of women chant and dance while plastering the floor of the front court in a house; or the way the different cultures counteract or harmonize with one another—these are the everyday rhythms and music of life. In such environments one realizes how much modern society is based on compartmentalization—the mentality colonialism has spread.

MacDonald: On the sound track, the statements about Africa are presented in such a way that the deepest voice seems to speak from within the cultures being discussed, the highest voice speaks—as you said in the introduction to the text—"according to Western logic and mainly quotes Western thinkers," and the medium-range voice (yours) speaks in the first person "and relates personal feelings and observations." But while the speakers vary, their statements often overlap. Were you suggesting that what you hear about any given culture, or within any culture, is a combination of what it says about itself and what it knows is said about it by others?

Trinh: One can see it that way, certainly. Some viewers have told me, "If you had fictionalized these voices a little bit more (which probably means they want the voices to be more in opposition rather than simply "different"), it would be easier to understand the role of these voices." But I find it informative that a number of people have difficulty hearing the differences between the voices, even though their tonal ranges, their accents, and their discursive modes are so distinct. In the media we consume one, unitary, narrating voice-over. It is not surprising then, that it may take some viewers more than one viewing to hear several voices in their differences. A viewer thought the difficulty comes from the fact that the voices are "disembodied" (meaning that the narrators do not appear on screen), which may be true. But I think there are other factors involved, because this same viewer may have no difficulty whatsoever listening to a "disembodied" omniscient voice-over on a TV program.

Any person who has had prolonged interactions with country people and villagers—whether from their own culture or from another culture—knows that you have to learn to speak differently in order to be heard in their context. So if you listen carefully to your own speech in your interactions with them, you recognize that even though you may both speak the same language—the case is further complicated when you don't—you speak differently. This sounds like a very banal statement until you find yourself in a situation where you wish to relate what the villagers say, to your audience—in other words, to translate them. Translation, which is interpellated by ideology and can never be objective or neutral, should here be understood in the wider sense of the term—as a politics of constructing meaning. Whether you translate one language into another language, whether you narrate in your own words what you have understood from the other person, or whether you use this person directly on screen as a piece of "oral testimony" to serve the direction of your film, you are dealing with cultural translation.

To give an example: a villager may say, while pointing toward the front court of her dwelling: "Calabash, we call it the vault of heaven." The local interpreter may translate: "The calabash is the vault of heaven." But when outsiders to the culture try to translate this to their audience back home, it might come out, "The calabash is like the vault of heaven" or "stands for the vault of heaven." There are all these little devices in language that "explain" instead of stating "this, this" or "this *is* this" with no explanation added. When you translate, you automatically rationalize what people say according to the logic and habits of your own language or mode of speaking. This tendency, which seems to me to be particularly naturalized in the media, is dealt with in *Naked Spaces* by assigning the explanatory logic and its ensuing linguistic devices to the voice of the woman (Linda Peckham) whose English accent (actually South African) is easily detectable. It was a real challenge for me to try to bring out these subtleties of translation and to remain consistent in the distinction of the three discursive modes. Moreover, the only voice in the film that can afford to have some kind of authority (not media or academic institutionalized authority, but rather a form of insider's assertion) is the mediated voice of the people, the low voice that quotes the villagers' sayings and other statements by African writers. My voice gives little anecdotes and personal feelings.

The distinction made between the voices is not a rigid one; the voices of the women of color at times overlap in what they say and how they speak. All three voices are joined together in the last third of the film, when the viewers see images of the Fon's lake-dwellings. The two voices of the women of color (Barbara Christian and myself) meet here in the sequence about this village, whose people's income thrives on tourism. The meeting concerns the controversy of giving and taking. As is fairly well-known, in the first-world/third-world relationship, what may assert itself in appearance as "giving" very often turns out to be nothing but a form of taking and taking again. The problematic of donor and acceptor is thus played out in that part in the sound track: for example, the Linda Peckham voice says, "They call it giving"; my voice says, "We call it self-gratification"; the Barbara Christian voice says, "We call it self-gratification." This can be said to be the only place in the film where the first-world and third-world voices work in opposition. Most of the time, it was important for me that the voices meet or not meet, but that they are not just set up in opposition to one another.

The voice of Western logic quotes a number of Western writers, including Cixous, [Gaston] Bachelard, and Éluard. For me, these quotations are very relevant to the context of the dwelling I was in. I don't situate myself in opposition to them just because the writers are Westerners. Actually, in a public debate, a white man resentfully asked me why I quoted Heidegger and added, "Why not let *us* quote him?" This is like saying that I have encroached on some occupied territory and that the exclusive right to use Heidegger belongs to Euro-Americans. Such ethnocentric rationale is hard to believe (although not the least surprising) when you think of such figures of modernity as Picasso or Brecht (to mention just two): what would their works be like without their exposure to African sculpture or to Japanese and Chinese theater? History constantly needs to be rewritten. In fact, whether I like it or not, Heidegger is also part of my hybrid culture.

MacDonald: In effect the sound track is a nexus for *all* these voices. And all these voices meet in you; you're not only a first-person observer, you have internalized many voices.

Trinh: Exactly. The place of hybridity is also the place of identity.

MacDonald: Actually, different forms of culture are present in Africa; there's no point in pretending that African peoples live in isolation from the world.

Trinh: Sometimes you can never win. On the one hand, I encounter reactions such as "Why don't you show more of the trucks and the bicycles we see all the time in African villages?" When I hear such questions, I can tell the type of villages the questioner is familiar with; he may have been to rural Africa, but he seems to have no idea of the villages I went to, which are fairly remote and difficult of access. On the other hand, some viewers ask, "Why show all the signs of industrial society in these villages?"—referring here to the way the camera lingers, for example, on the white doll a child is playing with in *Reassemblage,* a red plastic cup, or a woman's pink plastic shoe in *Naked Spaces.*

At the same time as it is reassuring for certain Western viewers to see evidence of their industrial society spreading over third-world rural landscapes, it is irritating for others to see the camera gazing at some of these industrialized objects a few seconds too long. The shooting of *Reassemblage* informed me of the potential of a cultural difference whose manifestations neither oppose nor depend on the West—in other words, neither succumb to assimilation nor remain entirely pristine in its traditions. My decision was precisely to work in the remote countryside where circulation was mainly either on foot, by bicycle, or by pirogue. As a result of this choice, whenever any element of industrial society was found in such context, it was very visible.

MacDonald: One thing that's been said about anthropologists is that, essentially, by going into "primitive" cultures and gathering information, they are "scouts" for the dominant culture, leading the way toward the destruction of indigenous people.

Trinh: There is some truth to that metaphor, although it is a dangerous one because none of us who have gone to the cultures in question can claim to be free of that effect. I would use another metaphor: sometimes anthropologists act as if they were fishermen. They select a location, position themselves as observers and then throw a net, thinking that they can thereby catch what they look for. I think the very premise of such an approach is illusory. If I apply that metaphor to myself, I have to be *the net,* a net with no fisherman, for I'm caught in it as much as what I try to catch. And I am caught with everyting that I try to bring out in my films.

MacDonald: You were saying yesterday that some people who like the African films were unpleasantly surprised by *Surname Viêt Given Name Nam.* There are common elements in all three films, but your decision to explore what we might consider your own experience, your own heritage, requires you to more obviously distance yourself, to more overtly question your own position of authority with regard to your culture. One of the centers of the film is the set of interviews that were originally recorded in Vietnamese by someone else, then translated into French, and are finally reenacted in your film by women who have come to the United States from Vietnam. In at least one sense, the film is more about the process of translating meaning from one culture to another than it is about Vietnam.

Trinh: You raise several questions. That some poeple are reacting differently to my last film is true, but I would not say this is only due to a difference between my African films and this film. There has already been a split reaction between *Reassemblage* and *Naked Spaces.* A num-

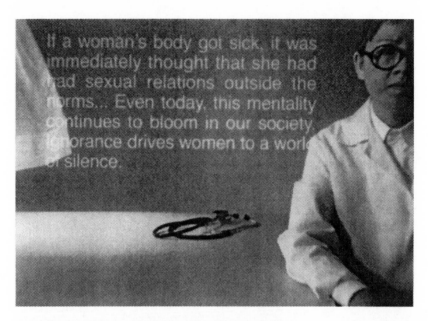

From Trinh's Surname Viêt Given Name Nam *(1989).*

ber of people who really loved *Reassemblage* had problems with *Naked Spaces* when it first came out. I guess everything has its own time. When *Reassemblage* was released, I had to wait a whole year before the film really started circulating and before I got any positive feedback from viewers. It was such a hopeless situation, for I was piling up, one after the other, rejections from film festivals and other film programs. People "didn't know what to do" with such a film; it was totally misunderstood. Then unexpectedly, the film started being picked up simultaneously in diverse places. Viewers were bewildered but enthusiastic. This unanticipated circulation of the film continues to expand. A somewhat similar process happened with *Naked Spaces*. Although the film got to be shown almost immediately to some packed audiences, the disappointment from those who came expecting another *Reassemblage* was quite apparent. Most of the praise and positive reactions I obtained in the first few months were from people who had not seen *Reassemblage*. One sympathetic viewer at a festival told me that when she shared with others her admiration for the film, she was told that she should see *Reassemblage* first before offering any comment. *Reassemblage* had become a model! And yet, since then, I have had very, very moving and elating feedback on *Naked Spaces*—sometimes well beyond any expectations I had for that film.

MacDonald: Was the objection some people had to *Naked Spaces* the fact that it is less overtly feminist than *Reassemblage,* that it doesn't put the role of women in African cultures in the foreground as obviously as the earlier film?

Trinh: I don't think so. The most obvious problem people have with *Naked Spaces* is the length. The notion of time and of duration are worked on in a way that makes the experience quite excruciating for some. Time not only as the result of editing, but time made apparent within the frame itself by the camera's slow unstable movement across people and their spaces, by the quiescence and contemplative quality of many of the scenes shown, and moreover by the lack of a central story line or guiding message. Moviegoers do not mind sitting a couple of hours for a narrative feature. But to go through two hours and fifteen minutes of a nonaction film with no love story, no violence, and "no sex" (as a viewer reminded me) is a real trial for many and a "far out," unforgettable experience for others. It was important for me, on the one hand, to bring back a notion of time in Africa that never failed to frustrate foreigners eager to consume the culture at a time-is-money pace (one of them warned a newcomer: "You need immense, unlimited patience here! *Nothing is happening!*"). On the other hand, it was also critical to bring about a different way of experiencing film.

Some of the objections to *Naked Spaces* also have to do with the fact that certain viewers prefer the overt politics of *Reassemblage. Naked Spaces* seems to appeal to people who are aware of the predicament of dwelling in modern society and are tuned to the inseparable questions of aesthetics, spirituality, sociality, and environment. I have had, for example, intense and exalted feedback from a few native-American viewers. I could never have anticipated this when I made the film.

For a while, I didn't quite know how to locate some of the hostilities toward *Surname Viêt Given Name Nam,* although in making it, I was well aware of the risks that it was taking and the kind of difficulties it might encounter. Now that I have participated in more public debates on the film than I could ever have wished, I can identify two kinds of viewers who have problems with it. Actually, the problems are fundamentally related. These are the viewers who either feel antagonistic toward the feminist struggle, or are simply unaware of its complexities in relation to other struggles of liberation. Many of these viewers may think of themselves as pro-feminist, but they are not really into the feminist struggle, and this slips out in the questions they raise, in the lack of concern they show for any earnest inquiry into gender politics.

There are other viewers who identify themselves as belonging to the antiwar movement and who do not really see *women* in *Surname Viêt* (just as many male radicals in the sixties could not take seriously their female co-workers and the feminist struggle that was burgeoning independently right in the midst of their struggle for freedom of speech). These viewers tend to deny, or worse—to *obscure* entirely—the question of gender by constantly casting the Vietnam reality back into the binary mold of communism and anticommunism. They also seem to be preoccupied with what they militated for, eager to preserve an idealized image of a Vietnam they supported, and unwilling to look at the actual situation of postrevolutionary Vietnam. As with many libertarian movements, there are people who are genuinely fighting for change and remain sensitive to the complexities of the feminist struggle, and there are those who only work to consolidate a position of authority and feel threatened by any form of resistance other than the one they are familiar with. Right now in Vietnam, the leaders are acknowledging some of the failures of the system and are raising questions pertaining to the transformation of socialist society. But even when the people who are directly involved see the necessity for change, you have people from the outside still holding fast to a past image of Vietnam, where for example, all the women involved in the revolution are upheld as "heroines." The work of critical inquiry cannot be content with fixed anti-positions, which were, in their own time, necessary in regard to the war in Vietnam but need to be problematized in the context of contemporary histories of political migration.

The struggle will never end, and we women still have a long way to go. The more I discuss these questions, the more I realize how little is known of the historical debates within the feminist struggle, not to mention the Sisyphean efforts of women of color across nations to expose the politics of gender within revolutionary movements.

After this long detour, let me end by responding to the point that *Surname Viêt* is as much about the process of translating as it is about Vietnam. To unravel the "name" of Vietnam in the context of translation is to confront the much debated politics of identity—female identity, ethnic identity, national identity. For translation, as I suggested earlier, implies questions of language, power, and meaning, or more precisely in this film, of women's resistance vis-à-vis the sociosymbolic contract—as mothers, wives, prostitutes, nurses, doctors, state employees, official cadres, heroines of the revolution. In the politics of constructing identity and meaning, language as translation and/or film as translation is necessarily a process whereby the self loses its fixed boundaries—a disturbing yet potentially empowering practice of difference. For me, it is precisely in fighting on more than one front at a time, that is, in fighting not only against forms of domination and exploitation but also against less easily locatable forms of subjection or of binarist subjectivity, that the feminist struggle and other protest movements can continue to resist falling back into the consolidation of conformism.

Godfrey Reggio

At the time of our interview, Godfrey Reggio had made only two films—
Koyaanisqatsi (1983) and *Powaqqatsi* (1988)—but he had accomplished
something rare in the annals of independent cinema: he had developed a
considerable popular audience for feature-length, nonnarrative film experiences. After a reasonable success in commercial theaters, *Koyaanisqatsi* has become one of the most frequently rented films on the American college circuit, an almost inevitable Earth Day presentation, and in
1990 *Powaqqatsi,* though it had failed to live up to commercial expectations in 35mm release, was able to fill Alice Tully Hall at Lincoln Center
more than once: Philip Glass and his ensemble performed the *Powaqqatsi* sound track live. Reggio's success is due to several factors. First, he
has been able to exploit a form of viewer pleasure most commercial and
critical cinema has ignored, and he has been able to invest this pleasure
with a spirit of social concern and spiritual mission. Second, he has
developed a productive working relationship with Glass, whose music
energizes both Reggio films.

Koyaanisqatsi attempts to develop a provocative contrast between the
natural world, as epitomized by the American Southwest, and modern
technological society, as epitomized by the contemporary American city.
Though it is not structured as a day in the life of either of its primary urban
subjects, New York and Los Angeles, it has much in common with the
tradition in independent cinema of the "city symphony"—Alberto
Cavalcanti's *Rein que les heures* (1926), Walter Ruttmann's *Berlin: Symphony of a Great City* (1927), Dziga Vertov's *The Man with the Movie
Camera* (1929), Arne Sucksdorff's *Symphony of a City* (1948), Francis

Thompson's *N.Y., N.Y.* (1957)—and in particular, with the frequent use of time-lapse photography to reveal the patterns of city life, evident in *The Man with a Movie Camera,* as well as in Marie Menken's *Go Go Go* (1964), Hilary Harris's *Organism* (1975), and Peter von Ziegesar's *Concern for the City* (1986).

After a mysterious opening shot that is not explained until the conclusion of the film, *Koyaanisqatsi* presents gorgeous, real-time and time-lapse aerial imagery of spectacular Southwestern landscapes, including remarkable imagery of Monument Valley that reveals its contours in a manner strikingly different from the way John Ford used the same spaces in so many Westerns. Having created a sense of the grandeur and dignity of these landscapes, Reggio moves toward the city (by way of strip mines, a nuclear power plant, and electric power lines), and by combining telephoto shooting and time lapse, reveals the modern city as a gigantic machine and the human beings who live there as its moving parts. *Koyaanisqatsi* emphasizes a paradox: Reggio's use of time lapse discovers, again and again, the remarkable degree to which the city-machine *does* function—traffic zooms along expressways; cars and crowds pulse across New York streets; the day's work gets accomplished—but at the same time, the primary product of the machine seems to be the destruction of individuality and serenity. The commercial cinema focuses on individuals, singing the beauties of particular faces and bodies, and honoring individuals' abilities to effect resolutions to whatever problems they face. In *Koyaanisqatsi* Reggio critiques this central dimension of the popular cinema, by revealing that our trust in individuality is often a function of our ability to blind ourselves (really and cinematically) to the larger patterns within which what we call individuality is subsumed.

The conclusion of *Koyaanisqatsi* provides a completion of the mysterious opening shot, revealing it to be the thrusting jets of a rocket that subsequently blasts off and explodes, its fragments tumbling slowly back to earth, and a definition of the film's title: "ko yaa nis qatsi (from the Hopi language) n. 1. crazy life. 2. life in turmoil. 3. life out of balance. 4. life disintegrating. 5. a state of life that calls for another way of living." The frame provided by the rocket image and the definition are Reggio's implicit critique of the commercial cinema's general reliance on optimistic resolution and its reconfirmation of the commodification of contemporary life.

While *Koyaanisqatsi* cinematically recontextualizes the individual in modern, industrialized society, placing him or her in the background and bringing to the foreground the larger social-industrial machine, *Powaqqatsi* cinematically recontextualizes the masses of women and men in third-world societies, removing them from the background to the foreground of our attention and allowing us to observe them not as cine-

decoration for the mythic adventures of Western swashbucklers, but as individuals functioning in day-to-day life. In order to effect this change in perspective, Reggio uses a different set of techniques. Instead of time lapse, which almost inevitably reduces individual actions to patterns, Reggio exploits slow motion, which not only allows us to see individual motions in precise detail, but reveals the grace and dignity of forms of physical labor rendered trivial or repellent in conventional cinema. *Powaqqatsi* is an immense montage of individuals laboring—and to a lesser degree, celebrating, worshiping, relaxing—in Peru, Brasil, Kenya, Egypt, Nepal, and India. The focus on third-world labor is contextualized by sequences that represent the allure of the industrialized world, especially as it is marketed on television, an allure that, as *Powaqqatsi* reveals, is already transforming the Southern Hemisphere: one of the film's organizational principles is the juxtaposition of the beauty of life and labor in natural settings and the frenzy of labor in the third-world city.

Reggio has frequently been criticized for his naïveté in participating in the very patterns he pretends to abhor: *Koyaanisqatsi* is an antitechnology film *but* it was produced not only with technological means but with the most technologically advanced cinematic means available; *Powaqqatsi* sings the dignity of the laboring, third-world individual *but* provides no information about the individuals filmed, rendering them socially decontextualized exotics: indeed, Reggio's "adventure" in filming his second feature can be seen as a form of swashbuckling. As is clear in the discussion that follows, Reggio has thought about these charges, but whether the reader is satisfied with Reggio's explanations or not, he must be given credit for what he *has* accomplished. He has made visually arresting nonnarrative feature films that generate considerable thought and discussion in the audiences that see them, and he has brought his vision to a substantial audience, while refusing to reconfirm crucial ideological conventions of much of the commercial cinema.

I spoke with Reggio in Santa Fe, New Mexico, in March 1990.

MacDonald: I understand that before you became a filmmaker, you were a member of the Christian Brothers, a Roman Catholic monk.

Reggio: Until I was twenty-eight.

MacDonald: I'm curious about how you went from that life to making a 35mm feature film.

Reggio: Well, one of the vows you take as a Christian Brother is to

teach the poor gratuitously. That was the original spirit of the brotherhood, though that spirit is long since gone. There were all sorts of
rational and "correct" reasons why the brothers were not able to teach
the poor: it wasn't practical; if they *did* teach the poor, they couldn't
sustain their life-styles. In fact, almost all the children in the schools
where I taught were middle-class kids, and yet I lived in *this* community
[Santa Fe] where about forty percent of the people had no access to
primary medical care, and where the barrio was being eroded out from
under the poor. There was great social disintegration. A lot of the people who were and are in the barrio come from the little villages in
Northern New Mexico that were pushed out because of welfare laws. So
there was a huge community of poverty, and I felt drawn to give some
kind of assistance if I *could.*

When I started to work in the community, it became apparent that
there were huge neighborhood-based gang structures, nine in number. I
dedicated myself to dealing with that situation, and that got me in trouble with my order because they felt that I was acting in a singular, rather
than a communal, way.

During the course of that activity, a friend turned me onto a film. I
had not seen many films, to be truthful. I went into the brotherhood at
the age of fourteen; we were told to shun the world, or were made to
shun the world.

MacDonald: Was it your choice to join the order?

Reggio: Yes, it was. I had a desire to pursue an idealistic life. I think
children, especially adolescents, pursue as much meaning as they have
access to, and this looked like a very meaningful thing for me to do. I
lived in a very stratified racist society, New Orleans, and I don't want to
say I had lived la dolce vita, but I had lived a pretty fast life already by
that time, and I wanted to leave it for something more meaningful. My
family wasn't so happy about my choice, but they gave me the freedom
to do what I wanted to do. So that meant being away from them from
that time forward.

Anyway, during the course of my life in Santa Fe, my friend turned
me onto this film by Luis Buñuel, *Los Olvidados* [1950]. It was shot in
the barrios of Mexico City, though it could have been shot here. Santa
Fe isn't a big city, but the barrios are similar. That film touched me
deeply, and I used it as a tool to help organize the gangs into a super-
family called Young Citizens for Action. I felt if *I* could be touched that
deeply by this medium, it was worth exploring.

I don't make films like Buñuel's, but I decided then that if I could
imagine the kind of films I wanted to make, I might be able to make
them—if I wouldn't get mystified by the tools.

The analysis that makes up the metaphysical base for the *Qatsi* Trilogy came not from academia or from intellectual study, but from reading the sad reality that I was encountering daily for almost nine years working on the streets. I had become frustrated that the *causal* elements of deprivation, disenfranchisement, violence—all of the accoutrements that go with the kind of life I witnessed—came from the overall society, from everything being commoditized and transformed into a spectacle removed from reality. I could see I couldn't create any alleviation of that syndrome, unless I had a broader relationship with the larger society. Of course, I couldn't change the whole society, but I could think about it, I could feel about it, and I could work with the medium that I feel is the language of this time—the image.

The larger society had changed—cultures of aurality had given way to cultures of literacy, and more recently, to the culture of image. I realized that if I wanted to communicate to the larger society about the world I was seeing—recognizing that people learn in terms of what they already know—the most appropriate thing I could do would be to communicate with my audience in the form they had come to accept: film.

I make a critical distinction between Reality and the Truth. I think the *eye* observes Reality; the *word* struggles to name the Truth. I felt that printed language had lost its power, its original charge. That's not to say I don't love language. I feel that we approach the Truth through language. Language is a critical part of what gives us our nature as human beings. But I also felt that for many people language was a technology that had become a use form only, rather than a meaningful form. Consequently, I felt it would be not useful for my purposes to pursue a form of film that centered on dialogue, and that's how I arrived at the idea for the nonverbal structure. I wanted to produce an iconography of image that would provide an experience of reality that could not come by way of English.

I felt differently about what I knew of the Hopi language. There the word had not been devalued. You might say that in my films I reverse the Napoleonic axiom that one picture is worth a thousand words. My "thousand pictures" are a means of expressing the Truth of the single Hopi words "koyaanisqatsi" and "powaqqatsi." The Hopi in no way motivated the nature of what I was seeing or my visions for the films, but I felt a certain synchronicity with them, in world view. Everything that we call normal, they call abnormal. Everything we call sane, they call insane. Our moment of the Truth, is their moment of the False. I decided to go to a language that had no cultural baggage and use their subjective categories to observe the world, and by doing that, offer people a way to re-see the world, to revisit their sense of ordinary daily living. So the Trilogy is really a metaphysical effort, an effort to rename the world. In naming something, we can empower ourselves so that we're not controlled by what surrounds us.

MacDonald: You mentioned that *Los Olvidados* was pivotal for you. The bulk of my research has been into nonnarrative film. Ordinarily, filmmakers who do long nonnarrative films start with short films and work toward larger projects. Am I correct that *Koyaanisqatsi* is your first film?

Reggio: Yes, it is.

MacDonald: Between seeing the Buñuel film and making *Koyaanisqatsi,* did you see a lot of nonnarrative film? Did you see Hilary Harris's *Organism* [1975] or other independent films that use time lapse as their central device? Harris has a credit on *Koyaanisqatsi.*

Reggio: I knew nothing about film before beginning *Koyaanisqatsi.* I tried to turn my zero film literacy into an advantage. As a child I'd seen Randolph Scott movies and stuff like that, and that was the extent of my viewing. As a Brother, I saw a few religious films. I remember that *Monsieur Vincent* [Maurice Cloche, 1947] moved me greatly. But I had no real background, and I felt that that was a unique preparation: I didn't have to unlearn anything to do what I was doing. To be quite candid, Scott, I felt a bit like a blind man having to work through the hands of other people: I didn't know camera equipment or technology, but what I had clear from the beginning was a pre-visualization of what I was concerned with. It was more than a concept; it was a feeling, and what I could feel, I could see.

I did a lot of traveling from the mid sixties through the early seventies to large cities in this country, Canada, and Mexico, and my observations led me to the structure of *Koyaanisqatsi.* My work in the barrio had ceased, but it had led me to media. With three other persons, I formed this media collective [Institute for Regional Education, where my interview with Reggio was recorded], which is now in its nineteenth year. While I didn't make films before *Koyaanisqatsi,* I did make a series of nonverbal public interest spots as part of a large media campaign, sponsored by the American Civil Liberties Union.

The campaign dealt with invasions of privacy and the use of technology to control behavior. Rather than use public service announcements, which had no visibility, we bought spots for the period of one month, in all media windows—television, newspapers, billboards, radio. For each of the television network affiliates, we had three spots in prime time per night, plus others during the talk shows. These ads were so visible and so popular that the viewing public was calling the station to see what time the next *ad* would be on. The technicians began to throw them in whenever they had an open spot, so we got a lot more than we paid for. We also had over thirty billboards in high traffic-density areas, and radio spots in "drive time." And we wrote a book, but instead of publishing it in the usual way, we inserted it into New Mexico's largest newspaper as a

Billboard near Santa Fe, New Mexico (1974)—part of Reggio's publicity campaign against governmental invasion of privacy.

Sunday supplement. We had hot air balloons (that's a big thing in Albuquerque) with eyes draped on them.

MacDonald: How did you fund this campaign?

Reggio: We went through traditional Left foundation sources, people who were interested in social justice.

MacDonald: What were the billboards like?

Reggio: We had several different kinds, actually. We tried to use nonverbal communication. We had analyzed—as best we could, albeit from a great distance—the nature of billboard advertising, and we found that really it was not competitive; it was all pretty much the same. So we designed billboards that were in diametric opposition to most billboards, which gave us a new kind of recognition. Usually, if you're passing a billboard, you have anywhere from seven to fourteen seconds to have some recognition of it. Because our billboards were so unusual and because they were on main arteries in high-traffic-density areas, they stuck out. In fact, we tried to put them next to other boards so their difference would have a real effect, a *conscious* effect. One of our billboards had a huge eye on it; that one was particularly effective. I'd sit behind the billboards with some of my colleagues and check out the drivers; we could *see* that we were having an impact on people.

MacDonald: [Reggio shows me a photograph of one of the billboards.] There's a "seed" for *Koyaanisqatsi* in this image. Here's this incredible landscape and in the middle, a horrifying image that undercuts the landscape's beauty.

Reggio: Definitely. That campaign was extraordinarily successful. We hadn't predicted what the outcome would be; we wanted to see what simultaneity could do. But the result was the elimination of Ritalin as a behavior-modifying drug in many school districts in the state. Knowing that politicians often do the right things for the wrong reasons—they live by polls—we coordinated the campaign to happen when the state's Democratic and Republican conventions were held. While I don't believe in polls as a way to exercise democracy, I knew that politicians did, so *we* had a poll done by the University of New Mexico. The issue we were focusing on went from a fourteen percent recognition rate up to a sixty-seven percent. Politicians adopted almost all of the issues that were built into the campaign, and two of our congressional delegates in Wash-ington cosponsored bills that eventually led to the elimination of psychosurgery in all federal institutions in the country.

Next, I tried to use what we had developed in this campaign as a prototype and take the issues into a national forum. A conference was being developed at the University of Chicago for principal lawmakers around the country. Senator Sam Irvin was going to keynote it. We had worked with Lawrence Baskir, who was the chief consul and researcher for the Senate Subcommittee on Constitutional Rights. We had given them a lot of material and felt we were in a position to launch a national campaign. We wanted to show that this was a pattern *endemic* to the information society, that in fact *everybody* had extensive files on them, and that police and planning bureaucracies were using computers, aggregate statistics, to do all of their prognosis and policy development, that drugs were being used, from Ritalin in schools to Prolixin [a strong tranquilizer] in the prisons.

That campaign didn't work out, but I wanted to continue to explore media and I felt that film might give me more access to the public. Of course, having never made a film, having no credibility, I found it agonizing to get support. Basically, I found "angel support," people who were not interested in the return on their investment, but loved our project. *Koyaanisqatsi* took seven years.

MacDonald: Let's do a timetable. When did you form this collective?

Reggio: In the early seventies.

MacDonald: This local campaign that was so successful was in . . .

Reggio: 1974. We worked on *Koyaanisqatsi* from 1975 to 1982.

MacDonald: When you look at the film now, can you see its history? Were certain kinds of things shot at certain times?

Reggio: Well, we started to shoot the film in 16mm because at first that was the only film technology we could command—though we always wanted to go to 35mm. I was so excited by what we garnered in 16mm that we went back to some of the people who had shown interest in the project. They shared our excitement and said we should shoot in 35mm. What began as a forty-thousand-dollar, thirty-minute, 16mm film became a demo. I put Tomita's rendition of Mussorgsky's *Pictures at an Exhibition* on what had been shot and used that to show people what the power of this project could be. That got me the money to work in 35mm. I went back and reshot a lot of the locations, although in one case, 16mm footage remains in the 35mm film: the material on Pruit Igoe—the first example of a mass housing development in response to poverty. Housing and Urban Development (HUD) built this monstrosity in Saint Louis, and we were fortunate to be able to film it in 16mm once it was abandoned. I use it as a metaphor. When we were ready to shoot in 35mm, most all those buildings had been torn down, so we took that original 16mm, cleaned it up with an opal glass and wet gate process at Disney, and blew it up to 35mm. The grain structure held up.

MacDonald: You mentioned "angel support." Was that local here?

Reggio: No. It was support that had been identified and located during the ACLU campaign. I'd guess upward of seventy people put in money, but it was the faith of one person putting in close to two million dollars that got this film made. That person has requested—and I have honored that request—to remain anonymous. That same person continued to support us through *Powaqqatsi* (a 4.2-million-dollar film), putting in two million dollars. Cannon put in the other two million, for a paper deal—meaning we got bank financing and they had negative pickup. Cannon [Releasing Corporation] got all the rights, so in fact this gentleman was willing to make a bad deal for love of the project. He got net points way down the line but will probably never realize anything off it. Cannon will take most of whatever profits there are. Though, I must say, Menahem Golan and Yuram Globus at Cannon were very fine to me: they *never* interfered and gave me full creative control, which of course I required.

MacDonald: Let's go back to *Koyaanisqatsi*: it must have felt strange to be involved in such a big project.

Reggio: Well, after the ACLU campaign, I was not mystified by media, but from ten-, thirty-, and sixty-second spots to a 35mm feature *is* quite a jump. In fact, no one who worked on *Koyaanisqatsi* had ever made a feature. The cinematographer had only shot 16mm . . .

MacDonald: Ron Fricke?

Reggio: Yes, I was sure if he had the right tools, and if he could hear what I was asking for (which, it turned out, he could; we were able to work together quite well), he would do a fine job. By *not* becoming mystified, we were able to get on top of the project; in fact, we were able to come from a more original place than we might have, had we gone to film school and learned the "correct" procedures.

The opportunity to collaborate with Ron Fricke was unique. Ron is a gifted artist and technical designer. He has the rare capacity for brilliant composition and a masterful command of the camera system as a tool. Indeed, any success that *Koyaanisqatsi* enjoys is the result of a fruitful collaboration between Ron, Philip, myself and the provocative and intelligent crew that was assembled for the film: Alton Walpole, Michael Hoenig, Walter Bachauer, Anne Miller, and Dennis Jackob. All of us in our own manner added vital energy.

MacDonald: At what point did Hilary Harris become involved?

Reggio: During the editing of the film, which took place in Venice, California, someone called me up one night from New York, very hysterical, and said he had seen a film on channel thirteen in New York: "You gotta check this out immediately!" So I looked at *Organism* and called Hilary.

MacDonald: This was after you finished shooting?

Reggio: Well, the shooting never stopped. We had stumbled onto the time-lapse technique in some low-visibility commercial work, and it became clear to me and Ron that this was the language that we were missing. We became focused on time lapse as a way to create the experience of acceleration. So we shot all the way through the editing; we were still shooting in 1982, the year the film was released.

I got a copy of *Organism,* looked at it, and was very pleased. I *felt* that I saw—and after conferring with Hilary, I was *sure* that I saw—a very different intention in his footage. His intention was to celebrate the city: *Organism* is a celebration of modernity. He had none of the metaphysical concerns that I have—that's no put-down of Hilary; it's only an indication of a different point of view.

Also, Hilary's shots were very short. Now, of course, with time lapse, it might take you a long time to shoot a six-second piece, but I was looking for much longer shots. Though Hilary was willing to sell me footage, most of the footage he had was unusable in our film. I asked if we could employ him to do some of the shooting. He said he would be delighted.

MacDonald: How much of the New York material is his?

Reggio: Several of the most powerful pattern shots of people and traffic were shot by Hilary. However, most of the New York shooting was done by Ron Fricke.

MacDonald: Have you seen Fricke's *Chronos*?

Reggio: Yes, I have.

MacDonald: That's another instance of a time-lapse film where the metaphysics seem very different from yours. In fact, ideas seem to have been eliminated in *Chronos*. What's left is everything *but* ideas or politics.

Reggio: It's a triumph of technique, lavishly shot, but perhaps with*out* the presence of an Entity. It ended up as beautiful pictures, as a technical tour de force.

MacDonald: In *Koyaanisqatsi* you use time lapse more extensively than anyone I know of.

Reggio: Certainly we didn't pioneer time lapsing; it's been around practically as long as the camera's been around, but it's remained basically a technique for emphasis. By using it as a main drive language, I think *Koyaanisqatsi* picked up on something new. But since *Koyaanisqatsi*, it's inundated the media.

MacDonald: You've built your approach from the ground up, without extensive experience with other films. Not surprisingly, your films recall the beginnings of cinema, in two ways. One has to do with Muybridge and his idea of motion study: time lapse allows you to do "motion studies" of one kind and slow motion, which is the central device of *Powaqqatsi,* of another kind. Second, your interest in *Powaqqatsi* in going around the world and recording footage of people and places that for a standard audience would be exotic or unusual is reminiscent of early Lumière programs.

Reggio: Well, I think we're only at the beginning of the potential of the image. I think as we transit even more fully into the language of image, we're going to see more and more exploration of the potential of these tools for doing more than telling a story. Since I didn't want to use dialogue, I had to look at the camera as the paintbrush. In the case of *Koyaanisqatsi*, we were looking at a very accelerated world, a world of density, of critical mass, and I felt that the technique of time lapse would be extremely important in articulating an experience of the subject. In the case of *Powaqqatsi*, we're looking at a world that is intrinsically slow, that lives with the rhythms of nature, that is diversified, that is the opposite of the high kinetic energy of the industrial world. In *Powaqqatsi*, the intention was to create a mosaic, a monument, a frozen moment of the simultaneity of life as it existed in one instant around the Southern Hemisphere. We used slow motion, or very fast shooting, as the norm, and long lenses, not to romanticize the subject, but to monumentalize it so that we could look at it from a different point of view. In both *Koyaanisqatsi* and *Powaqqatsi*, the intention was to see the ordinary from an extraordinary perspective. In the case of *Powaqqatsi*, we went out with a sense of style and form that motivated the kinds of equipment we got, the kinds of lenses that we took with us.

I think a lot of people were expecting *Powaqqatsi* to be a *Koyaanisqatsi 2*. I'm very pleased that the films do not repeat each other. Both are nonnarrative, but they have a different visual language. *Koyaanis-qatsi* was intrinsically exciting because of the spectacle that we've made out of the world. *Powaqqatsi* is more like a long poem. I know there are problems with both films—and I've learned from what I consider mistakes—but I feel very fortunate about both films. They have a life of their own.

MacDonald: Is it fair to say that the films reverse a set of traditions in commercial narrative films? Most movies focus on upper-middle-class individuals and their adventures, whereas *Koyaanisqatsi* reveals how all these theoretically "big" people are really little parts of a giant machine. *Powaqqatsi* does the opposite: it's normal in American entertainment movies to depict third-world people as background or, at best, as side-kicks, but you make them the center of attention.

Reggio: Exactly. The human being has more dignity in the South, because the South turns on the presence of human beings and their work. In *this* world, in the North, the human being is no longer the measure of life: we've been crushed into a synthetic environment that is no longer human. Even major characters of history—Hitler, Stalin, Churchill, Roosevelt—are unimportant. What is important is the nature of the mass—mass man. But in the South, which represents maybe two thirds of the planet's population, the human being is still the measure of life.

MacDonald: Koyaanisqatsi is framed by a long, continuous shot of a rocket taking off and then exploding and descending. Within that frame, there's a movement from rural to city with an increasingly frenetic pace until the final section where you slow down for several portraits of individual street people. One of the things that troubles me, and one of the things critics talked about, is that until you know that that rocket *is* going to fall and until we see the definition of "koyaanisqatsi," there's no way to know what the message of the city material is. It could pro-voke one to say, "Oh, this is wildly frenetic anti-technology footage," *or* to say, "Isn't it incredible how well this all works!"

Reggio: What I wanted to reveal was the beauty *of* the beast. People perceive this as beautiful *because* there's nothing else to perceive. If one lives in this world, in the industrialized city, all one can see is one layer of commodity piled upon another. There's no ability to see beyond, to see that we've encased ourselves in an artificial environment that has re-placed nature. We don't live *with* nature any longer; we live above it; we look at it as *resources* to keep this artificial environment going. I was trying to raise questions, and I worked on the premise that there must be an ambiguity built into the films if they're going to be art. Otherwise, they would become driving, didactic, propagandistic pieces. I look at the structure of each film in a "trilectic" sense. There's the image, there's the music, and there's the viewer, each with a point of view, casting a particular shadow. It's impossible to totally eliminate the sense of didacticism, but I wanted to make the films as pliable and as amorphic as possible. I tried to take the things we see as our glories and turn them on a slight edge. In that sense I feel the film is successful.

As I got into *Koyaanisqatsi,* I started to see more films. This sounds very simplistic, but one of the obvious things I noticed was that in most films the foreground was where the plot and characterization took place, where the screenplay came in, and how you directed the photography. Everything was foreground; background (music included) basically supported characterization and plot. In my films I try to eradicate all the foreground of traditional film and make the background, or what's called "second unit," the foreground, give *that* the principal focus. I was trying to look at buildings, masses of people, transportation, industrialization as *entities* in and of themselves, having an autonomous nature. Same thing with nature: rather than seeing nature as something dead, something inorganic like a stone, I wanted to see it as having its own life form, unanthropomorphized, unrelated to human beings, here for billions of years before human beings arrived on the planet, having its own Entity. That's what I tried to put into the film; what people get out of it is another matter. I was trying to show in nature the presence of a life form, an Entity, a Beingness, and in the synthetic world the presence of a different entity, a consuming and inhuman entity.

MacDonald: So, you meant to leave the experience open, but reveal, at the end (when we see what happens to the rocket and discover what "koyaanisqatsi" means) what *you* have concluded from what you've shown us?

Reggio: I started off with the lift off of this rocket, a metaphor for the celebration of modernity, progress, and development, and then I impose my own point of view, clearly, by including footage of the rocket exploding.

MacDonald: Do you see your position as filmmaker as ironic? Film is, after all, the great technological art form, and yet, you use it to attack the problems of modern technology. Your enterprise in making *Koyaanisqatsi* seems to be part of what you take a position against.

Reggio: The film is using as high a base of technology as was possible at that time. In fact, that contradiction lost me money, and got me accused of being hypocritical, confused. I don't see it that way. If I could have presented my point of view by just *thinking about it,* then I would have done so and saved myself the effort. Obviously, that's impossible: no Immaculate Conception is taking place. I felt that I had to embrace the contradiction and walk on the edge, use the very tools I was criticizing to make the statement I was making—knowing that people learn in

Monument Valley as seen in Reggio's Koyaanisqatsi *(1983).*

terms of what they already know. In that sense, I saw myself, if I may be so bold, as a cultural kamikaze, as a Trojan horse, using the coinage of the time in order to raise a question about that very coinage.

My films are based on the premise that the question is the mother of the answer. Giving people answers does them no service; I found out as a pedagogue that the intrinsic principle of learning is the *learner,* not the teacher. All the teacher can do is set the environment. I believe in the Socratic method, that basically the best you can do for a person—if you're interested in *them* learning—is to raise questions. Through that process of questioning, they can come to an answer. I felt it was important to create an experience of the subject from which conceptualization could start to take place. I'm not interested, during the course of the one hundred or eighty-seven minutes that one sits and watches these films, in creating an intellectual dialogue. I'm hoping that people can let go of themselves, forget about time, and have an experience. Once the experience is had, and held, which is certainly not going to happen for everyone—these films are not for everyone, but they are for some people—*then* the process of reflection can start to take place. I feel these images can keep coming back to people.

Obviously, I can't (and don't want to) control people's reactions. I've been criticized severely for both films. In fact, I was spat upon in Berlin when *Powaqqatsi* was shown there, for aestheticizing poverty.

I'm pleased that the film had such a strong response. That's not to say that everybody felt that way, but some people did. Some people felt, who am I to deny the opportunity of the Third World to make their lot better through industrialization. The Left especially took after this film in Berlin. But I feel there's a *fundamental* confusion between poverty and the norms of simple living. It's a distinction that some in the Left have not digested yet. Witness the collapse of repressive ideology in the East and everyone opting for a market economy as the way to bring about some kind of sanity. Yet, the market economy only further removes them from sanity and leads toward bigger problems down the line. This is not a popular position to take, especially right now. East Berlin has this sinister, bureaucratic Stalinist architecture; you can feel the ghost of the Nazis. But the Disneyland of West Berlin is no answer: people are addicted to the materialization of all values through the market economy. We've created a need that we've become addicted to.

My persuasions are also of the Left, but of a Left deeper than the ideological Left or the bureaucratized or the movement Left. Mine is more of an anarchist's Left.

MacDonald: Has *Powaqqatsi* been shown in the Third World?

Reggio: Yes, first at Tashkent, which is the biggest third-world festival, and later in Sao Paolo. It had a great response. In Sao Paolo it won Best Film, an audience award. *Koyaanisqatsi* won the same honor five years previous to that. I felt that was the real test of how the Third World responds to the film. I recently showed *Powaqqatsi* in India and had a great response. About thirty percent of the image is from India, and people from India felt that they were able to re-see the world they live in through someone else's eyes. I felt gratified by that.

MacDonald: There's an irony in the Left having a problem with the film. The opening sequence, and much of the film actually, is full of respect for the act of labor. The opening suggests two metaphors at the same time: on one hand, it's a Sisyphus metaphor . . .

Reggio: Absolutely!

MacDonald: And that opening sequence concludes with a crucifixion metaphor. It's as though you're saying that while it may indeed be horrifying to spend your life going up and down the side of this mine, on another level, this incredible effort and sacrifice should be respected. What comes through most obviously in *Powaqqatsi* is the grace of the labor. I think the image that moves me most—although a lot of them are powerful—is right after the credits, where we see two people carrying gigantic bundles. Their labor creates a magical dance.

Reggio: Yes. It's a woman and a little boy, coming onto the Ganges at Varanasi at sunrise. The Ganges was low at this point so they were walking in the silt. We shot with the 300mm lens at something like seventy frames a second. That gave us a choreographed image.

MacDonald: Do you know Trinh T. Minh-ha's films?

Reggio: No.

MacDonald: Her *Naked Spaces—Living Is Round* was filmed in West Africa, in a number of different cultures. That film confirms your statement about simple living and poverty. Her premise is that to confuse the two is disastrous for the indigenous people and for the visitors.

Reggio: It is. It's patronizing. Poverty for me *is* the equivalent of violence, and there *is* driving poverty in the South, but that's because the people are being pulled as if by a magnet out of their societies into a cash economy, rather than into a use economy. Tremendous poverty is created by this, which I tried to show in *Powaqqatsi* after the train sequence when we go into the city. There we see essentially the same people, but the looks on their faces have been transformed into a stoic resignation to the hardness of life. Life was not easy in the country, but there was a sense of joy, a sense of dignity. I'm not in any way advocating going back to the teepee or the cave. That's over with. But I do think we need to go to more convivial, decentralized, diversified forms. That's where real progress lies.

MacDonald: *Koyaanisqatsi* is a national film; it focuses on the United States as, at least at this point in history, the ultimate market economy. *Powaqqatsi* is international; it moves across national boundaries. But since there's no way to know *where* in the Third World these people are from, the film tends to render them all distant exotics, rather than people we can place within particular cultural contexts.

Reggio: Well, I did that consciously. The shots in Peru, as an example, had to interact with the shots of Hong Kong, with the shots in Africa, with the shots in India. My intention was not to make a travelogue, but a mosaic that could communicate the simultaneity of life. I was not trying to document how people live in Peru. I was trying to show that the unity of people in the South was achieved through diversity, whereas in *Koyaanisqatsi* the unity was achieved through homogenization: the machinery of commoditization renders everyone essentially the same. Had I had the money, I would have shot *Koyaanisqatsi* in Europe and Japan as well as in the States, because I feel that what was lensed here is equally true for any industrial zone.

MacDonald: *Powaqqatsi* focuses on children. You create a sense of simultaneous horror and admiration: horror that kids, particularly the city kids, have to grow up so fast, and astonishment that they *do*.

Reggio: There are a number of reasons for the focus on children. Half or more of the population of the South is under twenty-five. By the time children are four or five, they're already part of the work force.

Another reason I used so many children is that people's hearts are

Child stares at camera in Iquitos, Peru, from Powaqqatsi *(1988).*

opened by seeing children. I found that, unlike American children who almost automatically perform for the camera, children from the South are not ego-bound in relation to the camera. I found a striking innocence and curiosity. They looked *right into* the camera, and I felt that the screen became the medium through which they could turn that look onto the audience.

MacDonald: Is it fair to say that the title of *Powaqqatsi* [the translation of *powaqqatsi*—"(from the Hopi language, *powaq* sorcerer and *qatsi* life) n. an entity, a way of life that consumes the life force of other beings in order to further its own life"—is presented at the end of the film] refers to you as filmmaker? Do you see yourself as sorcerer, and film as the life consuming other lives?

Reggio: It has something to do with that. I can't produce a film *without* using the camera, so I had to freely accept that as a contradiction.

MacDonald: There are moments in the film that seem to have nothing to do with the Third World. Perhaps the most obvious (and maybe I just don't understand what I'm looking at) is the shot where you're in some kind of car on a track: the experience is very like the roller-coaster ride World's Fair films take audiences on.

Reggio: Well, that was shot in Brazil, in Cubatao, which is probably the single, densest industrial zone in the Third World, and the most polluted—so polluted that some children are born without brains. That was a power plant, and we were in a car on a long cable track. It was going very slow, but we were shooting at very slow frame rates to produce acceleration. Along with the aerials over the high rises in Sao Paolo, that shot is an introduction into modernity as a consuming force. It makes way for the shot of the huge El Globo Television Tower in Sao Paolo, followed by the video dream—the video advertising images showing the seductive nature of this "sorcerer." I wanted to be true to the term *powaqqatsi*: the method of operation of a powaqqa, a black magician, is seduction and allurement. It's not an out-front aggression; it's subtle. I feel that's the way modernity operates: it doesn't say, "This is going to be bad for you"; it creates desires that become "necessities."

MacDonald: How much did you shoot and how much did you use of what you shot in *Koyaanisqatsi* and *Powaqqatsi*?

Reggio: The ratio was fifty to one in *Powaqqatsi*: for a film of about ten thousand feet we shot five hundred thousand feet of footage. The reason, of course, is that you only get one shot at going around the world. I wanted a year to shoot; I got six months. So instead of using one crew, I used two. Also, when you're shooting at very fast frame rates—our norm was anywhere from 36 to 129 frames a second—footage adds up quickly. Without a screenplay, with a dramaturgical structure, I had to be sure to get enough material because I didn't know how the film would edit together until we saw what we actually had. Of course, the footage not used in one film may be useful to me for other productions, or for other people's films. It's available. I have a library.

In the case of *Koyaanisqatsi,* we shot more like thirty to one. Time-lapse makes for very slow frame rates, so we used less footage for more impact. We shot about three hundred thousand feet.

MacDonald: Did you personally supervise all the shooting?

Reggio: In the case of *Powaqqatsi,* I had contact with the cinematographers here for several months in advance. We worked on the dramaturgical concept of the film, as well as on the language of the cinematography. During the shooting, two crews always stayed in the same city or the same region. I would scout every other day with the directors of photography (we didn't shoot every day); then I would divide my time between the two crews. I would say my participation was about seventy-five percent. We would collaborate on what the image would be, but I choose cinematographers who I feel are artists at heart, and I like to give them as much freedom as they feel they can use.

MacDonald: What had Zourdoumis and Berry done before?

Reggio: Leo Zourdoumis, who died in a plane crash two years ago in Zurich, was an I-Max specialist. He had done a lot of work at the Canadian Film Board. Graham Berry was an aerial specialist, an underwater specialist, and a portrait specialist.

I should also mention that without the tremendous organizational capacity of Mel Lawrence, who was one of the directors of Woodstock, I couldn't have got *Powaqqatsi* done. Mel and I had gone around the world once before, looking for locations, while we showed *Koyaanisqatsi,* and used that as a way to find people we could work with as production crews in each of the countries where we were planning to film. We went to thirteen countries with virtually no screw-ups. We lost one piece of equipment between Peru and Brazil and that was it, and we had two and a half tons of equipment going around the world! Without his ability to organize local crews, locations, permissions, getting stock in and out of the countries for processing, dealing with customs, the film would never have happened. The other producer was Lawrence Taub; without his ability to maintain the budget and the schedule, we'd have had all kinds of problems. So I feel really well served by the producers I worked with.

MacDonald: May I go back to a comment you made a while ago about mistakes you felt you made in the first two films? What mistakes are you referring to?

Reggio: In the case of *Koyaanisqatsi,* I feel that the experience was perhaps too intense. At one point in the film, we were dealing with eleven polyrhythmic musical structures colliding all at once, for twenty-one minutes! That was a bit much. I can remember, having attended many public screenings of *Koyaanisqatsi,* that at the end of that sequence, you would hear an enormous sigh from the audience. Now on the one hand, that motivated me to say, "Well, we probably did the right thing," but on the other, I feel I may have battered the audience a bit too much. I also feel I could have placed more focus, albeit in a mass form, on human beings caught inside this vast machine we call modernity. The film could have had a more human focus.

In the case of *Powaqqatsi,* I tried to be very conservative, especially in terms of the possibilities of juxtaposing images. What I learned from *Koyaanisqatsi* is that you can't just do a hundred-minute montage: it won't work; you can't sustain interest. The montage form is good for a half hour to forty minutes *max*—if there's a master working on it. Looking at *Powaqqatsi* now, I feel that if I could have made it a little shorter, it would be stronger. And I would like to have intercut some things to suggest other dimensions of the issues raised.

MacDonald: Do you mean more mini-montages, like the one about religious observances?

Reggio: That's correct. On the new film, *Naqoyqatsi,* I feel I can be more adventurous. We can diversify ourselves a bit. I don't want to repeat *Powaqqatsi* or *Koyaanisqatsi.* I want to hold to the metaphysical point of view, but I want to develop it in a different form.

MacDonald: Did you assume from the beginning that you were going to do a trilogy?

Reggio: No. It was only during the editing of *Koyaanisqatsi,* when Philip and I became so excited about the language we felt we had struck upon, that we decided we wanted to flesh out our point of view.

MacDonald: How did you originally connect up with Glass?

Reggio: Through two friends, one known in the film world actually—Rudy Wurlitzer, a screenwriter—and Jeffrey Lew, a Buddhist friend of Philip, who set him up with his first recording studio at 112 Green Street. I had done a study with a woman in Santa Fe who is a composer and pianist—Marcia Mikulak. But after listening to various music, I felt Philip's music was what I wanted. It had a trance element built into the rhythm structures that would fuse with the image. Getting to Philip was difficult. After my first inquiry through Rudy, Philip said, "I don't like movies, I don't see movies. I have no real interest. I'm not putting down your effort; it's just not what I do." Then I said to Rudy, "Let's try this: I'm going to put some images to some music Philip has done—specifically, *North Star*—and I'll have a little screening for him at Anthology Film Archives," which was on Wooster Street at that point. Philip was kind enough to come to the screening, as a favor to Rudy, I think. He told me afterward that he had intended to duck out, but he became very entranced by the relationship of my images to his music, and from that moment on, we've had a very productive and convivial relationship. We're able to be very critical with each other and yet maintain a mutual respect.

Within the production group here, the choice of Philip Glass was the single most controversial thing I did. People here *hated* his music. They said, "If you wanted to choose the *worst* composer in the world, you'd get this person who has broken-needle syndrome." Of course, I disagreed and persevered. My colleagues wanted me to use the great musics of the world, Bach and Mozart, et alia. My own clear feeling, which I trust explicitly, is that if the music is truly half of what's happening, it has to be written with the charge of the intention of this film: we can't be borrowing music that had another intention. That I'm able to collaborate with such a great composer gives me a real edge. I'll give Philip a poetic understanding of my feeling, and he'll try to translate it back through composition, through mathematics, which a lot of composition is, so that the *feeling* comes through. I should mention that I don't know anyone who worked on *Koyaanisqatsi* who doesn't feel Philip's music was the right choice now.

MacDonald: Does Glass look at material as you shoot it?

Reggio: He's integrated into the whole process. Usually, as you well know, a composer scores background to plot and characterization and is not integrated into the life of the film. Maybe he's involved for as long as a month. Philip is involved with the concept; he goes on location, looks at all of the rushes, is collaborating on a daily basis with me. I set up my studio in New York for *Powaqqatsi* because I realized in doing *Koyaanisqatsi* that we should have been closer together. Ours is a hand-in-glove operation, one medium motivating the other. In fact, I think that's what gives Philip the opportunity to come to the fore: there's so much focus and attention given to the score that it allows him to produce his best work.

MacDonald: It's funny that your other collaborators thought his music wouldn't work with the film, because the serial approach to music that's evident in compositions by Glass, Terry Reilly, Steve Reich, and others relates very directly to film's serial arrangement of frames.

Reggio: It was so obvious to me that I couldn't believe I was getting that response, but then again, I *can* understand. When you listen to *Music in Twelve Parts,* there's a certain demand on the listener to let go; it's almost like taking acid, which can be a very frightening experience if you're not willing to die. I know I'm being dramatic, but listening to Philip's music can produce a tremendous emotional movement inside the listener. Philip abandoned the twelve-tone Western scale for the inspirational power of Vadic Hindu chants, which are trancelike; they open up the conscious and the unconscious mind to another space, another dimension.

MacDonald: In *Powaqqatsi,* there are intermittent sound effects—the waterfall and so on. At what point does that level of sound get into the film?

Reggio: Well, to work with Philip is to work with his crew, which is a real advantage for me. He has a music director, Michael Riesman, and a producer, Kurt Munkacsi, and all the musicians who have worked with him. The sound effects were developed by Kurt Munkacsi along with me, the editors, and Philip's crew. Sound effects were more important in *Powaqqatsi* than in *Koyaanisqatsi,* though there are some in the earlier film too. The music director of *Koyaanisqatsi,* by the way, was Michael Hoenig (an early member of Tangerine Dream and now a composer on his own in Los Angeles). We want to do much more with sound effects in the third film, and have the sound design move to the forefront at certain points. We want to create a musical "bed" where other sounds fit in. We're going to hire a sound designer to work with Philip and me.

MacDonald: Powaqqatsi has done less well at the box office than *Koyaanisqatsi.* Has that seriously affected the third film?

Reggio: Well, it hasn't helped raise money. You're only as good as your last film. I want to congratulate Yoram Globus and Menahem Golan for giving me the creative space to be totally independent. They've given me great respect, and they're true lovers of *Powaqqatsi.* They're proud to have their name on it. But I think the way the film was *handled* in exhibition was a problem. They tried to handle it as a big film. In New York they released at the Ziegfeld. Well, that's the flagship of the City. It's also a desert at night because of its location on Fifty-fourth Street. We wanted to put it in a small theater with a great sound system, a theater where the house gross might be smaller, but where word of mouth could have time to generate a larger overall audience. *Koyaanisqatsi* opened at the Fifty-seventh Street Playhouse and had a twelve-week run. In Los Angeles we premiered at the Century City Plaza for two weeks, and then moved it to the Royale, where it stayed for more than five weeks—the overall run in the L.A. area was twenty weeks. After being at the Ziegfeld for, I think, five weeks, *Powaqqatsi* opened at ten New York area theaters. Well, you don't do that with this kind of film. Maybe it was to meet some financial imperative for the video deal, where they had to make so many theater play dates, but it didn't help us. I think Yoram, big person that he is, is going to allow us to rerelease *Powaqqatsi* in a different way.

MacDonald: Who made the connection with Coppola and Zoetrope [Zoetrope Studios, Francis Ford Coppola's production studio]?

Reggio: I made the connection through Tom Luddy, who was Director of Creative Affairs at Zoetrope. We had just finished the final mix of *Koyaanisqatsi*. Francis was off to shoot *The Outsiders* [1983] and *Rumble Fish* [1983] in Oklahoma, and he asked if I could do a special screening. So Francis saw the film with his crew at a private screening and stood up afterward and spoke highly about the film. And the next day, Francis offered (gratuitously) to be involved. He was very generous to offer his name to the film. In fact, I think most people see that film and think it's a Coppola film, which works well in terms of the distribution.

MacDonald: Does he still feel connected to the project?

Reggio: Francis requested that he somehow be involved with the second film, so he and George Lucas share presentation credits. George also allowed us to use, at cost, the facilities at Sprockets, his post-production facility, for the mix, which was invaluable; and he and Francis will serve as presenters for *Naqoyqatsi*. George is acting as our co-executive producer, helping us put together the package for the new film. If I call someone, that's one thing. If Francis Coppola or George Lucas does, it's quite a different thing, and I'm very fortunate to have their patronage. It was actually Francis Coppola who set up the deal for *Powaqqatsi* with Menahem Golan and Yoram Globus.

MacDonald: I was involved in the production of a film called *The Journey* [1987], an attempt at a global film. Peter Watkins, the director, was concerned that his earlier films had, to a degree, functioned within the timetable of commercial film and TV, and his goal for this film was to interrupt that expectation, to make the film so long that you'd have to invent new contexts for showing it. In a way, your decision to do a trilogy comes out of an urge to resist feature-length consumption patterns. Does it concern you that individually the parts of the trilogy still fit within the standard time structure for consuming film?

Reggio: Well, no, it doesn't. That's something that I consciously dealt with during the media campaign for the ACLU. People learn in terms of what they already know. I cannot change the industry of consumption. I cannot change the world. Obviously. If I want to have this film seen, I have to make certain concessions. If I made this film sixty-five minutes, there'd be no venue for it. If I'd made it three hours long, it wouldn't have floated. You're right in saying that in doing a trilogy, I can avoid this need to consume things in predetermined bites, but I felt, and feel, that my objective, not only as a filmmaker, but as an organizer, must be to get these films before the public. The films are unusual to begin with. They must have the chance to be consumed, and in that consumption, transform. I don't think it's the *right* thing; it's the given. And it's something that I have to try to work with.

Douglas Trumbull approached me to do *Powaqqatsi* in Showscan. Well, I thrilled to the concept, but I couldn't go that route. Douglas's intention was to make Showscan theaters multiply all over the world, but that was only an intention. The image is just about one third smaller than I-Max, but with *tremendous* luminosity because it projects at sixty frames per second. The image has almost a surreal quality. But I felt that as wonderful an opportunity as it would have been for my purposes—given that the impact of the image is extraordinary and I could have used magnetic tape for six-track Dolby sound—there might have been no place to show it.

MacDonald: Using slow motion and Glass as a soundtrack sets *Powaqqatsi* apart from standard movies anyway.

Reggio: It does, though with Showscan you can invade the viewer in a more total way. At certain increments of quantity, you change the qualitative possibilities of what happens. I think that's generally true in the world: we've quantified everything to such an extent that we've changed the quality of life.

MacDonald: I don't agree—especially in a context of your films. When you go into a special screening situation, like I-Max, you're psychically prepared for an overwhelming experience, and to some degree, perhaps, you achieve it. When you go into a normal theater, you're prepared for the level of "awesomeness" that the image normally gives you. Since most film centers everything in the middle of the image, you're really not looking at the entire screen. Your films tend to create a larger experience than most 35mm films, as a result.

Reggio: That's interesting. That offers me something.

MacDonald: What's the current state of *Naqoyqatsi*?

Reggio: We have a concept and a dramaturgical structure. We know how long the film will take to produce and post-produce. In fact, Philip and I have been working on the film since Christmas of 1985, so we're ready to move. I've gotten a third of the money earmarked from European sources, and I'm working with George Lucas, who is the co-executive producer on this film, to interest other sources. My problem is that the box office projections, as a result of the last film, don't add up to six million dollars (my budget for *Naqoygatsi*)—though all of us feel that neither film has really been exploited to its full potential. What I am clear and happy about is that the films can have longevity, and are "repeatables"—that's an industry term: people can see them more than once, and I think both films will stay around a long time. When the third film is finished, there'll be a trilogy to offer.

MacDonald: What will the new film be like?

Reggio: Fifty to seventy percent of the film, assuming I get the images I want, will be stock and archival footage. We'll print that footage; we'll recompose it; we'll cross frame it; we'll do opticals on it; we'll extend or constrict the grain structure; we'll manipulate it. And then we'll shoot the other fifty percent of the film. The principal photography will be the "outside look," seeing the present from the point of view of the past. The stock and archival footage will be the "inside look," the visual vernacular that people's minds, eyes, imaginations are drenched in by virtue of being part of Media World. We'll try to reposition the context of those stock and archival images so they can be looked at in a new way.

Naqoy means "war"; *qatsi* means "life"—in its compound: "war as a way of life." But this is not a film about the battlefield. It's a film about sanctioned aggression against the force of life, how we confuse human freedom with our pursuit of technological "happiness" or material affluence. Essentially, the film will be about the death of nature—not in an ecological sense, though that'll be included—but the death of nature as the *host of life,* as the place where life is lived, and how it has been replaced with the synthetic world we live in. I think the film will be timely. I hope it will allow us to rename the world we live in, albeit with the very limited resources of a film.

Peter Watkins

Peter Watkins has been directing films that critique the commercial cinema in general, and television news in particular, since the late fifties. Even in his early "amateur films"—as they were called in England—he dealt with the issues of war and revolution in unconventional ways. By the time he went to work for the BBC in 1963, Watkins was a recognized talent (*The Diary of an Unknown Soldier,* 1959, and *The Forgotten Faces,* 1961, had won "Oscars" in the then-annual Ten Best Amateur Films Competition) with a desire to use film as a means of changing conventional ways of seeing and understanding history and current developments. Watkins's first two directorial projects at the BBC caused considerable controversy. The first of these to be completed was *Culloden* (1964), a dramatization of the final major battle between the Scottish and the British and the subsequent destruction of the Highland Clans as a political force. The film was based on John Prebble's history of the events, *Culloden* (London: Secker & Warburg, 1961), but while *Culloden* is rigorously true to the facts, it in no way conforms to the cinematic forms standard at the time—even at the BBC—for "recreating" history. For *Culloden* Watkins extended the methods he had explored in the amateur films, especially the use of the camera as part of the action, rather than detached observer, and the reliance on close-ups of characters who look directly at the camera/audience. As the Highlanders look out at the viewers, they defy the conventional limits of history and geography, confronting our tendency to fantasize about the "heroic" past and ignore the problematic connections between past and present.

Watkins's break with convention in *Culloden* resulted in both awards and protests; at the BBC it catalyzed an opportunity to follow through on a project he had suggested before *Culloden,* a dramatization of the potential horrors of nuclear war. In the years since its controversial release (the BBC initially banned the film from television, and maintained the TV ban for more than twenty years), *The War Game* (1965) has become a widely influential "documentary," and it remains a film of considerable power and insight. The irony is that the film's very effectiveness as a form of horrifying entertainment has obscured its brilliance as a critique of conventional filmmaking and of mass media in general. While the subject of *The War Game* is nuclear war—the film dramatizes events leading up to a nuclear holocaust, the moment when the holocaust begins, and its seemingly unending aftermath—the focus of its critique is the emptiness of the "involvement" promoted by commercial media fiction and of the "detachment" of documentary film and TV news. The passages in *The War Game* that look and feel most like candid documentary—the sequences of people experiencing a nuclear detonation and its gruesome results—are acted fictions; and the passages that seem most ludicrous—a churchman explaining that one can learn to love the Bomb, "provided that it is clean and of a good family"; ordinary citizens revealing their utter ignorance about strontium 90—are either candid or based on real statements. *The War Game* emphasizes the fact that both entertainment films and documentaries are fabrications, the function of which is to maintain the system through which more products of both kinds can reach consumers.

In the years immediately following *The War Game,* Watkins completed a series of feature films that, in one way or another, elaborated on the critique of mass media he had developed in *Culloden* and *The War Game*: *Privilege* (1967), *The Gladiators* (1969), and most notably perhaps, *Punishment Park* (1970), the one Watkins film produced entirely in North America. Like earlier Watkins films, *Punishment Park* takes place in a potential near future: the war in Southeast Asia has expanded and China has become involved, fueling an even more fervent resistance at home and causing President Nixon to use the authority given him by the 1950 Internal Security Act to establish a set of Punishment Parks, where war resisters are punished and law enforcement personnel trained, simultaneously. The film reveals what happens to one group of resisters who have been found guilty of treason, while the next group is being tried and found guilty by a citizens' tribunal. Watkins used nonprofessional actors, most cast according to type: people in sympathy with the war resistance "played" the resisters; people committed to "law and order" "played" law enforcement personnel. Their dialogue was improvised. The finished film is a relentless, candid psychodramatization of the attitudes and language of a large group of Americans in 1971.

Watkins's next project, *Edvard Munch* (1974), critiqued conventional

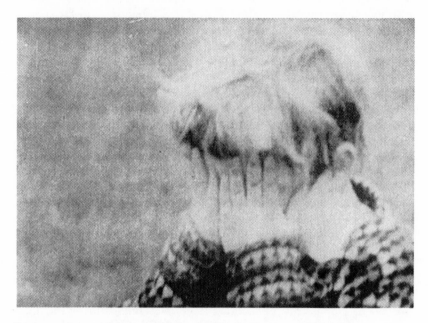

Boy's eyes burned by atomic flash in Watkins's The War Game *(1965).*

film and television biographies. *Edvard Munch* is, simultaneously, an explicit, carefully researched biography of the Norwegian expressionist *and* an implicit autobiography. Like *Culloden, Edvard Munch* recreates a historical period on the basis of careful research, but "modernizes" the period by interviewing citizens of nineteenth-century Norway and Germany as if they are our contemporaries. Again, the result is a negation of the conventional cinematic boundaries between past and present and between different nations. *Edvard Munch* was followed by two films and a video—*The 70s People* (filmed in Denmark in 1975), *The Trap* (videotaped in Sweden in 1975), and *Evening Land* (filmed in Denmark in 1977)—none of which received widespread attention or distribution. Several other projects collapsed, including film biographies of Russian composer Alexander Scriabin, Italian futurist poet Filippo Tommaso Marinetti, and Swedish playwright August Strindberg, and a proposed remake of *The War Game*.

By the early eighties, Watkins had become convinced that film and television production organizations were essentially so inflexible—in terms of their means of production and in terms of the media language they use—that there was no longer any point in trying to change them from the inside. He began to develop plans for a new kind of project, which was to become his magnum opus: the 14½-hour *The Journey* (1987). By the end of 1983, Watkins had organized a grass-roots, voluntary, international system committed to the production of an openly political film. Many of those who agreed to work with Watkins were programmers and exhibitors who had presented his work on the college circuit. Watkins had challenged them to commit—at least in this one instance—to the *production* of an openly political media critique. In fourteen countries, local organizations formed to raise money, to assemble local crews, and to find local citizens willing to be the focus of interviews and community dramatizations. During 1983 and 1984 Watkins filmed in three American locations (Portland, Oregon; Seattle, Washington; and Utica/Ilion, New York); in France, West Germany, Norway, the Soviet Union; in the Hebrides Islands and Glasgow, Scotland; in Mexico, Mozambique, and Tahiti (despite some French government resistance); and in several Australian and Japanese locations. He did not travel protected by a personal or professional entourage; he moved from one nation to the next, from one language system to the next, alone, relying almost entirely on the good will of the people in the locales where he filmed.

When Watkins arrived at the National Film Board of Canada early in 1985 to edit the film, he had shot over a hundred hours of material, and more important, had demonstrated that a filmmaker could interrogate contemporary systems not simply by working within them, but by moving across them, continually exceeding their limits, and finishing a complex, expensive project (the *The Journey* cost the equivalent of more than a million dollars). His individual achievement in seeing the film to completion was a way of suggesting that all of us, whether we're involved in media or not, can and must do a good bit more than we tell ourselves we can do, if we care about delivering a more humane, progressive world to our descendants.

The 14½ hours of *The Journey* are organized into an immense filmic weave that includes candid discussions with "ordinary people," mostly family groups from around the world, about international issues; community dramatizations of the absurdities of contemporary civil defense planning; a variety of forms of deconstructive analysis of conventional media practices; presentations of critical films and photographs by others; portraits of people and places; and a wealth of specific information about the knot of contemporary issues that include the world arms race and military expenditures in general, world hunger, the environment, gender politics, the relationship of the violent past and the present, and, especially, the role of the media and of modern educational systems with regard to international issues.

Since 1987, Watkins has worked on a variety of projects related to *The Journey* and he has begun to formulate new projects. His commitment to critique has led him to undertake an extensive exploration of *The Journey* itself. With the assistance of Vida Urbonavicius, he has developed an epic "teaching guide" for the film, a critique of the widespread tendency among filmmakers of all kinds to move on after each film project without considering, in any sustained public way, the meaning and impact of the previous work: to become, in other words, obsessed with production itself while ignoring how this production fits into the larger network of events—the way those who produce nuclear weapons focus on each new job at hand, rather than its wider implications. Watkins has also continued to work with community and student groups in Sweden, Canada, New Zealand, and the United States.

Two interviews with Watkins follow. The first was recorded in Toronto in 1981, soon after Watkins had spent a summer teaching at Columbia University and not long before his Strindberg project collapsed (though, as this is written, Watkins expects to work with a Norwegian student group on a new version of the project in 1992–93). The second was recorded in Utica, New York, in November 1983 and January 1984, soon after *The Journey* (it was called "The Nuclear War Film" at the time the interview was recorded) had gotten underway.

Part 1

Watkins: Let's start with that *Roots* experience I had at Columbia. It was a summer session. There were about thirty-five students, a very interesting bunch. I selected four subjects for us to deal with: two were *Roots* [1977] and *Holocaust* [1978]. Then there was the material we were able to get from the Television News Archive at Vanderbilt University. They've been off-air recording all the major network news broadcasts every night since 1968. For a minimal fee, you can ask them to send you a copy tape of any item of the news, providing you can identify it. [The Television News Archive publishes a monthly index to the evening news—*Television News Index and Abstracts*—which provides summaries of individual news items. Tapes of news stories can be rented from the Archive. In addition to several thousand hours of evening newscasts from ABC, CBS, and NBC, the Archive includes presidential speeches (since 1970), coverage of political conventions, the Watergate hearings, and other materials]; it so happened that someone had ordered every item relating to Iran from three months prior to the fall of the Shah to his leaving the country—twelve hours of one- and two-minute segments. We pounced on that. Then we ordered everything about Three Mile Island transmitted for a month after the accident. So we had four great subjects, each relating to history—either contemporary history or past history. What we wanted to see was what modern media is doing to change our perceptions of history past or present. We found that the distortions of past history in *Roots* and *Holocaust* are almost identical to the distortions of our perception of modern events.

Anyway, we got this mass of material, and these thirty-five people broke up into four groups. We used a very open methodology, which I would like to see become part of the educational system and part of normal community activity. It has to do with analyzing and participating in the way you receive information, which is something we have to get into very, very heavily now. The theories for everything I'm doing are based on that kind of practice. I gave the group various ideas of how they could work with the material, and they added many of their own, splayed off in many directions: one would go and interview the guy who produced a show; another would count the cuts and look at various audiovisual rhythms; somebody else would look at the historical value, or analyze the text looking for hidden messages or subtexts; another would look at the advertising. The *Roots* group was the strongest. One thing we found was that the values that come out underneath this superficially rather liberal, unusual, first-time look at the institution of slavery were really worrying, and it's not that we were being communistic or hyper-radically paranoid.

MacDonald: Can you give me an example?

Watkins: The students immediately pounced on the fact that the only suggestions of overt rebellion on the part of the black people in the entire run of *Roots* was a single reference to the Nat Turner Rebellion: you see a body half covered in a ditch. That's the nearest you come to anyone rebelling, not only against slavery but against the values that are imposed in this series. The real message is that you must fit into the iron-cast American family values. I can't go into the whole analysis the students gave, which was brilliant, but they illustrated time after time that same message: know your place in American society.

They also noticed that when the white people were making love or kissing each other or just being romantic, the scene was always filmed like a deodorant commercial: very pristine images were used; the lovers never really did anything outrageous with each other; it was all soft focus. Now when the black people were being romantic, that was all in the dark, half hidden, and filmed in an entirely different way. When you saw naked people, you saw black people. The white ladies were always kind of dressed up—not the black; the producers used them to provide sexual titillation. But the values about knowing your place and conforming, the celluloid was dripping with that.

I also talked with them about cutting rhythms and production decisions. I asked them to really look at the role of actors, and at the pat narrative structure, with the violins playing and the guy coming back home after twenty years away from his slave family and the tears, the synthetic tears, rolling down the faces of the black ladies. It's puke-making. I really can't look at a narrative film anymore—not one with these traditional rhythms going on. The manipulation is so obvious and so patent. I got the students to think about what these rhythms might be doing in terms of their perception of history, their perception of themselves, and their sensitivity to the black and white issue.

We didn't meet Alex Haley, but we met his counterpart in *Holocaust*, Gerald Green. He came along and spoke; we were lucky to get him. Everything I've said about *Roots* you could say about *Holocaust*. The people who make these shows are so proud of their research, but when you start to press them about it, they back off immediately and say, "Well, you know, we're not doing documentary; we're making a show; we're making drama; we never pretend that we're being historians." But they do! The Learning Corporation of America, the distributor of *Holocaust*, is constantly saying in the blurbs that this *is* reality, this *is* accuracy, that it represents an incredibly high academic standard, that this is for people who don't have time to read anymore. I remember Green saying, well, we don't think of ourselves as historians; this is entertainment. It's fantastic the way these people yo-yo between the two. As soon as you hold them to some responsibility for what they're doing, they do a quick Pontius Pilate and say no, no, we're only entertainers.

MacDonald: Well, I think they feel proud because they've done *some* research; most TV is entirely fantasy.

Watkins: And unfortunately it's just that that allowed *Roots* to scrape through in America, because it was the first time—which just proves the absolutely appalling standard of American television—the *first* time anything on the subject had even been seen. According to most people I've talked with, black people welcomed it with open arms. But in my opinion, it is overt racism of a most virulent form, to take the suffering of the slave experience and the suffering of the whole experience of being black in America today and wrap it up in this conservative, if not neofascist, schmaltz! I would go so far as to say that to put the black experience into a conventional narrative structure is racist—today. Because you are feeding it into a language that neutralizes it. How many people say, "I can't even remember the film I saw last night." You put the slave experience through the same rhythms as *Kojak* and *Love Story*

[1970] and . . . well, I think that's a real problem now. And the other problem is that few people are even criticizing this phenomenon.

MacDonald: How do you account for the fact that *Roots* was so popular? I believe some episodes had the largest audiences in the history of American TV. Do you think that's a function of people's hunger to deal with that issue?

Watkins: I don't know what goes on in the minds of other people. All I can do is guess. I think it's certainly partly what you said; in fact, it must be very strongly what you just said—especially on the part of black people. I regret to say I also think it is part of the whole attraction that film has these days for people. I think we're on a high as far as film is concerned, but I think this high is going to break sooner or later, because the rhythms are getting faster, and people are being over-stimulated by more and more audiovisual stuff now. I think it's got to break sooner or later. But I also speculate whether the Hollywood people have found a pattern of rhythms that from a film language point of view simulates a kinetic experience. You've got so much happening; the cutting is going so rapidly; you've got so many climaxes; you never have silence; you have dialogue thrown backwards and forwards, cut, response, cut, response, whang, climax, car chase, violence; you're hauled around, cutting, cutting, cutting. I'm beginning to think we're being attracted to television and cinema by a kind of flicker.

MacDonald: It's kinetic enough to keep you watching, without getting you deeply involved.

Watkins: I think it's important to keep throwing one's mind over one's shoulder to the cinema. I'm getting to be more worried now about the cinema, because I think many people have an in-built reservation about television. Of course, if you watch *I Love Lucy,* you take that on your own shoulders, but when you're watching something about history, or the news—that's where it really gets bad. But at the same time, I think the cinema is getting into a terribly dangerous state. It's so obviously picking up these rhythms from TV, though you can really speculate which came first. One of the things we talked about in the Columbia course was a theory I had, that the cutting rhythm of somewhere between five to seven seconds average shot comes from television. Well, I thought I had better check this out, so we studied a series of films: *Birth of a Nation* [1915], some silent newsreels of the pre–First World War period, some American newsreels of the early sound period, and the German newsreels of the Second World War. And I was wrong. It was pretty constant all the way through. As I remember, even the silent newsreels cut every eight seconds. Here's a good stopper of conversation: when you look at Nazi propaganda films—Leni Riefenstahl, for example—you're looking at the basic cutting rhythms that you see today in *Roots.*

MacDonald: When I show Larry Gottheim's *Blues* [1969] and *Fog Line* [1970] in class, many people react strongly—at least at first—almost entirely because of rhythm. I mean they're not anti-blueberries or anti-fog (though some people don't feel that such things are fit topics for movies); it's primarily the fact that they're being expected to watch an eight-and-a-half-minute continuous shot from a single camera position. It's like I'm asking them to be involved in a system of belief that they know to be false because it doesn't obey the rhythms of a system of belief they're accustomed to.

Watkins: Well, in having said that, you've partly answered your question about the public response to *Roots*. *Roots* is challenging but reassuring at the same time, which is one of the really worrying things. If I made a film about the slave experience, you'd have a totally different reaction simply because the experience would be so difficult and complex to observe. In *Roots,* you're given a seemingly bleak or radical look at history, which in fact isn't at all because you're swimming along in this warm reassuring Jell-O: the narrative form in which it's given to you.

MacDonald: And the context . . .

Watkins: And the context in which it's given to you. Absolutely. Double layers of Jell-O. It's a very clear form of pollution—"pollution" actually is not a strong enough word. When I talk to people now, I ask them to think about the way these rhythms cut up the time continuum, like a chip fryer slicing french fries. I try and have people think about that as breaking up, slicing through, our psychic continuity. I mean if we normally relate to things, or should relate to things, in gentle curving flows as we progress and grow, this is the opposite. It fragments our learning process, and our psyches. But there's a dilemma: it's hard to keep this whole topic from being just a kind of abstract aesthetic to discuss with students; we have to really start dealing with it in the body politic, in the social process.

MacDonald: Is the Strindberg film to a stage where you know how you're going to deal with these problems?

Watkins: No, not really. I have theories about it, but I'm quite worried because there's been so much research to do on the subject itself. It's been two years nonstop; I haven't had as much time as I would have liked to feel my way through certain ideas. And I guess anything I say is affected by the fact that I'm really strongly aware of the limitations of film now—for me. I'm so aware of the manipulative process, and no matter what I do, I'm only moving to another level of the same process. I might go to an infinitely more complex level, and I might allow—I deliberately use that word *allow*—people to have more variety in their responses, more complexity of response, more individuality of response, but I'm under no illusions about what's happening: that I am *still* shaping the film. What I don't know yet about the Strindberg film is how much I'm going to try and fight against responding to my own rhythms, those I've built into myself as an editor and director: someone stops talking, one, two, cut. I mean it's almost like when you take a sandwich, it goes towards your mouth—these things become so instinctual. I started to break away from that in *Edvard Munch* by cutting *against* the beat in the music, which I really enjoyed. Normally when you put music on a film, you get your wax pencil out, and as the film is running through the machine, you're marking the beats, so that all you need to do is cut on the places you've marked on the track. But to the best of my memory, I didn't do that with the Munch film, and what I really liked was putting in a piece of music and then just suddenly stopping it. It created such a tension in me, and I think in the audience, because it breaks the usual rhythmic expectancy. I do want to work with time, and our perception of time. I feel that the basic Hollywood narrative structure is totally antithetical to the way we experience life. We don't experience things in synch; we don't think in synch. Our bodies may go through a basic rhythm during the day, but we certainly don't do so inside, particularly inside our feelings. We can look at someone and be thinking about something else. You can be hearing something, but seeing something else, et cetera, et cetera. Your thoughts can be a mixture of past, present, and future, all in a highly complex individual pattern.

MacDonald: Of course, to the extent that one is being practical— working toward an end, concentrating—one is imposing synch onto life. Right now, I'm concentrating on listening to you talk. There are a lot of other things going on here, but to the extent I'm being practical, I'm forcing myself to work as though things were in synch. So, one might say that—and TV does this more than film—to make shows that are entirely in synch is like presuming that a go-get-'em practicality is the only way of functioning in life.

Watkins: That's right. The point that I keep trying to hammer home these days is not only that the ideas on TV are conservative, but that the *form* with which they're presented (even if they *were* ideas with which you and I might politically agree) defuses them.

MacDonald: In other words, if you put radical subject matter into a conventional form, it's as though you're teaching people to have ideas they don't act on, to think about things they would never take action to change.

Watkins: That's right, yes. If I could wage full-time war, I'd wage it on such words as "objectivity" and "propaganda." I mean *The War Game* has been shot down for being propaganda, and this by the BBC, which has transmitted pro-government, pro-nuclear-weapon films. I mean this is how fucked up Western society has become in its perception of reality.

I think so much of what is happening today is stemming from the way we're being affected by film and television. How can we go on ignoring the effects of these forms of media, generation after generation?

It's impossible not to have a message in a film or TV show. The way you cut a film, the way you shape it, is highly subjective. Even if you have someone sitting in a chair facing the camera, the moment you touch the bloody button that starts the celluloid through the gate, you're manipulating, because you've had to decide where to put the camera. These are all dilemmas when you make a film. I think Godard has fallen into traps by believing that he can work out these problems within films. I'm not really sure that you can. Well, the structuralists or minimalists, or whatever one should call the filmmakers you mostly work with, Scott, seem to me to be working in extremely interesting ways with film, in ways that really challenge this basic language. Even so, whether you take that route or you take the other routes—the ones I took with *Munch* and my other films, for example—you are participating in a manipulative experience, which you must continually reevaluate.

MacDonald: Also, avoiding traditional forms can make you seem more manipulative than people whose methods of manipulation are accepted as normal.

Watkins: That's quite right; I hadn't thought of it like that.

MacDonald: I think that's why it's important to do the other kind of work; even if it's not seen by everybody, it's seen by some, and whenever it *is* seen, it immediately recontextualizes the more "normal" films. If the normal film manipulation is all that exists, then it does seem to be inevitable. But once students have seen *The War Game* or *Blues,* I have to think that there's a seed in their brains that will sooner or later undermine their ability to accept the normal narrative pattern as the only way of interpreting human experience.

Watkins: What I'm going to try to do with the Strindberg film so that I won't end up doing some of these things is really complicated: I'm going to have a go at the normal narrative structure: I'm going to shred it. What makes this subject so right for what I want to do (and which is one of the primary reasons why I've stuck through all this nonsense I've been experiencing in Sweden) is this man's complex character. He's completely different from Munch, though Munch was complicated too. Strindberg wrote novels, plays, short stories, political articles; he wrote on all kinds of things, on astronomy, astrology, biology; he studied language systems, the Chinese, the Runic, the Arabic, Japanese, Javanese; he studied plant life; he studied optics; he studied sound. He's a renaissance figure, and, of course, he was the grand amateur in a sense, but sometimes he went a long way. What makes him especially interesting is that at times he became very depressed by writing. He doesn't talk about manipulating, and he doesn't go as far in his analysis as I might have liked. But he does talk about writers being parasites.

Strindberg married three times, but the first marriage was the main one. His first wife's name was Siri von Essen. She was Swedish-Finnish, and they were married for about fourteen years, though the marriage was breaking up after about ten. He wrote two autobiographies. One was written in 1886; it's called, in English, *A Madman's Defense*. It's this incredible story about his marriage. Strindberg is attacked by feminists as the greatest sexist, but in fact he isn't, if you really think about it. He does really attack his wife, and it's awful—no doubt about it. He's calling her a whore and he's having really paranoid fantasies that she's having affairs with other people, which as far as I've been able to learn, she was not. She put up with murder being with this guy.

They had married in 1876, after a fantastic love affair. She was married to a royal guards' officer who gave her over to Strindberg because he himself wanted a flirtation with his cousin. Strindberg was the knight in shining armor to this woman, also because via him she could get to be an actress, which she couldn't do while married to a guards' officer. A fantastic love affair. The first part of *Madman's Defense* is full of the most amazing lyricism and tenderness, but at the same time, it was *written* when the marriage was falling apart. That in itself sets you thinking. What complex forces were underneath in him?

He also wrote another autobiography, *The Son of a Servant*, in 1886. He called it that because his wife—sorry, Freudian slip—his *mother* had been his father's housekeeper. She had given illegitimate birth to the first couple of children before Strindberg was born in wedlock. Part of the film will be based on his writing about his childhood. I'm going to illustrate his life from his birth up to 1875 when he first meets Siri von Essen, which is fantastically romantic. That is where the film will stop. The film will *also* start when he *meets* Siri von Essen and, based on *A Madman's Defense*, will wend a certain course. And I'm *also* going to center on the period when he wrote *A Madman's Defense*. It's going to be so tremendously complex, and not knitted together—I'm not looking for the bridges. I've done a script. I just wrote letting things come, jumping backward and forwards between the three periods just to see what fell against what. I've deliberately forced only one meeting of the structures during the body of the film: when he divorces Siri von Essen, his mother dies in his childhood. But the other events will come where they come. It's really exciting; it means that in the editing, when the stuff starts to drop together, there'll be all kinds of complex relationships.

There's another layer I haven't told you about yet. It's an important part of all this, the sociological part. I'm going to trace the development of the increasing rigidity of Stockholm as a city. Now *this* I'm expert on!

A really fantastic historian is helping me trace the development of the Stockholm press and the way the structure of information *on the page* settled into a pattern by the 1860s, and had become completely commercialized by the 1880s. I'm indirectly laying that against a social tracing of the increasing rigidity of the social pattern of Stockholm, which was never a free city. It was a city ruled by the king. Kings have played an extremely autonomous role in the Swedish society, and the Swedes have rarely looked at that. They always go goo goo over the king, like we do in England. Well, in the film the king is going to emerge as something of a tyrant. Swedish kings interfered strongly in politics, and several were really reactionary.

Stockholm was an agricultural city dominated by the court; there was a large underprivileged class. Very rapidly it was hauled into the industrial era—probably more rapidly than any other city in the Western world. Within fifteen years, heavy production came in, and so on. And the Swedish soul began to develop—unfortunately, the modern soul. The city became more and more rigid. The police force developed. By 1879, the city was broken up into zones of control, which interestingly is just about when the press had become spatially systematized. Each zone contained ten thousand people, and there was a guy in charge of registering the population. This was seen as a more sophisticated censor process—oops, sorry, another slip—*census* process; they registered the birth, death, and occupation of every person within each district. They also listed prison sentences, and other reported irregularities in moral behavior. From this time on, you can look at the way juvenile delinquents are treated, the increasing stress on more penal sentences. I won't bore you, but there are so many things that you can see are part of the development of "modern civilization." The town is architecturally destroyed. Stockholm is a fantastic model for how our society's completely fucked itself up with more and more structures and blocks. And, of course, there's also what the words of the news stories are *saying,* which will add other complexities.

I'm even going to try and talk about cutting rhythms at a certain point in the film. I may try and cut a sequence one way, and then cut it another way—not just for the didactic hell of that, but to try and flow a bit with Strindberg's own decentralization as a person. Do we need a center inside ourselves or don't we? Strindberg was so all over the place that one could theorize that he never really had an internal center to his psyche, which was both a strength and, unfortunately, a weakness for him. He suffered all his life, and he could never really flow with his relationship with Siri von Essen. At the same time, he was always trying to break out of conventional structures, particularly in his plays. He made highly condensed, highly charged pieces, where a lot is done just with looks or one short sentence. He does in a few sentences what people had spent pages doing before. So he's breaking out of convention, but he's trapped by it, because he's quite a bourgeois man in many ways. He's very trapped by money, although he never had much.

This film will be far less syrupy than the Munch film. I don't identify with Strindberg the way I did with Munch, and there's no point in doing the same film again anyway. I've done a lot of developing since I made the Munch film; that was in 1973. And I really want to work with all this media stuff now. I want to create abysses into which people can fall and tumble where they want; if I can ever do that in a film, then I'll stop making films—I'll have arrived. I do think there's a self-terminating point. I'm not in love with film anymore, and that's one of the most liberating things that's happened to me. I don't need it as a means of expression. In fact, if I could be a professional researcher for the rest of my life, I'd probably do that. I love doing research. Film is not my "high" anymore.

MacDonald: I would hate to see you out of film. Your films are some of the few that are based on serious research. The Munch film is as powerful as it is, partly because you clearly know as much about Munch as anybody alive. The film is not a fantasy about Munch, it's an attempt to deal with material that took a tremendous effort to compile.

Watkins: But, you understand the trap there, which is the trap we've been talking about. The more I become an "expert," the more I am creating for people their image of Edvard Munch. A well-known historian of Strindberg (he's a very nice guy who's been very helpful) said to me, "Well, I must say"—and he meant this as a compliment—"I must say, your *Edvard Munch* is what Edvard Munch *is* to me now." I was really happy that he said that, but I thought to myself afterwards, "Ugh! God!"

MacDonald: I think you're being too hard on him and yourself.

Watkins: Oh, I'm not being hard on him. I'm really glad he said it. But, still, because I am worried about the *whole* role of the media, I cannot lift myself out as some kind of elitist who's somehow found the eternal secret of being the perfect researcher and the perfect complex filmmaker, who's removed from this. I'm not. I'm right in the middle of it.

Part 2

MacDonald: Many people would say it's madness for you to think you can complete this new project [what was to become *The Journey*]. I know of no film that has been substantially funded by the donations of individuals in various countries.

Watkins: Well, nobody has actually said, yet, that such a thing is madness. And I don't see it as madness at all—quite the contrary. It is *because* we've gotten used to the media being so damned centralized that we think of such a project as unusual. You can find many aspects of the social process where the public should be involved but aren't. But here's a clear example where receivers are almost completely uninvolved in the creation of what they are receiving. It's fantastically off-balance. What I'm doing should be quite normal, as far as the process is concerned.

I'm quite sure the film will get done. It may be that for one reason or another I won't be able to shoot the film in all the countries I hope to, but I don't think that will be for financial reasons. It may be because this country or that makes it too bureaucratic for me to function.

MacDonald: How exactly are you raising money?

Watkins: I'm building up a several-tier process. In some countries we've applied for public funds. In France, for example, we're applying for a national grant, though the support for the film there is coming from the Midi-Pyrenees Regional Film Production Center in the south of France. I've applied for funds to cover the cost of the equipment and filming. But a local regional board has said that even if I don't get the grant, they will lend me the equipment for nothing. Wherever I can, I'm trying to cover my bets, so that if we get less than full funding, I'll have emergency plans to fall back on.

MacDonald: How much are you trying to raise?

Watkins: If you add up the target allocations I've set for each country, it comes to nearly five hundred thousand dollars, but I have a safety margin built in. Even if you were trying to raise money in just this country over the next year from public and cultural funds, five hundred thousand dollars would not be impossible. We're trying to raise it in countries all over the world.

MacDonald: What's your goal for the two U.S. episodes you plan to shoot?

Watkins: About a hundred and fifty thousand dollars, a bit more than a third of the budget. Another third will be coming from Sweden: the Swedes are trying to raise about a million crowns [approximately $150,000]. The other third will be raised elsewhere, in eight countries or so. In Sweden we've applied for two main grants. The National Film Board of Canada has offered to provide me with stock and costs, which I think means stock and equipment. But even if it means stock, that will be very helpful.

MacDonald: But, even should you get some of the grants, much of the money will still come from individuals and groups in the various countries trying to raise money on their own?

Watkins: Yes, the public process. A large amount of money will come from that.

MacDonald: When you were in this country in spring of 1983 you spent some time trying to get money from Hollywood, from Canadian commercial TV, and other commercial sources. But I had a sense even then that part of you wanted to generate funds on a more local basis, on principle.

Watkins: That's right. I wasn't ambivalent about the principle at all, but at that point I was concerned about the practice. It takes a long time to raise money. You can't be quite sure, until you're underway and really rolling, how people will respond to a particular project. It's a very special and individual chemistry, dependent on the time you're in, on the nature of the subject, on so many things. I tried to raise money publicly in England last year when I wanted to remake *The War Game.* That project was stopped by Central Television. We had started the public fund-raising there, though I'm not sure if it's fair to judge the results or not. At the time the project was stopped, we had raised around thirty-five thousand dollars. That was a national appeal concentrating mostly on England, but it went on for only about two months, and I think it tended to peter out once people thought that Central Television was paying for the film. So it's hard to say whether that rather small amount of money was a warning or not, but it did show me that the process could take a tremendous amount of time. We were trying to find several hundred thousand dollars.

MacDonald: At what point did the idea for this film become international?

Watkins: So much has happened in the last year and a half. I've been around the world twice just this year. So I can't remember exactly, but the idea was already germinating by the time we tried approaching Home Box Office and Hollywood last spring.

MacDonald: I know you want to shoot in the Soviet Union. How do you mean to arrange that? Do you know other filmmakers who have worked that way?

Watkins: There are Western filmmakers who have worked in Soviet-bloc nations, of course. There have even been some international television linking arrangements, and I think they're trying now to link citizens of Lawrence, Kansas, and citizens of Leningrad for *The Day After* [1983]. I'm not sure which citizens. But I don't know anyone who's done what I'm trying to do: deal with a major subject, with different yet common perspectives from all the major countries involved.

I don't know if the Soviet Union has ever been involved in this kind of process before. We're approaching the state authorities. It's very difficult because Soviet state authorities are extremely slow-moving; they're

like the Indian state authorities—extremely bureaucratic, very much
wanting to make sure that what comes out is favorable to the existing
regime, or whatever. I'm approaching them saying that I don't want to
have to deal very much with constraints. This is a film that can't function
with the usual constraints. I told the Soviets that I wanted to film with a
non-party family. After all, I'm not filming with a U.S. "party" family:
some Washington family, fresh out of some Republican committee.
There may lie the crunch. They've never had to deal with a nonstruc-
tured project like this before, something that isn't all detailed on paper.
They just don't understand it.

Western television doesn't understand that approach either: to work
without a script would be unheard of. That you might have a learning
process out of which the film develops is total anathema. I am very
strongly aware of how revolutionary this project is going to be in terms
of the existing mass media. I can't really talk much about some of the
internal meaning of the project for fear it will sound too abstract. I talk
most about the way in which the film will very, very publicly ask people
to challenge the way the media is functioning. One of the aims of the
film is to compel the film establishment and the media to actually deal
not only with "content," the nuclear issue in this case, but with the
effects of conventional media language on the issue and on the widespread feeling of powerlessness about the issue.

Anyway, if you can understand that there are difficulties *here* in dealing with this process, you can image how difficult it is in the Soviet
Union. We're dealing with the Soviet Peace Committee, which is the
internal peace organ in charge, I think, of all internal peace arrangements and all peace people who visit the Soviet Union. I'm going to sit
down in front of these people, and I'm going to be quite open about
what this film is about. I'm going to ask them to help us give the film top
priority, to say that the film is absolutely essential. If they won't do that,
I won't go there: I'll find some way of doing it outside the Soviet Union.
[The Soviet Union agreed to a family sequence which was shot in Moscow in August 1984.]

MacDonald: The War Game is a painful, powerful film. Will this new
film be similar?

Watkins: I've never repeated any film I've made. And I'm not interested in doing that. I won't think about *The War Game*. This film will
make me work in different ways. The blending of the various elements
will be entirely different. One thing I plan to do, that I've not done as
overtly before, is to deconstruct some scenes. I'd like to show the effects
a cut has, how a scene is constructed.

MacDonald: You mean that the film will move back and forth between narrative and self-reflexive examination of narrative.

Watkins: Yes, though I think you can use "narrative" here only in the very loosest sense. The film will be constantly moving from one set of people to another. There will be a certain chronological drive which will be interrupted from time to time by self-reflexive moments.

I really wouldn't like to project how television companies are going to react when asked to show the film, a self-reflexive film which is not just a didactic exercise on the blackboard, but which confronts the issue in the context of nuclear war. But the film will be put on the desks of all the television organizations, in each of the countries where we film. And you can be quite sure there will be people ready to make a strong challenge when any of those companies reject the film. I'm quite sure there will be a sizeable rejection. The only thing I cannot project is who will do the rejecting. Neither can I be sure about the cinema distributors, some of whom are very conservative, some of whom are very helpful.

I'm going to try it all, because that's the only means one has of reaching large numbers of people. And I want the film to earn money, because it's important that money comes back into the groups that helped—and into the movement toward demilitarization. But I can't rely on that, as I know from bitter experience. So we're going to try to set up an alternative distribution—it's just a theory at this point—asking different groups to start a series of showings in local halls, in churches, at universities, in *public* places where there can be rigorous debate on the material the film is dealing with. I want that to happen a great deal. I'm going to aim for that, because that's the nearest equivalent in distribution to the way in which the film is being made. It's organized to be part of a discussion that explodes upwards and outwards.

MacDonald: In this country most films that have tried to deal self-reflexively with film and media language and to provide alternatives to it have tended to be shown in the art ghettos in big cities; despite the wishes of many of the filmmakers, the audience never expands very far. For me, what sounds remarkable about this project is your attempt to bridge the gap. You're not just talking about film, or about making a film about film; you're using the making of a film to demonstrate and develop new kinds of relationships between producers, films, and audiences.

Watkins: There are filmmakers concerned in examining form; quite a lot of them do that. Some do very interesting work. But many of them don't seem anxious to go further with what they do, by taking it into the actual social process. You can't just talk about nuclear weapons blowing people up anymore. You have to talk about the society that is creating them, the society that is seemingly pushing down people's ability to be able to respond to them. The issue is going to be everywhere, and you cannot deal with it, as the peace movement has often tended to, as

Watkins and crowd preparing scene for The Journey *(1987). Production still by Sylvia de Swaan.*

something destructive which one has to simply pluck out, like plucking out the core of a malignancy. Here the core is not a lump. It's got obscene roots going everywhere now. And the moment you understand that, you have to start dealing with why people are not reacting. And *that* leads to why people know so little.

We have to deal with the way we are receiving our information (and our entertainment, because the two are linked together) and with how that process is intricately interwoven into the quality of life. We all know this in theory, but we never move on it. We just go on letting it happen, without any kind of public reflexivity, which is really what I'm talking about: public participation in the processing of information.

I suppose one way of saying it is that I think the process I'm trying to get going in this film is one model, just one, of the kinds of ways in which I think the media should be working with the public. There should be a psychological and intellectual relationship, a working relationship, between the media and the public, not simply a closed masonic secret language coming from one kind of power source to the receiving public who don't quite understand the language of manipulation. This is *totally undemocratic*.

As things are, the media is a fantastic metaphor. The United States fires off nuclear missiles, including the MX missiles they test, from the

Vandenberg Air Force Base in California. They fire the missiles into an atoll in the Marshall Islands. It's called the Missile Firing Range. The islanders are moved away, so the missiles presumably don't hit them. But the image of firing this stuff off towards a clump of islands thousands of miles away is just parallel to the way the media works. Just launch the stuff towards the public, and say good-bye.

I find the usual process pretty horrifying, and I'm really looking forward to working with families without a centralized script, and I'm looking forward to showing the film publicly. I'm hoping it will send tremors through certain sections of the media. Part of the media's way of not dealing with the public is to make production a secretive, elitist process. The professional does everything. He or she writes it, films it, and there's no relationship at all with the receivers. My god, there are as many possible ways of making film as there are blades of grass. But the media still clings virtually to one form, the theatrical mode, which has become a form of political constraint, of political power.

Filmography

In the following listing, each film's title is followed by the year in which the film was completed, the film's gauge, the length of the film to the nearest quarter minute, and an indication of whether the film is black and white and/or color, silent or sound. In parentheses I have listed primary rental sources. The following abbreviations are used:

ACGB (Arts Council of Great Britain, 105 Piccadilly, London W1V 0AU)

AFA (American Federation of Arts, 41 East 65th St., New York, NY 10021)

BFI (British Film Institute, 21 Stephen St., London W1P 1PL)

CC (Canyon Cinema, 2325 Third St., Suite 338, San Francisco, CA 94107)

CFDC (Canadian Filmmakers Distribution Centre, 67A Portland St., Toronto, Ontario, M5V 2M9)

Circles (113 Roman Road, London E2)

FACETS (video only: 1517 W. Fullerton Ave., Chicago, IL 60614)

FMC (Film-makers' Cooperative, 175 Lexington Ave., New York, NY 10016)

FR (First Run, 153 Waverly Place, New York, NY 10014)

LFC (London Film Makers' Co-operative, 42 Gloucester Ave., London, NW1)

MoMA (Museum of Modern Art, Circulating Film Program, 11 W. 53rd St., New York, NY 10019)

WMM (Women Make Movies, 225 Lafayette St., Suite 207, New York, NY 10012)

Major distributors of commercial features (New Yorker, Films Incorporated . . .) are indicated by name only. In some cases, films are available from the filmmakers. In those instances, I include the filmmaker's address only once, with the listing of the earliest of such films.

Bruce Baillie

On Sundays. 1961. 16mm; 26 minutes; black and white; sound (FMC).

David Lynn's Sculpture. 1961. 16mm; 3 minutes; black and white; sound.

Mr. Hayashi. 1961. 16mm; 3 minutes; black and white; sound (CC, FMC, MoMA).

The Gymnasts. 1961. 16mm; 3 minutes; black and white; sound (CC, FMC).

Friend Fleeing. 1962. 16mm; 3 minutes; black and white; sound.

Everyman. 1962. 16mm; 6 minutes; black and white; sound.

The News No. 3. 1962. 16mm; 3 minutes; black and white; sound.

Have You Thought of Talking to the Director. 1962. 16mm; 15 minutes; black and white; sound (FMC).

Here I Am. 1962. 16mm; 10 minutes; black and white; sound.

A Hurrah for Soldiers. 1963. 16mm; 4 minutes; color; sound (CC, FMC).

To Parsifal. 1963. 16mm; 16 minutes; color; sound (CC, FMC).

Mass for the Dakota Sioux. 1964. 16mm; 24 minutes; black and white; sound (CC, FMC, LFC, MoMA).

The Brookfield Recreation Center. 1964. 16mm; 6 minutes; black and white; sound.

Quixote. 1965. 16mm; 45 minutes; black and white/color; sound (CC, FMC, MoMA).

Yellow Horse. 1965. 16mm; 8 minutes; color; sound (CC, FMC).

Tung. 1966. 16mm; 5 minutes; color; silent (CC, FMC, LFC).

All My Life. 1966. 16mm; 3 minutes; color; sound (CC, CFDC, FMC, LFC, MoMA).

Still Life. 1966. 16mm; 2 minutes; color; sound (CC, FMC).

Termination. 1966. 16mm; 6 minutes; black and white; sound (CC).

Port Chicago Vigil. 1966. 16mm; 9 minutes; black and white; sound.

Castro Street. 1966. 16mm; 10 minutes; black and white/color; sound (CC, CFDC, LFC, MoMA).

Show Leader. 1966. 16mm; 1 minute; black and white; sound (CC, FMC).

Valentin de las Sierras. 1968. 16mm; 10 minutes; color; sound (CC, CFDC, FMC, LFC).

Quick Billy. 1970. 16mm; 56 minutes; black and white/color; sound (CC, FMC, LFC).

Roslyn Romance (Is It Really True?). 1977 (Introduction Part I and II; ongoing). 16mm; 17 minutes; color; sound (CC, FMC).

The Cardinal's Visit. On-going. 16mm/video; 120 minutes; color; sound (Baillie, 669 W. Kodiak Ave., Camano Island, WA 98292).

Dr. Bish Remedies. 1987 (No. I; Nos. II and III in progress). Video (VHS); 60 minutes each; color; sound (Baillie).

The P-38 Pilot. 1990. Video (VHS); 15 minutes; color; sound (Baillie).

James Benning

did you ever hear that cricket sound? 1971. 16mm; 1 minute; black and white; sound (Benning, 30718 San Martinez, Val Verde Park, CA 91384).

Time and a Half. 1972. 16mm; 17 minutes; black and white; sound (FMC).

Art Hist. 101. 1972. 16mm; 17 minutes; black and white; sound (Benning).

Ode to Musak. 1972. 16mm; 3 minutes; color; sound (Benning).

57. 1973. 16mm; 7 minutes; color; sound (Benning).

Michigan Avenue (co-made with Bette Gordon). 1973. 16mm; 6 minutes; color; sound (FMC).

Honeyland Road. 1973. 16mm; 6 minutes; color; sound (Benning).

8½ X 11. 1974. 16mm; 32½ minutes; color; sound (FMC).

Gleem. 1974. 16mm; 2 minutes; color; sound (Benning).

I-94 (co-made with Bette Gordon). 1974. 16mm; 3 minutes; color; sound (FMC).

The United States of America (co-made with Bette Gordon). 1975. 16mm; 27 minutes; color; sound (FMC).

Saturday Night. 1975. 16mm; 3 minutes; color; sound (Benning).

An Erotic Film. 1975. 16mm; 11 minutes; color; sound (Benning).

3 minutes on the dangers of film recording. 1975. 16mm; 3 minutes; black and white/tinted; sound (Benning).

9-1-75. 1975. 16mm; 22 minutes; color; sound (FMC).

Chicago Loop. 1976. 16mm; 8½ minutes; color; sound (FMC).

A to B. 1976. 16mm; 2 minutes; color; sound (Benning).

11 X 14. 1976. 16mm; 83 minutes; color; sound (CFDC, FR).

One Way Boogie Woogie. 1977. 16mm; 60 minutes; color; sound (CFDC, FR).

Four Oil Wells. 1978. 16mm film installation; continuous; color (Benning).

Grand Opera. 1978. 16mm; 90 minutes; color; sound (CFDC, FR).

Oklahoma. 1979. 16mm film installation; continuous; color; sound (Benning).

Double Yodel. 1980. 16mm film installation; continuous; color; sound (Benning).

Last Dance. 1981. 16mm film installation; continuous; color; sound (Benning).

Him and Me. 1982. 16mm; 88 minutes; color; sound (CFDC, FR).

American Dreams. 1984. 16mm; 58 minutes; color; sound (CFDC, FR).

Pascal's Lemma. 1985. Computer installation; continuous; color; silent (Benning).

O Panama. 1985. 16mm; 28 minutes; color; sound (CFDC, FR).

Landscape Suicide. 1986. 16mm; 95 minutes; color; sound (FR).

Used Innocence. 1988. 16mm; 95 minutes; color; sound (FR).

Lizzie Borden

Regrouping. 1976. 16mm; c. 80 minutes; black and white; sound.

Born in Flames. 1983. 16mm; 90 minutes; color; sound (FR).

Working Girls. 1986. 35mm; 93 minutes; color; sound (Miramax, FACETS).
Love Crimes. 1992. 35 mm; c. 90 minutes; color; sound.

Robert Breer

The most complete filmography for Breer was compiled and annotated by David Curtis for *Robert Breer,* the catalogue for an exhibition organized by the Cambridge Animation Festival and the Arts Council of Great Britain in 1983.

Form Phases I. 1952. 16mm; 2 minutes; color; sound (ACGB; FMC, LFC).
Form Phases II & III. 1953. 16mm; 7½ minutes; color; silent (FMC, LFC).
Form Phases IV. 1954. 16mm; 4 minutes; color; silent (FMC).
Untitled. 1954. 16mm; loop; color; silent.
Un Miracle. 1954. 16mm; ½ minute; color; silent (FMC, LFC, MoMA).
Untitled. 1955. 16mm; 3 minutes; black and white; silent (Breer, 80 Sparkill Ave., Tappan, NY 10983).
Image by Images. 1956. 16mm; 2½ minutes; color; sound (BFI, FMC, LFC).
Motion Pictures. 1956. 16mm; 3 minutes; color; sound (Breer).
Cats. 1956. 16mm; 1½ minutes; color; sound (BFI, FMC, MoMA).
Recreation. 1956. 16mm; 2 minutes; color; sound (AFA, ACGB, CC, FMC, LFC, MoMA).
Recreation II. 1956. 16mm; 1½ minutes; color; silent (Breer).
Jamestown Baloos. 1957. 16mm; 5 minutes; color; sound (BFI, CC, FMC, LFC, MoMA).
A Man and His Dog Out for Air. 1957. 16mm; 2 minutes; black and white; sound (ACGB, BFI, CC, FMC, LFC, MoMA).
Par Avion (unfinished). 1958. 16mm; 3 minutes; color; silent (Breer).
A section of Michel Fano's *Chutes De Pierres, Danger Du Mort.* 1958. 16mm; 3–5 minutes; color; sound.
Eyewash. 1959. 16mm; 5 minutes; color; silent (FMC).
Trailer (for Cinema 16). 1959. 16mm; 1 minute; black and white; silent (lost).
Inner and Outer Space. 1960. 16mm; 5½ minutes; color; sound (AFA, FMC).
Homage to Jean Tinguely's Homage to New York. 1960. 16mm; 9½ minutes; black and white; sound (CC, FMC, LFC, MoMA).
Blazes. 1961. 16mm; 3 minutes; color; sound (ACGB, CC, FMC, LFC, MoMA).
Kinetic Art Show Stockholm. 1961. 16mm; 15 minutes; color; sound (David Brinkley's Journal, NBC).
Horse Over Tea Kettle. 1962. 16mm; 8 minutes; color; sound (AFA, FMC, LFC, MoMA).
Pat's Birthday. 1962. 16mm; 13 minutes; black and white; sound (CC, CFDC, FMC, LFC, MoMA).
Breathing. 1963. 16mm; 6 minutes; black and white; sound (CC, FMC, LFC, MoMA).
Fist Fight. 1964. 16mm; 11 minutes; color; sound (CC, CFDC, FMC, LFC, MoMA).

66. 1966. 16mm; 5 minutes; color; sound (FMC, LFC, MoMA).

69. 1968. 16mm; 5 minutes; color; sound (AFA, ACGB, CC, FMC, LFC).

PBL 2. 1968. 16mm; 1 minute; color; sound (FMC, MoMA).

PBL 3. 1968. 16mm; 1 minute; color; sound (Breer).

70. 1970. 16mm; 5 minutes; color; silent (FMC, LFC, MoMA).

Elevator. 1971. 16mm; 1 minute; color; sound (Produced for Children's Television Workshop).

WHAT? 1971. 16mm; 1 minute; color; sound (Produced for Children's Television Workshop).

Gulls and Buoys. 1972. 16mm; 7½ minutes; color; sound (AFA, CC, FMC, LFC, MoMA).

Fuji. 1974. 16mm; 8½ minutes; color; sound (CC, FMC, MoMA).

Rubber Cement. 1975. 16mm; 10 minutes; color; sound (CC, FMC, MoMA).

77. 1977. 16mm; 7 minutes; color; sound (Arts Council of Great Britain, CC, FMC, MoMA).

LMNO. 1978. 16mm; 9½ minutes; color; sound (ACGB, CC, FMC, MoMA).

TZ. 1978. 16mm; 8½ minutes; color; sound (AFA, ACGB, CC, FMC, LFC, MoMA).

Swiss Army Knife with Rats and Pigeons. 1981. 16mm; 6 minutes; color; sound (AFA, CC, FMC, LFC).

Trial Balloons. 1982. 16mm; 5½ minutes; color; sound (AFA, ACGB, CC, FMC, LFC).

Carrot Fork Bottle. 1985. 2 screen 16mm; 3½ minutes; color; sound (FMC).

Carrot Fork Bottle. 1985. Spectacolor electronic lightboard, Times Square, New York; ½ minute; color; silent.

Bang! 1986. 16mm; 10 minutes; color; sound (FMC).

Blue Monday (co-made with William Wegman). 1988. Video; 4 minutes; color; sound (Warner Brothers).

A Frog on the Swing. 1989. 16mm; 5 minutes; color; sound (CC, MoMA).

Su Friedrich

Hot Water. 1978. Super-8mm; 12 minutes; black and white; silent.

Cool Hands, Warm Heart. 1979. 16mm; 7 minutes; black and white; silent (CC; Friedrich, 222 East 5th St., #6, New York, NY 10003; FMC, WMM).

Scar Tissue. 1979. 16mm; 7 minutes; black and white; silent (Friedrich).

I Suggest Mine. 1980. 16mm; 6 minutes; black and white/color; silent.

Gently Down the Stream. 1981. 16mm; 14 minutes; black and white; silent (CC, CFDC; Cinenova, 113 Roman Rd., London E2 OH2, U.K.; Circles; Drift, 83 Warren St., #5, New York, NY 10007; FMC, Friedrich; Lady Slipper, 613 Vickers Ave., Durham, NC 27701; LFC, MoMA, WMM).

But No One. 1982. 16mm; 9 minutes; black and white; silent (CC, FMC).

The Ties That Bind. 1984. 16mm; 55 minutes; black and white; sound (CC, CFDC, Cinenova, Circles, Drift, MoMA, WMM).

Damned If You Don't. 1987. 16mm; 42 minutes; black and white; sound (CC, CFDC, FMC; Frameline, 347 Dolores St., #205, San Francisco, CA 94110; Friedrich, LFC, MoMA, WMM).

Sink or Swim. 1990. 16mm; 48 minutes; black and white; sound (CC, CFDC, Drift, Friedrich, LFC, MoMA, WMM).

First Comes Love. 1991. 16mm; 22 minutes; black and white; sound (CC, CFDC, Drift, Friedrich, LFC, WMM).

Anthony McCall

Landscape for Fire. 1972. 16mm; 7 minutes; color; silent (McCall, 11 Jay St., New York, NY 10013).

ABCD. 1973. 16mm; 30 minutes; color; silent.

Line Describing a Cone. 1973. 16mm; 30 minutes; black and white; silent (CC, LFC, McCall).

Conical Solid. 1974. 16mm; 10 minutes; black and white; silent (LFC, McCall).

Cone of Variable Volume. 1974. 16mm; 10 minutes; black and white; silent (McCall).

Partial Cone. 1974. 16mm; 15 minutes; black and white; silent (McCall).

Long Film for Four Projectors. 1974. 16mm (4-projector environment); 360 minutes; black and white; silent (McCall).

Four Projected Movements. 1975. 16mm; 75 minutes; black and white; silent (McCall).

Long Film for Ambient Light. 1975. Installation; continuous.

Letters I–VI. 1975–76. Super-8mm; 3 minutes, each letter; color; sound.

Ear. 1976. Super-8mm; 3 minutes; color; sound.

Carnage (directed by Ken Burns; cinematography by McCall). 1976. Super-8mm; 90 minutes; color; sound.

Argument (co-made with Andrew Tyndall). 1978. 16mm; 75 minutes; color; sound (McCall).

Sigmund Freud's Dora (co-made with Claire Pajaczkowska, Andrew Tyndall, Jane Weinstock). 1979. 16mm; 40 minutes; color; sound (BFI, McCall).

Ross McElwee

20,000 Missing Persons. 1974. 16mm; 30 minutes; color; sound.

68 Albany Street. 1976. 16mm; 24 minutes; color; sound.

Energy War (directed by D. A. Pennebaker, Pat Powell, Chris Hegedus; some cinematography by McElwee). 1977. 16mm; 300 minutes; color; sound (Pennebaker, 56 West 45th St., New York, NY 10036).

Charleen. 1978. 16mm; 59 minutes; color; sound (Artificial Eye, 211 Camden High St., London NW1 7BT, U.K.; FR).

N!ai: Portrait of a !Kung Woman (directed by John Marshall; some cinematography by McElwee). 1978. 16mm; 60 minutes; color; sound (1980).

Space Coast (co-made with Michel Negroponte). 1979. 16mm; 90 minutes; color; sound (Artificial Eye, FR).

Resident Exile (co-made with Alex Anthony, Michel Negroponte). 1981. 16mm; 30 minutes; color; sound (Artificial Eye, FR).

Backyard. 1984. 16mm; 40 minutes; color; sound (Artificial Eye, FR).

Sherman's March. 1986. 16mm; 155 minutes; color; sound (Artificial Eye, FR).
Something to Do with the Wall (co-made with Marilyn Levine). 1990. 16mm; 88
  minutes; color; sound (Artificial Eye, FR).

Jonas Mekas

Guns of the Trees. 1961. 35mm; 75 minutes; black and white; sound (FMC).
Film Magazine of the Arts. 1963. 16mm; 20 minutes; color; sound (FMC).
The Brig. 1964. 68 minutes; black and white; sound (CC, CFDC, FMC).
Award Presentation to Andy Warhol. 1964. 16mm; 12 minutes; black and white;
  sound (FMC).
Report from Millbrook. 1966. 16mm; 12 minutes; color; sound (CFDC, FMC).
Walden. 1969. 16mm; 177 minutes; color; sound (FMC).
Hare Krishna. 1966. 16mm; 4 minutes; color; sound (CFDC, FMC).
Notes on the Circus. 1966. 16mm; 12 minutes; color; sound (AFA, CC, CFDC,
  FMC).
Cassis. 1966. 16mm; 4½ minutes; color; sound (CC, CFDC, FMC).
The Italian Notebook. 1967. 16mm; 14¾ minutes; color; silent (FMC).
Time and Fortune Vietnam Newsreel. 1968. 16mm; 4 minutes; color; sound (FMC).
Reminiscences of a Journey to Lithuania. 1972. 16mm; 82 minutes; color; sound
  (CC, FACETS, FMC).
Lost Lost Lost. 1976. 16mm; 178 minutes; black and white/color; sound (CFDC,
  FMC).
In Between. 1978. 16mm; 52 minutes; black and white/color; sound (FMC).
Notes for Jerome. 1978. 16mm; 45 minutes; color; sound (FMC, MoMA).
Paradise Not Yet Lost (a.k.a. "Oona's Third Year"). 1979. 16mm; 96½ minutes;
  color; sound (FMC).
Street Songs. 1983. 16mm; 10½ minutes; black and white; sound (FMC).
Cup/Saucer/Two Dancers/Radio. 1983. 16mm; 23 minutes; color; sound (FMC).
*Erick Hawkins: Excerpts from "Here and Now with Watchers"/Lucia Dlugo-
  szewski Performs.* 1983. 16mm; 5¾ minutes; black and white; sound (FMC).
He Stands in a Desert Counting the Seconds of His Life. 1985. 16mm; 150
  minutes; color; sound (FMC).

Laura Mulvey

Penthesilea (co-made with Peter Wollen). 1974. 16mm; 90 minutes; color; sound
  (Mulvey, 207 Ladbroke Grove, London W11, U.K.; Wollen, 11005 Strath-
  more Dr., Los Angeles, CA 90024).
Riddles of the Sphinx (co-made with Peter Wollen). 1977. 16mm; 92 minutes;
  color; sound (BFI, MoMA; New Cinema, 75 Horner Ave., #1, Toronto,
  Ont., M8Z 4X5 Canada).
Amy! (co-made with Peter Wollen). 1979. 16mm; 33 minutes; color; sound (BFI,
  MoMA).
Crystal Gazing (co-made with Peter Wollen). 1981. 16mm; 90 minutes; color;
  sound (BFI).

Frida Kahlo and Tina Modotti (co-made with Peter Wollen). 1983. 16mm; 30 minutes; color; sound (ACGB; MoMA).

The Bad Sister (co-made with Peter Wollen). 1983. Video; 90 minutes; color; sound (Channel 4, U.K.).

New Horizons (co-made with Chris Welsby). 1987. 16mm (transferred to video and presented on 36-monitor video wall); 2½ minutes (longer in video wall version); color; sound (Mulvey).

Andrew Noren

A Change of Heart. 1965. 16mm; 81 minutes; black and white; sound (lost).

Say Nothing. 1965. 16mm; 30 minutes; black and white; sound (Noren, 76 Cypress Lane, Aberdeen, NJ 07747-2222).

Recognitions (a series of eight portraits). 1965–67. 16mm; 240 minutes (30 minutes/portrait); black and white; sound (all lost except *Say Nothing:* see separate listing).

The New York Miseries. 1966. 16mm; 180 minutes (in interchangeable 3-minute, 100-foot, single-take rolls); black and white; sound (lost).

Untitled. 1966–67. 16mm film loops; indeterminate running times; black and white/color; silent (lost).

Untitled. 1966–67. 16mm (found footage compilation films); various running times; black and white/color; sound (lost).

Bathing. 1967. 16mm; interchangeable 10-minute, 400-foot, single-take rolls; color; sound (lost).

The Wind Variations. 1969. 16mm; 18 minutes; color; silent (Noren).

Huge Pupils (Part I of *The Adventures of the Exquisite Corpse*). 1968. 16mm; 61 minutes; color; silent (LFC, Noren).

Scenes from Life. 1972. 2 screen 16mm; 30 minutes; color; silent (Noren).

False Pretenses (Part II of *The Adventures of the Exquisite Corpse*). 1974. 16mm; 67 minutes; color; silent (Noren).

The Phantom Enthusiast (Part III of *The Adventures of the Exquisite Corpse*). 1975. 16mm; 70 minutes; color; silent (Noren).

Charmed Particles (Part IV of *The Adventures of the Exquisite Corpse*). 1979. 16mm; 78 minutes; black and white; silent (FMC).

The Lighted Field (Part V of *The Adventures of the Exquisite Corpse*). 1987. 16mm; 61 minutes; black and white; silent (FMC).

Yoko Ono

During the sixties and seventies, Ono conceptualized and, in some cases, executed installation pieces and works in other forms, often in connection with Fluxus. Many included film (including some that recycled films listed here). For a description of Ono's installations and of all her work with Fluxus, see Jon Hendricks, *Fluxus Codex* (New York: Harry N. Abrams, 1988), pp. 415–426.

Eyeblink (a.k.a. *One* and *One Blink, Fluxfilm* #15 and #19). 1966. 16mm; 5 minutes; black and white; silent (FMC, as part of *Fluxfilm Program*).

No. 1 (a.k.a. *Match, Fluxfilm* #14). 1966. 16mm; 10 minutes; black and white; silent (in Gilbert and Lila Silverman Fluxus Collection Foundation, Detroit, MI).

No. 4 (a.k.a. *Fluxfilm* #16). 1966. 16mm; 5½ minutes; black and white; silent (FMC, as part of *Fluxfilm Program*).

No. 4 (Bottoms). 1966. 16mm; 80 minutes; black and white; sound (AFA).

Film No. 5 (Smile). 1968. 16mm; 51 minutes; color; sound (AFA).

Two Virgins (co-made with John Lennon). 1968. 16mm; 19 minutes; color; sound (AFA).

Bed-In (co-made with John Lennon). 1969. 16mm; 61 minutes; color; sound (AFA).

Rape (co-made with John Lennon). 1969. 16mm; 77 minutes; color; sound (AFA).

Apotheosis (co-made with John Lennon). 1970. 16mm; 18½ minutes; color; sound (AFA).

Fly. 1970. 16mm; 25 minutes; color; sound (AFA).

Freedom. 1970. 16mm; 1 minute; color; sound (AFA).

Up Your Legs Forever. 1970. 16mm; 70 minutes; color; sound (AFA).

Erection (co-made with John Lennon). 1971. 16mm; 20 minutes; color; sound (AFA).

Imagine (co-made with John Lennon). 1971. 16mm; 70 minutes; color; sound (AFA).

The Museum of Modern Art Show. 1971. 16mm; 7 minutes; color; sound (AFA).

Ten for Two: Sisters, O Sisters (co-made with John Lennon). 1972. 16mm; 4 minutes; color; sound (AFA).

Walking on Thin Ice. 1981. Video; 6 minutes; color; sound (AFA).

Woman. 1981. Video; 3½ minutes; color; sound (AFA).

Goodbye Sadness. 1982. Video; 2½ minutes; color; sound (AFA).

Yvonne Rainer

Volleyball. 1967. 16mm; 10 minutes; black and white; silent (Castelli-Sonnabend, 420 West Broadway, New York, NY 10012).

Hand Movie. 1968. 8mm/16mm; 5 minutes; black and white; silent (Castelli-Sonnabend).

Rhode Island Red. 1968. 16mm; 10 minutes; black and white; silent (Castelli-Sonnabend).

Trio Film. 1968. 16mm; 13 minutes; black and white; silent (Castelli-Sonnabend).

Line. 1969. 16mm; 10 minutes; black and white; silent (Castelli-Sonnabend).

Lives of Performers. 1972. 16mm; 90 minutes; black and white; sound (BFI, CFDC; Zeitgeist, 200 Waverly Pl., New York, NY 10014).

Film About a Woman Who . . . . 1974. 16mm; 105 minutes; black and white/color; sound (BFI, CFDC, Zeitgeist).

Kristina Talking Pictures. 1976. 16mm; 90 minutes; black and white/color; sound (BFI, CFDC, MoMA, Zeitgeist).

Journeys from Berlin/1971. 1980. 16mm; 125 minutes; black and white/color; sound (BFI, CFDC, FACETS, MoMA, Zeitgeist).

The Man Who Envied Women. 1985. 16mm; 125 minutes; black and white/color; sound (CFDC, MoMA, Zeitgeist).
Privilege. 1990. 16mm; 100 minutes; black and white/color; sound (Zeitgeist).

Godfrey Reggio

Koyaanisqatsi. 1983. 35mm; 87 minutes; color; sound (New Yorker, FACETS).
Powaqqatsi. 1988. 35mm; 99 minutes; color; sound (New Yorker).
Anima Mundi. 1991. 35mm; 29 minutes; color; sound (World Wildlife Fund).

Anne Robertson

Robertson makes a distinction between films that are "in progress"—unfinished films she will bring to conclusion at some future date—and films that are "on-going": films she assumes will continue to develop as long as she lives.

Spirit of '76. 1976. Super-8mm; 10 minutes; color; silent (Robertson, 69 Dennison Ave., Framingham, MA 01701-6418).
Subways. 1976. Super-8mm; 13 minutes; black and white; sound-on-tape (Robertson).
Dawn. 1979. Super-8mm; 13 minutes; color; silent (Robertson).
Snoozalarm. 1979. Super-8mm; 10 minutes; color; sound/sound-on-tape (Robertson).
Locomotion. 1981. Super-8mm; 7 minutes; color; sound (Robertson).
Out a Window. 1981. Super-8mm; 3 minutes; color; sound (Robertson).
Going to Work. 1981. Super-8mm; 7 minutes; color; sound (Robertson).
Lonely Streets. 1981. Super-8mm; 10 minutes; color; silent (Robertson).
Diary. 1981 to present (ongoing). Super-8mm; 2040+ minutes; black and white/color; sound/sound-on-tape/voice narration (Robertson).
Magazine Mouth. 1983. Super-8mm; 10 minutes; color; sound-on-tape (Robertson).
Windows. 1985. Super-8mm; 40 minutes; color; sound-on-tape (Robertson).
Talking To Myself #1. 1985. Super-8mm; 3 minutes; color; sound (Robertson).
Kafka Kamera. 1985. Super-8mm; 3 minutes; color; sound/sound-on-tape (Robertson).
Rotting Pumpkin. 1985. Super-8mm; 13 minutes; color; silent (Robertson).
Fruit. 1985. Super-8mm; 8 minutes; color; silent (Robertson).
My Obsession. 1986. Super-8mm; 16 minutes; color; sound/filmmaker-in-performance (Robertson).
The Nude. 1987. Super-8mm; 17 minutes; color; sound-on-tape/filmmaker-in-performance (Robertson).
With Clothes. 1987. Super-8mm; 17 minutes; color; sound-on-tape/filmmaker-in-performance (Robertson).
Seasons. 1987 to present (in progress). Super-8mm; 40 minutes; color; sound-on-tape (Robertson).

Talking To Myself #2. 1988 to present (in progress). Super-8mm; 3+ minutes; color; sound/filmmaker-in-performance (Robertson).
Talking To Myself #3. 1988. Super-8mm; 17 minutes; color; sound/filmmaker-in-performance (Robertson).
Weight. 1988. Super-8mm; 55 minutes; color; sound-on-tape (Robertson).
Measurements. 1988. Super-8mm; 20 minutes; color; sound (Robertson).
Diet. 1988. Super-8mm; 24 minutes; color; sound (Robertson).
The Sign of Jesus Is the Fish. 1989 to present (in progress). Super-8mm; 3+ minutes; color; sound (Robertson).
Apologies. 1990. Super-8mm; 16 minutes; color; sound (Robertson).
Suicide. 1990. Super-8mm; 8 minutes; color; sound (Robertson).
Melon Patches, or, Reasons to Go On Living. 1990 to present (in progress). Super-8mm; 24+ minutes; color; silent/voice narration (Robertson).

Anne Severson (Alice Anne Parker)

I Change I Am the Same. 1969. 16mm; 40 seconds; black and white; sound (CC).
Riverbody. 1970. 16mm; 7 minutes; black and white; sound (CC).
Nineteen Bygone Sweethearts. 1971. 16mm; 47 minutes; color; sound (Severson, 59075 Paula Rd., Haleiwa, HI 96712).
Introduction to Humanities. 1972. 16mm; 5 minutes; black and white; sound (CC).
Near the Big Chakra. 1972. 16mm; 17 minutes; color; silent (CC).
Animals Running. 1974. 16mm; 23 minutes; black and white; sound (CC).
The Struggle of the Meat. 1974. 16mm; 4 minutes; color; sound (CC).

Michael Snow

A to Z. 1956. 16mm; 4 minutes; black and white; silent (CFDC, FMC).
New York Eye and Ear Control. 1964. 16mm; 34 minutes; black and white; sound (CFDC, FMC).
Short Shave. 1965. 16mm; 4 minutes; black and white; sound (FMC).
Wavelength. 1967. 16mm; 45 minutes; color; sound (BFI, CC, CFDC, FACETS, FMC, MoMA).
Standard Time. 1967. 16mm; 8 minutes; color; sound (CFDC, FMC, LFC).
←—→(*Back and Forth*). 1969. 16mm; 52 minutes; color; sound (CC, CFDC, FMC, LFC, MoMA).
Dripping Water (co-made with Joyce Wieland). 1969. 16mm; 10½ minutes; black and white; sound (CFDC, FMC).
One Second in Montreal. 1969. 16mm; 26 minutes (17 minutes, if projected at sound speed); black and white; silent (CC, CFDC, FMC, LFC, MoMA).
Side Seat Paintings Slides Sound Film. 1970. 16mm; 20 minutes; color; sound (CFDC, FMC, LFC).
La Région Centrale. 1971. 16mm; 190 minutes; color; sound (CC, CFDC, FMC, LFC, MoMA).
Two Sides to Every Story. 1974. 16mm film installation, using two 8-minute loops

projected on opposite sides of the same screen, simultaneously; color; sound (owned by the National Art Gallery of Canada).

"Rameau's Nephew" by Diderot (Thanx to Dennis Young) by Wilma Schoen. 1974. 16mm; 267 minutes; color; sound (CFDC, FMC).

Breakfast (a.k.a. "Table Top Dolly"). 1972, 1976. 16mm; 15 minutes; color; sound (CC, CFDC, FMC, LFC, MoMA).

Presents. 1980. 16mm; 98 minutes; color; sound (CC, CFDC, FMC, LFC).

So Is This. 1982. 16mm; 47½ minutes; color; silent (CC, CFDC, FMC, LFC).

Seated Figures. 1988. 16mm; 40 minutes; color; sound (CFDC, FMC).

See You Later/Au Revoir. 1990. 16mm; 18 minutes; color; sound (CC, CFDC, FMC).

To Lavoisier, Who Died in the Reign of Terror. 1991. 16mm; 53 minutes; color; sound (CFDC, FMC).

Trinh T. Minh-ha

San Francisco. 1980. Super-8mm; 12 minutes; color; silent.

Calligraphy. 1981. Super-8mm; 10 minutes; color; silent.

The Wedding. 1982. Super-8mm; 15 minutes; color; silent.

Reassemblage. 1982. 16mm; 40 minutes; color; sound (Circles; Idera, 2524 Cypress St., Vancouver, BC V6J 3N2, Canada; MoMA, Third World Newsreel, 335 West 38th St., 5th Fl., New York, NY 10018; WMM).

Naked Spaces—Living Is Round. 1985. 16mm; 135 minutes; color; sound (Circles, Idera, MoMA, WMM).

Surname Viêt Given Name Nam. 1989. 16mm; 108 minutes; color; sound (Circles, Idera, MoMA, WMM).

Shoot for the Contents. 1991. 16mm; 101 minutes; color; sound (WWM).

Peter Watkins

A complete Watkins filmography is included in James Michael Welsh, *Peter Watkins: A Guide to References and Resources* (Boston: G. K. Hall, 1986), pp. 45–63. It is all-inclusive through 1977.

The Web. 1956. 8mm; c. 20 minutes; black and white; sound (Institute of Amateur Cinematographers, 63 Woodfield Lane, Ashstead, Surrey, KT21 2BT, U.K.).

The Field of Red. 1958. 16mm; ? minutes; black and white; sound (lost).

The Diary of an Unknown Soldier. 1959. 16mm; 20 minutes; black and white; sound.

The Forgotten Faces. 1961. 16mm; 17 minutes; black and white; sound (Institute of Amateur Cinematographers).

Culloden. 1961. 35mm; 75 minutes; black and white; sound (FACETS, Films Incorporated; New Cinema, 75 Horner Ave., #1, Toronto, Ont., M8Z 4X5 Canada; University of California, Extension Media Center, 2223 Fulton St., Berkeley, CA 94720; University of Michigan, Media Resources Center, 416 Fourth St., Ann Arbor, MI 48109).

The War Game. 1965. 35mm; 47 minutes; black and white; sound (EmGee, 6924 Canby Ave., Suite 103, Reseda, CA 91335; FACETS, Films Incorporated; University of Illinois, Film Center, 1325 South Oak St., Champaign, IL 61820; New Cinema; Syracuse University, Film Rental Center, 1455 East Colvin St., Syracuse, NY 13210; University of Michigan).

Privilege. 1967. 35mm; 103 minutes; color; sound (Swank, Twyman).

Gladiatorena ("The Gladiators"). 1969. 35mm; 105 minutes; color; sound (New Cinema, New Line).

Punishment Park. 1971. 35mm; 88 minutes; color; sound (Joseph A. Gomez, Dept. of English, Box 8105, North Carolina State University, Raleigh, NC 27695).

Edvard Munch. 1974. 35mm; 210 minutes (original TV version)/167 minutes (16mm U.S.A. release version); color; sound (New Yorker; Norsk Rikstringkasting, NRK television, Norway; Sveriges Radio AV Productions, SR2 television, Sweden).

70-Talets Manniskor ("The Seventies People"). 1975. 35 mm; 127 minutes; color; sound.

Fallan ("The Trap"). 1975. Video; 65 minutes; color; sound (Gomez).

Aftenlandet ("Evening Land"). 1977. 35mm; 110 minutes; color; sound.

The Journey. 1987. 16mm; 873 minutes; color; sound (CC, DEK, 394 Euclid Ave., Toronto, Ont., M6G 2S9 Canada; FACETS).

Bibliography

General References

The first volume of *A Critical Cinema* includes a listing of selected general references. The following listing is an addendum to it. When a book is listed in the General References section of *A Critical Cinema 2,* a shortened citation is used if that book is cited in one of the individual filmmaker bibliographies that follow.

Beauvais, Yann, and Miles McKane, eds. *Mot: dites, image.* A catalogue for a show of films that use visual text, Musée National D'Art Moderne, Paris, Oct. 19–Nov. 13, 1988. Paris: Scratch/Musée National D'Art Moderne, 1988.

Brakhage, Stan. *Film at Wit's End.* Kingston, N.Y.: Documentext/McPherson & Co., 1989.

Elder, R. Bruce. *Image and Identity: Reflections on Canadian Film and Culture.* Waterloo, Ontario: Wilfred Laurier University Press, 1989.

Erens, Patricia, ed. *Issues in Feminist Film Criticism.* Bloomington/Indianapolis: Indiana University Press, 1990.

Film-makers' Cooperative Catalogue, no. 7. New York: Film-makers' Cooperative, 1989.

Fischer, Lucy. *Shot/Countershot: Film Tradition and Women's Cinema.* Princeton, N.J.: Princeton University Press, 1989.

Gidal, Peter. *Materialist Film.* London/New York: Routledge, 1989.

Hoberman, J. *Vulgar Modernism: Writing on Movies and Other Media.* Philadelphia: Temple University Press, 1991.

International Experimental Film Congress. A catalogue for a conference in Toronto, May 28–June 4, 1989. Toronto: Art Gallery of Ontario, 1989.

James, David. *Allegories of Cinema: American Film in the Sixties.* Princeton, N.J.: Princeton University Press, 1989.

Katz, John Stuart, ed. *Autobiography: Film/Video/Photography.* A catalogue for a show at the Art Gallery of Ontario, Nov. 1–Dec. 7, 1978. Toronto: Art Gallery of Ontario, 1978.

Kuenzli, Rudolf E. *Dada and Surrealist Film.* New York: Willis Locker & Owens, 1987.

MacDonald, Scott. "Putting All Your Eggs in One Basket: A Survey of Single Shot Film." *Afterimage* (U.S.A.) 16, no. 8 (March 1989): 10–16.

———. "Text as Image in Some Recent North American Avant-Garde Films." *Afterimage* (U.S.A.) 13, no. 8 (March 1986): 9–20.

Mellencamp, Patricia. *Indiscretions: Avant-Garde Film, Video and Feminism.* Bloomington/Indianapolis: Indiana University Press, 1990.

Pines, Jim, and Paul Willemen. *Questions of Third Cinema.* London: British Film Institute, 1989.

Rabinovitz, Lauren. *Points of Resistance: Women, Power and Politics in the New York Avant-garde Cinema, 1943–71.* Urbana/Chicago: University of Illinois Press, 1991.

Schwartz, David. *Independent America: New Film 1978–1988.* A catalogue for a film show at the American Museum of the Moving Image, October–November 1988. New York: American Museum of the Moving Image, 1988.

Silverman, Kaja. *The Acoustic Mirror: The Female Voice in Psychoanalysis and Cinema.* Bloomington/Indianapolis: Indiana University Press, 1988.

Bruce Baillie

Brakhage, Stan. "To Bruce Baillie." In *Brakhage Scrapbook,* ed. Robert A. Haller, pp. 146–155. New Paltz, N.Y.: Documentext, 1982.

Callenbach, Ernest. *Bruce Baillie.* A Film in the Cities Monograph. Minneapolis/St. Paul: Film in the Cities/Walker Art Center, 1979.

Film Culture, no. 67–69 (1979). Includes a sixty-four-page Baillie section: letters by Baillie, essays by Ken Kelman, Paul Arthur, Anthony Bannon.

Fischer, Lucy. "*Castro Street:* The Sensibility of Style." *Film Quarterly* 29, no.3 (Spring 1976): 14–22.

Sitney, P. Adams. *Visionary Film.* New York: Oxford University Press, 1974, chaps. 6, 7.

Whitehall, Richard. "An Interview with Bruce Baillie." *Film Culture* 47 (1969): 16–19.

Williams, Alan. "The Structure of Lyric: Baillie's *To Parsifal.*" *Film Quarterly* 29, no. 3 (Spring 1976): 22–30.

James Benning

Benning, James. "Sound and Stills from *Grand Opera.*" *October,* no. 12 (Spring 1980): 22–45.

Lehman, Peter, and Stephen Hank. *"11 X 14*: An Interview with James Benning." *Wide Angle* 2, no. 3 (1978): 12–20.

Rosenbaum, Jonathan. *Film: The Front Line/1983*. Denver: Arden Press, 1983, pp. 49–61.

Lizzie Borden

Borden, Lizzie. "Trisha Brown and Yvonne Rainer." *Artforum* 11, no. 10 (June 1973): 80–81.

De Lauretis, Teresa. *Technologies of Gender.* Bloomington/Indianapolis: Indiana University Press, 1987, chap. 8. Also available as "Rethinking Women's Cinema: Aesthetics and Feminist Theory," in *Issues in Feminist Film Criticism,* ed. Patricia Erens.

Ehrenstein, David. *Film: The Front Line/1984*. Denver: Arden Press, 1984, pp. 114–119.

Fusco, Coco. "Working Girls: An Interview with Lizzie Borden." *Afterimage* (U.S.A.) 14, no. 5 (December 1986): 6–7.

Jackson, Lynne. "Labor Relations: An Interview with Lizzie Borden." *Cineaste* 15, no. 3 (Fall 1987): 4–9.

Judge, Maureen, and Lori Spring. "An Interview with Lizzie Borden." *CineAction!* 8 (Spring 1987): 69–76.

Robert Breer

Breer, Robert. "Robert Breer on His Work," *Film Culture,* no. 42 (1966): 112–113.

———. "Robert Breer: On Two Films." *Film Culture,* no. 22–23 (1963–1964): 163–164.

———. "A Statement." *Film Culture,* no. 26 (1962): 57.

———. "A Statement." *Film Culture,* no. 29 (1963): 73.

———. "What Happened." *Film Culture,* no. 26 (1962): 58.

Burch, Noel. "*Image by Images, Cats, Jamestown Baloos, A Man and His Dog Out for Air.*" *Film Quarterly* 12, no. 3 (1959): 55–57.

Cote, Guy L. "Interview with Robert Breer." *Film Culture,* no. 27 (1962–1963): 18–20.

Film Culture, no. 56–57 (Spring 1973): 23–72. A special section in honor of Breer's receiving the Eleventh Independent Film Award, includes the award announcement; P. Adams Sitney, "Robert Breer—From 'The Visionary Film-makers,' " pp. 24–38; Jonas Mekas and P. Adams Sitney, "An Interview with Robert Breer Conducted by Jonas Mekas and P. Adams Sitney on May 13, 1971—in New York City," pp. 39–55; "An Interview with Robert Breer Conducted by Charles Levine at Breer's Home, Palisades, N.Y. Approximate Date July 1970," pp. 55–69; "Letter from Robert Breer to Jonas Mekas 5/25/70," pp. 69–70; and Robert Breer, "Robert Breer—Filmography" (annotated), pp. 70–72.

Fischer, Lucy. "Independent Film: Talking with Robert Breer." *University Film Study Center Newsletter* 7, no. 1 (October 1976): 5–7.

Hoberman, J. "Robert Breer's Animated World." *American Film* 5, no. 10 (September 1980): 46, 48, 68.

Klüver, Billy, Julie Martin, and Barbara Rose, eds. *Pavilion by Experiments in Art and Technology*. New York: E. P. Dutton, 1972, pp. 5–11, other references.

Mekas, Jonas. *Movie Journal*. New York: Collier Books, 1972. Includes reviews of Breer's work—"On the Cinema of Happiness and Robert Breer" (p. 176), "On the Changing Nature of Avant-Garde Film Screenings" (pp. 342–343)—and other references.

Mendelson, Lois. *Robert Breer: A Study of His Work in the Context of the Modernist Tradition*. Ann Arbor, Mich.: U.M.I. Research Press, 1981.

Moore, Sandy. *Robert Breer*. A Film in the Cities Monograph. Minneapolis/St. Paul: Film in the Cities/Walker Art Center, 1980.

Renan, Sheldon. *An Introduction to American Underground Film*. New York: E. P. Dutton, 1967, pp. 129–133, other references.

Russett, Robert, and Cecile Starr, eds. *Experimental Animation*. New York: Van Nostrand Reinhold Co., 1976. The Robert Breer section (pp. 131–136) includes Guy L. Cote, "Interviews with Robert Breer" (reprinted from *Film Culture*); Breer, "A Statement" (reprinted from *Film Culture*, no. 29); and "Interview with Robert Breer" (reprinted from *American Film Institute Report* 5, no. 2 Summer 1974).

Sitney, P. Adams. "The Achievement of American Avant-Garde Cinema 1960–1970." In *"The Pleasure Dome," American Experimental Film 1939–1979*, eds. Jonas Mekas and Sitney, pp. 24–26. A catalogue for a show at Moderna Museet, Stockholm, Sweden, February 16–April 4, 1980. Stockholm: Moderna Museet, 1980.

———. "The Films of Robert Breer." In *New Forms in Film*, ed. Annette Michelson, pp. 45–49. A catalogue for an exhibition of North American avant-garde film, Montreux, Switzerland, Aug. 3–24, 1974. Montreux, Switzerland: Imprimerie Corbaz, 1974.

———. *Visionary Film*. New York: Oxford University Press, 1974, pp. 313–332, other references.

Su Friedrich

Beroes, Stephanie. "Interview with Su Friedrich." *Cinematograph*, no. 2 (1986): 68–71.

Camper, Fred. "Daddy's Girl." *Chicago Reader* 20, no. 18 (Feb. 8, 1991): 12, 17–18.

Friedrich, Su. "Radical Form: Radical Content." *Millennium*, no. 22 (Winter/Spring 1989–90): 118–123.

———. "(Script) for a Film without Images." *Feminism/Film*, no. 1 (Spring 1984): 1–11.

Hanlon, Lindley. "Female Rage: The Films of Su Friedrich." *Millennium*, no. 12 (Fall/Winter 1982–83): 78–86.

Jenkins, Bruce. "Gently Down the Stream." *Millennium*, nos. 16–18 (Fall/Winter 1986–87): 195–199.

Kruger, Barbara. "The Ties That Bind." *Artforum,* no. 23 (October 1984): 89.
MacDonald, Scott. "Su Friedrich: Reappropriations." *Film Quarterly* 41, no. 2 (Winter 1987–88): 34–43.

Anthony McCall

Ehrenberg, Felipe. "On Conditions." *Art and Artists* (March 1973): 39–43.
McCall, Anthony. *anti-catalogue.* New York: The Catalogue Committee of Artists Meeting for Cultural Change, 1977.
———. "Interview: Formalist Cinema and Politics." *Performing Arts Journal* 1, no. 3 (Winter 1977): 51–61. Includes statements on *Line Describing a Cone* and other "Cone" films, on *Long Film for Four Projectors* and *Long Film for Ambient Light,* and an interview with McCall by Gautam Dasgupta.
———. "Film as a Connective Catalyst." Paper delivered at International Forum of Avant-Garde Film, Edinburgh Film Festival, 1976.
———. "Two Statements." In *The Avant-Garde Film,* ed. P. Adams Sitney, pp. 250–254. New York: New York University Press, 1978.
———, and Andrew Tyndall. *Argument.* A catalogue published in several versions on the occasion of screenings of the film *Argument.* First edition: August 1978 (for Edinburgh International Film Festival and London Filmmakers' Co-operative); Second edition: October 1978 (for The Collective for Living Cinema and Millennium Film Workshop in New York and Media Study-Buffalo); Third edition: March 1979 (for Temple University Conference on Culture and Communication, International Film Theory Conference 5, University of Wisconsin-Milwaukee, and Chicago Filmmakers). The final edition includes essays by McCall and Tyndall, Jane Weinstock, David Himelfarb, and Claire Pajaczkowska.
MacDonald, Scott. "Text as Image." P. 13.

Ross McElwee

Edelstein, David. "A Date with History." *Voice,* September 9, 1986, pp. 54–56.
Hoberman, J. "I Sync Therefore I Am." *Voice,* September 9, 1986, pp. 54–56.

Jonas Mekas

Briggs, Judith E. *Jonas Mekas.* A Film in the Cities Monograph. Minneapolis/St. Paul: Film in the Cities/Walker Art Center, 1980.
Film Culture. Mekas is the founder and editor of *Film Culture.* He has written many editorials for the journal and has conducted many interviews. An index to *Film Culture* is available at Anthology Film Archives, 32–34 First St., New York, N.Y. 10003.
James, David. *Allegories of Cinema.* Pp. 100–119.
MacDonald, Scott. "Lost Lost Lost over *Lost Lost Lost.*" *Cinema Journal* 25, no. 2 (Winter 1986): 20–34.
Mekas, Jonas. "Anti-Workers Manifesto." *Downtown Review* 2, no. 3 (Fall 1980): 14–15.

————. "A Call for a New Generation of Film-makers." *Film Culture,* no. 19 (1959): 1–2.

————. "Diaries. Installment One"; "Diaries. Installment Two." *No Rose* 1, no. 3; 2, no. 1 (Spring 1977; Winter 1979): 33–52; 33–45.

————. "The Diary Film." In *The Avant-Garde Film,* ed. P. Adams Sitney, pp. 190–198. New York: New York University Press, 1978.

————. "From the Diaries." In *The American New Wave: 1958–1967,* ed. Melinda Ward, Bruce Jenkins, pp. 4–11. Buffalo/Minneapolis: Media Study—Buffalo/Walker Art Center, 1982.

————. *I Had Nowhere to Go.* New York: Black Thistle Press, 1991.

————. "Independent/Avant-Garde Film Dissemination and Other Issues: A Critique of Two Recent Texts." *Downtown Review* 7, no. 2 (Spring 1980): 3–10.

————. Letter to Dave Lee. *Downtown Review* 3, no. 1–2 (Fall–Spring 1981–82): 48.

————. *Movie Journal: The Rise of the New American Cinema 1959–1971.* New York: Collier Books, 1972.

————. "Notes on Some New Movies and Happiness." In *Film Culture Reader,* ed. P. Adams Sitney, pp. 317–325. New York: Praeger Publishers, 1970.

————. "Where Are We—The Underground?" In *The New American Cinema,* ed. Gregory Battcock, pp. 17–22. New York: E. P. Dutton, 1967.

Ruoff, Jeffrey K. "Movies of the Avant-Garde: Jonas Mekas and the New York Art World." *Cinema Journal* 30, no. 3 (Spring 1991): 6–28.

Laura Mulvey

Fischer, Lucy. *Shot/Countershot.* Chap. 2.

Flitterman, Sandy, and Jacqueline Suter. "Textual Riddles: Woman as Enigma or Site of Social Meanings? An Interview with Laura Mulvey." *Discourse,* no. 1 (Fall 1979): 86–127.

Friedman, Lester D. "An Interview with Peter Wollen and Laura Mulvey on Riddles of the Sphinx." *Millennium,* no. 4–5 (Summer/Fall 1979): 14–32.

Kaplan, E. Ann. *Women and Film: Both Sides of the Camera.* New York: Methuen, 1983. Chaps. 11,12.

Mulvey, Laura. "British Film Theory's Female Spectators: Presence and Absence." *Camera Obscura,* no. 20–21 (May–September 1989): 68–81. Also, in the same issue, "Individual Responses" includes a Mulvey section, pp. 248–252.

————. "Pandora: Topographies of the Mask, the Box, and Curiosity." In *Space and Sexuality,* ed. Beatriz Colomino. Princeton, N.J.: Princeton University Press, 1992.

————. *Visual and Other Pleasures.* Bloomington/Indianapolis: Indiana University Press, 1989. Reprints fifteen Mulvey essays, including "Visual Pleasure and Narrative Cinema," "Afterthoughts on 'Visual Pleasure and Narrative Cinema' inspired by King Vidor's *Duel in the Sun* (1946)," and "Film, Feminism and the Avant-Garde."

Mulvey, Laura, and Peter Wollen. "*Penthesilea: Queen of the Amazons*—Interview." *Screen* 15, no. 3 (1974): 120–134.

———. "*Riddles of the Sphinx* script." *Screen* 18, no. 2 (Summer 1977): 61–77.

———. "Script of *Amy!*" *Framework*, no. 14 (1981): 38–41.

Silverman, Kaja. *The Acoustic Mirror.* Pp. 129–140.

Andrew Noren

Cahmi, Gail. "The Films of Andrew Noren." *Film Culture,* no. 70–71 (1983): 100–118.

Carson, L. M. "Introduction" to *David Holzman's Diary* (screenplay). New York: Farrar, Strauss & Giroux, 1970. Pp. viii–ix.

Hoberman, J. "Lust for Light." *Village Voice,* March 12, 1979. "Streets of Fire." *Village Voice,* Oct. 6, 1987.

Kardish, Larry. *Of Light and Texture: Andrew Noren and James Herbert.* A catalogue for a retrospective of the two filmmakers. New York: Museum of Modern Art, 1981.

Mekas, Jonas. "On Andrew Noren, the Master of Texture." In *Movie Journal,* by Mekas, pp. 369–371. New York: Collier Books, 1972.

Yoko Ono

As one of the world's most visible personalities, Ono has been interviewed many times about a wide variety of projects and about John Lennon. This listing focuses on her film work only.

Hanhardt, John, and Barbara Haskell. *Yoko Ono: Objects, Films.* A catalogue for a show of films and objects at the Whitney Museum, Spring 1989. New York: Whitney Museum of American Art, 1989.

Hendricks, Jon. *Fluxus Codex.* New York: Harry N. Abrams, 1988, pp. 415–426.

Mekas, Jonas. "Films of Yoko Ono and John Lennon." In *Movie Journal,* by Mekas, pp. 411–413. New York: Collier, 1972.

Ono, Yoko. Filmscripts. In Scott MacDonald, "Yoko Ono: Ideas on Film (Interview/Scripts)," *Film Quarterly* 43, no. 1 (Fall 1989): 16–21.

———. *Grapefruit.* Tokyo: Wunternaum Press, 1964. Reprinted, New York: Simon & Schuster, 1964, 1970. A paperback edition was published by Simon & Schuster/Touchstone in 1971.

———. *Museum of Modern FArt: Yoko Ono—One Woman Show.* A catalogue for an installation at the Museum of Modern Art, Dec. 1–15, 1971. New York: Yoko Ono, 1972.

———. "Yoko Ono" (interview). In *The Guests Go In to Supper: John Cage, Robert Ashley, Yoko Ono, Laurie Anderson, Charles Admirkhanian, Michael Pepper, K. Atchley,* ed. Melody Sumner, Kathleen Burch, Michael Sumner, pp. 169–213. Oakland, Calif.: Burning Books, 1986.

———. "Yoko Ono on Yoko Ono." *Film Culture,* no. 48–49 (Winter–Spring 1970): 32–33.

Ono, Yoko, and John Lennon. "John Lennon, Yoko Ono: Our Films." *Filmmakers Newsletter,* no. 6 (June 1973): 25–27.

──────. *This Is Not Here.* A catalogue for a retrospective show at the Everson Museum, Syracuse, N.Y., 1971. Syracuse: Everson Museum, 1971.

Yvonne Rainer

An extensive listing of publications by and about Rainer and her films was compiled by Patricia White for *The Films of Yvonne Rainer* (Bloomington/Indianapolis: Indiana University Press, 1989), which includes the scripts for *Lives of Performers, Film About a Woman Who . . . , Kristina Talking Pictures, Journeys from Berlin/1971,* and *The Man Who Envied Women,* along with "Yvonne Rainer: An Introduction," by B. Ruby Rich; "Impossible Projections," by Bérénice Reynaud; and "Interview with Yvonne Rainer," by Mitchell Rosenbaum.

Camera Obscura, no. 1 (Fall 1976): 53–75. Includes "Yvonne Rainer: An Introduction" and "Appendix: Rainer's Descriptions of Her Films."

Carroll, Noel. "Interview with a Woman Who . . . ." *Millennium,* no. 7–9 (Fall/Winter 1980/81): 37–68.

De Lauretis, Teresa. *Technologies of Gender.* Bloomington/Indianapolis: Indiana University Press, 1987, chap. 7.

Fischer, Lucy. *Shot/Countershot.* Chap. 10.

Lippard, Lucy. "Yvonne Rainer on Feminism and Her Film." In *From the Center: Feminist Essays on Women's Art,* by Lippard, pp. 265–279. New York: NAL-Dutton, 1976.

Mekas, Jonas. "Interview with Yvonne Rainer." *Village Voice,* April 25, 1974, p. 77.

Rainer, Yvonne. "Annotated Selections from the Filmscript of *Kristina Talking Pictures.*" *No Rose* 1, no. 3 (Spring 1977).

──────. "Beginning with Some Advertisements for Criticisms of Myself, or Drawing the Dog You May Want to Use to Bite Me With, and Then Going On to Other Matters." *Millennium Film Journal,* no. 6 (Spring 1980): 5–7.

──────. "Conversation Following Screening at Cinematheque of *Kristina Talking Pictures,* April 6, 1978." *Cinemanews* 78, nos. 3–4 (1978): 16–17.

──────. "Incomplete Report of the First Week of the Edinburgh International Film Festival, August 17–30, 1980 and Musings on Several Other Films." *Idiolects,* nos. 9–10 (Winter 1980–81): 2–6.

──────. "Looking Myself in the Mouth." *October,* no. 17 (Summer 1981): 65–76.

──────. "More Kicking and Screaming from the Narrative Front/Backwater." *Wide Angle* 7, nos. 1–2 (Spring 1985): 8–12.

──────. "Some Ruminations around the Cinematic Antidotes to the Oedipal Net(tles) While Playing with De Lauraedipus Mulvey, or He May Be Off Screen, But . . . ." *The Independent* 9, no. 3 (April 1986): 22–25.

──────. "Thoughts on Women's Cinema: Eating Words, Voicing Struggles." *The*

Independent 10, no. 3 (April 1987): 14–16. Reprinted in *Blasted Allegories: An Anthology of Writings by Contemporary Artists,* ed., Brian Wallis, pp. 380–385. New York/Cambridge, Mass.: New Museum of Contemporary Art/MIT Press, 1987.

————. *Work 1961–73.* Halifax/New York: Press of the Nova Scotia College of Art and Design/New York University Press, 1974.

Rich, B. Ruby. *Yvonne Rainer.* A Film in the Cities Monograph. Minneapolis: Walker Art Center, 1981.

Wallace, Michele. "Multiculturalism and Oppositionality." *Afterimage* (U.S.A.) 19, no. 3 (October 1991): 6–9.

Walworth, Dan. "A Conversation with Yvonne Rainer." *Psychcritique* 2, no. 1 (1987): 1–16.

Godfrey Reggio

Dempsey, Michael. "Quatsi Means Life: The Films of Godfrey Reggio." *Film Quarterly* 42, no. 3 (Spring 1989): 2–12.

Ebert, Roger. *"Koyaanisqatsi."* In *Roger Ebert's Movie Home Companion,* pp. 399–400. Kansas City: Universal Press Syndicate, 1990.

Anne Robertson

Schwartz, David. Program notes for Anne Robertson. In *Independent America: New Film 1978–1988,* pp. 55–56. Includes a statement by Robertson.

Anne Severson (Alice Anne Parker)

Severson, Anne. "Don't Get Too Near the Big Chakra." *Spare Rib,* no. 20 (February 1974): 7–9. Reprinted in *Spare Rib Reader,* ed. Marsha Rowe. New York: Penguin Books, 1982.

————. Authored and co-authored a series of essays on dreams and other topics in *Metapsychology* (P.O. Box 681, Clinton, WA 98236): "Turning Bad Dreams into Good Ones" (Spring 1985), "Beneath the American Dream: A Conversation with Menos" (Summer 1986), "The Three Breath Exercise" (Winter 1986–87), "The Morning After: Discarnate Dream Analysis" (Spring 1987), "On the Evolution of Consciousness" (Summer 1987), "Visits from the Higher Self" (Winter 1987–88), "Interpreting Your Dreams" (Autumn 1987), "The Morning After: Trees of Growth, Houses of Self" (Autumn 1987).

————. *Understand Your Dreams: 1001 Basic Dream Images and How to Interpret Them.* New York: H. J. Kramer, 1991.

Michael Snow

Cornwell, Regina. *Snow Seen: The Films and Photographs of Michael Snow.* Toronto: Peter Martin, 1980.

De Lauretis, Teresa. "Snow on the Oedipal Stage." In *Alice Doesn't: Feminism*

Semiotics Cinema, by De Lauretis, pp. 70–83. Bloomington: Indiana University Press, 1982.

Dompierre, Louis. *Walking Woman Works: Michael Snow 1961–67.* Catalogue for a traveling show. Kingston, Ontario: Agnes Etherington Art Centre, 1983. Includes extensive photo documentation of the Walking Woman, a detailed Walking Woman chronology, and essays by Snow, Peter Morris.

Elder, R. Bruce. *Image and Identity.* Chaps. 8, 10, 12, 14.

Field, Simon, Guy L'Eclair, Michael O'Prag, eds. *Afterimage,* no. 11 (1975, "Sighting Snow"). Includes a detailed, annotated filmography by Snow, "A Conversation between Snow and R. Bruce Elder," and essays by Field, Nicky Hamlyn, O'Prag, and Jonathan Rosenbaum.

Film Culture, no. 46 (Autumn 1967—published October 1968). Includes Ninth Annual Film Award (to Snow); a statement and a letter by Snow; a conversation with Snow, Jonas Mekas, and P. Adams Sitney; and an essay on *Wavelength* by Bob Lamberton.

Gidal, Peter, ed. *Structural Film Anthology.* London: British Film Institute, 1978. Includes an interview by Simon Hartog, a letter to Gidal from Snow, and essays by Annette Michelson and Gidal.

Lehman, Peter. "The Nature of the Material: An Interview with Michael Snow." *Wide Angle* 7, nos. 1 & 2 (1985): 92–100.

Sitney, P. Adams. "Michael Snow's Cinema." In *The Essential Cinema,* ed. P. Adams Sitney, pp. 219–229. New York: Anthology Film Archives, 1975.

Snow, Michael. *Cover to Cover.* Halifax/New York: Press of Nova Scotia College of Art and Design/New York University Press, 1975.

———. *Michael Snow/A Survey.* Catalogue for show at Art Gallery of Ontario, February 14–March 15, 1970. Toronto: Art Gallery of Ontario, 1970. Includes extensive photos by Snow and others, and essays by Robert Fufard, Dennis Young, Richard Foreman, and P. Adams Sitney.

———. "Two Letters and Notes on Films." In *The Avant-Garde Film: A Reader of Theory and Criticism,* ed. P. Adams Sitney, pp. 184–189. New York: New York University Press, 1978. Volume also includes Annette Michelson, "Toward Snow."

Trinh T. Minh-ha

Trinh includes a bibliography of her writings in her *Women, Native, Other* (Bloomington/Indianapolis: Indiana University Press, 1989), pp. 167–168.

Trinh, Minh-ha T. "Mechanical Eye, Electronic Ear and the Lure of Authenticity." *Wide Angle* 6, no. 2 (Summer 1984).

———. "Questions of Images and Politics." *The Independent* 10, no. 4 (May 1987).

———. "On the Politics of Contemporary Representation." In *Discussions in Contemporary Culture,* ed. Hal Foster. Seattle: Bay Press, 1987.

———. "Outside In Inside Out." In *Questions of Third Cinema,* by Jim Pines and Paul Willemen, pp. 133–149.

———. "On *Naked Spaces—Living Is Round.*" *Motion Picture,* no. 1 (Spring 1986): 13.

———. Script of *Reassemblage. Camera Obscura,* no. 13/14 (1985): 104–111.

———. Script of *Naked Spaces—Living Is Round. Cinematograph* 3 (1988): 65–79.

———. *When the Moon Waxes Red: Representation, Gender and Cultural Politics.* New York/London: Routledge, 1991.

———, and Jean-Paul Bourdier. *African Spaces: Designs for Living in Upper Volta.* New York: Holmes & Meir, 1985.

Peckham, Linda. "Peripheral Vision: Looking at the West through *Reassemblage.*" *Cinematograph,* no. 2 (1986): 1–5.

Stephenson, Rob. "Interview with Trinh T. Minh-ha." *Millennium,* no. 19 (Fall/Winter 1987–88): 122–129.

Peter Watkins

James M. Welsh's *Peter Watkins: A Guide to References and Resources* (Boston: G. K. Hall, 1986) provides a complete, annotated listing of publications by and about Watkins, and interviews with him, up through 1985. Welsh's book also includes the most detailed Watkins filmography up through 1977, and a biographical and a critical survey.

Gomez, Joseph A. *Peter Watkins.* Boston: Twayne, 1979.

MacDonald, Scott. "Conspicuous Consumption: The 1987 Flaherty Film Seminar." *The Independent* 11, no. 2 (March 1988): 12–17.

———. "The Means Justify the Ends: Peter Watkins, from *The War Game* to *The Journey.*" *Afterimage* (U.S.A.) 14, no. 9 (April 1987): 4–7.

Nolley, Ken. "Making *The Journey* with Peter Watkins." *CineAction,* no. 12 (Spring 1988): 60–71.

———, ed. *The Journey: A Film in the Global Interest* (Willamette Journal of the Liberal Arts, Supp. Series 5). Includes Watkins's "The Journey: A Voyage of Discovery" and essays by Nolley, Scott MacDonald, James Welsh, Mary Ann Youngren, Gregg B. Walker, and Catherine Collins.

Watkins, Peter. *The War Game.* New York: Avon Books, 1967.

———, and Vida Urbonavicius. Study Guide for *The Journey.* 1991. Available from Canyon Cinema, 2325 Third St., Suite 338, San Francisco, CA 94107.

Index

All films are listed individually by title, rather than with the filmmaker's name.

449

Printed in the United States
73963LV00005B/38